ECONOMIC ARTICLES AND CORRESPONDENCE

The Collected Writings of John Maynard Keynes

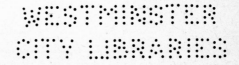

Keynes in 1912
(From Dr Milo Keynes's collection)

THE COLLECTED WRITINGS OF
JOHN MAYNARD KEYNES

VOLUME XII

ECONOMIC ARTICLES
AND
CORRESPONDENCE

INVESTMENT AND
EDITORIAL

EDITED BY

DONALD MOGGRIDGE

MACMILLAN

CAMBRIDGE UNIVERSITY PRESS

FOR THE

ROYAL ECONOMIC SOCIETY

Published for the Royal Economic Society

throughout the world, excluding the U.S.A. and Canada, by

THE MACMILLAN PRESS LTD

London and Basingstoke
Associated companies in Delhi Dublin Hong Kong Johannesburg Lagos
Melbourne New York Singapore Tokyo

ISBN 0-333-10731-4

and throughout the U.S.A. and Canada by

THE SYNDICS OF THE CAMBRIDGE UNIVERSITY PRESS

32 East 57th Street, New York, NY 10022, U.S.A.

ISBN 0-521-23070-5 (the U.S.A. and Canada only)

Printed in Great Britain by the
University Press, Cambridge

CONTENTS

v

GENERAL INTRODUCTION

This new standard edition of *The Collected Writings of John Maynard Keynes* forms the memorial to him of the Royal Economic Society. He devoted a very large share of his busy life to the Society. In 1911, at the age of twenty-eight, he became editor of *The Economic Journal* in succession to Edgeworth: two years later he was made secretary as well. He held these offices without intermittence until almost the end of his life. Edgeworth, it is true, returned to help him with the editorship from 1919 to 1925; Macgregor took Edgeworth's place until 1934, when Austin Robinson succeeded him and continued to assist Keynes down to 1945. But through all these years Keynes himself carried the major responsibility and made the principal decisions about the articles that were to appear in *The Economic Journal*, without any break save for one or two issues when he was seriously ill in 1937. It was only a few months before his death at Easter 1946 that he was elected president and handed over his editorship to Roy Harrod and the secretaryship to Austin Robinson.

In his dual capacity of editor and secretary Keynes played a major part in framing the policies of the Royal Economic Society. It was very largely due to him that some of the major publishing activities of the Society—Sraffa's edition of Ricardo, Stark's edition of the economic writings of Bentham, and Guillebaud's edition of Marshall, as well as a number of earlier publications in the 1930s—were initiated.

When Keynes died in 1946 it was natural that the Royal Economic Society should wish to commemorate him. It was perhaps equally natural that the Society chose to commemorate him by producing an edition of his collected works. Keynes himself had always taken a joy in fine printing, and the Society, with the help of Messrs Macmillan as publishers and the

Cambridge University Press as printers, has been anxious to give Keynes's writings a permanent form that is wholly worthy of him.

The present edition will publish as much as is possible of his work in the field of economics. It will not include any private and personal correspondence or publish many letters in the possession of his family. The edition is concerned, that is to say, with Keynes as an economist.

Keynes's writings fall into five broad categories. First there are the books which he wrote and published as books. Second there are collections of articles and pamphlets which he himself made during his lifetime (*Essays in Persuasion* and *Essays in Biography*). Third, there is a very considerable volume of published but uncollected writings—articles written for newspapers, letters to newspapers, articles in journals that have not been included in his two volumes of collections, and various pamphlets. Fourth, there are a few hitherto unpublished writings. Fifth, there is correspondence with economists and those concerned with economics or public affairs. It is the intention of this series to publish almost completely the whole of the first four categories listed above. The only exceptions are a few syndicated articles where Keynes wrote almost the same material for publication in different newspapers or in different countries, with minor and unimportant variations. In these cases, this series will publish one only of the variations, choosing the most interesting.

The publication of Keynes's economic correspondence must inevitably be selective. In the day of the typewriter and the filing cabinet and particularly in the case of so active and busy a man, to publish every scrap of paper that he may have dictated about some unimportant or ephemeral matter is impossible. We are aiming to collect and publish as much as possible, however, of the correspondence in which Keynes developed his own ideas in argument with his fellow economists, as well as the more significant correspondence at times when Keynes was in the middle of public affairs.

Apart from his published books, the main sources available to those preparing this series have been two. First, Keynes in his will made Richard Kahn his executor and responsible for his economic papers. They have been placed in the Marshall Library of the University of Cambridge and have been available for this edition. Until 1914 Keynes did not have a secretary and his earliest papers are in the main limited to drafts of important letters that he made in his own handwriting and retained. At that stage most of the correspondence that we possess is represented by what he received rather than by what he wrote. During the war years of 1914–18 and 1940–6 Keynes was serving in the Treasury. With the opening in 1968 of the records under the thirty-year rule, the papers that he wrote then and between the wars have become available. From 1919 onwards, throughout the rest of his life, Keynes had the help of a secretary—for many years Mrs Stephens. Thus for the last twenty-five years of his working life we have in most cases the carbon copies of his own letters as well as the originals of the letters that he received.

There were, of course, occasions during this period on which Keynes wrote himself in his own handwriting. In some of these cases, with the help of his correspondents, we have been able to collect the whole of both sides of some important interchanges and we have been anxious, in justice to both correspondents, to see that both sides of the correspondence are published in full.

The second main source of information has been a group of scrapbooks kept over a very long period of years by Keynes's mother, Florence Keynes, wife of Neville Keynes. From 1919 onwards these scrapbooks contain almost the whole of Maynard Keynes's more ephemeral writing, his letters to newspapers and a great deal of material which enables one to see not only what he wrote but the reaction of others to his writing. Without these very carefully kept scrapbooks the task of any editor or biographer of Keynes would have been immensely more difficult.

The plan of the edition, as at present intended, is this. It will total thirty volumes. Of these the first eight are Keynes's published books from *Indian Currency and Finance*, in 1913, to the *General Theory* in 1936, with the addition of his *Treatise on Probability*. There next follow, as vols. IX and X, *Essays in Persuasion* and *Essays in Biography*, representing Keynes's own collection of articles. *Essays in Persuasion* differs from the original printing in two respects: it contains the full texts of the articles or pamphlets included in it and not (as in the original printing) abbreviated versions of these articles, and it also contains two later pamphlets which are of exactly the same character as those included by Keynes in his original collection. In *Essays in Biography* there have been added a number of biographical studies that Keynes wrote both before and after 1933.

There follow two volumes, XI–XII, of economic articles and correspondence and a further two volumes, already published, XIII–XIV, covering the development of his thinking as he moved towards the *General Theory*. There are included in these volumes such part of Keynes's economic correspondence as is closely associated with the articles that are printed in them. A supplement to these volumes, XXIX, prints some further material relating to the same issues, which has since been discovered.

The remaining fourteen volumes deal with Keynes's *Activities* during the years from the beginning of his public life in 1905 until his death. In each of the periods into which we divide this material, the volume concerned publishes his more ephemeral writings, all of it hitherto uncollected, his correspondence relating to these activities, and such other material and correspondence as is necessary to the understanding of Keynes's activities. These volumes are edited by Elizabeth Johnson and Donald Moggridge, and it has been their task to trace and interpret Keynes's activities sufficiently to make the material fully intelligible to a later generation. Elizabeth Johnson has been responsible for vols. XV–XVIII, covering Keynes's earlier years and his activities down to the end of World War I reparations and reconstruction. Donald Moggridge is responsible for all the remaining volumes recording Keynes's other activities from 1922 until his death in 1946.

The record of Keynes's activities during World War II is now complete with the publication of volumes XXII–XXVII. The volumes dealing with Keynes's activities between 1906 and 1946 are now complete, as is the volume dealing with his social, political and literary writings. There remain two volumes, of which this is the second, containing certain of Keynes's professional articles and reviews, along with related correspondence, as well as materials relating to his career as an investor and investment adviser. An index to the whole edition, plus a full bibliography of Keynes's writings, will appear later as volume XXX.

Those responsible for this edition have been: Lord Kahn, both as Lord Keynes's executor and as a long and intimate friend of Lord Keynes; able to help in the interpreting of much that would be otherwise misunderstood; the late Sir Roy Harrod as the author of his biography; Austin Robinson as Keynes's co-editor on *The Economic Journal* and successor as Secretary of the Royal Economic Society. Austin Robinson has acted throughout as Managing Editor; Donald Moggridge is now associated with him as Joint Managing Editor.

In the early stages of the work Elizabeth Johnson was assisted by Jane Thistlethwaite, and by Mrs McDonald, who was originally responsible for the systematic ordering of the files of the Keynes papers. Judith Masterman for many years worked with Mrs Johnson on the papers. More recently Susan Wilsher, Margaret Butler and Leonora Woollam have continued the secretarial work. Barbara Lowe has been responsible for the indexing. Since 1977 Judith Allen has been responsible for much of the day-to-day management of the edition, as well as seeing the volumes through the press.

xi

EDITORIAL NOTE

In this volume and its companion volume XI we bring together
the remainder of Keynes's published writings not included in the
Activities volumes (XV–XXVII), the volumes relating to the composition and defence of the *Treatise* and the *General Theory*
(XIII, XIV and XXIX), or in his *Social, Political and Literary
Writings* (XXVIII). As well, we print some previously unpublished
correspondence relating to Keynes's own articles; his Adam
Smith prize essay on Index Numbers of 1909; a selection from
his pre-war lecture notes and a selection of editorial correspondence relating to *The Economic Journal* which Keynes edited from
1911 to 1945. Finally in this volume we print a longer essay,
interleaved with correspondence and memoranda, on Keynes's
activities as an investor.

The organisation of this rather disparate material has presented something of an editorial problem. With the exception of
the materials relating to investments and to *The Economic Journal*,
it would have been possible to present all the material in chrono-
logical order of publication. Such an arrangement would have the
advantage of showing the range of Keynes's interests in any
particular period and the ways in which several of his activities
were interrelated. However, it would have the disadvantage in
several cases of obscuring what seem to the editors strong links
between Keynes's successive treatments of a particular subject.
This disadvantage is perhaps less strong here than in the various
Activities volumes, but seems sufficiently strong to us to suggest
that we follow previous practice in grouping the material around
certain themes. For the reader interested in following every one
of Keynes's publications chronologically throughout the edition,
a suitable guide will be available in volume XXX.

As in all other volumes in this edition, in general, Keynes's
own writings are printed in larger type. Keynes's own footnotes,

as well as those of his correspondents, are indicated by asterisks or other symbols to distinguish them from the editorial footnotes indicated either by numbers, or, in tables, by small italic letters. All introductory material and all writings by others than Keynes are printed in smaller type. The only exception to this general rule is that occasional brief quotations from Keynes in the introductory passages to clarify a situation are treated as similar introductory matter and are printed in smaller type.

Most of Keynes's letters included in this and other volumes are reprinted from the carbon or manuscript copies remaining in his papers. In most cases he has added his initials to the copy in the familiar fashion in which he signed to his friends. Except in those cases where we have obtained the top copy from the papers of friends or colleagues, we have no way of knowing whether the top copy sent to the recipient of the letter carried a more formal signature.

Chapter 1

KEYNES AS AN INVESTOR[1]

It is appropriate to approach Keynes's investment career by dividing it into the same two parts that prove useful in discussing many of his other activities —up to his resignation from the Treasury in June 1919, and afterwards.

In the earlier period, Keynes was operating on his own account on a modest scale and providing investment advice for his friends.[2] His dealing activities were limited and most of the increase in the value of his portfolio came from savings. After 1919, on the other hand, Keynes was operating in financial markets on a very much larger scale, both on his own account and on the account of others. For example, Keynes was a Bursar of King's College, Cambridge, Chairman of the National Mutual Life Assurance Society (1921–38), a director of the Provincial Insurance Company, a director of various investment trusts—the Independent Investment Company (1923–46), the A.D. Investment Trust (1921–7), the P.R. Finance Company (1924–36, Chairman 1932–6)—and an instigator of the Syndicate of 1920. During these years his income came to depend much more on his financial than his academic activities, as Table 1 indicates.

In what follows, I shall first concentrate on Keynes's activities as an individual investor over both periods, before looking more widely to the financial dealings which he undertook in collaboration with other, equally forceful personalities in the City, and on behalf of King's.

---

[1] In preparing this chapter, I have had the assistance of many people. In particular I should like to thank Professors S. K. Howson and W. B. Reddaway, Sir Anthony Burney, the late W. H. Haslam, A. G. A. Mackay, Ian Macpherson, Jack Peters and J. J. H. Wormell for helpful comments on an earlier draft. As well, Buckmaster and Moore provided some old Stock Exchange figures and J. Reisenstein and Wayne Lewchuck spent much time extracting material from Keynes's own records and those of King's. The Canada Council and the Social Sciences and Humanities Research Council of Canada provided research support.

[2] The exceptions to this generalisation are his dealings for a family trust after 1913, a speculation in U.S. Steel shares in 1913 with his own funds and those of J. T. Sheppard, and an arrangement made with Roger Fry on 3 April 1914, whereby Fry loaned Keynes £1,000, repayable at 6 months' notice on either side, at 4½ per cent per annum. Any profits or losses on the fund, after payment of the 4½ per cent, were to be shared equally. The arrangement ceased in January 1920, when Fry loaned the money to Duncan Grant for investment in the Syndicate.

Table 1. *Keynes's income (£) by tax years, 6 April 1908 to 5 April 1946*

Year	Income[a] Total	(of which academic[b])	Allowance from J. N. Keynes	Total
1908–9	200	115	180	380
1909–10	595	580	110	705
1910–11	595	575	135	730
1911–12	664	623	105	769
1912–13	815	726	95	910
1913–14	906	741	85	991
1914–15	992	702	80	1,072
1915–16	1,214	358	65	1,279
1916–17	1,303	248	55	1,358
1917–18	1,390	275	—	1,390
1918–19	1,802	324	—	1,802
1919–20	5,156	3,819	—	5,156
1920–1	3,935	3,324	—	3,935
1921–2	3,794	2,786	—	3,794
1922–3	5,929	4,950	—	5,929
1923–4	4,414	1,177	—	4,414
1924–5	5,963	1,403	—	5,963
1925–6	5,523	1,690	—	5,523
1926–7	6,648	1,636	—	6,648
1927–8	5,558	1,436	—	5,558
1928–9	3,764	1,498	—	3,764
1929–30	3,725	1,657	—	3,725
1930–1	4,502	1,406	—	4,502
1931–2	6,420	2,561	—	6,420
1932–3	5,447	3,296	—	5,447
1933–4	7,750	3,356	—	7,750
1934–5	6,528	2,229	—	6,528
1935–6	6,552	1,703	—	6,552
1936–7	15,194	1,248	—	15,194
1937–8	18,801	1,388	—	18,801
1938–9	6,192	1,337	—	6,192
1939–40	10,080	1,262	—	10,080
1940–1	11,774	1,127	—	11,774
1941–2	14,353	1,403	—	14,353
1942–3	12,657	1,117	—	12,657
1943–4	13,302	1,122	—	13,302
1944–5	14,392	971	—	14,392
1945–6	11,801	867	—	11,801

[a] The primary source is Keynes's own tax calculations in the Keynes papers, supplemented by other information in the papers so as to assign income to the year in which it actually accrued.

[b] Includes income from lectures, Fellowship, examining, the Royal Economic Society, books and articles and his position as a Bursar of King's College, Cambridge.

Sources

The basic source for what follows is Keynes's own papers. He kept in a series of notebooks records of all his investments (including a continuous series of valuations of his portfolio at market prices and cost on 31 December of each year from 1922–46), of dividends received, of sources of income and of commodity transactions. These records are supplemented by a full run of bank books, contract notes, brokers' correspondence and accounts. As well, there are various files of correspondence, balance sheets and memoranda, covering his involvement with the companies mentioned above. We also have the records of King's College, Cambridge, helpfully made available by permission of the Council.

I. *Personal Investments*

1905–1919

Keynes's career as an investor began with what he, in his records, referred to as his 'special fund' or 'special account'. This was the repository for his birthday money, various academic prizes and the like which J. N. Keynes had kept for his son. Keynes used the proceeds for loans to his friends (Bernard Swithinbank, Lytton Strachey, John Strachey, J. T. Sheppard, H. T. J. Norton and George Mallory), for furniture and for books on probability, but from July 1905 its major role was as the basis for his investments. At the time of his first transaction, the fund stood at just over £181.

Keynes's first purchase occurred on 6 July 1905 when he bought 4 shares in the Marine Insurance Company for £160 16s. 0d. His next came just under six months later when he bought 4 shares in the engineering firm Mather and Platt for £49 7s. 9d. He made no further investments until 1910. From the records that survive in the Keynes Papers, it would seem that this reflected the fact that he was living up to his income and saving no more than a few pounds a year. Once his income rose to a level that permitted larger savings, Keynes expanded his portfolio by buying shares in Horden Collieries and Eastern Bank in 1910. The next year saw his first switches in the market, while in 1913 he was involved in a brief speculation in shares of U.S. Steel which netted him £5 15s. Generally during this period Keynes's dealing activities were limited and purchases of additional securities were the order of the day. Table 2 provides a summary of Keynes's financial position at the end of each calendar year during the period.

Table 2. *Keynes's gross and net assets (£) 1905–19*

Year (31 Dec.)	Gross assets			Loans	Net assets
	Securities	(No.)	Other[a]		
1905	158	(1)	62	—	220
1906	203	(2)	53	—	256
1907	195	(2)	57	—	252
1908	197	(2)	120	—	317
1909	218	(2)	246	—	464
1910	539	(4)	66	—	605
1911	940	(6)	87	—	1,027
1912	1,463	(6)	23	—	1,486
1913	1,691	(5)	254	—	1,945
1914	4,617	(9)[b]	—	115[b]	4,502
1915	3,818	(9)[b]	—	69[b]	3,749
1916	4,598	(9)[b]	—	253[b]	4,345
1917	6,201	(11)[b]	10	—	6,211
1918	9,428	(5)[b]	—	1,964[b]	7,464
1919	14,453	(4)[b]	17,360[c]	15,498[b]	16,315

[a] Bank balance, when positive, plus remainder of special fund not invested in securities.
[b] Both these items exclude the Roger Fry arrangement referred to above.
[c] Includes book profits on speculations.

1919 and after

After his departure from the Treasury, Keynes became much more active in financial markets. In many of his activities,[3] both immediately after the War and for most of the next decade, Keynes was closely associated with O. T. Falk, a former colleague from A Division of the Treasury, who was a partner in Buckmaster and Moore, the London stockbrokers. At first, however, Keynes's activities were on his own account when he began his career as a speculator in August 1919.

Although he engaged in some speculation in shares, Keynes's activities were centred on the foreign exchange market. His strategy was straightforward: to sell short in the forward market the currencies of France, Italy, Holland and, after March 1920, Germany, and to go long in U.S. dollars, Norwegian and Danish krone and Indian rupees. Initially, he was quite successful, for by 2 January 1920 his realised profits amounted to £6,154. The result was an even larger scheme.

[3] The National Mutual, the Provincial, the Independent Investment Company, the A.D. Investment Trust, the P.R. Finance Company and the Syndicate.

4

The Syndicate was an arrangement whereby Keynes and O. T. Falk might use their own capital, plus that of their friends, to speculate successfully on the foreign exchanges. The scheme involved initially a capital of £30,000, half provided by Keynes and his friends and relations, half by a group around Falk. Keynes's group had three risk-taking principals: himself (using loans from J. N. Keynes, A. V. Hill, Walter Langdon Brown and Margaret Keynes), Geoffrey Keynes and Duncan Grant (using his own funds plus loans from Roger Fry, David Garnett, Vanessa Bell, Alix Sargent-Florence and his mother).[4]

The Syndicate began operations on 21 January 1920, going short in French francs and lire and long in rupees. In March the group closed out the lira position and went long in dollars. At the end of the month, the problems of dealing in such large sums in very thin markets[5] led Falk to suggest that his group leave the Syndicate, which they did, leaving only the Keynes group, which by this time was short in marks and French francs and long in dollars. There the Syndicate remained until mid-May when it went short in lire again as well.

Initially the Syndicate had been quite successful. By the end of April, the Keynes group's realised profits totalled almost £9,000 and book profits ran to almost £8,000. The group then ran into problems when European currencies strengthened against sterling, sterling rose against the dollar and the rupee fell against sterling in a context of wide daily swings in rates. The *dénouement* was rapid. On 14 May, the Syndicate had realised profits of £10,408, and book losses of £3,146. By 19 May the position was so bad that Falk warned Keynes that book losses exceeded realised profits, that the available cover was now under 10 per cent of the outstanding commitments and that it was necessary either to increase the available cover or close out some positions. Keynes's personal speculative position was similarly threatened. Keynes moved quickly to put the position in order[6] by closing out contracts, realising securities from his own portfolio, arranging with Macmillan for an advance payment of sums due on sales of *The Economic Consequences of the Peace* and borrowing £5,000 from Sir Ernest Cassel. When Keynes closed out the Syndicate's position, losses totalled £22,575; whilst on his own speculative account, which had been running since August 1919, gains

---

[4] Grant's position as a principal was ambiguous, as Keynes provided his brokers with a guarantee against Grant 'sustaining any loss' in respect of his funds.

[5] At the time, margin requirements were 10 per cent. Thus the fund could take up forward positions up to an amount equal to ten times their capital and realised capital gains.

[6] Buckmaster and Moore eased the position in the transition by not interpreting their rules quite strictly.

roughly equalled losses plus dealing expenses (the deficit came to £133 8s. 0d.). The Syndicate's closing position showed losses in every currency dealt in, but the largest losses proved to be in marks, lire and French francs.

On several occasions during the summer of 1920, Keynes took stock of his own position. The most complete—and most bleak—came on 1 August, after J. N. Keynes had written off £2,000 from his Syndicate loan of £5,000.

Assets	Liabilities	
Securities £19,000	Bank loan	£4,618
	Buckmaster and Moore	£3,619
	Sir Ernest Cassel	£5,000
	J. N. Keynes	£3,000
	A. V. Hill	£2,400
	W. Langdon Brown	£1,000
	M. E. Keynes	£1,200
		£20,837

To add to his deficiency, Keynes also had what he regarded as 'moral' debts to other participants in the Syndicate as follows:

Duncan Grant	£2,860
Geoffrey Keynes	£2,000
Basil Blackett	£400
Vanessa Bell	£1,490
	£6,750

In such circumstances, it was obvious that it would take Keynes some time to rebuild his position.

Some indication of his state of mind at the time, and his optimism, comes from the letter to Sir Ernest Cassel that resulted in the £5,000 loan mentioned above. At the top of it, Keynes noted 'This proposal meant a capital of £60,000. It would have won a profit of £50,000 by today. JMK. 4. 11. 20.'

To SIR ERNEST CASSEL, *26 May 1920*

Private

Dear Sir Ernest Cassel,

Some time ago you encouraged me to apply to you in the event of my having any financial venture in view, where I needed your assistance. The present demoralised condition of the foreign exchange market offers, in my judgement, an unequalled opportunity for speculation. At the time of writing, the quotations are about as follows

Marks	127
France	48
Lire	63

The quotations are rather nominal and bear no relation to real values. Speculators are being squeezed out everywhere and the prices quoted are absurd. I am practically certain that there is nothing brewing for the Brussels and Spa Conferences which justifies this position. Indeed the rumoured international loan is pure deception.

My proposal is, therefore, as follows—that you authorise me to *sell* marks, francs and lire *forward* on your behalf and to close the transactions at my discretion, subject to your overruling instructions at any time. I would keep you informed daily as to the position. I am well accustomed to this business and know the ropes. I suggest as amounts

Marks	5,000,000
Francs	5,000,000
Lire	3,000,000

or smaller or larger amounts as may commend itself [*sic*] to you. It would be necessary for you to put up (say) 20 per cent margin of the liability and to maintain 10 per cent intact.

The profits would be shared between us in such proportion as you may deem fair. I anticipate very substantial profits with very good probability if you are prepared to stand the racket for perhaps a couple of months.

I must add, what I should like to have been able to explain to you in person if you had been in London, that I am not in any position to risk any capital myself, for the reason that I was a bear of these currencies at higher values than now current and have, at present prices, quite exhausted my resources. But the prospects for anyone who comes in at the present low shake-out

7

level are very good. I am miserable at my own bad management in not being able to take advantage of the situation and hence apply to you at a moment when your aid would be of the greatest help to me.

I don't know if this is at all the kind of thing you had in mind when you spoke to me. But it is far the most promising opportunity which has occurred. I probably speak with about as much knowledge of the circumstances as anyone else has, and I am in a position to take the whole responsibility of the necessary operations. If you feel able to come in, I shall be immensely beholden to you.

As prompt action is desirable, I beg you to let me know immediately on receipt of this letter, either by telegram to 46 Gordon Square, London, W.C. or by telephone to Museum 3875.

If necessary I could come down to see you at Bournemouth tomorrow.

Sincerely yours,
[Copy initialled] J.M.K.

Keynes rebuilt his fortune in the same way he had lost it, through speculation. By the end of 1920 he had repaid Blackett and Sir Ernest Cassel. He repaid the rest during 1922, with the exception of Margaret Keynes who left her £1,200 with him until 1936. (In most cases other than Blackett's and Cassel's, those involved left the funds repaid under Keynes's indirect control, first in the A.D. Investment Trust and then the P.R. Finance Company, where they were to lose and regain their fortunes again in the years after 1927.[7] Thus by 31 December 1922, Keynes had cleared off his Syndicate debts and become a substantial investor with the net assets in excess of £21,000 recorded in Table 3. The bulk of the restoration, leaving aside reported savings of £10,336, came from speculation in currencies and commodities, with realised capital gains as follows between 1 August 1920 and 31 December 1922:

Exchange	£16,638
Cotton	£3,672
Metals	£2,113
Securities	£2,947

[7] See below pp. 31–2.

8

Thus from the end of 1922 onwards we are dealing with Keynes as a substantial investor.

The tables below set out Keynes's experience as an investor in several ways. Table 3 continues the earlier series for net assets down to 31 December 1945, whilst Table 4 presents a summary of Keynes's investment income from dividends, realised capital gains and speculation. (One should note, however, that from April 1926 Keynes hived off his speculative activities for tax reasons into the Tilton Company and that whilst the results of the speculations continue to appear in Table 4 only the net position of the company appears in the year-end valuations of Table 3 thereafter.) Finally Table 5 attempts to compare Keynes's experience as an investor in securities in London and New York with the behaviour of various stock market indices.

What can we say in a general way about Keynes's investment activities on his own account? The first thing that strikes one in Table 5 is that he was not uniformly successful as an investor. In the 1920s, for example, in five of the seven years between 1922 and 1929 Keynes did *worse* than the *Bankers' Magazine* index. On the other hand, in the years after 1929, his investments outperformed the market in 21 of 30 accounting years and did so cumulatively by a large margin.[8] As well, the figures indicate that he was much more likely to beat the market when it was rising. From the detailed records available, it is also clear that he was an extremely active investor. Within most of the years between 1923 and 1940, the value of the securities Keynes sold exceeded the market value of the securities he held at the beginning of the year. In most years as well until the outbreak of war in 1939, Keynes was also active in both the commodity and foreign exchange markets (when sterling was not on the gold standard). As a result of the volume of his transactions, snapshots of the state of his portfolio at particular dates are less illuminating than with a less active investor. Nevertheless a rough breakdown appears in Table 6. One must remember, though, that in addition to the problems of interpretation arising from the volume of dealing, indications of the numbers of securities held and their types are also rather unhelpful, for Keynes tended not to work in units of particular size. More often than not, especially after the late 1920s, the securities of a few firms would dominate Keynes's portfolio.[9] If we use as a criterion of concentration the number of firms whose securities at current

---

[8] Of course the amount of skill involved in outperforming Wall Street after 1939 owed little to Keynes's activities after that date, as most of his sales were to the authorities under Treasury vesting orders and any sales of his remaining American securities meant the repatriation of the dollar proceeds to London under the exchange control regulations then in force.

[9] For the reasoning behind Keynes's behaviour see below, pp. 57, 78, 82–3, 97–9, 107.

9

market prices accounted for half the portfolio, we get the following results for selected years:

Valuation of 31 December	£ securities	$ securities
1929	4	–
1931	2	–
1937	4	3
1945	3	1

Nor were such concentrations atypical, for individual holdings larger than 10 per cent of the value of the whole portfolio were common.

It was, perhaps, another reflection of Keynes's tendency to back his long-term judgement on a substantial scale when he had the resources to do so. The same tendency led him on occasion to take delivery of future contracts in the commodity market, despite the costs of storage, often with favourable results. This stubbornness led Keynes in 1936 to estimate the cubic capacity of King's College Chapel when he was about to take delivery of several loads of wheat on his account. According to Jack Peters, then a clerk in the King's Bursary, Keynes was most annoyed that it was too small! Macpherson's memory of the incident runs as follows.

'I can add to the wheat story. As K's position recovered and the firm was able to create a proper system for watching and regulating margin accounts I put a young executive, Mark Clayton, on to looking after and handling K's business personally and one Monday morning he came into my room saying "I was playing golf in Sandwich at the week-end and saw all those ships going round to enter the Thames". On my asking what on earth he was talking about he said "Did you not know K in one form or another has acquired about one month's supply of wheat for the whole of this country?", which he should never have been allowed to do without the partnership being informed. From the firm's point of view this was a very grave matter because this particular commodity deal which started as a hedge in Chicago and ended up in Buenos Aires had been done through us and at that time it was not clear that members of the Stock Exchange in London were allowed by the Council to deal in commodities without a full disclosure. While I was wondering how to handle the matter, K walked into my room saying he thought I might want to see him, which I did, that he had measured up King's College Chapel during the weekend and could take half of the wheat and what could we do about the other half. After some protest from myself he explained that as each cargo came in he proposed to object to its quality and was assured that such cargoes from the Argentine would have to go to

Table 3. *Keynes's gross and net assets (£) 1919, 1920 (August), 1922–1946*

Year (31 Dec.)	Gross assets			Loans	Net assets
	Securities	(No.)	Other[a]		
1919	14,453	(4)	17,360	15,498	16,315
1920 (1 Aug.)	19,000	(4)	—	20,837	−1,837[b]
1922	14,288	(7)	10,050	2,720	21,558
1923	26,839	(12)	8,725	1,200	34,364
1924	56,976	(18)	8,021	1,200	63,797
1925	26,507	(19)	18,303	1,200	43,610
1926	27,550	(22)	15,450	2,200	40,800
1927	78,500	(21)	12,400	46,900	44,000
1928	35,480	(20)	3,370	25,790	13,060
1929	18,165	(20)	3,650	14,000	7,815
1930	20,565	(19)	56,960	65,000	12,525
1931	19,488	(17)	7,575	11,965	15,100
1932	23,994	(19)	17,552	19,774	21,722
1933	78,925	(21)	55,156	78,859	55,222
1934	299,363	(75)	11,987	165,343	146,007
1935	377,450	(79)	31,440	188,271	220,619
1936	692,059	(87)	113,950	299,347	506,522
1937	346,697	(80)	58,582	190,035	215,244
1938	250,285	(70)	37,732	106,470	181,547
1939	267,605	(62)	41,026	109,136	199,495
1940	188,353	(56)	43,392	60,655	171,090
1941	193,992	(49)	40,042	28,753	205,281
1942	243,057	(45)	30,736	19,720	254,073
1943	308,058	(49)	36,956	31,643	313,371
1944	365,864	(44)	35,613	46,167	355,310
1945	436,194	(39)	13,930	38,886	411,238

[a] Includes book profits on speculations, net assets of the Tilton Company, personal loans, cash, farm capital, Arts Theatre (Cambridge), insurance policies, leases, etc.
[b] Excludes the 'moral' debts resulting from the Syndicate of £6,750.

be cleaned and that the available machinery could only handle one cargo for some period of days at a time because the great millers, Ranks, Spillers and the Cooperative normally cleaned their own cargoes. The method of judging a cargo at that time was to spread out a cubic foot of wheat on the floor and count the weevils which had to be under some figure such as 30. As usual K was absolutely right in his opinion: every cargo had to be cleaned; it took over a month to clear the position; I understood at the time with no loss or profit to him. I myself had a hair-raising experience on the same Monday because one of my friends was Managing Director of Spillers with whom I

Table 4. *Keynes's investment income by source 1920–45*

Year	Sterling dividends (gross) (£)	Dollar dividends (gross) ($)	Sterling capital gains (£)	Dollar capital gains ($)	Currency speculation (£)	Commodity speculation (£)	Misc. speculation[a] (£)	Other[b] (£)
1920	815	—	−602	—	−10,632	—	—	—
1921	885	—	−1,638	—	9,677	2,155	—	—
1922	346	—	−1,180	—	3,335	6,729	13	—
1923	654	—	3,618	594	4,946	13,702	299	65
1924	1,581	—	1,038	—	4,817	15,245	610	103
1925	2,649	250	−356	—	−335	−5,627	−2,298	142
1926	1,804	400	−3,333	—	419	6,570	—	124
1927	2,119	500	850	—	188	10,525	—	146
1928	2,791	100	4,325	3,250	—	−23,267	—	252
1929	1,517	—	3,440	—	—	−70	—	78
1930	2,190	—	−973	—	—	−3,009	—	48
1931	2,470	—	1,583	—	—	1,550	—	35
1932	1,078	—[c]	−4,044	−443	—	404	—	20
1933	1,805	—[c]	33	11,142	83	2,364	—	25
1934	3,056	8,251	20,559	−799	−466	8,820	—	151
1935	6,191	11,039	22,404	5,600	−2,092	−4,304	682	204
1936	11,795	19,217	30,169	92,432	12,362	36,009	407	373
1937	17,353	37,884	54,884	234,097	1,056	−8,141	−2,299	546
1938	5,961	13,997	−18,572	−140,819	−1,844	−3,612	−315	504
1939	3,209	5,555	−3,548	30,900	−1,668	−3,138	−554	544
1940	8,189	8,241	1,005	3,517	—	—	—	797
1941	12,729	1,527	−58	−62,923	—	—	—	748
1942	11,074	1,112	11,432	—	—	—	—	978
1943	8,657	879	7,925	12,183	—	—	—	863
1944	11,402	548	−838	—	—	—	—	1,152
1945	5,156	2,277	9,052	56,766	—	—	—	863
Total			£137,175	$245,497	£19,846	£52,905	−£3,455	

[a] Options, stags, etc.
[b] Income, etc., on unlisted securities.
[c] Some small dollar dividends in sterling.

was lunching that day who spent the whole time saying that he was short of wheat and some infernal speculator had got hold of most of the next month's supply. All I could reply was that I was a stockbroker and not a corn merchant.'

Finally, Keynes normally carried a substantial portion of his portfolio on borrowed money—frequently more than half. This combination of longer-

Table 5. *Keynes's stock market experience in London and New York 1922–45*

	London (£000)							New York ($000)						
	Index[a]	Net cost[b]	Market value	Change in market value	New[c] funds	Index change[d]	Residual[e]	Index[f]	Net cost	Market value	Change in market value	New funds	Index change	Residual
1922	117·6	13·5	14·3	—	—	—	—	—	—	—	—	—	—	—
1923	115·9	27·5	26·8	+12·5	+14·0	-0·2	-1·7	—	—	—	—	—	—	—
1924	126·9	50·3	57·0	+30·2	+22·8	+2·5	+4·9	—	—	—	—	—	—	—
1925	132·5	29·1	26·5	-30·5	-21·2	+2·5	-11·8	—	—	—	—	—	—	—
1926	135·7	30·9	27·5	+1·0	+1·8	+0·6	-1·4	—	—	—	—	—	—	—
1927	146·9	81·8	78·5	+51·0	+50·9	+2·3	-2·2	—	—	—	—	—	—	—
1928	158·8	45·3	35·5	-43·0	-36·5	+6·4	+0·1	—	—	—	—	—	—	—
1929	147·1	34·0	18·2	-17·3	-11·3	-3·3	-2·7	—	—	—	—	—	—	—
1930	118·5	28·8	26·6	+8·4	-5·2	-3·6	+17·2	—	—	—	—	—	—	—
1931	90·7	30·6	19·5	-7·1	+1·8	-6·2	-2·7	58	3·4	3·4	—	—	—	—
1932	95·8	31·0	18·3	-1·2	+0·4	+1·1	-2·7	49	13·3	19·3	+15·9	+9·9	-0·5	+6·5
1933	108·4	61·5	70·5	+52·2	+30·5	+2·4	+19·3	73	8·9	35·0	+15·7	-4·4	+9·5	+10·6
1934	113·5	151·8	249·3	+178·8	+90·3	+3·3	+85·2	72	223·9	247·5	+212·5	+215·0	-0·5	-3·0
1935	120·1	72·3	222·6	-26·7	-79·5	+14·5	+38·3	103	442·6	774·3	+526·8	+218·7	+106·7	+201·4
1936	137·7	119·7	415·2	+192·6	+47·4	+32·7	+112·5	131	676·8	1,359·5	+585·2	+234·2	+209·8	+141·2
1937	115·5	-45·8	199·2	-216·0	-165·5	-66·8	+16·3	82	334·5	626·5	-733·0	-342·3	-508·5	+117·8
1938	104·4	-75·5	118·9	-80·3	-29·7	-19·3	-31·3	98	362·4	533·6	-92·9	+27·9	+12·9	-133·7
1939	100·8	-12·3	180·5	+61·6	+63·2	-4·0	+2·4	96	79·6	236·6	-297·0	-282·8	-10·7	-3·5
1940	93·5	-47·2	117·8	-62·7	-34·9	-13·0	-14·8	85	23·5	189·1	-47·5	-56·1	-27·2	+35·8
1941	99·6	-44·0	151·8	+34·0	+3·2	+7·7	+23·1	71	-28·7	64·7	-124·4	-52·2	-31·2	-41·0
1942	106·6	-55·5	189·6	+37·8	+11·5	+10·6	+38·7	77	-29·4	68·5	+3·8	-0·7	+5·5	-1·0
1943	113·5	-65·9	232·3	+42·7	-10·4	+12·3	+40·8	93	-63·6	129·6	+61·1	-34·2	+14·2	+81·1
1944	119·9	-42·3	274·2	+41·9	+23·6	+13·1	+5·2	104	-64·0	171·2	+41·6	-0·4	+15·4	+26·6
1945	125·4	-33·8	330·7	+56·5	-8·5	+12·6	+52·4	140	-225·4	201·5	+30·3	-161·4	+59·2	+132·5

[a] *Bankers' Magazine* for shares.　　[b] Cost of securities less realised capital gains.　　[c] Change in net cost from previous year.

[d] Change in value if the value of securities held at the end of the previous year had moved with the relevant index.

[e] Residual = Change in Market Value − (New Funds + Index Change).　　[f] *Federal Reserve Bulletin* (Standard Statistics) for shares.

Table 6. *The distribution of Keynes's security portfolio 1920–45 (at market prices)*

	% distribution of total							% distribution of quoted securities				
Year[a]	Sterling ordinary shares	Sterling pref. shares	Sterling bonds	Dollar ordinary shares	Dollar pref. shares	Dollar bonds	Unlisted[b] sterling securities	Sterling securities	Dollar securities	Ordinary shares	Pref. shares	Bonds
1920	94·9	—	5·1	—	—	—	—	100	—	94·9	—	5·1
1921	80·8	—	11·2	—	—	—	8	100	—	81·8	—	12·2
1922	62·0	—	16·0	—	—	—	22	100	—	79·5	—	20·5
1923	82·7	10·3	—	—	—	—	7	100	—	88·9	11·1	—
1924	91·7	3·0	—	—	—	—	5·3	100	—	96·8	3·2	—
1925	85·5	0·9	—	—	3·2	—	10·4	96·4	3·6	95·4	4·6	—
1926	81·7	—	—	—	4·8	—	13·5	94·4	5·5	94·5	5·5	24·2
1927	71·5	—	23·5	—	2·0	—	2·9	97·8	2·2	73·7	2·1	1·2
1928	75·4	15·8	1·1	—	—	—	7·7	100	—	81·7	17·1	5·3
1929	80·4	2·2	4·6	—	—	—	12·8	100	—	92·2	2·5	1·9
1930	90·0	—	1·8	—	—	—	7·3	100	—	98·1	—	4·4
1931	77·1	4·6	3·8	—	—	—	14·5	100	—	90·2	5·4	55·3
1932	29·5	1·2	51·2	10·4	0·3	—	7·4	88·4	11·6	43·1	1·6	11·5
1933	66·7	4·0	10·4	5·9	3·6	0·2	9·4	89·5	10·5	80·1	8·4	18·6
1934	48·9	3·2	16·6	11·9	9·5	0·2	9·7	76·1	23·9	67·3	14·1	1·9
1935	48·7	5·4	1·6	16·8	18·7	—	8·6	60·9	39·1	71·7	26·4	21·2
1936	35·7	2·2	20·3	16·8	21·0	0·1	3·9	60·6	39·4	54·6	29·2	3·6
1937	47·5	1·7	3·5	26·6	16·4	n[c]	4·1	55·0	45·0	77·3	18·9	5·4
1938	40·8	5·6	3·6	19·9	20·0	1·3	8·7	54·8	45·2	66·6	28·0	22·1
1939	24·8	15·9	20·2	19·6	11·1	0·1	8·2	66·3	32·7	48·4	29·4	6·6
1940	29·5	22·3	5·6	14·8	15·1	0·2	12·5	65·6	34·4	50·6	42·7	7·9
1941	37·5	33·6	6·5	4·8	3·5	0·3	13·7	89·5	11·1	49·0	43·0	0·2
1942	52·1	26·2	n	3·4	2·0	—	16·3	93·5	6·5	66·3	33·7	0·2
1943	51·3	21·3	0·1	6·5	5·3	—	15·4	85·9	14·1	68·3	31·4	—
1944	58·2	16·9	0·1	5·5	5·3	—	13·9	87·3	12·7	74·0	25·8	
1945	65·6	12·2	—	7·6	0·8	—	13·8	90·3	9·7	84·9	15·1	

[a] At 31 August for all years except 1931 (1 November) and 1939 (31 October).
[b] Includes P.R. Finance Company, Provincial Insurance Company, A.D. Investment Trust, etc.
[c] n = less than 0·1%.

term concentrated holdings, large loans and considerable short-term speculative activity could bring problems. On all of the occasions when Keynes
suffered a substantial diminution in his net worth, these factors played an
important role. This role will become clearer as we examine Keynes's
experience in two periods, 1928–31 and 1937–8.

(a) 1928–1931

The collapse in security prices in London following September 1929 after
they had rested on a plateau for almost 18 months came at the end of a period
of difficulties for Keynes. By then his net assets were under a quarter of
what they had been two years earlier.

The origins of Keynes's difficulties lay in the commodity markets. By the
end of 1927 he had been dealing in commodities for more than six years.
From April 1926 for tax reasons, Keynes channelled all his commodity and
exchange transactions through the Tilton Company. In its first financial
year, which lasted until 31 December 1927, it continued Keynes's earlier
successes in the market, realising profits of over £16,000. It was, in fact, in
a position to lend Keynes £7,500 for his other financial activities at the end
of 1927.

The following year was to prove more difficult for the Tilton Company.
Its profits became losses and its loan of £7,500 to Keynes became a loan of
£15,000 from Keynes. Over the year realised losses came to over £23,000,
of which £15,185 arose in rubber. There were also large losses in corn,
cotton and tin. However, rubber played the most important role.

The large losses on rubber were associated with the ending of the Stevenson Rubber Restriction Scheme, organised in 1922 and covering Ceylon,
Malaya and the Straits Settlements, but not the Dutch East Indies. At the
end of 1927, Keynes had seven forward purchase contracts for a total of 177
tons maturing between April and December 1928, 12 tons maturing in 1929
and 12 tons maturing in 1930—all entered into at prices ranging from 1s. 8¼d.
to 2s. 6d. per pound. During the three months from 1 November 1927 to
31 January 1928, the spot price of rubber had averaged just over 1s. 7d. per
pound with forward prices slightly higher. However, prices drifted slightly
lower during January and spot rubber stood at 1s. 6½d. per pound early
in February.[10] Then on 9 February, the Prime Minister, Mr Baldwin,
announced in the House of Commons that he had asked the Committee of
Civil Research to look into the working of the export restriction scheme. This
immediately took 1½d. off the spot price and affected futures prices. During

---

[10] Prices had been lower in the course of 1927, averaging 1s. 4·6d. in the quarter 1 August
to 31 October.

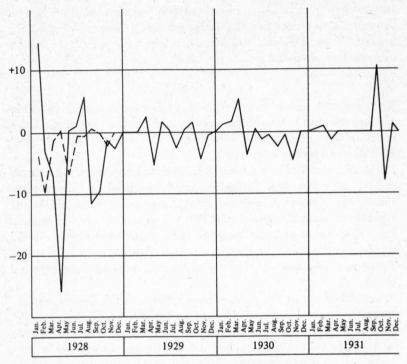

Figure 1. Net transactions in securities, monthly, 1928–1931, and net income from commodities, monthly, 1928 (£000). Securities, ———; commodities, – – –.

the Committee's deliberations, prices eased further to stand at just over 1s. per pound spot on 4 April, when the Government announced that having received the Committee's report it would end restrictions on 31 October 1928. Prices immediately fell further and spot prices averaged 8½d. to 9½d. per pound during the rest of the year.

The development of Keynes's realised losses in commodities in 1928 is set out in Figure 1. With these losses came the need for further loans to continue his operations at a time when he was, himself, carrying much of his security portfolio on borrowed money. Thus he began to lighten his position in March. However, matters became even more difficult in April when his brokers asked for a 20 per cent margin on his commodity position rather than the previous 10 per cent. Just over a month later they asked for more cover on his loan against securities. As a result of these pressures, Keynes made large sales of securities, as is clear from Figure 1. Again in August his cover

16

became inadequate, and he made further large sales. These continued throughout the autumn. In fact, from the beginning of April to the end of the year his net sales of securities amounted to almost £45,000.

Although Keynes's problems with commodities were less serious during 1929, his loan position and his need for cover often left him worried, his heaviest net sales coming in months when his cover was inadequate. Only at the end of the year did he sell heavily on a falling market, and he realised substantial capital gains over the year as a whole. His sales left a rather unbalanced portfolio, dominated by his large holding of shares in the Austin Motor Car Company, whose fall from 21s. to 12s. during 1928 and to 5s. in 1929, markedly affected his overall investment results, as he held 10,000 shares by January 1928. (On the other hand, their recovery in 1930 to 35s. in April, when Keynes sold 2,000 shares, and to 28s. 3d. by the end of the year, had the opposite effect.)[11]

When the market recovered during the first months of 1930, Keynes returned as a net buyer on a small scale, but after April he was again a seller. From 13 October 1930 his dealing activities virtually ceased: the sum of all his transactions between that date and 23 September 1931 came to just £2,676. Probably the best reasons for his lack of activity appeared in a short memorandum he prepared for the Board of the National Mutual in February 1931.

Memorandum for the Board of the National Mutual, 18 February 1931

In response to a request to me from Mr Marks[12] to write for the Board a short memorandum of my general views, I offer the following:

(1) There is a great deal of fear psychology about just now. Prices bear very little relationship to ultimate values or even to reasonable forecasts of ultimate values. They are determined by indefinite anxieties, chance market conditions, and whether some urgent selling comes on a market bare of buyers. Just as many people were quite willing in the boom, not only to value shares on the basis of a single year's earnings, but to assume that

---

[11] Keynes's concentration on Austin shares meant that in May 1931 this holding amounted to 47·5 per cent of his security portfolio. If one added his holding of Leyland Motors to his Austins, almost two-thirds of his securities portfolio was in two shares and in one industry! It certainly worried his brokers.

[12] The National Mutual's actuary.

ARTICLES AND CORRESPONDENCE

increases in earnings would continue geometrically, so now they
are ready to estimate capital values on today's earnings and to
assume that decreases will continue geometrically.

(2) In the midst of one of the greatest slumps in history, it
would be absurd to say that fears and anxieties are baseless. As
I have constantly said, I consider the prospects of 1931 to be
extremely bad. It is indeed only too easy to feel frightened, and
to find plausible reasons for one's fears.

(3) But I do not draw from this the conclusion that a responsible investing body should every week cast panic glances
over its list of securities to find one more victim to fling to the
bears. Both interest and duty point the other way. I do not
consider it impossible that there may be in the ensuing weeks
something which might be called a flight or semi-flight from
sterling, or a flight from British Government securities. But I do
not think it will last, even if it occurs. Nor do I think that we are
called on to lead the way towards flight. If insurance companies
and investment trusts generally were to adopt this policy, it
would necessarily in a sense justify itself—in the sense that those
who both got out first and got back first would make money. But
the repercussions would not be advantageous to any of us. It is
much better and wiser to stand reasonably firm.

(4) Moreover, the situation is quite capable of turning round
at any time with extreme suddenness. Our fundamental position
remains extraordinarily strong. The introduction of a tariff, a
change of Government, and all sorts of things quite unpredictable in advance will suddenly cause people to turn right round,
to appreciate how very cheap almost everything is, and to discover that the market is completely sold out.

(5) I believe, therefore, that we should do well to make no
more sales of securities except for very special reasons. I feel this
with much more confidence because we have so thoroughly overhauled our list of late. Subsequent falls in price are an increased
reason for *not* selling, and not the opposite. Our list is well
chosen on the whole.

(6) This does not mean that I should not reconsider a good many things in the event of a substantial recovery. If the market were to turn round violently for political reasons, or if Wall Street were to carry to any length one of its usual spring booms, so that there were buyers about at decidedly higher prices than at present, then I should like to go through our list again. But meanwhile 'Be Quiet' is our best motto.

18 February 1931   J.M.K.

(b) 1937–1938

These two years are of considerable interest as far as Keynes is concerned. We have not only our usual records of his transactions but also a more complete series of statements of his views on the evolving situation than at any other time. This wealth of statements of view was a result of his illness, which kept him both from King's and from meetings of his insurance companies, most importantly the Provincial, and obliged him to set his views down on paper.

At the end of 1936, Keynes could look back on a run of extremely successful years. His net assets had risen by over £450,000 over the previous three years. His speculations in currencies and commodities during the previous twelve months had brought capital gains of over £48,000. At the turn of 1937, he was heavily involved in both Wall Street and Throgmorton Street, carrying much of his portfolio on credit as his loans came to almost £300,000. During the next two years, the value of his net assets was to fall by almost two-thirds and he was to suffer large losses on commodities and currencies.

At the end of 1936, Keynes was reasonably optimistic about the future, as he told F. C. Scott, the managing director of the Provincial on 3 December.

From a letter to F. C. SCOTT, *3 December 1936*

My feeling is that nothing can really stop improvement in America in the coming months, though, so far as we can see now, it will be prudent to revise one's investments very considerably before the end of the year.

If such a substantial recovery in America duly comes to pass, I think that this should outweigh all other influences in sustaining the situation elsewhere. This will be the case particularly if, as seems to me not unlikely, a further recovery in America should bring about a more definite upturn in the prices of commodities than has occurred hitherto. I am a little sceptical of Great Britain moving further forward on her own initiative, assuming, of course, that existing policies are substantially unchanged. But strong commodity prices based on the improving position in America should certainly hold the position.

As regards immediate policy as to American holdings, I am beginning to think that the preferred stocks and bonds, which we have held successfully up to date, might be sold fairly soon and that a portion of the proceeds might be reinvested (or even invested a little in advance of the sales of the others) in more marginal securities such as the common stocks of the investment trusts. We already have a fair, though not a very large, holding of the latter, and when the markets turn downwards they are a hopeless market and, being marginal stocks, are necessarily somewhat speculative. How would you feel about the above policy in the light of this? My feeling is that we ought to try to participate in the American position at least another six months, but that, if we could do it with less capital engaged there by moving into more marginal stocks, this might be a sensible thing to do.

To summarise Keynes's activities during the months that followed, I have set out in Figure 2 a record of his net month-to-month transactions in sterling and dollar securities and the realised results of his commodity transactions. These indicate that during the first months of 1937 Keynes moved more heavily into America and enjoyed substantial gains from commodities, although by early May he seems to have decided to lighten his position slightly. At this point came his heart attack, which kept him out of action for over a month but from the second half of June he resumed his activities as an investor on a limited scale.

At this stage Keynes's commodity transactions showed signs of problems with a small monthly loss of £2,962. However, the book position was perhaps more worrying, for by 25 June the weekly return for the Tilton Company

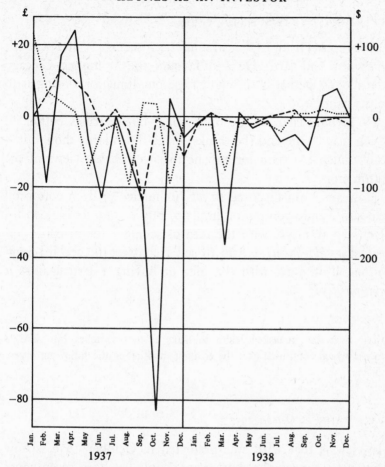

Figure 2. Net transactions in securities and net income from commodities, monthly, 1937–1938. £ securities (£ooo), ——; commodities (£ooo), – – –; $ securities ($ooo), · · · · ·.

showed book losses of £11,134 gross (£10,353 net) the bulk of which were on lard and cotton oil for which it held forward purchases for 3,400,000 and 2,400,000 lbs respectively. King's was also heavily involved in the same commodities as well. At this point, however, Keynes was not worried. As he told Richard Kahn, Second Bursar at King's,[13] on 30 June

[13] Kahn soon became a director of the Tilton Company as well.

From a letter to R. F. KAHN, *30 June 1937*

I have reports from Lydia, who has been seeing [Walter] Case,[14] on wheat and lard. He still favours the Winnipeg–Chicago straddle; so perhaps we might raise our limit for closing it to 20 pts gain.

He favours lard for the time being, but distrusts cotton oil which may in the end (he thinks) bring down lard; though it is really much too soon for anyone to have reliable views of the cotton crop.

However I am disposed to *job* (unhurriedly) from cotton oil into lard. Could you put on limits to buy 1 contract [50,000 lb] Decr lard at 11.75, with the idea of selling 1 (or 2) cotton oil against it *subsequently*? And to sell 1 contract [60,000 lb] Septr cotton oil at 9.25, with the idea of buying 1 lard against it *subsequently*?

The next day he asked Kahn to make further switches into lard, a process which continued over the ensuing months, as the following letters indicate.

To R. F. KAHN, *26 October 1937*[15]

My view is that what was predicted in October 1936 is now happening, though the shortage of supply has been accentuated by the fact that lard is so cheap relatively to other pig products that as little as possible of the animal is being converted into that form, so that the present output of lard from a given hog is much below normal. At the same time the price relatively to substitutes is not high enough to lead to much substitution. Consumption now appears to be running at a fully normal figure, and is about twice production.

If Piero [Sraffa] had ever seen a pig, he would know that the

---

[14] *JMK*, vol. X, pp. 324–5.
[15] Kahn's comments appear as footnotes.

live animal cannot be kept in cold storage waiting till its food stuffs are cheaper. It is marketed at about 8 months old, and none of the pigs now coming into the market could have been held over to be finished on cheaper maize.[16] All that could happen is that the light hogs, which would otherwise have been marketed at the end of September, at 6 months, might be kept on for another 2 months.[17] But the price of light hogs[18] is very satis-factory, as distinct from the price of lard, so that there is no great motive to do this.

On the other hand, I should have thought that Piero's argu-ment would be plausible in the case of pigs which are now very young, so that there would be a more abundant supply by next May. Yet the market does not seem to take this view, May lard being at a contango instead of at a material backwardation, as one would have expected.[19]

J. M. K.

lb

	Consumption & exports	Production	Reduction of stocks
August	73,000,000	35,000,000	38,000,000
September	91,000,000*	45,000,000+	46,000,000

* My estimates on consumption looks too high to be possible. Hog slaughter has only fallen 20 per cent, but lard per hog has fallen 25 per cent, so that lard output has fallen 40 per cent, whilst consumption and exports has increased.

From PIERO SRAFFA *to* R. F. KAHN [*October 1937*]

In October 1936 the argument for buying was that the stocks were rising so fast, that all the young pigs and sows must have been slaughtered, and there would be none left to produce lard in the spring. At present, every lb of lard

[16] 'But the pigs which are not coming onto the market might have.'
[17] 'Exactly—that is the point.'
[18] 'Dead or alive?'
[19] 'Why not sell May and buy January?'

that fails to go into stock will be fattened into two or ten lbs. which will come on the market in a few months. The less lard there is in stock, the more (with a multiplier) there is under the skin of pigs.

P.S.

From R. F. KAHN, *29 October 1937*

JMK

What Piero means is that the reason why stocks are running low is because half-grown pigs, which were born on the expectation of cheap maize coming to their rescue, are now being held off the market as a result of the cheap maize.

R.F.K.

Keynes persisted in his view. His losses continued, by the end of 1937 totalling £27,210 on lard. He also lost over £17,000 on cotton oil.[20]

As for his securities position, Keynes remained relatively inactive. As he told Richard Kahn on 17 July:

I am not keen to sell at the moment, though I hope the chance of diminishing a bit in America will occur some day. (If only like the gents on Wall Street one could take profits on a falling market! That must be the explanation why they are so rich.)

By late August he was much more pessimistic. Initially, on 20 August, he put his change of view down to 'acidosis', but his pessimism continued as he had 'less confidence in a substantial autumn recovery'. By 26 August he was definitely in 'a liquidating mood'. As he told Kahn on 2 September:

For several years I have always felt during a recession that it was worth hanging on, and, provided one's cover position was all right, all one had to do was to wait; so that if I felt the cover position was quite safe, I didn't bother. But today I don't feel like that. I don't want to have a big loan, even though the cover

[20] There were also substantial losses for the College (below, p. 90).

position is perfectly good. I've not got to the point of being a bear, but I am *much* more disinclined to be a bull on borrowed money. And to bring loans down sufficiently is necessarily a tedious and difficult process. On the other hand, yesterday's prices in U.S.A. seem quite unnecessarily low.

Two days later Keynes set his views out in more detail in a letter to Francis Scott from Ruthin, where he was still convalescing.

To F. C. SCOTT, *4 September 1937*

My dear Scott,

If all goes well, I shall leave here in the last week of the month, and shall be hopeful of being able to attend a Board meeting towards the end of October. It would be better if it were on a Thursday than a Wednesday, so as not to overlap with the National Mutual.

Meanwhile, since there has been some significant change in my angle of view, I might perhaps try and summarise what I now feel.

I am not expecting a significant recession of trade and employment. In the United States I still think that some recovery in the autumn or next spring is more likely than not. If the persisting lack of momentum, both here and in the U.S.A., leads to a certain recession, I should not at all expect it to develop into a slump, certainly not in the U.S.A., and the recession would probably appear to the future historian as merely an incident in the upward movement. In this sense, my pessimism does not go particularly deep for the time being.

On the other hand, in spite of the above, I am much less optimistic of the markets than I was. I feel that they will require, not merely reasonably good trade, but continual fresh stimulus, if they are to go higher; and they would be very sensitive to a

25

recession, even if it were only of the character suggested above. I think that for some time to come what in another context I have called liquidity preference will rule very strong. Almost all holders of speculative and semi-speculative securities believe that there will be another slump sooner or later, during which their holdings will not keep their present prices. Since the recovery has now lasted a good long time, they are almost hysterically anxious in the matter. The international situation also preys on their minds, naturally enough; and in the U.S.A. the political possibilities, rightly or wrongly, tend to undermine confidence. Thus, I think it would take a very material change in the situation to carry markets any great distance upwards. There will be, too, many people who will look for recovery as the longed-for opportunity to get out. On the other hand, sinking spells, for good reason or for bad, may quite likely be recurrent phenomena. Thus, even though trade really is quite respectably good, speculative and semi-speculative markets have more to fear than to hope.

Anyone who is banking on getting liquid during a higher level of market boom than we have yet experienced is assuming that the market is more liable to an error of optimism than an error of pessimism. My feeling is that, for some little time, the errors the market will make will be definitely of pessimism and that prices will be often lower than the underlying situation really warrants rather than higher.

To give a numerical illustration, one would usually expect that a thoroughly sound base metal share would, at some time during the recovery, rise to a price at which its current earnings did not represent more than 6 or 7 per cent. I doubt if that will occur this time. It may well be that they will still yield 8 or 9 per cent on current prices at the peak of their prosperity; or even 10 or 11 per cent.

The qualifications which I make are two:—

1. I still feel that the prospects in relation to current prices are much more hopeful in the U.S.A. than they are here. The

sinking spells may be worse, but the recoveries may also be more marked. It would certainly be surprising if there is not some moment before next April at which the market is not a good deal better than it is today.

2. I feel moderately happy about gold shares. It seems to me unthinkable that the price of gold can be lowered in the present atmosphere. The change could only occur in the event of a boom and of a soaring tendency of commodity prices. For their present yield I think they remain an excellent way to insure against pessimism in other directions.

Perhaps I should add a further influence, which should surely be favourable in the long run, namely, the relative abundance of gold. But my feeling now is that influence is likely to be deferred. My expectation is that there will be some significant recession, though not a violent one, before the abundance of gold is allowed to produce its proper effect. If, in the next two years, there is some moderate recession of activity, I should expect that some of the gold now sterilised would be set free, and efforts be made to reduce the rate of interest. It is, therefore, on the next journey, and not on this one, that I should expect the abundance of gold to have its effect on price levels. Quite likely it will be just this abundance of gold which will prevent the next recession from developing into a slump. This is a further reason why I expect more violent fluctuations in market prices than in trade and employment.

How rightly to govern one's current investment policy in the light of the above is another matter.

Yours sincerely,
[copy not initialled or signed]

To lighten his position Keynes proceeded to do as Figure 2 indicates, although on occasion, when particular Americans looked cheap, he re-entered the market to a limited extent—as 'a very dubious bargain hunter' as he told Richard Kahn on 9 September. He may have been relieved to have sold so much, since at the end of September, Buckmaster and Moore asked for an increase in cover on their loan to Keynes. Initially the terms had been 30 per cent on the first £100,000 and a minimum of 50 per cent on the excess, but they now asked for 50 per cent on the entire loan position from 1 April 1938.[21] Such excess cover requirements, combined with the behaviour of share prices, made Keynes a more willing seller, but by mid-November he was more sanguine. As he told G. H. Recknell of the National Mutual on 16 November:

Of course the right time to sell was in the spring, but that was *very* difficult to detect. By August it was fairly easy to see the bearish factors, and it was still not too late to sell. But since October that opportunity has passed. And at today's prices I do not see much to be afraid of.

Or at least he did not see anything for the moment. He soon became some-what uncertain again. As he told Richard Kahn on 16 January 1938:

In practice I find myself torn between hanging on for a rise in the near future, a fair amount of confidence about the ultimate prospects, and a considerable amount of doubt and hesitation about the intermediate prospects. If only Wall Street would continue for another week or two as heretofore,[22] you will, I hope, find me liquidating on a fair scale.

With further declines in the market and the prospect of the new cover requirements coming into operation, Keynes explained the position to Richard Kahn on 29 March:

The last week or so has been a time of considerable anxiety, for I still have a huge American position and the valuations at bid prices for some of the shares bring out grotesque values. The

---

[21] This was later postponed, given the state of markets to 1 May 1938. The cover require-ments were also altered after discussion to 60 per cent on the upward journey (40 per cent on the downward) on the first £100,000 and 100 per cent (50 per cent on the down-ward) above that. However, Buckmaster and Moore gave Keynes some leeway as to the beginning of the arrangement.

[22] Prices had recovered during the first two weeks of the month.

problem has been whether to sell hard or to use the iron ration of unused liquid resources which I had vowed to keep intact. In the main I sold (some £40,000 to £50,000 in securities in the last fortnight which took some selling in these markets) and still have the greater part of my private reserves still in hand and not with the brokers.

None too good for health with continuous anxious work on the telephone, but I've got through pretty well considering.

By then the worst was over in Wall Street, although London remained nervous for some months to come. Moreover, Keynes became more sanguine.

To R. F. KAHN, *13 May 1938*

R.F.K.

If I sell Americans at this juncture, what am I aiming at?—
(1) buying back at a substantial profit
(2) buying back at a loss when the bull market is more clearly established
(3) not buying back at all
(4) helping the brokers with their overhead or
(5) enjoying the pleasurable sensations of activity?

It is only (5) that really appeals to me. (3) is next best but isn't it too soon for that?

JMK

The chicken feed *profit* which you advise me to take is a loss of about £5,000. Where there *was* a decent jobbing turn—Cities Service and El P and L [Electric Power and Light]—I have taken it.

With the end of difficult markets, Keynes also became more philosophical about investing in general and set down his thoughts in a series of memoranda and letters. As these also concerned his activities on behalf of King's and his insurance companies, we print them below (pp. 92–109) after looking at his other activities.

II. *Keynes and the City*

Most of Keynes's City activities grew out of his friendship with O. T. Falk, who had joined A Division of the Treasury on a part-time basis in 1917 and had founded with Keynes and others a dining and discussion club for City men, civil servants and academic economists called the Tuesday Club. Falk, who had started his City career as an actuary with the National Mutual Life Assurance Society, was a partner in Buckmaster and Moore, a firm of stock brokers, and, after 1932 a member of O. T. Falk and Partners, a firm of investment consultants. Keynes's City connection initially took the form of a directorship of the National Mutual in September 1919. He subsequently became chairman in May 1921, a post which he held until his resignation from the firm in October 1938. There followed connections with a series of investment companies organised by Falk, the A.D. Investment Trust (July 1921), the P.R. Finance Company (January 1923) and the Independent Investment Company (January 1924). At the end of 1923, Keynes also joined the board of the Provincial Insurance Company, initially to assist Falk with investment policy, but subsequently as a full replacement for Falk.

In the 1920s and 1930s, Keynes's relations with Falk had their ups and downs. Both men were strong personalities with a tendency to take up firm positions. As well, as the articles of association of companies such as the A.D. and P.R. and stories of his behaviour towards his own clients indicate, Falk tended to resent any interference in investment matters, insisting on his right to act without consultation with his clients.[23] Although the two men remained friends to the end, marked divergences in their views developed from 1929 onwards and, coupled with their differing operating styles, made collaboration extremely difficult, if not impossible. By 1938 they had severed all business connections with the exception of the Independent Investment Company, where effective control lay in other hands.

In dealing with Keynes's City activities, we cannot go into great detail about every company. Nor is it really necessary, as Keynes was less actively involved in the affairs of some firms than others. Also, in most cases Keynes did not have a free hand in investment policy, for he was in some cases a junior partner of Falk's and in others a member of a board where there was little discussion of investment policy. There were exceptions, however, and we shall take one of the largest first.

[23] For an affectionate portrait of Falk see N. Davenport, *Memoirs of A City Radical* (London, 1974), pp. 44–7.

(a) The P.R. Finance Company[24]

This company was founded in January 1923 with a capital of £115,000 in £1 shares. The original directors were Falk (chairman), Keynes, Rupert Trouton and W. H. Haslam. Trouton and Haslam left in 1927 and Maurice Bonham Carter, a partner of Falk's joined the board. The company was intended to provide a means of increasing the capital of the promoters' friends along the same lines as the earlier A.D. Investment Trust without diluting the capital of the latter by expansion. One surviving list of shareholders, dated 15 October 1931, provides an indication both of the personal nature of the company and of those involved. They included Clive Bell (3,000 shares), David Garnett (2,000), Roger Fry (2,000), Lytton Strachey (500), Walter Langdon Brown (2,000), Geoffrey Keynes (1,200), John Neville Keynes (2,500) and A. V. Hill (1,200). Other individuals involved included Geoffrey Fry, Andrew McFadyean, J. C. C. Davidson (all old Treasury colleagues of Keynes and Falk), F. C. Scott and Geoffrey Marks. Keynes originally held 300 shares, but bought another 2,200 in December 1927.

At first the company seemed somewhat successful, paying dividends for 1923, 1924 and 1927, but in 1928 things went wrong as the firm's speculations in commodities, its main activity, were unsuccessful. The upshot was that the results for 1928–31 saw a series of losses of £30,537, £50,659, £15,938 and £1,874 respectively.

After the first year of losses, there was a change in the P.R.'s management arrangements. Keynes took responsibility for managing one-third of the remaining assets, this sum roughly representing the proportion of the firm's capital which had come from his friends, while Falk took responsibility for the rest. In the first year of this regime, Keynes's initial fund of £28,000 suffered a depreciation of £4,000, while Falk's fund fell from £56,000 to £20,000. This divergence in performance continued over the next eighteen months with the result that Falk offered Keynes complete control of the remnants of his fund as well and sold him 6,000 of his shares at the firm's break-up value of 2s. 11½d.—a far cry from the issue price.

There matters rested uneasily for a few months. Then, in February 1932 Falk finally fell out completely with his partners at Buckmaster and Moore. All the active partners, other than Ian Macpherson, left the firm; Falk to form O. T. Falk and Partners. The break up of the firm raised the problem of whether its former clients, including Keynes and the P.R., would continue to place their business through the firm. At first Buckmaster and Moore offered to buy all of Keynes's and his friends' interest in the P.R. and manage

---

[24] The name came from πάντα ῥεῖ, all things are flux.

it themselves. Keynes refused, saying he felt morally bound to restore his friends' capital. Thus it happened that Falk and his associates took over the management and interest in the A.D. while Keynes with the support of the continuing firm of Buckmaster and Moore became wholly responsible for the P.R. Falk and Bonham Carter, two of the resigning Buckmaster and Moore partners left the P.R. board. At the same time, Keynes offered to take up to 25,000 shares in the P.R., at a break-up value of 3s., from individuals who had not come into the company at his suggestion. He received offers of just over 4,000 from Falk, Bonham Carter and two others.[25] With Rupert Trouton as his other director, Keynes set out to retrieve the position. During 1932 recovery was slow, with profits running to £5,034 and net assets rising to £21,508. During the next fifteen months, profits amounted to £81,091 and net assets rose to £102,599. Eventually, in May 1935, the company went into voluntary liquidation. Each shareholder received £1 7s. 7·68d. per share.

(b) The A.D. Investment Trust

The firm was founded in July 1921 with a capital of £50,000 in £1 shares. The original directors were all associated with A Division of the Treasury: Falk (chairman), Keynes, J. C. C. Davidson, Geoffrey Fry, H. A. Siepmann and Rupert Trouton. The company was successful: so much so that many of the same group became involved in the P.R. to spread the benefits of such success more widely without diluting the original equity. Keynes remained a director until 23 November 1927 when he sold all his shares in the company. His papers give us no indication why he did so. During the period 1923–7, dividends ran at 10 per cent per annum, largely as a result of the high returns of the years 1921–4. The firm, also caught up in Falk's departure from Buckmaster and Moore, did not survive the 1929–32 slump.

(c) The Independent Investment Company

The company issued its prospectus to potential subscribers in January 1924. Its authorised capital was £350,000 in £10 shares. The original directors were Falk, Keynes and T. Carlyle Gifford, an adviser to and director of several Edinburgh investment trusts. The prospectus made its originators' aims clear, though there is no indication as to whether it was written by Keynes or Falk.

[25] In October 1934, Keynes was offered a further 1,500 shares. He took them at 18s. This purchase took his total holding to 14,344 shares.

32

From the prospectus of The Independent Investment Company, January 1924

This Company has been formed with the objects specified in its Memorandum of Association, and in particular to carry on the usual business of an investment company, aiming at obtaining a higher return on the capital employed than is open with safety to the individual investor, and also having special regard to certain principles of investment which are now well recognised but have as yet been acted on in only a limited measure. It is now known that fluctuations in the relative values of long-dated and short-dated fixed-interest securities and also of fixed interest securities generally and of ordinary shares are all affected by a periodic credit cycle. Changes in the short-period rate of interest affect the value of long-dated securities to a greater degree than should strictly be the case, with the result that considerable profits can be made by changing from one class to another at the appropriate phases of the credit cycle. Similar periodic changes also take place in the relative values of money on the one hand and of goods and real property on the other, which are reflected in the relative values of bonds and of shares, representing as these do respectively money claims and property, so that here also the same principle of changing from one class to another at appropriate times can be applied.

The result of accumulated experience on these matters is to make it clear that the course of events is sufficiently regular to enable those who are in close and constant touch with the financial situation in certain instances to anticipate impending changes in the course of the credit cycle.

Whilst the directors will carry on the business of the Company on the stable lines recognised by sound investment companies, they intend in addition to avail themselves of the above principle by moving from one category of investment to another whenever the general situation indicates such a change to be advisable. This does not imply any intention to adventure the funds of the Company upon investments which would not be considered suitable for a prudently managed investment company. Indeed the policy of moving from time to time from one category of investment to another will require that the funds of the Company should in the main be employed in investments which are readily marketable, and which are among the leaders of their class. It will be the object of the directors to create an organisation which will enable the ordinary investor who is unable or does not desire to pay constant attention to his individual holdings to obtain all the advantages of close supervision of his investments.

33

In 1926 the company's authorised capital was raised to £500,000, of which £420,000 was actually subscribed. In January 1928 it was further increased to £1,000,000. At the same time each existing share was converted into 60 per cent 5 per cent cumulative preference shares and 40 per cent ordinary shares. None of the additional capital authorised was issued in Keynes's lifetime.

The company was moderately successful initially, the appreciation reaching £63 per £100 ordinary shares on 31 March 1929. This compares with a rise in the London and Cambridge Economic Service's index of ordinary shares of 50·3 per cent over the same period. As well, dividends ran between 5 and 7¾ per cent each year during the period.

However, the slump caught the firm. The appreciation per £100 of ordinary shares fell to £34 12s. 8d. by 31 March 1930 and then lapsed into depreciation as follows (all values per £100 originally invested).

	Ordinary shares	Preference shares
30 September 1930	−£43 9s.	0
31 December 1930	−£86 12s.	0
31 March 1931	−£71 7s.	0
30 September 1931	−£100	−£32
31 March 1932	−£100	−£52 4s.

The decline in the firm's fortunes coincided with and reflected disagreements between Keynes and Falk. In the summer of 1928 Falk had decided that money rates had risen so far that the wise investor would sell ordinary shares and invest in Treasury bills and did so for many of his clients. In the summer of 1929 he partially reversed his position and suggested that the United States was the market of the future and that investment should occur there rather than in Britain. He followed his suggestions in dealings for clients. Late in the autumn of 1929, after the Wall Street crash, Keynes suggested that a major slump was in the offing and that the Independent should sell shares and repay overdrafts. Falk disagreed and with such disagreements a clear board policy was impossible as the third director refused to take a view. The situation was further complicated by Falk's continuing his previous tendency to act without consulting his colleagues. At first, one proposed solution to meet the deadlock was to increase the size of the board and to get Falk to bind himself to the views of the majority on matters of policy. Keynes, however, realised that the only way to achieve long-term peace was agreement between him and Falk. The attempt to expand the board proved a failure, as the additional director died soon after taking office and Gifford resigned in the course of a contentious board meeting. The problems continued, despite another agreement between Keynes and Falk in July 1931 that the board would consist of 3—Keynes, Falk and one of Falk's partners acceptable to the other two—that decisions must be unanimous and that Falk would receive very limited powers to act. Meanwhile, declining prices meant forced sales as cover became inadequate.

Sterling's depreciation following Britain's departure from the gold standard on 21 September 1931 produced further problems for the firm. In January 1931, taking advantage of lower American interest rates, Falk had borrowed dollars in New York to repay a sterling overdraft using some of the firm's remaining American securities as cover. On 17 September 1931, Falk proposed replacing this loan with a sterling overdraft. Keynes refused to close the next day in the following terms.

From a letter to O. T. FALK, *18 September 1931*

What you suggest amounts in present circumstances to a frank bear speculation against sterling. I admit that I am not clear that this would be against the national interest; for it may be better that the special credits[26] should be used up by Englishmen than by foreigners. All the same, I am clear that an institution has no business to do such a thing at the present time. I should like to see exchange dealings controlled so as to take away the opportunity of choice. But meanwhile one is not entitled to take matters into one's own hands. One has to fall in with the collective decision whether one agrees with it or not. I am confident that this would be the wish of our shareholders if we could consult them.

The existence of the loan complicated matters for the firm and caused problems for the accountants. As American share prices continued to fall, the cover for the loan became impaired. To restore the cover position or reduce the loan, the Independent would then need to make forced sales of securities essential for its recovery. Added to the problems associated with

[26] The Bank of England and the British Government had raised £130 million in New York and Paris in August.

the loan were the difficulties caused by Falk's departure from Buckmaster and Moore and his resumption of his tendency to deal without consulting his fellow directors, often, they thought, to the company's disadvantage. Eventually, Geoffrey Marks and three other insurance company managers asked for a meeting with the board to discuss the position since so much of their capital had been lost. The upshot was a reorganisation, part of which included provisions for a debenture issue of £50,000 which the insurance companies would underwrite,[27] additional outside directors and a change of investment managers to Herbert Wagg. Keynes and Falk remained on the board, but they had little to do with the actual management apart from suggestions they made at board meetings. Keynes became even less involved after his illness in 1937 and his return to the Treasury in 1940. Herbert Wagg adopted the method of an orthodox investment trust and recovery proceeded. By the time of Keynes's death, the funds underlying the ordinary shares had almost returned to their original issue price. The firm is still in existence.

(d) The National Mutual Life Assurance Society

Keynes joined the board of the National Mutual in September 1919. He became chairman in May 1921 and remained such until October 1938.

During his years as chairman, Keynes's speeches to the Society's annual meetings became an important part of City life—and often a source of controversy in the press. On several occasions [*JMK*, vol. XXI, p. 312] they had a marked impact on the prices of gilt-edged securities. Although some extracts from Keynes's speeches have appeared as background material in the Activities volumes, we reprint the whole series below (pp. 114–239).

During the years Keynes was associated with the Society, its board contained a number of strong personalities. One, of course, was O. T. Falk, but there were also the Society's actuaries Geoffrey Marks (later a director) and G. H. Recknell, as well as C. T. Burchall, F. M. Curzon, Nicholas Davenport and Walter Layton.[28] This combination of personalities, plus the determination of Falk and Keynes that the Society should be more adventurous than its competitors in investing in industrial shares and in issuing policies, most notably by making annual rather than quinquennial valuations, inevitably produced conflicts and disagreements, with actual or threatened resignations not uncommon. Many of the disagreements occurred during the slump, which played havoc with the newly instituted annual valuations,[29]

---

[27] Debentures for £100,000 were issued in 1935.
[28] See Davenport, *Memoirs of a City Radical*, pp. 43–4, 53, and 'Keynes in the City', in Milo Keynes (ed.), *Essays on John Maynard Keynes* (Cambridge, 1975).
[29] In 1932 the Society postponed its valuation. It subsequently reverted to biennial valuations.

and brought sharply to the fore the disagreements already mentioned between Keynes and Falk on investment policy. Many of the disagreements on insurance policy are clearly documented in the Keynes papers, as most of those involved were vigorous draughtsmen. On the Society's investment policy, less documentation exists, partially as a result of the board's weekly meetings. In consequence, one cannot always obtain from the papers a clear view of Keynes's influence on investment philosophy and practice. However, some documents do survive as the one printed above[30] from 1930 indicates.

Perhaps the most interesting of Keynes's letters on the National Mutual were written in the aftermath of the 1937–8 recession. When the accounts for 1937 revealed a capital loss of £641,000, F. N. Curzon, acting chairman in Keynes's absence, initiated a discussion of investment policy and urged further liquidations. Keynes was not at all happy with what followed and unsuccessfully tried in correspondence to restrain the board. On 13 March, Curzon sent Keynes a 14 page letter criticising the investment policy of previous months and suggesting further liquidations of doubtful shares. Keynes replied.

To F. N. CURZON, *18 March 1938*

Dear Curzon,

Thank you for your very full letter. I was hoping to hear from you, and am glad to have this careful explanation of your general point of view. I admit that, being out of touch and not fully informed, some of my criticisms have been ill-directed.

My attitude is governed by the following general considerations, and I fancy that, whilst we do not see eye to eye, you do not disagree with some at least of these.

1. I do not believe that selling at very low prices is a remedy for having failed to sell at high ones. The criticism, if any, to which we are open is not having sold more prior to last August. In the light of after events, it would clearly have been advantageous to do so. But even now, looking back, I think it would have required abnormal foresight to act otherwise. In my own case, I was of the opinion that the prices of sterling securities

[30] Pp. 17–19.

37

were fully high in the spring. But I was prevented from taking advantage of this, first of all by the gold scare,[31] and then by the N.D.C.[32] scare, both of which I regarded as temporary influences for the wearing off of which one should wait. Then came the American collapse with a rapidity and on a scale which no one could possibly have foreseen, so that one had not got the time to act which one would have expected. However this may be, I don't feel that one is open to any criticism for not selling after the blow had fallen. As soon as prices had fallen below a reasonable estimate of intrinsic value and long-period probabilities, there was nothing more to be done. It was too late to remedy any defects in previous policy, and the right course was to stand pretty well where one was.

2. I feel no shame at being found still owning a share when the bottom of the market comes. I do not think it is the business, far less the duty, of an institutional or any other serious investor to be constantly considering whether he should cut and run on a falling market, or to feel himself open to blame if shares depreciate on his hands. I would go much further than that. I should say that it is from time to time the duty of a serious investor to accept the depreciation of his holdings with equanimity and without reproaching himself. Any other policy is anti-social, destructive of confidence, and incompatible with the working of the economic system. An investor is aiming, or should be aiming primarily at long-period results, and should be solely judged by these. The fact of holding shares which have fallen in a general decline of the market proves nothing and should not be a subject of reproach. It should certainly not be an argument for unloading when the market is least able to support such action. The idea that we should all be selling out to the other fellow and should all be finding ourselves with nothing but cash at the bottom of the market is not merely fantastic, but destructive of the

---

[31] On rumours that the official American price of gold would be reduced.
[32] The National Defence Contribution was introduced in the 1937 Budget. It was later substantially modified. See *JMK*, vol. XXI, pp. 409-13.

whole system. I do not believe you differ from me on this. But I repeat it because it is profoundly the basis of my general attitude.

3. I do not agree that we have in fact done particularly badly. I have been carrying on for my own benefit a post mortem into results and making such comparison with other institutions as are open to me.[33] Recknell, who has helped me with these investigations, would agree, I think, that, whilst we do not come out particularly well, we do not come out particularly badly. As far as I can judge, there is extremely little difference between our results and those of other people. If we take the Prudential, for example, with its very large holdings of ordinary shares, I should say that, though they may have done just a trifle better than we have, there is extremely little in it. Moreover, if our results are compared with those of the Index, for a period, they are extremely good. We have done a very great deal better than the Index, and have in that way shown power of management and have justified the capacity of insurance offices to undertake constructive investment. If we deal in equities, it is inevitable that there should be large fluctuations. Some part of paper profits is certain to disappear in bad times. Results must be judged by what one does on the round journey. On that test we have come out successfully. If, on the other hand, we do not hold equities, we must either be content with earning a definitely lower rate of interest, or we shall be tempted, in my judgement, into risks which, while they may be less apparent and take longer to mature, are really much more serious than those of equity holders.

As I began by saying, I think it is easy to exaggerate the extent of the divergences of our opinions. I feel sure that you agree with a great deal of the above, and on several occasions you have shown yourself a supporter in practice of a steady policy as against some other members of the Board. One main difference lies, I fancy, in your taking a less favourable view as to our

[33] See below pp. 92–9 for the results of this.

experience over the whole swing of recent years. And I believe that, if full comparisons were available, you would find yourself greatly comforted.

Yours sincerely,

J. M. KEYNES

Curzon, however, kept up his pressure to sell, fuelled in his pessimism by the Society's capital loss for the first quarter of 1938 of £231,000 and President Roosevelt's decision to increase public works expenditure in the United States. At this stage, as well, O. T. Falk became strongly bearish as regards ordinary shares, even in America. Keynes maintained a running commentary.

To G. H. RECKNELL, *30 April 1938*

Dear Recknell,

I have your letter of April 28th reporting to me Falk's bearish views and arguments. It would take more than a letter to deal with them thoroughly, but I certainly do not find them at all convincing. Your own reply, which you briefly outline, seems to me very much sounder indeed.

As regards this country, I certainly see no reason whatever to expect any kind of catastrophe, and the way in which the market has taken the Budget surely shows that a confidence crisis engendered by force of the budgetary position is a fantasm. It appears to be virtually certain that government expenditure will prevent any serious recession of business in the near future below the present level.

In the case of the United States, the immediate prospect is more obscure. But there it is surely a case for patience and fortitude. Both the forces of natural recovery and those of official assistance may take a bit of time to work. But, after reading innumerable reports and statistical analyses of the American position, I can see no reason for expecting a very serious further recession and every reason for believing that things will be a great deal better than they are now by the end of the year. I think it would be a disastrous mistake to choose this moment for taking up an ultra-bearish position.

I agree with you that our resources are fully adequate to meet any probable loss. Moreover, a fall in ordinary shares due to a confidence crisis and not to a decline in yield, will surely be temporary; and a drastic decline of yield in the light of the present vast expenditures, does not seem to me to be something for a reasonable man to expect.

There is, moreover, a further reason against a further diminution in our ordinary share portfolio, which should I think weigh with us all, namely, the question of yield. The worst thing that could happen would be that we should be tempted into low-grade fixed-interest stocks and real estate in an effort to recover the yield lost by turning out ordinary shares. If one is to run any equity risk at all, first-class ordinary shares are by far the safest way of running it. The alternative is to stick to interest stocks. But that would mean a reduction in the rate of interest, which would mean an immediate drastic reduction in our rates of bonus. No doubt, if catastrophe is ahead, we should have to face that. But the whole prognostication seems to me to be based upon a wholly mistaken view of the prospects. The world today is certainly one in which catastrophes can occur. But it is impossible to predict their character (they might, for instance, take the form of a loss in the value of money, which would mean that a portfolio consisting of interest stocks and no equities would suffer disastrously). Indeed, as you say, against such things it is useless to legislate.

Yours sincerely,
[copy initialled] JMK

To G. H. RECKNELL, *5 May 1938*

Dear Recknell,

There seem to be profound underlying contradictions in Falk's argument. I note that he expects with a high degree of probability a progressive recession of trade in this country, in spite of the armament expenditure and although he is hopeful for recovery in the United States before very long. This means, I think, that he has returned to the expectation of a secular decline in this country to a state of general ruin which he used to forecast, as you will remember, a few years ago. At that time it was a corollary of this argument that we should invest as heavily as possible in U.S.A. and other investments outside this country. And, if he were right, that, apart from national considerations, would appear to be the corollary today.

I notice that, on the first page of his letter of the 4th May, he expects the recession of trade in this country to be along the lines of the normal trade cycle, but, on page 2, he gives himself the next few years for the realisation of his prediction. So that here he is returning to the idea of secular rather than cyclical decline, i.e. the view I am attributing to him above.

If, however, general ruin lies ahead of us, it seems to me vain to suppose that we can escape it by increasing our purchases of government stocks. A prolonged period of progressively increasing unemployment and the decline of the revenue, coupled with heavy armament expenditure, would obviously produce a fiscal and political situation from which gilt-edged securities could not possibly escape. No doubt it is my absence from the Board which has prevented me from hearing any reasons by which he backs up his forecast; in the documents circulated to me none are given beyond his bare opinion and the mentioning of heavy odds. If, however, his pessimism should prove well founded, it surely is a case of a situation against which, as you say, it is impossible to legislate.

I can only hope that the Board will retain their level-headedness and that the process of weeding out from our remaining holdings those that are considered highly vulnerable will not take the form of weeding out those which have the prospects of the biggest recovery in the event of the pessimists proving to be wrong.

My own view remains what I described it before, and is easily summed up. I do not know how many months will elapse before a real recovery in America takes full effect. So long as there is no recovery in America, the effect on the prices of certain leading raw materials will be adverse to the interests of many sterling companies. But if and when there is a genuine recovery in America, this, combined with the level of armament expenditure, is capable of making 1939 quite a good year.

Could you circulate copies of this letter to the Board?

Yours sincerely,

[copy initialled] J.M.K.

From E. H. DAVENPORT, *16 July 1938*

My dear Maynard,

I would very much like to have your views of Wall Street. I am fighting a lone battle at the National Mutual Board against the rest who appear to want to sell every American at once. I take the view that the pump-priming, catching traders with low inventories, is bound to cause the consumer goods to recover so that practically every business index will turn upwards for the next few months. Whether a capital goods revival will follow on depends largely on confidence, on a deal between Mr Roosevelt and the utilities and on other political matters. But no one else on the Board seems to think that even a consumer goods revival is possible. Certainly Wall Street has risen too fast and whenever it oversteps the mark it will have to come back, but I should have thought that the trend is upwards for the next few months.

I would be very glad if you would send a line as to whether you agree. I hope all goes well with your progress. My love to Lydia.

Yours ever,

NICHOLAS

To E. H. DAVENPORT, *16 July 1938*

My dear Nicholas,

I regard the N.M. as almost past praying for and do my best to avert my eyes from what is going on. Full sympathy in your lone battle. My view is that a material improvement in U.S.A. in

43

the course of the next six months is practically certain. But I am not attempting to make any confident forecast as to the timing. A market reaction is, of course, possible. I doubt whether it is worth going for, partly because it may not go far enough, and partly because, if it does, it is extremely likely that no advantage will be taken of it to get back—the bears would simply feel that it confirmed their worst fears. On the other hand, I am not against selling a little on the way up. For example, I was not against the sale of U.S. and Foreign Common, or even of U.S. Steel; though perhaps I should have preferred to replace with other sound and more promising shares. Undoubtedly there are some shares in the market which look pretty high. On the other hand, there are many outstanding bargains.

My impression is that the behaviour of the market is being very considerably dominated by the new rules against short sales. This is preventing the traders from tipping off stop-loss limits. I do not believe that the market would have maintained its stability for the last two or three weeks, if this had not been so. Otherwise the market recession would have been sufficiently enlarged to frighten the newly fledged bulls (for bulls certainly have wings). In the actual circumstances, probably the best thing one can do is to stand more or less pat without resisting moderate selling of the less attractive items. But, as I say, the odds on still higher prices before the end of the year are, I consider, very high.

Won't you come over here for a night in the course of the next week or two and tell us the news—not July 21, but most other days probably free.

Yours ever,
[copy initialled] J.M.K.

To G. H. RECKNELL, *23 July 1938*

Dear Recknell,

Many thanks for your letter of July 21st about American investments. My view is that the American recovery is a genuine one and is likely to go further. Whether the improvement will come fast enough to prevent any reaction from present prices it is impossible to say. There is also the risk of a reaction nearer the November elections, which are surely likely to turn out favourably to the President. What is perhaps of most importance to us is the real possibility of a fairly favourable political decision concerning utilities. In the long run, the great question will be whether recovery, when it comes, will go far enough or last long enough to be really satisfactory. But that is a consideration to be taken into account, not now, but when prices are again looking pretty good. Personally I regard *that* as the real risk, but think there is a likelihood of prices appreciably higher than the present some time in the course of the next 6 or 9 months. Accurate timing in such cases is beyond anyone's ability.

This does not mean that I am against selling gradually on the way up, just as I am in favour of buying gradually on the way down. The precise tinge of my own reactions (if this is a permissible metaphor) is best indicated perhaps by what I have done in other connections. I was buying modestly all the way down from October to March, having failed to make more than modest sales prior to October, with the result that book values of American investments reached their maximum on March 31st. From May to the present time I have been selling gradually on the upward journey and have cleared out more than the equivalent of the purchases made between October and March. I should say that the percentage of the common stock sold is higher than the 14 per cent which you mention as applicable to the National Mutual. On the other hand, the net reduction of the position is a good deal less than this, since about half the sales of common stocks have been reinvested in bonds and preferred. Indeed, up to date I have been taking advantage of the improvement much more to raise the quality than to diminish the quantity. From now onwards, however, I am inclined not to make replacement purchases, and to make a net reduction on every improvement. With an increase of the market generally up to 10 or 20 per cent, I should expect my rate of selling to be slow.

45

But when the market generally has risen a further 20 per cent, it would get a good deal brisker. I doubt if one really gets into the danger zone until the market has risen another 20 to 30 per cent, apart, of course, from the perennial risk of temporary reactions. That probably conveys my general attitude to the position as clearly as is possible.

In regard to details, I was in favour of the sale of U.S. and Foreign, which is a very vulnerable share and seems to me to have risen out of relation to the other investment trusts. But I regret the sale of Atlas, which I consider about the cheapest of the lot. I have bought more of them than you have sold during the current period. I also have a pretty good opinion of General American and would myself have put the selling limit at about 2 points higher than those suggested. In the case of Chicago Pneumatic Tool Pref. I should have put my limit above, rather than below, 40. I agree with the sales of Steel shares. You will see that I am putting my ideas 10 or 20 per cent higher than yours. In some of the other cases, however, I have no particular views one way or the other.

I strongly support the proposal to reinvest some of the proceeds in Courtaulds, and I agree with your suggestion that we are approaching a position when the hoped for opportunity of lightening the American holdings in favour of the English is arriving.

I am glad that the Board did not go any further this week, but, as I have indicated, I personally should be extremely ready to reconsider the position after a further 20 per cent rise.

Yours sincerely,
[copy initialled] J.M.K.

Finally, Keynes resigned from the National Mutual. He gave his reasons to O. T. Falk.

From a letter to O. T. FALK, *11 October 1938*

Now that I am able tentatively to return to work, I have to decide what it is most prudent to give up. One naturally chooses that part of one's activities in which one finds least satisfaction. And that, in present circumstances, is I feel the National Mutual. I do not think it lies in my power to cure the faults of the management, and I am reluctant to continue to take the responsibility for them.

Even after leaving the National Mutual, Keynes was still consulted on occasion.

From G. H. RECKNELL, *18 January 1939*

My dear Keynes,

I have had rather a depressing afternoon, and am writing to you for reassurance. Falk has been here, and has been preaching again his usual doctrine of general desolation and ruin, and the 'Decline and Fall' of England. As you know, he has put forward these views before, notably a year ago and more particularly in 1930 in his famous printed memorandum.

His general thesis from the point of view of our investment policy is the avoidance of equities or prior charges depending on profits, and exercising a predilection for shorter-term gilt-edged stocks. He does not, I think, go so far as to want a general slaughter of existing holdings, and I agree with him in not wishing to increase our existing stakes in equities or preference shares, but I dislike this predisposition for short-dated securities at a time when our investment spread generally is shorter than it was a year ago and such as to give us in my view all the protection we can hope for.

I cannot feel convinced that economic activity in this country can decline much further in face of such enormous and increasing armament expenditure. Nor do I think, if his fears about war next week or next month are realised, can we hope to avert the investment consequences by confining ourselves to gilt-edged. Our ordinary stocks are fundamentally a long-term holding and hedge against inflation. Falk is fearful about the rate of interest because of his political views and because of his views about the Budget situation, but here again I think he overlooks the importance of the new found power which the Bank of England now possesses to sell its £200 million Treasury bills

47

and buy long-term gilt-edged. The money market is crying out for the former, and the Stock Exchange for buyers of the latter; and £200 million is comparable, I find, in order of magnitude with the increase in total bank investments over the relevant 1931–4 when bank buying was a prime factor in bringing about the rise in the gilt-edged market. The long-term factors it seems to me still make for a cheapening in money rates and I am fearful of missing the boat.

It is most improper of me to write to you like this, but I hope you will give me some comfort and reassurance. I hope also that you are well, and are enjoying the relief from 'National Mutual' affairs.

With kind regards to Mrs Keynes and yourself,

Yours sincerely,

G. H. RECKNELL

To G. H. RECKNELL, *19 January 1939*

My dear Recknell,

This is indeed like old times. I wonder how many such letters you (and Marks before you) have written me in the past in almost identical terms! How relieved I am that I have not to grapple with it.

If war actually comes there is, in my opinion, not much to be afraid of. There will doubtless be fixed prices in the gilt-edged market, and I cannot imagine the Government borrowing in such circumstances at a rate of interest above $3\frac{1}{2}$ per cent; while such an event is surely certain, in the long run, to produce inflationary conditions which will be highly favourable to equities, if the system of private capitalism survives at all.

One has much more reason, as an investor, to be afraid of a long drawn out period of anxiety and depression, without war actually coming; but I doubt if one does much good either to oneself or to the community by searching for better holes. Unquestionably, the really right policy would be to aim at as high an income as possible, and not to trouble too much about capital valuations. I do not consider that the profits now being earned are particularly bad, nor are they likely to be. The Actuaries' Index shows that the fall in value of equities has been altogether out of proportion to any decline in profits. What we are suffering from is an intense phase of liquidity preference, and no wonder either! Such a phase has to be lived through with as much patience and courage as may be. There is no escape whatever for a permanent investment institution; nor indeed should there be. One can comfort oneself by the consideration that, if during the next year or so there is a further sagging of prices so that the market as a whole has fallen another 10 or 15 per cent or more, everyone's margin will have run off, and there will be nothing to be ashamed of. This is surely a case where one can accept the common fate with equanimity and not struggle too hectically to be a miraculous exception.

As regards encouraging points, I entirely agree with the important possibility to which you call attention in the third paragraph of your letter. I also have high, but restrained, hopes of America. A real recovery there would not merely raise American prices, but sharply improve a great number of commodity stocks over here. Moreover, the London market looks extremely sold out and, if there were to be a bit of good news, there would be a very sharp reaction.

It would probably be quite unpractical to make what I should consider the best individual suggestions. As on previous occasions, I should say that the best course for the Board of the N.M. is to stand pat and do the least possible. It will be much easier to persuade the Board to acquiesce in this than to take any positive measures or look round for sound switches.

Am I right, by the way, in having the impression that the Prudential are handling the situation with high courage and public spirit? There can be no possible question, but that composure is in the public interest; and the fact of being responsible for a public investment institution does not, in my opinion, lay any overriding obligation on one to act in an un-public-spirited manner.

I am getting on very steadily and as quickly, I suppose, as I can expect. I am now spending term time back at Cambridge, and am able to undertake more than half of a normal day's work.

Yours sincerely,
[copy initialled] J. M. K.

Keynes sent a copy of his letter to Recknell to Francis Scott of the Provincial.

From a letter from F. C. SCOTT, *January 1939*

Thank you so much for sending me Recknell's letter, and your reply, which is very typical of you in its sanity and robust faith in the ultimate rightness of a policy based on reason and common sense. If war comes nothing matters, whatever we do would be wrong, but, short of that, some day I feel convinced we shall look back on this time as only just another instance of the incredible folly of the financial world.

(e) The Provincial Insurance Company

Keynes and Falk joined the board of the Provincial in December 1923 at the suggestion of W. H. Haslam, an old Kingsman who had acted as Keynes's secretary at Genoa and who had heard good reports of the financial advice they were giving Sir Ernest Debenham. Initially Falk bore the larger share of responsibility in dealing with investments, but he left the board at the end of 1926 in favour of his partner Sir Maurice Bonham Carter. From then onwards, although Falk continued in an advisory role, Keynes took more responsibility and from 1930 the main burden was his as Falk's connection with the firm ended.[34]

The Provincial was a small, family controlled company based at Kendal, Westmorland. As a result, much more of Keynes's involvement took the form of correspondence, largely with Francis Scott the firm's managing director but also with A. G. A. Mackay the investment secretary.[35] Both

---

[34] During World War II, Keynes's Treasury position often made it impossible for him to act as an adviser. During such periods, Ian Macpherson of Buckmaster and Moore took over much of the responsibility.

[35] Mackay was investment manager of Binder Hamlyn C.A. and worked for the Provincial on a part-time basis between 1931–45. He recalls an investment committee meeting when a member suggested buying Indian Government bonds. 'By all means', said Keynes, 'but timing is important. Wait 'til a Viceroy has been assassinated!'

Scott and Keynes were vigorous correspondents on particular shares, the general outlook and the problems of the company. Both were also great speculators although quite different in character. Scott believed that Keynes's advice had been sufficiently useful to be worth collecting together after the latter's death. Keynes also valued his Provincial connection, for he was an extremely active director throughout the years after 1930, except when constrained by his Treasury connection during the Second World War. On investments, Keynes had fairly complete discretion within the guidelines set by the board at its monthly meetings and successfully persuaded the firm of the virtues of equities. Keynes's surviving Provincial papers after 1930 greatly exceed those from the National Mutual, even when he was chairman of the latter. As he frequently attempted to persuade the Provincial to hold shares in which he had an interest on his own account, his correspondence also throws light on his own portfolio.

We print below a selection of letters from the Provincial files, dated largely from after 1938. Where necessary we have added the relevant explanatory matter.

When South Africa left the gold standard, Keynes began buying South African gold mining shares on his own account. His purchases between 1 February and 11 May came to over £32,000. Almost immediately he also started buying similar shares for the Provincial.

From F. C. SCOTT, *3 February 1933*

Dear Keynes,

I confess I am a little bit startled by the purchase of South African mining shares as an investment for the Provincial, although perhaps the Union Corporation at all events should not be regarded wholly as interested in the Rand mining field. While I am very definitely in favour of an Industrial Index, I am not sure that I quite contemplated including mining shares in this or that I have too much confidence in the flare-up in the mining market consequent on South Africa going off gold.

Just as a matter of interest, two criticisms from Vickers' letters to me rather confirm my own view:

Feb 1st 1933

I had lunch to-day with Esmond Harmsworth and he described the movement in the Kaffir market as a 'Dance of Death'. I certainly cannot find any serious people who are taking part in this particular movement.

We do know the mining houses are selling large blocks of shares with calls, and the people will buy anything at the moment, but I do not feel tempted to operate as there are too many unknown factors.

Feb 2nd 1933

It is almost impossible to write about the mining market. It is up one minute and down the next. I believe they started dealing in the street before the Stock Exchange opened this morning, and the movements are such as to worry anybody but a real gambler. The future of this market depends entirely upon whether the public are really going to buy or not. The few speculators who are in the market at present are making a bold bid for public support, and they have the press well in hand, and people are being attracted by the wonderful figures which are being held up before their eyes. You know what these markets are like once the public really goes for them, nothing can stop them, although the shops and professionals are selling very freely. At present I am more bullish than otherwise.

As the orders have been placed it is rather on a matter of principle than the particular transactions that I am inclined to question.

Yours truly,

F. C. SCOTT

To F. C. SCOTT, *5 February 1933*

My dear Scott,

I am sorry you are shocked about the mining shares. I will look into the matter when I am in London next week. If you feel in this way I think we ought to sell them again. But in my own opinion what has happened is a very trustworthy event and I do not feel investment in this direction to be more speculative than in any other, indeed, probably much less so. It may amuse you to read the very popular account which I have written for Tuesday's *Daily Mail*.[36]

The quotations you give from Vickers' letters strike me as rather superficial. I doubt if he can have looked into the thing much. As regards Esmond Harmsworth, it is rather amusing that

[36] See *JMK*, vol. XXI, pp. 225-9.

I lunched with him on the day following Vickers' lunch, when I found him of quite a different opinion. My own belief is that it is a very big event, and the notion that it is a spurious thing worked up by the big mining houses is surely absurd. Also this is not in the least like an ordinary mining proposition where one is speculating as to what will come out of the hole in the ground. The element of uncertainty in this case is solely a question of the exchange and of the division of profits. But that there is a large increment of profit on any reasonable anticipation I have no doubt.

Yours sincerely,
[copy initialled] J. M. K.

From F. C. SCOTT, *8 February 1933*

Dear Keynes,

With further reference to your letter of the 5th inst., I read your *Daily Mail* article with much interest, and logically there seems a great deal in the argument in favour of gold mines at the present moment.

I am afraid I am one of those people who think that a reasoned argument is not by any means the safest guide in regard to investment, and I think one has a little illustration of this in the memorandums which were so freely distributed at one time by Buckmaster & Moore; all admirable in their facts and their deductions, and which yet, in the light of subsequent events, have been made to look so extraordinarily wide of the mark.

I remember once a very successful speculator who amassed and managed to retain a large fortune telling a friend that one lesson he had learnt from bitter experience was to keep right out of the South African mines market as the South African Jew is recognised as a past master in the art of selling the public, and I believe these horse-sense maxims are worth all the reasoned logic in the world.

I confess that as we are in I should be inclined to keep the shares and give them a modest run, but I should not be a bit surprised myself to see the public left to hold the baby and the gold boom a very minor thing on paper.

Yours faithfully,
F. C. SCOTT

From a letter to F. C. SCOTT, *9 February 1933*

I dare-say you are right to be wary of gold mines. I have never bought one in my life or advised anyone else to buy one, until the last month; but I regard recent developments as not really primarily within the mining sphere itself, but an adjustment to a new exchange situation—and that is something I can pretend to understand—and not a speculation about the contents of a prospective hole in the ground. One is dealing today with a highly developed and routined industry, the doubts being almost entirely concerned with exchange and taxation prospects and not with mining prospects. If your heart were to melt towards them, I should very strongly recommend, apart from the question of principle, the purchase of 300 Crown Mines. Personally I think this is an absolutely suitable investment for an insurance company. I know it has been thought so in other cases—one of the greatest properties in the world, capitalised today at about £15,000,000.

From a letter from F. C. SCOTT, *13 February 1933*

With regard to the South African mines, I think your reply is a perfectly fair one, and is largely the answer to my objections, though I think you will probably admit that you cannot altogether rule out the possibility of factors coming into play which might largely upset the calculations upon which the anticipated rise in the profits of the mines has been based.

I am certainly more inclined to buy now, on the reaction, as I think it is probably a more favourable moment and there is pretty certain to be a rebound the other way again. I should not mind adding another £1,000 or thereabouts to our small holding.

Seventeen months later, Keynes was having to reassure Scott about the position.

To F. C. SCOTT, *15 August 1934*

Dear Scott,

Union Corporation

My strong feeling in favour of retaining our holding in this is based on the following considerations:

1. 2,500 shares at 7 are worth £17,500, scarcely more than 1½ per cent of our assets. It is also legitimate, I think, in this connection, to consider what a holding cost as well as what it might fetch and on this test the amount involved is less than £11,000, or less than 1 per cent of our assets. Thus I do not feel that the holding can be considered dangerously high in itself, if other factors favour it, and if the investment itself amounts to a spreading of risks.

2. The present market capitalisation of Union Corporation is more than £6,000,000, so that it is a very substantial concern. We are far from having our eggs all in one basket in as much as the Corporation controls at least six South African gold mines in addition to which it has substantial interests in the Rhodesian copper mines (which it was in from the beginning and holds at a very satisfactory price), the San Francisco lead silver mines and important interests in Australia. Its two industrial interests, namely, British Enka Silk and the Polyphon Gramophone Company which were only moderately successful ventures are now an entirely negligible portion of its interests. The Corporation itself holds a substantial amount of shares in its companies, but it is primarily concerned, of course, in their financial and technical management, in which it has been outstandingly successful. In addition to this it does a considerable and growing banking, foreign exchange and stock exchange business, partly in connection with its interest in gold and partly arising out of the fact that like all South African houses it is the 'shop', i.e. the principal jobber, for its own companies. In order to enable it to take advantage of banking and exchange business opportunities it has been accustomed to hold in cash and British Government securities a large sum—probably about £3,000,000 at the present time.

55

3. The dividend policy of the Corporation has been immensely conservative by which it has built up the value of its shares from 12s. 6d., to which sum they were written down in 1917, to £7 at the present time. I may mention that it was a German company before the War, which was taken over during and on account of the War and has been rebuilt into its present state during the last 17 years. It is accustomed to show no more profits than are required to pay the dividend with a margin for reserves. I should estimate that its actual income may easily be two or three times what it shows. It has many concealed assets, valuable options etc. One of its most important and successful mines has not yet reached the dividend stage and another one has only just reached it and is not yet at full strength, so that there is much more income to come by the mere efflux of time. It is important to estimate accurately the present break-up value of the shares on the basis of the current market values of its constituent assets, but my guess would be that the break-up value could scarcely be far short of £10 a share. The Corporation still has to get the full benefit of its conservative and farsighted management. In my opinion it is the up-to-date and coming South African house, much more alive, more efficient and much more honest than any of the others.

4. I consider that the management has the highest standards and exercises extreme industry and care. I have known Sir Henry Strakosch, the managing director, who is the virtual creator of the Corporation in its present form, intimately for 15 years. He has also been for some time the financial member of the India Council and one of our representatives on the Financial Committee of the League of Nations. I feel that that part of one's resources which one is willing to embark in gold and other metals cannot be better handled than by leaving him to manage them for one from his position of exceptional advantage.

5. The business is one with a strong compound interest element in it. If nothing goes wrong with the gold situation, I see no reason why the shares should not reach 20 in 3 or 4 years.

They have increased 12-fold in value in the last seventeen years and yet, as I have said above, are only now beginning to get the full advantage of their farsightedness. There would, therefore, be nothing at all surprising in their trebling in value in the next 3 or 4 years. I am convinced that one's interests would be sufficiently spread for there to be no serious risk, except the general risk, which I do not underestimate, of gold mines as a whole. If one's opinions changed about the prospects of gold, that would alter the situation altogether. But, in so far as one is prepared to continue to hold investments in the metal, I have decided for myself and for other accounts for which I am responsible, to concentrate practically the whole of what I am prepared to invest in this way in the Union Corporation, and then to hold the shares obstinately for a period of years for a really large appreciation,—unless, as I have said, the gold position as a whole shows signs of change.

As time goes on I get more and more convinced that the right method in investment is to put fairly large sums into enterprises which one thinks one knows something about and in the management of which one thoroughly believes. It is a mistake to think that one limits one's risk by spreading too much between enterprises about which one knows little and has no reason for special confidence. Obviously this principle ought not to be carried too far. The real limitation, however, on its application in practice is in my experience the small number of enterprises about which at any given time one feels in this way. One's knowledge and experience are definitely limited and there are seldom more than two or three enterprises at any given time in which I personally feel myself entitled to put *full* confidence.

Yours sincerely,
[copy initialled] J.M.K.

To F. C. SCOTT, *23 August 1934*

Dear Scott,

Gold Shares

I have your letters of August 15th and 16th. I do not disagree from the view that in face of the very large rise which has taken place it is prudent to diminish somewhat one's holding of gold shares. Also I think that optimistic market expectations based upon a further devaluation by Roosevelt are, to say the least, very premature.

We have, however, substantially reduced our holdings recently; and whilst I think that the prospects of further capital appreciation are much reduced, the shares are still excellent yielders on a pure investment basis. Indeed the return is much better than can be got elsewhere and for this reason the shares have been passing, I should say on a very large scale in recent months, from the hands of speculators and speculative investors into the hands of permanent investors and investment institutions. The above does not apply, of course, to new flotations with the great majority of which I would certainly have nothing to do.

I think Vickers is wrong in thinking that the rise in the cost of living and costs generally will interfere with the profits of gold mines within the next twelve months. Indeed the argument in the first paragraph of the extract you sent is, I think, rather muddled.

As regards your letter of August 16th about Union Corporation, I should go some way with you in considering the sale, if I saw some *general* set-back in gold shares. On the other hand, it seems to me to be most important not to be upset out of one's permanent holdings by being too attentive to market movements. Unless one believes the market movement to be well founded, taking a long view, I should like in a case where I felt real confidence to disregard it. It is indeed awfully bad for all of us to be constantly revaluing our investments according to market movements. Of course, it would be silly to ignore such things, but one's whole tendency is to be too much influenced by them.

In the matter of English Electric you have, I think, misunderstood what I meant to say. I have no desire to buy back the preference shares we sold.

Yours sincerely,
[copy initialled] J. M. K.

Late in 1933 the issue under discussion was the firm's American investments.

From a letter from F. C. SCOTT, *17 November 1933*

American Position. Do not in any way think that I am putting the responsibility on you. I recognise that I assented as much as anyone else, and if it is to be considered a mistake, I am equally responsible, but, in fact, have we really not got to recognise that we have made a loss of £26,000 through the holdings of our American investment list since the 1st January 1930, and ought we not really to contrast with this the fact that we should, instead of having made a loss at date, have probably had a profit of not far off the same amount had we invested this money in the home gilt-edged market, which probably would have been the case otherwise, and therefore there is a difference of not far short of £50,000.

That we have been wrong is not necessarily an argument for reversing our decision now, and it may be the entirely wrong thing to do, but in looking back on our policy, I think it is not an unfair summary of the position.

Now, as regards the future. While I agree that the fall in the exchange is automatically reducing our American position, so long as we are covered, assuming the American dollar is going to run away still further, we should actually recoup our position quicker if we were to sell a substantial part of our American investments and still retain the exchange cover, but this you may regard as gambling.

I cannot quite accept the view that a fixed interest bond is the best form of investment if we are building on a trade recovery there by inflation, and if we really think that, logically, we ought to be out of the fixed interest bond and into the equity share.

Personally, I still feel that while I should be reluctant to realise our holdings in total and to write off a loss of £25,000, I should steadily reduce our commitments where we could do so without any appreciable loss and rather look to going back into the equity market there again if and when the time came that we felt more reasonably certain that the inflation plans were going to succeed.

Events are moving so quickly that I feel hesitant to suggest that we should leave the matter over to discuss at our next meeting, and I think really that if you and Binder and Haslam could have a talk together and come to a decision we, my brother and I, would willingly acquiesce in whatever you decided to do.

To F. C. SCOTT, *23 November 1933*

Dear Scott,

I saw Haslam last night, and on his telling me that you pressed strongly for a sale of some American securities, I agreed to a selection for sale which should realise about £10,000. They were taken, as previously suggested, from those of the very highest class, showing, though high, nevertheless the least yield. I repeat that I do not agree with this decision, because with the dollars hedged it does not appear to me that we are in the long run exposed to any material risk on the securities in question, and I doubt if it really reduces our risk in the event of the American position deteriorating.

However, I consider it by no means unlikely that the next movement of these and other American fixed dated securities may quite conceivably be downwards, and I must console myself with the hope that I may perhaps later on, when the outlook is less uncertain, be able to persuade you to reinvest this money, or some part of it, on terms not less favourable than those on which we are realising.

As regards the past history, I cannot quite accept the summary you give in your letter of November 17, though since all the relevant data were given in Mackay's letter of November 14, it is only a question of interpretation.

If we leave out the securities purchased before January 1st

1930, which represent the remnant of a policy which I did not agree with at the time, particularly in regard to the selection of certain securities which have almost completely disappeared in value, the depreciation as at the date of Mackay's letter, after deducting profit on exchange, was about £8,000 on securities costing £68,000, or less than 12 per cent. If some allowance is made for the high yield which has been obtained on these securities, for the expenses of getting in, and for the fact that the valuation is on the basis of middle prices, a good deal lower in some cases than the price at which we could in fact buy today, I should judge that if we had never touched an American security since January 1, 1930, and were then to seek to set up our existing position today, the advantage to us would not be above about 5 per cent on the money; which considering all the things which have happened, is not very material.

Thus I am inclined to claim that the selection of investments made has stood up to events pretty well so far. But the real question, of course, is how they are going to behave for the future. In this respect I think that our existing list may prove an advantageous one, because it mainly consists of preferred stocks which are now hopelessly out of fashion with American investors and heavily depressed below their real value. I agree, of course, that one must not in such uncertain circumstances risk too much in one direction, but I still believe that some of the American preferred stocks offer today one of those outstanding opportunities which occasionally occur of buying cheap into what is for the time being an irrationally unfashionable market.

Let me quote again the two examples which I am fondest of citing, because I happen to know their figures better than the others, but do not really differ from the general average of our selection, namely National Power and Light Preferred and United States and Foreign Preferred.

At present prices the former yield about 15 per cent. The results, both quarterly and monthly, up to September 30th last have just been published. These show that the profits for the year ending September 30, 1933 were very little below those of the year ending September 1932, and also that for the three months ended September 30th the results were better than for the preceding year. Thus the company is slightly on the up-grade. It is in a highly liquid condition, holding in cash and its equivalent nearly $15,000,000. On the profit of the year to September 30 the preferred dividend is covered about five times. The cover is also quite substantial if one takes it as a percentage of the total operating revenues of all the company's subsidiaries taken into a consolidated account.

I know that there are all sorts of scares about inflation and public utilities generally, which influence the American public. But one is surely [in] with a pretty good chance when one can purchase a preference share, which never in recent years has been covered less than five times, to yield you 15 per cent.

The United States and Foreign Company is an investment trust, well managed in my opinion, which holds a widespread selection of the best bonds, preferred stocks and common stocks of the most marketable character quoted on Wall Street. It has lately paid up all arrears of preferred dividends. Taken at current market prices, the assets of the company cover the present price of the preferred shares twice over, and the yield on them at current prices is 10 per cent. The preference share of an English investment trust equally well covered (and many English investment trusts hold a large amount of American securities) would sell for at least twice the price.

The stocks which we have actually decided to sell do not, of course, yield so high a price as the above. But this is because the security behind them, both of capital and income, is quite overwhelming. The amount of cover, for example, behind Tobacco Products which we are selling, which is a first charge on the American Tobacco Company, must be quite astronomical. These securities are yielding not far short of twice what one would get on comparable securities in this country.

I am far from blind to the uncertainties of the American outlook. But in the first place these prices discount an enormous amount. The prospects of profit in my judgement, if things do not go utterly to smash, far outweigh the reasonable risks of loss; and in the second place I am at a loss to see how the inflationary programme of the President is really injurious to stocks of this character. For any rise of prices which he engineers will necessarily increase the proportion of equity cover behind the preferred claim.

Yours sincerely,

[copy initialled] J. M. K.

From F. C. SCOTT, *28 November 1933*

Dear Keynes,

American Securities

Many thanks for your very interesting letter of the 23rd inst. So far as past history is concerned, it is perhaps not very profitable to pursue this, except that I personally always value these inquisitions as perhaps helping one to acquire a greater wisdom for the future and I am a little doubtful if you really make full allowance for the appreciation which we should have made in gilt-edged holdings, or the cost of renewing our exchange transactions, as for instance 7 points in our profit exchange has gone in the further three months' renewal.

What I am interested in is your comment on certain of the American securities which have been particularly disastrous and which you say that you did not agree with. I must confess this is rather a surprise to me as I do not recollect that you expressed any disagreement with the selection at the time, but this may have been possibly due to the temperamental difficulties of our one-time financial partner. However the real problem is the immediate policy, and I note that in this connection you are not really in agreement with our views.

While I admit all that you say in support of the individual investments and in cover and yield there is everything to be said in favour of them, I personally feel that the question of retaining an interest in the American market or not rests on much bigger issues. I do not think it is a question of whether an investment yields 5 or 10 per cent or whether it is covered 2 or 10 times by assets, but rather whether you feel confident that the country is heading for financial recovery or financial disaster, and while I certainly cannot claim any sufficient knowledge to be able to arrive at a reasoned and sound opinion, I do think there is sufficient uncertainty on this major issue to make it wiser for us to have a very minor stake in the country.

I cannot help thinking that if recovery is going to come, we shall eventually have a much clearer indication of it than we have at the moment and that although we may not be in at the bottom, there will be more than enough profit to be made when we can go in with more real confidence.

It is on these broad grounds that I personally should not be in the least bit sorry to be wholly out of America at the moment.

Yours truly,

F. C. SCOTT

From a letter to F. C. SCOTT, *29 November 1933*

3. I would by no means deny that you might not turn out right about America. At any rate I completely concede that the real issue is the major one as to the future of the country, rather than the prospects of particular securities, and it is really on this rather than on details that we make different estimates. I feel that general disaster for a great country like United States is a far more unlikely event than disaster for particular firms or industries, and that nine times out of ten it is a safe bet that the extremes of misfortune will not occur.

On this point of detail in your letter of November 28, the estimate I made already allows for the cost of renewing exchange transactions so far as they have been incurred up to date. And it seems to me rather a severe test that more profit could have been made in other directions, especially as the Board was until fairly lately extremely doubtful, not only about increasing its holdings of long-dated gilt-edged securities, but even of retaining those we already had. As to what I said about some of Falk's investments, I may be more explicit than my own memory justifies, since I sank towards the end into tacit acquiescence, especially as regards individual securities. I only meant really that I did not intend to be taking any personal responsibility about the selection, since in a number of cases I knew nothing whatever about the securities and did not pretend to do so.

Sorry for all this post mortem discussion, which we really oughtn't to go in for; except that it is useful, as you say, to try to get clear as to what one's real reasons are when there is a difference of opinion. The more I have to do with investment, the more I believe in a certain continuity of policy. The danger of Board management, against which one has to be on one's guard, is lest one should succeed in persuading the Board rather against its better judgement in the first instance, and then have to suffer the penalty of their faint-heartedness at a later date, just when the virtues of continuity of mind are most required if one is to be successful in the long run.

However, I think we can now feel that our stake in America is so small as not to be any occasion of major concern either way.

In the spring of 1938, Keynes drafted a series of post mortems on the previous year's investment results. The first was designed for the Provincial, although it also saw limited circulation at the National Mutual. In these cases he circulated a preliminary draft in February and a final draft in March. Since it also concerns the experience of King's, we reprint the final draft below along with the document Keynes designed for the Estates Committee of King's on 8 May.[37]

On reading Keynes's post mortem, Francis Scott on 2 May wrote Keynes a long letter wondering whether a more conventional investment policy would have avoided the Provincial's depreciation of £420,000 between the 31 December 1936 and 31 March 1938. He also wondered whether future investment policy might be guided by a scheme that limited investments in particular groups of securities to fairly fixed percentages. Keynes replied.

To F. C. SCOTT, *7 June 1938*

My dear Francis,

I now have time to reply in detail to your letter of May 2.

[37] Below, pp. 92–109.

I

It is important in conducting a post mortem to be sure what is one's test of success. One important test is the avoidance of 'stumers' with which many investment lists are disfigured. I mean by this definite mistakes where the fall in value is due not merely to fluctuations, but to an intrinsic loss of capital. These are in an altogether different category from fluctuating securities, since there is no particular reason to expect a subsequent recovery. There is apt to be great confusion of mind between depreciation arising out of fluctuations and depreciation arising out of serious mistakes in the choice of individual securities.

On this test I think we can claim very good success. Our list includes a proportion of the above sort of mistake, but the amount of capital involved is not large. It is particularly useful for future guidance to make a list of these and remember how they arose. The following is my list, in which I have not attempted to include Americans since it is particularly difficult at the present time to analyse them accurately from this point of view:— Omes; Petters Preference; British and Dominions Film; Carbo Plaster; Enfield Rolling Mills; Grand Union Canal; South African Torbanite; Universal Rubber Paviors; Mortgage Bank of Chile.

You will notice that these are practically all specialities and rather obscure concerns, mostly bought on private advice. Omes was due to Trouton; Carbo Plaster and South African Torbanite to Falk; Enfield Rolling Mills and Grand Union Canal to Brett. I am sure experience shows that private and personal recommendations of this class of security tend to turn out wrong in the long run. I am not quite sure whether Enfield Rolling Mills is justifiably included in that list, since it may succeed in getting over its preliminary difficulties. But perhaps our holding of Textiles bought on Hunter's advice ought also to be included, since one rather doubts whether they will recover fully, even when industry is again at a peak.

The other chief test must be, I would urge, against representative index numbers. A valuation at the bottom of the slump tends to bring out an unduly unfavourable result as against an investment policy which on the whole avoids equities; since it allows nothing for the nest egg in hand arising out of the fact that such a valuation is assuming in effect that one has purchased a large volume of equities at bottom prices. As long as you are beating the index number by a satisfactory percentage on the round journey there is, I am sure, not too much to worry about. For provided that you are avoiding stumers and beating the index number, you are bound to do brilliantly in the long run.

The modern habit of concentrating on calculations of appreciation and depreciation tends to interfere with what should be the proper habit of mind that the object of an investment policy is averaging through time. Insurance policy is, of course, doing that a little bit; but on the whole investment [insurance?] policy is averaging over a number of items which are in the same position in time, but in different positions in place. Investment policy which is successful in averaging through time will produce the same good results as insurance policy which is successful in averaging through place; and one must not be deflected from the sound principles of that kind of averaging any more than one must be deflected in an insurance policy by a heavy loss in a particular place.

II

I come next to the question of the percentage of aggregate funds which it is prudent to hold in different classes of investments. We certainly need minimum percentage in government securities and maximum percentage in ordinary shares. This is required partly for appearances; partly in the case of government securities to provide a satisfactory margin over our large volume of deposited securities, and in the case of ordinary shares to avoid the risk of excessive fluctuations exceeding our investment reserves.

But apart from these two general principles I am strongly opposed to rigidities in other respects. Fixed percentage—particularly within each group of industry etc.—is surely altogether opposed to having an investment policy at all. The whole art is to vary the emphasis and the centre of gravity of one's portfolio according to circumstances. Subject to a minimum in government securities and a maximum in ordinary shares I would strongly urge the desirability of the greatest possible flexibility.

Proceeding to details, I am in sympathy with your suggestion for some increase in our holding of British Government securities. At present we hold a rather larger percentage than the average of all the insurance companies measured as a percentage of total assets. (At the end of 1936 insurance companies as a whole held 23·1 per cent in British Government securities as against our holding of 24·82 at the end of 1937 and 26·44 in March 1938.) Since, however, other offices held a much larger percentage of non-Stock Exchange assets their percentage of British Government securities measured as a percentage of Stock Exchange assets was higher than ours. There is, I agree, a good deal to be said for raising our percentage to some such figure as you propose—33 per cent. An alternative way to look at it would be to include public boards and railway debentures and aim at 40 per cent in British Government securities, British public boards, municipal securities and railway debentures taken altogether.

As regards colonial government and foreign government securities, I should be quite ready to cut them out altogether as a normal policy, apart from investments made on quite special considerations and those required for the purpose of insurance deposits.

In the case of ordinary shares there ought to be a fairly wide margin of fluctuation in the percentage held: say between 20 and 30 per cent and without any fixed percentages as between different classes of ordinary shares.

This would leave between 30 and 40 per cent on fixed-interest securities (debenture and preference taken together) in transport, industrial and financial concerns at home and abroad.

The above are intended as percentages of Stock Exchange securities rather than of total assets. We mainly differ, of course, from other offices in having a much smaller percentage of non-Stock Exchange assets. I should imagine that the average percentage of non-Stock Exchange assets to total assets is between 20 and 30 per cent. Including Capital and Country Estates and mortgages we might aim at increasing our non-Stock Exchange holdings towards 10 per cent. But I should not be very keen on going beyond this. They are very unliquid; by no means free from risk, and involve difficult problems of management. I doubt if, generally speaking, they offer a yield sufficient to compensate for these disadvantages.

III

As regards the time for change, I agree with you that we should not be too precipitate. A better opportunity will be given when markets are more active and have shown some recovery. The present inactivity of markets makes exchanges of securities exceptionally expensive. Moreover, when the time comes for diminishing our holding in Americans—of which when it does arrive I should wish to take advantage—this may offer a suitable opportunity for a general re-adjustment of percentages.

There is, however, one immediate step which might, I suggest, be helpful and facilitate some immediate re-adjustment as well as acting as a guide to the Board in general and to myself in detail. I suggest that a complete list of our holdings should be circulated to all the members of the Finance Committee, and that they should mark those securities about the continued holding of which they feel definitely enthusiastic at present prices —i.e. those securities which they feel clearly it would be a mistake to sell in present conditions. This would enable us to discover which securities none of us holds a brief for. It is a leading fault of all institutional investors that their portfolio gradually tends to contain a long list of forgotten holdings originally purchased for reasons which no longer exist and for which no one holds a brief.

This might also provide an opportunity for some concentration of holdings by exchanging the forgotten holdings in order to increase the stake in those companies about which some of us at least have an instructed enthusiasm.

IV

One final *caveat*: Compared with their predecessors, modern investors concentrate too much on annual, quarterly, or even monthly valuations of what they hold, and on capital appreciation and depreciation generally; and too little either on immediate yield or on future prospects and intrinsic worth. I would plead, therefore, that the question of yield should not be overlooked. Over a period of time this is at least as valuable a test of sound investment as those tests with which I began this comment.

In 1937 we earned $5\frac{1}{2}$ per cent on book value—or say 5 per cent on market value. Presumably there will be some setback in 1938 at any rate on book value, though not perhaps on market value. This yield is the result of a steady improvement in recent years amounting in aggregate to more than 1 per cent on book value, and I should guess approaching $\frac{1}{2}$ per cent on market value.

I should like to continue to aim at something approaching 5 per cent on market value. If we hold 40 per cent in gilt-edged securities not yielding on the average much more than $3\frac{1}{2}$ per cent, this implies a substantial holding at much higher yields. I believe myself that the safest and soundest average yield basis is arrived at as an average of high and low yielding securities and that the intermediate securities yielding between 4 and 5 per cent are in the long run less satisfactory than the strictly gilt-edged securities on the one hand and the high yielding equities on the other. And I should be sorry to see a change in investment policy which tended either to result in a considerable reduction in yield and interest earnings or alternatively a greater concentration in the class of securities yielding between 4 and 5 per cent. I should, in short, like to balance a holding of equities larger than the average (though not so much larger as appears at first sight if real estate is included with the equities) by holding more gilt-edged securities than the average.

Yours ever,
[copy initialled] J. M. K.

The next letter of Keynes's we print was written soon after the outbreak of war.

To F. C. SCOTT, *20 September 1939*

My dear Francis,

Investment Position

Until recently technical difficulties were still in the way of doing much in America. But permission has now come through without the least difficulty. Sales up to date come to about $28,000, and there are any number of limits outstanding, not much above the market, which will be touched off day by day, if the present upward movement continues.

Now that you have reassured me as to the amount of liquidity you will need this year, and in the light of Barber's[38] latest figures as to the bank position, my own view is rather strongly that I should like to reinvest a considerable proportion of American sales in this market.

I agree with you that the latter may easily go lower. It is at present friendless. The clearing up of pre-war positions, plus the deadlock in gilt-edged, plus the compulsory insurance scheme,

---

[38] J. A. Barber was the secretary of the Provincial.

plus the fear of new taxation, is deterring most buyers. The result is that the very prime industrials which have usually looked too dear can now be got to yield 7 per cent or better. Taking a long view, I believe we ought to have them. If we try to hit the bottom, we shall certainly not get them. I don't feel that in wartime one ought to hold more cash than one really needs for one's own prospective purposes. For surely the one thing that is certain is that it is money, rather than equities, which must in the end depreciate in value.

The kind of shares I have in view are Barclay's Bank, 'A', fully paid, fixed interest; Imperial Tobacco (we sold these the other day at 6½ and could now repurchase them at 5); even the electricity shares, such as County of London, which are being valued on the basis that because people will be cutting their use of current for the time being they will do so permanently; Marks and Spencer; Woolworth; iron and steel shares. Indeed one could make a long list. They have all fallen 20 or 30 per cent or more.

I wonder also what you think about insurance shares. There has been a huge drop in Prudential, to give an example. The highest price of the year was 35¾. On August 23rd they stood at 31. The present price is 21. Do you really think that the Prudential has lost 40 per cent of its assets? We sold our Pearl shares not long ago at 19. We could repurchase them at 12½. I consider these shares really more attractive than the raw commodity shares which are popular and are standing up well.

Or take the armament shares, where the fear of taxation seems to me beyond all reason. John Brown which, apart from its intrinsic merits, is, of course, overwhelmed with work, has fallen 25 per cent. The aeroplane companies have fallen about 50 per cent, since the beginning of the year, and are now priced on the basis that they cannot possibly hope to repeat the average of their pre-war profits. Turning back to electricity shares. County of London have fallen from a highest of the year of 46s. 9d. (highest of 1938—51s. 9d.) and a price of 41s. 6d. from August 23rd, to a price of 28s. 9d.; surely all this is rather nonsense.

The position is that the sterling value of our American shares has, in many cases, gone up 40 per cent or more and the price of the very primest British shares has fallen 25 to 30 per cent or more. In other words, the relative price of American shares in terms of British shares has risen 100 per cent in the last few weeks. (Americans, which were worth 100, can be sold for 140; British, which were worth 100, can be bought at 70.)

In the light of the present prices of British shares, I feel that there is a good case perhaps for selling the Americans more rapidly than one had intended and not being too greedy about the price, and reinvesting in prime British stocks. On the other hand, if one is going to keep one's proceeds in cash, I should be inclined to go slow with American sales, hoping for higher prices yet. And very considerably higher prices in America are, of course, on the map.

I shall be at Cambridge for the week-end and letters should be sent there. I don't pretend that the problem is easy. Though I am convinced by the above argument, I find it quite difficult to act on it in my own case or in that of King's. But, undoubtedly, if America goes 10 per cent higher in the course of the next week, as they well may if the neutrality legislation goes through, and British shares do not rise, I should find it much easier to get moving.

I have been seeing a lot of people here[39] and had a long conference at the Treasury yesterday. We are gravely over-organised and there is much chaos. I suppose things will shake down. At present the home front is one grand mess. We are still just running on pre-war momentum. But, if nothing is done, much of the economic life of the country will be at a standstill in a month's time. I suppose we shall get near that and then finally pull ourselves together and do what is sensible.

On the cheering side, I had a visit yesterday from the Elmhirsts,[40] who had flown over and only left Washington a few days

---

[39] Keynes was writing from London.   [40] See *JMK*, vol. XXII, p. 22.

ago. They are in close touch with the President and the Administration. They are convinced that the neutrality legislation will go through (as to that we shall soon get the right answer) and, according to them, practically everyone in Washington and New York is perfectly certain that America would come in in some shape or form if we got into any difficulties or if there was any bombing of London and Paris. But what would be easy, if we handled ourselves properly, would be to get a complete economic front with America, whilst not asking them to send troops. They say that emotionally people in America, precisely, I expect, because they cannot act, have let themselves go more than we have, and that the anti-German emotion is universal and vehement. They said that almost everyone they saw in either party was passionately on our side.

Yours ever,
[copy initialled] J.M.K.

Just over a month later, he was explaining his recent investment activities to Scott—an indication of the discretion Keynes enjoyed.

To F. C. SCOTT, *20 October 1939*

My dear Francis,

As you may be rather perplexed about what I am doing in the gilt-edged market, I had better report briefly in advance of next week's Board meeting.

You will remember that I was firm against accepting the sacrifice of income which would have been involved any time in the past two years in moving out of our long-dated securities, such as Consols, into the dated securities of comparatively short term. For, as you will remember, I was not convinced that the risk of heavier depreciation on the former was great enough to justify the sacrifice of the existing position.

As things have turned out, the position is more paradoxical. During the last week or two, Consols, which is our principal holding, has risen about $7\frac{1}{2}$ per cent above its minimum price, whereas several of the most attractive short-dated securities can still be purchased at the minimum. The result is that, for the first time in history that I am aware of, you can actually get a higher net redemption yield on the short-dated securities than on the undated securities of the Consol type. It seems to me that this situation is the result of the disorganisation of the market and cannot possibly last as soon as managers of Life offices etc. have had time to study their yield tables. I have, therefore, rather paradoxically as I say, found this the right moment for moving, on a modest scale, out of the long-dated into the short-dated. This means a slight sacrifice of running income as contrasted with redemption income, but it does represent a considerable safe-guarding of the position without real sacrifice. For example, I have been selling Consols at a price to give a gross redemption yield of £3 15s. 4d. and a net redemption yield of £2 7s. 0d., and re-investing part of the proceeds in National Defence Loan at 3 per cent, which must be repaid at par in 1958, to yield £3 12s. 0d. gross redemption and £2 7s. 6d. net redemption (actually a few pennies better than Consols!); and I have actually been able to purchase quite a few thousand pounds of London Electric Transport $2\frac{1}{2}$'s, which has to be repaid in 1955 at latest and $2\frac{1}{2}$ per cent Railway Finance, repayable in 1952 (only 13 years hence), to yield, in the first case £3 17s. 7d. gross redemption and £2 16s. 0d. net redemption, and in the second case £3 17s. 8d. gross redemption and £2 16s. 0d. net redemption, or actually nearly 10s. per cent net redemption yield higher than Consols. These two securities are, of course, Government guaranteed stocks and have nothing to do with the credit of the railways. I never saw anything so topsy-turvy in my life. There is an additional reason for the switch, in that we obtain quite a substantial realised loss on the Consols for income tax purposes. In fact we shall recover on income tax an amount very nearly equal to the whole of our depreciation on Consols since the end of last year, i.e. the mere act of switching our large holding of Consols into some other

Government stock would cause a tax saving nearly equal to the whole of this year's depreciation on our gilt-edged holding.

I have in fact only operated so far on a relatively small scale, partly because the market does not allow large-scale operations. I also have bought rather more than I have sold, since I am not up to date in the bank position. This can, however, easily be rectified as soon as I know the position at next Wednesday's meeting. Perhaps you could let me have a wire on Monday morning, if, after some sales I hope to make today, we seem to be too heavily over-invested. I should also like to have your views about proceeding on a much more substantial scale, if suitable opportunity offers. I have now really quite a good hope, if nothing bad happens in the rest of this year, of ending the year without any depreciation on book values. But, undoubtedly, a further move in the above direction would consolidate the position a good deal.

Thanks for your letter of October 16th with two or three suggestions. The prices given in your Manchester stockbroker's list, however, relate to the buying opportunities of a fortnight or three weeks ago. For the Grand Trunk, which you call 80, one would have to pay about 90, and for the Distillers Pref., which you call 24s., the price would not be less than 27s. On the other hand the Watney Preferred may be in the neighbourhood of your price, and I have put on a buying limit today to test the market.

Yours ever,
[copy initialled] J. M. K.

In April 1940 after Scott wondered about reducing the Provincial's holding of Electric Power and Light Preferred and United Gas Preferred, Keynes tried to reassure him, after going into a bit of back history.

To F. C. SCOTT, *10 April 1940*

Dear Francis,

Electric Power and Light

I am always in danger of getting into disgrace about the securities where we have made most money! And I am afraid that Electric Power & Light is going to get settled in your mind, like Austins, as one of our grand mistakes.[41]

But I do not think you can really judge it properly unless you go into the back history. These are shares I have been following more closely than anything else in the American market for the last six years, and we have been in and out at various times. So I got Mackay to prepare a history of the whole thing, which I append.[42]

You will see from this that so far we have made a profit, realised or on paper, in the Electric Power & Light Preferred and the United Gas Preferred, of approximately £31,000. It is true that the present value of our remaining holding is £48,000. But, if you think of £31,000 of this as having been provided out of profits, the actual amount of cash we have put into these stocks is only £17,000, or a little more than one-third of the gross figure. Yet this is in spite of the fact that the main event for which I have been waiting all this time has not yet happened, so that even with this disappointment we have not done too badly. I am still convinced that one is doing a fundamentally sound thing, that is to say, backing intrinsic values, enormously in excess of the market price, which at some utterly unpredictable date will in due course bring the ship home.

I am rather encouraged to keep this correspondence going, since the Electric Power & Light Preferred have in fact risen about 40 per cent since we began it, the $6 Preferred being, I think, 22½ when you first wrote to me a few weeks ago, and are now, according to the latest quotations, 31 bid, as you will see

[41] Keynes's holdings of these shares had also been very successful.
[42] Not printed.

from Mackay's statement. We have also, since I last wrote to you, sold a further 100 United Gas Preferred which rose high enough to reach an old-standing limit.

My latest information is that this rise is probably due to a change for the better in the prospects of the funding scheme for the arrears of United Gas First Preferred. There is now said to be a much better chance of this. But I am not backing this in the very near future. I am only saying that it is bound to happen sooner or later. Very few American investors buy any stock for the sake of something which is going to happen more than six months hence, even though its probability is exceedingly high; and it is out of taking advantage of this psychological peculiarity of theirs that most money is made.

You won't believe me, I know. But it is out of these big units of the small number of securities about which one feels absolutely happy that all one's profits are made. I fancy it is true that practically the whole of the appreciation of the Provincial since we started is accounted for by the profits on Austins, and the profits on Electric Power & Light and on United Gas. At any rate, I am sure I could pick out six of my pets, and that much more than the whole of our profit would have been made out of them. Out of the ordinary mixed bag of investments nobody ever makes anything. And if one breaks more or less even, it is the best you can possibly hope for. This has been my uniform experience in all investment connections. Exactly the same thing is true in the case of King's. And in the case of my own personal investments, which have done a great deal better than the Provincial's, the sole explanation is that I have held my pets in relatively larger proportions, often holding myself even larger units than the Provincial, out of a fund which is, of course, only a small fraction of the size.

Yours,

[copy initialled] J. M. K.

When he moved to the Treasury in 1940, Keynes's involvement in the Provincial lessened, especially once he became more closely involved in advising the Government on taxation and new issue policy. However, he still provided advice on occasion.

For example, in January 1942, Keynes purchased 10,000 shares of Elder Dempster Holdings for the Provincial. He reported this to Scott on 10 January. On 13 January, Scott replied that he 'did not see the justification for such a large and exceptional unit' and suggested that the holding be halved over the next six months. Keynes replied.

To F. C. SCOTT, *16 January 1942*

My dear Francis,

Sorry to have gone too large in Elder Dempster. But, finding a security which was good, which we had not got and of which a large block could actually be purchased—an accumulation of circumstances I had not come across for months—I lost my head. I was also suffering from my chronic delusion that one good share is safer than ten bad ones, and I am always forgetting that hardly anyone else shares this particular delusion. The price has, I think, now gone up about 6*d*, so you can get rid of any surplus without loss that you would like to.

Yours,
[copy initialled] J.M.K.

From F. C. SCOTT, *28 January 1942*

Dear Maynard,
Elder Dempster

Thanks for your letter, which I put on one side to answer some time, when I could make up my mind whether it really called for an answer or was even intended to invite one, but having to spend some hours in the train I have been ruminating on it.

I always remember Falk declaiming with irresistible logic (for once he was quite lucid) on the position of the Jute Industries Preference and proving they were an essentially sound purchase and yet in its degree I suppose we had no more disastrous investment. I remember at the time reflecting that I had been brought up by a very intelligent father to distrust figures and to remember that other factors—management, competition, slumps and booms, and all kinds of unforeseen factors—so often completely upset the most convincing array of figures.

So I feel inclined to challenge your assumption that on such figure information as we have in the Elder Dempster papers, you are entitled to say you have picked a winner or that ten other investments picked with some reasonable care might not prove a sounder choice. You know perfectly well you villainously beg the question in the form in which you put it! At least if I had given £20,000 into your hands to invest, I should with reason feel easier in my mind if I knew you had spread it over four investments rather than one.

But I am not sure the issue may not go deeper, and that you and I may not be to some extent at variance on the fundamental principles of investment policy. My conception of our responsibility is that our first primary duty is to so invest our funds, which are the security we offer our policy-holders for the fulfilment of our contracts, that the public confidence will never be impaired. Our second task is to ensure that the bulk of them are in semi-liquid form, and the third is to earn a reasonable rate of interest return. Only as an incidental to these considerations have we the right to consider capital profits, and our major concern is to reduce the swing of the pendulum between high and low market valuations to the minimum.

I am sometimes tempted to think that you would pervert my morals and encourage me in my secret vice to regard capital profits as a definite part of our investment plan and in fact to regard the investment of our funds, not as incidental to our main business—insurance—but as an equally important contributor to the profits of the Company. I have little doubt you will indignantly deny my accusation, and, if you can find the time and the energy, will riddle my impeachment with devastating argument, but all the while I shall still have more than a suspicion that your and my profit-motive devil has only made a strategic and temporary retreat, biding his time.

Seriously, I am entirely convinced that we are right in keeping to certain investment limits both in broad categories of class and in the individual investments within those categories. As regards our equity holdings, I am prepared to regard £5,000 as a minimum limit for a sound industrial unit, and to increase this to £10,000 or even £20,000 where there is such a spread of risk and variation of market as to justify this differentiation. I know it is a matter of opinion just where such an investment as Elder Dempster would come in these gradations, but I should have thought that a shipping company, such as this, which is primarily dependent on one route—the West Coast trade—was not a widespread risk and as such was probably suitable for a normal limit of £5,000 or £7,500 at most. The fact that the shares are on a favourable price basis does not seem to me an argument for increasing our acceptance limit, or if admitted as an argument only for some modest increase. All this will be anathema to you, but you must have patience with my insurance mind and its train of thought, the reduction of everything to some kind of methodical practice, with a law of average as its basic principle.

I have no fear we can come to any harm with this particular investment, and am content to leave it at all events until we think some other shipping shares equally or more attractive, but your letter was provocative, and as I utterly absolve you from the need for any reply till we meet, you will probably forgive my outburst.

Yours sincerely,
F. C. SCOTT

To F. C. SCOTT, *6 February 1942*

My dear Francis,

Elder Dempster

I have even less leisure than usual, and you must forgive me if I do not reply to your letter of January 28th at any length. It raises a subject which it would need a long essay to answer. Moreover, it is a subject on which we both of us have often expressed our views before. So may I limit myself to the following few points?—

(1) I confess that I bought too much of this particular security and would have done better to buy less.

(2) In saying that I preferred one good security to ten bad ones, of course, as you say, I was begging the question. I ought to have said that I preferred one investment about which I had sufficient information to form a judgement to ten securities about which I know little or nothing.

(3) I consider capital profits and accruing income as the measure of success. But it is not the case that I aim at capital profits as such. There are very few investors, I should say, who eschew the attempt to snatch capital profits at an early date more than I do. I lay myself open to criticism because I am generally

trying to look a long way ahead and am prepared to ignore immediate fluctuations, if I am satisfied that the assets and the earning power are there. My purpose is to buy securities where I am satisfied as to assets and ultimate earning power and where the market price seems cheap in relation to these. If I succeed in this, I shall simultaneously have achieved safety-first and capital profits. All stocks and shares go up and down so violently that a safety-first policy is practically certain, if it is successful, to result in capital profits. For when the safety, excellence and cheapness of a share is generally realised, its price is bound to go up. The Elder Dempster case is a very good example of this. I have no particular expectation of this share going up at any early date. I picked it because it seemed to me exceedingly safe and, apart from short-term fluctuations, unlikely to go down in the years ahead.

I am quite incapable of having adequate knowledge of more than a very limited range of investments. Time and opportunity do not allow more. Therefore, as the investible sums increase, the size of the unit must increase. I am in favour of having as large a unit as market conditions will allow and, apart from a small group of securities, this generally means a smaller unit than would be made necessary by the size of the investible fund.

(4) As good examples of speculative attempts at capital profits I should instance South American shares and oil companies within the area of hostilities. I should not deny for a moment that such investments may result in capital profits. My objection is that I have no information on which to reach a good judgement, and the risks are clearly enormous. To suppose that safety-first consists in having a small gamble in a large number of different directions of the above kind, as compared with a substantial stake in a company where's one information is adequate, strikes me as a travesty of investment policy.

(5) The units we actually work to in the Provincial represent a very expensive concession from what I personally think the counsel of perfection. There has been an extremely good experimental test of this in a comparison of results in the accounts of

the Provincial and King's over the last twenty years. The spread of the King's investments between gilt-edged and others is much the same. The arguments against undue risk and in favour of stability of income are at least as great for a college as for an insurance company. Since I have been so closely concerned with both, the leading shares purchased by both have been very much the same in both cases. Where one institution has held a large stake in a particular direction in almost every instance the other one has also.

Nevertheless, King's has done immeasurably better than the Provincial. I am quite sure the reason for this is that our unit of investment, which has been practically the same size as for the Provincial, though our investible funds are only about one-third as large, has been so much larger. We have been much more strictly limited to shares where I have felt myself in a position to have a sound judgement. We have not lived up to this as much as we should. We should have done better still if we had lived up to it more. Looking back, I feel this applies particularly to purchases in the American market as distinct from the London market, though on the whole the American investments have worked out all right.

The other day we were looking at our back records with a view to conducting a little bit of a post mortem and to discover whence the satisfactory results came. The answer seemed to be that (with one or two minor exceptions in the American market) there had scarcely been a single case of any large-scale loss. There had been big fluctuations in market prices. But none of the main investments had, in the end, turned out otherwise than all right. Thus, against the profits which inevitably accumulate, there were comparatively few losses to offset. Virtually *all* our big holdings had come right.

Now that is what I call a safety-first policy as judged by results. Where King's has made profits the Provincial has nearly always made profits too. But they have not been an equally high proportion of the total invested funds.

Yours ever,
[copy initialled] J.M.K.

Scott replied on 9 February reporting that 'All you write is intensely interesting and causes me to think furiously'. He asked Keynes to meet him in London, which he did on 12 February.

Our final letter comes from the end of the war, when Scott had suddenly decided to increase the Provincial's bank balance. Keynes initially questioned the decision and on receiving what he regarded as an unsatisfactory reply continued the correspondence.

To F. C. SCOTT, *25 July 1945*

Dear Francis,

I still do not see how we can be short of cash for currently accruing taxes, since they are necessarily on profits, which come to us in cash. Moreover, we never have to take account from the cash point of view both of arrears and prospects, since the paying over of taxes is always the same amount in arrear. Surely, therefore, the question really comes down to the issue whether Workmen's Compensation and Marine are likely to shrink more than Motor and other departments increase. On this I was simply going on your figures. They show there is not much in it, namely that the shrinkage will exceed the growth by some £50,000, which will be more than offset by current profits after deduction of tax. In fact, I think we shall both be rather surprised if things really work out like this, but that is another matter.

However, in whatever way these particular figures may work out, the argument, as I see it, is rather different. If there is a liability to shrinkage, it means that we should be to a fair extent in marketable securities. The distinction of marketable and unmarketable is quite different between short-dated and long-dated. I think there is an argument for being in marketable securities, not perhaps so much on a possible temporary position, but in general an insurance company should be liquid in the sense of being marketable.

I have always myself aimed rather definitely at this in thinking of policy. I should say that we are considerably more liquid than most insurance companies, since we have so much less in real estate, mortgages and other sticky stuff. In fact, at the last Board Meeting we expressly took steps to clear out a few securities which seemed particularly unmarketable.

The choice as between cash or near-cash and investments proper seems to me to depend primarily on other considerations. There is first of all the general issue of risk, and that we are dealing with by the rather high proportion of the Stable Fund. The second consideration is whether at any given date our judgement is that the market is high or low.

A situation may easily arise in which I should be greatly influenced in favour of near-cash on these grounds. I should not be at all surprised if that is not the position, let us say, two years hence. But the present position seems to me most definitely of the opposite character. The incidence of E[xcess] P[rofits] T[ax][43] and other war measures has prevented equities from reflecting, as in the long run they must, the change in the value of money. I feel great confidence that there is no likelihood of a reversal of the trend towards a falling value of money in the foreseeable future. Thus, when we move into clearer peace-time conditions, I should predict with a very high degree of confidence that a well-selected group of equities is bound to do well. Furthermore, the real risk of the future, about which it is difficult to predict for certain, is whether we may not be in for a further rise of prices due either to internal reasons (i.e. increases of wages) or external reasons (i.e. a general rise in international prices of food and raw materials). These are the real, genuine risks ahead of us, against which wise investment should endeavour to hedge.

Much the same applies to the rate of interest. Gilt-edged rates have trended downwards, to the surprise of a good many people. It is much more likely that this trend will be continued, though

[43] Then at 100 per cent with a provision for a post-war credit of 20 per cent.

perhaps not very decidedly, rather than that it will be reversed. Here again the eventual effect of the falling rate of interest has not been fully reflected, in my judgement, in the prices of equities.

My expectation would be that, in due course, these tendencies and potentialities, which are now latent, will become more obvious to the common-or-garden investor. And, when that happens, it will very likely be carried too far.

In our own case, moreover, there is a very tiresome consideration which, whether we like it or not, tends in the same direction. That is the effect of the way in which we are taxed. For the present, at any rate, that has a quite enormous stabilising effect on our profit position as determined by our investments, as distinct from the insurance business. It means, as you are well aware, that it is very difficult for us to retain any worthwhile realised profits. Equally it means that we are protected from the incidence of realised losses. Our present difficulty is that, if we were in fact to have to realise a substantial sum of money, we should at the same time have to realise a substantial amount of profit, a large part of which would disappear in taxation. But the fact that practically the whole of our investments stand above, and often considerably above, what we paid for them is scarcely an argument for not investing. And if the moment at which we had to realise (though personally I believe that the arrival of such a moment is exceedingly improbable) should happen at a time when some, at least, of our securities have been falling a bit, it would not do us much harm to make a careful selection for sale of the least attractive, and the realised losses that we should then bring in would be substantially offset by the effect of the tax position.

In fact the real perplexity, as I see it, is somewhat different. In the relatively near future it is exceedingly difficult in the event of realisation either for us to profit from appreciation or to lose from depreciation. We are willy-nilly in a rather stable position. Looking further ahead, one hopes that this situation will no longer apply in its present intensity. Thus we are in an exceptionally strong position for making purchases now with almost complete exemption from risk in the near future, if we make mistakes, since we can then retrace our steps with very little loss, if any, to ourselves, whilst if we do not make mistakes, we shall in general be able to hold on and postpone realisation until a time of more favourable tax position.

You will see that I regard the situation in rather a more complicated fashion than as simply a matter of whether or not our funds will continue swelling as they have of late or will experience a reaction. In anything remotely resembling present circumstances a reaction in the size of our funds could scarcely result, for the reasons just explained, in any significant capital loss. Whereas, if we keep in near-cash on anything more than a modest scale at the present juncture, what is likely to happen, in my judgement, is that such cash resources will after a bit increase quite excessively, and we may then find ourselves being forced into the market in much less favourable conditions. If we keep rather fully invested before the dangerous period is imminent, that will be extremely wholesome for us, since it will make it much easier to reverse operations and have a policy more suitable to the changed conditions when the change arises.

In practice, of course, we can, and should, compromise about all this. But the above is the best investment advice I can give, and I should, therefore, give it.

I am sending a copy of this letter to Macpherson.

Yours,
[copy initialled] J. M. K.

P.S. The above was written before the General Election, but I purposely refrained from posting it so that I could add a postscript in the light of the Election. Obviously the results will make markets a bit queasy for the time being.[44] But, except on a very

[44] The election brought the Labour Party to power with a majority of 146 over all other parties.

short view, my belief is that they reinforce the general conclusions arrived at above, for the following reasons:

(1) the new Government will be, if anything, more wedded to
cheap money than the old;

(2) the chances of inflation through a rise in wage rates are, I
should say, a little greater, rather than a little less, than they
were before; and

(3) the maintenance of a system of taxation which will continue to have a highly stabilising effect on our results, depriving
us at the same time of the benefit of our profits and of the
incidence of our losses, is also greater, rather than less, than it
was.

It was partly because I felt that the results of the Election,
whatever they were, could not forcibly weaken the arguments I
was using that I wrote as I did. However, we shall have to take
stock of all this at the next board meeting. No need to do anything meanwhile. I held up earlier in the week the ordering [of]
Leylands which were approved in principle at the last board
meeting, but have realised it today at a low limit. So far from
having increased our investment in ordinary shares by upwards
of £20,000, as we were contemplating at the last board meeting,
we have in fact actually reduced our holdings, apart from the
order for Leylands, not yet executed.

27.7.45

Immediately after this letter, Keynes's Treasury position with a change of
Government required him 'to retire into silence and inactivity'. Then, with
the loan negotiations and other calls on his time, he devoted relatively little
time to the Provincial's investments during the rest of his life.

III. *Keynes and King's*

Keynes became involved in the financial affairs for the College almost
immediately after his election as a Fellow, when his colleagues elected him
an Inspector of Accounts for 1909. This meant that he and his fellow
inspector had to examine the College's accounts for the year and report to

the Fellows on any irregularities, or on any suggestions for changes in practice. In 1911 he was made a member of the Estates Committee.

In the three reports of the Inspectors with which he was associated, there were requests that the Bursars consider the more profitable employment of the sums which they held on current account. In 1909 the request was muted; in 1910 the Inspectors presented a reasoned case for better management by pointing out that for only two weeks of the year did the College's cash balances fall below £3,000, whilst for all but 8 weeks they stood above £4,500 and for nearly a third of the year they stood above £6,000—this in the face of regular payments. In 1911 with no further action there were even sharper comments from the Inspectors. In 1911 there were also some suggestions for investigating the possibility of further improvements and economies in the administration of the kitchens. In this light it is less surprising that in the autumn of 1912, after another year's experience and Bursarial inactivity, after organising the younger Fellows into a Junior Caucus, Keynes moved three motions in the Annual Congregation. The first renewed the attack on the Bursar's large cash balances. It was carried. The second asked for a committee to consider the integration of prices and contracts in the kitchen, buttery and combination room departments and to enquire into the staff's employment conditions. It too was carried, and Keynes appointed to the committee. The third proposed an increase in the Fellowship dividend from £120 to £130 a year, thus implying a lack of confidence in the Bursar's advice on the matter. It was heavily defeated, but Keynes was elected to the College Council at the same meeting. There matters rested until after the War, although Keynes did become a member of a committee in 1913 to consider the Bursar's resignation.[45]

After his return to King's from the Treasury, Keynes again became closely involved in the financial affairs of the College. In November 1919 he became Second Bursar and from 1924 First Bursar, a post which he retained until his death. The first result of his influence came in June 1920, when the College agreed to authorise an investment of £30,000 'in foreign government and other government non-trustee securities'. This was the origin of the Chest, whose remit was subsequently broadened to include shares and currency and commodity speculation.

To set out his experience as a Bursar-investor, Table 6 provides certain summary statistics. In examining these, one must remember that the College's investment possibilities were constrained in that certain large funds, almost half the portfolio in the 1930s, were restricted to investing in trustee securities. Only one fund (the Chest) after 1920, and two further investment

[45] The First Bursar, C. E. Grant, remained in office until 1919.

funds (Funds B and C) were not so restricted. The results for these funds, plus Fund A which was restricted to trustee securities, are listed separately. Finally, for information we must note that Keynes's Bursarship saw the College involved in substantial property transactions. In every year in the 1920s, except 1925 when he bought farmland in North Lincolnshire,[46] Keynes disposed of property, with total sales coming to just over £200,000. Disposals continued in the early 1930s, but over the decade as a whole there were net purchases of just over £6,000. Between the 1939 and 1945 Audits, on the other hand Keynes was a net purchaser of property, spending just over £140,000.

In his College investing, as elsewhere, Keynes was extremely active. An examination of his transactions for the Chest, excluding shares still held at the time of the 1945 Audit, reveals that almost 30 per cent were held for three months or less, just under 15 per cent were held for longer than three years. However, as in the case of his personal portfolio, his dealing activity declined towards the end of his life: an examination of the securities in the Chest at Audit 1945 shows that the average security had been held for almost six years. To some extent this long-holding policy reflected the fact that, under the exchange control regulations introduced during 1939–40, any sale of a dollar security required the seller to remit the proceeds to the Treasury. Thus the regulations effectively locked Keynes into those parts of the dollar portfolio under his management that were not subject to vesting orders.

As noted above Keynes's activities on behalf of King's also involved some currency and commodity speculation. As regards the former, the sums do not seem to have been all that large: profits or losses only exceeded £1,000 on four occasions.[47] In the case of commodities, Keynes was more active after 1931, with realised profits exceeding £1,000 in eight of the nine years concerned. As with his personal account, profits reached a peak in 1936–7 at just over £17,000, with losses peaking the next year at just over £12,600. In the College's case, as in Keynes's personal dealings, losses on lard played an important role.

In the case of Keynes's College activities, we have two statements of his investment philosophy in the form of post mortems on his 1937–8 results. Both appear below. The first was designed for the board of the Provincial

[46] The idea was to let the 22 farms at Worlaby-cum-Elsham, but in 1928 renewed agricultural depression meant that many tenants could not cope. Thus the College came to farm 3,000 acres on its own account. The experiment produced fine breeding stock and led to Keynes's own experiment in farming at Tilton, but the financial returns were low. The farms were sold in 1956.

[47] Keynes was involved in forward exchange transactions for the Chest during 12 years after 1922, sometimes as a speculator and sometimes to hedge the Chest's dollar dividend income. Overall, the results showed a loss of £339.

Table 7. *Indices of King's College investments in securities 1920–45*

Year (ending 31 Aug.)	Total investments[a] (1)	Appreciation since 1920 as a percentage of (1)	The Chest (net)[b]		Fund A[c]	Fund B[d]	Fund C[e]	Income as a percentage of (1)
1920	100	—	100		—	—	—	2·6
1921	106	5·8	n.a.		—	—	—	4·5
1922	120	16·7	n.a.		—	—	—	5·0
1923	126	20·0	n.a.		—	—	—	5·4
1924	117	23·5	n.a.		—	—	—	5·9
1925	114	26·8	n.a.		—	—	—	6·9
1926	120	26·6	n.a.		—	—	—	6·2
1927	121	23·7	234		—	—	—	5·8
1928	127	24·5	226		—	—	—	5·5
1929	128	23·5	228		—	—	—	5·2
1930	131	15·3	154		—	—	—	5·9
1931[f]	120	3·9	116		—	—	—	6·2
1932	137	7·8	168		—	—	—	5·2
1933	164	30·0	227	100	100	100	100	4·2
1934	185	38·9	302	133	116	115	110	4·1
1935	197	48·1	436	192	120	130	110	4·3
1936	229	57·4	680	300	126	150	115	4·5
1937	230	56·8	738	325	120	160	105	4·9
1938	208	38·2	442	198	95	130	98	5·3
1939[g]	200	37·1	499	220	89	123	108	5·0
1940	183	33·2	421	186	83	104	130	6·5
1941	222	44·3	562	248	105	129	164	5·5
1942	235	45·1	557	246	113	135	179	5·2
1943	273	52·9	857	378	119	166	211	4·7
1944	293	54·8	981	433	121	175	220	4·3
1945	346	50·7	1,124	496	119	189	238	4·5

n.a. = not available.

[a] The figure for total investments includes the Chest, Funds A, B and C, the Trustee Account, funds supervised by the Ministry of Agriculture. It does not include property.

[b] The figure given for the Chest is net of its liabilities to other College funds. With these deposits netted out and allowing for the fact that the Chest normally spent all its income in the year received, the index for the Chest is an index of capital appreciation or depreciation on the original investment of 1920.

[c] A general College fund restricted to trustee securities.

[d] A general fund restricted to British shares (see p. 94 below).

[e] A general fund which only just exceeded £10,000 at the end of the period, which was restricted to investments in wasting assets.

[f] 1 November.

[g] 31 October.

(and, secondarily the National Mutual), while the second was for internal King's consumption. In the case of the latter, we have not printed certain appendix tables which provided exact figures for various aspects of the College's investments.

Memorandum for the Provincial Insurance Company, 7 March 1938

INVESTMENT RESULTS

I. *Comparison of the Provincial with the National Mutual*

1. *Sterling Ordinary Shares*

Detailed statistics are available for the Provincial from the beginning of 1929. On Dec. 31, 1937 the appreciation on cost amounted to 53 per cent of the average capital invested, or 5·79 per cent per annum over the nine years. Dividends received amounted to an average of 5·45 per cent per annum on the capital invested; so that the total return worked out at 11·24 per cent per annum. The amount invested increased substantially during the period, the final investment being a little more than 2½ times the average. Thus the amount invested during the three good years 1933–6 was substantially larger than in the three bad years 1929–31. On the other hand the amount was largest of all in the bad year 1937. As is shown in a subsequent table the gain from the investment of a level sum would have been a good deal less; on the other hand, that way of calculating entirely eliminates gains from buying and selling at the right time.

In the case of the National Mutual the return from appreciation works out at just under 1 per cent per annum on the average capital invested.

2. *Dollar Securities*

The Provincial statistics do not distinguish between preferred and common stocks, and they do not begin in a form from which these calculations can be made before Jan. 1, 1931. The aggregate depreciation on Dec. 31, 1937 was 5·75 per cent of the final capital invested; but here again the capital invested had grown considerably, and the depreciation worked out at about 11·5 per cent of the *average* capital invested, i.e. about 1·65 per cent per annum. The above is after deducting exchange profits from hedging, part of which was in francs and guilders. If only the exchange profits from dollars are included, the aggregate depreciation would be about 2·75 per cent greater.

In the case of the National Mutual, after crediting *all* exchange profits, the depreciation works out at 8·9 per cent on the average capital investment or 1·26 per cent per annum, and at 7·78 per cent on the final investment. This is a little better than the Provincial on the average investment and a little worse on the final investment.

3. *Total Investments*

In the case of the Provincial for the eight years Jan. 1, 1930 to Dec. 31, 1937 the aggregate appreciation works out at 16·3 per cent of the final book value and at 23·2 per cent of the average capital invested, or 2·9 per cent per annum.

For the National Mutual over the same period the aggregate appreciation came to 14·4 per cent of the final investment* and about the same figure of the average capital invested, or 1·8 per cent per annum.

II. *Comparisons with King's College*

The College has five investment funds, three of which are restricted to trustee securities. The other two we will call Fund I and Fund II. The sterling investments in these two funds are mainly ordinary shares, although a few preference shares are held and occasionally a temporary holding of other stocks; but the dollar securities include a number of preferred stocks. Fund I, however, has included *no* American stocks, has contained a somewhat larger (though not a large) proportion of preference

* Calculated at market value on Jan. 1, 1930, and subsequent net cost.

and other stocks, and generally speaking has been more conservatively invested, stability of annual income being more important than in the case of Fund II, where it is a matter of indifference whether the profit arises on capital or income account and irregularity of results is of no great consequence.

The College financial year ends on Aug. 31. At the commencement of the period this does not make much difference as compared with January 1st, since there was no great change in values between those dates. But at the end of the period an important adjustment is necessary, which has been made below, to allow for the substantial depreciation between Sept. 1, 1937 and Jan. 1, 1938.

Fund I (mainly sterling ordinary shares). Figures are only available since Sept. 1, 1933, when this Fund was constituted in its present form, so that they are not very useful for purposes of comparison. In the four years up to Jan. 1, 1938 the aggregate appreciation amounted to about 43·5 per cent on the initial value. Since the capital of the fund increased very little during the period, no adjustment is necessary on this head, and the average appreciation works out at 10·9 per cent per annum.

Fund II (including a substantial investment in American preferred and common stocks). Here the figures are available from Sept. 1, 1928. The aggregate appreciation up to Jan. 1, 1938, amounted to 166 per cent of the fund's initial value. In this case the Fund somewhat overspent its income, so that the net capital declined; on the other hand it was frequently over-invested. Allowing roughly for these factors, the average appreciation over the 9 years works out at about 14 per cent per annum.

Total Investments

If the other three funds, which are limited to Trustee securities, are included, the total appreciation over the nine years amounts to about 58 per cent of the initial investment. The amount invested (taken at net cost) increased so little over the period that no adjustment is required for this, and the average appreciation works out at about 6·4 per cent per annum.

Summary of Appreciation per annum for 9 years
ending Dec. 31, 1937

	Sterling ordinary		Dollar	Total appreciation per annum
National Mutual	+1·0		−1·3	+1·8
Provincial	+5·79		−2·75	+2·9
King's College	Fund I*	Fund II		
	+10·9	+14·00		+6·4

* Four years only.

The National Mutual Fund was about four times as large as the Provincial's, and the Provincial Fund (say) two and a half times that of King's. This has some bearing on the comparative results, as we shall see below.

In the case of the Provincial interest earnings over the nine years averaged almost exactly 5 per cent per annum (before deduction of tax); so that the total return on the investments from interest and appreciation averaged 8 per cent per annum. This is a stringent test, since the final valuation is taken at a low point of values.

III. *Comparisons with the Prudential etc.*

In April 1937 Mr Raynes read a paper before the Institute of Actuaries on the results over a period of investment in British Industrial Ordinary shares. In the discussion a representative of the Prudential gave their results for the period 1926–36 in terms of index numbers. These lead up to the following comparison [see next page]:—

This table is extraordinarily interesting for the closeness of the recent results between the Prudential and the Provincial. For the purpose of comparison with the National Mutual the value of the table is much impaired by the much greater increase in the capital so invested by the Prudential (the N.M. having been a

Proportion of market value to book value

	Prudential	N.M.	Provincial
Dec. 31, 1928	129	123	114
29	119	99	110
30	98	84	89
31	78	58	73
32	93	77	89
33	115	98	115
34	131	119	130
35	141	130	142
36	151	144	160
37			119

pioneer in this respect). But for comparison with the Provincial this is not so serious, the Prudential having rather more than trebled and the Provincial rather more than quadrupled its investment in ordinary shares at book cost during the period.

If we consider the results of investing a level £100 book value throughout the period, which eliminates the element of growth but also eliminates the effect of purchases or sales of ordinary shares made at the wrong stage of the credit cycle, the result (subject to my errors of arithmetic!) is as follows:—

End of	Prudential	N.M.	Provincial	Investors' Chronicle Index	Actuaries Index
1928	100	100	100	100	100
29	96	85	90	76	83
30	80	73	70	61	66
31	63	52	57	49	50
32	74	69	66	58	56
33	92	86	83	72	69
34	105	104	97	80	74
35	116	114	111	87	80
36	129	129	137	97	90
37			110	[79]	74

Here again the closeness of the results of the three insurance offices is striking. In the early part of the period the Prudential did best, and the Prudential representative mentioned at the discussion that they had had some exceptional investment opportunities. But by the end of the period the Provincial was slightly ahead. It is noteworthy that all three insurance companies gave a good thrashing to the two indexes.

IV. *General observations*

The Prudential figures relate only to sterling ordinary shares. On the one hand they enjoy certain exceptional opportunities of investment, but on the other hand their size must stand in the way of their taking advantage of swings except on a modest scale. For the latter reason it is unlikely that their experience in 1937 was much better than other people. The experiences of the three insurance offices in this class of investment scarcely differ from one another sufficiently to represent more than the luck of the green. At most one can say that the Provincial is 2 up on the Prudential after 36 holes (or quarters!), having been one down at the start; and the Prudential 1 up on the National Mutual. But the amount by which all three have beaten the index numbers is very reassuring. Using the last table as the basis of comparison, at the end of 1937 the Actuaries' Index was back to the same figure as at the end of 1934; whereas the Provincial had retained an appreciation of 13 per cent, i.e. one-third of the maximum shown at the end of 1936. (I suspect that the admixture of gold shares, not included in the Actuaries' Index, is a part of the explanation. Other shares held, which are not included in the index, are not likely to have helped much.)

Since, through my common influence, there were large resemblances both in the general policy of all three institutions and in the actual shares held, it is interesting to consider some possible explanations. I think that they must be found mainly in the three factors following:—

(i) King's and the Provincial have pursued a more steadfast

policy in favour of the longest-dated gilt-edged and semi-gilt-edged securities; whereas in the case of the National Mutual the emphasis, though in the same direction, has been more fluctuating. Apart from any results of this up to date, I remain convinced that this policy, which is not to be judged one way or the other over short periods, will be the major factor in determining profits over the next decade. If the long-term gilt-edged rate of interest rises well above $3\frac{1}{2}$ per cent as its normal mean figure (and it is only on this hypothesis that the above policy can lose as compared with that of holding fixed-date maturities yielding at present below $3\frac{1}{2}$ per cent), the existing economic structure cannot possibly survive in time of peace; and even the contingency of a war would increase the necessity for keeping down the cost of government borrowing.

(ii) I think that King's has gained somewhat over the two insurance offices by holding practically no sterling second-grade fixed-interest securities at home or abroad; its assets being either in securities of the trustee class or in equities (including marginal preferences) and Americans. No doubt the College was in part driven to this policy by the fact of being compelled by law to invest so large a proportion in the trustee class. But I believe that this has proved an advantage. There is no sufficient uncovenanted profit in the above class of investment to compensate for the uncovenanted loss in respect of those which, in spite of every care in selection, go wrong. This is broadly a class of securities, which, apart from changes in the rate of interest which affect first-class securities equally, cannot go up and can only go down.

The Provincial may have gained a little on the N.M. in this respect, since the proportion of its assets in this class of security is, I think, somewhat less. As in the case of King's, the law, in the shape of the various deposits required, forces the Provincial to hold a large volume of gilt-edged, in addition to which the semi-gilt-edged holding is also large; whilst the rate of interest earned is a matter of more indifference to the Provincial than it can be to the N.M. (A good holding of mines is the most riskless way in the long run of keeping up the average rate of interest.)

(iii) The Provincial has lost, compared with the other two, by having too small a unit of investment in particular securities. Although the funds of the Provincial are almost two and a half times those of King's, the average unit of investment for the two institutions is about the same, the Provincial investments being about two and a half times as numerous as those of King's. What is even more striking, although the funds of the N.M. are nearly four times those of the Provincial, the number of the Provincial's separate investments exceeds those of the National Mutual by about 50. (King's 130 investments, Provincial 325, N.M. 275 in round numbers.) Now it is vastly easier to find 130 satisfactory investments than to find 325; particularly if you are largely depending on the repertory of one man (the N.M. has a greater variety of sources of information). I myself follow fairly closely, or think I have some knowledge, of upwards of perhaps 200 investments; and whilst, say, 50 others (at the outside) may be followed closely by other members of the Finance Committee, I should say that the Provincial holds 50 to 100 securities about which none of the Board know much. Now out of the 200 which one tries to follow more or less, there are probably less than 50 in all classes about which, at any given time, one feels really enthusiastic. I am convinced that the good results shown by King's are *mainly* due to the large proportion of its assets held in the less than 50 favourite securities. To carry one's eggs in a great number of baskets, without having time or opportunity to discover how many have holes in the bottom, is the surest way of increasing risk and loss.

As an institution grows, the number of separate investments must necessarily increase. But the N.M. seems to me to have pursued a better policy in this respect than the Provincial. I cannot but believe that the Provincial would gain by reducing the number of its separate investments by upwards of 100.

When Keynes had completed a revised version of his 'Post Mortem', he sent it to Richard Kahn with a covering note.

To R. F. KAHN, *5 May 1938*

POST MORTEM

I have now prepared the revised version attached. Could you get this cyclostyled and send me four copies? Circularisation to the Estates Committee might be held up until we have settled about the meeting.

The question about policy is very interesting. I daresay there is more temperament than logic in the solution. I can only say that I was the principal inventor of credit cycle investment and have seen it tried by five different parties acting in detail on distinctly different lines over a period of nearly twenty years, which has been full of ups and downs; and I have not seen a single case of a success having been made of it. In addition to this experience, the most logical followers of the policy whom I know are some of the American investment trusts, and their results are not encouraging. As regards individuals, I know one or two who make a modest livelihood by jobbing on general short-term principles without perhaps too much regard to the longer swings, but the credit cyclers have not by now enough capital left to be much of a recent guide.

Credit cycling means in practice selling market leaders on a falling market and buying them on a rising one and, after allowing for expenses and loss of interest, it needs phenomenal skill to make much out of it.

My alternative policy undoubtedly assumes the ability to pick specialities which have, on the average, prospects of rising enormously more than an index of market leaders. The discovery which I consider that I have made in the course of experience is that it is altogether unexpectedly easy to do this, and that the proportion of stumers amongst one's ultra favourites is quite small. Moreover, this practice does, in my opinion, in fact enable one to take at least as good an advantage of fluctuations as credit cycling, though in a rather different way. It is largely the fluctuations which throw up the bargains and the uncertainty due to fluctuations which prevents other people from taking advantage of them. The refusal of the American investment trusts to pick up bargains as long as they believe that it is still broadly speaking a bear market is typical of credit cycling mentality. For it is an essential of a logical carrying out of this not to allow exceptions or be carried away by having fancies about specialities.

The whole thing is really summed up in something that I said in the original version of my memorandum. It is a much safer and easier way in the long run by which to make investment profits to buy £1 notes at 15s. than to sell £1 notes at 15s. in the hope of repurchasing them at 12s. 6d.

[copy initialled] J. M. K.

P.S. I am, of course, in favour of being more heavily invested at the bottom than at the top, if one can manage it (which I never have yet in spite of trying—and (formerly) trying *mainly* for this). But I say that it won't make a big difference to one's final result.

One can put the distinction like this: By credit cycling I mean buying and selling according as you think shares cheap in relation to *money*. By my alternative I mean acting according as you think them cheap in relation to *other shares*, with particular reference to the possibilities of large relative appreciation;—which means buying them on their intrinsic value when, for one reason or another, they are unfashionable or appear very vulnerable on a short view. One may be, and no doubt is, inclined to be too slow to sell one's pets after they have had most of their rise. But looking back I don't blame myself *much* on this score;—it would have been easy to lose a great deal more by selling them too soon.

Memorandum for the Estates Committee, King's College, Cambridge, 8 May 1938

POST MORTEM ON INVESTMENT POLICY

In the short period of four months between Audit (Aug. 31) 1937 and January 1, 1938, the College investments in ordinary shares and American securities depreciated fully 20 per cent and there was some further depreciation after that date, most of which has been subsequently recovered. This means that the greater part of the paper appreciation earned in the two years ended Audit 1937 has since disappeared. Most members of the Estates Committee have probably been uneasily aware of this, and, indeed, on a rough general impression the depreciation may have seemed likely to have been even greater than the above. They may, therefore, welcome an approximate interim report on the situation. The experiences of this period have also stimulated me into attempting a post mortem covering a longer period, partly with a view to comparing our experiences with those of other investors and partly to discover what lessons were to be learnt.

I

There are not many institutional investors who publish their results in a form which permit of a close comparison. The following figures are based on two institutions (much larger investors than the College) where, being concerned with the management, I am in possession of the actual figures, on the Prudential (the largest investor in the world) which has disclosed partial information covering the period up to the end of 1936, and on the published index numbers of security values. In the case of the College the initial capital invested (apart from appreciation earned subsequently) has not changed much over the period considered. But in the case of the above institutions the comparison is complicated, though not I think greatly affected taking the period as a whole, by the fact that their funds invested in ordinary shares have been increasing largely year by year.

The chief object of this enquiry is to compare results in respect of ordinary shares and American securities. But it is interesting to begin with a comparison of results over the whole body of investments during the nine years from January 1, 1929, to January 1, 1938, which covers the previous slump, the latest recovery, and the recent slump. (In the case of the College the period covered is from Audit, September 1, 1928, to January 1, 1938, but there was no significant change in the value of our investments between September 1, 1928, and January 1, 1929.)

	Aggregate appreciation at Jan. 1, 1938, as a percentage of market value at Jan. 1, 1929, and subsequent net cost	Average appreciation
Institution X	14 per cent*	1·56 per cent
Institution Y	6·9 per cent	0·77 per cent
The College	64·4 per cent	7·2 per cent

* But about 21 per cent of *average* capital invested.

I have reason to think that Institutions X and Y have not done worse than the average of such institutions over this period. The superior aggregate results obtained by the College were, I calculate, mainly due to our better experience with sterling ordinary and dollar securities as shown below, the results from our fixed-interest investments being much the same as those of the others. We earned (very roughly) about 25 per cent in the nine years, Institution X 20·5 per cent (perhaps 30 per cent on average capital) and Institution Y 11·5 per cent (say 16 per cent on average capital).

Substantially all the College American investments have been held by the Chest. Thus the figures for the Chest are a mixed result of sterling ordinary shares, commodities and Americans;

whilst the figures for Investment Fund B relate mainly to sterling ordinary shares.

Rate of appreciation (or depreciation) per annum for 9 years ending January 1, 1938

	Sterling ordinary	Dollar securities
Institution X	+ 5·79	− 1·65*
Institution Y	+ 1·0	− 1·3
K.C. Investment Fund B†	+ 10·9	
K.C. Chest		+ 14·00

* On *average* capital invested during *seven* years from Jan. 1, 1931.
† Covers the period from Audit 1933 only when Fund B was first constituted.

Thus it is clear that, *after* allowing for the recent depreciation, the College investments in ordinary shares and in Americans have been on balance very profitable, and much more successful than the average. Including interest, the average earnings of the Chest over the nine years seem to have been well in excess of 20 per cent per annum on the initial investment.

The following table gives the basis for a further comparison,

Proportion of market value to book value

	Institution X	Institution Y	The Prudential	The Chest* (Audit 1928 = 120)	Fund B	Investors' Chronicle Index	Actuaries Index	New York Stock Exchange Index
Jan. 1, 1929	114	123	129	121		100	100	149·0†
30	110	99	119	122		76	83	—
31	89	84	98	97		61	66	—
32	73	58	78	85		49	50	—
33	89	77	93	106		59	56	45·8†
34	115	98	115	157	100	73	69	52·5†
35	130	119	131	199	114	79	74	50·5
36	142	130	141	276	129	87	80	71·1
37	160	144	151	395	148	97	90	87·8
38	119	126		315	143	79	74	54·6

* The figures for the Chest given for Jan. 1, 1929, is the average of Audit 1928 (120) and Audit 1929 (122); those for the Chest and Fund B for the subsequent years up to 1937 are for the previous Audit; and the figures for Jan. 1, 1938, are based on an estimate for that actual date.
† Average of year.

but not for a very clear one. The two indexes are mainly restricted to *home* industrials and do not include e.g. gold mines which are included in the sterling ordinary industrials of the institutions; whilst the results for the Chest also cover our holdings of dollar securities.

It will be noticed that the three investment institutions have all done much the same and decisively better than the published indexes for the average of home industrials. Over the whole period the indexes fell 20 to 25 per cent, whereas the institutions gained $2\frac{1}{2}$ to 5 per cent. The Chest, however, gained 150 per cent, rising to two and a half times its initial value. Thus in spite of its unfavourable experience in the past year, mainly due to the preposterous fall in American securities, the net results of the Chest are very good. The comparison is much more favourable than I expected when I set out to make it.

Nevertheless serious mistakes were made in the year from Lady Day 1937 to Lady Day 1938. How far they were avoidable it is difficult to say. We were over-invested at the former date and remained over-invested throughout the year. It would have been much better to have been under-invested at the low prices of Lady Day 1938. But it is easy to exaggerate how much difference this would have made. If we had sold one-fifth of each of the investments of the Chest (i.e. if we had sold say £50,000 altogether) at the former date which was practically the top, and re-invested this amount at the latter date, which was literally the bottom, we should have gained perhaps £20,000 or, say, 8 per cent averaged over the entire holdings of the Chest. In fact no-one could have been so clever as this, and to have saved 5 per cent would have been very clever indeed. Yet, looking back, it does not seem to me that either the particular evidence or general considerations could at any time have been held to justify more drastic action than the above. I did in fact foresee in August 1937 (though not earlier), as I recorded in writing at the time, the likelihood of trouble ahead, and blame myself for not having acted more drastically on this expectation; but I console myself by the calculation that the most drastic action one was at all likely to have taken, having regard to all the circumstances, would not have made a really significant difference to the final result.

II

In fact the chief lesson I draw from the above results is the opposite of what I set out to show when, what is now nearly 20 years ago, I first persuaded the College to invest in ordinary shares. At that time I believed that profit could be made by what was called a credit cycle policy, namely by holding such shares in slumps and disposing of them in booms; and we purchased an industrial index including a small holding in an outstanding share in each leading industry. Since that time there may have been more numerous and more violent general fluctuations than at any previous period. We have indeed done well by purchasing particular shares at times when their prices were greatly depressed; but we have not proved able to take much advantage of a general systematic movement out of and into ordinary shares as a whole at different phases of the trade cycle. In the past nine years, for example, there have been two occasions when the whole body of our holding of such investments have depreciated by 20 to 25 per cent within a few months and we have not been able to escape the movement. Yet on both occasions I foresaw correctly to a certain extent what was ahead. Nevertheless these temporary severe losses and the inability to take substantial advantage of these fluctuations have not interfered with successful results.

As the result of these experiences I am clear that the idea of wholesale shifts is for various reasons impracticable and indeed undesirable. Most of those who attempt it sell too late and buy too late, and do both too often, incurring heavy expenses and developing too unsettled and speculative a state of mind, which, if it is widespread, has besides the grave social disadvantage of aggravating the scale of the fluctuations. I believe now that successful investment depends on three principles:—

(1) a careful selection of a few investments (or a few types of investment) having regard to their cheapness in relation to their probable actual and potential *intrinsic* value over a period of years ahead and in relation to alternative investments at the time;

(2) a steadfast holding of these in fairly large units through thick and thin, perhaps for several years, until either they have fulfilled their promise or it is evident that they were purchased on a mistake;

(3) a *balanced* investment position, i.e. a variety of risks in spite of individual holdings being large, and if possible opposed risks (e.g. a holding of gold shares amongst other equities, since they are likely to move in opposite directions when there are general fluctuations).

On the other hand, it is a mistake to sell a £1 note for 15s. in the hope of buying it back for 12s. 6d., and a mistake to refuse to buy a £1 note for 15s. on the ground that it cannot really be a £1 note (for there is abundant experience that £1 notes *can* be bought for 15s. at a time when they are expected by many people to fall to 12s. 6d.).

Another important rule is the avoidance of second-class safe investments, none of which can go up and a few of which are sure to go down. This is the main cause of the defeat of the average investor. The ideal investment portfolio is divided between the purchase of really secure future income (where future appreciation or depreciation will depend on the rate of interest) and equities which one believes to be capable of a *large* improvement to offset the fairly numerous cases which, with the best skill in the world, will go wrong.

The following is an illustration of how much more is to be made by picking the right shares than by wholesale shifts between market leaders and cash through a correct anticipation of the major swings. If the latter is aimed at then (if one is responsible altogether for a *large* body of investment) specialities which cannot be sold in quantity on a falling market must be avoided and the holding must be widely spread amongst the highly marketable leading shares, which means that the movements of the index numbers can be taken as a good guide to the actual movements of values relevant to such an investment policy. Now the index numbers quoted above show (for Jan. 1) two peaks in 1929 and 1937 and two bottoms in 1932 or 1933 and 1938. British shares fell from 100 to 50, rose again to 90 and fell to 74; Americans fell from 149 to 46, rose to 88 and then fell to 55. These figures for Jan. 1 are, of course, not the absolute tops and bottoms; but anyone who managed to sell all his British shares at an average of 100 reinvesting his money at 50, sold again at 90 and reinvested at 74 (and similarly with his American shares selling at 149, reinvesting at 46, selling again at 88 and reinvesting at 55) would have shown almost superhuman skill in predicting credit cycle movements. Now if he had held half his money in sterling and half in dollar securities, allowing for loss of interest at 5 per cent during the periods when he was liquid, he would have raised the value of his investments from 100 to 182 in the nine years. In fact the Chest investments were raised during this period from 100 to 262, so that the appreciation (162 per cent) was almost exactly double that earned by the credit cycle genius (82 per cent).

In the main, therefore, slumps are experiences to be lived through and survived with as much equanimity and patience as possible. Advantage can be taken of them more because individual securities fall out of their reasonable parity with other securities on such occasions, than by attempts at wholesale shifts into and out of equities as a whole. One must not allow one's attitude to securities which have a daily market quotation to be disturbed by this fact or lose one's sense of proportion. Some Bursars will buy without a tremor unquoted and unmarketable investments in real estate which, if they had a selling quotation for immediate cash available at each Audit, would turn their hair grey. The fact that you do not know how much its ready money quotation fluctuates does not, as is commonly supposed, make an investment a safe one. Until recently tithe was a much more dangerous investment than tin mines, and Worlaby-cum-Elsham has been, since we bought the property, a much more speculative as well as a much less profitable and more trouble-some holding than the investments of the Chest in ordinary shares. But it is true, unfortunately, that the modern organisation of the capital market requires for the holder of quoted equities much more nerve, patience and fortitude than from the holder of wealth in other forms. Yet it is safer to be a speculator than an investor in the sense of the definition which I once gave the Committee that a speculator is one who runs risks of which he is aware and an investor is one who runs risks of which he is unaware. The management of stock exchange investments of any kind is a low pursuit, having very little social value and partaking (at its best) of the nature of a game of skill, from which it is a good thing for most members of our Society to be free; whereas the justification of Worlaby and Elsham lies in its being a con-structive and socially beneficial enterprise, where we exercise a genuine entrepreneurial function, in which many of our body can be reasonably and usefully interested. I welcome the fact that the Estates Committee—to judge from their poker faces and imperturbable demeanour—do not take either gains or losses from the Stock Exchange too gravely;—they are much more depressed or elated (as the case may be) by farming results. But it may be useful and wise nevertheless, to analyse from time to time what is being done and the principles of our policy.

J.M.K.

8.5.38

IV. *Minor Activities*

The above account does not exhaust Keynes's financial activities. In collab-oration with two treasurers, Alfred Hoare and R. G. Hawtrey, he provided advice on the finances and investments of the Royal Economic Society. As Honorary Treasurer, he stretched the meagre resources of the Camargo Society to cover its ambitions. Finally, when he became a Fellow of Eton to represent the Masters on the Governing Body in October 1940, his interests turned to the finances of the College almost immediately and by the end of that month he was providing the Bursar with advice. He summed up his views to the Provost, Lord Quickswood in February 1942.

From a letter to LORD QUICKSWOOD, *19 February 1942*

I doubt if Eton's finances have been what one could call *well* managed for at least half a century and it may be one has to go back to the seventies of the last century, when Bursar Carter was in his prime, to find anything really good. To judge from my knowledge of what happened at King's, I believe that the Eton–King's Fellows were greatly interested in estate and financial management in the sixties and seventies of the last century. It was in those two decades that the transition was made from medieval arrangements. They were absolutely up-to-date on the standards of that age and looked after matters well from every point of view; being both good landlords and efficient financiers. In the case of Eton, I doubt if the same thing could be said of any subsequent date. I do not mean that the management has been very bad; only that it has not been as good as it should have been.

Inevitably, Keynes became more involved with the College's finances, both with Chalcots, its property in Hampstead, London, and with its investments, going first on a sub-committee to manage the estates in July 1943, and joining an investments sub-committee in March 1944. His influence was, however, limited, for he met with the opposition of Jasper Ridley, a banker, on most of his unorthodox views. Thus early in March 1944 when Ridley opposed Keynes's suggestion of buying Australian dollar bonds because of fears for the future of the dollar and Australia's reputation, Keynes made two comments.

From a letter to R. E. MARSDEN,[48] *8 March 1944*

I confess I was a little bit annoyed about Ridley changing his mind on the Australian Dollar Bonds. But, as I have written to him, I really have no reason to complain and cannot expect to get things both ways. If orthodox opinion in the city thought

[48] The Bursar of Eton.

better of these bonds, then no doubt the price would inevitably be too high, and I should take no further interest in them. So one has the dilemma. All orthodox suggestions are too expensive, and all unorthodox are too unorthodox, so I am rather discouraged about making any further suggestion.

To SIR JASPER RIDLEY, *undated* [*March 1944*]

Dear Jasper,

Sorry to be so quarrelsome on the telephone. My central principle of investment is to go contrary to general opinion, on the ground that, if everyone is agreed about its merits, the investment is inevitably too dear and therefore unattractive. Now obviously I can't have it both ways—the whole point of the investment is that most people disagree with it. So, if others concerned don't feel enough confidence to give me a run, it is in the nature of the case that I must retire from the unequal combat. And you may legitimately argue that it is wrong for an institution to be, even successfully, clever—the proper course is to receive a little money. But in that case why waste one's pains?

Yours ever,
[copy not initialled or signed]

From SIR JASPER RIDLEY, *8 March 1944*

Dear Maynard,

Thank you very much for your note of some days ago. You certainly were cross on the telephone, but there it is—you feel it is a proper risk for Eton and I hesitate to think so.

Certainly I could not differ from your principles of buying against the stream in the investment of personal funds or the funds of certain businesses, and I am certain you are clever at this. I would be indeed foolish if I did not appreciate your skill and experience. But I doubt if the Trustees of a great school can rightly take the same sort of risks, partly because there *is* the extra risk, and partly because the successful management of such an investment policy demands consistent management by the right man at the centre. I do

III

not see how such consistent skilful management at the centre can be ensured at Eton.

But I am only one of several Fellows, and I am well enough acquainted with committee operations to accept decisions which may be made contrary to my own. I dare say my opinion would not be supported in this matter, especially in the face of your very lucid persuasiveness. I can only hope that you are not so cross with me that you will think it necessary to abandon putting up ideas. Honestly, I feel that that part of your little lecture to me was hardly what I would have expected of you. Forgive me for saying so.

Yours,
JASPER RIDLEY

To SIR JASPER RIDLEY, *12 March 1944*

My dear Jasper,

Thanks for your letter and renewed apologies for being so tiresome. But it is just the point, which in your last paragraph you say you do not like, which seems to me sensible on my part and not tiresome. The sort of investment policy I favour can only be carried through with the free acquiescence of all those intimately concerned. The experience I have had with it in various contexts has always gone to enforce that. So if there is not that free acquiescence, I am sure that much the best plan is to drop it altogether.

Yours ever,
[copy initialled] M.K.

Despite disagreements such as the above, investing with Keynes did have its enjoyable side as everyone's memories make clear. Perhaps it is best to conclude with a letter from a contemporary observer, the Provost of Eton.

From a letter from LORD QUICKSWOOD, *17 December 1943*

I find Governing Bodies meetings usually very entertaining. I like to hear the naked covetousness with which you recommend Southern Preferred Stock, the austere puritanism with which Lubbock[49] meets such suggestions

[49] Cecil Lubbock, Deputy Governor of the Bank of England, 1923–5, 1927–9; a member with Keynes of the Macmillan Committee on Finance and Industry.

and the tergiversation of Ridley, who, agreeing with Lubbock, nevertheless votes with you because it is a poor heart that never rejoices and one must have a flutter sometimes. Altogether it is delightful.

Table 8. *Summary table for Keynes's investment activities*

	Keynes		King's		Prices	
	Income[a] (1920 = 100)	Net assets[b] (1922 = 100)	Net securities[c] (1920 = 100)	Chest[c] (1920 = 100)	Final[d] expenditure (1920 = 100)	London[e] industrial shares (1920 = 100)	New York[f] common stocks (1920 = 100)
1920	100	—	100	100	100	100	100
1921	96	—	106	n.a.	85	70	86
1922	106	100	120	n.a.	72	80	105
1923	112	159	126	n.a.	68	95	108
1924	152	296	117	n.a.	67	105	113
1925	140	202	114	n.a.	67	110	140
1926	169	189	120	n.a.	66	115	158
1927	141	204	121	234	64	135	192
1928	96	61	127	226	64	130	250
1929	95	36	128	228	63	105	326
1930	114	58	131	154	61	85	264
1931	163	70	120	116	58	80	172
1932	138	101	137	168	57	95	87
1933	197	256	164	227	55	120	113
1934	165	677	185	302	55	130	124
1935	166	1023	197	436	56	150	133
1936	386	2350	229	680	57	140	195
1937	478	998	230	738	60	115	193
1938	157	842	208	442	60	110	145
1939	274	925	200	499	62	90	151
1940	299	794	183	421	70	95	138
1941	364	952	222	562	78	105	124
1942	322	1178	235	557	83	125	109
1943	338	1454	273	857	88	140	145
1944	366	1648	293	981	93	145	157
1945	300	1908	346	1124	95	160	190

[a] Tax year beginning April—Table 1.
[b] 31 December—Table 3.
[c] 31 August—Table 6.
[d] C. H. Feinstein, *National Income, Expenditure and Output of the United Kingdom 1865–1965* (Cambridge, 1972), Tables 2 and 5.
[e] London and Cambridge Economic Service, *The British Economy: Key Statistics 1900–1970* (London, n.d.), Table M.
[f] Standard and Poor's 500 Average—*ibid.* Table O.

Chapter 2

INVESTMENT POLICY AND INSURANCE

Keynes's experience as an investor naturally spilled over into his publications, initially in the 'Finance and Investment' column of *The Nation* (*JMK*, vol. XIX). It also resulted in a series of reviews, which we reprint below. Most importantly, as the 1920s progressed, his experience plus his position as Chairman of the National Mutual, made his speech to the Society's annual meeting something of a City event.

We begin, therefore, by reprinting the published texts of Keynes's remarks annually from 1922 to 1938 with some related press controversies.[1]

Speech to the Annual Meeting of the National Mutual, 18 January 1922

Gentlemen,

Before moving the formal adoption of the annual report and accounts, I will comment, in accordance with the usual custom, on points of special interest arising out of them.

The directors regret to report the death during the year of their Chairman, Colonel Villiers. He was a loyal supporter of the Society, and after serving on the board for 45 years, he had been for the last 18 months of his life the Society's Chairman, a position which he filled with dignity and with the respect of all his colleagues. My fellow-directors have done me the honour to elect me his successor, an honour which I naturally much appreciate.

Mr W. T. Layton, whose name and reputation in economic and in business circles are well known, has been appointed to the board, subject to confirmation by the members at this meeting.

---

[1] Copies of Keynes's remarks appeared in several places in the financial press. The versions printed below are the complete texts which the National Mutual placed in *The Times*. The same or abbreviated versions appeared elsewhere. The records of the National Mutual do not contain a full list of all the places where the remarks appeared, much less of all the variants used.

The new business of the year is set out in the report. It is about 16 per cent less than last year, but is in excess of the new business obtained in any year previous to 1919. Some diminution in our new business is not surprising in view of the general depression of trade throughout the past year. A similar experience is shown in nearly all the returns of life assurance so far published, and in the case of some of the best and strongest offices the decline has been relatively larger than our own.

Premium income and expenses

Nevertheless, the depression has not prevented our securing more than enough business to replace the claims, surrenders and lapses of the current year, with the result that our premium income is increased by about £13,000.

Last year the Chairman called attention to the increase in the expense ratio, and gave the reasons for it. This year you will be pleased to learn that, our expenses having been practically the same as in 1920, whilst the premium income has increased, the ratio of expenses to premium income has fallen by more than 1 per cent of the latter.

Claims

The claims by death exceed those of 1920 by approximately £34,000, but 1920 was in this respect the most successful year which the Society has ever experienced, while 1919 was nearly as good. Some increase in claims, as compared with these years, was therefore inevitable, and is no cause for any uneasiness as to the character of the lives assured in the Society. In spite of the heavier claims, the year's results still show us a small profit under the heading of mortality.

Rate of interest

The rate of interest, both gross and net, again shows a satisfactory increase, being better than last year by rather more than 4s. per cent over the whole of our securities, excluding reversions.

The net rate of interest, after deduction of income tax, was £4 13s. per cent, as compared with the rate of 3 per cent, on the basis of which we value our liabilities. This difference represents a profit of about £56,000 in the year, which goes to swell the surplus which will be divisible amongst the members at the end of 1923. It is possible, however, that the current year may see some diminution in the rate of interest obtainable.

Stock exchange securities

You will see on the left-hand side of the revenue account that there is a balance of profit on assets realised and revalued of nearly £179,000. Of this sum, £162,000 is represented by profit actually realised in cash, and only £17,000 is attributable to an increase on balance in the reassessment of book values. Nearly all—namely, £172,000—of this profit is due to the capital gains on our stock exchange securities, which represents about 8 per cent over the whole of our assets of this description. A considerable part of this is, of course, attributable to the general improvement in the values of gilt-edged securities which occurred in the latter part of last year. But the exceptionally satisfactory result recorded above could have been secured only by the special care which the board have bestowed on this part of their duties and the active policy which they have pursued in taking quick advantage of the opportunities which have presented themselves.

Comparison of values

The members can best judge, I think, of the success which has attended the efforts of the board in this direction by considering together the results of the two years 1920 and 1921. This period happens to be a particularly convenient one for purposes of comparison, because the leading British Government securities stood at almost the same prices at the beginning and at the end of the period. For example, Five per Cent War Loan stood at $91\frac{7}{16}$ at the beginning of the two-year period, and at $92\frac{1}{4}$ at the end of it; Funding Loan at 75½ and 76¼; Victory Bonds at 80⅜ and 81⅜; and Local Loans at 55½ and 56. In fact, the average of these four standard securities fell 10 per cent in 1920 and rose 11 per cent in 1921, so that the depreciation of the first year was almost exactly balanced by the recovery in the second year, the net result over the two years being an appreciation of almost exactly 1 per cent. National War Bonds did a little better than this, the recovery in 1921 bringing them to about 4 per cent above what they had been two years earlier. On the other hand, many other classes of securities, particularly ordinary shares, showed a heavy depreciation on balance over the two years.

Balance of appreciation and realised profit

The test of success in an active investment policy is to be found in an ability to avoid losses when security values are falling, whilst, nevertheless, obtaining profits when they are rising. Anyone can make profits in gilt-edged investments when gilt-edged investments are all going up; and we must look, therefore, to the net result of the two years 1920 and 1921 taken together. Over these two years our Society has a balance of appreciation and realised profit over the whole of its stock exchange securities of approximately 6 per cent. I do not think that any other Society can show an equally good result, and I am certain that it could not have been obtained by an inactive policy, however well and carefully the investments had been selected in the first instance.

Assurance societies and investment policy

I venture to say that at the present time life assurance societies must stand or fall mainly with the success or failure of their investment policy. The labours of the great actuaries of the 19th century have carried actuarial science to a point where great improvements or striking innovations are no longer likely. All well-conducted societies now follow almost the same established actuarial rules. They work on mortality tables based on past experience, which, by reason of the improvements in medical science and public sanitation, are likely to yield some profit on the actual claims falling due over a period of years. The rise in the rate of interest, even when allowance is made for the depreciations of income tax, the present incidence of which on life assurance is open to objection both on principle and on grounds of public policy, provides an automatic profit over the rate assumed in the valuation. These factors are in favour of all societies alike, and tend to put them in a strong position, unless these advantages are thrown away by a defective investment policy. But investment, on the other hand, provides both more pitfalls and also more opportunities than formerly. The wide fluctuations even in securities of the highest class, which have occurred in recent years, are likely to continue in the near future; while the range and choice of investments now available afford opportunities for an active policy which did not exist previously.

New problems

Until comparatively lately, insurance companies generally employed a large proportion of their funds outside stock exchange securities in mortgages, reversions, ground-rents, house property and loans; and when they ventured into stocks and shares, those in which it was suitable or convenient to keep a large holding were few and lacking in variety. The requirements of government and municipal finance have now led to the creation of stocks of the greatest possible variety and of all maturities, from perpetual stocks to short-dated bonds. The new problems of investment thus presented are, in the opinion of your board, the most difficult and the most important with which the insurance world is now faced. They believe that the gradual building up of a sound investment policy is the most vital part of their duties. It is too soon to speak confidently as to what can be done on these lines. But at any rate the results which your board has obtained in the past two years are not an accident, but are attributable to a conscious and deliberate policy.

Funds and valuation

The funds of the Society have increased during the year by £277,000, the largest addition which they have ever received in a single year. This year, as in previous years, we have made a valuation of our liabilities for our own information, with a view to determining how much of this increase represents surplus. These valuations are made on exactly the same basis as those which are made quinquennially for the purpose of bonus distribution. The fact that, although our annual meeting is being held a week earlier than usual, the whole of the valuation results are already available, is greatly to the credit of the staff, and the conduct of the routine side of our work with so much punctuality and good order helps to give the board confidence that, if increased business were to come our way, we have an organisation which could handle it with promptitude and accuracy.

The increase in net surplus

This valuation discloses that our net surplus has increased during the year by £231,000, bringing our aggregate surplus up to nearly £409,000, with two more years still to run before the close of the current quinquennial period. At our valuation in 1913, which concluded the most successful quinquennium in the society's history, there was a surplus of £341,000, on which result a compound reversionary bonus of 36s. per cent was declared and more than £100,000 carried forward. The cost of a similar bonus would now be greater, owing principally to the increase in the number of endowment assurances. But, after making allowance for this factor and for certain adjustments which may be necessary in 1923, the prospects for the Society's policyholders are decidedly good.

Production and consumption

I look for a revival of trade in the coming year, irrespective of political developments here and in Europe, because I attribute the exceptional severity of the recent trade depression by no means entirely to the falling-off in consumption, but also in large measure to a financial and credit situation which has held up production and has kept it far below the rate of current consumption. This means that stocks of commodities, particularly invisible stocks, have been falling, a process which cannot go much farther without leading to scarcity and a reaction towards higher prices and busy production. Let me quote two figures so striking as to be almost incredible. In 1921 Lancashire's export of piece goods was the lowest for 60 years; Great Britain's production of pig iron was the lowest for 70 years. In spite of the War and the state of Europe, nothing like this can be true of consumption.

Growing popularity of endowment assurances

In conclusion, I should like to say a word about possible developments in the future. The growing popularity of endowment assurances points the direction, I think, in which insurance can develop most fruitfully. Life assurance, in its origin, sought to provide an organisation to mitigate the injury to a man's family from his premature death, and to accumulate the savings which he desired to transmit to his heirs. With the development of endowment assurances, provision is now also made for accumulating the savings which are to care for his own old age. I believe that if the boards of assurance societies can gain enough public confidence in their investment policies, we shall come, even more than at present, to look on such societies as providing the best available organisation for looking after the savings of the middle class.

Investments of the middle classes

We ought, I think, to improve the facilities for making funds available to the policyholder in case of need in advance of the maturity of the policy. With that and other improvements, I do not see why societies such as ours should not become the main channel for the investments of the savings of the middle classes.

After all, the man who saves £50 to £100 a year usually stands at an immense disadvantage if he tries to invest these small sums in stock exchange securities. The expenses of such investment are relatively large; he generally finds it difficult to obtain good advice; and he cannot easily average his risks. What a considerable part of such savings are often lost! During the past two years this Society has earned on its stock exchange investments in interest and appreciation 7½ per cent per annum clear of income tax. How many policyholders have done as well for themselves? I am sure that there is no better investment for small annual savings than our with-profits endowment policies.

A well-managed mutual society, where the profits all belong to the policyholders, is surely an ideal institution for the investment of small annual savings. If only the mutual societies of this country can improve their principles of investment as successfully as they have perfected actuarial science, their social usefulness will be even greater in the future than it has been hitherto.

I now beg formally to move the adoption of the annual report and accounts.

Speech to the Annual Meeting of the National Mutual, 29 January 1923

Gentlemen,

In moving the adoption of the annual report and accounts, I need not comment at much length on the various points of interest, which are sufficiently evident in the documents themselves. New business and premium income are well maintained. The net rate of interest and the expense ratio are practically the same, and, though the claims are only slightly less in amount, our profit from mortality amounts to about £30,000, which is well above the average. We have a balance of nearly £263,000 appreciation and realised profit on our investments. All except a few hundreds of this has been obtained from our stock exchange securities, and amounts to 10·6 per cent of the funds thus invested, which, added to the net interest earned—namely, 4·6 per cent—represents a total contribution for the year of 15·2 per cent, free of tax. The large appreciation secured materially increases the strength of our position. Nevertheless, it is nothing out of the way in the special circumstances of the year, being almost exactly the average appreciation of fixed-interest-bearing securities generally. The board's investment policy has enabled them, over the last three years, to combine the avoidance of serious loss when markets were falling with taking full advantage of the opportunities of a rising market. Possibly we might have made somewhat more. But the political and business outlook was, and is, uncertain, and we have been more concerned to retain the handsome profits which we have made than to risk losing a part in the attempt to increase them further.

Upward tendency of trade

My own view is that the strong tendency towards the revival of trade and confidence in this country, which has already begun, will need facts, and not merely fears, to hold it back. Many favourable conditions are now developing, and, although the growth of confidence about the level of prices has been necessarily retarded here, as compared with the United States, so long as the rise of the sterling exchange has continued to depress sterling prices in relation to dollar prices, the end of this movement must come sooner or later. Whether political developments are good or bad, I expect a rise, rather than a fall, of prices, which, however, is not necessarily the same thing at all as general prosperity. The number of men in employment is now about the same as before the War, which is something to set against the depressing facts that no work is at present available for the substantial increase in the employable population since 1913, and that those who are employed are probably producing on the average about 10 per cent less than formerly for approximately the same real wage. Without great improvements in the technique and intelligence of trade and industry, it looks doubtful whether, on these terms, we shall be able to employ the whole employable population except at the very top of the periodic booms. The above estimate is in conformity with the indications of several other groups of statistics that the general turnover of trade is now on the average somewhere round about 10 per cent below the pre-war level.

'Critical situation in the Ruhr'

So far as Europe is concerned, our chief concern must obviously be the critical situation in the Ruhr. A few weeks ago a settlement would have been possible by which, in the long run, substantial payments might have been secured from Germany. Now that France has chosen herself to tear up the Treaty and to break the peace of Europe, I much doubt whether any substantial reparation will ever be paid at all. The European system created by the Peace Treaties is rapidly breaking up, and France has embarked on a course, the final results of which on the continuance of high civilisation in Europe are not yet calculable. From our own selfish point of view, fortunately the world is large; and we must hope that those are right—and within certain limitations they may be—who believe that this country can, by prudence, maintain a decent life, in spite of violence and disorder across the Channel. We in England are, I think, a united people at the present time on the main issue, that we stand for peace, to a degree that only exists at important crises of our history.

Valuation and analysis of profit

The valuation and analysis of profit, which we make each year for our own information, show that the net surplus has been increased during the year by more than £337,000, and that the total surplus now amounts to £734,000, of which all but about £98,000 is realised profit, with one year of our quinquennium still to run. This is mainly due to the fact that over the last three years we have earned in interest and appreciation on our stock exchange securities an average of 10 per cent per annum, free of income tax. At the conclusion of the most prosperous previous period in the Society's history—namely, the quinquennium which ended in 1913, our total surplus represented rather less than 12½ per cent of our actuarial liability. The surplus now disclosed is rather more than 24 per cent of the present liability, or nearly double the proportion at the end of 1913, although, as I have just reminded you, there will be a further year's profits to be brought in before the distribution of bonus at the end of this year. This is an exceptionally favourable position for any society to be in, and, whilst there are many adjustments to be made and an adequate sum to be reserved as a carry forward, it is clear that the prospects for our with-profit policyholders are unusually good.

Popularity of endowment assurance

Last year I referred to the growing popularity of endowment assurance, and expressed the opinion that in this form of assurance, supported by a sound investment policy, the most fruitful development of life assurance was to be anticipated. That the popularity of this class of policy has not diminished is shown by the fact that last year about 40 per cent of our new business came from endowment assurances. This has no doubt been influenced by the consideration that, as you all know, a rebate of income tax at one-half the standard rate is allowed, subject to the usual limitations, on all premiums paid on life assurance policies; whilst, at the same time, under the new income tax arrangements, any member whose taxable income exceeds £225 pays tax at the standard rate on the balance of his income, so that to the extent that his income exceeds that sum he loses nothing from the fact that the Society have to pay at the standard rate on the income from investments in their hands. But if we are to develop this form of thrift fully, we must make it clear to policyholders that savings by means of an endowment policy can be regarded as a provision not only against death and old age, but also against all the other sudden contingencies of life which require a financial reserve. The average investor must obviously be at a hopeless disadvantage in looking after his savings as compared with a well-managed mutual society. It ought to be considered as imprudent for such a man to make his own investments as to be his own doctor or lawyer. I should like to see by far the greater part of the moderate savings of the middle class invested through the best mutual offices. To encourage our own members to go further than they do in this direction, let me state clearly the existing facilities as regards borrowing against the surrender values of their policies.

Surrender value of policies

It is true that the amount of the surrender value sometimes seems disappointing to the policyholder, especially in the earlier years of assurance. This must inevitably be so, partly because the initial expenses have to be written off the earlier premiums received, and also because payment for the risk of death during the period already expired, the cost of which in respect of those who die untimely must be averaged over the whole number of policyholders, has to be deducted from the gross accumulated value of the premiums paid. But against the sum thus calculated, we make it as straightforward and as cheap as possible for our members to obtain cash advances to meet sudden contingencies or to pay up their premiums during a period of temporary loss of income. We are always ready to inform a policyholder as to the surrender value of his policy up to date, so that he can know exactly where he stands; and we are prepared to make advances up to 90 per cent of this amount, at short notice and without inquiry as to their purpose, at a rate of interest which is at present 5 per cent, and is not likely at any time in the near future to exceed 1 per cent over Bank rate, subject to a minimum of 5 per cent. Moreover, it is always open to a policyholder, who finds it necessary to obtain an advance, to cover it by taking out at the same time an additional policy on the usual conditions for the amount in question. I urge every one of our policyholders, who is not specially well situated for looking after his own investments, to take our endowment policies up to the maximum rather than up to the minimum of his capacity to save. There must be a great volume of saving which does not, at present, find its way to the leading mutual societies, yet could advantageously do so.

Right line of future development

Excluding colonial offices, there are now 15 mutual societies in the United Kingdom, of which 10 had total funds of less than £8,000,000 each at the date of their latest published returns. This seems to me a healthy state of affairs. I am sure that the right line of future development is towards closer friendship and co-operation on many matters of common interest between existing societies, rather than the further aggrandisement of a few at the expense of the rest. There must be, I think, an ideal size for a mutual life office, a point at which its funds, its income, its outgo, its membership, its administrative staff, and its directorate are all in harmonious relationship one to the other, and so capable of their highest economic efficiency. In particular, practical experience of investment indicates that there is a definite limit to the amount of funds which an office can control to the greatest advantage, and I should put this limit not higher than £10,000,000 or £15,000,000. I am assuming that the investment policy of the office is an active one, in the sense in which I used the words last year. If our holdings in any particular security or class of security were very large, market limitations would come in to prevent the completion of our plans, for I need not tell you that there are times when even the London Stock Exchange is not anxious to buy or sell great blocks of securities, however good they may be. We could, of course, deal on a larger scale than we have any need to do at present, or are likely to need to do for many years. But I am sure that a society which does not go beyond the limits which I have indicated above has a very real advantage in the management of its investments over the vast insurance and banking aggregations which have grown up in recent years.

Principles of investment

There is another factor where compactness and concentration are likely to be advantageous—in the directorate. You will no doubt have noticed the marked tendency in recent years, in financial and investment companies especially, but also in industrial and commercial companies, towards smaller boards, mainly composed of experts in the businesses which the companies are formed to exploit. The directors of a life assurance company will not usually be experts on the actuarial and the medical sides of the business, and, as regards the acquisition and selection of new business, their usefulness must be limited. But on the investment side, where lies, as I said last year, the chief part of the directors' duties, there is room for the application of the principles which, in other forms of enterprise, commend themselves to those who are responsible for their control. In the last few years we have taken some steps in the direction indicated, and later on—probably at our next annual meeting—we hope to be able to submit to you our considered proposals as to the future.

Business prospects

We do not seek to grow too big or too fast. Nevertheless, as a result of our present strong position, we are hoping, I think justifiably, for a substantial increase in our business. We have prepared for it by taking over and reconstructing the upper part of the next house, thus securing more and greatly needed accommodation for our staff. We are now in a position to handle, even more rapidly than in the past, the business which may come our way.

Keynes's speeches for 1922 and 1923 were the subject of comment by Sir William Schooling. In an article in *The Daily Telegraph* for 10 April 1923, he compared Keynes's remarks on the previous year's realised capital gains with those of Sir Walter Runciman at the annual meeting of the more conservatively managed United Kingdom Provident Institution and suggested that the National Mutual might be impairing the future position for the sake of the present unless it carried such realised profits into its reserves. Moreover, it went on to praise traditional 'safety-first' insurance principles. Keynes replied.

To the Editor of The Daily Telegraph, *14 April 1923*

Sir,

My attention has been called to an interesting article by Sir William Schooling in your issue of April 10th, which comments on some remarks I made as Chairman of the National Mutual Life Assurance Society on an 'active investment policy'.

Following Mr Runciman, Sir William Schooling lays down the principle that an active investment policy is not preferable to an inactive policy unless in the long run a larger income is derived from the former policy than from the latter. I think it would be more accurate to say 'unless a larger surplus is derived' from it. But since a larger surplus will yield a larger income, Sir William Schooling's criterion can be accepted. Indeed, the point is obvious. It is true that when the general rate of interest is falling investments appreciate without any increase in income. (I do not agree that appreciation even of this kind does not strengthen a life office. I am sure it does.) But appreciation which comes to everyone alike is precisely the kind of appreciation which is not peculiar to a policy of active investment. An active policy is not successful unless over a period of years it makes more appreciation (or escapes more depreciation) than the average run of high-class securities, and consequently leads to an increased income.

Sir W. Schooling remarks that last year the National Mutual gained 10·6 per cent appreciation on its investments in stock exchange securities, in addition to 4·6 per cent net interest, and asks what effect this has had on the income of the society. The answer is that the society's income is higher by 10·6 per cent on its stock exchange investments than if this appreciation had not been earned. Does Sir W. Schooling suppose that we leave our profits uninvested?

I do not understand why so plain a point should be thought to require such elaborate discussion. But if there is any intention to suggest that a society of which the investment policy leads to a surplus larger than that of another society is not that much better off, I suspect a fallacy. And whilst it is true that it is safer for some people to go to sleep over their investments than to deal actively with them, ought such persons to be directors of insurance companies? If, however, the only point is that an active policy ought not to take credit for appreciation merely due to a lowering of the general rate of interest, then I cordially agree.

When it comes to a question of distributing surplus, the problem arising out of a fall in the prevailing rate of interest during the quinquennium is the same for all offices, and is in no way connected with the investment policy pursued. If the rate of interest assumed in calculating the society's liabilities is the same at both quinquennia, whereas the rate of interest actually obtainable has fallen between the two dates, I agree that the increase of surplus arrived at by this method of valuation is not the true increase. But the calculation of the true increase, whilst not difficult, is not correctly given by the too simple method employed by Mr Runciman in the passage quoted by Sir W. Schooling.

I am, &c.,

J. M. KEYNES

Sir William Schooling returned to defend his position, but Keynes did not reply further until his next speech.

Speech to the Annual Meeting of the National Mutual, 30 January 1924

Gentlemen,

Before proceeding to our main business of today—the results of this quinquennium—I will deal briefly with the figures of the past year.

The amount of new business obtained slightly exceeds that of 1922, but the more than proportionate increase in the amount of new premiums indicates that our business has been more largely of the type of endowment assurance and other forms of investment assurance than was the case in 1922. The claims by death are a little up, but there remains a substantial actuarial profit on the mortality of the year. The small, but satisfactory, decrease of ½ per cent in the ratio of expenditure to premiums is due principally to a growth in the premium income of more than £13,000. The accumulated funds have increased by more than £140,000. The average gross rate of interest earned on these funds, excluding reversions, which are valued on a 6 per cent basis, was £5 2s. 5d. per cent before deduction of income tax, as compared with £5 1s. 1d. in 1922. The net rate of interest was £4 6s. 3d. per cent, as against £4 12s. in 1922, the difference being accounted for by the fact that in 1922 there was brought into credit a considerable sum reserved against a claim for income tax, which was finally decided in favour of the Society.

Since we were criticised in some quarters last year for bringing into account what are called 'unrealised profits', I may explain that your board act on the principle that the balance sheet of the Society should show its exact position at the close of each year as nearly as it can be ascertained. The members are entitled to this information without any concealment or reservations, and when the position has been exposed, as it is in the valuation balance sheet included in the actuary's report, they are in a position to see for themselves the true surplus at the disposal of the board.

Investment policy

The revaluation of the Society's assets, carried out on this principle, shows a total appreciation of £72,200 on the year, of which £28,300 has accrued on stock exchange securities.

The average prices both of gilt-edged securities and of other investments, as shown in the index numbers compiled by various authorities, were almost the same—within 1 per cent—on January 1, 1924, as they were on January 1, 1923. This is in accordance with our own experience. But in spite of this relative stability of prices, the year has not been an easy one for investment. Throughout almost the whole year your board have been pursuing what can be best described as a waiting policy. Underlying conditions have been strongly in favour of a marked revival of trade, and last spring it looked as though these were asserting themselves. Political conditions, particularly abroad, but more recently at home also, have, however, operated in the opposite direction. In face of such conflicting tendencies it has been difficult to see one's way clearly. We have regarded the avoidance of loss on the Society's investments as our first object; and, as things have turned out, your board's hesitation to take a decided view has been justified by the facts. It will be seen in the report that approximately half of our stock exchange investments are British Government securities. It is interesting to recall that ten years ago this Society held no British Government securities.

The net result of the year, all sources of profit being taken into account, is an addition of £143,000 to our surplus—a highly satisfactory figure.

Revision of articles

There have been no changes in the directorate during the year, but Mr A. K. Tharp, the deputy-chairman of the Society, intimated to his colleagues at the close of the year that he would prefer not to seek re-election. Mr Tharp has been connected with the Society for 35 years, for the last 13 of which he has been deputy-chairman. His colleagues have accepted his resignation with great regret, and I am sure that you would like me to convey to him your good wishes for him in his retirement. I may mention that the actuary has told the board that he has contemplated for some time a revision of the Society's articles of association, and possibly the promotion of a new Act of Parliament. It is probable, therefore, that you will be called together later in the year to consider the alterations in our constitution and certain other matters, which must be submitted to you at two special general meetings.

Profit of the quinquennium

I now come to the results of the quinquennium as a whole. I am in the fortunate position of being able to announce to you one of the largest surpluses (in proportion to liabilities) in the history of life assurance—namely, £912,360, being 28·8 per cent of our liabilities—a sum far exceeding anything in the previous history of the Society, and, I believe, far larger than any surplus which has been previously shown by an office of the size of the National Mutual. Deducting the surplus brought in—namely, £184,668 —the profit of the quinquennium amounts to £727,692, equivalent to a net return on the mean fund—in addition to 3 per cent, the valuation rate of interest—of £4 12s. 6d. per cent per annum, so that during the past five years our aggregate earnings, after paying all expenses, have been at the rate of £7 12s. 6d. per cent. per annum, free of tax.

Special provisions

In dealing with this unusually large sum, your board have considered, in the first place, whether there were any special provisions or writings down to effect which it would be proper to take advantage of at this opportunity. The result is shown in the actuary's report. We have appropriated a sum of £65,000 to form a fund which will cover present and prospective liabilities in respect of staff pensions. We have further effected special writings down, beyond those required by the valuation, to the amount of £29,771. These mainly consist of two items: (1) In 1902 we made a large advance on mortgage, repayable only by instalments, the last of which is not due until 1952. The rate of interest then obtainable on mortgage securities of the highest class was very low, and the board have decided to write down the book value of this security to such a figure that the interest paid by the borrowers will yield a return of 5 per cent on the adjusted value, the instalments of principal being accumulated at $3\frac{1}{2}$ per cent net. There is no doubt whatever that we hold ample security, but we take the view that mortgage securities which cannot be called in must fluctuate in value with the current rate of interest, just as redeemable bonds or debentures fluctuate, and that in valuing them as assets it is preferable to adjust them according to that standard. (2) The other item, nearly £10,000, has been written off the Society's premises. It is approximately the amount which we have expended on the alterations made when we took over the house at the corner of Cheapside, and although we are advised that the total value of the property has increased by more than this amount, we have decided not to take credit for the sum in question. A further sum of about £42,500 has also come out of the surplus of the quinquennium and been paid away in interim bonuses to those policies which became claims during the last five years. After deducting these various sums, there remains an available balance of £775,101.

The proper and prudent disposal of this surplus has been the subject of much anxious thought and discussion between the board and their actuary. Their final conclusion is expressed in the valuation report.

Class A policyholders

Class A, which is treated separately, is a closed series into which no new policyholders have been admitted for many years. The method of division in this class is prescribed by our Act of Parliament, and has been followed as in the past, but the directors are considering whether it would not be to the interest of the remaining policyholders in the class that they should be absorbed in the general body of participating policyholders, possibly with a guarantee that their future profits should never be less than would be sufficient to extinguish the annual premiums during the remainder of their duration. I may add that no action of this sort will be taken without the consent of the policyholders in the class.

Rate of reversionary bonus

The reversionary bonus on National Mutual policies will be at the rate of 42s. per cent per annum compound, that is to say, calculated on sums assured and bonuses existing at the end of 1923. The usual adjustment for differences of premium on policies dated prior to the amalgamation will be made. The interim bonus on policies which may become claims before December 31 next will be at the full rate now declared, if a whole year's premium has become due and been paid during the year and prior to death or maturity.

The board have further considered the advisability of giving a retrospective bonus for the period of 1913–18—a course the possibility of which was contemplated in the actuary's report of 1918. The board have, however, decided against this course, partly on general grounds, and partly in view of the declaration in the following paragraph from the annual report for the year 1919 which was adopted by the members:—

'The directors have given the most careful consideration to the question of a distribution of surplus in respect of the quinquennium 1914–18. The continued depreciation in values and the general uncertainty of the outlook have made them decide to follow the course adopted by other offices of the highest standing and not to add to the Society's liabilities by declaring a bonus for that quinquennium. They have, therefore, finally determined to make no general distribution of surplus in respect of the valuation period 1914–18.'

Annual distributions of surplus

The existence of an unusually large surplus, such as we have on this occasion, is bound to give rise to difficult questions of distribution policy, how to assess the just claims of the present policyholders against the interests of the Society as a permanent institution, older than the existing members yet with longer prospects of life; and how best to combine the advantage of continuity and regularity with the rapid fluctuations of the modern world. Such considerations, amongst others, have weighed with us in reaching the decision, which will probably commend itself to all of you, that, in future, distributions of surplus shall be made to the policyholders annually instead of at five-year intervals as in the past. Not only will this arrangement give members the satisfaction of receiving a definite bonus every year, but it will afford an opportunity for more frequent stock-taking and for closer and more continuous examination of all the conditions which should be considered in determining the problems of a distribution of surplus.

'Position of unexampled strength'

At any rate, carrying forward an undistributed surplus equal to about 15 per cent of our liabilities, we are in a position of unexampled strength to meet the ups and downs of the next few years. These figures entitle me to emphasise again the opportunities which our institution offers for the management of the savings of its members, and to urge each of you to increase his stake in so well-secured a property by taking out additional endowment or other policies up to the full capacity of your income.

I beg to move the adoption of the report and accounts.

Speech to the Annual Meeting of the National Mutual, 28 January 1925

Gentlemen,

I am happy to be able to announce exceptionally satisfactory results for this first year of our new policy of annual valuations and declarations of bonus. Our gross profits for the year amount to £215,902, made up as follows:—

	£	£
Net miscellaneous profits from mortality, etc.	28,551	
Interest earnings in excess of 3 per cent on mean fund, excluding carry-forward	49,508	
		78,059
Capital appreciation on securities sold or revalued		117,019
Interest earned on the carry-forward from the previous year		20,824
Total		£215,902

The reversionary bonus

We have declared out of this a reversionary bonus for the year of 42s. per cent, the same as for the quinquennium which ended last year. This bonus will cost, inclusive of interim bonuses at the same rate paid during the current year, £77,786. Thus the payment of a rate of bonus which, relatively, is high will absorb not much more than one-third of the earnings of the year. It is covered by the miscellaneous trading profits and interest earnings, without touching the capital appreciation or the interest earned on the surplus carried forward.

There are, however, certain other deductions to be made before calculating the net addition to our carry-forward. In accordance with my anticipations last year, we have been able to deal with the Class A policyholders. The offer which the board was able to make to this class proved, however, so satisfactory to its members that the settlement has been completed by paying off the policies and thus winding up the class, instead of amalgamating it with the existing with-profit class. The sums paid to the Class A policies in excess of the reserves held amounted to £21,456, which is entirely a charge on the funds of Class A included in the accumulated surplus of previous years, and does not in any way prejudice the policyholders in the other classes.

We have also decided to strengthen the basis of valuation of the non-profit policies (Class C) by raising the provision for expenses from 6½ to 10 per cent of the office premiums at a cost of £8,401. After deducting these items and the valuation expenses of £1,500, the amount carried forward is increased by £106,759 to £575,290, which is 16⅔ per cent of our liabilities.

Interest and appreciation

As regards the separate items, the net rate of interest earned, after deduction of income tax on assets other than reversions, has amounted to £4 11s. 3d. per cent, which is a satisfactory increase on last year's figure of £4 6s. 3d. per cent. Our expense ratio has fallen from 16·7 per cent to 15·3 per cent, which is also satisfactory, but may not be maintained, since it is due to an unusual proportion of single premiums received during the year. New business shows a total of £672,038, which is considerably the highest figure in the society's history.

There remains the important item of £117,000, which represents capital appreciation—namely, about 3 per cent of the mean fund of the year. Thus in interest and appreciation together we have earned at the rate of about 7½ per cent per annum free of income tax. We cannot hope to maintain so high a rate of earnings year in year out in future. Nevertheless, we have now earned at this rate as an average over a period of no less than six years. We have continued our investment policy on the same general lines as before. Our list of investments shows no material changes from last year's list. The largest increase is under the heading of 'securities not otherwise classified'. These consist mainly of high-class notes, carrying a fixed rate of interest and approximating to debentures in type.

Bonus outlook

Since we are bound to have downs, as well as ups, in future, it is worthwhile to point out that the maintenance of the present rate of bonus is in no way dependent on the recurrence of such good fortune with our investments as we have had lately. It will be observed that, for the past year, it has not been necessary to use any part of our capital appreciation for the payment of bonus. But this has also been the case during the whole period of the past six years during which capital appreciation has been accruing. So far we have not drawn upon this source for the payment of bonuses, but have used all of it for strengthening our general position in various ways, as, for example, by the establishment of a fund for staff pensions, and, mainly, by adding to our carry-forward. I may add, since some people attach importance to the point, that almost the whole of this capital appreciation has been realised.

The result is that the interest alone on our surplus funds carried forward now amounts, calculated at $4\frac{1}{2}$ per cent net, to nearly £26,000 per annum, which by itself is the equivalent of a bonus of 14s. per cent per annum on our policies now outstanding. Thus, apart from any future earnings out of capital appreciation, and apart from the safeguard which this carry-forward gives us against the results of any depreciation of capital which we are likely to suffer from time to time in future years, we are in an unusually strong position as regards our capacity to earn bonus.

Minimum of £500 for new policies

This position, however, satisfactory as it must be to our members, raises questions of great difficulty and perplexity for the board, of which, in my opinion, we have not yet found the final solution. It is obvious, in the light of the figures which I have just given to you, that we are selling new policies much too cheap. We are admitting newcomers without charge to the benefits of the large surplus which the Society has now accumulated. This is, of course, always so to a moderate extent in the case of the with-profit policies of any prudently conducted office which has built up a sound position. The question is one of degree. But I do not know of any recent precedent for the right solution of this problem in the degree in which it now presents itself to your board. Should we distribute much larger bonuses at irregular intervals? Or close the present series of policies and raise our rates of premium to new members, to which there are many technical objections? Or take steps, in other ways, to limit the amount of new business?

On the present occasion your board have decided to take tentative steps towards the limitation of the amount of new business and to concentrate our efforts on securing larger policies and on obtaining these as cheaply as possible. We shall thus reduce both our initial costs and our running expenses. We propose this course, not only because it will prevent too great an influx of new members coming in to claim a share in past accumulations, but also because, apart from this particular difficulty, it will not be many years, if we go on at our present rate of development, before our aggregate funds reach a total greater than, in the opinion of your board, we can manage to the best advantage.

The cost of new business in the case of small policies is disproportionately heavy, and we have, therefore, decided not to accept new assurances for smaller amounts than £500, although existing policyholders will be privileged to take out further with-profit assurances of not less than £250. Measured by the premium payable and by the income which the sum assured will produce when invested, a policy for even £500 makes but a small provision. In this connection I do not think it is realised how greatly the people of this country are under-insured in comparison with other progressive countries. It is estimated that the life assurance per head of our population is only £39, whilst in the United States of America it is nearly £109 and in Canada £74. An expansion in the amount of assurance carried by the individual policyholder here is, therefore, much to be desired.

Proposed variation in risks

As regards the upper limit of the risks we accept, we propose to apply to the Court to vary the memorandum of association scheduled to our Act of Parliament to the intent that we shall be authorised to hold at our own risk such a sum as makes the total amount at risk on any one life not more than £20,000 at any one time. We have been inconvenienced for some time by the fact that the memorandum, in strict conformity with which we have to work, provides that no greater sum than £10,000, exclusive of bonus additions, shall stand at the Society's own risk on a single life. This limit of £10,000 was fixed in 1895, when our total funds were only 60 per cent of their present amount.

Further, we are examining ways and means of keeping down commission costs, and of cutting off sources of business which, though costly, have proved unproductive. Finally, as a further precaution, if the total of new business in any year should reach a figure which the board considers to be the maximum in the interests of the Society, we shall reserve a discretion to impose a limit on the total with-profit business to be accepted in that year.

We have also resolved to reduce our rates of premium for non-profit policies, in order to encourage a class of business advantageous to the with-profit members, which has been shrinking in recent years to a low figure.

Before concluding, I should like to explain that, to save time and expense, the amount of previous bonus will no longer be stated on the bonus notices posted to the members. It is hardly necessary for me to say that the new bonus is in addition to any previous bonus which there may be, and I mention the matter only so that the members may not misunderstand the notices which they will receive to-morrow.

General prospects

The prospects for general prosperity appear much more secure than they did a year ago, but the perturbations which may attend the restoration of the gold standard, and the possibilities of dearer money will give your board plenty to think about in the never easy but always interesting task of conducting the affairs of the National Mutual Society.

I beg to move the adoption of the report and accounts.

Speech to the Annual Meeting of the National Mutual, 27 January 1926

Gentlemen,

The National Mutual Society has again experienced a satisfactory year. Our gross profits amount to £153,864, made up as follows:—

Net miscellaneous profits from mortality, etc.	£32,360
Interest earnings in excess of 3 per cent on mean fund, excluding carry-forward	51,347
Capital appreciation on securities sold or revalued before special adjustment	44,650
Interest earned on the carry-forward from the previous year	25,507
	£153,864

We have declared out of this a compound reversionary bonus for the year of 44s. per cent, 2s. more than for the previous six years, and the highest in the history of the society. This bonus will cost, including interim bonuses already paid, £89,667, thus leaving a balance of about £64,000 for strengthening the society's position in various ways, and adding to the carry-forward.

Out of this balance we have added £31,483 to the actuarial reserves. This is made up of a number of items, in particular an increase in the reserve for annuities in accordance with the newest tables. We are also writing off about £11,000 from our stock exchange securities. These securities are usually valued at their selling prices at the end of the year, less accrued interest. But we have thought it prudent to make some further provision in the case of securities where the dealings are not very active, with the result that a seller who comes to market runs the risk of having to take something less than the quoted selling price. After making these provisions there remained a balance of £20,358 to be added to the carry-forward, which is thereby raised to £595,648, being 15·9 per cent of our liabilities.

Capital appreciation of investments

We have had a long series of successful years as regards the capital appreciation of our investments. But a year is bound to come sooner or later when we shall suffer some degree of depreciation, possibly for reasons quite beyond our control. Our large carry-forward, mainly built up out of capital appreciation, places us in an exceptionally strong position to meet any such circumstances.

Our expense ratio has fallen from 15·3 per cent to 12·7 per cent. But, as was also the case, though in a less degree, last year, this is largely explained by the abnormal swelling of our premium income from single-premium policies. Apart, however, from this disturbing factor there has been a real reduction in our expense ratio, which would have fallen by about ½ per cent if single premiums were eliminated from the revenue accounts of the last two years and equivalent annual premiums substituted. The expenses of management, apart from commission, which has naturally increased with the new business, and the large amount of single premiums, are actually about £1,000 less than last year.

As is stated in the board's report, we have not during the year written directly a single policy on the now popular basis of lending to the policyholder 90 per cent of his single premium at 5 per cent interest or thereabouts. Two or three reassurances of this kind, which we have taken from other offices, are special cases, where the terms regarded as a whole were advantageous to the Society. If, however, we were to do any large proportion of our total business on the terms usual for this class of policy, we could not earn profits at our present rate or even earn our present bonus, so that, with-profit policies of this type, since they cannot contribute proportionately to the Society's surplus, are not to the Society's advantage.

Our efforts during the year to reduce the expenses involved in new business by increasing the average size of our policies, and in other ways, have been successful, the average policy rising in amount from £846 in 1924 to £1,176 in 1925. We have twice lowered the rates for non-profit policies, with a view to encouraging such business, and have increased those for with-profit endowment policies, which were too low relatively to those for whole-life policies. We have also closed down during the year one branch which has proved expensive in proportion to the business obtained.

Increased rates of interest

Let me now turn to the investment side of our business. Both the gross and net rates of interest earned are very slightly better than last year—at £5 6s. 9d. gross and £4 11s. 6d. net. We should have earned a higher rate of interest if we had not held an unusually large proportion of our assets in British Government securities —at the end of the year more than two-thirds of our total investments in stock exchange securities were so held. It is not the policy of the board to hold so large a proportion of our funds in this way as a general rule, and the possibility of a transfer into other securities, which will yield on the average a somewhat higher rate of interest, represents a considerable reserve of potential earning power.

Net capital appreciation has amounted this year to £33,800, being about 16s. per cent on the mean fund of the year. Thus in interest and appreciation together we have earned about $5\frac{1}{4}$ per cent per annum, free of income tax. This is not so high as the corresponding rate of about $7\frac{1}{2}$ per cent per annum, free of income tax, which we earned on the average of the preceding six years. Nevertheless, your board are well satisfied to have achieved so good a result in the somewhat difficult conditions for investment which have marked the past year.

How difficult it has been to secure a satisfactory net return, after allowing for appreciation and depreciation during the year and for income tax, is shown by the indexes of securities currently compiled, which indicate that typical gilt-edged investments and other first-class fixed-interest securities have depreciated in capital value on the average by not less than 2 per cent. For example, the net return on Three-and-a-Half per Cent Conversion Loan for the year, after writing-off depreciation, has worked out at a negative figure; on Five per Cent War Loan it is only about 3 per cent; and on Commonwealth of Australia Five per Cent (1934–45) it is slightly less. I estimate that first-class, long-dated, fixed-interest securities have not yielded, on the average of the whole class, above 2 per cent for the year, after writing-off depreciation and allowing for income tax. In face of such conditions, your board has again pursued throughout the year an ultra-cautious policy chiefly aimed at the avoidance of depreciation, and this policy has again been justified by its results.

The London money market

Moreover, the difficult conditions are by no means at an end. Success in the investment of insurance funds mainly depends on anticipating, so far as possible, the course of the rate of interest. Unforeseen fluctuation in this rate is the one factor which is capable of seriously upsetting our calculations. If only we knew for certain what the course of the rate of interest was going to be, whether high or low, we could act without hesitation. But as things are, it is particularly difficult to take up a confident attitude.

On the one hand, the view is commonly held—though I am not sure that I myself agree with it—that with the buying on account of sinking funds and the unceasing flow of new savings, the long-period trend of interest rates will be assuredly downwards. On the other hand, the London market is at present out of equilibrium with the rest of the world, and the events which will attend the gradual restoration of equilibrium are far more important for the time being than any considerations which relate to the long-period trend.

This country is not yet in financial equilibrium, and that is the central financial fact of the moment which it would be rash to ignore. The terms on which London is ready to lend overseas are so attractive to borrowers that the outflow of investment exceeds the surplus which our exports are capable of providing—after making allowances for other items—so long as British gold costs of production, as resulting from the re-establishment of the exchange at the pre-war parity, remain at their present relatively high level. Unless the United States comes to offer more attractive terms to borrowers than ours, or unless gold costs of production abroad, particularly in Europe, rise materially, it is evident that sooner or later we shall be compelled to raise our terms as lenders or to force down our costs as producers, or both. Now it is difficult to see how either of these results is to be attained except through a régime of dear money, which will have other undesired consequences. A period when interest is rising and profits are falling hits the owner of previously invested funds both ways; for the prices of both bonds and shares will tend downwards. The mere possibility of a development along these lines must naturally breed a high degree of caution in anyone who is responsible for the handling of large funds.

Influence of increased Bank rate

But this is not the end of our perplexity. If we knew when the readjustments required to restore equilibrium were coming, we could lay our plans accordingly. But the experience of the past year has shown that the final adjustments may possibly be delayed for some little time. Only a very slight progress has been made towards the adjustment of interest rates in the past year, and almost none at all towards the adjustment of gold costs of production. We have been enabled to put off these adjustments owing to the attraction to London of international bank balances, partly as a result of the restoration of the gold standard and partly by the maintenance of dearer money here than in New York. The increase of Bank rate has been very ineffective in deterring foreign investments and in lowering costs of production, but very effective indeed in attracting floating balances. But obviously it is not possible to go on indefinitely balancing the national account in this manner.

We have made two additions to the board during the year, of which we shall invite your confirmation in a moment—Mr Geoffrey Marks and Sir William McLintock. Mr Geoffrey Marks has been actuary and manager of the Society, a post which he will still retain, since 1893. You are all aware of the great services which he has rendered to the Society, and how the foundations of its exceptional prosperity have been entirely laid during his long régime and in accordance with his conceptions. All the other members of the board are his juniors in the service of the Society, and most of us, I think, have owed our first introduction to the society to his friendly offices. Sir William McLintock, who was a member of the Royal Commission on the Income Tax, and has given to the state much other valuable service, is one of the most eminent and accomplished accountants in London. He will bring to the board a type of knowledge and experience which we have hitherto lacked.

I will now move the adoption of the report and accounts.

Speech to the Annual Meeting of the National Mutual, 26 January 1927

Gentlemen,

We are again able to say that the National Mutual has experienced a satisfactory year. Our new business has slightly increased, our average policy is larger, and our profits from trading and interest exceed those of last year by nearly £20,000. The decrease in the premium income and the increase in the expense ratio are due, in accordance with the explanation I made last year, to the smaller sum which we received in single premiums in 1926 as compared with 1925. If in both years we were to substitute equivalent annual premiums for the single premiums received, we should find that our annual premium income had increased by about £7,000, while the expense ratio had decreased by about 6s. per cent and was nearly 1 per cent below the average of the post-war years. Moreover, our total expenditure on commission and expenses of management is somewhat less than in 1925 in spite of the increase in the new business.

The gross profits

Our gross profits for the year from all sources amount to £150,465, as compared with £153,864 in 1925, and are made up as follows:—

Profit from mortality	£35,353	+£12,500
Profit from miscellaneous sources	9,487	
Interest earnings in excess of 3 per cent on mean fund, excluding carry-forward from 1925	58,162	+ 7,000 (nearly)
Capital appreciation on securities sold or re-valued (before making special allocation)	19,691	− 25,000
Interest earned on the carry-forward from the previous year	27,772	+ 2,250
	£150,465	
Net rate of interest	£4 13 3	+ 1s. 9d. per cent

I have given the mortality profit separately as it is a large amount for us and is due to our remarkably light mortality. I also state it as a separate definitely ascertained figure, because it is a too common practice to give the difference between actual and expected claims, leaving it to be inferred that this difference represents the profit on mortality. It is nothing of the sort, since the total of actual claims thus stated treats equally claims falling on young lives and policies recently effected with claims falling on old lives and policies of long standing.

Value of invested funds

In respect of our invested funds, we have secured on the year only a small appreciation in capital value—about £20,000. This is not so large as in recent years, but, as I pointed out a year ago, capital appreciation is bound to be an irregular item, in respect of which we cannot hope to repeat year by year the figures of our best years. However, we have now been on the right side for six consecutive years, and have accumulated altogether from this source the sum of £665,000, or about 16 per cent of our mean fund during this period, the whole of which has been employed so far in strengthening our resources in various ways, mainly by additions to the carry-forward, which now yields us an interest income of about £28,000 a year, quite apart from the results of any year in respect of current business.

In obtaining this small appreciation during the year, amounting to about 0·4 per cent of our mean fund, we cannot claim to have done appreciably better than the average. The securities index of *The Investors' Chronicle* shows that gilt-edged securities fell during the year 1926 by 0·5 per cent, whilst stock exchange investments generally rose 0·3 per cent on balance. In fact, apart from a few small groups and individual securities, the net changes on the year have been remarkably small as compared with previous periods.

Investment problems

I called attention last year to the unusually large proportion of our assets which we were holding in British Government securities, and I added that it was not the policy of the board to hold so large a proportion of our funds in this way as a general rule. During the past year this figure has been slightly reduced— namely, to £2,112,000. Your board have been proceeding slowly and carefully with the task of finding an outlet for the Society's funds in securities yielding on the average a somewhat higher rate of interest. They will do their best to proceed further in the same direction during the current year, for our British Government securities still represent 58 per cent of our stock exchange securities and 44 per cent of our total invested funds.

The heavy investment of life offices generally in British Government securities is, of course, entirely a post-war phenomenon, and, on the average of the leading offices, the tide has already begun to turn in the opposite direction. Figures published in the *Journal of the Institute of Actuaries* show that for 26 leading offices the proportions of British Government securities to total investments have been as follows:—

1913	1922	1924
0·23	40·30	35·87

It is right for the Treasury to proceed on as optimistic a hypothesis as possible as to the future rate of interest at which they will be able to borrow, but it will be prudent to remember that, with the vastly increased volume of outstanding debt, Consols, new or old, are bound to stand on a more strictly competitive basis with alternative investments than was the case formerly. Policyholders have become accustomed to bonuses which presume, in most cases, that the office is earning on the average a net rate of interest of not much less than 4½ per cent after payment of income tax. If an attempt is made to put British Government securities on a basis appreciably below 4 per cent net, it is certain that in many quarters a powerful stimulus will be brought into play to find more profitable outlets for invested funds. In seeking these outlets no doubt mistakes will be made, just as they were before the War. Your board will not forget that the depreciation of investments has been the plague of insurance finance in past years, and that avoidance of this kind of loss must be their first consideration.

Future rate of interest

Guessing at the future rate of interest is, in my opinion, one of the most puzzling problems in the world. I am quite unable to take a confident view either way. Before the War Great Britain, France, and Germany set the pace in the international loan market. Henceforward it will be the United States. Is the United States going to have such a surplus of savings over her own needs and such confidence in the prevailing conditions of the outside world that she will be prepared to subscribe heavily year by year to first-class international securities at a yield of less than 5 per cent, as we used to do? The answer to this question is going to determine by its indirect reactions the equilibrium price of British Government long-dated securities far more than anything the British Treasury can do by ingenious methods of funding or by powerful sinking funds. Nevertheless, for the first time in more than three years past I incline to agree with the prevailing opinion that, so far as the near future is concerned, the signs seem to be set in favour of a somewhat lower rate of interest.

Bonus declaration

I come now to our declaration of bonus for the past year, particulars of which are already in your hands. We maintain last year's figure of 44s. per cent compound on all classes of with-profit policies, and we are giving an additional bonus for this year of 6s. per cent compound, making 50s. altogether, on whole-life with-profit policies. The total cost of this is covered by the ordinary profits of the year, excluding capital appreciation and interest earned on the carry-forward. The change from previous practice in the method of distribution requires some explanation.

The relative terms which we and other offices quote for endowment assurance policies and whole-life policies respectively are based, amongst other things, on certain assumptions as to the rate of mortality to be experienced and the rate of interest to be earned. The assumptions are cautious, and, in so far as we can do better, with-profit policyholders reap the benefit in the shape of bonuses. In course of time, however, these assumptions have come to differ from actual experience by far more than the margin of reasonable precaution which they represented when this method was first adopted. The rise in the rate of interest and the fall in mortality as compared with the life tables still in use, which is all that actuaries have to work on pending the completion of the new tables, have been so considerable as seriously to upset the parities between the existing premiums on the two leading classes of policies. Put very roughly, the decline in mortality brings us more surplus profit in the case of whole-life policies than it does in the case of endowment assurance policies. Thus, if we pay the same rate of bonus to both classes we are in danger of paying out to holders of the latter profits which we have really earned on our whole-life business.

The compound reversionary bonus system cannot pretend, any more than any other method of distributing surplus at present in use, to do mathematically precise justice all round; nor with the information at present available is it possible to make exact calculations as to what is precisely just. Nevertheless, two striking papers read before the Institute of Actuaries during the past year, one of them by Mr C. R. V. Coutts—whom we are glad to see here today—a former assistant actuary of our own society and now the distinguished actuary of the Provident Mutual Life Assurance Association, and the other by Mr G. H. Recknell, our present assistant actuary, have made it clear that, with the existing relative with-profit rates of premium, the anomalies of an equal bonus on endowment assurance policies and on whole-life policies are becoming altogether excessive. I refer anyone who is interested in the details, and thinks he can understand them, to the *Journal of the Institute of Actuaries* for July, 1926, wherein both papers are printed.

In the light of these calculations your board have decided, without binding themselves as to their future action, that they will be doing no more than justice to their with-profit whole-life policyholders if they award them for this year an additional bonus of 6s. per cent compound. I venture to congratulate these members of the Society both on their longevity and on its reward. I should add that this differentiation will involve no injustice to the holders of endowment assurances. Indeed, we calculate that the balance of advantage is still, if anything, very slightly in their favour. This is true even in the case of those policies which have been granted since the beginning of last year at the increased premiums which then came into force. *A fortiori*, it is true of entrants before that date.

Encouragements to whole-life business

There is a further advantage in this course in that the proportion of whole-life business done by the leading life offices had fallen off seriously since the War, and the special bonus may do something to restore the whole-life policy to favour. The popularity of endowment assurance has been based, indeed, on sound foundations. In past years I have strongly advocated it as a means of investment, especially for the man of moderate means and little financial training or experience, and I still do so where the main consideration is the safe investment of small savings. But for the proper balance of a life office's business as a whole, a due proportion of whole-life business is highly desirable.

The tendency of chairmen of life offices to deplore in their annual speeches the falling off in whole-life business, when actuarial science has been able to show that they are offering these policies on relatively unfavourable terms, is surely not quite consistent. In their preference for endowment assurance on the existing terms the public have been showing, doubtless by accident, the shrewder actuarial instinct. Other encouragements to whole-life business, which we have already put into practice, have resulted in the proportion of this type of our assurances to our total new business increasing from 27½ per cent in 1925 to 40 per cent in 1926. With the additional bonus now declared, and having regard to our rates of premium and the general strength of our position, we can now claim, I think, to be the most attractive office in the country to the applicant for a whole-life policy.

The Report of the Board of Trade Committee on the revision of the Assurance Companies Act, 1909, will shortly be published, and it is probable that, as a result of their report, considerably wider disclosures as to the exact position of the companies will have to be made in official returns. In this connection I should like to re-state our own position, which I described in my speech three years ago. We act on the principle that the balance sheet should show the exact position at the end of each year as nearly as it can be ascertained. We disclose the whole of our surplus, and we state the present values of our assets and the bases on which these values are arrived at. We hold no concealed reserves to act as a curtain for any future mismanagement or future losses. Our financial and actuarial results are fully exposed to the skilled outside critic.

This is our 97th annual meeting, and the report before you is the 97th annual report. Our centenary meeting will be held early in 1930, and the annual report will then deal with our position at the end of our 100th year of existence, counting from the date of the foundation of the old 'National'.

Speech to the Annual Meeting of National Mutual, 25 January 1928

Gentlemen,

Both in trading profit—i.e., profit apart from capital gains— and in total profit the past year has provided the highest totals which the National Mutual Society has so far experienced. Our gross profits amount to £226,481, made up as follows:—

Net miscellaneous profits from mortality, etc.	£44,264
Interest earnings in excess of 3 per cent on mean fund, excluding carry-forward	65,981
Capital gains on securities sold or revalued (before making special allocation of £1,702)	86,065
Interest earned on the surplus carried forward from the previous year	30,171
	£226,481

The corresponding total last year was £150,465. After increasing the reversionary bonus to 45s. per cent compound on endowment assurance policies and to 51s. per cent compound on

153

whole-life policies at a total cost of £115,441, including the interim bonus, and allowing for a small special writing down of certain securities below market price (£1,702) and for valuation expenses, we are adding £111,040 to our undistributed surplus carried forward, bringing this up to a total of £751,246, which is now 17·8 per cent of our liabilities as compared with 16·0 per cent at the end of 1926.

Bonus rates and costs

The broad results of the nine years since the War can be summarised as follows:—

I. *Rate and cost of compound bonus*

Year	Rate of compound bonus	Cost of compound bonus
		£
1919–23 (annual average of the 5 years)	42s.	60,314
1924	42s.	76,530
1925	44s.	88,797
1926	44s.	100,928
	+ 6s. whole life	
1927	45s.	111,416
	+ 6s. whole life	

II. *Profits earned*

Year	(1) Trading profit	(2) Capital gains on investments	Total profit (1+2)	Rate of bonus earned
1919–23 (annual average of the 5 years)	£	£	£	s. d.
	73,186	72,352	145,538	101 6
1924	98,882	117,020	215,902	118 6
1925	109,214	44,650	153,864	76 6
1926	130,772	19,693	150,465	69 0
1927	140,416	86,065	226,481	96 6

Thus the cost of the bonus declared during these nine years has not exceeded on the average 80 per cent of the trading profit, excluding altogether the capital gains on investments, which have aggregated £629,000. One further significant figure—we have earned in interest and capital gains together on the average of the nine years more than 6 per cent per annum, free of income tax, notwithstanding the large sums written off against depreciation at the end of 1919 and 1920, and more than 7 per cent, free of income tax, on the average of the last seven years.

Success of investment policy

An investment policy which has shown these profits can fairly claim to have passed the test of results.

On several previous occasions I have had something to say about the principles underlying this policy. Speaking very broadly, it has consisted in constant care and activity—a line of action which was the object of much more criticism when we began than it is now. We have acted in agreement with the following quotation from the annual report of the Carnegie Corporation:—

'The funds of a great endowment can be kept intact only by a systematic revision month by month of all the securities of the endowment and by a continuous process of sale and exchange as circumstances may affect the financial soundness of this or that security.'

In particular, we have been pioneers amongst the life offices in the practice of employing a substantial part of our funds in the purchase of ordinary shares. The proportion of our funds so employed at the end of each year has been as follows:—

1918	3·04 per cent
1923	16·35 per cent
1924	18·67 per cent
1925	9·56 per cent
1926	15·66 per cent
1927	18·33 per cent

This is materially divergent from the prevailing practice. The Board of Trade returns for life assurance companies—which include total funds in the case of the composite offices—show the following average results:—

Board of Trade returns published in year (1)	Total of balance sheets (2)	Holding of ordinary stocks and shares (3)	Percentage of (3) to (2)
1911	£467,000,000	£18,000,000	3·9
1926	946,000,000	41,000,000	4·3

Since papers read before the Institute of Actuaries by Mr Raynes, of the Legal and General, and by others elsewhere during the past year have directed the general attention of the insurance world to a closer consideration of this policy, it may be in place if I enlarge somewhat upon it in the light of our own experience.

Market capitalisation of ordinary shares

The arguments in favour of holding a certain proportion of ordinary shares are, from the point of view of the individual office, broadly two—one of them of a permanent character, the other possibly temporary. The permanent reason is to be found in the advantage of spreading the fund between assets such as bonds, expressed in terms of money values, and assets representing real values. Formerly, this result could be secured by means of investments in real estate; and, until recently, it was not practicable to invest in real values on a large scale in any other way. Today, however, the position is quite different. On the one hand, real estate as an investment is subject to serious drawbacks, and few insurance offices would wish to invest heavily at the present time either in agricultural land or in urban house property. On the other hand, the public joint stock company has taken a tremendous leap forward and now offers a field for the investment of funds which simply did not exist even 20 years ago.

Leaving out for the moment railways and public utilities, there are now quoted in the London Stock Exchange Official List about 188 commercial and industrial British companies each having an ordinary share capitalisation which amounts at present market prices to £1,000,000 or over, and 60 companies producing primary raw materials, mostly operating abroad, which satisfy the same test. The present market capitalisation of the ordinary shares of the commercial and industrial companies comes to about £1,177,000,000, or an average of £6,000,000 per company, and that of the produce companies to £342,000,000, which also gives an average of nearly £6,000,000 per company. In each category the average is greatly raised by the giants which head the list.

Now, when we speak of the new policy of investing a certain proportion of an insurance fund in ordinary shares, we have primarily in view—without any intention of excluding investments in railways and public utilities—these (in round figures) 250 companies with a total ordinary share market capitalisation of about £1,500,000,000. These represent the live large-scale business and investment world of today, and any investment institution which ignores or is not equipped for handling their shares is living in a backwater.

In addition to the above, there are about 70 railway and other public utility companies—many of them with a much longer investment history behind them—which have on the same tests a market capitalisation of about £392,000,000, or an average of more than £5,000,000. Finally, there are the ordinary shares of companies overseas, particularly in the United States.

Railway security values

In order to correct the old-fashioned sense of the perspective, it is worth remarking that the nine oil companies included in the produce companies with a market capitalisation of £169,000,000 compare with seven home railway companies with £143,000,000; whilst 35 rubber, tea, and coffee companies with £81,000,000 compare with 12 foreign railway companies with £83,000,000. Thus 44 oil, rubber, tea, and coffee companies centred in London have an ordinary share market capitalisation nearly equal to that of all the 30 home, foreign, Indian, and colonial railway companies having a sterling capital. One could give many other startling illustrations. The ordinary share market capitalisation of Courtaulds at the end of 1927 exceeded by nearly 15 per cent that of all the 12 foreign railway companies which satisfy our test added together, and the ordinary shares of Courtaulds and Imperial Chemicals are together worth more than those of all the British railway companies. (Let it be remembered that I am taking ordinary share capitalisation, not total capitalisation.) In short, the centre of gravity of business, and therefore of investment, is not where it was. A 'conservative' investment policy is apt to mean in practice backing the enterprises which were in the van 50 years ago, instead of backing the new ones which are the characteristic achievement of the best business brains of today.

The second reason for investing in ordinary shares is the fact that they are undoubtedly under-valued relatively to bonds after making all due allowance for risk and other relevant considerations. The fact that most well-managed and progressive concerns divide substantially less than they make introduces a cumulative, compound interest element which is often overlooked. Calculations made by Mr E. L. Smith in America and Mr Raynes here, confirmed by common experience, fully bear this out. For example, the results published during 1926 of 1,572 companies and analysed in *The Economist* show that in the aggregate the allocations to reserves equalled 2·02 per cent of the ordinary share market capitalisation. Whether this under-valuation will still remain by the time that all our friends and colleagues in the insurance business have followed our example (i.e., have invested some 20 per cent of their total funds in this way), I am more doubtful.

Arguments against ordinary investments

What are the arguments on the other side? For there are undoubtedly important objections. To judge from our own experience, they are mainly two. In the first place, the knowledge
required and the care and attention which must be given are
much greater, with the result that the burden of work and
responsibility which is thrown on the board and on the executive
is increased. It means that the directors have serious duties to
perform, and in cases where the directors have not performed
serious duties for many years, and are perhaps between 70 and
90 years of age, there must always be a doubt whether it is wise
to put new duties on them. Moreover, however much care
and attention is given, it is extraordinarily difficult to acquire
enough information to justify a substantial investment. The
next great step forward in the evolution of joint stock enterprise of widely diffused ownership will follow, I think, from
a revised company law which will insist on much greater
publicity of accounts and will strengthen the hands of the
auditors.

The second objection is to be found in the relative narrowness
of the market—in spite of the fairly large total capitalisation—
except in a few cases. Out of some 250 commercial, industrial,
and produce companies, you will have your work cut out to
discover 50 which are *prima facie* attractive and about which
you can acquire adequate information. The National Mutual,
although our total fund now exceeds £5,000,000, is one of the
smaller units amongst insurance offices. With a larger fund the
dilemma would soon be reached between having to invest an
amount in given companies which is rather too large for the
market and having to go outside the range of the detailed
information at the disposal of the office. We have sometimes
tried to overcome this difficulty by deciding to back an industry
rather than a particular business, dividing our investment between all the leading firms in the business, even though we might

not know much about them individually. We have had considerable success along these lines. But the difficulty still remains.

National finance

In conclusion, I venture to urge that there are important grounds of public policy why institutions such as insurance offices and investment trusts, which are now responsible for administering an ever-increasing proportion of that part of the national savings which finds its way to the Stock Exchange, should be encouraged to develop their policy, their organisation, and their experience along these lines.

In the first place, it is extraordinarily important that we as a nation should not become, as time goes on, a *rentier* nation depending on interest from bonds and cut off from the living enterprises of the day, where constructive things are being done and today's wealth is being earned. In a sense there is always a risk in doing anything new, but there are at least gains to balance losses, whereas the bondholder sometimes loses and can never win. At any rate, it would be a great misfortune if we were to see others, let us say the Americans, owning the ordinary shares, in other words, the equities, of the new enterprises of each generation—today, for example, oil, motors, artificial silk—whilst the life offices of Great Britain were diverting the savings of their policyholders almost exclusively into the bonds of the old things, which, as it is politely expressed, 'have stood the test of time'.

In the second place, the insurance offices might, if between them they held large blocks of ordinary shares in leading companies, do much to remedy one of the greatest difficulties and evils of the present stage in the evolution of joint stock enterprise —namely, the complete impotence, when things are going wrong, of the shareholders, separated from one another, each with only a tiny stake in the concern, and practically incapable of joint action, against a board of directors who may, as shareholders, have no great sum at risk. There may be important future possibilities in co-operative action between insurance offices, and a committee representing them might be able to play the part of the reasonable, well-informed shareholder able to make his views and wishes felt, which is at present so signally lacking in the existing scheme of things.

In short, I believe that considerations of public and of private advantage are in this instance happily combined. It will increase the wealth and efficiency of this country if those responsible for the investment of large funds come to consider it a part of their duty to participate as ordinary shareholders—to a moderate extent and within the due bounds of prudence—in the leading enterprises of their day and generation.

Gentlemen, I move the adoption of the report and accounts.

Speech to the Annual Meeting of the National Mutual, 30 January 1929

Gentlemen,

Our profit of 1927 has been exceeded in 1928 by a comfortable margin, a small reduction in trading profits being more than balanced by increased capital profits. Our gross profits amount to £249,445, made up as follows:—Net miscellaneous profits from mortality, &c., £26,280; interest earnings in excess of 3 per cent on mean fund, excluding carry-forward, £70,955; capital gains on securities sold or revalued, £117,555; interest earned on the surplus carried forward from the previous year, £34,655, making a total of £249,445.

The corresponding total was £226,481 in 1927 and £150,465 in 1926. After paying the same reversionary bonus as last year— namely, 45s. per cent compound on endowment assurance policies and 51s. per cent compound on whole-life policies—and allowing for sundry outgoings specified in the actuary's valuation report, we are adding £126,278 to our undistributed surplus carried forward, bringing this up to a total of £877,524, which is 20·7 per cent of our liabilities as compared with 17·8 per cent at the end of 1927. This valuation report has been signed for the first time by Mr G. H. Recknell, previously assistant actuary, whom the board have had the pleasure to promote to the position of actuary, Mr Geoffrey Marks retaining the position of general manager.

The abnormal volume of maturities of endowment assurance policies, as shown in the annual report, is due to £266,071 falling due in respect of special non-profit war bond policies issued ten years ago. This has had the effect of decreasing the increment of our total funds below its normal figure.

The year has not been an easy one for investment. Your board has pursued a somewhat hesitant policy, and has slightly reduced the Society's holding of ordinary shares, but in the result our capital gains have turned out the highest for several years past. Our total assets have yielded over the year, in interest and appreciation, approximately 7 per cent per annum free of income tax, which means that the yield on our stock exchange securities has been somewhat better than this. We have now earned annually a total return on our assets of not less than 7 per cent free of income tax on the average of the last eight years.

Comparison with previous quinquennium

The year 1928 completes a quinquennium of annual distributions since the declaration of the last of our quinquennial distributions—in respect of 1919–23. It is interesting, therefore, to compare the aggregated results of the five years, 1924–8, with those of the previous five years. Our efforts to diminish the cost of new business by increasing the average amount of our policies have been markedly successful, the average policy for the past five years being about £1,200, compared with £650 in the previous quinquennium, with the result that we have written 25 per cent fewer policies for an aggregate amount which is nearly 40 per cent higher. The other principal comparisons are as follows:—

	Five years ending	
	Dec. 31, 1923	Dec. 31, 1928
Amount of funds at the end of the period	£3,940,268	£5,231,907
Average net rate of interest earned	£4 8 6%	£4 13 0%
Expense ratio	17·0	13·7
Trading profit	£365,932	£611,174
Balance of profit on securities realised and revalued	£361,760	£384,983
Amount distributed in bonuses	£301,570	£498,248
Rate of bonus earned	101s. 6d.	91s. 6d.

The approaching centenary

It follows that over a period of no less than ten consecutive years we have earned an average annual bonus in excess of 95s. per cent, whereas the amount which we have actually distributed to with-profit policyholders has been about half this sum. Each year we have hesitated to regard our good success as other than abnormal, and, in particular, we have reserved the whole of our capital gains so that they should be available to meet a possible depreciation of our securities. It is obvious, however, that this piling up of reserves cannot go on indefinitely, and that it would be unfair to the existing generation of policyholders—and, indeed, contrary to the principles of mutual life assurance—not to divide the excess beyond the reserves—actuarial and otherwise—which are properly required to secure the Society's financial stability. I am, therefore, authorised by the board to make to you a preliminary announcement as to our intentions.

We are now entering our 100th year. At the conclusion of this year we propose to distribute a large special centennial bonus in addition to the ordinary bonus of the year. This bonus will not be at a uniform rate, but will be distributed with due regard to all the equities, and I hasten to add that new policies taken out in 1929 will not participate in the special bonus, unless it be in respect of profits earned during 1929. The details of this exceptional distribution have not yet been determined by the board, and will not be announced until the occasion of our centennial meeting next year.

Proposed new policies

We are also celebrating our entry into the 100th year of our activities by initiating a new series of policies—in addition to our existing series, which will be continued for the present unchanged —on lines which will, I think, be of high interest to intending policyholders, and to the life assurance world generally. We have not revised our rates of premium for with-profit whole-life policies for over 30 years, while the only changes in the rates for with-profit endowment assurance policies have been in an upward direction so as to bring them more into line with the whole-life terms. Yet the diminished rates of mortality, the better initial selection of lives as a result of the progress of medical science, and increased opportunities for employing advantageously the fund represented by the accumulated premiums, have combined to reduce materially the rates of premium which it is necessary to charge to secure a given initial sum assured.

The result is that we, in common with other life offices, have drifted into a situation in which too much of the benefit of a given rate of premium is given in the shape of bonuses which will accumulate only in the course of years and too little in the shape of the initial sum assured—too much and too little, that is to say, from the point of view of those whose primary object is protection against the risk of premature decease. In short, life offices have not revised their terms proportionately to the change of conditions, with the result that the margin between the amount of the policy which they contract at the outset to pay for a given premium, and the amount for which they could afford to contract, has become much greater than is required by considerations of caution. This does not matter in the end to the policyholder who lives a long time, for he gets the excessive margin back again in the form of reversionary bonuses. But it matters very much in the beginning to a policyholder—even though he does in fact live to a ripe old age—who wants security in the years immediately after he takes the policy out.

Professional man's needs

Take the case of a professional man not yet middle-aged who has a good earned income but not, as yet, much invested savings. What he wants, when he assures his life, is the certainty of leaving behind him in the event of his dying in early or middle life a sum sufficient to provide for his family. He is much more interested in this than he is in his heirs receiving a large sum in the event of his surviving to the age of 80, for if he lives to be 80, his family will not need so much provision, and what provision they do need will be more probably covered by his other savings.

The type of policy which we and most other offices have been issuing hitherto is, indeed, ideal for those who live to be 80. A policyholder who survives to old age may get more than twice the amount which the office contracted to pay him when he first assured. But it is very far from ideal for the man who wants to be assured against risks, who wants to be certain of leaving a proper provision behind him if he does not survive to old age. In fact, the object of providing against a married man's premature death, which ought to be one of the principal tasks of life assurance, has been falling a little into the background in favour of a kind of policy which provides plums for the heirs of octogenarians.

New with-profit policies

We propose, therefore, to institute a new series of with-profit policies, the rates of premium on which are calculated with reference to modern life assurance experience. Bonuses on this series will be paid over a period of years in accordance with what the series is able to earn, the rate of bonus for the first year being guaranteed at the rate of 15s. per cent compound. This enables us to offer a whole-life with-profit policy on which the initial sum assured for a given premium is from 30 per cent to 20 per cent greater than for a corresponding policy in the old series. In effect we are offering with-profit policies at rates of premium practically equal to those which were quoted until recently for non-profit policies. To give a single example, the annual premium in the old series for a man aged 30 next birthday to secure a with-profit whole-life insurance of £1,000 is £21 15s., after allowing for income tax rebate. The same premium will provide a similar assurance in the new series for £1,247. Such figures should, I think, impress the young married man with the solid advantages in the shape of security for his family which can be obtained in return for a very modest outlay.

'Cheaper life assurance'

Public opinion has shown of late some slight signs of restiveness about the reluctance of life offices to modify their terms in accordance with changed conditions. With these new policies the National Mutual will be doing something to meet the popular demand for 'cheaper life assurance'. But it must not be supposed that we do not at the same time adhere to views which I have previously expressed as to the great and growing part which life assurance should be able to play as a medium for the investment of savings as well as for protection against risk. The point is that different would-be assurers properly attach different degrees of importance to the element of investment and to the element of protection, in accordance with their different circumstances and needs, with the result that a single type of policy, even when it is differentiated into whole-life and endowment assurance, cannot provide every one with just what he wants. The trend in recent years has been towards offering investment facilities rather than protection. With the National Mutual new series of 'reinforced' or 'married men's' policies, offered concurrently with policies of the former type, we are able to meet both types of requirement.

General economic conditions

The business of life assurance is so sensitive to economic and industrial conditions that it will not be out of place for me to say a little, as in former years, about the general economic prospects. In 1923 I said: 'Those who are employed are probably producing on the average about 10 per cent less than formerly for approximately the same real wage. Without great improvements in the technique and intelligence of trade and industry, it looks doubtful whether, on these terms, we shall be able to employ the whole employable population except at the very top of the periodic booms.' In 1926 I pointed out that almost no progress at all had been made towards the adjustment of gold costs of production which the return to the gold standard had rendered necessary. The question of the relationship of wages to the efficiency of production still seems to me to lie at the heart of our problem.

Recent calculations by Professor Bowley have made possible some very interesting generalisations. Between 1914 and 1924 average real wages for the normal week (full employment) rose by more than 8 per cent. During the same period the weekly hours of work were reduced by more than 10 per cent. The result was that employers were set the task, if they were to maintain their pre-war position, of increasing efficiency by nearly 20 per cent. The Census of Production of 1924 indicates that the increase of efficiency up to that date was just about sufficient to balance the shortened hours, but was not able to make, in addition, any contribution towards meeting the increased weekly wage. Thus already in 1924 employers, in those industries in which the increase of efficiency had not been above the average, were making heavy weather. Between 1924 and 1928 money wages have remained practically unchanged, whilst the return to the gold standard at the pre-war parity has had the effect of increasing real wages by a further 8 per cent.

The employers' task

It follows that employers have been faced with the task of improving efficiency by 16 per cent, as compared with 1924, before they can recover their pre-war position. Now it is not over-optimistic, I think, to suppose that efficiency is, in fact, being increased at the rate of, say, 1½ per cent per annum over the average of the whole field of industry, which, if it is the case, is a considerable achievement. This means that today, in 1929, the deficiency has been reduced from 16 per cent to about 10 per cent. But the depressing feature of the situation is the fact that at this rate it may be another five or six years before we are quite straight. The change in the value of our money in 1924-5, coming on the backs of industrialists, already weakened by the course of events since 1914, has naturally contributed to prolonged unemployment in all those industries of which the strength is not above the average.

Since it is impracticable and unwise to reduce wages, the only solution is to be found in accelerating the increase of efficiency and in so conducting our international monetary diplomacy as to avoid a further fall in the level of world prices. But we might also mitigate unemployment if we were to endeavour—for a time—so to conduct our national investment policy as to direct our savings into those channels which are likely to provide immediate employment at home, rather than into those which are likely, in the first instance, to embarrass the reserve position of the Bank of England by the burden which they throw on the foreign exchange.

Speech to the Annual Meeting of the National Mutual, 29 January 1930

Gentlemen,

We are celebrating today the completion of the 100th year of the business life of our society. I will therefore deal somewhat briefly with the figures of last year, so as to leave myself time for some more general remarks.

Our net new business for the year has fallen a little short of last year's record figures, though it exceeds all years previous to that. The small decline is due, however, only to our having given out during the year more reassurance than we have received back. The new insurance business obtained direct by this office is, in fact, the largest in our history. The new with-profit policies which I described to you last year have made an important contribution to these record figures. I have no doubt that, as time goes on, and as their advantages to certain classes of policyholders become fully appreciated, they will represent a steadily increasing proportion of our total business.

Our expense ratio as shown in our annual report differs very little from last year's. The corrected figure, adjusted so as to exclude the effect of single premiums, is slightly reduced. Our total trading profits for the year, exclusive of appreciation or depreciation on investments, have amounted to £149,403, as compared with £131,890 last year, made up as follows:—

Net miscellaneous profits from mortality, etc.	£33,850
Interest earnings in excess of 3 per cent on mean fund, excluding carry-forward	£73,317
Interest earned on the surplus carried forward from the previous year	£42,236
	£149,403

Larger interest earned

This improvement has been partly due to the fact that the average gross rate of interest earned on our funds, excluding reversions, is no less than 5s. per cent higher than last year and has reached the high figure of $5\frac{3}{4}$ per cent. The increase as compared with previous years results in part from our having carried out the policy, which I have announced at previous annual meetings, of a substantial changeover of investments in British

Government securities to other investments, mainly higher yielding fixed-interest securities. But it is also in large degree attributable to the depreciation in the capital value of our securities which we have suffered during the past year in common with all other investment bodies. To this I shall return in detail in a moment. The full effect of this depreciation on the rate of interest has been only partly felt in the year 1929, and it is possible, therefore, that there may be a further increase in the rate to report next year.

On the other hand, any future capital gains which we may obtain as the result of the appreciation of our investments will, of course, operate to reduce the rate of interest. Nor is it wise, in my judgement, to be too much influenced in pursuing an investment policy by the desire to obtain as high a current yield as possible, since those investments which are most satisfactory in the long run are often those which yield a comparatively low running income at the moment. It must not, therefore, be considered necessarily a sign of retrogression if the rise in the rate of interest earned, which I have now reported to you for a number of years in succession, is ultimately reversed. It should also be borne in mind, when our results are being compared with those of other offices which do not write the value of their investments up and down in accordance with their market value, that the fluctuations in interest earnings will appear in our results more obviously than in theirs, though the underlying facts may be the same.

Fall in investment values

The most important event of the year, however, on the investment side has, of course, been the serious fall in the general level of investment values—the most important movement, indeed, which has taken place since 1921. For a considerable number of years we have shown an unbroken series of gains through the appreciation in the capital value of our stock exchange securities. I have repeatedly stated in my annual speeches that this source of profit could not be regarded as a reliable one year by year, and I have warned you that the time was sure to come when a general movement of investment values in a downward direction would wipe out some part of our previous gains. For this reason we have hitherto distributed to our members no part whatever of our profits from capital appreciation, holding the view that any distributions made out of this source of profit should be carefully averaged over a period of time. We have in fact now decided to make a special distribution to with-profit policyholders in respect of our profits through capital appreciation over the last decade, partly because we think that the time has come for such a distribution, and partly as a suitable celebration of our centenary year.

It is, I think, in some respects fortunate that the setback in the investment market which was bound to come some day should have materialised before we had actually made our distribution of capital profits, for it enables us to do so while taking into account one bad year along with many good ones, and so to obtain an average which is more likely to be typical of what can be achieved in the long run than a distribution would have been which was based on an unbroken succession of upward movements.

'Every reason for moderate satisfaction'

Turning to the actual amount of the depreciation we have suffered, I think that we have, on the whole, every reason for moderate satisfaction that our losses are not much larger. The capital value of our fund has depreciated by a sum of £317,420, or approximately 6 per cent of its mean value during the year. Taken by itself this is a substantial loss, but viewed in relation to our previous capital gains it leaves us in a position of immense financial strength; for after writing down our securities to their value on December 31 last we are still strong enough to divide out of the remaining balance of capital appreciation the large centennial bonus to which I shall come in a moment, and to carry forward against future contingencies the sum of £386,000. But the main test in judging the success or otherwise of our investment policy during the past year must be made on the basis of a comparison with the decline of investment values generally.

The indexes compiled by the financial press and other authorities indicate that practically every class of investment securities has suffered a severe setback during 1929. For example, if the whole of our funds had been invested in long-dated British Government securities, we should have suffered a depreciation of 5 to 6 per cent, as compared with an actual figure of 6 per cent on our funds as a whole and 8 per cent on our stock exchange securities. I should estimate that non-gilt-edged fixed-interest securities must have fallen on the average by something like 10 per cent, while investments in industrial ordinary shares have fallen from 20 to 30 per cent in value according to the particular selection made by different authorities.

Holdings of ordinary shares

In spite, therefore, of our well-known policy of investing in ordinary shares to a greater extent than the majority of insurance offices, we have, in a year in which ordinary shares have suffered a quite exceptional depreciation, managed to get through with a percentage of loss which is not only far below the fall in ordinary shares generally, but is much less than the amount of depreciation of non-gilt-edged fixed-interest securities, and is only a little greater than has been suffered by long-dated British Government securities. I am not sure that, rightly viewed, this does not represent a greater measure of success for the long-run prospects of our general policy than the results of some former years which have looked much better. I may add that we have actually increased our holding of ordinary shares during the year 1929 from £729,792 to £1,090,959. We stand, therefore, in a strong position to obtain important advantages as soon as the tide turns. In fact, the date at which our valuation was taken—

namely, December 31 last—came almost at the bottom of the decline, and in the brief period that has since elapsed we have already recovered an important proportion of last year's depreciation.

The moral is that no body which is responsible for the investment of large sums of money can hope to be immune from the major movements of the market as a whole, whether upwards or downwards, and we shall be very content if in the long run we can earn more appreciation than the average on the up-swings and lose less on the down-swings—which we have undoubtedly succeeded in doing in the past year. After writing off the whole of last year's depreciation we have earned annually a total return on our assets—from interest and capital appreciation—of nearly $6\frac{1}{2}$ per cent, free of income tax, on the average of the past nine years.

Profit-sharing scheme

Among other occurrences of the past year which deserve some remark is the institution of a profit-sharing scheme for the management and staff of the Society. I believe that we are the first among mutual offices to introduce such a scheme. We had some little difficulty in arriving at an appropriate formula applicable to the profits of a mutual life office. It may be, therefore, of some general interest for me to say that the profit-sharing system is based on a percentage of the total salaries of the staff in proportion to the excess of the trading profits above what is necessary to provide a standard rate of compound reversionary bonus, together with a further small percentage similarly calculated in respect of the capital profits in excess of a datum line. Apart from this, we have thought it appropriate to mark our centennial year by an additional distribution to members of the staff, in the division of which we are paying much regard to length of service as well as to the level of salary.

The new Companies Act has involved very few changes in our established form of accounts, the only material additions being the mention of the amount of the directors' fees and of the basis of valuation of the assets other than stock exchange securities.

For the past year we are repeating, as you have already been informed, the same rate of bonus as in the two previous years for the Old Series of policies, and giving a bonus of 15*s*. per cent compound to the New Series. The trading profits of the year are £21,512 in excess of the cost of this bonus. There are, however, certain other provisions which we have made, partly out of the surplus of the year's trading profits and partly out of our general carry-forward. These are shown in detail in the actuary's report, which has been circulated, the most important being the sums required to meet the staff profit-sharing scheme for 1928 and 1929, the special centenary bonus to the staff which I have already mentioned, and a contribution of £18,417 to the staff pension fund.

The centenary bonus

I now turn to our special centenary bonus, of which the details have already been communicated to you in the actuary's report. We are proposing to take this opportunity of distributing to with-profit policyholders an important portion of that part of the accumulated profits from the appreciation of our investments which have arisen during the past decade and have not been distributed in the annual bonuses declared during this period. It is obviously right that these profits should not be permanently retained by the Society in excess of the sum which it is prudent to reserve in our carry-forward against contingencies. On the other hand, it is undesirable that an irregular and uncertain source of income should be looked on as a normal source of annual bonus, or should be dealt with except over a sufficiently long period to allow of the averaging of results.

For this reason a special occasion like the present one offers an appropriate opportunity for dealing with that part of our accumulated surplus which we can prudently spare, without creating a precedent which might be dangerous, or arousing expectations which it might not be possible to fulfil in future. Our idea is, however, that if circumstances warrant it the general policy of a special distribution should be considered from time to time in future, and in the future we shall review the state of our aggregate surplus from this point of view at intervals of not less than five years.

Benefits for older members

The actual details of the bonus which we are declaring show that we have employed a method which has been specially devised to protect the interests of the older members. We have felt that it was essential to do this inasmuch as the accumulated profits which we are now distributing, while earned entirely in the post-war period, accrued to quite an important extent a few years ago, so that it is those members, the reserves against whose policies have stood at a relatively high figure in proportion to the sum assured over the last 10 years, who are primarily entitled to what we are distributing. In accordance with my declaration last year, members who have entered the Society since 1928 are excluded from participation, and other members are to share on a sliding scale according to the date at which they took out their policies. For example, policies taken out in 1920 will receive a special reversionary bonus at the rate of 70s. per £100 sum assured, policies taken out in 1910 will receive a bonus of 145s. per cent, and policies dating from 1900 or previously will receive the handsome addition of 200s. per £100 sum assured.

The total cost of this special bonus will be £162,421, and it will leave us with an undivided surplus of more than double this sum, namely, £386,019, to be carried forward. The ordinary annual bonus notices will be sent out forthwith, but there will be a little delay, owing to the time occupied in their preparation, before members will receive their individual bonus notices relating to this special distribution.

History of 100 years

We have prepared an exceedingly interesting history of the course of our affairs during the past hundred years, of which copies have been already sent to the large policyholders. We shall be happy to send a copy to any other policyholder who would be interested to have one and will send a post card to the secretary. It is wonderful how vast a fund can be accumulated over a period of years from small beginnings. In the light of the principles and practices of caution which we can afford today, the risks taken by our predecessors, particularly in their inadequate basis for reliable averaging, seem rather terrifying. Yet it was by them, largely in the period 1820–50, that the foundations of British mutual life assurance as it exists today were well and truly laid. I attribute the success with which they surmounted their early difficulties mainly to the absolute honesty of the promoters and to the public spirit which prompted them to give thought and trouble without a prospect of any appreciable financial profit to themselves.

Tribute to the Society's founders

Two personal references are suggested by a review of the long years behind us. The old 'Mutual' largely depended for 50 years on the staunchness of James and William Burchell, founders of the Society, whose portraits hang on these walls and whose grandson and great-nephew is our deputy chairman today. Mr Geoffrey Marks, our present chief officer, has been in the service of our society for 45 years out of the century of its existence and has been our chief officer for 37 years of that period. Mr Marks entered our service one year after the death of James Burchell and three years before that of William Burchell, so that he and they between them span the whole period of the old 'Mutual', which is four years less than that of the old 'National', from the amalgamation of which by Mr Marks the present office springs. It is fair to say that the National Mutual, as it exists today, is mainly the creation of James and William Burchell and of Geoffrey Marks.

The future

It has been my custom at these annual meetings to cast an inquiring eye on the future, but today there has been so much to say about the past that I must be brief. I pointed out last year that the disparity of movement between prices and wages since 1924 had faced employers with the task of increasing efficiency by 16 per cent if they were to hold their own. I ventured to guess that efficiency was perhaps increasing at the rate of $1\frac{1}{2}$ per cent per annum, with the result that they might have reduced their relative disadvantage from 16 per cent to 10 per cent in the four years ended in 1928. Unfortunately the course of events during 1929 has further aggravated their problem instead of mitigating it; for prices have fallen by a further 4 to 5 per cent, while wages are unchanged.

Moreover, while the difficulties in which the return to gold involved our own industries in the period after 1924 were mainly local to this country, the fall in the wholesale prices of raw materials has now taken on the character of a world wide disaster. The storm centres are to be found today, in my judgement, neither in Great Britain nor in the United States, but in the great producers of raw materials overseas. For significant signs of recovery or of further deterioration it may not be so important today to consider London or New York as to watch Australia, South America, and Asia, and also Central Europe, for these areas are being reduced to very grievous distress by the combined circumstances of the fall in the prices of their chief products and the difficulty of obtaining funds on the international loan market.

Consequences of fall in wholesale prices

Between 1921 and 1924 the reaction from the great post-war inflation was practically completed, but since 1924 our wholesale index number has fallen by a further 20 per cent. This rate of fall, lasting over a period of four or five years, otherwise than as a reaction from an immediately preceding inflation, is, I believe, unparalleled in modern economic history. The consequences have already reached the dimensions of a first-class disaster. Nor is it by any means certain that a further movement in the same direction is going to be avoided.

I believe that these events, so inimical to the wealth and happiness of the whole world, are avoidable and remediable. But they are to be attributed to the want of collective wisdom on the part of the central banking authorities of the world taken together, and are not now wholly remediable by the isolated action of any single country. The internecine struggle for gold stocks must cease and the market rates for money in the leading financial centres of the world must be reduced to a really low figure— which presents no difficulties if they all move together—in the neighbourhood of, say, 3 per cent, and must remain there for some time, before it is reasonable to expect a recovery of enterprise and confidence throughout the world and the general enjoyment of that measure of prosperity which the ever-increasing achievements of scientific and business technique would make possible, if only the government, or want of government, in international monetary affairs would at last permit.

Speech to the Annual Meeting of the National Mutual, 28 January 1931

Gentlemen,

Before proceeding to our ordinary business I have to record with the deepest personal sorrow the death during the year of our youngest director, Mr Sidney Russell Cooke. Mr Russell Cooke was fast making for himself a position of great esteem in the City. The premature loss of his brilliant and engaging personality will be a source of lasting regret to those who knew him well.

The year's business

The new life assurance business which we obtained in 1930 was the greatest in the history of the society, and the number of new policies written was substantially greater than last year. But as the result of our having reassured a little more than before, in pursuance of our policy of carefully limiting our risk on any one life, the net business shows a slight reduction. Our expenses remained at almost exactly the same figure as in each of the previous two years, though their proportion to premium income was somewhat increased by the decrease of single premium business (from £63,000 to £18,000) as a result of the new legislation—business, however, which we have never welcomed and which has never played an important part in our activities. Our rates of bonus on the various classes of policies have been maintained at the same high level as in the previous year.

Our total trading profits for the year, exclusive of appreciation or depreciation on investments, have amounted to £141,487, made up as follows:—

Net miscellaneous profits from mortality, etc.	£39,323
Interest earnings in excess of 3 per cent on mean fund, excluding carry-forward	83,577
Interest earned on the surplus carried forward from the previous year	18,587
	£141,487

The first two items in the above statement are larger than last year, and the reduction in the last item is partly due to the effect of the centenary bonus on the carry-forward.

Gross rate of interest

The gross rate of interest earned has—as I forecast in my speech of last year—again increased substantially—from £5 15s. 11d. per cent to £5 19s. 10d. per cent—and is now no less than 10s.

179

per cent higher than it was three years ago. The gain on the year has, however, been required to offset the increase in the rate of income tax. There may be yet a further increase in the gross rate of interest during the current year, partly as a result of our having written down our securities to a lower figure. But looking further ahead I should be disposed to predict, with great confidence, the beginning of a substantial downward movement, which may, in course of time, exert a considerable influence on the policy of life offices and set them a new problem of a kind which events have enabled them to forget for some years past.

One of the main preoccupations of the past year has naturally been the question of investment policy. We have suffered a depreciation on the year in respect of securities realised or revalued of £179,733, which represents about 3½ per cent on our mean fund. Having regard to the fact that we have been passing through one of the greatest slumps in economic history, I think that even the critics of our well-known investment policy will agree that we have no occasion for serious disappointment. The indexes of the prices of securities, now currently compiled by various authorities, including the Institute of Actuaries, show conclusively that we have been a great deal more successful than we should have been with an average sample of the leading securities similarly distributed between the different categories. Nor has anything occurred, even in the present exceptional circumstances, to upset the principles of our policy over the period during which it has been operating. For, after writing off the whole of the depreciation of 1929 and 1930, we have earned over the last 10 years an average annual return on our assets— from interest and capital appreciation together—of nearly 6 per cent, free of income tax.

Holdings of securities

It will be seen on reference to our balance-sheet that our holdings of ordinary shares stand at £254,000 less than a year ago, and there has been a further reduction since the close of the year;

while at the same time our holdings of British Government securities have increased by £220,000. This movement reflects an opinion on the part of your board that it would not be safe to assume that the end of the slump is yet in sight—a matter to which I will refer in a few minutes. Our view is that we are still in the phase of the investment cycle at which it is prudent to exercise extreme caution, and we have repeatedly overhauled our list of securities from this point of view, retaining only those where we feel the price fully discounts the prospects. We have taken particular precautions to avoid risk on foreign government securities.

It may be interesting to mention that we have now reduced our holding of European government securities to very small dimensions, and that for many years past we have held no securities of the Australian Government or States. It is a striking testimony to the Society's strength that, in spite of a period of two years of unprecedented difficulties, we start the year 1931 with a carry-forward of over £200,000, after writing off all our depreciation, and declaring not only the usual high rate of annual bonus, but also the special centenary bonus of £162,000. In addition, although the Society's basis of valuation is that which is conventionally known as the 'O^m 3 per cent net premium valuation', in reality the reserves include in a number of ways a considerable sum in excess of what is strictly required to satisfy the conditions of that basis, which is in itself extremely strong.

New business developments

Before proceeding to other matters I would like to refer briefly to certain developments in relation to our new business which have taken place during the year. The Society is now prepared, within certain limits, to issue policies without the usual medical examination. This has been done for some years by many of the life offices, and we thought the time had come when your society should offer this facility to those who are eligible. We have also during the year brought out a new form of policy—the reinforced income policy—an extension of the new series of low-premium policies which I referred to in my speech in 1929.

From our short experience of this new scheme I can say that it appears to supply a want. Most people can make provision for their dependents in the event of untimely death only by means of life assurance, but viewed in the light of the income produced by the capital sum assured the provision is generally quite inadequate. This inadequacy could hardly be avoided under an ordinary policy, as the cost of providing a sufficient capital sum was in many cases prohibitive. This difficulty has now been overcome. Under the reinforced income policy a substantial income on death is provided at a low cost, during the years when it will be most needed. For in addition to the payment of the capital sum assured with bonuses immediately on death, there is also payable an income of 12 per cent of the sum assured until the expiry of a period of 20 years from the date of the policy. For example, assuming that the capital sum is invested at 5 per cent, a man of 25 for an annual premium of £21 3s. 4d. can, in the event of his premature death, secure for his dependents an annual income of £170 for the period stated, whilst they will still retain the capital sum of £1,000 at the end of that period. This new policy, therefore, carries us a considerable step forward in fulfilling the main function of life assurance—the adequate financial protection of dependents in the event of the premature death of the breadwinner.

With regard to our new business it may interest you to know that quite a substantial proportion of it is derived from introductions by our policyholders, and I take this opportunity of thanking them for the practical interest they thus show in the Society's welfare. We have always been particularly fortunate in our policyholders. They appear to realise that they are members of a mutual society, conducted solely in their interests, and to appreciate that the word mutual connotes reciprocity. They, on their part, carry out their mutual obligations not only by effecting any further assurances on their own lives with the Society, but also by introducing their relatives and friends. This is a great help to the management, and I hope that the new policyholders will maintain this good tradition.

International trade and finance

Turning from our own affairs to those of the world at large, I am sorry that my gloomy prognostications of a year ago have been more than fulfilled. I then forecast that the storm centres would be found, not in Great Britain or in the United States, but in the great producers of raw materials oversea, and that we had to watch with anxiety Australia, South America, Asia, and Central Europe. I added that the fall of wholesale prices had 'already reached the dimensions of a first-class disaster', and that 'it was not by any means certain that a further movement in the same direction was going to be avoided'. These warnings, which were widely commented on at the time, have proved to be a serious understatement. Nor do I see much reason for being cheerful about the immediate future. In particular, I would emphasise that the mere lapse of a few more months of time will not by itself bring about a lasting recovery. For one thing, on the basis of our experience of past disturbances relatively little time has yet passed by. But, apart from this, the recovery will only come, in my opinion, after the emergence of some definite new factor.

The worst of it is, moreover, that, while we can still do something to help ourselves out of the slough of inactivity and negative-mindedness into which we have fallen—I made, a week or two ago, some rash confidences about this to the ether,[2] which staggered, I am told, under the impact—the main root of the problem is international in character. If I were asked to sum up briefly the essence of the present position, I should say that it is to be found in the behaviour of the creditor countries in pursuing a course of action which is calculated to bankrupt the debtor countries.

[2] See *JMK*, vol. IX, pp. 135–41.

Credit of debtor countries

We have always known that the whole course of international trade and finance depends on a steady flow of lending, equal to the amount of their surplus resources, from the creditor countries as a whole to the debtor countries as a whole. If this flow is interrupted, we know that there is no means whatever by which the whole body of debtor countries, unable either to sell their goods or to borrow, can possibly pay in gold the amount of their annual indebtedness. The contraction of credit and purchasing power attendant on their efforts to do so, in combination with the tremendous falling off in the production of capital goods in the United States and a consequent reduction in their demand for goods from the rest of the world, was bound to produce the catastrophic fall of prices which has actually occurred. Besides, a vicious circle is set up. For the fall of prices destroys the credit of the debtor countries and it becomes increasingly unsafe, from the point of view of the individual investor, to lend to them.

I told you a few minutes ago about the ultra-cautious attitude of your own board towards foreign bonds, and from our own individual standpoint it is a wise and necessary precaution. Yet, from another point of view, it is absolutely the opposite of what is needed to put things right. For *someone* must lend to these countries if a catastrophe is to be avoided. Nevertheless, our own policy coincides, I think, with the interests of this country. For it is not any holding back on our part which has caused the trouble. Indeed, quite the contrary. London's difficulties have been due to her efforts—experienced and considerate creditor that she is—to save the position by carrying more of the responsibilities of the creditor countries as a whole than properly belongs to her. Now we, too, are feeling that we must sit back until someone else takes up the running. In spite of present appearances to the contrary, it is not very unlikely, I think, that, as a result of London also becoming a reluctant lender, the Bank of England may find herself with more gold at the end of 1931 than at the beginning.

Need for joint action

It is, therefore, becoming increasingly important that some sort of joint action should be taken to prevent the further deterioration of the credit of the debtor countries. Or, alternatively, the creditor countries must find an outlet in home investment— which, failing an early revival in general confidence, might require a very great fall in the current rate of interest—for the savings which they are no longer lending to debtor countries; for this, also, would bring considerable relief to the debtor countries by increasing the demand for their products at an improved price.

Speech to the Annual Meeting of the National Mutual, 2 March 1932

The new assurance business which we obtained in 1931, following upon a record year, showed a modest falling off at £705,979 net. Our expense ratio at 13·7 per cent, compared with 14·7 per cent in the previous year, showed a very satisfactory reduction, though this was caused to some extent by the smaller amount of new business transacted. The gross rate of interest earned was £5 11s. 1d. per cent, a rate satisfactory in itself but not quite so good as in the previous year, owing partly to a transfer of resources from ordinary shares to gilt-edged securities. As a consequence of our unusually small holdings of foreign bonds the loss of interest due to defaults was negligible, amounting to about 1 per cent of our total interest receipts.

The investments—increased government holdings

Owing to our decision not to make an actuarial valuation on this occasion, a matter to which I will return in a few minutes, the usual valuation of our stock exchange securities at their market values on December 31, 1931, does not appear in the report which you have received. But the decision to postpone the actuarial valuation is no reason for altering our practice, long established in our case, though there are many offices which do not follow it, of stating annually the market valuation of our assets. During the year 1931 our depreciation and realised loss combined were equal to 15·8 per cent of the mean fund invested in stock exchange securities or 11·8 per cent of the mean total assets. These figures leave out of account both the carry-forward at the end of 1930 and the trading profit of 1931. The principal changes in the distribution of our securities between different classes of investments have been a reduction of our ordinary shares from 16·2 per cent to 14·3 per cent of the total assets, and an increase of British Government securities from 15·8 per cent to 18·8 per cent. Our holdings of foreign government and municipal securities are, as I have said, very small at 4·3 per cent. Our investments in the United States have never been large, and were 5·1 per cent at the beginning of the year and 5·3 per cent at the end of it.

The past year has been, of course, one of extraordinary anxiety for all those concerned with the safe investment of large funds. The actual degree of depreciation suffered by every class of security has been unprecedented. Moreover, our difficulties have been considerably increased by the 'badness' of markets, in the sense that it has often proved impracticable to carry out desired changes of investments, whether by buying or selling, at the ostensible market price or sometimes even at any reasonable figure. It has been, in particular, a testing time for a society such as ours, which has been a pioneer of methods of investment approaching more closely to those of an investment trust than is the case with most life offices; which holds an unusually large proportion of its funds in market securities subject to a fluctuating valuation, as compared with mortgages, for example, the book value of which is kept unchanged irrespective of market conditions; which has always taken pride in stating the exact market value of its investments, and which, therefore, has had no concealed investment reserve behind which the board could take refuge in bad times.

Investment and market values

How have we emerged from this test? In comparison with leading investment trusts we have certainly done extremely well, with a much lower percentage of depreciation than the typical trust company. A comparison with the average of the life offices can, unfortunately, never be made, since too few of them state exact figures of the market value of their investments at the end of each year. But I should suppose that we have done slightly worse than the average, since one would expect the market valuation of investments distributed as ours are to be somewhat lower, at the bottom—or at what one hopes may be near the bottom—of the greatest industrial slump in history, than that of a holding in which ordinary shares are a much smaller proportion and mortgages and properties a much larger proportion of the whole. Nor need this disturb us. For if the slump continues no kind of asset, however insensitive its nominal valuation may be over a short period, will escape calamity in the end; while if recovery comes, the former relative valuations will be restored. Even today one would wonder what the consequences would be if all properties and mortgages had to be valued on the basis of an actual 'bid' price on the analogy of stock exchange securities. Moreover, it may be considered a point in favour of our policy under existing conditions that we should be holding a fair proportion of ordinary shares which represent 'real' values, reduced though it is from the figure of two years ago.

At the moment of extreme deflation, such as the present, when commodity prices are at so low a level that a substantial recovery in them, sooner or later, is the only alternative to a widespread default of obligations expressed in terms of money, our holding of ordinary shares represents, for the policyholder who has committed his savings to our care, a stake in the future recovery of things—failing which all investments alike will lose their basis of security—which should prove valuable when the recovery comes. Meanwhile it is remarkable how comparatively little our holding of ordinary shares has affected the final results even in present conditions. Our aggregate depreciation on stock exchange securities amounted, as I have said, to 15·8 per cent, whilst the depreciation on our fixed interest securities amounted to 13·5 per cent, so that, if we had held no ordinary shares at all, the amount of our depreciation would have been less by little more than 2 per cent.

An interesting comparison

As a more absolute test it is interesting to compare the results with those shown by the leading index numbers of security prices. Taking the Actuaries' Index as the most comprehensive and modern index available, we may make the following comparison:—

	Actuaries' Index per cent	National Mutual per cent
Fixed interest securities	12	13·5
Ordinary shares	23·3	24·9

This comparison, however, does less than justice to our position, since the Actuaries' price indexes do not purport to cover the whole field of investments in which the funds of typical British institutions have been placed. In particular they include no foreign bonds, the losses on which last year were particularly severe; so that we get no credit for our small holdings of these bonds and our avoidance of loss in respect of them. Nor in regard to ordinary shares is the comparison adequate, since the Actuaries' Index, being limited to concerns operating at least partially in this country, takes no account of the much heavier depreciation suffered by shares of an international character. Lastly, they include no American securities, and therefore fail to reflect the catastrophic fall in their values.

Looking back on the year's operations, we could, of course, have saved depreciation by a wholesale disposal of our ordinary shares and long-dated fixed-interest securities, reinvesting the proceeds in short-dated securities such as Treasury bills. But even apart from the fact that such a course would have resulted in a certain loss in interest yield of at least 2 per cent per annum, it would have remained a gamble whether we could have got back again into permanent investments at just the right moment. Indeed, I am sure that this is not a course which an institution ought to pursue which depends on earning a satisfactory rate of interest over a long period of years. My own candid opinion, for what it is worth, may be summed up by saying that we might, with a little better luck or a little better management, have suffered 2 per cent less in depreciation, but that, in view of the universal character of the collapse in values, we could not, by any reasonably practicable selection of securities compatible with general long-term policy and the maintenance of our interest income, have done much better than that.

Postponement of the actuarial valuation

I now turn to the actuarial side. As regards the postponement of our actuarial valuation I need not add much to what I said at the special general meeting, at which this course was approved by the members. The prudence of not making final decisions as to distribution based on the momentary conditions of December 31 last has been confirmed by subsequent developments, which have, of course, increased the quotations of our stock exchange securities by a very considerable sum. Meanwhile, members may be glad to have the information that after allowing for the appreciation experienced this year up to date, our carry-forward and trading profits virtually suffice to cover the whole of the remaining depreciation without any change in our basis of valuation as published heretofore.

As regards our departure, at least for the time being, from annual valuations, which we and two others amongst life offices not transacting industrial business have been alone in making in recent years, old-fashioned people can legitimately point to the change as being a return to the wisdom of our ancestors. But the root of the matter, as I see it, is one of great importance to all life offices and deserving of even fuller discussion than it has already had. The difficulty lies in combining on the one side conventional and rigid methods of valuation and distribution, which take little or no account of changing circumstances, and on the other, highly sensitive methods of valuation, easily affected by the circumstances of the moment.

Actuarial methods

As time has gone by, the bases of actuarial valuation have remained largely conventional. An actuary does not base his expectations of mortality on the rate which he and his fellows are actually experiencing. His provision for expenses is not the rate which he is actually incurring. Above all—and of particular importance for my present argument—a rate of interest is assumed which is not only widely different from the rate of interest which the office is actually earning, but, since it never changes, is not only different from the facts but bears no steady relation to them. Over and above these main items, individual actuaries introduce various minor excess provisions into their calculations, and, provided the errors are all on the right side, i.e., on the side of over-statement of liabilities in relation to assets, as, of course, they always are, valuations become a sort of competition in unveracity, the most praiseworthy being those which are based on assumptions the most remote from the facts and which are the most rigidly maintained irrespective of changes in the facts. On the top of this, rates of bonus have also a tendency (which is, however, weakening) to become stereotyped and to respond most reluctantly either up or down to changing circumstances.

Now it is evident that for institutions whose contracts extend over a period as long as human life and for which absolute security is not only a matter of pride but a necessity if they are to perform the functions for which they exist, some (though not, I think, all) of the above customs and practices have great virtue, in so far as they promote caution and the understatement of favourable results, when these results have not yet stood the test of time. But in practice they do not effect these objects in a steady and regular way if they are combined with a totally different method of valuation on the asset side of the balance-sheet. A conventional valuation of liabilities on one side and an actual valuation of assets on the other may lead to highly misleading results. I am not sure that an awareness of this has not sometimes given actuaries a bias in favour of assets which lend themselves to a conventional valuation, because, as there is no published market price for such assets, no obligation is felt to change their book value at every breath of wind that blows upon the stock exchange. Mortgages are, of course, a leading example of this type of investment, which also includes, however, most investments other than stock exchange securities. But, looked at with an unprejudiced eye, it ought not to be regarded as an outstanding merit in an investment that it has no market price.

The illogical consequences of the prevalent methods are best illustrated by what happens when there is a change in the rate of interest, assuming that capital changes are shown in the revenue account. A fall in the rate of interest actually earned narrows the margin between the actual rate and the assumed conventional rate, i.e., it weakens the basis of valuation. But as in normal circumstances it is accompanied by an appreciation in the market value of fixed-interest securities, it increases the carry-forward and thus increases the ostensible strength. On the other hand, a rise in the rate of interest has the opposite effect. It strengthens the valuation, but diminishes the ostensible strength by lessening the carry-forward. I have no solution to offer for this dilemma, but I commend it to the continued attention of the insurance world.

'The most prosperous country in the world'

I have sometimes ventured at these meetings on some general remarks on the economic situation. This year I find myself moving uneasily between a cautious optimism when I consider the position of this country and a very helpless pessimism when I look abroad. Great Britain today is decidedly the most prosperous country in the world, and here the trend seems to me to be slightly in the right direction. But this is not saying much. It is a relief to see the United States at last taking measures to quieten their financial panic. But it is a long step from that to industrial prosperity. As I have said elsewhere, the outstanding difference between the problem of today and the problem of a year ago arises out of a financial crisis having been superimposed meanwhile upon the industrial crisis.

The financial crisis

Today it is, of course, an indispensable preliminary that we should relieve the financial crisis. Unless the really desperate situation in Central Europe upsets things, it is legitimate to hope that the first steps in this direction have now been taken. But to me it is unthinkable that we can step straight from the relief of the financial crisis to the relief of the industrial crisis without a cheap money phase intervening. As soon as we have found our feet again and feel ourselves masters of our own position and with our power of international initiative regained, I hope that we shall move with courage to the relief of international credit, lending boldly and ourselves expanding boldly. For that will be by far the safest course and will offer the best chance of salving the immense sums which we have embarked in foreign investment in former years. The pre-war gold standard worked because it was in truth a sterling standard. When gold went off sterling last September it doomed itself as a currency, at least for the time being. We have been forced, it is true, to step down for the moment from the position of international leadership in finance. But our place has not been taken by anyone else, and I feel confident that, unless we lack the pluck, we shall soon be strong enough to resume our old position with the heightened prestige of holding it in virtue of having surmounted present difficulties and not merely as an inheritance of past accomplishment.

Speech to the Annual Meeting of the National Mutual, 1 March 1933

Gentlemen,

It now falls to me to move the adoption of the report and accounts. The new business which we obtained in 1932 shows an appreciable falling off, compared with recent years, at £536,806. Our new business organisation has not had an easy task during the past year, as, apart from the abnormal conditions which have prevailed, there is no doubt that the postponement a year ago of our valuation and bonus distribution has affected our new business. I am hopeful, however, that these special difficulties may now be at an end, since my statement of our position to-day is, I think, one of the most satisfactory which it has fallen to me to make since I have been Chairman.

In connection with our new business, I would draw your attention to several new schemes of assurance introduced during the past year and described in the annual report. In particular we have introduced, in conjunction with an old-established building society, a scheme for granting mortages on house property, which combines the benefits and protection of life assurance with the facilities provided by a building society.

Improved position

It will be within your memory that in my speech last year I stated that we had suffered during 1931 a depreciation and realised loss on our investments equal to 15·8 per cent of our stock exchange securities and 11·8 per cent of our total assets. I expressed the belief, however, that this might be the reflection of purely temporary conditions and that it would be wise to postpone our valuation until the real position was clearer. I am glad to report that the advisability of postponement has been borne out by the subsequent course of events.

During the past year we have not only recovered the whole of the depreciation and realised loss incurred in 1931, but have also secured a useful balance of profit, amounting to £33,527 over the two years taken together. Indeed, the appreciation and realised profit on our investments which we have secured during 1932 amounts to no less than £642,541, being 18·3 per cent of the mean fund employed in stock exchange securities and 14·1 per cent of our total mean assets. It may be interesting to mention that the appreciation has been fairly evenly spread over our fixed-interest securites and our ordinary shares, having been 17·6 per cent in the case of the former and 22·8 per cent in the case of the latter.

Comparison between the assets in the balance sheets of 1931 and 1932 is affected by the fact that the 1931 figures are based on the market prices of December 31, 1930. On this basis, the principal changes have been an increase in British Government securities from £985,000 to £1,329,000, a further reduction in foreign government securities from £219,000 to the very small figure of £45,000, and a decrease in our ordinary shares from £747,000 to £679,000, which is about 12 per cent of our assets. Our investment in British Government securities is considerably greater than we should consider advisable in normal times, and we propose to reduce it as favourable opportunities offer.

I have been accustomed in past years to state our average earnings over the post-war period from interest and capital profits combined after writing off the whole of any realised losses and depreciation. Over the past 12 years this figure works out at 5·65 per cent, free of income tax, and the interest included in this figure is the main source out of which our substantial bonuses have been paid.

Rate of interest earned

Turning to the items which make up our trading profit during the past year, the net rate of interest earned has declined from £4 9s. 11d. per cent in 1931 to £4 5s. 8d. per cent. Since our funds at the beginning of the year were taken for the purpose of calculating the amount of the mean fund at the prices of December 31, 1930, the 1932 interest yield approximately reflects the present level of fixed-interest securities, though any further fall in the general level of interest would naturally affect our interest yield in 1933. On the other hand, our unusually large holding of British Government securities represents a potential source of increased income in the future as and when we are able to reinvest in higher yielding securities.

I may add that our long-established practice of showing our stock exchange securities at market prices has the effect of throwing up a rate of interest return which, by fully reflecting current conditions, may tend, in times of rising prices, to compare somewhat unfavourably with that shown by companies which use their appreciation to form a separate investment reserve fund or allow it to remain as a hidden reserve. Nevertheless I feel that the maintenance of interest yields at a satisfactory level may be the severest task facing the managements of life offices in the next few years. On grounds of public policy one hopes to see a further substantial reduction in the current level of interest, which, apart from income tax deductions, is still somewhat high even on pre-war standards, and much too high in present circumstances. But the decline will, if it occurs, present the business of life assurance, which is so dependent on the results of compound interest, with a serious problem affecting the relationship between existing rates of premium and of bonus.

I may add that your board have been fully alive to this prospect for some time past and have done what they could to protect the Society against the risk involved. In my annual speech two years ago I said 'I should be disposed to predict with great confidence the beginning of a substantial downward movement' in rates of interest; and last year I remarked that, while by selling our long-dated securities we might have avoided some of the depreciation then incurred, and have given in this way a superficial appearance of caution, 'it would have remained a gamble whether we could have got back again into permanent investments at just the right moment'. It is sometimes the case that activity to avoid the appearance of temporary depreciation is, on a long view, the opposite of caution; and the satisfactory results of last year have been largely due to our steadfastness.

Substantial mortality profits

Our mortality profits in 1932 were substantial—more than double those of the previous year—the incidence being unusually favourable and the actual amount paid in claims by death—namely £149,311—the lowest in any year since 1926. Both expenses and commission payments show an absolute saving, though the reduction in the latter is due to the decline in the volume of new business. The result is seen in a decline in our expense ratio from 13·7 per cent of premium income in 1931 to 12·7 per cent in 1932.

Bringing the above and other sundry items together, our trading profit for the two years 1931–2, calculated on the same basis as in previous years, has been as follows:—

Net miscellaneous profits from mortality, etc.	£124,877
Interest earnings in excess of 3 per cent on mean fund excluding carry-forward	136,764
Interest earned on the surplus carried forward from 1930	18,076
	£279,717

In view of these results your board have felt sure that you would wish them to make the valuation and distribution of bonus, postponed from last year. It would be foolish to pretend that the prospects are yet clear or that we have escaped for certain from the phase of violent fluctuations in the financial and economic world. But on any test, however stringent, which can be reasonably applied to the actual results of the past two years, the bonus has been comfortably earned, and it should, therefore, be distributed. A board which sought to make provision against wholly uncertain and unpredictable contingencies, arising not out of its own affairs but out of those of the world at large, might never declare a bonus at all.

Bonus reserve valuation

This being so, our actuary has given anxious consideration to the question whether the time has not come for changing over from the old-fashioned and now somewhat misleading methods of valuation, in which we have followed tradition for many years past, to the more scientific method, already adopted by one or two offices, known as bonus reserve valuation. In accepting his advice that we should make this change we have done so with the more satisfaction from the fact that the originator of the new method, Mr Coutts, now manager and actuary of the Provident Mutual, was formerly a member of our staff.

The technical details of the new method have been explained at length by the actuary in his valuation report, which you have already received. You will have seen that, while the reserves required by the new method do not differ very greatly from those required by the old method, they are slightly more stringent, requiring us to set aside out of profit an additional sum of nearly £20,000.

The change summed up

If I may venture as a layman to sum up the essence of the change I should do so as follows:—

The estimated liability under a life policy consists in the excess of the present value of the sum assured, together with bonuses already declared, over the present value of the future premiums payable, the 'present value' being calculated on the basis of certain assumptions which may or may not be realised. There should, therefore, be a substantial margin over and above the sum thus estimated in order to provide for unforeseen contingencies which might upset the expectations upon which the estimate has been based.

When a life office values its liabilities in order to ascertain what surplus is properly available for present distribution, it must not take credit for this margin, because if bonuses were to be declared corresponding to it the margin would be used up and the provision would have disappeared. Thus actuaries have to devise some method of distinguishing between this undistributable margin and the surplus over and above it, which is properly available for immediate distribution. The method most commonly adopted in the past has ensured that the margin required to meet future contingencies is withheld from immediate distribution, by adopting arbitrary assumptions as to rates of interest, mortality, etc., so much less favourable than those actually experienced as to bear but little relation to them.

The result has been to make it difficult even for an expert to assess what the net provision arrived at in this way really amounts to. For this reason it has become common for actuaries to make at the same time for their own guidance a supplementary valuation based on assumptions which, while distinctly conservative, are in reasonably close relationship to the facts. There is then no difficulty in setting up an additional specific reserve against unforeseen changes in terms of the future rate of bonus for which this margin will provide each year if no adverse circumstances arise. This method, which is appropriately known as the bonus reserve method of valuation, gives a scientific measure of what the provision which the office is making really amounts to. In our own case the reserve which we are making is one which will provide bonuses of 30s. per cent per annum during the lives of our fully participating policies, and 15s. in the case of our low premium policies, if the assumptions on which the valuation is based are realised.

A more adaptable method

I have said that the assumptions as to future rates of interest, mortality, and expenses, while in a definite relationship to present experience, are made conservatively. This is illustrated by the fact that we are now able to declare for the years 1931 and 1932 bonuses, not of 30s. per annum, but of 42s. 6d. on our whole-life and 37s. 6d. on our endowment assurance fully participating policies. Moreover, these rates are comfortably within what we are earning in present conditions, and have been declared without drawing upon the results of our favourable mortality, our low expenses, or our capital appreciation in the current year. Our actuary is satisfied that they can be maintained in future, unless there is a considerable further fall in the net rate of interest or serious developments, affecting all institutions alike, in the financial circumstances of the world and of this country. Furthermore, if important changes occur hereafter which appear to be of an enduring character, our new method of valuation is more readily adaptable to them than were the rigid assumptions used previously.

I may mention that if, as we hope, we can maintain the rates of bonus now declared, the results will be even more advantageous to policyholders than are those of policies which have been in force for a period of years and are now maturing for payment.

Your board have considered carefully whether we should now return to the routine of annual valuation and distribution, which, on general grounds, we much prefer. But, for the reasons given in the actuary's report, we think that it would be better not to do so at present. We cannot be sure that we are yet immune from violent, temporary fluctuations in security values, and we believe that it conduces to greater equanimity in investment policy if we have less anxiety as to the precise market value of our securities over short periods; but we shall, of course, continue as in the past (though there are but few offices which follow this course) to inform you at each annual meeting of the market value of our securities at the end of each year.

Retirement of Mr Marks

During the year Mr G. H. Recknell, who had succeeded Mr Geoffrey Marks as actuary in 1928, has also succeeded him as our chief officer. I am glad to say that Mr Marks remains on the board, but he has ceased to be our chief officer, after holding that position for nearly 40 years. The National Mutual, as it is today, is largely his creation. He has been, indeed, our second founder. At the close of today's proceedings I shall ask you to approve the acquisition by the society of an admirable portrait of Geoffrey Marks, hung in this room today, painted by Mr Henry Lamb. Mr Marks has devoted all his gifts of mind and character and temperament to this institution and its problems and to the individuals who, even in the case of so abstract a thing as a life office, really constitute it. He has been a great educator, as the personnel of other life offices in this country exist to testify, a wise innovator and pioneer, and a beloved human being. He carries with him into his retirement our affectionate best wishes.

Speech to the Annual Meeting of the National Mutual, 21 February 1934

Gentlemen,

Our net new business of £700,935, showing the substantial increase of 30 per cent on the previous year's, bears out, I think, the hope which I expressed at our meeting a year ago that the abnormal conditions which were adversely affecting us had come to an end. This year's business has been well spread among the various classes of assurance and the Society's new schemes have received a good measure of support. This is particularly the case with our house purchase scheme introduced about 18 months ago in conjunction with the Burnley Building Society. The 'All clear' income policy providing for the payment of the capital sum assured by annual instalments free of income tax, which was introduced in the course of last year, has also met with a satis-factory response.

I may mention that the new business completed could have been increased if we had cared to encourage the issue of sinking fund policies and short-term endowment assurances particularly by single premiums. We have, however, thought it advisable to stiffen the terms on which we are prepared to transact these classes of business—partly for reasons arising out of the prospec-tive rate of interest, to which I will return in a few minutes.

Claims and expenses

The claims by death are above the exceptionally low figure of 1932, but less than in 1930 or in 1931. The increase of claims by maturity is, of course, the natural outcome of a gradually in-creasing volume of business. I am glad to say that the number of policies surrendered during the year has fallen very greatly—less than half the amount of either of the two previous years measured by the sums assured on the surrendered policies. It is a sign of improving conditions that this figure has now returned to within what may be expected in normal times. Our expenses show a reduction, although the expenditure ratio has risen slightly, merely as a reflection of the fact that the premium income on which the calculation is made includes on this occasion a smaller volume of single premiums than last year.

As I intimated to you a year ago, valuations with a view to distribution of surplus are to be made, for the time being at any rate, biennially instead of annually as heretofore. Nevertheless, a valuation for internal purposes has been made which shows that the trading profits, exclusive of appreciation on securities, have covered the rates of bonus declared last year with a sub-stantial margin. The board has not, therefore, hesitated to declare an interim bonus on claims arising this year at the full rates as before.

Valuation of investments

Although our actuarial valuations are no longer published annually, we are maintaining the practice, which we have long pursued, of disclosing each year the result of the current valuation of our stock exchange securities and other investment assets. I am able to report a satisfactory result. The balance of appreciation in 1933 was £363,963, equal to 6·6 per cent of the total mean funds and to 8·3 per cent of the stock exchange securities. This works out somewhat better than the indexes in the case both of fixed-interest securities and of ordinary shares, the percentages of appreciation on the mean funds so employed being 5·9 per cent and 23·6 per cent respectively. In 1932 a large proportion of our appreciation was earned on British Government securities. During the past year the further appreciation under this heading has been comparatively small, and the appreciation has been mainly earned on our other securities.

Taking the two years together, the aggregate appreciation has amounted to more than £1,000,000, which is a large sum in proportion to our resources, exceeding 25 per cent of our mean holding of stock exchange securities. In view of this material improvement in the position the board has considered it advisable to create a reserve fund out of the surplus resources thus accumulated; and the sum of £250,000 has been transferred from the life assurance fund for this purpose. As and when circumstances permit, it is the board's present intention to increase this fund from time to time. In creating a separate reserve fund, instead of showing the whole of our surplus in the carry-forward, the board has been influenced by the undesirability of including large temporary fluctuations in capital values in a revenue account primarily intended to show the result of current trading operations. We think it will be useful, therefore, to put a cushion, so to speak, between the fluctuations in capital values and the results of our current trading operations.

Our previous practice has lent itself to misunderstanding, since many other offices do not show any part of the fluctuations in capital values in their revenue accounts. The method now adopted will allow the board to continue its practice of publishing the amounts of these fluctuations from year to year, without, however, the whole of them being allowed to swamp the normal trading figures which are much less susceptible to violent changes. I should add that the existence of this fund will in no way interfere with the board's discretion to utilise it for any purpose which seems in the best interests of the Society, whether it be to meet future fluctuations in the value of our investments, to strengthen the basis of our valuation, or for any other purpose.

Interest earnings

The average net earnings from interest and capital profits combined over the past 13 years work out at 6 per cent per annum after deduction of income tax. The net rate of interest which we are now able to earn on our investments is, however, much less than this, having declined during the past year from £4 5s. 8d. per cent to £4 1s. 10d. on our aggregate funds. If we reckon our interest earnings as a percentage on the assurance funds exclusive of the reserve fund, last year's figure is £4 3s. 9d. per cent, which is more comparable with the figures published by other offices, few of which write up their assets as we do to accord with market values. The decline of the net rate of interest which we are able to earn on the investment of new money to a figure not much in excess of 4 per cent raises, however, questions of the greatest possible importance and interest to all investment institutions and not least to insurance offices, and I should like to take this opportunity of considering the general problem which this phenomenon presents in a little more detail.

In 1932 long-term British Government securities moved from a 5 per cent to a 3½ per cent basis. This was largely the result of the steps taken by the Bank of England to facilitate the conversion of the War Loan, including open-market operations on an unprecedentedly large scale, which raised the resources of the

London clearing banks by £246,000,000, out of which they invested £176,000,000 in British Government securities.

In 1933 Government securities marked time, improving in price by only some 2 per cent, and the year was occupied by other fixed-interest securities rising to their usual parity with Government securities, and in some cases beyond it. This was in spite of a further increase of £93,000,000 in the investments held by the banks—no longer out of additional resources provided by the Bank of England, but through the shrinkage of their other assets. Meanwhile the Treasury bill rate has averaged less than 1 per cent, and for more than a year there has been a spread of $2\frac{1}{2}$ per cent between the yield on long-term Government securities and the rate at which the money market has been able to borrow against them. This abnormal and anomalous relationship indicates a grave doubt in the mind of the market as to whether the existing price of long-term securities will be maintained.

Two views

Two views can be held. Those who are afraid of holding long-term securities point out with truth that the rise in their prices is largely due to the purchases of the banks; and they invoke, again with truth, the evidence of past experience to the effect that, as trade recovers, the banks have been accustomed to sell their investments to provide the means for increased advances to industry. They argue, therefore, believing that history will repeat itself, that long-term Government securities will fall in price as soon as there is a material improvement in the demand for advances. It would be rash to affirm that the course of events will be different this time. But I would like to give some grounds for this conclusion, before passing to what seem to me to be more fundamental reasons for expecting a further fall in the long-term rate of interest.

In pre-war days the resources of the banking system were somewhat rigidly linked to the gold reserves of the Bank of England. Open-market operations were unimportant and, broadly speaking, the assets of the clearing banks went up and down according as gold was moving into, or out of, the Bank of England. Now in times of good trade this country tended to expand, and in bad times to contract, its foreign lending more rapidly than its favourable balance; the effect of which on movements of gold was to prevent the assets of the banks from increasing in good times, while sometimes the tendency for these assets to increase was actually stronger in times of depression. It is not to be wondered at, therefore, that with improving trade it was often impracticable for the banks to accommodate industry except by selling their investments. This is the historical origin of the expectation that Consols will fall when trade recovers.

Resources of the banks

Today, however, there is no necessity for events to follow this course. The resources of the banks depend at least as much on changes in the volume of securities purchased by the Bank of England as on changes in the Bank's stock of gold. Thus the technique of management lately evolved by the Bank puts it in its power to adjust the resources of the clearing banks to the needs of trade and employment. We are no longer at the mercy of the blind and perverse forces which ensured in pre-war days that, as soon as we began to move towards prosperity and optimum employment, factors would begin to be generated which would shortly throw us back again into the pit which we had lately climbed out of.

Moreover, in present circumstances the increased basis of credit which the Bank of England would have to provide might prove to be moderate in amount. In the first place, part of the clearing banks' existing advances represents frozen rather than active credit, so that increased demands for current credit will be partly met by the repayment of old advances; while some of the largest concerns in the country are now much less dependent on bank borrowing than was the case with the constituent businesses out of which they have been formed. But, apart from this, an increase of (say) £20,000,000 in the Bank of England's assets would enable the clearing banks to increase their aggregate advances by 25 per cent, which should be fully adequate to all requirements unless there is to be a large rise in wages and other costs.

It is clear, therefore, that there is no necessity for reviving trade to break the gilt-edged market unless the authorities desire this to happen. So I return to the fundamental reasons, as I see them, why the authorities should in fact desire just the contrary.

Return on gilt-edged stocks

There is, surely, overwhelming evidence that even the present reduced rate of $3\frac{1}{2}$ per cent on long-term gilt-edged stocks is far above the equilibrium level—meaning by 'equilibrium' the rate which is compatible with the full employment of our resources of men and of equipment. It is often forgotten that $3\frac{1}{2}$ per cent is much in excess of the average yield on Consols, which ruled over the 40 years previous to the war—namely, just under 3 per cent —or even the average yield which ruled over the 80 years from 1835 to 1914—namely, just over 3 per cent.

The argument that this comparison is vitiated by the income tax which the lender must now pay is quite invalid if we are considering the 'equilibrium' rate, rather than the actual market rate; for the rate which the borrower can afford to pay depends in the long run on the yield of capital assets and is not increased by reason of taxes on the lender. Yet during the nineteenth century the annual amount which the community was disposed to save when it was fully employed was much below what it is today, whereas the outlets for profitable investment were vastly greater on account of the rapid growth of population and the opening up of new worlds oversea.

Curtailment of the investment field

With the opportunities for safe and profitable investment abroad greatly curtailed, as much by the unfortunate results of past investment as by the diminished opportunities for new investment, Great Britain and the United States would, if they were to return to the full employment of their resources, save sums so vast that they could not possibly be invested to yield anything approaching $3\frac{1}{2}$ per cent. No one can foretell at what point the rate of interest will reach its equilibrium level until we actually approach it. But it is highly probable that the equilibrium rate is not above $2\frac{1}{2}$ per cent for long-term gilt-edged investment, and may be appreciably less. In the early days of a recovery, while working capital is being restored and various postponements of renewals and fresh development are being overtaken, it is true that business can temporarily stand a higher rate. But the longer the recovery lasts the further will the appropriate long-term rate of interest have to fall. If when the recovery is well on its way the Bank of England so manages the basis of credit as to force the clearing banks to sell their investments on a substantial scale or otherwise to weaken the long-term loan market, then, indeed, it is as certain that depression will follow recovery as that night follows day.

Downward tendency of interest rates

But why, in making our prognostications, should we attribute such disastrous ideas to our financial authorities? No institution is more interested than the Treasury in a falling rate of interest. The further we move from the abnormal rates of the war period, the clearer, I believe, will it become to every one that our economic health needs a rate of interest appreciably below, and not above, the nineteenth-century level. There is no harm in the fall of the rate of interest being gradual, but it is a necessity for the epoch into which we are now entering that there should be a steady movement in the downward direction. In each of the last three years, I have ventured, in addressing you, to predict a falling rate of interest. I say today with undiminished conviction that we are still some way from the end of the journey, and that the course of events which I forecast three years ago will still continue in the same direction.

Board's conservative policy

I hope that I have not burdened your attention with so long a disquisition on general matters. But I need scarcely emphasise how important it is for those who are responsible for the conduct of a life office to ponder these matters, since our business consists in entering into long-term contracts the fulfilment of which depends on our earning not less than a certain assumed rate of interest. And I may add that, however the result may turn out, the course of prudence for a life office undoubtedly lies in leaning towards a conservative view as to the future rate of interest and in taking such measures as are possible to protect the position in the event of this rate moving steadily downwards. That is the policy of your board; and while, if my forecast proves correct, we shall not be able to avoid many perplexities, yet you may feel assured that we shall be as fully protected as we know how.

Speech to the Annual Meeting of the National Mutual, 20 February 1935

Gentlemen,

The report, which is already in your hands, shows that the volume of new business, at £839,273 after deduction of re-assurances, was well above the 1933 total, and has returned to the figures of some four or five years ago. The number of new policies issued has kept pace with the volume and the business has been well spread among the Society's various connections. The fall in the rate of interest has had the effect of encouraging annuity business, and the consideration money which we have taken for immediate annuities has risen from £26,410 in 1933 to £45,287 last year, in spite of our having found it desirable on two occasions to stiffen the terms on which such contracts are granted. We have also found it advisable to discourage business in the form of single premium sinking fund policies and short-term endowment assurances on terms which might prove unremunerative.

Our mortality experience during the year has proved exceptionally favourable. The aggregate amount paid under claims by death—namely, £135,087—is lower than in any year since 1926, in spite of the increase since that date in the volume of policies outstanding, and the mortality profit earned has been substantially higher than that to which we are accustomed. The small increase in our expense ratio has been mainly due to the increased volume of new business.

Appreciation of invested funds

The appreciation on our invested funds in 1934 was £532,351, equal to 8·7 per cent of the total mean funds, and to 10·5 per cent of the portion invested in stock exchange securities. This result follows upon a corresponding figure of £363,963 in 1933, so that in the two years combined the Society has gained in this way a sum of nearly £900,000, equal to 16 per cent of the mean funds. The principal changes in our investments during the year are a shift of some part of the Society's holdings of British Government securities into the item 'british public boards', and a substantial reduction in our relatively small holding of foreign government bonds.

The net rate of interest has declined further from £4 1s. 10d. per cent on the mean total fund to £3 18s. 6d. per cent, and the current return on the valuation of our assets as at the end of the year would be still lower. This decline is, however, wholly due to the appreciation in our securities, the absolute amount of our net interest income showing an increase of some £16,000, with the result that the net interest income as a percentage on the mean assurance funds has in fact risen from £4 3s. 9d. per cent to £4 5s. 5d. per cent. It is the latter rate which is more comparable with that shown by many other offices which do not write up their assets as we do to accord with market values. In continuation of the figures which I have given in previous years I may mention that our average earnings from interest and capital profits over the past 14 years work out at 6·63 per cent per annum after deduction of income tax.

Result of valuation

This, as you know, is for us a year for the valuation of assets and liabilities and for the declaration of bonus. The outcome of the various factors, which I have just outlined, has put us in an excellent position. The operations of the two years since our last valuation have accumulated a surplus of assets over liabilities, reckoned on the same basis as before, amounting to £1,456,899, or more than 25 per cent of our liabilities. The board consider that the portion of this—namely, £896,314—which is due to profits on and appreciation in the value of our investments, should be wholly applied to strengthening our position in various ways. Accordingly we have utilised £123,110 to strengthen our actuarial reserves by introducing the new Institute of Actuaries mortality table; £600,000 has been transferred to a general reserve and £150,000 to an investment reserve, and the balance has been added to the carry-forward. Including these last two appropriations the total surplus which we shall be carrying forward into the next valuation period will amount to £1,028,947 in excess of what is required for our actuarial reserves, or a margin of nearly 19 per cent.

We have considered it advisable to hold by far the greater part of this sum in a general reserve and in the carry-forward, both of which are applicable to any purpose, rather than to make a more specific allocation, owing to the uncertainty as to which of two opposite contingencies we may have to provide for in the future. If the movement in the rate of interest is reversed, we shall inevitably lose some part of the existing appreciation on our investments. If, on the other hand, the rate of interest continues to fall, the terms on which we shall be able to accumulate the current and prospective premiums paid by our policyholders will fall below the figure upon which we have been counting, with the result that we may have to make a substantial transfer to our actuarial reserves.

Effects of decreased interest rates

A life office gains from a fall in the rate of interest in the appreciation of its existing funds, but it loses, if, as in the case of most offices, its aggregate funds are steadily increasing, by reason of the lower rate of accumulation of future premiums in respect of existing obligations. A narrowing of the margin between the actual current rate of interest and the rate assumed in calculating the actuarial reserves has, therefore, the effect of flattering the apparent position by bringing into the open reserves which were previously concealed. It is important that members should appreciate that during the last two years our own position has been flattered in this way, and that an important part of the apparent increase in our surplus resources—though not the whole—is merely an improvement on paper.

Nevertheless, your board feel that the capital position is so well protected that they would not be justified in withholding the current trading profits from distribution as bonus. The bonuses now declared, therefore, not only repeat the 1932 scale of distribution, but include a special addition such that the total compound reversionary bonuses on the various classes of policy are the highest in our history—namely, 52s. 6d. and 45s. per cent per annum on whole life and endowment assurances with full profits respectively, and 17s. 6d. per cent per annum on low-premium policies with reduced profits. Our favourable recent experience in respect of mortality has played a considerable part in making possible the special distribution now made, and policyholders must not count on our being in a position to repeat it.

Conflicting forces

A year ago I gave reasons for expecting a further fall in the long-term rate of interest. Since then Government securities definitely redeemable within 25 years have fallen to a yield well below the level of $2\frac{1}{2}$ per cent, which then seemed to me to be within sight, while the yield on longer-dated securities or securities with no fixed date of redemption is now below 3 per cent. Today, however, the prospects are by no means so clear, for we are now, in my judgement, between two sets of strong conflicting forces.

On the one hand, the evidence indicates that the maintenance of the national prosperity and the improvement of employment still require a lower rate of interest than we have yet enjoyed. So far from the falling rates of interest having proved excessively stimulating to new enterprise, it has been disappointing to notice how comparatively few large-scale opportunities for the investment of new savings have as yet disclosed themselves under the influence of the low rate of interest, though we must not underestimate the predominant part which new building and new electrical developments, both of them relatively sensitive to the rate of interest, have had in bringing us such measure of prosperity as we have attained. I am, therefore, confirmed in the opinion that we shall require, for our economic health, a rate of interest gradually falling to levels much lower than we have known in the past, whereas the present reduced rates are even now no lower than those which often prevailed in pre-war days.

But, on the other hand, there are serious obstacles in the way of an immediate further reduction. British rates of interest have already fallen much below those which rule elsewhere. At present our domestic rates are protected by the extreme lack of confidence in the economic position of foreign countries. We must hope that a revival of confidence elsewhere will be accompanied by a fall in their interest rates towards a normal parity with our own levels. But meanwhile the existing disparity of rates may make our own position slightly precarious. Far more important than this, however—for I do not expect an early return to anything which one could call an international rate of interest—is the attitude of British institutional investors to the future of the rate of interest. The current long-term rate of interest is a highly psychological phenomenon which must necessarily depend on what expectations we hold concerning the future rate of interest. In the mind of the typical professional investor today the current return does not offer much of a premium against the possibility of a turn in the tide. Investors are watching more anxiously for a change than they would if the position was considered stable.

A difficult task

Thus the task of maintaining a rate of interest sufficiently low to be compatible with national prosperity and good employment is likely to present increasing difficulty. Indeed, one may feel some doubt whether it is capable of solution by 'normal' traditional methods in an industrially advanced community, which is, for various reasons, no longer in a position to invest large sums abroad and of which the population is no longer advancing rapidly.

I would suggest, however, that, for the moment, the wisest course on the part of those in authority is to consolidate the position which has been won, rather than to aim at an immediate further advance. Fixed-interest securities outside the class of British Government securities and the like have not yet fully adjusted themselves to the price of the latter, as the Institute of Actuaries' Index clearly shows: while there are other important rates of interest, in particular mortgage interest, the terms on which building societies lend and borrow, and the rates charged by the banks, which have lagged much further behind. For the encouragement of enterprise a fall in these rates is more important than a further decline in the yield on Government securities.

Moreover, a rate of interest must persist for some time before it has its full effect on business decisions which involve a new technical programme only made possible by the fall in the rate. I feel not less strongly than before the importance of a declining long-term rate of interest, but a greater degree of confidence than now exists in the maintenance of the rates of interest we already have at a level not above their present figure is our most pressing need.

Suggestion to the Treasury

There is, I suggest, an important contribution to this object which it lies within the power of the Treasury to make—namely, that they should themselves show confidence in the expectation of a declining rate of interest in the future. Advice is often offered them on the lines that the present is a golden opportunity for trapping the investor, so to speak, into lending to them for an indefinite period on terms which he will subsequently regret. This advice seems to be based, like most advice, on the extremely improbable assumption that the future will resemble the past. But in any case it is bad advice, for the major purpose of the Treasury should be to establish stable conditions with a gradually declining rate over a long period of years ahead, a necessary condition of which is the creation of a reasonable expectation that this is, in fact, the probable course of events.

To act along these lines will not only increase confidence, but is likely to be profitable to the Treasury and to the taxpayer. I would urge, therefore, that, in future funding or refunding schemes, securities should be offered having fixed terms of redemption well spread over dates from five to 25 years hence. Local Loans are particularly well suited to this treatment, since the bulk of the money advanced by the fund will be repaid to it at dates already fixed within this period.

This policy has everything to recommend it. The Treasury will borrow more cheaply; they will help the psychology of the market by themselves showing confidence in the maintenance of low rates of interest, and they will improve the structure and stability of the banking system by supplying a type of security suitable to institutions which are themselves borrowing the bulk of their funds on short terms. The present position, in which the greater part of the available supply of Government securities is in the form either of three-month Treasury bills or of securities having no fixed date of redemption within the next 50 years, is technically very defective.

An essential factor

I would emphasise the fact that there is no reliable way of establishing a low long-term rate of interest except by fostering a reasonable expectation that the rate of interest will continue low in the future, and by offering fixed dates of redemption to those who, rightly or wrongly, remain doubtful; but, if the Treasury themselves pursue a policy which implies a belief that the current rates of interest are abnormally low, they cannot expect institutions and the public to feel that degree of confidence which is essential to further progress.

After this long digression I must return to our own domestic affairs. In two important respects this meeting marks a break with the past. The Society acquired the site of the building in which we meet today nearly 90 years ago, and the greater part of the premises we occupy was built for us nearly 80 years ago at the modest cost of £6,000. It no longer meets modern requirements or makes the best use of a valuable site, and your board have decided to rebuild it. The additional accommodation provided will exceed what we shall require for ourselves, and, after allowing for the rentals obtainable from outside tenants, we shall possess more commodious premises at but small cost to the society. Your board has commissioned as architect Mr Campbell Jones, F.R.I.B.A., who has had much experience in the erection of office buildings in the City.

Retirement of Mr Burchell and Mr Marks

A much greater break for all of us will be the retirement from the board of Mr Charles Burchell and Mr Geoffrey Marks, both of whom have been associated with the Society for nearly fifty years. I played a part some years ago in effecting the change in our articles which introduced an age limit for directors. I still believe that the change was advisable, but when one sees it operating in particular cases one cannot but regret it—not least when it causes us to lose our two best-loved directors. A hundred years ago

Mr Burchell's grandfather and grand-uncle, whose portraits you see to the left and to the right, founded the old 'Mutual', which nearly forty years ago Mr Marks joined with the 'National' to create the 'National Mutual'; and Mr Burchell's years as a director have completed the full century for which his family has served the society with integrity and assiduity and wisdom. We shall greatly miss him.

If we lose with Mr Burchell, the representative of our first founders, we lose with Mr Marks, our second founder. The society, as it exists today, is largely his creation, and it must be a great satisfaction to him to leave it in so strong a position. Mr Marks has never sought to make the National Mutual into an organisation of vast size and impersonal character. His object has been rather to use his great gifts of nature to serve his generation by educating in the way that they should go the many eminent actuaries who have served under him in their youth, by moving in the vanguard of new ideas, and by building up a life office which should be a model of his own conceptions of excellence, never allowing the pursuit of size and volume to deflect him from his model.

It is a measure of his success that those policyholders who entrusted their savings to his management 30 years ago have actually earned over the whole period bonuses superior to those which they could have obtained from any other English or Scottish office. Yet this might not have been the case, I think, if he had aimed at a more rapid rate of expansion. The growth of business shows itself quickly, but careful selection and the avoidance of unnecessary expense only justify themselves in proved results over a length of years.

I move the adoption of the report.

Speech to the Annual Meeting of the National Mutual, 19 February 1936

Gentlemen,

Our annual report shows a substantial increase in the volume of our new business to a figure just less than £1,000,000. The total has, however, been swollen by an exceptional volume of non-life business. In order that the figures may be quite clear, we have, for the first time, shown separately the volume of life business on the first page of the report. There is also a substantial increase in the volume of annuity business, a class of business which, as I indicated last year, we undertake with a certain amount of hesitation; and the increase has taken place in spite of our having made our terms a little less favourable to the purchaser. Perhaps the most trustworthy guide to the progress of the business is the yearly premium income, and this has shown a larger increase than for many years past.

Mortality experience

Last year our mortality experience was exceptionally favourable. This year the tide has turned, and has left us with a greatly diminished, though not unsatisfactory, mortality profit. The National Mutual is not a large enough office to average mortality results accurately over a single year, which may be regarded, incidentally, as a reason against our recurring too hastily to annual valuations. On the other hand, the surrenders have been unusually light, lighter, indeed, than in any year since 1927, which is a welcome indication of the improved financial position of our policyholders. The expense ratio for the year at 11·5 per cent is artificially low on account of a substantial single-premium business effected this year; though we are satisfied that there is some real reduction after allowing for this.

Valuation of investments

The results of our investment policy during the year may be considered, I think, as very satisfactory. This is not for us a valuation period, but it has been usual in the past for me to give you annually the exact results of the revaluation of our investments at the end of each year. This shows capital profits of £203,000, equal to 3·5 per cent of our stock exchange securities and 2·9 per cent of our total assets. We are content with this result in a year in which gilt-edged securities have slightly declined and other fixed-interest stocks as a group have shown no significant movement. On the average of the past 15 years, our net earnings from interest and capital profits combined have been 6·7 per cent per annum, free of income tax. I know of no other investment institution which has published so good a return over a period of years.

Though it has not been easy to find satisfactory alternative investments, we have succeeded in making a further reduction in our unnecessarily large holding of British Government securities. On the other hand, the increase in our holdings of ordinary shares is mainly accounted for by appreciation and our direct stake in British industrial shares, a matter to which I shall recur, is today much diminished. We have somewhat increased our holdings of non-stock exchange assets, including various forms of real estate, but it has required much patient selection to discover reasonably priced properties.

As a result we have just succeeded in maintaining the rate of interest at which we have been able to invest the new funds accruing in our hands, and the decline in the net rate of interest on our total funds from £3 18s. 6d. per cent to £3 16s. 7d. per cent is entirely due to the effect of writing up the fund to correspond to the additional capital profits, and not to a decline in the absolute amount of the income receipts. The rate of interest earned on our net liabilities works out at over $4\frac{1}{2}$ per cent, compared with the rate of $3\frac{3}{4}$ per cent assumed in our actuarial valuation.

Interim bonuses

Although bonus distributions are now biennial instead of annual, the usual internal actuarial valuation has been made. While this has shown some diminution in the year's trading surplus as compared with 1934, almost wholly because of the reduced level of profits from mortality mentioned above, the trading surplus earned last year is much more than sufficient to cover the normal bonuses declared a year ago. Apart from this margin of trading surplus, the Society enters upon the current year, at the end of which a further distribution is due to be made, with a carry-forward of £279,000, together with capital profits earned last year of £203,000 and reserve funds totalling £750,000. Accordingly the board has had no hesitation in deciding to pay interim bonuses on claims arising this year at the full normal rates as before.

Long-term rates of interest

Two years ago I gave reasons for expecting a further fall in the long-term rate of interest. Last year I spoke more doubtfully since it seemed to me that we were between two sets of conflicting forces, and I concluded that we most needed a consolidation of the existing position coupled with a greater degree of confidence in the maintenance of the existing rates of interest. What is the prospect of the coming year?

In speaking of future prospects it is often difficult to make the distinction clear between what one considers the most desirable in the public interest and what one reckons to be the most probable in the actual circumstances. For unfortunately the course of events which is the most desirable is not always the most probable! Let me explain, therefore, that on this occasion I am primarily concerned with the question of what policy is most advisable.

If the present relatively (though not absolutely) satisfactory position is to be protected from subsequent reaction, I am sure that a further reduction in the long-term rate of interest—which, it must be remembered, will not produce its full effects for a considerable time—is urgently called for. But it is natural to ask by what means this result can be brought about. In attempting to answer this question there are certain considerations which I should like to call to your attention.

Treasury and short-term rates

Short-term money to-day is extremely cheap. But it is confidence in the future of short-term rates which is required to bring down long-term rates. Now the policy of the Treasury is not calculated to promote such confidence. They seem reluctant to issue bonds of from five to 10 years' maturity and anxious to reduce the short-term debt, in spite of the extraordinary cheapness with which it can be carried. They starve the banks and the money market of the type of security which the sound conduct of their business admittedly requires, and they pay a higher rate of interest than they need.

Take as an example their latest issue. They simultaneously borrowed at $1\frac{1}{2}$ per cent for five years and at $2\frac{3}{4}$ per cent for 25 years. They used part of the proceeds to repay short-term debt which was costing them about $\frac{1}{2}$ per cent. There can be no rational explanation of the longer-dated issue except that they themselves have no confidence in the short-term rate of interest remaining low. Since they largely control the situation, it is natural that humbler folk should be influenced by what the Treasury seem to expect. I suggest, therefore, that it is at least as important that the Treasury should themselves show confidence in the future of the short-term rate of interest as that they should maintain a low rate for the time being.

The supply of bank money

The other main factor (besides confidence in the future of short-term rates) in bringing down long-term rates of interest is a supply of bank money fully adequate to satisfy the community's demand for liquidity. The following figures are, I think, instructive. In the last quarter of 1932 the Bank of England's open-market policy had the effect of increasing the volume of bank deposits to a total 12 per cent higher than in the last quarter of the preceding year. During the same period both the index of production and the index of prices were slightly receding. As a result the price of fixed-interest securities rose during this period by 33 per cent.

Two years later the volume of bank money was practically unchanged, although the index of production had risen appreciably and the index of prices slightly. Nevertheless there was a further rise of some 12 per cent in fixed-interest securities, partly due to the delayed effect of the Bank of England's earlier measures. Last year the Bank of England again increased the volume of bank money by about 6 per cent. This was undoubtedly a move in the right direction; but it was not quite enough even to sustain the level of long-term Government securities, and not nearly enough to continue their upward movement in a year in which the London and Cambridge index of production (the Board of Trade index is not yet available) rose 10 per cent, the index of wholesale prices 4 per cent, and that of the cost of living 3 per cent.

The net result is, comparing the end of 1935 with the end of 1932, that, whereas the index of production has risen 33 per cent, wholesale prices nearly 8 per cent, and the cost of living nearly 4 per cent, the volume of bank money has risen only 6 per cent. There are, of course, many other factors of which account must be taken; and these must have been favourable to long-dated securities in view of the way in which the latter have maintained their prices. But it is evident that the time has come for another increase in the volume of bank money, if we wish long-term rates of interest to fall further. The increase should, of course, be very gradual and almost unnoticeable from week to week, and it should be accompanied by an increase in the supply of Government securities of a maturity suitable for the banks to hold in substantial volume.

Treasury and Bank of England steps

The Treasury and the Bank of England undoubtedly deserve great credit for the large steps which they have already taken in the right direction. That they have not achieved more is mainly due, I think, to their underestimating their own powers to achieve what they recognise as desirable. It is true that there exist certain important limitations on their power to influence the rate of interest. But I doubt if these limitations are yet operative. The two main limitations are, respectively, external and internal. So long as the public is as effectively free to lend abroad as to lend at home it is obvious that domestic rates of interest cannot fall far below their normal parity with foreign rates without seriously upsetting the balance of international payments.

In pre-war days this limitation was of great importance. But with our exchanges no longer tied to gold, with the admirable control over the pace of foreign issues which the Bank of England has established, and with the diminished credit of many former large-scale borrowers, the position is greatly changed. I do not believe that this factor need be regarded today as standing in the way of a further reduction in the rate of interest. If I were told that the resources of the Exchange Equalisation Fund are virtually exhausted, I might change my opinion, at least to the extent of advocating a stricter control of foreign investment, especially in American stocks. But I am hopeful that this is not the case.

The other, internal, limitation will come into operation when we have what is for practical purposes a state of full employment. In such circumstances a further fall in the rate of interest will merely stimulate a competition for current output, which will result in an inflationary rise of prices. Pre-war theory presumed that this was the normal state of affairs. Would that it were! But, in fact, this happy condition is not yet ours. When it is the rate of interest will have fallen far enough for the time being.

Industrial share prices

There is another feature of the financial situation which is not entirely satisfactory—namely, the very high relative level of the prices of British industrial ordinary shares. These prices presume not merely a maintenance of the present industrial activity for an indefinite period to come but a substantial further improvement. Not that many people actually believe this, but each is hopeful of unloading on the other fellow in good time. It is true that prices not much below the present level might be justified if the long-term rate of interest were to fall sufficiently to bring forward new types of capital development. But the present *relative* levels of gilt-edged securities and of industrial ordinary shares are calculated, unless they are revised, to bring ultimate disappointment to the holders of the latter.

To argue that, on a long view, first-class fixed-interest securities are cheaper today than the general run of British industrial ordinaries is not in accordance with the popular mood. The prospect of large government expenditure on armaments is thought to lead to precisely the opposite conclusion. The view that I am indicating may, indeed, be premature. But if it is not true now, it soon may be.

Once again, I have had to ask your patience for a long digression from our own domestic affairs; though the problems I have been examining are highly relevant to them. It has been a sad break with the past to meet today outside our own premises. But the rebuilding of our offices at the corner of Cheapside and King Street is making good progress, and we hope to welcome you next year in our new home.

I move the adoption of the report and accounts.

Speech to the Annual Meeting of the National Mutual, 24 February 1937

Gentlemen,

Our new business during the past year, with gross and net totals of £1,327,200 and £1,011,200 respectively, constitutes a record in the Society's history, whilst the life business proper—namely, £903,227 net—is only a little less than our previous best. With an old-established society such as ours, however, where the annual wastage from claims, etc., reaches a large figure, the progress of the yearly premium income is perhaps the best index of the extent to which new business is more than making good what we are losing by the efflux of time. It is therefore satisfactory to be able to report an increase in the yearly premium income of approximately 10 per cent during the last two years—namely, from £363,514 in 1934 to £397,117 last year. As I mentioned in a previous speech, we have stiffened our terms for annuities, with the result that we have taken somewhat less consideration money for this business—namely, £42,000 in 1936 as against £60,000 in 1935.

The total sum paid in claims by death and maturity—namely, £350,000—is rather less than in 1935. Although the total includes a larger aggregate of death claims, the incidence of those claims has been more favourable, with the result that the profits from mortality during the past two years show an improvement. The apparent increase in our expense ratio is largely due to the smaller amount received in single premiums.

Substantial appreciation of stock exchange securities

As a result of the annual valuation of the assets we are again able to report a substantial appreciation, amounting to £365,793, on our stock exchange securities, or 6·2 per cent of their mean value. We have taken the opportunity to write down substantially the cost of our own new building and also certain other real estate assets, whilst not taking credit for appreciation in these items where such is reported. The net result is to show a balance of capital profit on assets realised and revalued amounting to £310,758. During the past year the period of appreciation on gilt-edged and other fixed-interest securities has come to an end, and in these circumstances we consider so substantial a capital gain to be satisfactory.

In continuation of the figures which I have given in many previous speeches, the combined net earnings for interest and capital profits over the past 16 years have averaged 7·1 per cent per annum, free of income tax. This is not a method of calculation which is particularly significant over a short period, but over so long a series of years it is, I think, interesting.

For some time past your board has been aiming at effecting a reduction in what were our rather unduly large holdings of British Government securities. With the constant growth in our aggregate funds we have not found this easy. But some further progress has been made during the past year, particularly by increasing our investment in non-stock exchange assets, including mortgages, reversionary securities, and real estate. Partly by this means we have been able to arrest for the time being the decline in the net rate of interest on our funds, which has been maintained during the past year at practically the same figure as in 1935—namely, £3 16s. 4d. net, as against £3 16s. 7d. I should remind you that this figure is not comparable with the rate of interest published by other offices which do not write up their assets as we do to accord with market values, the more comparable figure being the interest calculated as a percentage on our insurance funds, which works out at £4 6s. 1d. per cent net. The increase in our holdings of ordinary shares is largely due to appreciation.

Strengthening the reserves

Under our present system of a biennial valuation of liabilities we have now reached the end of a valuation period, and the time for the declaration of a bonus. The details of the valuation are set out fully in the actuary's report, which is in your hands. Reckoned on the same basis of valuation as at the end of the previous biennium, our gross surplus comes out at £1,114,063. Of this sum the amount due to realised profits and profits from appreciation in the value of our capital assets in the two years is £513,646. It may prove, however, that the end of 1936 was a particularly favourable moment for the valuation of securities, and we have decided that virtually the whole of the above sum should be utilised to strengthen our reserves in various ways. In the first place we are taking the important step of strengthening the basis of the valuation of our liabilities by reducing the rate of interest assumed from 3¾ per cent to 3½ per cent. Under the system of so-called 'bonus reserve' valuation, which we, in common with a few other offices, are now employing, the object is to replace largely artificial assumptions by assumptions more closely related to the current facts. We have, indeed, in the last two years succeeded in earning a net rate of interest just in excess of 3¾ per cent. But the margin is excessively narrow, and we feel that it would be more prudent to provide some margin against a further fall in the rate of interest by basing our calculations on the prospect of earning no more than 3½ per cent. We have also increased the provision for expenses, the total cost of revising the basis of valuation in these two respects being £293,900. In addition, we have added £150,000 to the reserve fund, making this fund up to the total of £750,000, and £43,653 to the carry-forward. Thus we enter upon the new valuation period with total reserves £1,222,600 in excess of the actuarial reserves equal to 18·5 per cent thereof.

Record bonus distribution

The balance available, after making these special allocations, amounts to £661,693, out of which we are declaring bonuses, as shown in the actuary's report, of 52s. 6d. per cent and 45s. per cent compound per annum respectively for whole-life assurances and endowment assurances with full profits, and 17s. 6d. per cent per annum compound for low premium policies with reduced profits. This distribution, which repeats the distribution made two years ago, in 1934, is the highest in our history, and is, we believe, higher than the distribution by any other mutual office in this country which calculates bonuses on terms which can be compared with ours. I emphasise this point in order to make it clear that our very large accumulation of surplus resources has been compatible with a liberal treatment of our policyholders. It is no easy matter for the board of a mutual office to hold the scales level between a proper provision for future contingencies and the amounts currently distributed. But you may be assured that your board gives this matter the most constant and anxious attention, and does not purpose to withhold from distribution any more than a prudent view of the contingencies of the future makes necessary.

Rearmament and the gilt-edged market

I said a moment ago that the end of 1936 might prove to have been a specially favourable date for the valuation of our assets. For, on the one hand, industrial securities had probably felt by then the major effects of industrial recovery apart from any temporary top-knots due to actual boom conditions; while, at the same time, gilt-edged securities were still retaining the major part of their large gains. The subsequent disclosure of the Government's rearmament programme certainly seems to postpone for some time the prospect of an industrial recession. But the effect on the gilt-edged market has been severe; and an assurance society is, of course, much more largely interested in fixed-interest securities than in equities. Naturally, therefore, the assurance world is scanning the prospects of government finance with some anxiety. Are we entitled to take a cheerful view?

Treasury's need of a concerted policy

I feel no doubt that the sums which the Chancellor of the Exchequer proposes to borrow are well within our capacity; particularly if as much of the expendure as possible is directed to bringing into employment the unused resources of the Special Areas. It is incumbent on the Government to have a concerted policy for retarding other postponable capital expenditure, particularly in the near future, if temporary congestion is to be avoided; and there are other suggestions which could be, and have been, made. But over a period of five years there should be no difficulty in finding the resources required. The sinking funds of public boards and local authorities in respect of past expenditure, the huge repayments which the building societies are now collecting as the new houses of recent years are cleared of indebtedness by their owners, the steady growth of deposits in the Post Office and trustee savings banks in times of good employment, the large sums which industry will be able to put to reserves out of its profits—these alone should amount to something like £400,000,000, not in five years, but in one year. We must not estimate investible funds in a period of such large expenditures as are now contemplated on the basis of what they were in the years of depression.

Possibility of avoiding inflation

Thus it lies within the power of the Chancellor to get his money without producing conditions of inflation. But there remains the further question, what will he have to pay for it? This, to my mind, is entirely a matter of management and how the task is handled. If the Chancellor, weighed down by a sense of guilt, feels that for the sin of borrowing he must chastise himself (and us) by borrowing dear, markets will respond accordingly. But he will not find that this will make it any easier to borrow. On the contrary; it is much easier to borrow on a rising than on a falling market. The calls to be made on the gilt-edged market are a reason for encouraging the supporters of that market. And this, with their past experience to guide them, is what I should expect the Treasury to do.

In considering the terms on which new loans can be issued, it is interesting to compare the techniques of the British and the American Treasuries. In our own case by far the greater part of the debt (apart from Treasury bills) has no fixed date of repayment within the next 25 years—in round numbers £5,000,000,000 is long-dated in this sense and only about £1,000,000,000 of intermediate date. Moreover, nearly half of the securities of intermediate date stand above par, and are, therefore, inconvenient holdings to many investors for tax or other reasons. In the United States, on the other hand, practically the whole of the debt is repayable within 25 years; indeed, there is nothing

228

beyond 30 years. And within the next 25 years there are notes or bonds falling due for repayment in almost every year. Thus every taste is suited, the rate of interest rising slowly as the date of maturity becomes later; for example, the tax-free rates are about ¼ per cent for one year, 1 per cent for two years, 1¼ per cent for four years, 1¾ per cent for six years, 2 per cent for 10 years, rising to 2½ per cent for 15 years.

These rates do not greatly differ from the net redemption yields on British Government securities for comparable periods; but the arrangement of the maturities allows the American Treasury to borrow at a materially lower average rate. It is to be remembered that many holders of gilt-edged securities are primarily interested in security of capital; and whilst there are others who are attracted by security of income over a long period, it is unlikely that these latter are five times as numerous as the former. It is, therefore, expensive for the Treasury to keep the long-dated market in relative over-supply. They should profit from the anxieties of the public and save interest by supplying them with the potential liquidity which they demand.

Present interest rates not exceptionally low

In any case it is a popular error to suppose that the rate of interest today is exceptionally low. During the half-century preceding the War the average yield on Consols was approximately 3 per cent. Today the yield on War Loan is almost 3½ per cent. There was not a single five-year period between 1837 and 1914 when the average yield on long-term gilt-edged securities was as high as it is today. Yet our capital wealth per head is now half as great again as it was during much of that period; and in those years we were providing for a rapidly increasing population and were investing largely abroad. Even with the Treasury's requirements what we now know them to be I see no justification in the years to come for a long-term rate of interest higher than 3 per cent; and, indeed, it should be lower.

Nevertheless, the board of a life office must keep themselves prepared for disappointment and be more interested in what may be than in what should be. We have, therefore, preferred to assume that the end of 1936 was a particularly favourable date for our valuation. If two years hence our hopes have been fulfilled and our fears allayed, all the better.

The Society's new building

The most important domestic event of the year has been, of course, our entry into possession of our fine new building, after having been deprived of the use of our old site for 18 months. The new premises make much better use of this important position. They incorporate modern principles of planning and offer our staff a greatly increased standard of comfort. The cost has, for various reasons, substantially exceeded our early estimates, but we are carrying the building in our books at what we are advised is a moderate and conservative figure. Any members present who care to take this opportunity of inspecting the building after this meeting will be very welcome. I should like to mention in this connexion the very interesting booklet, written by Mr Recknell, on the history of the site and of our immediate surroundings during past centuries. Since we have occupied it ourselves for the better part of a century, we have been interested in tracing our predecessors. A copy of the book is available to any policyholder here present who would care to have one.[3]

We have experienced a great personal loss within the last few days through the death of Mr Charles Burchell, our deputy chairman until 1935, and a servant of the Society as solicitor and as director for 47 years. He was very much beloved by his colleagues, and his death severs a link between his family and the board which had existed since 1834.

I move the adoption of the report and accounts.

---

[3] For Keynes's preface to this book, see below p. 239.

Speech to the Annual Meeting of the National Mutual, 20 February 1938

Gentlemen,

It is pleasant to be able to record that during this past year every factor connected with the assurance business of the Society has been favourable, and we have again produced trading profits more than sufficient to provide the cost of the normal bonuses. For the first time in our history the net new life assurance business of the year has exceeded £1,000,000, and at £1,037,771 shows a substantial increase over that of 1936. This follows upon increases in each year since 1932. Moreover, if, as is preferable, we apply the more instructive test of the increase in the yearly premium income, this increase also constitutes a record in 1937. In reporting this increase of business we are glad to acknowledge the greater measure of support which the insurance broking community is now giving us, partly, no doubt, because of the Society's high bonus record, but also, I think, as a result of our strict attitude in regard to the payment of agent's commission.

Diminution of expense ratio

The amount absorbed by expenses and commissions showed less than the normal increase despite the larger volume of new business and the additional cost of maintaining our fine new head office premises, with the result that we are able to report a diminution in the ratio which the expenses bear to the premium income—from 14·6 per cent to 14·1 per cent. The amount paid in respect of policies surrendered has declined from £49,170 in 1936 to £42,894 in 1937, but the profit from this source was for various reasons greater last year than in 1936. We do our best to persuade those of our policyholders contemplating this course to adopt other steps than the irrevocable one of surrendering their policies. It is therefore of interest to mention that the sums assured on policies surrendered in 1937 amount to no more than 1·1 per cent of the total business in force.

Interest earnings

Calculated as a percentage on the total funds, excluding reversions, the net interest earnings last year were £3 17s. 1s. per cent, compared with £3 16s. 4d. per cent in 1936, in spite of the rise in income tax from 4s. 9d. to 5s. which, other things being equal, might have been expected to reduce the rate earned by rather more than 1s. I may mention, in continuation of the figures which I have given on many previous occasions, that over the past 17 years the combined net earnings from interest and capital profits or losses have averaged 6·4 per cent, free of income tax. I may add as an indication of the profits we earn from interest that the net interest earnings calculated on the actuarial liabilities come out at £4 5s. 6d. per cent. This margin between the rate earned on the liabilities and the rate assumed to be earned is a substantial one.

The changes in the disposition of our assets during the year are clearly shown in the balance sheet. Holdings of debentures show rather more than a normal increase, while those of preference and ordinary stocks show substantial reductions, partly because of depreciation but also because of the board's policy of reducing the Society's stake in British industry at a time when prices seemed high. The present greatly diminished holdings of ordinary stocks contain a relatively small stake in British industrial shares, and include considerable holdings of shares which though ordinary stocks in name are largely semi-fixed-interest in character, such as insurance shares, the shares of gas, water, and electrical undertakings. If the figures be examined it will be seen that the whole of the excess of income over outgo arising during the year has been invested in non-stock exchange securities such as mortgages, loans on public rates, and carefully selected real estate. This is in accordance with the board's policy of recent years of increasing the proportion of our assets in this class of investment.

Valuation of investments

In regard to the valuation of investments, I am afraid that this has been a dismal year for all institutional investors and we have not escaped the common fate. The year has been remarkable for the way in which practically every class of investment has been substantially affected in the downward direction. In our case, however, we have had the advantage of the large book and realised profits on investments recently earned and held in reserve. This year's decline has lopped off less than half of the previous precarious rise and leaves us with a large surplus in reserves and carry-forward. More precisely the loss on valuation over the year amounts to about $8\frac{1}{2}$ per cent of our assets. This still leaves intact an appreciation of about 10 per cent from the previous four years. How hard the lot has been even of the most cautious investor becomes evident when we calculate that if at the beginning of 1935 we had put all our assets into War Loan we should have lost 6 per cent, and old Consols actually depreciated by nearly 20 per cent, while during the same period the Actuaries' Index of industrial debentures has fallen by 4 per cent and their index of industrial preference shares has also fallen by 4 per cent. Nevertheless, our own depreciation over this period is only 1·73 per cent.

Financing of gold purchases

I have mentioned that the year has been remarkable for the similarity of the movement in the gilt-edged and the other markets. The fall in the gilt-edged market was particularly noticeable in the first three quarters of last year and has been commonly attributed to the Government's rearmament programme taken together with the increased demand for trade advances. I am disposed, however, to explain the decline mainly by reference to another factor which has been almost wholly overlooked.

This unsuspected factor is the particular technique by which last year the gold purchases of the Exchange Equalisation Fund

233

were being financed. Attention has been called to this in the January Bulletin of the London and Cambridge Economic Service, and I owe the following figures to Mr F. W. Paish, the Secretary of the Service, who has made a special study of the workings of the Equalisation Fund. In these days of large gold movements the policy of the Bank of England is indeed of small account in its effect on credit and liquidity compared with the policy of the Equalisation Fund, about which we know nothing until some months afterwards. The gist of the matter is as follows:—In the first nine months of 1937 the Equalisation Fund purchased about £190,000,000 of gold. How was this paid for? The sale of Treasury bills to the market might be regarded as the 'normal' method. But that course was not adopted on this occasion. Indeed the bills held by the market actually fell by about £36,000,000 in the first nine months of last year, a repayment which can be accounted for by the Exchequer's revenue surplus, not unusual at that time of year but earned on this occasion after meeting the whole of the rearmament expenditure of the period. Actually this surplus amounted to about £48,000,000, leaving in hand a sum of about £12,000,000 beyond what was employed in withdrawing Treasury bills.

Method of payment

How, then, was the gold paid for? It is not easy to draw up an accurate balance sheet, but, ignoring contra items within the Treasury accounts, the answer, roughly speaking, appears to be as follows:—£14,000,000 was raised by the re-sale of gold to the Bank of England; receipts on long-term capital account from the $2\frac{3}{4}$ per cent Funding Loan and National Defence Bonds exceeded capital repayments, etc., by about £104,000,000; there was a revenue surplus as above of £12,000,000 after repaying £36,000,000 Treasury bills previously held by the market; and the balance of about £60,000,000 would appear to have been provided out of the capital resources in the hands of various Government Departments, such as the Health Insurance Fund, the Unemployment Fund, etc., which took over Treasury bills from the Equalisation Fund, paying for them either out of current accruals or by the sale of longer dated securities to the market.

Thus, one way and another, over and above the £36,000,000 Treasury bills repaid, about £176,000,000 of liquid resources was withdrawn from previous domestic holders and placed at the disposal of the foreigners who were bringing to London their 'hot' money in the shape of gold. Now, in so far as the foreign holders of the 'hot' money were prepared to invest it in National Defence Bonds and other securities purchased on the London Stock Exchange, well and good—the circle was complete. The Treasury would have exchanged the National Defence Bonds for the gold, and the domestic credit situation would have been left unchanged. But it is surely improbable that this was the case.

Liquid 'hot' money

Much of the 'hot' money will have been kept liquid in the shape of bank deposits, Treasury bills, and the like. Now the *total* supply of liquid assets in the shape of bank deposits and Treasury bills held by the market was not increased. Thus the amount of liquid assets acquired by foreigners out of the proceeds of the £190,000,000 in gold which they sold to the Equalisation Fund were almost wholly at the expense of the liquid assets previously held by the domestic market. It would seem reasonable to put the amount by which domestically held liquid assets have been reduced at between £100,000,000 and £150,000,000 at least. Thus the gilt-edged and other markets had to fall sufficiently to induce domestic holders, who had previously preferred to keep liquid, to part with this amount of liquid resources in exchange for less liquid assets. The sums involved were so large that it is a matter for surprise that gilt-edged prices did not fall more. This must have been by far the most important factor in the credit market in the course of the year. To the Treasury it may have merely seemed a highly convenient process of getting the resources of the Government Departments more liquid. The hidden transactions of the Equalisation Fund served to obscure the fact that it was entirely at the expense of the supply of domestic credit; but, in conjunction with the policy of borrowing well before the money was wanted so that resources were being hoarded meanwhile, it produced the inevitable and observed results on the gilt-edged market.

Unwanted gold

I suggest that these facts offer considerable food for thought. The object of the Equalisation Fund should be to 'sterilise' an influx of unwanted gold, so as to avoid the inflationary effect of a credit increase up to as much as 10 times the amount of the gold, which might result if the proceeds of the gold were allowed, as in the pre-war system, to be added to the deposits of the Bank of England. It is clearly advisable in general that the liquid resources in the market should not be raised by a multiple of a large precarious gold influx. But if they are not raised at all, then assuming that the vendors of the gold desire to hold a proportion of the proceeds in a liquid form, the influx of the gold must have a strongly deflationary effect on the domestic credit situation; whilst if the same methods are used when the gold flows out again, the loss of the gold will be the signal for the inflation of domestic credit. This is, indeed, a topsy-turvy business; exactly the opposite of what happened with the pre-war gold standard. If the managers of the Equalisation Fund desire the ebb and flow of 'hot' money to have the least possible effect on domestic credit, they must arrange for the market supply of liquid resources to be increased to the extent of the increased demand from the holders of the 'hot' money—in the shape partly of bank deposits, partly of Treasury bills, in the appropriate proportions. As it is, they have largely depleted the liquid resources of the domestic market at a time when the international situation and the recession in America were disposing the market to become more, rather than less, liquid. And the result is that institutional and other investors, no matter what their policy, have had a dismal, and indeed an insoluble, task to keep their assets intact.

Events since September

What has happened in the five months since September 30, 1937, we have not as yet the data by which to tell. It may be that the recent improvement in the gilt-edged market is due to a cessation, if not a reversal, of the above forces. I do not know. The policy of our financial authorities is not, I am afraid, meant to be understood; and perhaps I should apologise for the impiety of this attempt. But I am convinced that there are several aspects of the flux and reflux of 'hot' money, and the perplexing problem of how best to handle it, which deserve a fuller examination than they have yet received. There is, for example, the question of what rate of interest it is advisable for the banks to allow on foreign deposits, to which Lord Wardington rightly directed attention. We need to segregate these funds from the domestic credit system, so far as is practicable, allowing them neither to flood, nor to steal from, the appropriate level of liquid resources in the hands of domestic holders.

What of the future? In spite of the unemployment figures and the depression on the Stock Exchange, I am prepared, for my part, to accept the repeated assurances of the Government and the bankers that no significant further recession is discernible in the very near future. Indeed, it would be disturbing if it were otherwise during a period before rearmament expenditure has reached its peak and after a period during which we have had no benefit from Government loan expenditure, and have, on the contrary, been forced, as I have just shown, to part with a large volume of liquid resources to the holders of foreign refugee funds. The fact that Stock Exchange prices for industrial securities seem to imply complete disbelief in the official forecasts does not mean that these prices are based on superior information.

The speculative markets

Speculative markets are closely linked and cannot escape American and European influences. Moreover, they are governed by doubt rather than by conviction, by fear more than by forecast, by memories of last time and not by foreknowledge of next time. The level of stock exchange prices does not mean that investors *know*, it means that they do *not* know. Faced with the perplexities and uncertainties of the modern world, market values will fluctuate much more widely than will seem reasonable in the light of after-events; and one would hope that in such circumstances insurance offices will show a good example of steadiness.

The notion of us all selling out to the other fellow in good time is not, of course, a practicable policy for the community as a whole; yet the attempt to do so may deflect prices substantially from a reasonable estimation of their intrinsic value, and become a serious impediment to constructive investment. Those of us who have helped to popularise talk about the trade cycle must bear part of the blame for this. I sympathise with the authorities in their appeal to the business community not to become unduly slump-conscious. What we need is that the roles should be reversed, and that they should become more slump-conscious. We could sleep more easily in our beds if we felt that they were sleeping less easily in theirs.

Appeal to Government

For the difficulty of avoiding disastrous depression in the modern world can scarcely be exaggerated. It will need all our knowledge, all our preparedness, all our precaution, all our skill, all our technical accomplishment, and all our endowment of public spirit. I appeal to the Government in fervour of heart to lose no opportunity of adding to our knowledge of the essential facts and figures which alone can make the working of the economic system intelligible and distinguish true theories from false by the test of results. A great deal is at stake. We are engaged in defending the freedom of economic life in circumstances which are far from favourable. We have to show that a free system can be made to work. To favour what is known as planning and management does not mean a falling away from the moral principles of liberty which could formerly be embodied in a simpler system. On the contrary, we have learnt that freedom of economic life is more bound up than we previously knew with the deeper freedoms—freedom of person, of thought, and of faith.

This is the last of Keynes's speeches to the Society, since he resigned late in 1938 (see p. 47). However, there remains one further short contribution from Keynes as Chairman.

In 1936 the National Mutual published a history of the site of its offices, drawing on information obtained in part during the rebuilding of 1935-6. Keynes provided a short foreword.

From King Street, Cheapside *by G. H. Recknell (1936)*

FOREWORD

There is no kind of business for which a mere decade means so little as for life assurance. Life assurance societies are no longer born and seldom die. Their contracts are for the term of human life. They are themselves mostly centenarians or there-abouts, and wish the same for their policyholders. They are trees of which the girth puts on one more ring a year with the sap of compound interest; and do not lightly change their address, once they have struck root.

It is appropriate, therefore, that they and their actuaries should think in terms of centuries and even of millenniums; and in this delightful essay Mr Recknell examines the soil into which we have now driven our second basement, to determine whether, on its records, it seems likely to sustain us for many bonus years to come. Already, it seems, we have sat here longer than any previous tenant since Julius Caesar; and now, in 1936, we have built ourselves a fine stone *le Cage*, from the corner windows of which we can survey in perspective for a few centuries yet the mighty edifices of the Bank of England and its attendant Five.

J. M. KEYNES
(*Chairman*)

In May 1924 *The Nation* published an Insurance Supplement. Keynes provided one signed article on investment policy and one unsigned one on bonuses.

From The Nation and Athenæum, *17 May 1924*

INVESTMENT POLICY FOR INSURANCE COMPANIES

The question of investment policy for life insurance companies has been much under discussion in the last year or two. The issues which have been raised are the result, not so much of new ideas, as of new facts. The problem of wise investment, as it has presented itself since the War, is largely a new one, and the life insurance world has been slowly feeling its way to new principles suited to the new conditions.

What was the pre-war field of investment? Leaving aside real property and reversions, advances on policies, and the like, the chief categories were (1) mortgages, (2) a limited selection of trustee securities, of which Consols was the main British Government stock, (3) American dollar securities, and (4) the better-class bonds of certain foreign governments and railways. If companies were to keep up their average interest earnings to a satisfactory level, compatibly with not placing too much capital outside the first two classes mentioned above, there was not a very wide scope for varying the proportions invested in the different classes; and within each class there was not much scope for gaining advantage from moving from one security to another. Some companies, however, were finding it difficult to keep up a satisfactory interest yield, which sometimes induced them to put a proportion of their resources into second-class bonds of various kinds—investments which on the average have not turned out well.

During the War there was, of course, a big movement, both on public and private grounds, into the various new types of British Government securities which were being issued. Many companies disposed of almost the whole of their dollar securities. Thus the end of the War found many companies with a far greater proportion of British Government securities in their hands than they had ever dreamt of holding in the past.

Not only is there now a much wider range of choice within the field of British trustee securities than there was before, but the comparative suitability of the pre-war classes of investment has greatly changed. The margin of yield between first-class mortgages and British Government securities has narrowed. The yield on American bonds no longer bears its old relation of superiority to the yield on sterling securities, apart from which doubts about the future course of exchange introduce a new and difficult factor. All our old ideas about the security of foreign government bonds have been entirely upset, and the element of political risk must now be given far greater weight than formerly. Even some British trustee stocks need a watchful eye, and doubts can reasonably be felt which before the war would have seemed unnecessary. Few investors, for example, care to hold a heavy amount of India stocks, and, as we have seen lately, circumstances can arise in which even colonial stocks do not seem perfectly safe.

Thus the question of security itself cannot be settled by the old rules of thumb which used to be deemed sufficient. The wise investor must now doubt all things, and constantly revise his ideas in accordance with changing events in the political world.

But not only do new risks require a more watchful eye. The range of choice within a given class of security gives new opportunities for obtaining an advantage through judicious transferences in accordance with the fluctuations which occur from time to time in relative prices. Above all, the choice between long-

and short-dated British Government securities inevitably raises a problem of a constantly varying aspect. I suppose that in old days the choice between mortgages and Consols had to be determined on much the same principles as the choice today between long- and short-dated securities. Essentially it is an eternal problem. But the range of choice actually available for investment, the shortest and longest dated securities and those of almost every intermediate date being available in large quantities, makes it practicable to act promptly on any considered opinion which may be reached.

Most companies compromise to a certain extent and never back any opinion, however plausible and well-founded it may seem, up to the full extent. Nevertheless, it is very unlikely that the same proportionate division of assets between long and short dated securities can always be right. It is bound to change in accordance with the fluctuations of the business world. Insurance companies have a special opportunity to take advantage of these fluctuations, because it seldom happens that they are under any necessity to diminish their aggregate holdings. An industrial firm which holds a portion of its liquid resources in gilt-edged securities, in order to enable it to finance its affairs in particularly brisk times, is inevitably a seller from time to time. In the same way banks are bound to vary the volume of their gilt-edged investments to balance corresponding variations in the opposite direction in the amount of their advances to their customers. When insurance companies sell, it is always to buy something else instead, which fact puts them in an extremely strong position for benefiting from the fluctuating demands of the rest of the market.

Thus it comes about that the management of an insurance company is almost inevitably driven, whether it likes it or not, into what has been termed lately 'an active investment policy'; which, after all, is merely another name for being alive to the fact that circumstances change. Unfortunately, it is not possible to make oneself permanently secure by any policy of inaction whatever. The idea which some people seem to entertain that an active policy involves taking more risks than an inactive policy is exactly the opposite of the truth. The inactive investor who takes up an obstinate attitude about his holdings and refuses to change his opinion merely because facts and circumstances have changed is the one who in the long run comes to grievous loss. Particularly in these days, no one is so wise that he can foresee the future far ahead. Anyone who obstinately takes up the view that over the next twenty years the rate of interest is bound to fall, or is bound to rise, is going beyond the evidence. If he is to be wisely guided he must take a shorter view and be prepared constantly to change it as the tide of events ebbs and flows.

It is equally false to believe that one form of investment involves taking a view and that another one does not. Every investment means committing oneself to one particular side of the market. The holder of long-dated securities lays himself open to losses, which may be very large, through the depreciation of his capital; whilst the holder of short-dated securities equally lays himself open to earn a lower rate of interest than that on which he has calculated. No one can get both security of capital and security of income; yet it is a great mistake to think that an insurance company, which depends on both, can neglect either. It was the neglect of these principles in the period which elapsed between the era of cheap money in 1896 and 1897 and the beginning of the Great War, which involved the companies in the serious capital losses which were then shown both in their annual accounts and in their valuation results. Capital depreciation is the great enemy of life assurance, and an 'active' investment policy has for its object the avoidance of capital loss at least as much as the making of capital profits.

The ideal policy for an insurance company is to put itself, so far as it can, into a situation where it is earning a respectable rate of interest on its funds, while securing at the same time that its risk of really serious depreciation in capital value is at a minimum. This, of course, is obvious. But it must be equally obvious that there is no golden rule for this, no invariable method. And this itself is the reason why constant vigilance, constant revision of preconceived ideas, constant reaction to changes in the external situation, in short, 'an active investment policy', seems to some of us an essential condition, and at the same time the most difficult and important branch, of the sound management of the great insurance societies and corporations which now administer so considerable a proportion of the national savings.

From The Nation and Athenæum, *17 May 1924*

THE MEANING OF 'BONUS'

There is hardly anything which it is more important for the ordinary man who is contemplating life assurance to understand than the meaning of the mysterious word 'Bonus', which figures so largely in all accounts of the subject. Yet even the insurance world itself might be astonished if it were to discover to how few members of the public this word conveys any definite idea whatever. Perhaps we may help a little to clear away the obscurity.

As has been pointed out in the preceding article, the rates of premium quoted by insurance companies for whole-life and endowment-assurance policies are very much on the safe side. This must be so, since the policies cover a long period of time, during which fundamental conditions may change materially. The insurance societies must be strong enough to meet even very improbable changes of circumstances. On the other hand, if matters go reasonably well the societies, or at any rate the non-mutual ones, would obviously make an altogether undue profit at the expense of their policyholders, if they were to retain the whole of the surplus income actually earned as compared with the very conservative estimate upon which they had reckoned in fixing the premiums. The system of bonus has been devised as a means of giving back to the with-profit policyholders either the whole of this surplus or the greater part of it, subject to a reasonable carry-forward.

In short, a with-profit policyholder who takes out a policy for £1,000 is in all probability insuring himself for a somewhat larger sum. The bargain which the insurance society makes with him is made up of two parts: a promise to pay him £1,000 on the maturity of the policy, together with a further undefined sum dependent upon the society's success during his period of membership of it.

There are, of course, many ways in which an insurance society could give its members the benefit of the surplus which it earns; for instance, by paying it out in cash, or by diminishing the annual premium payable. But after many years of experiment in different directions there is now a pretty general consensus in favour of what is called the 'reversionary' bonus system, by which additions are made from time to time to the sum assured, and are payable with it.

The declaration of a reversionary bonus at the rate of 1 per cent per annum means that the amount of the ultimate policy payable to the policyholder on maturity is increased by 1 per cent for each year in respect of which such a bonus is declared. For example, if a policyholder has taken out a policy for £1,000 and a bonus of 20s. per cent per annum is declared one year later, that means that without his having to pay any increased premiums the sum for which he is insured has been increased by 1 per cent, namely, from £1,000 to £1,010. He does not receive any immediate cash down or any reduction of premiums, but the amount of his policy is increased in the way described.

Simple versus compound bonus

There is one further complexity: some societies declare what is called a simple bonus, others a compound bonus. A simple bonus of 20s. per cent per annum means that the original sum insured, namely, £1,000 in the example given above, is increased by 1 per cent. A compound bonus of 20s. per cent means that not only the original amount of the policy, but that original amount together with the sum by which previous bonuses have increased it, is augmented by 1 per cent. Thus, if the policy was originally for £1,000, and has accumulated £100 of bonus in the course of time, then a simple bonus of 20s. per cent means that £10 is added to the total of the policy; whereas a compound bonus of 20s. per cent means that £11, namely, 1 per cent of £1,100, is added.

If bonuses are declared annually instead of triennially or quinquennially, then the benefit of the compound bonus as compared with the simple bonus is still more marked, since the sums are compounded annually instead of at intervals of three or five years.

The net result of the various systems can be illustrated as follows:—

A policy of £1,000 on which a simple bonus of 40s. per cent is declared annually for thirty years increases to £1,600 at the end of the period; if a compound bonus at the same rate is declared quinquennially, the total comes to £1,772; if a similar compound bonus is declared annually, the final result comes to £1,811.

Most societies, whilst encouraging their policyholders to take the benefit due to them in the form of reversionary bonuses as above, nevertheless give them the option of taking it immediately in cash or in reduction of premiums.

Keynes also managed a few reviews of financial studies or handbooks for *The Nation*, all but the first unsigned.

From the Nation and Athenæum, *2 May 1925*

AN AMERICAN STUDY OF SHARES VERSUS BONDS
AS PERMANENT INVESTMENTS*

The author of this interesting little book set out on his inquiry
with the idea that, whilst it was to be expected that an investor
in common stocks would do better than an investor in bonds
during a period of rising prices, yet the opposite would probably
be true during a period of falling prices. To test this he embarked
on a series of investigations to trace the history of the two classes
of investments over different periods between 1866 and 1922,
selecting his sample lists of securities by various objective tests,
such as those which were most actively dealt in at the date of
investment;—thus keeping to the best-known companies, in
which an intelligent investor would have been most likely to
invest at the dates in question, and avoiding any bias of the kind
sometimes known in this country as 'jobbing backwards', that is
to say, the selection of investments in the light of subsequent
events.

The results are striking. Mr Smith finds in almost every case
(in ten tests out of eleven), not only when prices were rising, but
also when they were falling, that common stocks have turned out
best in the long run, indeed, markedly so; whilst in the odd case
there was not much to choose between the two. Having got so far,
he applied a more rigorous criterion. Were the superior average
results obtained at the cost of an inconvenient irregularity of
income as between one year and another? On the contrary, he
found that, even in the worst years, his index of ordinary shares
gave, almost invariably, a better yield than his index of standard
bonds.

This actual experience in the United States over the past fifty
years affords *prima facie* evidence that the prejudice of investors
and investing institutions in favour of bonds as being 'safe' and

---

* *Common Stocks as Long-Term Investments.* By Edgar Lawrence Smith. Pp. ix+129.
(New York and London, Macmillan), 1925.

against common stocks as having, even the best of them, a 'speculative' flavour, has led to a relative over-valuation of bonds and under-valuation of common stocks.

It is dangerous, however, to apply to the future inductive arguments based on past experience, unless one can distinguish the broad reasons why past experience was what it was. Otherwise there is a danger of expecting results in the future which could only follow from the special conditions which have existed in the United States during the past fifty years. Mr Smith claims that the general causes for the relative advantages of common stocks are discoverable, and that they are of a kind as likely to operate in the immediate future as in the immediate past. I may summarise these causes, expressing some of them in my own way and some of them in his, as follows:—

(1) An investment in common stocks is an investment in real values. An investment in bonds is an investment in money values. Obviously there are advantages in the former, if the long-period trend of the value of money in terms of goods is downwards; and also contrariwise. Nevertheless, there is a presumption in favour of real values over money values: firstly, because the value of money can, in certain circumstances, fall indefinitely, as has happened in Europe since the War (and in the light of past history this is an appreciable risk against which it is worthwhile to be safeguarded), whereas a corresponding rise is out of the question; secondly, because, quite apart from catastrophes, the classes in the community who benefit from a falling value of money are stronger than those who benefit from a rising value,— 'All lenders of money, particularly bondholders, favour an appreciating currency. No other class is always actively in favour of an appreciating currency. In theory they all believe in sound or stable currency, but each, in his efforts to widen the margin of profit that he makes in relation to profits in other lines, at times subscribes to activities which tend towards depreciation' (p. 88).

(2) Even in the most carefully selected list of bonds, one or other of them will occasionally go wrong. But whilst the possibility of default cannot be ruled out, no bond ever pays *more* than the stipulated rate of interest. Thus there can be no exceptional successes to average out with exceptional failures. The purchaser of a selection of common stocks can afford to make an occasional mistake; the purchaser of bonds cannot. In other words, the actual average return from bonds, after allowing for unavoidable losses, is always somewhat less than the apparent average rate of interest at the date of investment.

(3) The 'human factor' in the management of the companies concerned favours the shares. 'The management of every company is on the side of the common stock and opposed to the interests of the bondholders. The management does not want the bondholders to get more benefit from the operation of the company than is absolutely necessary to make it possible for the company to sell more bonds if such additional sale of bonds can be made to show a profit to the stockholders' (p. 85). In particular, the management will avail themselves of their rights to repay bonds at dates most advantageous to the shareholders and most disadvantageous to the bondholders.

(4) 'In buying bonds, the investor agrees that the issuing companies may retain all earnings over and above the income return which he has agreed to accept. He establishes no reserves of his own, and relinquishes all title to the reserves that are established for him. Such reserves, while protecting his income, accrue to the benefit of the stockholders of the companies whose bonds he holds. The purchaser of a bond is an investor, but he exercises none of the functions of investment management with regard to his invested funds. He pays the corporation which issues the bonds a substantial sum for exercising this function for him, and a survey of the prices at which bonds in different industries sell discloses the fact that he pays on the average more for this service in those industries whose stabilised earnings call

for the least responsibility on the part of the issuing companies' (pp. 114, 115).

(5) I have kept until last what is perhaps Mr Smith's most important, and is certainly his most novel, point. Well-managed industrial companies do not, as a rule, distribute to the shareholders the whole of their earned profits. In good years, if not in all years, they retain a part of their profits and put them back into the business. Thus *there is an element of compound interest* operating in favour of a sound industrial investment. Over a period of years, the real value of the property of a sound industrial is increasing at compound interest, quite apart from the dividends paid out to the shareholders. Thus whilst an index of bonds yields, as we have seen, *less* in the long run than its initial apparent rate of interest, an index of shares yields *more* in the long run than its initial apparent rate of interest. So far, therefore, from the higher apparent rate of interest on shares, as compared with that on bonds, being required to compensate the greater risk of loss, the reverse is true. Shares work out better than bonds by more than the difference between the apparent rates of interest upon each.

Mr Smith has made an estimate of what this element of compound interest has amounted to upon the average. He finds that over a long period the average rise in market value of typical common stocks is approximately equal to the value which would have accumulated on the assumption that the concerns set aside annually out of current profits a sum equal to $2\frac{1}{2}$ per cent of their capital, and retained these sums to fructify in the business. This figure is not inconsistent with what one knows as to the actual practice of conservative business. But the effect of this accumulation over a period of years is, like all compound interest effects, of startling magnitude. It is sufficient to recoup after a moderate interval even those investors in common stocks who were so imprudent or so unfortunate as to make their initial investment at the top of a boom.

Mr Smith applies one final test of comparative advantage

which is the most overwhelming of all. He assumes that the ultra-prudent investor forms an investment reserve out of the surplus income of common stocks, as compared with that of an equal initial investment in bonds, regarding as income only that amount which he would have received from bonds and reinvesting the balance in additional shares. In this case the capital appreciation of his holding over a period of about twenty years varies from 104 per cent in the least favourable case to 355 per cent in the most favourable case—a calculation which certainly provides a big margin against the unexpected.

In working out his principles of investment, Mr Smith has not, particularly, in mind such institutions as insurance companies. Indeed, rather the contrary. He points out (p. 11) that, since the liabilities of an insurance company are fixed in terms of money, its criteria for safe investment must be somewhat different from those of other investors, and in particular that such a company has nothing to fear from the depreciation of money,—'The purchasing power of future dollars is of no concern to it. If dollars have shrunk in value, the beneficiary under its policies absorbs the shrinkage, the company does not.' This may have an important application to proprietary companies where the policyholders are not interested in profits. But its application to mutual life offices, for example, is, I think, very limited. In the case of these offices the object of the management must be to invest the funds to the best advantage of the members, subject to special care as to the absolute safety of the amount of the guaranteed policy. It would be poor consolation to the holder of a mutual with-profits policy, expressed in terms of francs, to know that the board have limited their attention to ensuring that he should receive at the maturity of his policy its full value in francs as stipulated before the War. If it is true that debentures are relatively over-valued, this is a conclusion of the highest interest and importance to those responsible for the investment of insurance funds.

It is unlucky for us in this country that Mr Smith's inquiry relates exclusively to American investments. It would be of great interest to know the results of a similar investigation applied to British investments. I have the impression that it might not turn out quite so favourably to ordinary shares, partly because our businesses have, for obvious reasons, not gone ahead at quite the same pace, and partly because American industrial concerns may have been rather more conservative than ours in the division of profits. I do not feel confident that the compound interest element would work out so high as $2\frac{1}{2}$ per cent per annum in the case of British ordinary shares. In any case, it is much to be hoped that the investigation will be made. It is not a particularly easy one to carry out. There is the initial difficulty of selecting a suitable index; and there is the recurrent difficulty of valuing bonus issues and other valuable 'rights', which are given to shareholders from time to time. Mr Smith puts emphasis on the importance of attending carefully to the latter, and points out that most charts of the values of ordinary shares over a long period are seriously vitiated on account of their compilers' slackness about this. But these difficulties are not insuperable, and the work would be of high educational value to anyone who aspires to understand ordinary shares. Will not the investment department of one of our great insurance companies put the work in hand? It is a task well adapted to the training and mentality of actuaries, and not less important, I fancy, to the future of the insurance industry than the further improvement of life tables.

From The Nation and Athenæum, *29 May 1926*

The Stock Exchange Official Intelligence for 1926. (London, Spottiswoode) 1926.

This splendid work of reference, produced under the sanction of the Committee of the Stock Exchange, has grown so fat that subscribers can now have it, if they like, in three volumes (for 12s. 6d. extra). The 450 new companies added this year would have brought it beyond 2,000 quarto pages, which must be nearly the maximum which can be contained within two covers, if the supplementary index of defunct companies, &c., had not been pushed out. This index can now be obtained separately for 2s. 6d. Room has been found, however, for the new Trustee Act as well as the usual statistical matter. Serious investors will spend their money well to have this book at hand, even if they cannot afford to renew it more often than every three or four years.

From The Nation and Athenæum, *19 April 1930*

The Stock Exchange Official Intelligence for 1930. (London, Spottiswoode) 1930.

This indispensable work of reference has succeeded in bringing itself up to date without becoming increasingly unwieldy. There is, however, one piece of additional information the inclusion of which would add to its value, namely, the Stock Exchange Rules as to the minimum commissions chargeable to clients. At present there is no source from which this information can be readily obtained; yet it is a matter on which members of the public may wish to reassure themselves without suggesting a discontent which they may not feel by applying to their brokers themselves. *The Stock Exchange Official Intelligence* generally aims at including each year a chapter on some matter of special interest. This year the matters dealt with relate to the recent reforms of local government and local taxation. The changes in methods of assessment effected by the Rating and Valuation Acts, 1925–1928, the Derating Act, and the Local Government Act of 1929 have between them effected a far-reaching reform in the principles and practice of local taxation. A full summary of the substance of the principal changes in law and practice adds to the usefulness of the volume.

From The Nation and Athenæum, *25 October 1930*

GLASGOW, GEORGE *The English Investment Trust Companies.* (London, Eyre & Spottiswoode) 1930.

This is a work of reference dealing with the *English* investment trust companies, though it is perhaps a pity that the title has been interpreted literally, so that the Scottish companies, which we usually think of as most characteristic of the investment trust, are excluded. The general introduction does not amount to much, and does not attempt any serious criticism of the way in which investment trusts have been managed. The bulk of the book is taken up by statistical tables, analysing the dividend record, etc., so far as it has been published, of seventy-six companies. It would have added a good deal to the interest of the book if there had been rather more material about the detailed policy of the companies. For example, the distribution of the investments of those which publish their lists might have been analysed, not only at the present time, but also at sundry past dates, so as to exhibit the changes of fashion which have passed from time to time over the investment trust world. However, Mr Glasgow has provided a succinct and convenient work of reference within the limits which he has set himself.

Chapter 3

COMMODITIES

Keynes's involvement in commodity markets did not end with his activities as an investor. From 1923 onwards, he contributed a number of articles on such markets to the press[1] and to the London and Cambridge Economic Service. In 1938, and again in 1942, he made specific proposals for the regulation of primary products (*JMK*, vol. XXI, pp. 456–70; vol. XXVII, ch. 3).

Keynes's first publication came in a *Manchester Guardian Commercial* Reconstruction Supplement, on 29 March 1923; we print it below with one correction noted in the issue of 26 April.

From The Manchester Guardian Commercial, *Reconstruction Supplement, 29 March 1923*

SOME ASPECTS OF COMMODITY MARKETS

The annual flow of commodities cultivated or extracted from the soil has a very large value in comparison with the capital resources of the cultivators and extractors. The value of the annual production is large even in comparison with the fixed capital required to raise it; and compared with the floating capital of the producers, available for financing the annual flow from the commencement of production up to the disposal of it to the consumers, it is very large.

This disparity, from which the precise form of the existing structure of finance and credit largely proceeds, has a significant bearing on the train of cause and effect which make the ups and downs of trade. The object of this article is to analyse one or two aspects of this state of affairs, which deserve attention from the practical point of view.

[1] In addition to the articles printed below, see *JMK*, vol. XIX, pp. 273–5, 546–52.

1. *The demand on banking accommodation*

We must make, first of all, the obvious but important distinction between the extracted commodities which come into existence at a more or less even rate throughout the year, as for example metals, and the crops which are harvested at a particular season. The maximum financial facilities required for carrying the former during the interval between production and consumption are obviously much less, in a normal state of trade, than the maximum facilities required for the latter, the value of which just after the harvest season may amount to nearly a year's supply; though this may be modified where the supplies for the international market are grown both in the Northern and in the Southern Hemispheres.

There is also a further distinction affecting the weight of the burden thrown on the financial system by different types of commodities. So far we have been considering stocks in the form of raw materials; but there are also the stocks of the same materials worked up into finished and semi-finished goods. Now a large proportion of some articles is manufactured in standard types and qualities, and made, as it is expressed, 'for stock'— whether manufacturer's stock or merchant's stock or retailer's stock; that is to say the process of manufacture can be set moving quite conveniently before the ultimate consumer of the goods is specifically in sight. Yarn is a good example of a semi-finished article of which this is true, and textiles generally of finished articles of this character. Other commodities cannot be conveniently produced on any considerable scale before the ultimate consumer is in sight, either on account of deterioration through time of which many animal food products are typical; or because of difficulty of storage as, for example, coal and oil; or because they are of the type of goods which are capable of so many minor but important variations that they must, generally speaking, be made 'to order', which is the case with very many finished and semi-finished iron and steel manufactures, including ships.

Thus for one reason or another, in their passage from the first processes of production to the eventual consumer, some commodities are liable to throw a much greater strain than others on the credit and financial system,—this strain being not necessarily proportionate to the value of the aggregate production of the commodities or to their importance in the economic life of the community. If I may venture to generalise without the support of precise data, I should say that an extraordinarily large proportion of that part of the demand for temporary credit, which arises out of the financing of goods, can be ascribed directly or indirectly to textiles and to food crops (including in the latter cereals, sugar and oil-seeds); and an extraordinarily small proportion to coal, transport, iron and steel products and non-ferrous metals, not nearly commensurate with the relative importance of the latter in the national economy.

Let me illustrate these contentions by some figures, selected from cases where I happen to have some data. On July 31st 1921 there were believed to be in the world about 8,700,000 bales of unspun American cotton; two months later the expense of cultivating and harvesting the current crop of 8,400,000 bales was practically complete. Thus allowing for current consumption, there was at that period something like 15,000,000 bales for which someone or other had to find the finance. At that time cotton was worth on the average more than £20 a bale, so that the total sum involved was more than £300,000,000. The value of the cotton produced elsewhere than within the United States means an addition of at least half as much again, to which must be added the value of stocks of yarn and piece goods in the hands of manufacturers, merchants and retailers, and afloat, throughout the world. Altogether in 1921 just after the new crop had been harvested, cotton textiles, not yet in the hands of the consumer, must have required financial resources amounting to something between £600,000,000 and £750,000,000 at least, possibly more, to carry them. If we add to this corresponding sums for wool, flax, hemp, jute and silk, so as to comprehend textiles as a whole, it is clear that an immense sum is involved. It follows that an important fluctuation in the price of these articles, or a big variation in the volume of stocks to be carried, makes an immense difference to the demand on the banks for accommodation. For example three months earlier American cotton was not worth more than £15 a bale, whilst a year earlier on the other hand it had been worth £40. At the present moment the amount of unspun American cotton in the world is less than half the amount assumed in the above calculation, whilst stocks of piece goods are also believed to be reduced. Fluctuations of this order in an item of such magnitude can exercise a decisive effect on the ease or the tightness of credit.

A calculation of the value of the world's stocks of cereals, etc. just after harvest also leads, obviously, to a huge figure. It must not be supposed that a demand for this amount of finance comes into existence suddenly at harvest time;—as the stocks of the previous crop run down, the sums expended on the preparation of the next crop are gradually increasing. Nevertheless a movement in prices or a marked variation in stocks has, here also, a huge reaction on the credit market.

Now for the other side of the story,—the case of the commodities which make small demands on the banks in comparison with their economic importance. At the present time the total stocks of tin, lead and spelter (zinc) in the world in the hands of producers, merchants and consumers and afloat, are not worth £10,000,000 altogether; all the mined, but unmanufactured copper in the world is not worth £25,000,000; the so-called vast stocks of rubber are not worth, even though the price has more than doubled recently, more than from £25,000,000 to £30,000,000. I feel confident that, at the moment when I write this article, all the unused stocks above-ground of copper, tin, lead, spelter, nickel, aluminium, rubber, coal, and pig iron in the world, taken all together, are not worth anywhere near what the stocks of sugar are worth. It would be a near-run thing whether all the ships in the world or the raw cotton available last autumn were worth the more. Would not these statements surprise most persons? Economists and the business world have not, I think, got a clear hold of such quantitative questions in their real proportion.

It follows from these calculations that index numbers of wholesale prices, as usually compiled, may be misleading for some purposes, in particular for measuring the effect of a change in prices on the demand for banking accommodation. In Sauerbeck's index number, for example, tin counts for half as much as all kinds of cotton, and lead for half as much as all kinds of sugar, whereas in each case the effect of a change in the price of commodity would be only from one fiftieth to one hundredth as great in its effect on bank advances. If all groups of prices are moving, under monetary influences, more or less equally, it makes, of course, but little difference in what way an index number is compiled. But if metals are moving differently from textiles and food crops, the effect may be material. It is broadly true to say that, apart from purely financial and stock exchange requirements, and (from time to time) those of the building industry, by far the greater part of the world's demand for short-period credit arises out of textiles and food crops, much greater than their proportionate importance in most index numbers. If the prices of these commodities rise sharply and at the same time the stocks of them increase even moderately, a situation is soon produced in which credit is strained to the breaking point and conditions tending towards crisis begin to mature. It must be remembered, however, that market prices must persist for some months at a high level before they produce their full effect on the demand for credit.

2. *The demand for speculative risk-bearing*

The provision of short-period credits for the producing and carrying of stocks of commodities during the period before they reach the eventual consumer is rightly regarded by banks as one of their chief duties, and such credits are made available on the most favourable possible terms and on narrow margins (often much too narrow adequately to protect the banks from loss). Indeed it would be better if in times of boom banks applied the brake harder and sooner. But something else is required besides finance, namely risk-bearing, of which the supply is far less adequate to what is sometimes required.

The banks are prepared to lend the money, or a considerable proportion of it, but they are not prepared (intentionally) to run the risk of a change in the price of a commodity between purchase and sale. This risk has to be carried between them by the producer, the merchant and the professional speculator. It is apparent from the illustrations given above that the amount of risk which in the aggregate such persons have to run at certain seasons of the year is formidable. If, for example, the supply of American raw cotton is worth £300,000,000 and may fluctuate in value 30 per cent or more within a few months, there is a big risk to be carried by someone. There has had to be developed in consequence, in the case of very big seasonal crops such as cotton, wheat and sugar, a special organisation to deal with this, namely the forward contract market. In most writings on this subject great stress is laid on the service performed by the professional speculator in bringing about a harmony between short-period and long-period demand and supply, through his action in stimulating or retarding *in good time* the one or the other. This may be the case. But it presumes that the speculator is better informed on the average than the producers and the consumers themselves, which, speaking generally, is rather a dubious proposition. The most important function of the speculator in the great organised 'futures' markets is, I think, somewhat different. He is not so much a prophet (though it may be a belief in his own gifts of prophecy that tempts him into the business), as a *risk-bearer*. If he happens to be a prophet also, he will become extremely, indeed preposterously, rich. But without any such pretensions, indeed without paying the slightest attention to the prospects of the commodity he deals in or giving a thought to it, he may, one decade with another, earn substantial remuneration *merely* by running risks and allowing the results of one season to average with those of others; just as an insurance company makes profits without pretending to know more about an individual's prospects of life or the chances of his house taking fire than he knows himself. The explanation is in the fact that, for the sake of certainty, the producer, not unnaturally, is prepared to accept a somewhat lower price in advance than what, on the balance of probability, he thinks the price is likely to be when the time comes. Suppose, for example, a cotton farmer has committed himself to expenditure on a cotton crop which he reckons will cost him 12*d*. a lb in the expectation that, when he places it on the market six months later, the price will very likely be round about 15*d*. a lb, nevertheless he will prefer to sell at any rate a considerable proportion of his stock forward at a price of (say) 14*d*. a lb; for no-one can say for certain in the case of such a commodity as cotton that the price may not have fallen to 10*d*. a lb six months later (although on the other hand it may rise to 20*d*.), and a loss of 2*d*. a lb on the whole of his production might cause him so much financial embarrassment that he is prepared to sacrifice a reasonable proportion of his prospective profit in order to avoid the risk and to make sure of a reasonable profit. Indeed his banker may make it a condition of lending him the necessary funds that he should keep his risks within the limit of his resources by selling forward a suitable proportion of his current output. It is true that the spinner who uses the cotton may also have occasion to protect himself, in the opposite direction, by buying forward. In so far as the producer and the spinner can accommodate one another, no outside assistance is required and no expense need be incurred. But generally speaking the producer needs to look much further ahead than the spinner, and whilst the latter may provide a good deal of assistance as regards the near future he is not so much help for more distant months.

The main point is that the financial resources of the producers are not adequate to carry the whole risk of price fluctuation as well as the expenses of production. What the producer requires of the speculator is not so much someone who knows better than he does the future prospects of cotton, as someone who will take off his shoulders at a reasonable probability of profit such part of the risk as he cannot afford to bear himself.

The same situation can arise in other cases than those of seasonal crops. For example a considerable part of the lead which reaches Great Britain comes from very distant sources of supply, Australia, Burma and Rhodesia, with the result that several months intervene between the time when the mining process commences and the time when the pig lead can be delivered to the consumer. The annual value of a mine's production is generally large compared with its free resources; and it is under precisely the same necessity as the cotton farmer to sell forward some part of its current production at some concession of price, if necessary, below what is considered the probable future price. The fact that there is a 'backwardation' in the price of a commodity, or in other words that the forward price is below the spot price, is, therefore, not necessarily an indication that the market takes a 'bearish' view of the price prospects.

3. *The supply and cost of risk-bearing*

What abatement below the probable future price, as he estimates it, must the producer accept in order to induce the speculative market to relieve him of risk? It is impossible to answer precisely, because it varies enormously according to the size and organisation of the market, and the special circumstances of the moment. I have examined a good deal of material relating to several different commodities, but it does not lend itself to tabulation. The general result is, however, that the price is very high,— much higher than is charged for any other form of insurance, though perhaps it is inevitable that a risk which only averages out over units spread *through time* should be less easy to insure than one which averages out over units which are nearly simultaneous,—for we have to wait too long for the actuarial result. I should doubt whether in the largest and most organised market the cost of a hedge-sale works out at less than 10 per cent per annum (e.g. 5 per cent for a sale six months forward) and often rises to 20 per cent per annum (e.g. 5 per cent for a sale three months forward) and even much higher figures.

I expect that many readers are not yet clear how I can isolate the remuneration of the speculator as a risk-bearer from his remuneration (or loss) as a prophet of the future course of prices, for which there can, of course, be no standard rate at all, since it wholly depends on the skill of the individual. My method of arriving at the former is to assume that market opinion of the future course of prices, as expressed in current quotations, is as likely to err in one direction as in the other, and the remuneration of risk-bearing is measured by the average excess of the spot price three or six months hence over the forward price today for three or six months delivery. If we take the example of cotton (which is not exceptional save in the fact that, owing to the better organisation of the market, the charge for risk-bearing is apt to be more moderate than in the case of many other commodities), and put the rate at (e.g.) 10 per cent per annum, this means that a speculator, who bought cotton forward and always transferred his contract into a more distant month when by lapse of time it was approaching maturity, would earn at this rate on the capital sum at risk (*in addition* to whatever interest he could obtain on this sum) over a period of years. It would not be necessary for such a speculator (or, rather, risk-bearer) to exercise any personal judgement as to the future course of cotton prices or indeed to give it so much as a thought. If he did, he might be tempted into the business of forecasting, for which he might have no special qualifications.

4. *The present position*

The present position as regards stocks of many stable commodities is abnormal and interesting in a high degree. It has certainly been a feature of the recent trade depression (I have not sufficient data to generalise about previous cases) that the production of staple raw materials has fallen off much more than the consumption. Broadly speaking, the order of events has been as follows: (1) The high prices of the boom period over-stimulated production and eventually reached a point at which they somewhat retarded consumption. (2) The process of production being a lengthy one, the resulting fall of prices did not immediately curtail the delivery of new supplies of materials. (3) Since normal stocks (or, in the case of seasonal crops, 'carryover') bear, in general, a small proportion to annual production,—in most commodities three months' stocks (or carryover) are considered substantial,—the more rapid curtailment of consumption than of production led to the heaping up of stocks much beyond normal. (4) The sight of such heavy 'visible supplies' drove prices not merely below the exaggerated boom price but below all reasonable anticipations of normal cost of production, with the result that new production was greatly curtailed and brought, in some cases, almost to a standstill. (5) Thus, whereas consumption during the slump did not fall, in many cases, by more than 10–20 per cent, production fell off at the minimum by as much as 30–50 per cent. (6) Consequently the surplus stocks have been steadily eaten into, production had been so hard hit that it has been slow to revive except for certain prospects of a higher price, and we now find ourselves with the stocks disappearing and consumption proceeding at a substantially higher level than production. (7) Even when production revives under the stimulus of higher prices, an interval must elapse before this can have its full effect on supplies coming forward, so that consumers may be confronted for a time with a famine of raw materials.

This is a broad diagnosis of the present position. Each individual commodity is, of course, affected by special circumstances, which render it to those in the trade a special case. Nevertheless a rough generalisation can be made, I think, on the above lines. To take some representative examples, I believe that, at the present time, current consumption exceeds current production in the cases of cotton, wool, jute, silk, rubber, tin, copper, and lead, and that stocks are disappearing.* This factor is the reason why prices are showing a decided upward tendency in spite of the European situation. Political uncertainties can prevent a price rise due to anticipatory speculation, by frightening speculators off with incalculable possibilities, but they cannot prevent a price rise due to a shortage of offerings of the actual commodity. Indeed political uncertainties, so far from hindering the price rise, are really, if we look back a little, partially responsible for it. For by deterring speculators from giving support at an earlier stage, they have postponed the revival of production until the danger point has been reached. A correct relative price level for raw materials, instead of being brought about by reasonable anticipation, has waited for the stimulus of impending famine conditions, with the result that prices of some materials may have to rise much more than would have been necessary otherwise before the balance can be redressed.

Many persons have a fixed belief that high prices are only the concomitant of prosperity and therefore that they are hardly to be expected in the present sad state of the world. This view is incomplete. High prices may be brought about by general confidence, or over-confidence, in business prospects. But boom high prices are not the only kind of high prices. There may also be famine high prices, due to a shortage of commodities in relation to purchasing power. High prices may indicate poverty as well as confidence. In the near future we may be in for a bit of both,—boom high prices due to business confidence in America and famine high prices due to the recent unprecedented curtailment of the world's production.

* I hope to examine this matter in greater detail in a *Bulletin* which I am preparing, and hope shortly to publish, for the London and Cambridge Economic Service on 'Stocks of Commodities' [Below, pp. 267–314].

Keynes's article was the subject of a letter from one 'S.R.', published on 12 April in *The Manchester Guardian Commercial Supplement*. In it he argued that by ignoring the futures market in cotton, Keynes had under-estimated the credit necessary to carry the cotton textile industry. He also elaborated on the difference between 'spot' and 'future' prices, where he thought he was able to modify Keynes's discussion of backwardation. The Editor of the *Commercial* printed a comment by Keynes immediately below the letter.

From The Manchester Guardian Commercial Supplement, *12 April 1923*

'S. R.' adds some interesting points, but there is a little mis-understanding between us on two particulars. (1) In speaking of the 'demand for credit' arising out of business in cotton futures, he is not using the term *credit* quite as I was; these transactions require 'credit' in the sense of 'guarantee' or 'security', but they do not involve, on balance, any bank funds or 'bank credit' beyond what is required to finance the actual cotton. (2) As regards the general tendency towards a 'backwardation' in the price of contracts for distant months, I was comparing distant months with near months, *not* distant months with spot. The option to the seller, to which 'S. R.' refers, applies just as much to contracts for near as for distant months.

In April 1923, the London and Cambridge Economic Service issued its first Special Memorandum by Keynes, who had been assisted by R. B. Lewis.

From London and Cambridge Economic Service, Special Memorandum No. 1
(April 1923)

STOCKS OF STAPLE COMMODITIES

The enquiry into stocks of commodities, of which the results are given below, covers a wider field than any similar investigation with which I am acquainted. It is, therefore, inevitably liable to error and open to criticism. As it is hoped to continue it at (approximately) six-monthly intervals, corrections and additions for future issues will be gratefully received by the authors.

The bulk of the statistics employed are unofficial and are based on trade estimates. They have had to be obtained, therefore, in the main, by reference to trade publications and by private enquiries from the leading merchant houses. As regards the latter, we beg to tender them collectively our sincere thanks for the remarkable willingness they have shown to take trouble on our behalf and to place their records at our disposal. I have the impression that the available returns are much fuller and more complete than they were before the War, and that the present is probably the earliest date at which it has been possible to put together such tables as are given below for a period of three or four consecutive years.

Accurate information as to the volume from time to time of surplus stocks of staple commodities is of the utmost interest both to businessmen and to economists. For reasons, which do not concern us in detail in this statistical enquiry, movements in the volumes of stocks have an immense influence on the course of price changes. In many commodities, for example, a reduction of stocks from three months' to one month's consumption or an increase from three months' to six months' is capable of affecting current prices to an extent which may seem disproportionate. But stocks, failing special explanations in particular cases, are the best index to impending instability of the price level, and there is nothing which it is more necessary for the merchant to gauge accurately than whether consumption is proceeding in excess of production or *vice versa*.

To the economist a statistical enquiry into fluctuations of stocks may, if it can be carried on over a long enough period, throw much light on the hidden mechanism lying behind cyclical movements, and prove decisive as between rival explanations, both of which are possible *a priori*. I have long believed that a certain amount of information (not hitherto available) as to the correlation between changes in the volume of stocks, and the successive phases of the trade cycle, is necessary to a full understanding of the latter.

I do not propose to enter here into the theoretical analysis of the facts disclosed in the following figures. But it is, I think, of obvious interest and importance that the stock statistics of widely varying commodities move on the whole together, so that broad generalisations can be made applicable to stocks of commodities as a whole. Of the 14 commodities examined below, 7 reached a maximum between the middle and the end of 1921, whilst 10 are at their minimum and 12 show a declining tendency at the present time. The statistics also exhibit a tendency towards an earlier minimum in the middle of 1920. The exceptions from the minimum and maximum of 1920 and 1921 are (1) three commodities, namely, wool, copper and lead, of which there were large post-war accumulations, and stocks of which have been continuously diminishing from an abnormal level throughout the period under review; (2) rubber and oil, stocks of which have been continuously increasing until just recently for reasons which are well known, and (3) wheat, stocks of which show no well-marked variations other than those of the seasons, but are at a fairly high level at present. The break in the last boom seems to have come when stocks began to mount up again. They continued to increase during the first phase of the depression. They diminished during its second phase (production having been curtailed by the break in prices to a level below that of current consumption). And by the beginning of 1923 they had fallen, or

	Am. cotton 1,000 bales (1)	Wool 1,000,000 lb (2)	Jute 1,000 bales (3)	Copper 1,000 tons (4)	Tin 1,000 tons (5)	Lead 1,000 tons (6)	Spelter 1,000 tons (7)	Rubber 1,000 tons (8)	Sugar 1,000 tons (9)	Coffee 1,000 bags (10)	Tea 1,000,000 lb (11)	Crude oil 1,000,000 barrels (12)	Nitrate 1,000 tons (13)	Wheat 1,000,000 centals (14)
1920														
1 Jan.	6,567	—	—	900	35	101	61	142	2,313	9,870	213	128	2,134	—
1 July	6,384	—	9,857	—	26	—	51	—	2,003	6,750	215	127	1,800	—
1921														
1 Jan.	7,417	1,200	—	822	27	72	81	207	2,389	8,765	214	134	2,235	279
1 July	8,623	—	8,190	—	44	—	99	—	3,312	8,700	219	151	2,405	—
1922														
1 Jan.	6,623	950	—	451	53	21	72	216	1,624	9,403	205	170	2,615	278
1 July	4,498	—	5,125	—	44	—	31	—	2,413	8,639	171	232	1,851	—
1923														
1 Jan.	2,875	300	4,105	319	38	1	17	248	1,548	8,257	168	248	1,891	309
1 Mar.	2,439	248	—	—	—	—	10	—	—	7,480	—	—	1,680	—

(1) Total supply seasonally corrected, exclusive of European and Asiatic mill stocks. (2) Total surplus supply not in manufacturers' hands. (3) Total supply. (4) Total supply outside hands of consumers. (5) Total supply outside hands of consumers. (6) Visible supply in U.K. and U.S. (7) Visible supply in U.K. and U.S. (8) Total supply outside plantations. (9) Total visible supply. (10) Visible supply in Rio, Santos, Bahia, Europe and U.S.A. (11) Stocks in bond in U.K. (12) Stocks in U.S. (13) Visible supply in Chile, U.S.A., Europe and Egypt. (14) Supply available for importing countries.

were falling, to a level in many cases dangerously low. It is noticeable throughout that the rate of production has fluctuated much more violently than that of consumption.

It is safe to say that during 1922 the world's consumption of raw commodities materially exceeded its production.* And it appears possible that political uncertainties in Europe by rendering speculation nervous and weakening the spirit of anticipation, may have caused the hint of rising prices to consumers and the stimulus of them to producers to be delayed dangerously long. The tardiness of speculative activity in response to a strong statistical position of stocks has also been due to recent memories of the disastrous slump and in some cases to the weakened financial position of the speculative merchant class.

Rising prices may result from general confidence in business prospects. But they may also be brought about by a famine of ready goods. We may be faced at the present time by the combined influences of a prosperity-boom in America and a famine-boom in Europe.

The table above summarises the figures given in detail below for each separate commodity. For the methods of compilation the reader is referred to the detailed statements.

COMMODITIES IN DETAIL

I. *American cotton*

At any given time stocks consist of the following:—

(1) Stocks up-country in the Southern States on plantations, compresses and railroads and in 'uncounted' interior towns.†

* The following figures compiled by the British Metal Corporation for the non-ferrous metals are striking (100 as index figure for 1913):

	Production		Consumption
	1921	1922	1922
Copper	43	86	91
Tin	75	83	97
Lead	73	79	77
Spelter	54	68	77

† I.e., towns not included in the figures for 'visible' supply.

(2) The 'visible' supply as shown weekly in the returns of the New Orleans and New York Cotton Exchanges.* This consists of (a) warehouse stocks in the more important interior towns (42 in number) and in the ports of the United States, (b) cotton afloat for Great Britain and the Continent, (c) warehouse stocks in the principal European ports, namely, Liverpool, Manchester, London, Havre, Marseilles, Genoa, Bremen, Ghent, Rotterdam and Barcelona.†

(3) Mill stocks in spinners' hands throughout the world, generally known as the 'invisible' or 'out of sight' supply.

The monthly table given below comprises (1) 'up-country' stocks *plus* (2) 'visible' stocks *plus* (3) the 'invisible' mill stocks in the U.S.A. but not the mill stocks in other countries, which are only known accurately at the half-yearly census. Aggregate figures are also given for *total* supply, including all mill stocks, at the end and in the middle of each season.

I define the 'up-country' stock as the 'up-country' carryover in the Southern States at the end of each season, *plus* the current year's crop, *minus* the amount of cotton which has come 'into sight', and has therefore been included in 'visible' supplies. It follows that the whole of the new crop is suddenly added to the 'up-country' stock in August of each year. This is corrected in the following table by the 'seasonal correction', which provides what would be the figure of 'up-country' stock if the current crop came into existence at an even monthly rate through the year. The weekly returns of cotton 'into sight' may be regarded as reliable.‡ The estimates of the current crop are reasonably accurate by the end of each calendar year. The 'up-country' carryover is the most doubtful item, and is always liable to be

---

* These various returns differ slightly from one another but not materially. Up to the end of the year 1921–2 I have taken the New York figures, and for the current year the Liverpool figures.

† Cotton afloat for Japan and in Japanese ports is not allowed for.

‡ Three estimates of this, compiled on somewhat different bases, are commonly quoted, namely, those of the New Orleans and New York Cotton Exchanges and *The Financial and Commercial Chronicle*. I follow the Liverpool Cotton Exchange in using the first-named.

Monthly table of supplies other than European and Asiatic mill stocks at end of each month (1,000 bales)

	'Up-country'	'Visible'	Total outside mills	Cor-rection for season	Cor-rected total	U.S. mill stocks†
1919						
July	2,193	3,214	5,407	—	5,407	
August	14,145	2,878	17,023	11,231	5,792	
September	13,386	2,740	16,126	10,210	5,916	
October	11,710	3,463	15,173	9,189	5,984	
November	9,573	4,227	13,800	8,168	5,632	
December	7,197	4,565	11,762	7,147	4,615	
1920						
January	5,632	4,658	10,290	6,126	4,416	1,952
February	4,547	4,791	9,338	5,105	4,233	1,869
March	3,765	4,501	8,266	4,084	4,182	1,854
April	3,141	4,205	7,346	3,063	4,283	1,812
May	2,850	3,876	6,726	2,042	4,684	1,699
June	2,576	3,275	5,851	1,021	4,830	1,554
July	1,703	2,944	4,647	—	4,647	1,358
August	14,810	2,612	17,422	12,254	5,168	1,131
September	13,959	2,754	16,713	11,140	5,573	901
October	12,450	3,513	15,963	10,026	5,937	940
November	10,782	4,243	15,025	8,912	6,113	1,118
December	9,159	4,805	13,964	7,798	6,166	1,251
1921						
January	8,165	4,842	13,007	6,684	6,323	1,264
February	7,238	4,725	11,963	5,570	6,393	1,327
March	6,384	4,549	10,933	4,456	6,477	1,337
April	5,733	4,497	10,230	3,342	6,888	1,316
May	4,879	4,553	9,432	2,228	7,204	1,281
June	4,092	4,442	8,534	1,114	7,420	1,203
July	3,713	4,113	7,826	—	7,826	1,111
August	11,192	3,753	14,945	7,293	7,652	1,006
September	9,791	3,940	13,731	6,630	7,101	1,118
October	7,826	4,474	12,300	5,967	6,333	1,398

Table (*cont.*)

	'Up-country'	'Visible'	Total outside mills	Cor-rection for season	Cor-rected total	U.S. mill stocks†
November	6,298	4,658	10,956	5,304	5,652	1,655
December	4,965	4,661	9,626	4,741	4,885	1,738
1922						
January	4,247	4,389	8,636	4,078	4,558	1,669
February	3,657	4,080	7,755	3,415	4,340	1,595
March	2,939	3,657	6,596	2,752	3,844	1,557
April	2,416	3,409	5,825	2,089	3,736	1,461
May	1,806	3,095	4,901	1,426	3,475	1,420
June	1,263	2,567	3,830	663	3,167	1,331
July	964	1,968	2,932	—	2,932	1,218
August	10,305*	1,611	11,916	8,800	3,116	1,025
September	8,830	2,238	11,068	8,000	3,068	1,065
October	6,758	3,386	10,144	7,200	2,944	1,380
November	4,660	3,952	8,612	6,400	2,212	1,721
December	2,799	3,755	6,554	5,600	954	1,921
1923						
January	1,967	3,460	5,427	4,800	627	1,987
February	1,557	2,860	4,417	4,000	417	2,022
March	1,097	2,452	3,549	3,200	349	

* 1922–3 crop taken at 9,738,000 bales.
† U.S. Bureau of the Census—figures for *all* kinds of cotton.

under- rather than over-estimated, with the result that very high prices may draw out a certain amount of unsuspected supplies. I have used for this the figures of Mr H. G. Hester, the Secretary of the New Orleans Cotton Exchange.

The consumption during the half-year ending Jan. 31, 1923, has been at a rate of not less than 13,000,000 bales per annum. Unless the 'up-country' stocks have been much under-estimated, the continuance of this rate of consumption up to the date when the new crop is available would bring stocks below the working

Annual table of total stocks at the end of each season (1 August)
(1,000 bales)*

	1918	1919	1920	1921	1922
'Up-country' carry-over in interior cotton belt	925	2,193	1,703	3,713	964†
U.S. warehouse stocks	1,450	1,965	1,547	2,463	797
U.S. mill stocks	1,465	1,304	1,357	1,065‡	1,141‡
Total in U.S.	3,840	5,462	4,607	7,241	2,902
European port stocks (including afloat for Europe)	347	1,247	1,394	1,695	1,167
European mill stocks	250	305	475	690	714
Asiatic mill stocks	?	?	267§	248	353
Total	4,437	7,014	6,743	9,874	5,136
Crop for year ‖	13,070	12,000	13,750	8,442	9,738¶
Total available	17,507	19,014	20,493	18,316	14,874
Total carried forward	7,014	6,476	9,914	5,136	
Consumption for year	10,493	12,538	10,579	13,180	

* Based on the returns of the New York Cotton Exchange, Mr Hester's Annual Reports to the New Orleans Cotton Exchange, and the Reports of the International Federation of Master Cotton Spinners.
† Of which about 450,000 estimated to be on plantations proper.
‡ Including Canada and Mexico.
§ Excluding China.
‖ I have here taken Hester's estimate of the actual growth, made at the conclusion of the season. The final official estimates, which are the figures usually quoted, are as follows:—
1918, 11,360; 1919, 12,252; 1920, 13,366; 1921, 8,283. There is a big discrepancy for 1918–19, the official figure being incompatible with the ginning returns.
¶ Provisional.

minimum—indeed almost to vanishing point throughout the world. It would seem, therefore (1) that the price of present-crop cotton must rise to a sufficient premium over new-crop prices to induce spinners to reduce their stocks below what they ordinarily consider convenient, and (2) that the price of American cotton

Annual table of total stocks in the middle of each season (1 February)
(1,000 bales)

	1920	1921	1922	1923
'Up-country' stocks	5,632	8,165	4,247	1,967
U.S. warehouse stocks	2,640	3,038	2,607	2,034
U.S. mill stocks*	1,936	1,212	1,613	1,937
Total in U.S.	10,208	12,415	8,467	5,938
European port stocks (including afloat)	2,018	1,650	1,575	1,302
European mill stocks	597	675	638	611
Asiatic mill stocks	117†	166†	351	189
Total available	12,940	14,906	11,031	8,040
Ditto 1 August preceding	19,014	20,226	18,316	14,874
Consumption for half-year	6,074	5,320	7,285	6,834

* Including Canada and Mexico.   † Excluding China.

must rise to a level which is to some extent deterrent, that is to say, which will cause a diversion or postponement of demand. In some markets (2) is said to be operating already; but it will have to proceed further. If, as seems likely, the demand for cotton in the U.S. is very inelastic, the major part of the curtailment of consumption might fall on the European mills.

II. *Wool*

The statistical position of this commodity has been dominated for several years by the holdings of the British-Australian Wool Realisation Association (BAWRA). During the War the large requirements of wool for clothing the Allied Armies on the one hand, and the difficulty of ordinary trade shipments of wool from Australia on the other, led to a vast scheme of Government purchase of the whole available supply, the one outstanding example of successful Government dealing on the grand scale. Buying began in November, 1916, and continued under

275

successive agreements between the British Government and the Australian wool growers until June 30, 1920, by which time £174,000,000 had been expended on the purchase of wool, and unsold stocks had accumulated to about 2,908,000 bales (= 930,560,000 lb, approximate). Since that date these stocks have been gradually disposed of, *pari passu* with the new clips, the profits being divided between the British Government and the Australian growers. The production of New Zealand was purchased, as well as that of Australia, and also a certain quantity of South African wool. The following table exhibits the progressive disposal of the BAWRA Stocks:

| | Australia and New Zealand | | South Africa | |
| | Merino | Crossbred* | | Total |
	(Bales of about 330 lb)			
30 June 1920	1,113,258	1,794,893	—	2,908,151
31 Dec. 1920	902,726	1,682,768	—	2,586,474
31 July 1921	659,870	1,549,213	—	2,209,083
31 Dec. 1921	422,241	1,487,488	80,655†	1,890,384
31 July 1922	164,782	1,039,267	14,828	1,218,877
31 Dec. 1922	76,239	837,006	Nil	913,245
28 Feb. 1923	51,000	701,284	Nil	752,284

* Including New Zealand scoured and slipes.
† 82,405 bales of South African wool were taken over at the end of Nov., 1921.
It will be observed that the stocks of Merino are practically exhausted.

The effect of these vast available surplus supplies has been to permit the wool consumption to exceed current production by a material amount during the whole period since the Armistice. But the end of this surplus is now in sight, and the wool trade seems to be faced with a situation in which consumption is stabilised at a higher figure than that of production, increase in which can only be effected by the gradual growth of the world's flocks. Thus wool is a commodity of which the available stocks have been falling continuously from an altogether abnormal initial figure during the whole of the period under review.

When we proceed to the consideration of stocks outside the published figures of BAWRA it is difficult to be precise. I am greatly indebted to the assistance of Sir Arthur Goldfinch, who has been in charge of the great Government scheme from its initial inception down to the present time.

Wool is, of course, grown for domestic consumption in all parts of the world, and we must limit ourselves in what follows to the holdings in the countries which are big producers of exported wool (Australasia, South America and South Africa), and those which are big consumers of imported wool (United Kingdom and United States).

(1) *Australasia*. Stocks, others than those in the hands of BAWRA, vary seasonally, no large amount being carried over at the end of the season, that is to say April. Figures of stocks in port at the close of the last two seasons were as follows:

30 June 1921	536,000 bales (= 178,000,000 lb)
30 June 1922	178,000 bales (= 59,000,000 lb)

At the end of Jan., 1923, the stocks had risen seasonally to 536,000 bales, which will probably shrink to zero by April and remain at a very low figure for about four months, being at a high point again by October.

The position in New Zealand is similar.

(2) *South Africa*. In the year ending 31 July 1921, a stock of 36,500,000 lb accumulated. Of this carryover about 27,000,000 lb was disposed of to BAWRA, as shown above. In the following year the disposals are estimated to have exceeded the current season's export surplus by about 9,000,000 lb, which liquidated the balance of the floating surplus, leaving no appreciable carry-over.

(3) *South America*. The accumulations after the War were considerable. By the end of the year 1920–1 (1 October 1921)

they had reached 264,000,000 lb (at Buenos Ayres and Bahia Blanca). In the following year the whole of this carryover was worked off, and there is now no accumulation over and above the current supplies passing into consumption.

(4) *The United States.* The U.S. Government collects a quarterly return of stocks from dealers and manufacturers. Out of 815 holders, 800 make returns; nevertheless, the unreturned stocks are believed to be as much as 20 per cent of the whole. The returns, together with those of the Government's own stocks, now exhausted, have been as follows:—

| | (million lb) | | |
	Commercial stocks	Government stocks	Total
31 March 1920	393	78	471
30 June 1920	382	68	450
30 September 1920	371	65	436
31 December 1920	426	57	483
31 March 1921	475	57	532
30 June 1921	443	47	490
30 September 1921	466	31	497
30 June 1922	374	nil	374
30 September 1922	420	nil	420

The probable present stocks are still about 420,000,000 lb, representing six months' consumption.

(5) *The United Kingdom.* Since the period of control came to an end, the trade has refused to make returns of its stocks. The amount held by dealers (a very small part only) and by manufacturers is believed to average about 350,000,000 lb and to be at present somewhat below 400,000,000 lb—rather above the figure of a year ago.

(6) *Other chief industrial countries.* Here also stocks in the hands of manufacturers are believed to average six months' consumption, that is to say, between 400,000,000 and 500,000,000 lb. They are probably somewhat greater than they were a year or two ago.

Thus there are now no surplus stocks in the exporting countries, except the BAWRA stocks amounting to 250,000,000 lb on 28 Feb. 1923; whilst the stocks in the industrial consuming centres are about 1,200,000,000 lb, representing a little less than six months' requirements.

Recently and at present the aggregate clip of the exporting countries has been about 1,500,000,000 lb per annum (of which half comes from Australasia); whilst the corresponding purchases of imported wool, in the wool year 1922, have probably reached 2,150,000,000 lb.* Consumption may have fallen a little short of this. Allowing 150,000,000 lb for increase of manufacturers' stocks, we have a consumption of imported wool of 2,000,000,000 lb, which is 33 per cent above current production.

Summing up, the surplus floating supply of wool, exclusive of wool passing out of the grower's hands at the normal rate, and exclusive also of manufacturers' stocks, may have been, roughly, as follows:—

1 Jan. 1921   1,200,000,000 lb
1 Jan. 1922   950,000,000 lb
1 Jan. 1923   300,000,000 lb

Clearly the limit of available supply must keep purchases of imported wool in 1923 below last year's figures by at least 10 per cent. Nevertheless, the position is safeguarded for the present by the size of manufacturers' stocks, a reduction of which by some 20 per cent would bridge the gap. Wool shares with jute the peculiarity that the mills themselves normally hold and finance a large proportion of the floating supply, and it is out of these 'invisible' stocks that a temporary shortage can be met. Nevertheless the level, at which the world's consumption of wool has been stabilised lately, cannot possibly be continued much longer without a substantial increase in the world's flocks.

* Both these figures omit wool consumed in the country of origin, which may be reckoned at 850,000 000 lb apart from Russia and Asia.

Even in the slump of 1921 consumption was exceeding the current clip.

III. *Jute*

In the case of this commodity most of the figures are little better than trade guesses. The opinions which have reached me from different sources of information have been so often discrepant, that the reliability of what follows is not to be regarded as high. Unlike the case of most other commodities, the bulk of the floating supplies seems to be held by the mills. The figure for mill stocks (based on returns made by the mills to the Bengal Chamber of Commerce) and port stocks out of India may be regarded as relatively accurate; those for the up-country stocks in India are specially doubtful. It is assumed in the tables below that the whole of the new crop is added to the up-country supply at the beginning of the season; but the 'seasonal correction' in the last column but one gives what the result would be on the assumption that the new crop came into existence at an even monthly rate through the year.

Annual table of stocks (1,000 bales)

	India up-country	Calcutta mills	Calcutta other stocks	Stocks outside India	Total	Seasonal correction	Corrected total
1 July							
1919	4,200	2,900	500	246	7,846	—	7,846
1920	4,700	3,900	300	957	8,857	—	9,857
1921	3,200	3,700	550	740	8,190	—	8,190
1922	550	3,150	125	1,200	5,125	—	5,125
1 Jan.							
1923	1,480	3,050	450	1,875	6,855	2,750	4,105

Experience shows that the Government crop figures are consistently underestimated. Their estimate for 1922–23 is 4,237,000 bales. The below figures assume a crop of 5,500,000. But even this may still be too low. The crop may turn out to be somewhere

Monthly table of stocks (end of month) (1,000 bales)

	India up-country	Calcutta mill stocks	Calcutta other stocks	Stocks outside India including afloat	Total	Seasonal correction	Corrected total
1922							
June	550	3,150	225	1,200	5,125	—	5,125
July	5,750*	3,000	50	1,200	10,000	5,040	4,960
August	5,200	2,900	200	1,075	9,375	4,582	4,793
Sept.	4,100	3,200	300	1,125	8,725	4,124	4,601
Oct.	2,880	3,425	300	1,475	8,080	3,666	4,414
Nov.	2,000	3,300	450	1,625	7,375	3,208	4,167
Dec.	1,480	3,050	450	1,875	6,855	2,750	4,105
1923							
Jan.	—	2,750	500	1,850	6,200	2,292	3,908

* Crop taken at 5,500,000 bales.

between 5,500,000 and 6,000,000 bales. The estimate for Calcutta mill stocks, which represent 7 months' consumption, may also be too low. Other authorities would place these at as much as 3,325,000 bales at the end of January, 1923, which would represent $8\frac{1}{2}$ months' consumption.

The European mills are believed to hold not more than two to three months' stock. The Germans mills in particular, which are still fully employed, are compelled by their financial necessities to live from hand to mouth. But Dundee probably has as much as a year's stock, that is at their present level of output, which is much below the pre-war figure, unequally distributed between different mills.

The position of jute is very similar to that of cotton,—abnormally large accumulations in the middle of 1921, followed by two successive very short crops, with the result that the accumulations have now been worked off. There is this difference, however, that the much larger stocks of the raw material normally held by jute spinners, as compared with cotton spinners, provides a more adequate reserve against temporary short supply. The ease with which the jute market will get through the rest of the season will depend on the willingness of the big mills to let their stocks run down. The level which prices will have to reach to produce this result will largely depend on the prospects of the next crop and the opportunities of replacing with new crop jute at lower prices.

World consumption at the present time is estimated by different authorities at rates varying between 7,000,000 and 8,750,000 bales a year. If the above table is correct, it seems to indicate a present consumption of about 7,600,000 bales, leaving a carryover of about 3,000,000 bales, or about $4\frac{1}{2}$ months' supply, on July 1 next. This is a far lower figure than the trade is accustomed to, but is by no means a definite shortage, provided a new crop is in sight on a scale fully adequate to requirements. The jute trade must remain perplexed until this question has been resolved one way or the other.

IV. *Copper*

Stocks of copper consist of (1) refined copper in the United States, which constitutes the main part of the world's floating supply, (2) rough and blister copper in transit between smelters and refiners in the U.S., and on hand or in process at refineries, (3) refined and rough copper in European and Japanese warehouses. In the years immediately after the War there were also large stocks in the hands of the Allied Governments and in the form of scrap metal.

The following estimates for the past five years are based on the figures of the U.S. Geological Survey, trade and expert estimates (especially those contained in *The Mineral Industry*, vols. XXIX and XXX), and the London Metal Exchange statistics. The figures for scrap metal are inevitably rather in the nature of a guess.

Tons

	1 Jan. 1919	1 Jan. 1920	1 Jan. 1921	1 Jan. 1922	1 Jan. 1923
United States					
Refined	80,000	281,000	294,200	205,000	124,000
In process, etc.	295,000	123,000	208,000	126,000	156,000
Allied Govt.		(say)			
stocks	281,000	180,000	82,000	trifling	nil
		(say)		(say)	
Scrap	361,000	270,000	183,000	90,000	trifling
U.K., Havre,					
Japan stocks	—	46,000	55,000	30,000	39,000
Total	1,017,000	900,000	822,000	451,000	319,000
production	993,000	945,000	533,000	840,000*	—
Available					
supply	2,010,000	1,845,000	1,355,000	1,291,000	—
Stock carried					
forward	900,000	822,000	451,000	319,000	—
Consumption	1,110,000	1,023,000	904,000	972,000	—

* Provisional.

It will be noticed that consumption has remained comparatively steady, whilst production in 1921 fell off nearly 50 per cent as compared with 1919. Thus the collapse was mainly due to the immense accumulations of stocks, amounting to the equivalent of about a year's consumption. The full weight of the stocks in the hands of the Allied Governments and in the form of scrap was only gradually appreciated, and did not exercise its full effect until some curtailment of consumption resulting from the break of the boom added its influence also.* In April 1921,† the bulk of the mines of the United States closed down and were only

* The fact was also important, that, as government and scrap stocks were gradually disposed of regardless of cost of production, a steadily increasing proportion of the aggregate stock had to be carried by the producers and refiners in U.S.
† By this date producers' stocks in America stood at their maximum figure of 550,000 tons.

gradually restarted in the course of 1922. At the present time consumption certainly exceeds 1,000,000 tons a year, and is probably at as high a rate as at any former period before or since the War.

In the case of a commodity such as copper, which is produced under conditions of widely varying cost, the problem of cost is obscure. Much copper, especially in South America, can be produced at costs far below even the lowest price ruling during the slump; a proportion of the North American supply can be produced comfortably below the present price; but the supply of relatively cheap copper is not equal to the present world demand, and it cannot be increased rapidly. It, seems, therefore, that the price must rise sufficiently to bring back into operation some of the more costly mines which were developed under the stimulus of war prices.* So lately as the beginning of 1923, however, the price of copper had scarcely reached the pre-war price,† and a substantial rise may be necessary to bring the real return to the producer up to the pre-war equivalent, regard being had to the increase of production costs in the United States. There is no reason to suppose that the production costs of copper in the United States have not risen more or less in the same proportion as the general index number. The chief new factor in the situation is the steadily increasing production of the cheap South American copper; but even now this cannot exceed

* Since more than 80 per cent of the world's copper has been produced in recent years in North and South America, costs in these mines dominate the situation. Of this 80 per cent, perhaps it might be said that 20 can be produced far below present prices, 30 comfortably below present prices, 20 round about present prices, and 10 above present prices; which suggests that elasticity of supply near present prices is greater than elasticity of demand, a condition favourable to sharp fluctuations.

† Average price of electrolytic copper in New York (in cents per pound):—

Average for 10 years preceding the War, 16.75.

1912	16.341	1917	27.180	1922	13.382
1913	15.269	1918	24.628	Jan. 1923	14.501
1914	13.602	1919	18.691	1 March 1923	17.000
1915	17.275	1920	17.456	1 April 1923	17.375
1916	27.202	1921	12.502		

15 per cent of the world's supply. Some time must still elapse before the Katanga copper can exert much influence on the market.

The following table gives some more detailed statistics for

[*Copper production*] (tons)

Beginning of month	U.S. refined	U.S. blister	U.K. all kinds	Havre	Japan
1921 January	294,000	208,000	11,646	5,968	37,500
April	295,000	255,000	13,628	6,026	—
July	302,000	—	19,656	5,834	12,300
October	255,000	161,000	19,485	4,124	9,600
1922 January	205,000	126,000	16,655	4,138	9,300
April	161,700	—	15,868	3,459	12,900
July	170,000	—	12,992	3,192	13,100
October	120,000	—	19,524	5,613	11,900
1923 January	124,000	156,000	26,780	3,345	9,122
February	118,000*	—	27,268	2,964	—
March	112,000*	—	27,632†	2,995	—

* Other authorities make the figures for February and March somewhat higher.
† Of which 7,926 tons refined and 19,706 tons rough.

Details of government copper stocks and scrap

	(In 1,000,000 lb)			
	1 Jan. 1919	1 Jan. 1921	1 Jan. 1919	1 Jan. 1921
	Allied Govt stocks		Scrap in brass, etc.	
United States	129	14	92	11
Great Britain	179	26	370	302
France	168	13	224	67
Italy	67	58	45	29
Germany	67	—	67	—
Japan	20	73	11	—
Total	630	184	809	409

recent dates. Some of the figures for intermediate months are unreliable, the producers tending to under-estimate stocks, with the result that there is an upward jump when the periodical figures of the U.S. Geological Survey come along.

European stocks are about normal as compared with 1913. Refined copper in producers' hands in the U.S. in 1913 (as published by the American Producers' Association) ranged between 13,300 tons and 55,900 tons.

V. Tin

Stocks of tin mainly consist of:—

(1) The 'visible' supply, as defined by the returns of Messrs Ricard and Freiwald, and of Messrs Strauss, namely warehouse stocks in Holland, U.K., and U.S., and tin afloat from the Federated Malay States, Netherlands Indies and Australia.

(2) Stocks of ore in Bolivia and Nigeria, and afloat from these countries to U.S. and U.K., and in course of smelting in U.S. and U.K.

(3) Stocks in the Federated Malay States and Netherlands Indies.

[*Monthly aggregates, world stocks*] (tons*)

End of month	1913	1919	1920	1921	1922	1923
January	14,875	7,758	20,980	18,104	25,346	22,598
February	13,348	6,981	21,472	16,900	24,434	22,183
March	12,117	6,431	18,279	15,764	21,040	21,703
April	10,814	5,113	18,716	15,131	21,244	—
May	14,663	5,279	20,801	17,767	22,235	—
June	12,903	6,208	18,883	16,953	22,558	—
July	13,713	12,697	18,482	19,852	20,364	—
August	12,841	18,157	20,152	19,037	21,753	—
September	14,673	21,292	18,326	20,777	20,488	—
October	13,049	22,807	19,442	22,891	19,975	—
November	16,112	19,585	19,065	22,247	22,131	—
December	15,543	21,491	18,479	24,273	22,155	—

* Figures of A. Strauss & Co.

(4) Stocks in China and afloat from China to U.S. and U.K.

Detailed monthly figures, of which the aggregates are given above, are available for (1) in the returns of the two firms mentioned, which are in fairly close agreement with one another.

(2) It is not necessary to take account of the normal flow of ore from Nigeria and Bolivia to the smelters. But there is believed to have been some considerable accumulation of stocks in Bolivia in 1919, and again in 1921. Accurate figures of shipments are available; but there are no reliable figures for production, so that estimates of stocks are largely guesswork.

Messrs Blum's figures for Bolivia indicate that the stocks may have been roughly as follows:—

End of 1918	6,000 tons
1919	7,500 tons
1920	Nil
1921	4,500 tons
1922	Nil

(3) On two recent occasions official pools have been formed for holding tin in the Malay States and Netherlands-Indies. The first was begun and liquidated between January and August, 1919. On the second and more important occasion the Government of the Federated Malay States began to buy on December 6, 1920, and finished buying on February 28, 1921, on which date the Bandoeng holding agreement was concluded between the following parties which at that time held stocks as follows:—

F.M.S. Government	9,508 tons
Netherlands Indies Govt.	4,000 „
Straits Trading Co.	2,680 „
Biliton Co.	2,800 „
Singkep Co.	150 „
	19,138 „

The Straits Trading Co. continued to add to its stocks but disposed of its additional stocks held outside the pool (1,350 tons) towards the end of 1921. In April 1922, and subsequently, the Billiton and the Singkep Companies were released from the agreement. The rest of the pool stocks were believed to be still in hand at the beginning of 1923.

(4) Chinese stocks, mainly held in Hongkong, can only be given from approximate trade estimates. They may have been somewhat as follows:—

End of 1919	6,000 tons
1920	2,000 ,,
1921	5,000 ,,
1922	Nil

Combining these figures, we have (very roughly) the following (in tons):—

	'Visible' supply	Bolivian ore stocks	Eastern pool	Chinese stocks	Total
1 Jan. 1920	21,500	7,500	Nil	6,000	35,000
1 July	18,900	3,500	Nil	4,000	26,400
1 Jan. 1921	18,500	Nil	6,000	2,000	26,500
1 July	17,000	2,500	20,000	4,000	43,500
1 Jan. 1922	24,300	4,500	19,100	5,000	52,900
1 July	22,600	1,500	17,000	2,500	43,600
1 Jan. 1923	22,200	Nil	16,200	Nil	38,400

The above table neglects Bolivian, Nigerian and Chinese tin afloat. Allowing for this, total stocks on 1 Jan. 1923, apart from consumers' stocks, may be put at the round figure of 40,000 tons.

The production of tin in recent years has ranged approximately from 110,000 tons to 125,000 tons per annum. Thus at their maximum stocks represented less than six months' supply, and stand at the present time at between three and four months' supply. Allowing for the fact that these figures include quantities afloat from distant sources of supply, present stocks do not show much surplus over the working minimum of (say) 20,000 tons.

VI. *Lead*

There are at present no surplus stocks of lead worth consideration outside the United Kingdom and the United States. As regards the former, monthly figures are available for the stocks in public warehouses, but in addition to these there are sometimes appreciable quantities in private warehouses and, of course, in the hands of consumers. As regards the United States I have only been able to obtain the annual estimates of the Geological Survey. There is also at any given time a month to six weeks' supply afloat to the United Kingdom from distant sources. In 1919, however, there were large accumulations, estimated at 180,000 tons, in Australia which it had been impossible to ship.

	Monthly stocks (tons) United Kingdom Private warehouses and Government stock			
End of month	1920	1921	1922	1923
January	47,348	19,777	622	414
February	40,435	19,129	589	648*
March	28,435	23,926	578	
April	26,250	18,127	522	
May	23,338	14,138	646	
June	25,192	13,278	268	
July	23,448	12,396	235	
August	21,521	11,515	686	
September	18,721	9,883	583	
October	15,335	5,161	281	
November	14,919	1,069	198	
December	19,045	284	518	

* One firm comments 'to which must be added a very large quantity at private wharves which it is estimated may reach into five figures'.

	Annual stocks (tons) United States*	United Kingdom	Total
1 January 1919	17,471	62,852	80,323
1920	45,710	54,975	100,685
1921	52,542	19,045	71,587
1922	20,548	284	20,832
1923		518	

* Mainly in the form of ore and base bullion.

	Other stocks not included in regular returns April 1919	December 1920	March 1921
Australia	180,000		
Spain		40,000	35,000
Belgium		4,500	33,000
Italy		18,000	
Germany		4,000	

There were also stocks in Spain (say, 35,000 tons) in 1920 and 1921. A few figures of these and other stocks, for which there are no regular returns, are given above.

The United States, which has recently raised the tariff on imported lead to the high figure of about £10 a ton, depends on her own supply and that of Mexico; the East on supplies from Burma and Australia; Europe mainly on the balance of the Burmese and Australian supplies, Rhodesia, Spain and Germany. The balancing factor is the Mexican supply which finds its way alternatively to the United States or to Europe according to the relative urgency of demand in these quarters.

The most striking feature of the situation is the extreme paucity of floating supplies. At the present time there are practically no such stocks, and throughout the post-war period they have never represented more than a very small proportion of the annual consumption.* As regards its supplies of lead the world has been living from hand to mouth, a state of affairs which may tend to continue in view of the fact that no important new sources of lead have now been discovered for some years, whilst its use tends to increase in paint, cables and storage batteries where no satisfactory substitute has become available.† Even under the extreme stimulus of war prices aggregate output barely reached the pre-war level and has never got within 20 per cent of it since the Armistice.

On the other hand, lead cannot, like tin and copper, be regarded as cheap relatively to other commodities on the basis of pre-war parities. In the United States, partly on account of the new tariff, prices (8.25 cents a lb in April, 1923, compared with averages of 4.5 cents and 4.4 cents in 1912 and 1913) are nearly double the pre-war level, whilst sterling prices are fully 50 per cent up (£28 5s. in April, 1923, compared with averages of £18 and £19 in 1912 and 1913). If we go back to the decade before 1912 £11–£13 per ton represented the normal price in London (except during the 1906–07 boom). It appears that the scarcity of new sources for lead may be slowly shifting its value relatively to commodities in general.

VII. *Spelter* (*Zinc*)

Monthly statistics are available of stocks in public warehouses in the United States and the United Kingdom as below [p. 292].

There are generally some stocks in Belgium, Germany and Poland, and a certain quantity afloat from Australia; also a trifle in France, Scandinavia, and elsewhere. Until recently these stocks represented a material addition to the world's supplies, e.g., in July, 1921, there were the following stocks in Europe: Germany, 20,000 tons; Belgium, 15,000 tons, besides 40,000

---

* World consumption since the Armistice has been very steady round about 900,000 tons per annum more or less, so that at their highest stocks have only represented about six weeks' supply.

† Except, at a price, zinc for paint.

Tons

End of month	1920			1921			1922			1923		
	U.S.	U.K.	Total	U.S.	U.K.	Total	U.S.	U.K.	Total	U.S.	U.K.	Total
January	35,880	25,000*	60,880	67,810	14,862	82,672	58,635	11,412	70,047	14,794	394	15,188
February	33,120	25,000*	58,120	69,660	13,606	83,266	57,250	8,335	65,585	9,700	197	9,897
March	27,695	25,000*	52,695	73,440	14,427	87,867	53,800	6,375	60,175	—	—	—
April	29,025	26,123	55,148	72,720	17,730	90,450	46,186	6,067	52,253	—	—	—
May	26,190	23,411	49,601	76,615	19,000	96,615	36,080	5,338	41,418	—	—	—
June	23,975	26,828	50,803	80,260	18,752	99,012	26,407	4,662	31,069	—	—	—
July	25,925	28,828	54,753	82,510	18,153	100,663	25,552	4,289	29,841	—	—	—
August	26,410	25,709	52,119	77,275	17,387	94,662	19,311	3,977	23,288	—	—	—
September	38,300	23,173	61,473	72,440	16,405	88,845	16,791	3,668	20,459	—	—	—
October	45,740	19,214	64,954	63,235	15,424	78,659	16,110	2,670	18,780	—	—	—
November	57,495	16,953	74,448	59,865	14,052	73,917	17,408	852	18,260	—	—	—
December	63,440	17,536	80,976	59,470	12,765	72,235	16,296	631	16,927	—	—	—

* Approximate. The Metal Exchange statistics only begin in April, 1920.

tons of sheets; Norway, 10,000 tons. A year ago (March 1922) such stocks were still appreciable, (say) 30,000 tons, of which more than half was in Germany. But they have fallen *pari passu* with the drop in U.K. and U.S. stocks, and are no longer important, amounting to (say) 15,000 tons altogether at the end of 1922 and at present (March 1923).

The quantity of mined material which awaits refining in the form of concentrates, slimes and ores is very large. In Australia there has been for some time past from 750,000 to 800,000 tons of concentrates and slimes, equivalent to 300,000 tons of metal. Part is being refined in Australia and part is being shipped under special arrangements made by the Board of Trade after the War for refining in Belgium and Great Britain. The limiting factor is the capacity of the refineries and not the supply of concentrates, which can only come on to the market in the form of metal gradually over a considerable time. Similar stocks in the United States are now reduced and do not represent above two months' supplies.

United States statistics for certain earlier dates are as follows:—Jan. 1, 1913, 4,038 tons; July 1, 1913, 19,514 tons; Jan. 1, 1914, 36,303 tons; Jan. 1, 1919, 36,821 tons; July 1, 1919, 53,183 tons.

The world's smelter output has been estimated* as follows:—

	1913	1919	1920	1921	1922
Belgium	204,220	19,860	77,245	63,121	108,294
Germany	278,800	85,000	94,241	92,000	103,840
France	67,890	10,800	19,822	23,973	39,811
Australia	4,187	8,281	9,665	1,763	23,724
United States	320,283	427,909	414,000	179,000	302,700
Canada	—	11,182	17,857	25,000	25,000
Other countries	35,382	83,465	67,222	47,042	57,664
Total	1,010,762	646,497	700,052	431,899	661,033

* 1913 and 1919 American Bureau of Metal Statistics; 1920-2, Messrs Rudolf Wolff and Co.

There is no difficulty in obtaining whatever amount of zinc may be required at an appropriate price. The present price is about 40 per cent above the pre-war figure in New York, and about 60 per cent in London.

VIII. *Rubber*

The stocks of rubber are held mainly:—

1. On plantations.
2. In Singapore and the East.
3. Afloat.
4. In London and Liverpool.
5. In U.S.A. ports and manufacturies.

Before the war Hamburg and Bordeaux were important centres, but they have not yet recovered.* Stocks in Holland have fluctuated in recent times between 7,000 and 2,500 tons (in February 1923, 2,849 tons), those in Antwerp, from 1,000 tons downwards (in February 1923, 20 tons). London now serves as the only important depository for Europe. The normal pre-war stocks in the Eastern ports were about 15,000 tons, so that, allowing for the increased production, the 25,000 tons actually held at the end of 1922 may be regarded as normal, the accumulations at the end of 1918, estimated at 70,000 tons, due to the shipping shortage, having been gradually worked off.

Only the figures for 3 and 4 are regularly available, and are as follows [see table opposite]:—

The adequacy of these monthly figures as an index to the situation as a whole can, however, be checked by the annual estimates which are compiled by the trade for the 'visible' supply as a whole, that is to say, the total supply exclusive of stocks on plantations. The table below [p. 296] is based on figures supplied by Messrs Symington and Sinclair† :—

---

* The stock of rubber in Bordeaux at the end of 1922, was reported to be three tons.

† These differ slightly from those used in the table on p. 295 and do not exactly tally with those in the following table.

1,000 tons*

End of month	1919			1920			1921			1922			1923		
	Plantation rubber afloat	Public warehouse stocks in U.K.	Total	Plantation rubber afloat	Public warehouse stocks in U.K.	Total	Plantation rubber afloat	Public warehouse stocks in U.K.	Total	Plantation rubber afloat	Public warehouse stocks in U.K.	Total	Plantation rubber afloat	Public warehouse stocks in U.K.	Total
January	24	20	44	45	23	68	28	63	91	40	77	117	43	81	124
February	29	18	47	42	24	66	30	65	95	39	76	115		71	
March	40	18	58	40	24	64	30	71	101	40	75	115		63	
April	48	24	72	35	25	60	29	76	105	33	78	111			
May	35	29	64	46	24	70	28	78	106	43	79	122			
June	43	31	74	38	25	63	32	78	110	44	80	124			
July	32	33	65	38	28	66	31	81	112	43	81	124			
August	34	33	67	36	33	69	30	82	112	44	81	125			
September	35	30	65	34	39	73	34	83	117	44	79	123			
October	38	28	66	36	46	82	32	79	111	47	77	124			
November	42	27	69	33	50	83	36	82	118	46	75	121			
December	37	25	62	37	55	92	32	80	112	45	79	124			

* Figures supplied by Messrs W. H. Rickinson.

Visible supply 31 December of each year (1,000 tons)

	1918	1919	1920	1921	1922
Singapore and Eastern ports	70	60	35	40	25
Afloat	35	37	37	37	45
United Kingdom	16	25	56	80	84*
U.S.A.	10	17	76	52	87
Brazil	5	—	—	—	2
Minor markets	—	3	3	7	5
Total	136	142	207	216	248

* Including 3 in private warehouses.

The most doubtful figures in the above are those for U.S.A. They are corroborated on the whole by the inventory of crude rubber in the United States and afloat for the United States ports on 31 October 1922, obtained by the Rubber Association of America. 357 manufacturers, who are estimated to represent 95 per cent of the trade, supplied information. The figures were as follows:—

	On hand (long tons)		Afloat (long tons)	
	Planta-tion	All other	Planta-tion	All other
American manufacturers (341)	54,574	5,383	12,881	335
Canadian manufacturers (16)	2,282	179	152	36
American importers and dealers (38)	21,341	1,223	29,375	735
Total	78,197	6,785	42,408	1,106

The sources of rubber supply being far distant from the localities of consumption, the working minimum of stocks is substantial. Formerly Messrs Symington and Sinclair put this at 135,000 tons. In view of the increased rate of consumption, they have now raised the figure to 150,000 tons, made up of 3 months' supply, namely 100,000 tons, on the move, i.e., afloat, in the East and in miscellaneous ports, and 50,000 tons for London and New York as the keepers of the trading stocks of their respective continents. Thus the 'true surplus' stocks at the end of 1922 represented about three months' consumption.

Production and consumption in recent years are estimated to have been as follows:—

Production and consumption*

Production	Tons 1919	Tons 1920	Tons 1921	Tons 1922
Malaya	180,000	190,000	170,000	238,000
Ceylon and India	35,000	40,000	40,000	48,000
Dutch East Indies	75,000	85,000	50,000	73,000
Other countries in the East	10,000	15,000	10,000	15,000
Total Eastern plantation rubber	300,000	330,000	270,000	370,000
Brazil	32,000	31,000	20,000	21,500
Wild	7,000	7,000	3,000	3,500
Total	339,000	368,000	293,000	399,000
Consumption				
U.S.A.	225,000	200,000	200,000	290,000
United Kingdom	33,000	25,000	18,000	20,000
France	22,000	16,000	14,000	25,000
Italy	14,000	6,000	5,000	5,000
Canada	9,500	11,000	9,000	9,000
Japan	—	7,500	12,500	13,000
Germany, Russia and Austria	5,500	11,000	18,000	29,000
Other countries	14,000	13,500	15,500	12,000
Total	335,000	290,000	292,000	403,000

* Symington and Sinclair.

Production during the current year is, of course, affected by the legislation for restriction in Malaya and Ceylon. The 'standard production' has been fixed at 270,000 tons for Malaya and 50,000 tons for Ceylon. The exportable quota is fixed at 60 per cent of this for the six months November, 1922–April, 1923, and at 65 per cent for the three months May–July, 1923.* If the price averages 1s. 6d. or over for the latter period, the quota will be raised in successive three-monthly periods to 70 per cent, 80 per cent, 90 per cent, 100 per cent.

Allowing for this, supply from these two countries in 1923 may be estimated at about 210,000 tons, which, with say 125,000 tons from other sources, makes a total of 335,000 tons. In view of the 1922 consumption, the corresponding figures for 1923 are not likely to fall below 415,000 tons.† Thus the restriction plan seems to allow approximately for the exhaustion of the 'true surplus' stocks during the current year.

IX. *Sugar*

In the case of this commodity it is necessary to restrict ourselves to 'visible' supplies, accurate estimates of stocks held up by producers in the fairly numerous different sources of supply not being available. Nevertheless, this limitation is not so serious as it would be in the case of many commodities, because, on the one hand, sugar being a semi-manufactured product, the agricultural producers send the bulk of the output forward to the centrals as soon as it is available, and, on the other hand, since it is in most countries a dutiable commodity, invisible supplies, on which duty has been paid, are not likely, as a rule, to be any larger than convenience dictates.

The 'visible' stocks naturally show a sharp seasonal fluctuation, falling to a minimum in November and rising to a maximum by about May (or a little earlier), at which date they may amount to about 20 per cent of the year's supply, or perhaps 30 per cent of the supply which comes on the world market.

The total monthly figures (supplied by Messrs Bagot & Thompson) have been as follows:—

* Assuming that the average price in London February–April, 1923, falls short of 1s. 6d. a lb.
† There is likely, however, to be an increased use of reclaimed rubber.

Total visible supply of sugar (1,000 tons)

First half of month	1913	1914	1920	1921	1922	1923
January	3,234	3,711		2,313	2,389	
February	4,043	4,323		2,816	2,898	
March	4,141	4,279	2,399	3,254	2,859	
April	4,006	4,192	2,433	3,331	2,961	
May	3,869	4,032	2,423	3,471	3,015	
June	3,732	3,792	2,075	3,382	2,580	
July	3,228	3,244	2,003	3,312	2,413	
August	3,426	2,668	1,788	3,141	2,231	
September	1,813	*	1,522	2,375	1,583	
October	1,259		1,338	2,039	1,195	
November	739		1,197	1,727	826	
December	1,900		2,103	2,258	1,548	

* No figures available between this date and March 1920.

The distribution of the stock between the different centres is shown by the following [p. 300] detailed table for selected dates. It will be observed that the abnormal accumulation of floating supplies in the autumn of 1921 was mainly accounted for by the huge carryover in Cuba.

The following table gives a very rough idea of stocks, production and consumption during the past three years:—

	1922–3	1921–2	1920–1
	Tons	Tons	Tons
Stock carried over on 1 Sept.	1,500,000	2,400,000	1,600,000
European beetroot crops	4,735,500	4,054,282	3,671,788
American beetroot crops	640,000	930,121	1,004,019
Cane crops	12,691,500	12,679,948	12,081,831
Totals	19,567,000	20,064,351	18,357,638
Deduct visible supplies on 1 September 1922 and 1921	—	1,500,000	2,400,000
Total consumption for year ended 31 August	—	18,564,351	15,057,638

1,000 tons

	January		April		July		October		December	
	1921	1922	1921	1922	1921	1922	1921	1922	1921	1922
U.K.	389	171	378	142	402	364	289	278	159	359
Germany	390	338	760	693	489	421	179	116	339	298
Czecho–Slovakia	619	480	558	384	394	198	70	15	479	468
France	213	140	262	177	110	76	31	86	140	176
Holland	103	95	148	128	74	83	15	53	95	82
Belgium	146	112	151	97	75	42	13	23	112	107
United States	97	62	126	179	185	200	117	128	31	12
Cuba	205	891	807	930	1,431	780	1,185	316	} 902	} 45
Estimated afloat	50	100	140	230	150	240	140	180		
	2,312	2,389	3,331	2,961	3,311	2,413	2,039	1,195	2,258	1,548

300

The United Kingdom and the United States are responsible between them for an extraordinary proportion of the consumption of exported sugar. Consumption in the United Kingdom is put at 1,420,000 tons in 1921 and at least 1,600,000 tons in 1922; United States consumption may amount to 5,000,000 tons or even a little more. The present situation is dominated by the fact that less Cuban and domestic sugar is available for the United States this year than last, whilst the consumption is increasing.

The short period demand for sugar appears to be very inelastic, with the result that price fluctuations since the War have been extremely violent. New York prices in May, 1920, rose to nearly three times the price current in the previous year, and then fell between that date and the end of 1921 by more than 80 per cent (i.e., to less than a fifth of the price of May, 1920). Early this year prices rose again within a very brief period to 50 per cent above the low level of 1922. It is noticeable that the increase in visible supplies from 2,423,000 tons in May, 1920, to 3,471,000 tons in May, 1921, was accompanied by a fall in price (New York) from 20.90 cents per lb. to 4.90 cents. It is easily calculated what huge banking resources were required to finance the stocks of sugar at the peak prices of May, 1920, shortly before the catastrophic break of prices in the latter half of 1920.

X. *Coffee*

About two-thirds of the supply of coffee for Europe and U.S.A. comes from Brazil. The following table is based on the figures supplied by Messrs Duuring and Zoon, the most important omissions from which are the stocks in the East and Eastern ports, in the interior of Brazil, and coffee from the East afloat to U.S.A.

The deliveries during the last four complete seasons are given below. For the first months (July 1st to Feb. 1st) of this year deliveries are slightly less (10,402,000 compared with 10,867,000) than those for the corresponding period in 1921-2.

Coffee (1,000 bags)*

Year	Beginning of month	Visible supply of Europe	Visible supply of U.S.A.	Stocks in Brazil	Total
1913	July	6,480	1,848	1,947	10,275
	August	6,392	1,639	2,451	10,482
	September	6,005	1,477	4,002	11,484
	October	6,019	1,393	4,769	12,181
	November	6,193	1,348	5,229	12,770
	December	6,703	1,379	5,059	13,141
1914	January	7,275	1,709	4,681	13,665
	February	8,556	2,206	2,514	13,276
	March	8,420	2,320	2,062	12,802
	April	8,702	2,172	1,743	12,617
	May	8,608	2,071	1,444	12,124
	June	8,353	2,056	1,207	11,616
1919	January	758	1,010	9,296	11,364
	February	1,288	1,463	8,904	11,655
	March	1,699	1,994	7,948	11,641
	April	2,755	1,964	7,060	11,799
	May	2,968	1,723	6,518	11,209
	June	3,357	1,389	6,274	11,020
	July	3,124	1,508	5,704	10,336
	August	3,311	1,562	5,352	10,225
	September	3,159	1,717	5,372	10,248
	October	2,821	2,057	5,540	10,418
	November	2,959	2,178	5,357	10,494
	December	2,973	2,007	5,088	10,068
1920	January	2,843	2,007	5,020	9,870
	February	2,928	1,766	4,615	9,309
	March	2,739	2,064	4,294	8,737
	April	2,573	2,209	3,392	8,174
	May	2,708	2,092	2,781	7,581
	June	2,553	2,111	2,324	6,988
	July	2,509	2,293	1,948	6,750
	August	2,495	2,326	1,908	6,729

Table (*cont.*)

Year	Beginning of month	Visible supply of Europe	Visible supply of U.S.A.	Stocks in Brazil	Total
	September	2,677	2,561	2,288	7,526
	October	2,955	2,640	2,387	7,982
	November	2,924	2,377	2,752	8,053
	December	2,861	2,347	3,241	8,449
1921	January	2,588	2,442	3,735	8,765
	February	2,480	2,359	3,938	8,777
	March	2,553	2,598	3,656	8,807
	April	2,533	2,765	3,389	8,687
	May	2,480	2,603	3,397	8,580
	June	2,575	2,252	3,748	8,575
	July	2,562	2,100	4,038	8,700
	August	2,682	2,191	4,319	9,192
	September	2,594	1,874	4,595	9,063
	October	2,564	1,838	4,589	8,991
	November	2,309	1,975	4,666	8,950
	December	2,195	2,237	4,680	9,112
1922	January	2,399	2,056	4,948	9,403
	February	2,669	1,824	4,796	9,289
	March	2,760	1,774	4,794	9,328
	April	2,977	1,583	4,580	9,140
	May	2,867	1,641	4,329	8,837
	June	2,991	1,497	4,414	8,902
	July	3,068	1,456	4,115	8,639
	August	2,948	1,353	4,313	8,614
	September	3,126	1,282	4,393	8,801
	October	3,007	1,182	4,292	8,481
	November	2,996	1,549	3,847	8,392
	December	2,921	1,603	3,733	8,257
1923	January	2,839	1,385	3,756	7,980
	February	2,764	1,402	3,573	7,739
	March	2,443	1,625	3,312	7,480

* G. Duuring and Zoon.

| | | Deliveries (1,000 bags) | | From | Other |
	Europe	U.S.A.	Total	Brazil	kinds
1918–19	4,376	8,985	13,361	8,589	4,772
1919–20	6,667	9,583	16,250	9,628	6,622
1920–1	5,899	9,631	15,530	9,837	5,693
1921–2	8,855	9,632	18,487	11,415	7,072

XI. *Tea*

The only figures available for the stocks of tea are of those in bond in the United Kingdom. Since, however, about three-quarters of the total world production passes through this country, these stocks should form a fairly reliable index of the position; in particular no less than 88 per cent of the 1921 crop in India, Ceylon and the East Indies, which countries provide nearly the whole of the tea in which there is a world market, were shipped to the United Kingdom for distribution.

Tea Brokers' Association : Report of tea in bond in United Kingdom
(1,000 lb)

End of month	1913	1919	1920	1921	1922	1923
January	136,057		215,175	224,415	216,117	
February	129,395		203,061	228,021	228,988	
March	121,477		212,645	236,300	222,727	
April	103,272		207,520	239,392	214,864	
May	87,568		212,152	234,001	192,585	
June	77,099		214,986	218,594	170,600	
July	72,665		212,759	207,399	151,094	
August	82,223		214,843	197,433	140,983	
September	99,717		215,251	190,799	149,686	
October	112,632	145,774	220,137	190,129	150,306	
November	125,434	169,861	223,229	196,534	156,986	
December	138,005	213,083	214,362	205,420	167,790	

Crops	1922	1921
India	312,500,000	272,000,000
Ceylon	168,000,000	162,500,000
Java and Sumatra	93,500,000	76,750,000
	574,000,000	511,250,000
World's total		600,000,000

A striking feature of the period since the War has been the immense increase in the consumption of tea in the U.K. which has risen 35 per cent since 1913 and has thus offset the collapse of demand from Russia.

Whilst there are believed to be no abnormal stocks in the countries of production, the unshipped crops on Dec. 31st, 1922, were 17,000,000 lb greater than on the corresponding date in 1921. Duty paid stocks in the U.K. are now lower than they were at Dec. 31st, 1913.

XII. *Petroleum*

The only figures of stocks regularly available are those for the United States. Since, however, nearly 80 per cent of the world's oil stocks are held in the United States, these figures can be regarded as reasonably representative.

The following table of stocks of crude petroleum in the United States is that published by the American Petroleum Institute:—[p. 306].

It will be seen that stocks of crude oil remained steady during 1919 and 1920, began to increase in 1921, and continued upwards throughout 1921 and 1922. At the end of 1922 they represented about $4\frac{1}{2}$ months' supply at the rate of consumption then current.

In addition to stocks of crude oil, there are also small stocks (rather more than a month's supply) of the principal refined

| Stocks at end | Crude petroleum (1,000 barrels) | | | | |
of month	1919	1920	1921	1922	1923
January	127,777	127,164	117,099	180,984	
February	126,982	126,329	121,713	191,471	
March	129,213	125,597	128,754	202,906	
April	130,729	124,991	134,719	213,371	
May	130,321	124,689	143,614	224,388	
June	133,995	126,763	151,339	232,032	
July	140,093	128,168	159,030	238,233	
August	136,467	129,043	162,903	242,635	
September	137,131	128,788	164,076	244,778	
October	135,461	129,451	163,335	246,625	
November	131,601	131,325	164,073	247,942	
December	127,867	133,690	170,350	248,413	

[*U.S.A. stocks of refined products*] (barrels)

End of month	Gasoline	Kerosene	Lub. oils	Fuel and gas oils
December 1918	7,079,213	9,050,425	3,306,033	15,690,510
June 1919	14,140,396	6,012,915	4,175,828	19,328,348
December 1919	10,637,939	8,079,040	3,269,498	17,002,963
June 1920	12,001,324	10,031,984	3,171,727	15,284,961
December 1920	11,009,091	9,358,831	3,821,964	19,938,200
June 1921	17,872,487	10,358,493	6,211,503	29,730,097
December 1921	13,954,456	8,119,251	5,161,084	31,696,796
June 1922	19,642,058	7,561,297	5,402,472	31,593,801
December 1922	21,042,687	6,691,675	5,612,733	31,064,949

products. The half-yearly figures of these stocks in the United States have been as follows:—[see above].

The relation of these stocks to current consumption of the various refined products (*not* consumption of crude oils by refineries) is shown by the following table:—

1,000 barrels

	Domestic consumption	Exports		Total
		General	Bunkers	
1919	349,565	62,853	14,031	426,449
1920	419,693	77,993	26,335	524,021
1921	418,963	70,723	27,027	516,713
1922	478,526	72,952	31,692	583,170*

* During the last quarter of 1922 the total of domestic consumption and exports was running at the rate of 660,000,000 barrels a year.

XIII. *Nitrate*

Nitrate statistics are comparatively simple since they all come from one part of the world. Very complete figures are regularly published by Messrs Aikman.

The figures for America include interior stocks but not those held by the American Government, which have gradually declined from round 300,000 tons in Dec. 1921, to 85,000 tons at the present time.

In normal times there is a considerable reduction in the visible supply in the early part of the year as the demand is somewhat seasonal.

In the hands of the American Government and not included in the above figures [pp. 308–9].

31 December 1921	300,000 tons	31 May 1922	175,000 tons
28 February 1922	210,000 ,,	31 December 1922	125,000 ,,
30 April 1922	190–200,000 ,,	31 January 1923	85,000 ,,

Deliveries (year ending 30 June) (1,000 tons)

	1914	1920	1921	1922
Europe and Egypt	1,984	861	706	895
U.S.A.	553	794	644	565
Japan and others	92	227	84	84
	2,629	1,882	1,434	1,544

Nitrate (1,000 tons)*

End of month	Visible supply (including afloat)		Stocks in Chile	Total
	Europe and Egypt	U.S.A.		
1913 January	1,128	89	490	1,727
February	921	86	495	1,517
March	686	97	527	1,326
April	484	140	579	1,219
May	378	138	692	1,218
June	416	84	754	1,265
July	430	83	687	1,215
August	510	77	734	1,337
September	571	79	752	1,414
October	739	89	671	1,511
November	868	71	636	1,588
December	1,098	71	498	1,685
1919 July	140	28	1,594	1,780
August	150	40	1,646	1,854
September	152	49	1,705	1,925
October	236	64	1,658	1,981
November	273	80	1,698	2,075
December	430	95	1,576	2,134
1920 January	545	226	1,348	2,180
February	518	274	1,258	2,121
March	368	253	1,218	1,914
April	312·5	308	1,186	1,869
May	343	317	1,160	1,846
June	317	216	1,248	1,800
July	337	135	1,319	1,813
August	404	170	1,347	1,937
September	495	194	1,303	2,008
October	565·5	182	1,320	2,073
November	629	130	1,372	2,139
December	782	132	1,304	2,235

Table (*cont.*)

End of month	Visible supply (including afloat)		Stocks in Chile	Total
	Europe and Egypt	U.S.A.		
1921 January	887	124	1,320	2,348
February	911	235	1,258	2,416
March	868	218	1,283	2,384
April	865	194	1,319	2,391
May	848	211	1,371	2,482
June	836	249	1,317	2,405
July	827·5	223	1,409	2,320
August	822·5	186	1,405	2,280
September	828	41	1,453	2,370
October	862	27	1,444	2,335
November	895	15	1,441	2,366
December	903·5	260	1,441	2,622·5
1922 January	869	261	1,459	2,618
February	750	182	1,482	2,434
March	520	115	1,504	2,149
April	394·5	80	1,496	1,982·5
May	282	111	1,549	1,948
June	227·5	38	1,582	1,851
July	244	58	1,564	1,900
August	260	119	1,519	1,940
September	277	148	1,482	1,940
October	314	152	1,396	1,899
November	402	182	1,313	1,924
December	427·5	192	1,231	1,891·5
1923 January	459	223	1,157	1,866
February	440·5	220	994	1,680
March				1,502

* Messrs Aikman.

Visible supply of wheat and flour in second hands (1,000,000 bushels)*

Beginning of	1919			1920			1921			1922			1923		
	1	2	3	1	2	3	1	2	3	1	2	3	1	2	3
January	231	?	?	170	77	247	148	67	215	184	54	238	232	53	285
February	240	58	298	143	82	225	120	68	188	161	51	212	220	65	285
March	230	63	293	130	80	210	116	79	195	146	67	213	207	72	279
April	192	63	255	123	77	200	92	80	172	133	77	210			
May	126	79	205	111	80	191	72	85	157	115	75	190			
June	76	90	166	97	92	189	51	101	152	92	69	161			
July	38	106	144	68	90	158	42	84	126	72	65	137			
August	56	91	147	51	93	144	65	69	134	62	58	120			
September	104	94	198	56	73	129	87	70	157	74	51	125			
October	169	85	254	99	71	163	137	63	200	133	43	176			
November	203	69	272	126	70	196	172	60	232	196	47	243			
December	195	81	276	144	68	212	184	57	241	215	64	279			

* *Broomhall's Corn Trade News.* 1. Visible supply in elevators and public stores in Canada and the United States. 2. Other visible supply, i.e. in the Argentine, afloat for U.K. and the Continent, and in U.K. (Details of each of these items separately are available.) 3. Total of 1 and 2.

310

XIV. *Wheat*

Wheat is a very baffling commodity to the compiler of comparative totals, because it is a seasonal crop, coming from many different sources, and harvested at many different times of year.

As in the case of other commodities, the statistics regularly available month by month are those of 'visible' supplies in 'second hands'; but, owing to the large amounts held on farms and elsewhere 'out of sight', these figures are only moderately useful as an index to the general situation. The figures in question are as follows:—[see page 310].

Perhaps the figures of the old crop carryover together with those of the new crop in the chief exporting countries, as published by the International Institute of Agriculture, are the most *complete* index to current supplies. These are as follows:—

Million centals (i.e., 100,000,000 lb)

		Canada			U.S.A.		
	1	2	3	1	2	3
1920	7·8	164·2	172·0	90·4	511·0	601·4
1921	8·2	180·5	188·7	69·2	476·9	546·1
1922	11·7	233·3	245·0	65·3	486·1	551·4

		Argentine			Australia		India
	1	2	3	1	2	3	2
1920	3·5	111·0	114·5	—	88·1	88·1	226·0*
1921	18·0	108·4	126·4	—	79·4	79·4	152·6
1922	5·8	129·6†	135·4	—	54·5†	54·5	219·8

1. Old crop carryover (July 1 for U.S., Sept. 1 for Canada and Dec. 31 for Argentine and Australia).   2. Current crop (crop of subsequent calendar year in case of Argentine and Australia).   3. Total available.
* Very poor crop, with the result that India instead of exporting a certain amount was under the necessity of importing.
† Preliminary forecasts.

Another way of approaching the question, favoured by the International Institute of Agriculture, is that of the exportable surplus in exporting countries on January 1 of each year (i.e., after allowing for domestic consumption, seed, and minimum carryover). On this basis the figures are as below (in this table supplies in all countries are worked out to the same date, which is a convenience). The Institute's figures for 1 January 1923, not

Quantities exportable from the exporting countries on 1 January (million centals)

	1921	1922	1923
Canada	35·7	68·3	80
United States	58·4	50·2	82
India	6·4	—	—
Argentine	71·3	74·7	83
Australia	66·7	59·7	34
Total	238·5	252·9	279
Stocks in U.K.	19·6	5·3	3·4
Afloat for U.K. and Continent	21·3	20·1	26·2
Grand total	279·4	278·3	308·6

being yet available as this goes to press, I have ventured to give in the 1923 column my own rough guesses, which must be regarded as strictly provisional. I have also supplemented the figures of exportable surplus by adding Mr Broomhall's figures for U.K. stocks and for the quantity afloat for Europe on the same dates, which gives as complete a total as is possible for the aggregate supplies available for the importing countries at the beginning of each calendar year.

The following supplementary tables may also be useful:—

Total stocks of wheat (both in first and second hands) in U.S.A. on 1 July million bushels)

1909	43	1912	78	1915	55	1918	28	1921	79
1910	88	1913	90	1916	163	1919	54	1922	57
1911	92	1914	76	1917	48	1920	151		

U.S. Dept. of Agriculture figures of farm reserves on 1 March (million bushels)

Year of harvest	Total crop	Stock in farmers' hands 1 March	Per cent of total crop	Consumed or distributed since harvest
1923		153	17·9	703
1922	856	131	16·1	684
1921	815	208	24·9	625
1920	833	166	17·1	802
1919	968	129	14·0	788
1918	917	111	17·0	540
1917	651	101	15·7	539
1916	640	242	23·9	770
1915	1,012	153	17·2	738
1914	891	152	19·9	611
1913	763	156	21·3	574
1912	730			

The general effect of these figures is to show that the aggregate supply of wheat to importing countries has been fairly steady in the last three years and that the stocks now on hand are fully as adequate as they have been at any time since the War. But it must be added that estimates of 'invisible' supplies of wheat are, inevitably, even more liable to error than other figures of the same kind, as became apparent when, during the War, it became necessary to frame policies on them.

Visible supplies in Australia (million bushels)

	1919	1920	1921	1922	1923
1 January	155	76	9	5	16
1 April	159	60	98	50	62*
1 July	170	34	36	5	
1 October	110	17	28	Nil	

* March.

Wheat is, however, relatively cheap compared with many other commodities, perhaps too cheap; and it remains to be seen whether the present level of relative prices is high enough to continue to call forth adequate supplies from the countries of export.

Keynes provided a second memorandum, not six but fourteen months later.

From London and Cambridge Economic Service, Special Memorandum No. 6 (June 1924)

STOCKS OF STAPLE COMMODITIES

The statistics given below are in continuation of a Memorandum published in April 1923. The same general lines have been followed as in the earlier Memorandum. An additional section has been added summarising the index of 'visible' stocks in the United States published by the U.S. Department of Commerce.

A year ago the Memorandum pointed out 'that during 1922 the world's consumption of raw commodities materially exceeded its production'. During 1923, especially in the first half of the year, the same tendency continued, but not quite so strongly. In the course of the year the world stocks of cotton, wool, jute, tin, rubber, coffee and nitrate fell materially. As against this, none of the commodities under review showed a material increase in stocks except petroleum. The same tendency has been continued during the first four months of 1924. American cotton, wool and tin stand out as commodities of which the level of consumption has been running for some time above that of production. This maladjustment is partly due to a reaction from the very excessive stocks of these commodities held three years ago. Foodstuffs, on the other hand—notably wheat and sugar—are in good supply.

The figures shown below for the four leading non-ferrous metals, compiled by the British Metal Corporation, are given in continuation of those printed in last year's Memorandum.

314

World production and consumption

Average 1911–13 = 100	Production			Consumption		
	1921	1922	1923	1921	1922	1923
Copper	57	91	123	59*	96	115
Lead	74	93	101	70	90	101
Tin	85	102	100	66	104	109
Spelter	46	73	100	47	79	95

* I do not agree with this figure. J.M.K.

Thus the aggregate world consumption of these metals has fully caught up the pre-war figures. Nevertheless the distribution of consumption is greatly changed, and the contrast between conditions in the United States of America and elsewhere is very marked. The United States consumed in 1923 72 per cent more copper, 33 per cent more lead, 35 per cent more spelter and 46 per cent more tin than in 1911–13; whilst the rest of the world consumed 13 per cent less copper, 15 per cent less lead, 21 per cent less spelter, and 14 per cent less tin. Nor is this feature limited to the non-ferrous metals. The proportion of the world's raw materials generally, consumed by the United States, is preposterously high.

It becomes remarkably apparent to anyone who follows such statistics as these, in conjunction with price movements, how sensitive the short-period price levels of many commodities are to maladjustments between the rates of production and of consumption of a comparatively small percentage amount. Over a period of a year or two demand and supply are generally quite elastic and can be reconciled by moderate price movements; but over a period of a few months they are apt to be inelastic, with the result of violent oscillations of price. It seems as if relative prices could be kept a good deal steadier if the organisation for carrying stocks at a moderate cost were on a larger scale.

The following table [p. 317] is a summary of the figures given in detail below for each separate commodity. For the methods of compilation the reader is referred to the detailed statements.

THE U.S. DEPARTMENT OF COMMERCE INDEX
OF COMMODITY STOCKS

This index has been recently revised and extended and now covers 45 commodities. It is weighted by reference to the value of the supply of each commodity in 1919. The table on page 318 shows the commodities chosen and the weights used (calculated in tens of millions of dollars).

The figures of this index are of much interest and deserve recording below. But it has two great weaknesses. In the first place, the statistics available are, generally speaking, for what is termed 'visible supply' in the U.S., and not for total supply even in the U.S.—far less in the world. In the second place, visible stocks of sugar, cereals, eggs and cotton, which between them make up a considerable part of the whole, are markedly seasonal; yet no correction has been made for the seasonal factor.

For the details month by month and for the definitions of 'visible' stocks, the reader is referred to the *Survey of Current Business* published by the U.S. Department of Commerce. The following tables [pp. 319, 320], however, give the annual averages for individual commodities and four-monthly averages for the total— these, in view of the above weaknesses, being really more valuable than the monthly figures. It will be noticed that visible stocks for the middle four months of the year are seasonally lower than those for the first or last months; also that, seasonal fluctuations apart, stocks rose from a minimum in the first half of 1920 to a maximum in the first third of 1922, falling again to a minimum in the middle of 1923 and rising somewhat since that time.

Stocks of staple commodities

	Am. cotton 1,000 bales (1)	Wool 1,000,000 lb (2)	Jute 1,000 bales (3)	Copper 1,000 tons (4)	Tin 1,000 tons (5)	Lead 1,000 tons (6)	Spelter 1,000 tons (7)	Rubber 1,000 tons (8)	Sugar 1,000 tons (9)	Coffee 1,000 bags (10)	Tea 1,000,000 lb (11)	Crude oil 1,000,000 barrels (12)	Nitrate 1,000 tons (13)	Wheat 1,000,000 centals (14)
1920														
1 Jan.	6,567	—	—	900	35	60	61	139	2,313	9,870	213	128	2,134	—
1 July	6,384	—	9,857	—	26	25	51	—	2,003	6,750	215	127	1,800	—
1921														
1 Jan.	7,417	1,200	—	822	27	19	81	204	2,389	8,765	214	134	2,235	279
1 July	8,623	—	8,190	—	44	13	99	—	3,312	8,700	219	151	2,405	—
1922														
1 Jan.	6,623	950	—	451	53	1	72	209	1,624	9,403	205	170	2,615	278
1 July	4,498	—	6,000	—	44	0	31	—	2,413	8,639	171	232	1,851	—
1923														
1 Jan.	2,875	420	—	296	41	1	17	271	1,548	7,980	168	248	1,891	391
1 July	2,480	—	4,000	—	35	0	17	254	—	5,340	127	327	1,255	—
1924														
1 Jan.	1,681	80	—	371	29	1	34	223	—	4,467	170	333	1,643	366
1 May	1,219	—	—	343	24	0	30	—	—	4,445	192	—	1,269	—

(1) Total supply seasonally corrected, exclusive of European and Asiatic mill stocks. (2) Total surplus supply not in manufacturers' hands (3) Total supply. (4) Total supply outside hands of consumers. (5) Total supply outside hands of consumers. (6) Visible supply in U.K. (7) Visible supply in U.K. and U.S. (8) Total supply outside plantations. (9) Total visible supply. (10) Visible supply in Rio, Santos, Bahia, Europe and U.S.A. (11) Stocks in bond in U.K. (12) Stocks in U.S. (13) Visible supply in Chile, U.S.A., Europe and Egypt. (14) Supply available for importing countries.

317

Table of weights used in this index

Raw materials	Domestic	Imported	Total	Manufactured products	Domestic	Imported	Final weight
Foodstuffs				Foodstuffs			
Sugar	6	39	45	Meats	164	—	164
Wheat	176	—	176	Wheat flour	144	—	144
Corn	70	—	70	Butter	52	—	52
Oats	21	—	21	Cheese	14	—	14
Eggs	66	—	66	Rice	8	—	8
Poultry	39	—	39				
Fish	10	4	14				
Apples	18	—	18				
Coffee	—	26	26				
Total	406	69	475	Total	382	—	382
Non-foodstuffs				Non-foodstuffs			
Cotton	201	—	201	Refined oils	163	—	163
Cotton seed	35	—	35	Cotton-seed oil	58	—	58
Flax seed	3	4	7	Cement	17	—	17
Rosin	2	—	2	Brick	20	—	20
Turpentine	1	—	1	Flooring	50	—	50
Crude petroleum	70	3	73	Lumber	139	—	139
Tin	—	5	5	Enamel ware	14	—	14
				Zinc	10	—	10
				Pig iron (merchant)	79	—	79
				Newsprint	10	4	14
Total	312	12	324	Total	560	4	564

Total index

(1919 Average = 100)			
1920	1st four months		96
	2nd ,,	,,	85
	3rd ,,	,,	107
1921	1st ,,	,,	138
	2nd ,,	,,	126
	3rd ,,	,,	131
1922	1st ,,	,,	143
	2nd ,,	,,	117
	3rd ,,	,,	119
1923	1st ,,	,,	128
	2nd ,,	,,	103
	3rd ,,	,,	127
1924	January		132

COMMODITIES IN DETAIL

I. *American cotton*

At any given time stocks consist of the following:—

(1) Stocks up-country in the Southern States on plantations, compresses and railroads and in 'uncounted' interior towns.*

(2) The 'visible' supply as shown weekly in the returns of the New Orleans and New York Cotton Exchanges. This consists of (*a*) warehouse stocks in the more important interior towns (42 in number) and in the ports of the United States, (*b*) cotton afloat for Great Britain and the Continent, (*c*) warehouse stocks in the principal European ports, namely, Liverpool, Manchester, London, Havre, Marseilles, Genoa, Bremen, Ghent, Rotterdam and Barcelona.†

---

* I.e. towns not included in the figures for 'visible' supply.

† Cotton afloat for Japan and in Japanese ports is not allowed for. All cotton consigned to Japan is considered by the leading Exchanges as 'consumed' or 'out of sight'.

Index of U.S. stocks

Monthly average	1919	1920	1921	1922	1923
Raw foodstuffs	100	89	161	192	144
Sugar	100	111	158	206	201
Wheat	100	60	64	84	108
Corn	100	147	528	649	284
Oats	100	74	225	224	87
Eggs	100	79	100	124	129
Poultry	100	71	78	84	105
Fish	100	73	72	57	58
Apples	100	123	121	132	171
Coffee	100	140	139	90	74
Raw materials for manufacture	100	106	147	110	111
Cotton	100	95	125	83	65
Cotton seed	100	72	101	87	90
Flax seed	100	607	1,288	185	351
Rosin	100	71	141	138	119
Turpentine	100	50	86	48	52
Petroleum	100	101	121	186	223
Tin	100	204	144	152	164
Manufactured foodstuffs	100	94	78	72	81
Meats	100	92	76	62	79
Wheat flour	100	95	76	77	81
Butter	100	89	78	76	70
Cheese	100	91	73	74	95
Rice	100	159	159	154	166
Manufactured commodities	100	98	135	118	130
Refined oils	100	98	143	156	174
Cotton-seed oil	100	97	88	53	57
Cement	100	74	104	99	94
Brick	100	105	112	117	129
Flooring	100	131	216	170	184
Lumber	100	113	126	120	119
Enamel ware	100	46	100	72	48
Zinc	100	108	213	97	54
Pig iron	100	60	132	67	115
Newsprint	100	99	127	97	95
Total index	100	96	132	126	119

(3) Mill stocks in spinners' hands throughout the world, generally known as the 'invisible' or 'out of sight' supply.

The table given below [p. 322] comprises (1) 'up-country' stocks *plus* (2) 'visible' stocks *plus* (3) the 'invisible' mill stocks in the U.S.A., but not the mill stocks in other countries, which are only known accurately at the half-yearly census. Aggregate figures are given on pp. 323–4 for *total* supply, including all mill stocks, at the end and in the middle of each season.

I define the 'up-country' stock as the 'up-country' carryover in the Southern States at the end of each season, *plus* the current year's crop, *minus* the amount of cotton which has come into 'sight',* and has therefore been included in 'visible' supplies. It follows that the whole of the new crop is suddenly added to the 'up-country' stock in August of each year. This is corrected in the following table by the 'seasonal correction', which provides what would be the figure of 'up-country' stock if the current crop came into existence at an even monthly rate through the year. The weekly returns of cotton 'into sight' may be regarded as reliable.† The estimates of the current crop are reasonably accurate by the end of each calendar year. The 'up-country' carryover is the most doubtful item, and is always liable to be under- rather than over-estimated, with the result that very high prices may draw out a certain amount of unsuspected supplies. I have based the figures below on those of Mr H. G. Hester, the Secretary of the New Orleans Cotton Exchange.

The consumption during the half-year ending Jan. 31, 1924, has been at a rate of nearly 12,000,000 bales per annum. The continuance of this rate of consumption up to the date when the new crop is available is not possible. Thus some curtailment of consumption is inevitable.

The present position is, therefore, approximately as follows. On February 1, 1924, there were about 7,250,000 bales of American cotton in the world, which allows for an under-

---

* The figures of 'into sight' include linters. This has been ignored prior to August 1923. From that date onwards, a correction is made by deducting 50,000 bales monthly from the gross figures of 'into sight'.
† Three estimates of this, compiled on somewhat different bases, are commonly quoted, namely, those of the New Orleans and New York Cotton Exchanges and *The Financial and Commercial Chronicle*. I follow the Liverpool Cotton Exchange in using the first-named.

Supplies other than European and Asiatic mill stocks
(1,000 bales)*

End of month	'Up-country'	'Visible'	Total outside mills	Correction for season	Corrected total	U.S. mill stocks§	Grand total‖
1919							
July	2,193	3,214	5,407	—	5,407		
Oct.	11,710	3,463	15,173	9,189	5,984		
1920							
Jan.	5,632	4,658	10,290	6,126	4,416	1,952	6,368
April	3,141	4,205	7,346	3,063	4,283	1,812	6,095
July	1,703	2,944	4,647	—	4,647	1,358	6,005
Oct.	12,450	3,513	15,963	10,026	5,937	940	6,877
1921							
Jan.	8,165	4,842	13,007	6,684	6,323	1,264	7,587
April	5,733	4,497	10,230	3,342	6,888	1,316	8,204
July	3,713	4,113	7,826	—	7,826	1,111	8,937
Oct.	7,826	4,474	12,300	5,967	6,333	1,398	7,731
1922							
Jan.	4,247	4,389	8,636	4,078	4,558	1,669	6,227
April	2,416	3,409	5,825	2,089	3,736	1,461	5,197
July	964	1,968	2,932	—	2,932	1,218	4,150
Oct.†	7,523	3,386	10,909	7,480	3,429	1,380	4,809
1923							
Jan.	2,732	3,460	6,192	4,960	1,232	1,987	3,219
April	1,475	1,871	3,346	2,440	906	1,889	2,795
May	1,048	1,432	2,480	1,600	880	1,621	2,501
June	784	1,111	1,895	760	1,135	1,345	2,480
July	184	866	1,050	—	1,050	1,089	2,139
Aug.‡	10,196	914	11,110	9,625	1,485	807	2,292
Sept.	8,836	1,061	9,897	8,750	1,147	773	1,921
Oct.	6,311	2,770	9,081	7,875	1,206	1,103	2,309
Nov.	4,356	3,292	7,648	7,000	648	1,439	2,087
Dec.	2,777	3,406	6,187	6,125	58	1,623	1,681
1924							
Jan.	1,815	3,078	4,893	5,250	−357	1,633	1,276
Feb.	1,457	2,782	4,239	4,375	−636	1,578	1,442
March	1,179	2,365	3,544	3,500	44	1,498	1,542
April	762	1,854	2,156	2,625	−109	1,328	1,219
May	446	1,441	1,887	1,750	137	1,158	1,295
June	154	1,153	1,307	875	432	951	1,303

* This table excludes linters, except that a small quantity (50,000–100,000 bales) is included in the 'visible' supply in U.S. The monthly figures prior to April 1923, were given in last year's *Bulletin*.

† 1922 Crop taken at 10,000,000 bales.

‡ 1923 Crop taken at 10,500,000 bales. The final Government estimate was 10,174,000 bales.

§ U.S. Bureau of the Census—figures for *all* kinds of cotton.

‖ Seasonally corrected and excluding Japanese and European mill Stocks.

Annual table of total stocks at the end of each season (1 August)
(1,000 bales)*

	1918	1919	1920	1921	1922	1923
'Up-country' carryover in interior Cotton Belt	925	2,193	1,703	3,713	964	184
U.S. warehouse stocks	1,450	1,965	1,547	2,463	762	416
U.S. mill stocks	1,465	1,304	1,357	1,065†	1,155	1,000
Total in U.S.	3,840	5,462	4,607	7,241	2,881	1,609
European Port stocks (including afloat for Europe)	347	1,247	1,394	1,695	1,083	390
European mill stocks	250	305	475	690	838	496
Asiatic mill stocks	?	?	267‡	248	381	185
Total	4,437	7,014	6,743	9,874	5,183	2,680
Crop for year§	13,070	12,000	13,750	8,442	10,000	10,500
Total available	17,507	19,014	20,493	18,316	15,183	13,180
Total carried forward	7,014	6,743	9,874	5,760	2,680	
Consumption for year	10,493	12,271	10,619	12,556	12,503	

* Based on the returns of the New York Cotton Exchange, Mr Hester's Annual Reports to the New Orleans Cotton Exchange, and the Reports of the International Federation of Master Cotton Spinners.
† Including Canada and Mexico.
‡ Excluding China.
§ For 1918–21 I have taken Hester's estimate of the actual growth, made at the conclusion of the season. The final official estimates which are the figures usually quoted were as follows: 1918, 11,360; 1919, 12,252; 1920, 13,366; 1921, 8,283. There is a big discrepancy for 1918–19, the official figure being incompatible with the ginning returns. For 1922 and 1923 I have taken round figures as above.

estimate of about 326,000 bales in the estimate of the current crop *plus* carry forward. I estimate the world consumption during February, March, April and May at about 920,000 bales

Annual table of total stocks in the middle of each season (1 February)
(1,000 bales)

	1920	1921	1922	1923	1924
'Up-country' stocks	5,632	8,165	4,247	2,732	1,815
U.S. warehouse stocks	2,640	3,038	2,607	2,034	1,810
American mill stocks*	1,936	1,212	1,638	1,958	1,588
Total in U.S.	10,208	12,415	8,467	6,724	5,213
European port stocks (including afloat)	2,018	1,650	1,575	1,302	1,268
European mill stocks	597	675	740	637	569
Asiatic mill stocks	117†	166†	390	206	203
Total available	12,940	14,906	11,031	8,869	7,253
Ditto 1 Aug. preceding	19,014	20,493	18,316	15,183	13,180
Consumption for half-year	6,074	5,587	7,285	6,314	5,927

* Including Canada and Mexico.   † Excluding China.

per month, leaving a world supply of 3,570,000 bales on June 1, 1924. Assuming a carryover of 1,800,000 bales on August 1, 1924, which must be near the minimum, there are 1,770,000 bales available for consumption in the two months following June 1,—an average of 885,000 bales per month. This compares with an estimate of 920,000 bales for the average consumption of the four preceding months, and 960,000 bales for the average consumption of the ten preceding months. It would permit of the consumption of 450,000 bales per month in America, 130,000 bales in England, and 305,000 bales elsewhere. This represents an appreciable, but not a sensational reduction below the present level of consumption. But it means that a current crop of anything less than 11,500,000 bales represents—famine. The first official estimate of conditions (as on May 25) indicates, however, a crop of less than 11,000,000 bales.

II. *Wool*

(1) Since the issue of last year's *Bulletin*, the stocks of the British–Australian Wool Realisation Association (BAWRA), which constituted the principal floating supplies of wool in the world, have been completely exhausted, the final sale being held in May 1924. The following table exhibits the progressive disposal of the BAWRA stocks:—

BAWRA stocks

End of month	Australia and New Zealand		South Africa	Total
	Merino	Crossbred		
	(Bales of about 330 lb)			
1920 June	1,113,258	1,794,893	—	2,908,151
Dec.	902,726	1,682,768	—	2,586,474
1921 July	659,870	1,549,213	—	2,209,083
Dec.	422,241	1,487,488	80,655	1,890,384
1922 July	164,782	1,039,267	14,828	1,218,877
Dec.	76,239	837,006	Nil	913,245
1923 Feb.	51,000	701,284	Nil	752,284
April	26,887	610,199	Nil	637,086
May	26,858	574,729	Nil	601,587
June	2,120	521,127	Nil	523,347
July	2,063	499,119	Nil	501,182
Sept.	1,985	431,322	Nil	433,307
Oct.	1,923	335,434	Nil	337,357
Dec.	220	209,397	Nil	209,617
1924 Jan.	71	130,219	Nil	130,290
May	Nil	Nil	Nil	Nil

(2) The only other wool stocks for which definite statistics are available are those held in the United States. The U.S. Government collects a quarterly return of stocks from dealers and manufacturers. Out of 815 holders, 800 make returns; nevertheless, amongst the unreturned stocks are those of the American

Woollen Company. The returns, together with those of the Government's own stocks, now exhausted, have been as follows:

U.S.A. stocks

End of month	Commercial stocks	Government stocks	Total
1920 March	393	78	471
June	382	68	450
September	371	65	436
December	426	57	483
1921 March	475	57	532
June	443	47	490
September	473	31	504
1922 June	479	Nil	479
September	525	Nil	525
December	519	Nil	519
1923 March	501	Nil	501
June	532	Nil	532
September	475	Nil	475

(million lb)

It will be seen that the stocks have been maintained at a fairly level figure, equivalent to between nine and ten weeks' consumption.*

(3) *The United Kingdom and other chief industrial countries.* No precise statistics are available. Manufacturers and dealers between them are believed to aim at stocks somewhere near six months' consumption at the commencement of the calendar year. The figures at the beginning of 1924 were probably much the same as at the beginning of 1923,—say 350,000,000 in the United Kingdom and between 400,000,000 and 500,000,000 bales elsewhere.

---

* The proportion of stocks to consumption was stated incorrectly in the previous Memorandum [above, p. 278].

(4) *Exporting countries*. At the end of 1923 there seem to have been no appreciable surplus stocks beyond the supplies normally passing into consumption. Sir A. Goldfinch thinks that the Argentine stocks were further reduced by 100,000,000 lb during the year, and that this almost exhausted the war accumulations. The amount carried over has been estimated at 20,000,000 lb.

Summing up the position as a whole, Sir Arthur Goldfinch estimates the total movement of wool during 1923 as follows:—

	lb
Year's clip	2,454,000,000
Reduction in BAWRA stocks	240,000,000
Reduction in Argentine stocks	100,000,000
Reduction in manufacturers' and dealers' stocks	96,000,000
Year's consumption	2,890,000,000

The surplus floating supply of wool, exclusive of wool passing out of the grower's hands at the normal rate, and exclusive also of manufacturers' and dealers' stocks, may have been, roughly, as follows:—

1 January 1921	1,200,000,000 lb
1 January 1922	950,000,000 ,,
1 January 1923	420,000,000 ,,
1 January 1924	80,000,000 ,,

The reduction in the number of sheep in the world seems to continue. According to one estimate the flocks in the chief wool-producing countries are now 89,000,000 below their figure in 1913. It seems that, as a result of this, the world consumption of wool has been running in recent years at 250,000,000 lb to 400,000,000 lb in excess of production. An adjustment between consumption and supply will have to be effected in the next two years. Fortunately the large stocks held by manufacturers and dealers, amounting altogether to something like 1,250,000,000 lb, or nearly six months' consumption, will provide a cushion sufficient to prevent any shock from sudden shortage.

III. *Jute*

In the case of this commodity most of the figures are little better than trade guesses. The opinions given by different sources of information are so often discrepant, that the reliability of what

Stocks of jute (1,000 bales)

		India up- country	Calcutta mills	Calcutta other stocks	Stocks outside India	Total
1 July	1919	4,200	2,900	500	246	7,846
„	1920	4,700	3,900	300	957	9,857
„	1921	3,200	3,700	550	740	8,190
„	1922	550	4,100	150	1,200	6,000
„	1923		2,350	225	1,150	
1 April	1924		2,900	300	2,025	
1 May	1924		2,600	250	1,950	

follows is not to be regarded as high. Unlike the case of most other commodities, the bulk of the floating supplies seems to be held by the mills. The figures for mill stocks (based on returns made by the mills to the Bengal Chamber of Commerce) may be regarded as relatively accurate; those for the up-country stocks in India are specially doubtful.

The stocks at the beginning of May 1924, represented between six and seven months' consumption.

Experience shows that the Government crop figures are consistently underestimated. On the average of the past five years the actual arrivals of jute in Calcutta have been 25 per cent in excess of the final Government forecasts for the total crop. In 1922–23 the final forecast was 4,236,000 bales and the actual crop probably about 6,000,000 bales. For 1923–24 the final forecast is 6,995,924, whilst the actual crop is now expected to reach 9,000,000 bales. Thus the Government of India's jute figures maintain their reputation of being amongst the worst statistics in the world.

World consumption is now estimated at somewhat in excess of 8,000,000 bales per annum.

IV. *Copper*

Stocks of copper consist of (1) refined copper in the United States, which constitutes the main part of the world's floating supply, (2) rough and blister copper in transit between smelters and refiners in the U.S., and on hand or in process at refineries, (3) refined and rough copper in European and Japanese warehouses. In the years immediately after the War there were also large stocks in the hands of the Allied Governments and in the form of scrap metal.

The estimates shown below [p. 331] for the past six years are based on the figures of the U.S. Geological Survey, trade and expert estimates (especially those contained in *The Mineral Industry*, Vols. XXIX and XXX), and the London Metal Exchange Statistics.

The most striking facts which emerge from this table are the enormous fluctuations in the volume of production and the comparative steadiness in the volume of consumption. Between the boom year 1920 and the slump year 1921, consumption only fell off 10 per cent, whereas production fell nearly 50 per cent. By 1922 consumption had already recovered to the 1920 level, and in 1923 it was 30 per cent higher than in any other post-war year. The violence of the fluctuation in production is even more marked if we confine ourselves to the U.S. mines, for which the figures during the last three years have been, approximately, as follows:—

329

1921	193,000 tons
1922	415,000 ,,
1923	745,000 ,,

Thus American production in 1923 was nearly four times as great as in 1921. At the end of the year and at the beginning of 1924 production was running at an even higher figure, but by February 1924 some curtailment was beginning to set in. In March 1924 current world production was estimated to be at the rate of 1,300,000 tons per annum.

The prices for these three years (electrolytic copper—cents per lb in New York) were as follows:—

	Average for year	Highest	Lowest
1921	12·5	13·7	11·7
1922	13·4	14·7	12·7
1923	14·4	17·4	12·5

Whilst it is rash to speak of normal prices without reference to the general price level (the Federal Reserve Board Index for U.S. rose from 100 in 1921 to 106 in 1922 and 110 in 1923), it seems at present that a price of 12 to 12½ cents per lb is very deterrent to production, and that a price of 15 to 16 cents per lb is very encouraging; that is to say, the margin of production for a considerable number of mines lies somewhere between these limits at the existing level of general prices. Copper is one of the commodities of which the relative price is much below the pre-war level.

As in the case of so many other commodities, the U.S. accounts for a prodigious proportion of the whole—62 per cent of the world's production and 56 per cent of the consumption. Seventy-eight per cent of the world's copper is mined in North and South America together, most of which is refined in the

Supplies and consumption of copper

Tons (2,240 lb)	1 Jan. 1919	1 Jan. 1920	1 Jan. 1921	1 Jan. 1922	1 Jan. 1923	1 Jan. 1924
United States:—						
Refined	80,000	281,000	294,000	205,000	96,000	114,000
In process, etc.	295,000	123,000 (say)	208,000	126,000	161,000	220,000
Allied Govt. stocks	281,000	180,000 (say)	82,000	trifling (say)	nil	nil
Scrap	361,000	270,000	183,000	90,000	trifling	trifling
U.K., Havre, Japan stocks	—	46,000	55,000	30,000	39,000	37,000
Total	1,017,000	900,000	822,000	451,000	296,000	371,000
Production*	856,000	871,000	479,000	800,000	1,300,000	
Available supply	1,873,000	1,771,000	1,301,000	1,251,000	1,596,000	
Stock carried forward	900,000	822,000	451,000	296,000	371,000	
Consumption	973,000	949,000	850,000	955,000	1,225,000	

* American Bureau of Metal Statistics.

331

Stocks of copper (tons of 2,240 lb)

Beginning of month	U.S. refined	U.S. blister	U.K. all kinds	Havre	Japan
January 1921	294,000	208,000	11,646	5,968	37,500
April	295,000	255,000	13,628	6,026	—
July	302,000	—	19,656	5,834	12,300
October	255,000	161,000	19,485	4,124	9,600
January 1922	205,000	126,000	16,655	4,138	9,300
April	161,700	—	15,868	3,459	12,900
July	170,000	—	12,992	3,192	13,100
October	120,000	—	19,524	5,613	11,900
January 1923	96,000	161,000	26,780	3,345	9,072
February	100,000	—	27,268	2,964	8,134
March	96,000	—	27,632	2,995	5,227
April	94,000	—	26,393	2,515	3,474
May	92,000	—	25,460	2,413	3,070
June	91,500	—	26,536	2,454	3,094
July	88,000	—	27,776	2,309	3,517
August	95,000	—	26,776	2,511	—
September	93,000	—	27,674	2,382	5,668
October	112,000	—	28,453	3,891	5,954
November	115,000	—	30,618	1,935	4,881
December	117,000	200,000	31,462	1,795	5,312
January 1924	139,000*	220,000	31,030	1,867	4,405
February	143,000	216,000	30,211	5,889	—
March	120,000	—	29,959	4,182	—
April	107,000	—	30,852†	5,281	—
May	98,500	—	33,700‡	6,380	—
June	100,500	—	34,699	9,520	—

* This is the figure of the American Bureau of Metal Statistics; the figure of 114,000 tons given in the preceding table is that of the U.S. Geological Survey.
† Of which only 2,491 tons was refined copper.
‡ Of which 4,243 tons was refined copper.

United States. Apparent consumption in the United Kingdom last year was only a little more than one-eighth of that in the United States—which seems surprisingly low.

The preceding table gives some more detailed statistics for recent dates.

An important event of the year has been the liquidation of the Copper Export Association which was formed in the U.S. at the depth of the depression to regulate the sales of copper for export. The sale of the 400,000,000 lbs. originally set aside was completed in June 1923, and the shipments a month or two later.

The American Bureau of Metal Statistics has recently commenced the publication of some useful monthly statistics for the United States as follows:—

U.S.A. supplies and stocks of copper (1,000,000 lb)

	Stock at beginning of month	Refinery output	Deliveries	Stock at end of month
November 1923	257	229	224	262
December	262	239	191	311
January 1924	311	224	215	320
February	320	205	234	291
March	291	220	271	239
April	239	216	234	221
May	221	—	—	225

It will be seen that the existing stocks of refined copper do not represent more than about a month's consumption.

Copper interests are naturally much affected by developments in Germany. In 1922 Germany recovered her position as the world's second largest consumer of copper, her imports reaching about 60 per cent of the pre-war figure of 114,000 tons. In 1923, however, the Ruhr occupation caused a falling off of some 20 per cent. At the present time there is a revival of consumption and the rate is probably not much below the 1922 figure. The

333

exhaustion of scrap, etc., which has been largely used in Germany tends to increase the demand for imported metal. The stocks of copper held in Germany have never reached a significant total. In the middle of 1923 some authorities put the stocks in the whole country at about 9,000 tons, which fell to a still lower figure later in the year.

V. *Tin*

Stocks of tin mainly consist of:

(1) The 'visible' supply, as defined by the returns of Messrs Ricard and Freiwald, and of Messrs Strauss, namely warehouse stocks in Holland, U.K., and U.S., and tin afloat from the Federated Malay States, Netherlands Indies and Australia.

(2) Stocks of ore in Bolivia and Nigeria, and afloat from these countries to U.S. and U.K., and in course of smelting in U.S. and U.K.

(3) Stocks in the Federated Malay States and Netherlands Indies.

Visible stocks of tin* (tons of 2,240 lb)

End of month	1913	1919	1920	1921	1922	1923	1924
Jan.	14,875	7,758	20,980	18,104	25,346	22,598	21,173
Feb.	13,340	6,981	21,472	16,900	24,434	22,183	18,428
March	12,117	6,431	18,279	15,764	21,040	21,703	19,247
April	10,814	5,113	18,716	15,131	21,244	19,058	16,227
May	14,663	5,279	20,801	17,767	22,235	18,263	17,030
June	12,903	6,208	18,883	16,953	22,558	17,543	
July	13,713	12,697	18,482	19,852	20,364	17,976	
Aug.	12,841	18,157	20,152	19,037	21,753	16,170	
Sept.	14,673	21,292	18,326	20,777	20,488	17,389	
Oct.	13,049	22,807	19,442	22,891	19,975	18,479	
Nov.	16,112	19,585	19,065	22,247	22,131	16,939	
Dec.	15,543	21,491	18,479	24,273	22,155	18,596	

* Figures of A. Strauss & Co.

(4) Stocks in China and afloat from China to U.S. and U.K.

Detailed monthly figures, of which the aggregates are given above, are available for (1) in the returns of the two firms mentioned, which are in fairly close agreement with one another.

(2) There are no longer any surplus stocks in Nigeria and Bolivia (as there were after the war and again in 1921) beyond the normal flow of ore to the smelters overseas.

(3) The most important event of the year has been the gradual disposal of the stocks of the official pool formed under the Bandoeng Agreement for holding tin in the Malay States and Netherlands Indies. The original purchases were made between December 1920 and February 1921. At the beginning of April 1923, the stock held was as follows:—

Netherlands East Indies Government Banka tin ingots	2,000 tons
„ „ „ „ „ „ in ore	2,000 „
F.M.S. Government tin ingots	10,000 „
Billiton Co. Straits tin ingots	1,000 „
Straits Trading Co. Straits tin in ore	2,600 „
	17,600 tons

The commencement of the scheme of liquidation was announced in April 1923 in the following official statement:

The scheme became operative on 1st April 1923, and 5 per cent of the amount of tin held by each of the four parties was released to them to hold or to sell at their discretion, and the same amount will be released on the first day of each succeeding month. The total amount released per month on the agreed basis will be 880 tons of tin, and a period of twenty months will elapse before the total amount of tin in the pool is released to the respective holders.

Up to the end of March 1924 the whole of the monthly quotas had been disposed of. But in April, as a result of the fall in the price of tin, the F.M.S. sold only 175 tons out of their quota of 500 tons for the month. The whole quantity will have been released from the agreement by November 1924.

(4) Chinese stocks, held in the Yunnan and in Hong Kong, can only be given from approximate trade estimates, as follows:—

Hong Kong	end of 1919	6.000 tons
	1920	2,000 ,,
	1921	5,000 ,,
	1922	nil
	1923	250 ,,
	May 1924	200 ,,
Yunnan	end of 1923	750 ,,

Combining these figures, we have (very roughly) the following (in tons):—

	'Visible' supply	Bolivian ore stocks	Eastern pool	Chinese stocks	Total
1 January 1920	21,500	7,500	Nil	6,000	35,000
1 July	18,900	3,500	Nil	4,000	26,400
1 January 1921	18,500	Nil	6,000	2,000	26,500
1 July	17,000	2,500	20,000	4,000	43,500
1 January 1922	24,300	4,500	19,550	5,000	53,350
1 July	22,600	1,500	17,600	2,500	44,200
1 January 1923	22,200	Nil	17,600	1,000	40,800
1 July	17,500	Nil	16,500	1,000	35,000
1 January 1924	18,600	Nil	9,680	1,000	29,280
1 June	17,030	Nil	6,105	800	23,935

Thus, ever since the high-water mark of stocks was reached in January 1922, consumption has been steadily running at a rate of about 1,000 tons per month in excess of production.

The world's output in tin in the past six years has been very steady, except in the slump year 1921, at a total between 120,000 and 125,000 tons per annum, and does not, at present, show much response to higher prices. The falling-off in European consumption since 1913 has been balanced by increased consumption in the United States, which now takes about 60 per cent of the world's output. The *Engineering and Mining Journal Press* summarises the situation as follows:—

Several times the world has been threatened with a famine in tin, and saved almost by a miracle. The first time was in the 'sixties, when tin consumption was cut in half by improved processes of tin-plating. The second was when the world depended on the insufficient Cornish production, and the shortage was relieved by development of the tin deposits of Malaya. A third time famine was averted by the 1907 panic in America, and a fourth time by the world collapse of 1920–1. What will avert it this time is the problem now confronting the trade.

VI. *Lead*

The most striking feature of the situation is the extreme paucity of floating supplies. At the present time, and for more than two years past, there are practically no such stocks. As regards its supplies of lead, the world has been living from hand to mouth.

The only precise statistics are those relating to those warehouses in the United Kingdom which are covered by the monthly returns of the London Metal Exchange, as follows:—

U.K. stocks of lead (tons)

| End of month | Monthly stocks United Kingdom Private warehouses and Government stock | | | | |
	1920	1921	1922	1923	1924
January	47,348	19,777	622	414	296
February	40,435	19,129	589	648	57
March	28,435	23,926	578	432	27
April	26,250	18,127	522	456	20
May	23,338	14,138	646	447	7
June	25,192	13,278	268	163	
July	23,448	12,396	235	1,815	
August	21,521	11,515	686	1,719	
September	18,721	9,883	583	1,439	
October	15,335	5,161	281	1,229	
November	14,919	1,069	198	1,233	
December	19,045	284	518	1,183	

Of the above stocks during the latter part of 1923, 1,000 tons was reported to be held by German interests on Russian account. This quantity was eventually exported. In the middle of 1923 German stocks were reported to be about 15,000 metric tons, equivalent to about a month's consumption.

Bonded stocks in the United States, mainly in the form of ore and base bullion, have been reported as follows:—

U.S.A. stocks of lead

	Metric tons		Metric tons
1 January 1919	17,471	1 January 1923	55,000*
1920	45,710	1 April 1923	40,000†
1921	52,542	1 November 1923	78,000‡
1922	19,533		

* Of which 40,000 tons lead content in ore stocks.
† Of which 25,000–30,000 tons lead content in ore stocks.
‡ Of which 38,000 tons lead content in ore stocks.

The production of lead in the chief sources of world supply is estimated* as follows:—

World production of lead (metric tons)

	1920	1921	1922	1923
United States	432,000	365,000	426,000	481,000
Canada	16,000	31,000	42,000	49,000
Mexico	85,000	61,000	121,000	167,000
Germany†	59,000	75,000	72,000	51,000
Spain	126,000	123,000	97,000	110,000
Burma	24,000	34,000	40,000	46,000
Australia	7,000	57,000	107,000	125,000
Rhodesia	15,000	18,000	21,000	11,000
Total	764,000	764,000	926,000	1,040,000

* American Bureau of Metal Statistics.   † Including Upper Silesia.

Sources of supply not included in the above produce about 100,000 metric tons per annum. Aggregate production in 1923 was back at about the pre-war level or a little higher. There have been large changes, however, in the distribution both of production and of consumption. Storage batteries, cables, and automobiles, as well as building and pigments, are now responsible for using large quantities of lead. As in the case of most raw materials, other than foods, the United States consumes nearly a half of the world's total supplies.

In April 1924 production in the United States was said to be running at the rate of 600,000 tons a year, and in Mexico at a rate of 180,000 tons a year—both somewhat in excess of last year and probably maximum figures.

VII. *Spelter (Zinc)*

Monthly statistics are available of stocks in public warehouses in the United States and the United Kingdom as given below.

These stocks throughout the last two and a half years have been almost negligible, since they never reached as much as a month's supply.

It is probable that stocks elsewhere than in the United States and the United Kingdom do not now exceed some 13,000 tons, of which at least half is in Germany.

Both production and consumption increased very largely during 1923. Of the two biggest producers, the United States increased from 339,000 metric tons in 1922 to 482,000 metric tons in 1923; and Belgium from 112,000 metric tons in 1922 to 148,000 metric tons in 1923. Total production was 456,000 metric tons in 1921, 732,000 in 1922, and 975,000 in 1923.

VIII. *Rubber*

The stocks of rubber are held mainly:—

(1) On plantations, etc., within the restricted area of Malaya.
(2) In Singapore and Penang.

339

U.K. and U.S. stocks of spelter (tons of 2,240 lb)

End of month	1920			1921			1922			1923			1924		
	U.S.	U.K.	Total	U.S.	U.K.	Total	U.S.	U.K.	Total	U.S.	U.K.	Total	U.S.	U.K.	Total
January	35,880	25,000*	60,880	67,810	14,862	82,672	58,635	11,412	70,047	14,794	394	15,188	36,330	1,088	37,418
February	33,120	25,000*	58,120	69,660	13,606	83,266	57,250	8,335	65,585	9,700	197	9,897	33,200	975	34,175
March	27,695	25,000*	52,695	73,440	14,427	87,867	53,800	6,375	60,175	8,947	838	9,785	28,600	858	29,458
April	29,025	26,123	55,148	72,720	17,730	90,450	46,186	6,067	52,253	8,014	1,238	9,252	29,270	673	29,943
May	26,190	23,411	49,601	76,615	19,000	96,615	36,080	5,338	41,418	11,624	1,702	13,326	37,820	628	38,448
June	23,975	26,828	50,803	80,260	18,752	99,012	26,407	4,662	31,069	15,333	1,679	17,012			
July	25,925	28,828	54,753	82,510	18,153	100,663	25,552	4,289	29,841	18,896	1,198	20,094			
August	26,410	25,709	52,119	77,275	17,387	94,662	19,311	3,977	23,288	23,635	1,007	24,642			
September	38,300	23,173	61,473	72,440	16,405	88,845	16,791	3,668	20,459	20,440	803	21,243			
October	45,740	19,214	64,954	63,235	15,424	78,659	16,110	2,670	18,780	23,024	1,034	24,058			
November	57,495	16,953	74,448	59,865	14,052	73,917	17,408	852	18,260	27,600	1,390	28,990			
December	63,440	17,536	80,976	59,470	12,765	72,235	16,296	631	16,927	32,660	1,190	33,850			

* Approximate. The Metal Exchange statistics only begin in April 1920.

Visible supply of rubber (1,000 tons)*

End of month	1919			1920			1921			1922			1923			1924		
	Plantation rubber afloat	Public warehouse stocks in U.K.	Total	Plantation rubber afloat	Public warehouse stocks in U.K.	Total	Plantation rubber afloat	Public warehouse stocks in U.K.	Total	Plantation rubber afloat	Public warehouse stocks in U.K.	Total	Plantation rubber afloat	Public warehouse stocks in U.K.	Total	Plantation rubber afloat	Public warehouse stocks in U.K.	Total
January	24	20	44	45	23	68	28	62	90	40	74	114	44	82	126	53	57	110
February	29	18	47	42	24	66	30	66	96	39	76	115	47	77	124	49	61	110
March	40	18	58	40	24	64	30	71	101	40	75	115	48	69	117		60	
April	48	24	72	35	25	60	29	76	105	33	77	110	51	64	115		59	
May	35	29	64	46	24	70	28	79	107	43	79	122	48	59	107			
June	43	31	74	38	25	63	32	78	110	44	81	125	52	55	107			
July	32	33	65	38	28	66	31	81	112	43	80	123	45	54	99			
August	34	33	67	36	33	69	30	83	113	44	80	124	45	53	98			
September	35	30	65	34	39	73	34	82	116	44	79	123	43	59	102			
October	38	28	66	36	46	82	32	79	111	47	77	124	47	63	110			
November	42	27	69	33	50	83	36	81	117	46	77	123	44	65	109			
December	37	25	62	37	55	92	32	80	112	45	81	126	52	60	112			

* Figures supplied by Messrs W. H. Rickinson.

(3) Afloat.

(4) In London and Liverpool.

(5) In U.S.A. warehouses and factories.

Monthly figures are only available for 3 and 4, and are as follows:— [see p. 341].

Estimates of the total stocks in the chief centres are available at yearly or half-yearly intervals, as follows:—

Total stocks of rubber (1,000 tons)

	31 Dec. 1918	31 Dec. 1919	31 Dec. 1920	31 Dec. 1921	31 Dec. 1922	30 June 1923	31 Dec. 1923	31 Mar. 1923
Malaya (restricted area)				12	30	25	14	
Singapore and Penang	} 70	60	35 {	28	25	21	24	21
Afloat	35	37	37	37	45	52	52	
United Kingdom	16	25	56	80	81	55	60	60
United States*	10	17	76	52	90	101	73	
Total	131	139	204	209	271	254	223	

* The returns represent about 90 per cent of the whole.

Messrs Symington and Sinclair estimate that stocks not covered by the above were at the end of 1923 as follows:—

Ceylon	4,000	tons
Dutch East Indies	10,000	,,
Holland, Belgium, etc.	2,500	,,
U.K. (private warehouses)	9,000	,,

This brings the aggregate stocks to 250,000 tons, in round figures, or nearly seven months' consumption.

The quarterly returns for the United States, which represent 90 to 95 per cent of the trade, have been as follows:—

U.S.A. stocks of rubber (1,000 tons)

	End of month							
	Dec. 1921	June 1922	Oct. 1922	Dec. 1922	Mar. 1923	June 1923	Sept. 1923	Dec. 1923
Manufacturers	69	60	60	72	65	79	69	54
Dealers	26	22	23	18	17	22	16	19
Total	95	82	83	90	82	101	85	73

The United States stocks of pneumatic tyres and inner tubes for automobiles are also important in this connection. These have been as follows:—

U.S. stocks of tyres and tubes (1,000,000)

End of month	Pneumatic tyres	Inner tubes
September 1921	3·3	3·8
December	3·7	4·7
March 1922	5·2	7·0
June	5·0	6·2
September	4·6	5·2
December	4·6	5·7
March 1923	5·7	7·7
June	7·0	8·9
September	5·4	6·5
December	4·3	6·3
January 1924	4·8	6·7
February	5·3	7·3

Thus at the end of June 1923, stocks of rubber in the United States, and also those of tyres and tubes, were standing at a decidedly high figure.

Stocks of rubber in Holland have varied recently between about 2,500 tons and 3,500 tons.

The following are the estimates of production and consumption in recent years:—

Production and consumption of rubber*

Production	Tons 1919	Tons 1920	Tons 1921	Tons 1922	Tons 1923
Malaya	180,000	190,000	170,000	238,000	165,000
Ceylon and India	35,000	40,000	40,000	48,000	40,500
Dutch East Indies	75,000	85,000	50,000	73,000	131,000
Other countries in the East	10,000	15,000	10,000	15,000	18,500
Total Eastern plantation rubber	300,000	330,000	270,000	370,000	355,000
Brazil	32,000	31,000	20,000	21,500	21,500
Wild	7,000	7,000	3,000	3,500	5,500
Total	339,000	368,000	293,000	399,000	382,000
Consumption	1919	1920	1921	1922	1923
U.S.A.	225,000	200,000	200,000	282,000	305,500
United Kingdom	33,000	25,000	18,000	25,000	27,000
France	22,000	16,000	14,000	27,000	30,000
Italy	14,000	6,000	5,000	6,000	7,500
Canada	9,500	11,000	9,000	9,000	14,000
Japan	—	7,500	12,500	16,000	12,000
Germany, Russia and Austria	5,500	11,000	18,000	31,000	25,000
Other countries	14,000	13,500	15,500	12,000	13,000
Total	335,000	290,000	292,000	408,000	434,000

* Symington and Sinclair.

Production in 1922 was probably somewhat higher than these figures indicate. Production in Malaya and Ceylon during 1923 has, of course, been affected by the legislation for restriction.

This has been offset, however, by the enormous increase in the unrestricted plantations of the Dutch East Indies. In last year's *Bulletin* we estimated the output from the restricted areas at 210,000 tons, as compared with the actual result of 205,000 tons. We estimated that the consumption was 'not likely to fall below 415,000 tons', as compared with the actual result of 434,000 tons. But the conclusion, that the restriction plan seemed to allow for the exhaustion of the true surplus stocks during 1923, has been confounded by the unrestricted areas producing 177,000 tons instead of 125,000 tons as anticipated.

Nevertheless there has been an appreciable reduction of aggregate stocks. During 1924 Messrs Symington and Sinclair forecast production and consumption as follows:—

Production	Tons	Consumption	Tons
Malaya	163,500	U.S.A.	320,000
Ceylon	34,000	U.K.	28,500
Dutch East Indies	150,000	Other countries	111,500
Other sources	57,500		
Total	405,000	Total	460,000

If this forecast is realised stocks may have been brought down by the beginning of 1925 to somewhere near the figure of 150,000 tons, which is considered to be the amount moving into consumption which time and convenience require. If the price remains below 1*s*. per lb. on the average of three months, which now seems likely, a further curtailment of output is enforceable in the restricted areas.

IX. *Coffee*

About two-thirds of the supply of coffee for Europe and U.S.A. comes from Brazil. The table following is based on the figures supplied by Messrs Duuring and Zoon, the most important omissions from which are the stocks in the East and Eastern ports, in the interior of Brazil, and coffee from the East afloat to U.S.A.

345

Coffee (1,000 bags)*

Year	Beginning of month	Visible supply of Europe	Visible supply of U.S.A.	Stocks in Brazil	Total
1913	July	6,480	1,848	1,947	10,275
	September	6,005	1,477	4,002	11,484
	October	6,019	1,393	4,769	12,181
1914	January	7,275	1,709	4.681	13,665
	April	8,702	2,172	1,743	12,617
	June	8,353	2,056	1,207	11,616
1919	January	758	1,010	9,296	11,364
	April	2,755	1,964	7,060	11,799
	July	3,124	1,508	5.704	10,336
	October	2,821	2,057	5,540	10,418
1920	January	2,843	2,007	5,020	9,870
	April	2,573	2,209	3,392	8,174
	July	2,509	2,293	1,948	6,750
	October	2,955	2,640	2,387	7,982
1921	January	2,588	2,442	3,735	8,765
	April	2,533	2,765	3,389	8,687
	July	2,562	2,100	4,038	8,700
	October	2,564	1,838	4,589	8,991
1922	January	2,399	2,056	4,948	9,403
	April	2,977	1,583	4,580	9,140
	July	3,068	1,456	4,115	8,639
	October	3,007	1,182	4,292	4,481
1923	January	2,839	1,385	3,756	7,980
	February	2,764	1,402	3,573	7,739
	March	2,443	1,625	3,312	7,480
	April	2,463	1,618	2,903	6,974
	May	2,438	1,197	2,488	6,123
	June	2,329	1,059	2,099	5,487
	July	2,296	1,075	1,969	5,340
	August	2,273	1,034	2,243	5,550
	September	2,449	1,387	2,016	5,852
	November	2,481	1,673	1,656	5,820
	December	2,453	1,750	1,182	5,385
1924	January	2,228	1,349	890	4,467
	February	2,153	1,088	979	4,220
	March	2,192	1,172	902	4,266
	April	1,935	1,075	954	3,964
	May	1,993	1,126	1,326	4,445

* G. Duuring and Zoon.

Deliveries during the last four years have been as follows:—

Deliveries of coffee (1,000 bags)

	To Europe	To U.S.A.	Total	From Brazil	Other kinds
1920	5,213	9,167	14,380	8,638	5,742
1921	8,094	9,958	18,052	11,356	6,696
1922	8,238	9,654	17,892	11,100	6,792
1923	9,240	10,585	19,825	13,516	6,309

The current year's crop (July 1923–June 1924) for the world is estimated at 21,200,000 bags, of which 14,700,000 will come from Brazil. A somewhat lower figure of output is anticipated for the year 1924–5. The carryover in the interior of the State of Sao Paulo at the end of June 1924, which is over and above the 'visible supply', is expected to be at least 4,000,000 bags. Thus the total world stocks at the end of the season may be equal to about five months' consumption.

X. *Tea*

The only precise figures available for the stocks of tea are of those in bond in the United Kingdom. Since, however, about three-quarters of the total world production passes through this country, these stocks should form a fairly reliable index of the position.

After April 1 1923, stocks held in the Irish Free State are excluded. These amounted to 1,310,791 lb on December 31, 1922, and are estimated at not more than 1,250,000 lb on December 31, 1923.

Messrs Harrisons and Crosfield estimated consumption as follows:—

The average consumption of tea in the United Kingdom during the years 1911 to 1913 amounted to just under 300,000,000 lb per annum. During

347

Tea in bond in the United Kingdom (1,000 lb)

End of month	1913	1919	1920	1921	1922	1923	1924
January	136,057		215,175	224,415	216,117	186,438	183,079
February	129,395		203,061	228,021	228,988	177,403	188,923
March	121,477		212,645	236,300	222,727	183,392	191,943
April	103,272		207,520	239,392	214,864	167,567	
May	87,568		212,152	234,001	192,585	141,513	
June	77,099		214,986	218,594	170,600	126,515	
July	72,666		212,759	207,399	151,094	113,198	
August	82,223		214,843	197,433	140,983	122,633	
September	99,717		215,251	190,799	149,686	134,350	
October	112,632	145,774	220,137	190,129	150,306	148,072	
November	125,434	169,861	223,229	196,534	156,986	152,748	
December	138,005	213,083	214,362	205,420	168,465	169,577	

the current year (1923) the consumption in the United Kingdom and the Irish Free State will probably amount to 410,000,000 lb, and that of other markets of the world as follows:—

	lb (1,000)
United States	100,000
Australasia	54,000
Canada	40,000
India	30,000
Russia and Poland	18,000
Europe (excluding the United Kingdom, Russia, and Poland)	38,000
Africa, Persia, etc.	33,000
South America	9,000

making a total of 732,000,000 lb. The average stock of tea in bond in this country at the end of July for the years 1911 to 1913 was about 74,000,000 lb. This can probably be looked upon as a normal stock at that time, and, if we make allowance for the increased consumption, the total stock at the end of July 1923 is very little in excess of the normal working stock. The stocks of tea which had accumulated, not only in this country but also in America and other places, largely on account of the disturbances caused by the War, have now practically disappeared, and the current consumption will have to be met from current production.

Production in the last three years has been as follows:—

Production of tea (1,000 lb)

	1921	1922	1923
Northern India	242,841	281,000	327,000
Southern India	27,389	29,500	37,000
Ceylon	162,347	171,392	183,500
Java	67,652	80,713	90,000
Sumatra	9,235	14,395	16,500
Nyasaland	259	737	1,000
China	57,007	76,745	80,000
Japan	15,862	28,856	24,000
Formosa	17,893	20,000	22,500
	600,485	703,338	781,500

Total production and consumption recently may be roughly estimated as follows (in lb):—

Million lb

	1921	1922	1923
Production	600	703	781
Consumption	620	718	750

The drop of about 150,000,000 lbs. in the consumption of Russia since 1913 has been compensated by increased consumption elsewhere. A revival of Russian consumption would greatly assist the market to absorb the increasing supplies which are now becoming available under the stimulus of high prices.

XI. *Petroleum*

The only figures of stocks regularly available are those for the United States. Since, however, nearly 80 per cent of the world's oil stocks are held in the United States, these figures can be regarded as reasonably representative.

The following table [p. 351] of stocks of crude petroleum in the United States is that published by the American Petroleum Institute.

At the beginning of 1924 these stocks represented about 164 days' supply as compared with 148 at the beginning of 1923.

In addition to stocks of crude oil, there are also relatively smaller stocks (rather more than a month's supply) of the principal refined products. The half-yearly figures of these stocks in the United States have been as follows:—[p. 351].

The relation of these stocks to current consumption of the various refined products (*not* consumption of crude oils by refineries) is shown by the following table:—[p. 352].

U.S.A. stocks of petroleum

Stocks at end of month	Crude petroleum (1,000 barrels)					
	1919	1920	1921	1922	1923	1924
January	127,777	127,164	117,099	282,875	180,984	333,742
February	126,982	126,329	121,713	191,471	283,498	334,585
March	129,213	125,597	128,754	202,906	289,871	
April	130,729	124,991	134,719	213,371	295,970	
May	130,321	124,689	143,614	224,388	304,668	
June	133,995	126,763	151,339	232,032	315,369	
July	140,093	128,168	159,030	238,233	326,635	
August	136,467	129,043	162,903	242,635	333,143	
September	137,131	128,788	164,076	244,778	339,961	
October	135,461	129,451	163,335	246,625	349,025	
November	131,601	131,325	164,073	247,942	350,000	
December	127,867	133,690	170,350	248,413	333,053	

[U.S.A. stocks of refined products] (barrels)

End of month	Gasolene	Kerosene	Lub. oils	Fuel and gas oils
December 1918	7,079,213	9,050,425	3,306,033	15,690,510
June 1919	14,140,396	6,012,915	4,175,828	19,328,348
December 1919	10,637,939	8,079,040	3,269,498	17,002,963
June 1920	12,001,324	10,031,984	3,171,727	15,284,961
December 1920	11,009,091	9,358,831	3,821,964	19,938,200
June 1921	17,872,487	10,358,493	6,211,503	29,730,097
December 1921	13,954,456	8,119,251	5,161,084	31,696,796
June 1922	19,642,058	7,561,297	5,402,472	31,593,801
December 1922	21,042,687	6,691,675	5,612,733	31,064,949
June 1923	30,085,000	6,293,000	5,360,000	31,524,000
December 1923	25,590,000	6,742,000	5,780,000	36,072,000
January 1924	28,632,000	7,480,000	5,828,000	36,365,000
March 1924	37,424,000	8,415,000	5,983,000	35,939,000

[*Refined petroleum*] (1,000 barrels)

	Domestic consumption	Exports		Total
		General	Bunkers	
1919	349,565	62,853	14,031	426,449
1920	419,693	77,993	26,335	524,021
1921	418,963	70,723	27,027	516,713
1922	478,526	72,952	31,692	583,170
1923	589,631	100,436	37,643	727,710

XII. *Nitrate*

Nitrate statistics are comparatively simple, since they all come from one part of the world. Very complete figures are regularly published by Messrs Aikman.

The figures for America include interior stocks, but not those held by the U.S.A. Government, which have gradually declined from round 300,000 tons in December 1921, to 85,000 tons at the present time.

In normal times there is a considerable reduction in the visible supply in the early part of the year, as the demand is somewhat seasonal.

The last column of the table below [p. 353] includes stocks in Japan and other countries, but excludes the following stocks in the hands of the U.S.A. Government:—

31 Dec. 1921	300,000 tons	31 Dec. 1922	125,000 tons
28 Feb. 1922	210,000 ,,	31 Jan. 1923	85,000 ,,
30 April 1922	190–200,000 ,,	31 Jan. 1924	85,000 ,,
31 May 1922	175,000 ,,		

COMMODITIES

Nitrate (1,000 tons)*

End of month	Visible supply (including afloat) Europe and Egypt	U.S.A.	Stocks in Chile	Total
1913 January	1,128	89	490	1,727
March	686	97	527	1,326
June	416	84	754	1,265
September	571	79	752	1,414
December	1,098	71	498	1,685
1919 January	140	28	1,594	1,780
September	152	49	1,705	1,925
December	430	95	1,576	2,134
1920 March	368	253	1,218	1,914
June	317	216	1,248	1,800
September	495	194	1,303	2,008
December	782	132	1,304	2,235
1921 March	868	218	1,283	2,384
June	836	249	1,317	2,405
September	828	41	1,453	2,370
December	903·5	260	1,441	2,622·5
1922 March	520	115	1,504	2,149
June	227·5	38	1,582	1,851
September	277	148	1,482	1,940
December	427·5	192	1,231	1,891·5
1923 January	459	223	1,157	1,866
February	440·5	220	994	1,680
March	348·5	238	898	1,502·5
April	234·5	184	884	1,344·5
May	159	107	992	1,280
June	170	66	983	1,255
July	208	109	1,001	1,372
August	287	125	949	1,409
September	360	114	939	1,446
October	390	62	974	1,457
November	458·5	99	987	1,564
December	551	199	881	1,643
1924 January	599	273	807	1,699
February	531	286	723	1,556·5
March	383	180	802	1,379
April	220	145	882	1,269

* Messrs Aikman.

353

Deliveries, year ending 30 June (1,000 tons)

	1914	1920	1921	1922	1923
Europe and Egypt	1,984	861	706	895	
U.S.A.	553	794	644	565	979
Japan and others	92	227	84	84	
	2,629	1,882	1,434	1,544	2,159

XIII. *Wheat*

Wheat is a very baffling commodity to the compiler of comparative totals, because it is a seasonal crop, coming from many different sources, and harvested at many different times of year.

As in the case of other commodities, the statistics regularly available month by month are those of 'visible' supplies in 'second hands'; but, owing to the large amounts held on farms and elsewhere 'out of sight', these figures are only moderately useful as an index to the general situation. The figures in question are as follows [see page 355]:—

Million centals (i.e, 100,000,000 lb)

	Canada			U.S.A.		
	1	2	3	1	2	3
1920	7·8	164·2	172·0	90·4	511·0	601·4
1921	8·2	180·5	188·7	69·2	476·9	546·1
1922	11·7	233·3	245·0	65·3	486·1	551·4
1923	7·1	281·9	289·0	66·8	469·0	535·8

	Argentine			Australia			India
	1	2	3	1	2	3	2
1920	3·5	111·0	114·5	—	88·1	88·1	226·0
1921	18·0	108·4	126·4	—	79·4	79·4	152·6*
1922	6·4	113·4	119·8	—	64·4	64·4	220·2
1923		150·6†		—	51†	51	221·6

1. Old crop carryover (1 July for U.S., 1 Sept. for Canada, and 31 Dec. for Argentine and Australia).   2. Current crop (crop of subsequent calendar year in case of Argentine and Australia).   3. Total available.

* Very poor crop, with the result that India instead of exporting a certain amount was under the necessity of importing.

† Preliminary forecasts.

Visible supply of wheat and flour in second hands (1,000,000 bushels)*

Beginning of	1919			1920			1921			1922			1923			1924		
	1	2	3	1	2	3	1	2	3	1	2	3	1	2	3	1	2	3
January	231	?	?	170	77	247	148	67	215	184	54	238	232	53	285	275	45	320
February	240	58	298	143	82	225	120	68	188	161	51	212	220	65	285	260	55	315
March	230	63	293	130	80	210	116	79	195	146	67	213	207	72	279	251	79	330
April	192	63	255	123	77	200	92	80	172	133	77	210	184	70	254	235	85	320
May	126	79	205	111	80	191	72	85	157	115	75	190	164	64	228	190	87	277
June	76	90	166	97	92	189	51	101	152	92	69	161	117	63	180			
July	38	106	144	68	90	158	42	84	126	72	65	137	88	59	147			
August	56	91	147	51	93	144	65	69	134	62	58	120						
September	104	94	198	56	73	129	87	70	157	74	51	125	104	48	152			
October	169	85	254	99	71	163	137	63	200	133	43	176	157	49	206			
November	203	69	272	126	70	196	172	60	232	196	47	243	217	58	275			
December	195	81	276	144	68	212	184	57	241	215	64	279	250	62	312			

* *Broomhall's Corn Trade News.* 1. Visible supply in elevators and public stores in Canada and the United States. 2. Other visible supply, i.e. in the Argentine, afloat for U.K. and the Continent, and in U.K. (Details of each of these items separately are available.) 3. Total of 1 and 2.

355

Perhaps the figures of the old crop carryover together with those of the new crop in the chief exporting countries, as published by the International Institute of Agriculture, are the most *complete* index to current supplies. These are as above.

Another way of approaching the question, favoured by the International Institute of Agriculture, is that of the exportable surplus in exporting countries on 1 January of each year (i.e. after allowing for domestic consumption, seed, and minimum carryover). On this basis the figures are as below (in this table supplies in all countries are worked out to the same date, which is a convenience). The figures for 1 January 1924, are those given by Mr Broomhall. I have also supplemented the figures of exportable surplus in each year by adding Mr Broomhall's figures for U.K. stocks and for the quantity afloat for Europe on the same dates, which gives as complete a total as is possible for the aggregate supplies available for the importing countries at the beginning of each calendar year.

Quantities exportable from the exporting countries on 1 January
(million centals)

	1921	1922	1923	1924
Canada	35·7	68·3	88⎫	197
United States	58·4	50·2	129⎭	
India	6·4	—	19·2	
Argentine	71·3	74·7	78·5	96
Australia	66·7	59·7	46·5	48
Total	238·5	252·9	361·2	341
Stocks in U.K.	19·6	5·3	3·4	5
Afloat for U.K. and Continent	21·3	20·1	26·2	20
Grand total	279·4	278·3	390·8	366

This year certain supplies have also been available from Russia, the Danube and North Africa. The exportable surplus

U.S. Dept. of Agriculture figures of farm reserves on 1 March
(million bushels)

Year of harvest	Total crop	Stock in farmers' hands, 1 March	Per cent of total crop	Consumed or distributed since harvest
1924		134	17·0	652
1923	786	153	17·9	715
1922	869	131	16·1	681
1921	815	208	24·9	625
1920	833	166	17·1	802
1919	968	129	14·0	788
1918	917	111	17·0	540
1917	651	101	15·7	539
1916	640	242	23·9	770
1915	1,012	153	17·2	738
1914	891	152	19·9	611
1913	763	156	21·3	574
1912	730			

in these countries on January 1, 1924, is estimated by Mr Broomhall at 19 million centals.

In 1925 J. W. F. Rowe began his collaboration with Keynes on the Special Memoranda—a partnership that continued, with the addition of G. L. Schwartz for the last issue, until the series ended in 1930.

From the London and Cambridge Economic Service, Special Memorandum, No. 12 (July 1925)

STOCKS OF STAPLE COMMODITIES

The statistics given below are in continuation of Memoranda published in April 1923 and June 1924.

The Memorandum of 1923 pointed out 'that during 1922 the

world's consumption of raw commodities materially exceeded its production'. The Memorandum of 1924 added to this the conclusion that 'during 1923, especially in the first half of the year, the same tendency continued but not quite so strongly'. We now have the figures for 1924 and some preliminary figures relating to the first half of 1925. They exhibit on the whole a stationary condition. By the end of 1923 stocks of several important staple commodities had reached normal levels and had in some cases fallen below them. In one or two cases stocks had reached a point below which no further reduction was practicable. Thus it is not surprising that the tendency of stocks to fall yet further should have been retarded during 1924.

In no case except in that of mineral oil has there been any material addition to stocks. In some cases, e.g. tin and rubber, the volume of stocks is now approaching the irreducible minimum.

Generally speaking the huge redundant stocks of the latter half of 1922 exist no longer; and in several cases stocks still in hand show little or no margin of safety. A distinction must be drawn, however, between commodities of which stocks are low merely for convenience, or as it were by choice, and commodities of which stocks are low from sheer necessity. Thus there is no doubt that stocks of copper can be increased at will, for production is far below the potential capacity of the existing mines. The same is probably true of spelter and nitrate, and also of sugar as the result of the recovery of beet sugar production. But in other cases stocks are low from necessity. The current cotton crop has started well, but it is not easy to see how stocks of cotton can be materially increased without either exceptional assistance from the weather, or a curtailment of consumption. In the cases both of tin and of lead supply is inelastic. While the restriction scheme lasts, a forcibly curtailed supply of rubber must be faced, and in the long period fully adequate supplies are by no means assured. This latter point applies also to mineral oils, especially the lighter oils. It is not suggested that in all these cases production cannot be increased if a substantial incentive is offered, except, perhaps, the production of tin. The real point is that as stocks are now at or near the working minimum, an increased consumption is only possible if it is accompanied by increased production, and that production will only respond slowly, in some cases very slowly. The fact that stocks are stationary at a low level does not necessarily mean that the business world holds an unchangingly pessimistic view as to the possibility of an improvement in industrial activity. In some cases stocks could not be accumulated, even if business men wished to prepare the way for increased production. If any material increase in manufacture and consumption were to develop in the near future, a shortage of many raw materials would inevitably ensue, and an appreciable interval would elapse before production could respond. The effect on prices might well be startling: recent events in the rubber market might be repeated in the case of other commodities. The longer the world continues to live from hand to mouth, the more delicate does the situation become; for consumption is far from stationary, and in one or two cases has recently shown its capacity for extremely vigorous expansion. There seems some danger that with certain commodities the requisite development of reserve productive capacity may be postponed too long.

The table below is a summary of the figures given in detail afterwards for each separate commodity. Wool and jute have not been included this year, as the available figures are not sufficiently comprehensive or reliable. On the other hand, it has now become possible to include sugar, which was omitted last year.

THE U.S. DEPARTMENT OF COMMERCE INDEX OF COMMODITY STOCKS

An addendum to Special Memorandum No. 6 was published in the *Monthly Bulletin* for July 1924. Statistics of this commodity index were there presented in a revised form, as the Department

Stocks of staple commodities

	American cotton* 1,000 bales (1)		Copper 1,000 tons (2)	Tin 1,000 tons (3)	Lead 1,000 tons (4)		Spelter 1,000 tons (5)	Rubber 1,000 tons (6)	Sugar 1,000 tons (7)	Coffee 1,000 bags (8)	Tea 1,000,000 lb (9)	Crude oil 1,000,000 barrels (10)	Nitrate 1,000 tons (11)	Wheat 1,000 quarters (12)
	A	B			U.K.	U.S.								
1 Jan. 1920	13,949	7,299	900	35	60	—	61	—	—	9,870	213	128	2,134	—
1 July 1920	7,255	6,468	—	26	25	—	51	—	2,003	6,750	215	127	1,800	—
1 Jan. 1921	16,197	—	822	27	19	—	81	219–229	2,313	8,765	214	134	2,235	183
1 July 1921	11,180	9,652	—	44	13	—	99	—	3,312	8,700	219	151	2,405	—
1 Jan. 1922	13,548	8,204	451	53	1	—	72	224–244	2,761	9,403	205	170	2,622	220
1 July 1922	6,009	4,790	—	44	0	—	31	—	1,903	8,639	170	232	1,873	—
1 Jan. 1923	9,182	3,471	296	41	1	—	17	286–306	2,433	7,980	170	248	1,912	199
1 July 1923	3,381	2,700	—	34	0	—	17	278	2,005	5,340	127	327	1,250	—
1 Jan. 1924	7,697	1,852	371	29	1	90	34	254	2,255	4,467	166	333	1,639	234
1 July 1924	2,758	2,083	—	25	0	97	45	208	2,086	5,071	139	392	1,250	—
1 Jan. 1925	9,989	2,205	389	24	0	78	19	181	2,708	5,384	206	391	1,709	210
1 June 1925†	—	1,611	350	20	0	94‡	19	138	3,053	5,228	191	393§	1,147	—
1 July 1925†	—	1,715	—	20	0	—	21	—	2,867	5,085	—	—	1,218	—

* The figures for cotton (1920–4 inclusive) are for 31 January and 31 July.   † Subject to minor revision in some cases.   ‡ February 1925.   § 1 May.   (1) A. Total supply.   B. Total supply, seasonally corrected, exclusive of European and Asiatic mill stocks.   (2) Total supply outside hands of consumers.   (3) Total supply outside hands of consumers.   (4) Visible supply in U.K., and stocks in U.S.   (5) Visible supply in U.K. and U.S.   (6) Total supply outside plantations.   (7) Total visible supply.   (8) Visible supply in Rio, Santos, Bahia, Europe and U.S.   (9) Stocks in bond in U.K.   (10) Stocks in U.S.   (11) Visible supply in Chile, U.S., Europe and Egypt.   (12) Supply available for importing countries.

of Commerce had corrected this index for seasonal variations. This removes one great weakness, though the value of the index is still reduced by its limitation of the series to 'visible supplies'.

Full details of the revised index are given in the *Survey of Current Business* for April 1924, published by the U.S. Dept. of Commerce. All the major groups register higher in 1924 than in 1923, when a minimum was reached after the peak of 1921. Figures are as yet available only for the first quarter of 1925, during which a further increase took place, particularly in raw foodstuffs and raw materials for manufacture.

I. *American cotton*

At any given time stocks consist of the following:—

(1) Stocks up-country in the Southern States on plantations, railroads, and in 'uncounted'* interior towns.

(2) The 'visible' supply. This consists of (*a*) stocks in public storage and at compresses (warehouse stocks) in the more important interior towns and in the ports of the United States, (*b*) cotton afloat for Great Britain and the Continent, (*c*) warehouse stocks in the principal European ports, namely, Liverpool, Manchester, London, Havre, Marseilles, Genoa, Bremen, Ghent, Rotterdam and Barcelona.†

(3) Mill stocks in spinners' hands throughout the world, generally known as the 'invisible' or 'out of sight' supply.

The first table in last year's *Bulletin* has been revised in accordance with an improved method of calculation. The 'up-country' stock is taken as the 'up-country' carryover in the Southern States plus warehouse and mill stocks in the U.S. at the end of each season, plus the current year's crop, minus the U.S. consumption to any particular date, minus the net exports to that date (i.e. exports minus imports), minus warehouse and mill stocks at that date. By this means it is possible to estimate

---

* I.e. towns not included in the figures of stocks in public storage and at compresses.

† Cotton afloat for Japan and in Japanese ports is not allowed for. All cotton consigned to Japan is considered by the leading exchanges as 'consumed' or 'out of sight'.

Course of commodity stocks in the United States, by major groups (seasonal variations eliminated)

TOTAL INDEX

Year	Monthly average	Jan.	Feb.	March	April	May	June	July	Aug.	Sept.	Oct.	Nov.	Dec.
1919	100	103	103	100	104	102	97	97	96	101	100	100	97
1920	98	99	96	91	93	93	93	95	95	96	107	106	109
1921	138	124	134	141	136	139	145	145	148	138	137	132	131
1922	126	131	131	131	127	133	130	128	119	126	116	119	117
1923	118	121	116	117	117	111	115	114	125	118	118	122	125
1924	136	136	135	136	136	141	134	130	134	135	137	136	145
1925	—	155	152	148	—	—	—	—	—	—	—	—	—

RAW FOODSTUFFS

Year	Monthly average	Jan.	Feb.	March	April	May	June	July	Aug.	Sept.	Oct.	Nov.	Dec.
1919	100	125	120	99	101	89	86	91	101	108	94	99	87
1920	97	101	91	73	82	85	86	98	94	103	135	114	104
1921	174	121	147	164	147	154	171	171	198	184	212	205	209
1922	192	191	195	206	203	233	220	214	174	190	150	163	163
1923	142	165	157	161	169	143	146	134	133	119	113	122	141
1924	163	164	173	169	164	178	157	151	160	148	154	153	190
1925	—	192	187	190	—	—	—	—	—	—	—	—	—

RAW MATERIALS FOR MANUFACTURE

Year	Monthly average	Jan.	Feb.	March	April	May	June	July	Aug.	Sept.	Oct.	Nov.	Dec.
1919	100	106	105	107	111	110	100	100	85	85	95	98	98
1920	104	96	97	94	89	95	98	99	103	102	109	123	139
1921	158	154	166	171	176	178	184	189	176	151	124	118	110

Year													
1922	108	110	107	105	105	100	100	96	102	121	120	116	111
1923	108	111	102	101	96	93	95	94	111	118	130	123	119
1924	116	125	118	110	109	105	98	95	100	118	129	141	142
1925	—	149	139	130	—	—	—	—	—	—	—	—	—

Manufactured Foodstuffs

Year													
1919	100	98	93	90	94	100	88	88	93	107	114	114	121
1920	95	113	114	115	113	99	95	87	85	82	78	79	78
1921	79	78	80	82	80	81	81	83	78	76	78	74	71
1922	72	66	68	63	58	66	75	80	80	77	75	76	75
1923	80	70	71	76	76	79	88	87	85	83	80	82	81
1924	84	74	74	79	86	86	87	89	87	90	87	84	88
1925	—	87	86	80	—	—	—	—	—	—	—	—	—

Manufactured Commodities

Year													
1919	100	88	95	103	110	110	109	107	100	100	98	92	89
1920	97	90	88	86	91	95	96	97	97	95	104	110	116
1921	136	141	142	144	143	144	145	141	140	133	124	120	120
1922	118	138	135	130	123	115	110	108	108	111	112	112	111
1923	129	124	121	117	113	117	121	128	136	140	141	147	146
1924	161	161	154	161	163	169	169	161	165	165	161	155	148
1925	—	175	174	171	—	—	—	—	—	—	—	—	—

Supplies other than European and Asiatic mill stocks (1,000 bales)*

End of month	Up-country	U.S. warehouse stocks†	U.S. mill stocks†	Total in U.S.A.	Correction for season	Corrected total in U.S.A.	Visible outside U.S.A.	Grand total, excluding mill stocks outside U.S.A.‡
1919 July	2,193	2,212	1,304	5,709	—	5,709	347	6,056
October	11,973	1,974	1,365	15,312	9,000	6,312	1,077	7,389
1920 January	3,780	3,760	3,677	11,217	6,000	5,217	2,082	7,299
April	3,252	2,967	1,809	8,028	3,000	5,028	2,034	7,062
July	1,703§	2,055	1,358	5,116	—	5,116	1,352	6,468
October	11,414	4,168	944	16,526	10,311	6,215	—	—
1921 January	6,788	5,645	1,273	13,706	6,874	6,832	—	—
April	4,961	5,029	1,316	11,306	3,437	7,869	—	—
July	3,713§	3,723	1,111	8,007	—	8,007	1,645	9,652
October	7,577	4,982	1,405	13,964	6,330	7,634	1,598	9,232
1922 January	4,550	4,618	1,675	10,843	4,220	6,623	1,581	8,204
April	3,484	3,214	1,458	8,156	2,110	6,046	1,436	7,482
July	964§	1,488	1,218	3,670	—	3,670	1,120	4,790
October	—	—	—	—	7,302	—	1,023	—
1923 January	1,569	3,486	1,988	7,043	4,868	2,175	1,296	3,471
April	667	1,966	1,878	4,511	2,434	2,077	804	2,881
July	280§	945	1,099	2,324	—	2,324	376	2,700

August	9,736	1,179	807	11,722	9,284	3,282	230	3,512
September	7,639	2,148	773	10,560	8,440	2,120	579	2,699
October	4,667	3,486	1,103	9,256	7,596	1,660	962	2,622
November	2,767	3,770	1,439	7,976	6,752	1,224	1,005	2,229
December	1,568	3,526	1,623	6,717	5,908	809	1,201	2,010
1924 January	1,049	2,966	1,633	5,648	5,064	584	1,268	1,852
February	658	2,485	1,578	4,721	4,220	501	1,207	1,708
March	490	1,983	1,498	3,971	3,376	595	1,121	1,716
April	341	1,512	1,328	3,181	2,532	649	966	1,615
May	213	1,127	1,158	2,498	1,688	810	765	1,575
June	110	882	951	1,943	844	1,099	648	1,747
July	160§	674	721	1,555	—	1,555	528	2,083
August	13,217	811	553	14,581	12,518	2,063	373	2,436
September	10,833	2,073	514	13,420	11,380	2,040	633	2,673
October	7,008	4,225	731	10,242	10,242	1,722	1,021	2,743
November	4,226	4,914	1,047	10,187	9,104	1,083	1,444	2,527
December	2,666	4,624	1,319	8,609	7,966	643	1,920	2,563
1925 January	1,780	3,863	1,434	7,077	6,828	249	1,956	2,205
February	1,174	3,075	1,546	5,795	5,690	105	1,958	2,063
March	656	2,237	1,645	4,538	4,552	−14	1,918	1,904
April	341	1,666	1,515	3,522	3,414	108	1,731	1,839
May	28‖	1,135	1,348	2,511	2,276	235	1,376	1,611
June	67‖	760	1,124	1,817	1,138	679	1,036	1,715

* This table excludes linters, except that an insignificant quantity is included in the import figures. † Figures for all kinds of cotton. ‡ Seasonally corrected and excluding European and Asiatic mill stocks. § The carryover according to the above method was as follows: 1920, 2,171; 1921, 3,779; 1922, 2,615; 1923, 356; 1924, 6. ‖ Provisional.

the location of all cotton in the U.S. month by month. But it follows that the whole of the new crop is suddenly added to the 'up-country' stock in August each year. This is corrected in the table [see pp. 364-5] by the 'seasonal correction', which provides what would be the figure of 'up-country' stock if the current crop came into existence at an even monthly rate through the year. The statistics of U.S. warehouse stocks and mill stocks are compiled by the U.S. Bureau of the Census, and may be regarded as reliable, as also may the 'visible' supply of Great Britain and the Continent.* The estimates of the current crop are reasonably accurate by the end of each calendar year. The 'up-country' carryover is the most doubtful item, and is always liable to be under-, rather than over-estimated, with the result that very high prices may draw out a certain amount of unsuspected supplies. The estimates of Mr H. G. Hester, the Secretary of the New Orleans Cotton Exchange, have been used until 1922, since when the estimates of the Shepperson Publishing Company (*Cotton Facts*) have been preferred. The monthly calculated figures for 'up-country' provide at best an estimate of the actual state of affairs, but in most years they tally reasonably well with the 'up-country carryover' estimates (see Note § below table).

At the beginning and in the middle of each season, statistics of European and Asiatic mill stocks, and of the world's actual consumption during the previous six months are available, and the position of the world's total stocks is shown in the two following tables.

The present position is, therefore, approximately as follows. On Feb. 1st, 1925, there were about 10 million bales of American cotton in the world, making a small allowance for an underestimate of the 'carryover' last year. The world's consumption during the half-year ending Jan. 31st, 1925, has been at the rate of roughly 12¾ million bales per annum. If this rate of consumption is maintained during the current half-year, there will be left on July 31st next, roughly 3½ million bales. The necessary

* As given by the Liverpool Cotton Exchange.

Annual table of total stocks at the end of each season (1 August) (1,000 bales)

	1919	1920	1921	1922	1923	1924
Up-country carryover in interior cotton belt	2,193	1,703	3,713	964	280	160
U.S. warehouse stocks	2,212	2,055	3,723	1,488	945	674
U.S. mill stocks	1,304	1,358	1,111	1,218	1,099	721
Total in U.S.	5,709	5,116	8,547	3,670	2,324	1,555
European port stocks (including afloat for Europe)	1,247	1,394	1,695	1,120	376	528
European mill stocks	305	475	690	838	496	502
Asiatic mill stocks	?	267*	248	381	185	173
Total	7,261	7,252	11,180	6,009	3,381	2,758
Crop for year†	12,000	13,750	8,442	9,738	10,128	13,650
Total available	19,261	21,002	19,662	15,747	13,509	16,408
Total carried forward	6,990	10,386	7,066	3,081	2,554	—
Consumption for year	12,271	10,616	12,556	12,666	10,955	—

* Excluding China.   † For 1919–21 Hester's estimate of the actual growth, made at the beginning of the season, as the official figures for these years are questionable.

Annual table of total stocks in the middle of each season (1 February) (1,000 bales)

	1920	1921	1922	1923	1924	1925
Up-country stocks	3,780	6,788	4,550	1,569	1,049	1,780
U.S. warehouse stocks	3,760	5,645	4,618	3,486	2,966	3,863
U.S. mill stocks	3,677	1,273	1,675	1,988	1,633	1,434
Total in U.S.	11,217	13,706	10,843	7,043	5,648	7,077
European port stocks (including afloat)	2,018	1,650	1,575	1,296	1,268	1,956
European mill stocks	597	675	740	637	578	755
Asiatic mill stocks	117*	166*	390	206	203	201
Total available	13,949	16,197	13,548	9,182	7,697	9,989
Total available 1 August preceding	19,261	21,005	19,622	15,747	13,509	16,408
Consumption for half-year	5,312	4,808	6,074	6,565	5,812	6,419

* Excluding China.

minimum world carryover may be put at 2 million bales. There is, therefore, no reason why consumption should not be maintained and even increased somewhat, provided that the world is content to risk a minimum carryover. Consumption in America from March to June was much the same as in the preceding months: in this country the forwardings to the mills continue

Finished cotton goods in U.S.

	1,000 yards		Cases	
	Production	Orders grey yardage	Shipments	Stocks
1921 monthly aver.	85,385	90,154	44,935	36,226
1922 ,, ,,	94,016	95,509	49,102	44,937
1923 ,, ,,	95,098	91,504	48,116	46,166
1924 January	92,714	86,888	54,291	48,007
February	85,823	81,680	47,856	45,883
March	85,110	80,300	46,469	43,948
April	79,776	80,530	42,170	44,959
May	76,574	65,610	39,035	43,395
June	64,761	55,955	33,397	43,586
July	58,322	59,514	33,514	42,378
August	63,895	71,630	35,951	41,850
September	70,547	74,213	39,753	39,325
October	86,765	90,601	44,331	40,664
November	75,822	81,689	39,052	41,516
December	91,686	84,652	46,531	42,162
1925 January	81,174	84,459	49,319	36,925
February	81,650	83,293	47,961	36,101
March	92,632	86,776	48,879	36,121

on a heavier scale than last year. The lower price level is encouraging the building up of more normal visible stocks here and in Europe. In spite, therefore, of the large crop it does not seem likely that there will be any material surplus above requirements at the close of the season.

There are no statistics relating to finished cotton goods except for the United States. While not by any means complete, these statistics afford an interesting comparable series, as will be seen from the table [see page 369].

II. *Copper*

Stocks of copper consist of (1) refined copper in the United States, which constitutes the main part of the world's floating supply, (2) rough and blister copper in transit between smelters and refiners in the U.S., and on hand or in process at refineries, (3) refined and rough copper in European and Japanese warehouses. In the years immediately after the war there were also large stocks in the hands of the Allied Governments and in the form of scrap metal.

The estimates shown below for the past seven years are based on the figures of the U.S. Geological Survey, the American Bureau of Metal Statistics, trade and expert estimates (especially those contained in *The Mineral Industry*, Vols. XXIX and XXX), and the London Metal Exchange Statistics.

Judging by the violence of the fluctuations in production as compared with the steadiness of consumption during the years 1919–23, it would hardly have been unexpected if the very considerable increase in consumption during 1924 had been accompanied by a small rise in price, and a much more than corresponding increase in production. In fact prices were lower than in 1923—the price of electrolytic in New York averaged only 13.0 cents per lb. as against 14.4 in 1923—and yet production just kept pace with the increased consumption. It is probable that the output of those mines which can produce at a decidedly low price is steadily increasing, and that the world is becoming less dependent on the mines which cannot make a profit at a price below 12½ to 13 cents per lb. (See last year's Memorandum.)

After a sharp rise of price beginning last October, there was some decline, followed by another rise, which has left the price

Supplies and consumption of copper (tons of 2,240 lb)

	1 January 1919	1 January 1920	1 January 1921	1 January 1922	1 January 1923	1 January 1924	1 January 1925
United States:—							
Refined	80,000	281,000	294,000	205,000	96,000	114,000	122,000
In process, etc.	295,000	123,000 (say)	208,000	126,000	161,000	220,000	212,000
Allied Govt. stocks	281,000	180,000 (say)	82,000	trifling (say)	—	—	—
Scrap	361,000	270,000	183,000	90,000	—	—	—
U.K., Havre, Japan stocks	—	46,000	55,000	30,000	39,000	37,000	55,000
Total	1,017,000	900,000	822,000	451,000	296,000	371,000	389,000
Production*	856,000	871,000	479,000	800,000	1,161,000	1,302,000	—
Available supply	1,873,000	1,771,000	1,301,000	1,251,000	1,457,000	1,673,000	—
Stock carried forward	900,000	822,000	451,000	296,000	371,000	389,000	—
Consumption	973,000	949,000	850,000	955,000	1,086,000	1,284,000	—

* American Bureau of Metal Statistics.

Stocks of copper (tons of 2,240 lb)

Beginning of month	American refined	American blister	U.K. all kinds	Havre	Japan
1921 January	249,000	208,000	11,646	5,968	37,500
April	295,000	294,000	13,628	6,026	—
July	302,000	255,000	19,656	5,834	12,300
October	255,000	161,000	19,485	4,124	9,600
1922 January	205,000	126,000	16,655	4,138	9,300
April	161,700	—	15,868	3,459	12,900
July	170,000	—	12,992	3,192	13,100
October	120,000	—	19,524	5,613	11,900
1923 January	96,000	161,000	26,780	3,345	9,072
April	94,000	—	26,393	2,515	3,474
July	88,000	—	27,776	2,309	3,517
October	112,000	—	28,453	3,891	5,954
1924 January	139,000*	220,000	31,030	1,867	4,405
February	143,000	216,000	30,211	5,889	4,170
March	120,000	220,000	29,959	4,182	5,200
April	107,000	212,500	30,852	5,281	5,300
May	98,500	220,000	33,700	6,380	6,700
June	100,500	215,000	34,699	9,520	7,900
July	100,000	216,000	36,515	10,225	8,600
August	113,000	221,000	37,298	9,176	8,900
September	114,500	223,000	37,614	9,066	—
October	122,000	209,000	37,387	7,885	—
November	—	—	38,078	5,832	10,081
December	—	—	37,455	7,213	—
1925 January	122,000	212,000	38,419	7,180	9,992
February	—	—	41,479	9,128	9,718
March	—	—	43,198	10,150	—
April	109,200	233,000	44,276	8,341	1,743
May	—	—	44,968	7,908	—
June	86,600	—	46,100	6,469	—
July	81,500	—	47,984	—	—

* The corresponding figure of 114,000 tons given in the preceding table is that of the U.S. Geological Survey.

definitely higher than last year's average. In some quarters the reason for the decline was attributed to too great activity in production, but this is not really borne out by the statistics to date. It was the fear, and not the fact, of over-production which caused the relapse; and the fear not being realised, a recovery has ensued. There is, however, no doubt that there will be ample supplies available without any considerable rise in prices.

For the first four months of 1925 the world's production of copper is estimated to have amounted to 476,000 tons, which is at the rate of 1,428,000 tons per annum, a further substantial increase on 1924 if it is continued throughout the year.

The increase in the world's consumption has not been confined to the U.S.A., though that country of course dominates the position—the mere increase in American consumption in 1924 being about one-half of the total consumption in Great Britain. However, the imports into this country last year exceeded those of 1913, 1920, and 1923, which were approximately constant, by no less than 30 per cent, and the low rate of consumption which had been prevailing—and was so surprising in view of the great development of the electrical industry—seems likely to be a thing of the past. Expectations that Germany would resume what may be considered a normal consumption have not been realised, but the increase as compared with 1923, when the Ruhr occupation dislocated her industrial activity, was very considerable, and seems certain to continue through 1925.

The table above supplies some more detailed statistics of the principal stocks.

III. Tin

Stocks of tin mainly consist of:—

(1) The 'visible' supply, as defined by the returns of Messrs Ricard and Freiwald, and of Messrs Strauss, namely, warehouse stocks in Holland, U.K., and U.S., and tin afloat from the Federated Malay States, Netherlands Indies and Australia.

(2) Stocks of ore in Bolivia and Nigeria, and afloat from these countries to U.K., and in course of smelting in U.K.

(3) Stocks in the Federated Malay States and Netherlands Indies.

(4) Stocks in China and afloat from China to U.S. and U.K.

Detailed monthly figures, of which the aggregates are given in the next table, are available for:—

(1) In the returns of the two firms mentioned, which are in fairly close agreement with one another.

(2) There are no longer any surplus stocks in Nigeria and Bolivia (as there were after the War and again in 1921) beyond the normal flow of ore to the smelters overseas.

Visible stocks of tin* (tons, 2,240 lb)

End of month	1913	1920	1921	1922	1923	1924	1925
January	14,875	20,980	18,104	25,346	22,598	21,173	21,155
February	13,348	21,472	16,900	24,434	22,183	18,428	21,809
March	12,117	18,279	15,764	21,040	21,703	19,247	18,320
April	10,814	18,716	15,131	21,244	19,058	16,227	16,770
May	14,663	20,801	17,767	22,235	18,263	17,030	19,567
June	12,903	18,883	16,953	22,558	17,543	19,143	19,535
July	13,713	18,482	19,852	20,364	17,976	19,223	
August	12,841	20,152	19,037	21,753	16,170	20,321	
September	14,673	18,326	20,777	20,488	17,389	19,124	
October	13,049	19,442	22,891	19,975	18,479	17,769	
November	16,112	19,065	22,247	22,131	16,939	19,684	
December	15,543	18,479	24,273	22,155	18,596	23,374	

* Figures of A. Strauss & Co.

(3) The most important event of the year has been the final disposal of the stocks of the official pool formed under the Bandoeng Agreement for holding tin in the Malay States and Netherlands Indies. The original purchases were made between December 1920 and February 1921. At the beginning of April 1923 the stock held was as follows:—

Netherlands East Indies Govt., Banka tin ingots	2,000 tons
„ „ „ „ „ in ore	2,000 „
F.M.S. Govt. Straits, tin ingots	10,000 „
Billiton Co. Straits, tin ingots	1,000 „
Straits Trading Co. Straits, tin in ore	2,600 „
	17,600 „

The commencement of the scheme of liquidation was announced in April 1923 in the following official statement:—

The scheme became operative on the 1st April, 1923, and 5 per cent of the amount of tin held by each of the four parties was released to them to hold or to sell at their discretion, and the same amount will be released on the first day of each succeeding month. The total amount released per month on the agreed basis will be 880 tons of tin, and a period of twenty months will elapse before the total amount of tin in the pool is released to the respective holders.

Up to the end of March 1924 the whole of the monthly quotas had been disposed of; but in April, as a result of the fall in the price of tin, the F.M.S. sold only 175 tons out of their quota of 500 tons for the month. The whole quantity, however, had been released from the agreement by November 1924, and had been actually sold by the end of the following month.

(4) Chinese stocks, held in Yunnan and in Hong Kong, can only be given from approximate trade estimates, as follows:—

Hong Kong:	end of 1919	6,000 tons
	1920	2,000 „
	1921	5,000 „
	1922	nil
	1923	250 „
	1924	100 „
Yunnan:	end of 1923	750 „
	1924	400 „

Combining these figures, we have (very roughly) the following (in tons):—

Total stocks of tin

	'Visible' supply	Bolivian ore stocks	Eastern pool	Chinese stocks	Total	Excess (+) of consumption over production per month
1 Jan. 1920	21,500	7,500	Nil	6,000	35,000	—
1 July	18,900	3,500	Nil	4,000	26,400	+ 1,430
1 Jan. 1921	18,500	Nil	6,000	2,000	26,500	—
1 July	17,000	2,500	20,000	4,000	43,500	− 2,830
1 Jan. 1922	24,300	4,500	19,550	5,000	53,350	− 1,640
1 July	22,600	1,500	17,600	2,500	44,200	+ 1,520
1 Jan. 1923	22,200	Nil	17,600	1,000	40,800	+ 570
1 July	17,543	Nil	14,960	1,000	33,503	+ 1,210
1 Jan. 1924	18,596	Nil	9,680	1,000	29,276	+ 700
1 July	19,143	Nil	5,725	500	25,368	+ 650
1 Jan. 1925	23,374	Nil	Nil	500	23,874	+ 250
1 July	19,535	Nil	Nil	500	20,035	+ 782

Thus, ever since the high-water mark of stocks was reached in January 1922, consumption has steadily exceeded production. By June 1925 the stocks were less than two-fifths of what they had been in January 1922, and during the forty-one intervening months consumption had exceeded production by an average amount of 800 tons a month. Since the 'visible' supply includes the tin 'afloat' on its long voyage from the East, the minimum figure of stocks is being rapidly approached. For example, in June 1925, 12,955 tons out of the total visible supply of 19,567 tons were afloat. Perhaps the minimum stock can be put at about 13,500 tons altogether.

The world's production and consumption of tin have been approximately as follows:—[p. 377].

The total production for 1924 was made up as follows:— [p. 377].

During the first five months of 1925, as compared with the same months of 1924, Bolivian shipments were reduced by 933 tons fine tin equivalent of ore, Nigerian shipments were practically unchanged but less rather than more, Australian shipments

	Production (Tons)	Consumption (Tons)
1922	128,000	141,000
1923	124,000	135,000
1924	132,000	137,000
1925 (Forecast)	136,000	145,000

[Total tin production for 1924] (tons)

Dutch Indies	28,000
Bolivia	30,000
Federated Malay States	43,000
Unfederated Malay States	2,500
Siam and Burma	9,000
Nigeria	6,000
Australia	2,000
South Africa	1,000
Cornwall	1,000
China	8,000
Elsewhere	1,500
	132,000

were reduced by 400 tons, and the exports of the Federated Malay States were 1,323 tons higher. Thus there is no sign of any material increase of production at present.

Tin is a pecular commodity in that both production and consumption are exceptionally insensitive to moderate changes of price, with the result that violent price fluctuations ensue whenever the difference between the two has to be absorbed into or out of 'stocks'. A firm of stockbrokers has recently summarised the position as follows:—

The cost of production of tin in the Straits is very low. The average company whose shares are quoted on the London Stock Exchange producing in the East has an all-in cost of less than £50 per ton of black tin (60 per cent pure). The lowest producer of all is at £23 a ton. Even with tin at a price as low as £200 a ton these companies make very large profits and naturally turn out as much as their dredge capacity. There is, therefore, no need for fear that an increase in price will be followed by an increase in production. There are only a few negligible producers, such as the Cornish mines, whose production is much influenced by the price of metal.

Between 40 and 50 per cent of the tin consumed in this country, and a somewhat smaller percentage of that consumed in America, is in the tin plate trade, whose prosperity is in no way dependent on the price of tin. The demand for tin in other uses, such as in white metal bearings, is practically independent of the price. The future course of the price of tin will, therefore, be determined almost exclusively by the progress of consumption, and especially by the absorption in the United States.

The average price of tin in 1913 was £200 per ton, and in recent years the price has varied as follows:—

Average prices of tin

	Highest	Lowest	Average
1921	£210½	£148	£165
1922	188	134	159
1923	240	176	202
1924	298	206	249
1925 (5 months)	278	229	252

IV. *Lead*

Stocks are still very small, as they have been for more than three years past. As regards lead supplies, the world has continued to live from hand to mouth.

The only precise statistics extending over a long period are those relating to warehouses in the United Kingdom which are covered by the monthly returns of the London Metal Exchange. These are shown in the following table below:—[p. 379].

Statistics of stocks of refined lead held in the United States and Mexico are available since the beginning of 1924, and have been as follows below:—[p. 379].

Bonded Stocks in the United States, mainly in the form of ore and base bullion, have been reported as follows below:—[p. 379].

U.K. stocks of lead (tons)

End of month	Monthly stocks United Kingdom Private warehouses and Government stock					
	1920	1921	1922	1923	1924	1925
January	47,348	19,777	622	414	296	130
February	40,435	19,129	589	648	57	136
March	28,435	23,926	578	432	27	14
April	26,250	18,127	522	456	20	34
May	23,338	14,138	646	447	7	74
June	25,192	13,278	268	163	6	141
July	23,448	12,396	235	1,815	3	—
August	21,521	11,515	686	1,719	19	—
September	18,721	9,883	583	1,439	65	—
October	15,335	5,161	281	1,229	1	—
November	14,919	1,069	198	1,233	3	—
December	19,045	284	518	1,183	58	—

Stocks in United States and Mexico

1924	Tons	1924	Tons	1925	Tons
January	89,759	July	94,161	January	90,112
February	90,376	August	92,372	February	94,475
March	92,292	September	87,747	March	—
April	98,585	October	87,028	April	—
May	98,145	November	87,822	May	—
June	97,107	December	77,854	June	—

Bonded stocks of lead in United States on 1 January

Year	Tons	Year	Tons
1919	15,599	1923	7,833
1920	40,812	1924	72,130
1921	46,912	1925	93,104
1922	17,440		

The following figures issued by the American Bureau of Metal Statistics apply to the principal lead-producing countries of the world, which, in 1923, furnished 83 per cent of the world's total lead output:—

Production of lead

	1923	1924
	Tons	Tons
United States	404,748	471,005
Mexico	164,502	158,796
Canada	48,124	75,298
Spain and Tunis	65,004	104,534
Italy	16,804	21,712
Australia	122,779	125,557
Burma	45,749	51,758
Rhodesia	10,859	6,253
Transvaal	4,816	4,477
Total	883,385	1,019,390

In the first four months of 1925 these same countries produced 365,800 tons, i.e. at the rate of 1,100,000 tons per annum. Thus the high prices recently prevailing have called forth increased production, sufficient to satisfy the high level of consumption. From the long-period point of view, the prospects of continued increasing production are not so favourable. The production of the seven countries, United States, Mexico, Canada, Spain, Australia, Burma, and Rhodesia (about 80 per cent of the world's output) has been approximately as follows in recent years:—

Production in principal areas

Year	Tons	Year	Tons
1920	629,464	1923	861,607
1921	615,178	1924	992,857
1922	762,500	1925*	1,093,750

* At rate for first quarter.

V. *Spelter* (*Zinc*)

Monthly statistics are available of stocks in public warehouses in the United States and in the United Kingdom as given below [p. 382].

While these stocks in 1924 showed a distinct increase on the previous year, they have never approached a month's supply and have been dwindling during the last few months.

Production and consumption in the United States show only a very slight increase in 1924 as compared with the previous year, which had registered a marked increase on 1922. But Belgium, the next biggest producer, increased by some 15,000 tons to a total of 163,000 metric tons in 1924. According to Rudolf Wolff & Company the world's output of virgin spelter was 451,800 tons in 1921, 688,520 in 1922, 960,168 in 1923, and 992,324 in 1924.

According to figures issued by the American Bureau of Metal Statistics the production of spelter by countries, which in 1923 furnished about 88 per cent of the world's output, has been as follows:—

Production of spelter (tons of 2,240 lb)

	1923	1924
United States	474,284	478,430
Canada	27,093	24,679
Belgium	145,733	160,411
Germany	110,396	102,989
Australia	40,248	46,601
Great Britain	31,279	38,480
Total	829,032	851,591

During the first quarter of 1925 these same countries produced 242,855 tons, i.e. at an annual rate of 971,421 tons.

U.K. and U.S. stocks of spelter (tons of 2,240 lb)

End of month	1921 U.S.	1921 U.K.	1921 Total	1922 U.S.	1922 U.K.	1922 Total	1923 U.S.	1923 U.K.	1923 Total	1924 U.S.	1924 U.K.	1924 Total	1925 U.S.	1925 U.K.	1925 Total
January	67,810	14,862	82,672	58,635	11,412	70,047	14,794	394	15,188	36,330	1,088	37,418	16,960	398	17,358
Feburary	69,660	13,606	83,266	57,250	8,335	65,585	9,700	197	9,897	33,220	975	34,175	14,910	331	15,241
March	73,440	14,427	87,867	53,800	6,375	60,175	8,947	838	9,785	28,600	858	29,458	15,350	315	15,665
April	72,720	17,730	90,450	46,186	6,067	52,253	8,014	1,238	9,252	29,270	673	29,943	16,370	227	16,597
May	76,615	19,000	96,615	36,080	5,338	41,418	11,624	1,702	13,326	37,820	628	38,448	18,940	389	19,329
June	80,260	18,752	99,012	26,407	4,662	31,069	15,333	1,679	17,012	44,360	671	45,031	20,460	506	20,966
July	82,510	18,153	100,663	25,552	4,289	29,841	18,896	1,198	20,094	47,060	352	47,412	—	—	—
August	77,275	17,387	94,662	19,311	3,977	23,288	23,635	1,007	24,642	45,470	442	45,912	—	—	—
September	72,440	16,405	88,845	16,791	3,668	20,459	20,440	803	21,243	40,820	814	41,634	—	—	—
October	63,235	15,424	78,659	16,110	2,670	18,780	23,024	1,034	24,058	34,330	675	35,005	—	—	—
November	59,865	14,052	73,917	17,408	852	18,260	27,600	1,390	28,990	24,030	541	24,571	—	—	—
December	59,470	12,765	72,235	16,296	631	16,927	32,600	1,190	33,850	18,930	396	19,326	—	—	—

VI. *Rubber*

The stocks of rubber are held mainly:—

(1) On plantations, etc. within the restricted area of Malaya.

(2) In Singapore and Penang.

(3) Afloat.

(4) In London and Liverpool.

(5) In U.S.A. warehouses and factories.

In addition relatively insignificant stocks are held:

(6) In Ceylon and India.

(7) In Dutch East Indies.

(8) In Para (Brazil).

(9) In Amsterdam and Antwerp.

Monthly figures are only available for 3 and 4, but since 1923 quarterly figures are available for all except 1. The following table

U.S. stocks of tyres and tubes (1,000,000)

End of month	Pneumatic tyres	Inner tubes
1921 September	3·3	3·8
December	3·7	4·7
1922 March	5·2	7·0
June	5·0	6·2
September	4·6	5·2
December	4·6	5·7
1923 March	5·7	7·7
June	7·0	8·9
September	5·4	6·5
December	4·3	6·3
1924 March	5·8	8·1
June	5·8	8·2
September	4·5	6·0
December	5·6	8·3
1925 January	6·0	8·7
February	6·7	9·8
March	0·1	10·7

[p. 385] is based on yearly and half-yearly estimates of the total world stocks in the chief centres at the end of 1920, 1921, and 1922: for 1923 some quarterly returns are available also; and since March 1924 the figures are reproduced from a table given in *The Rubber Quarterly*.

On the basis of consumption during 1924, the aggregate stocks at the end of 1924 were equivalent to between four and a half and five months' consumption, as compared with the equivalent of seven months' consumption at the end of 1923.

Stocks of rubber in the United States have continued to decline slowly, but stocks of tyres and tubes, which goods account for 80 per cent of the U.S. consumption of rubber, still stood at a high figure at the end of last March, as the table [p. 383] shows.

In this connection it may be remarked that while the U.S. output of motor-cars can scarcely be expected to increase much further, the adoption of balloon tyres may swell the replacement needs to some extent.

Stocks of rubber in the United Kingdom have declined very greatly, and there is now virtually no reserve on the Continent. By the middle of June visible stocks in the United Kingdom had fallen to the trifling figure of 5,360 tons.

The following table [p. 386] gives the estimates of production and consumption in recent years.

Production in Malaya and Ceylon has been and will continue to be affected by the legislation for restriction. In 1924 the more drastic provisions of the Stevenson Restriction Scheme came into operation as for three months the average price of rubber remained below 1s.

In their forecast for production in 1925 Messrs Symington and Sinclair state that they have 'gone on the assumption that buyers will have sufficient "horse-sense" to see that the average does not in any quarter fall below 1s. 6d.' (If the price is so maintained for another twelve months, the restriction scheme will automatically come to an end on May 1, 1926.)

Approximate total *World's rubber stocks (exclusive of stock on estates)* (1,000 tons)

End of:	United Kingdom*	United States†	Singapore and Penang	Ceylon and India	Dutch East Indies	Para (Brazil)	Amsterdam and Antwerp	Afloat	Approximate total
1920	56	76	35	?	?	?	?	37	(204)‡ 219§–229*
1921	80	52	40	?	?	?	?	37	(209)‡ 224§–244*
1922	81	90	55	?	?	?	?	45	(271)‡ 286§–306*
1923 March	79	87	21	3·5	9	0·6	1·0	48	249
June	64	101	46	?	?	?	?	52	(263)‡ 278§
September	68	90	27	4·0	10	0·9	1·2	43	244
December	75	73	38	4·0	10	?	2·5	52	254
1924 March	70	70	21	3·0	10	1·0	1·1	50	226
June	65	60	20	3·0	10	1·0	1·2	48	208
September	54	56	20	3·5	7	0·8	0·6	54	196
December	36	63	19	4·0	5	0·9	0·3	53	181
1925 March	23	51	17	4·0	5	1·2	0·1	50	151
May‖	6	52	16	?	?	?	?	56	138
June‖	5	—	—	—	—	—	—	—	—

* Including an estimate of stocks in private warehouses except in the figures for 1920, 1921, and 1922. The totals for these years were therefore certainly higher than the figures shown, and should perhaps be increased by 10,000 tons in 1920, and by 15–20,000 tons in 1921 and 1922.
† Returns cover 90–95 per cent of the whole.
‡ These figures in brackets give the actual total of stocks quoted.
§ These figures include an estimate of 15,000 tons for the unknown stocks in Ceylon, Dutch East Indies, Para, and at Amsterdam and Antwerp. This has been done in order to secure a more comparable series.
‖ Provisional.

*Production and consumption of rubber**

Production	1919	1920	1921	1922†	1923	1924
	Tons	Tons	Tons	Tons	Tons	Tons
Malaya	180,000	190,000	170,000	238,000	165,000	165,000
Ceylon and India	35,000	40,000	40,000	48,000	40,500	44,200
Dutch East Indies	75,000	85,000	50,000	73,000	131,000	162,000
Other countries in the East	10,000	15,000	10,000	15,000	18,500	19,300
Total Eastern Plantation:—						
Rubber	300,000	330,000	270,000	370,000	355,000	390,500
Brazil	32,000	31,000	20,000	21,500	21,500	23,500
Wild	7,000	7,000	3,000	3,500	5,500	6,000
Total	339,000	368,000	293,000	395,000	382,000	420,000
Consumption						
U.S.A.	225,000	200,000	200,000	282,000	305,500	335,000
United Kingdom	33,000	25,000	18,000	25,000	27,000	27,000
France	22,000	16,000	14,000	27,000	30,000	35,000
Italy	14,000	6,000	5,000	6,000	7,500	8,700
Canada	9,500	11,000	9,000	9,000	14,000	14,500
Japan	—	7,500	12,500	16,000	12,000	17,000
Germany, Russia and Austria	5,500	11,000	18,000	31,000	25,000	24,500
Other countries	14,000	13,500	15,500	12,000	13,000	13,300
Total	335,000	290,000	292,000	408,000	434,000	475,000

* Symington and Sinclair.
† Production in this year was probably somewhat higher than these figures indicate.

386

Their forecast of production and consumption in 1925 is as follows:—

Estimated production and consumption in 1925

Production		Consumption	
	Tons		Tons
Malaya	190,000	U.S.A.	360,000
Ceylon	44,000	U.K.	29,000
Dutch East Indies	193,000	Other countries	121,000
Other sources	61,000		
Total	488,000	Total	510,000

Excess of Consumption over Production 22,000 tons.

The above forecast of production was stated to be a maximum and of consumption a minimum. The latter qualification seems likely to be only too true, for in a recent report Messrs Symington and Sinclair state: 'The first six months of this year look likely, so far as figures are yet available, to show an actual consumption of about 280,000 tons. If we allow for a slight decrease in the second half, we still have to face a consumption this year of about 530,000 to 540,000 tons, which is well above all previous estimates.' Should this be correct, the position will be even more critical. If this forecast is realised, stocks at the end of 1925, according to the figures in the table on page 385, can scarcely exceed 150–160,000 tons. Since at least two months' consumption must always be afloat or in transit, this means that the actual available reserve will be under two months' supply, which is undoubtedly on the low side. Messrs Symington and Sinclair estimate stocks at the end of 1924 to be greater by 18,000 tons than the figure in the table on page 385, and yet they 'fail to see where the extra quantity is going to be found. The 22,000 tons may perhaps be spared from reserves, but even that is cutting matters very fine.'

387

VII. *Sugar*

In the case of this commodity it is necessary to restrict ourselves to 'visible' supplies, accurate estimates of stocks held up by producers in the fairly numerous different sources of supply not being available. Nevertheless, this limitation is not so serious as it would be in the case of many commodities, because, on the one hand, sugar being a semi-manufactured product, the agricultural producers send the bulk of the output forward to the centrals as soon as it is available, and, on the other hand, since it is in most countries a dutiable commodity, invisible supplies, on which duty has been paid, are not likely, as a rule, to be any larger than convenience dictates.

The total monthly figures of the visible supply are shown in the table below (up to December 1921 they were supplied by Messrs Bagot and Thompson, and since that date by Messrs C. Czarnikow, Ltd.: the two sets are only roughly comparable).

The distribution of the stock between the different countries is shown by the following detailed table for selected dates.

The total 'visible' stocks naturally show a sharp seasonal

Total visible supply of sugar (1,000 tons)

First half of month	1913	1914	1920	1921	1922†	1923	1924	1925
January	3,234	3,711		2,313	2,761	2,433	2,255	2,708
February	4,043	4,323		2,816	2,543	2,511	2,357	2,950
March	4,141	4,279	2,399	3,254	2,559	2,603	2,402	2,844
April	4,006	4,192	2,433	3,331	2,479	2,501	2,460	2,891
May	3,869	4,032	2,423	3,471	2,587	2,472	2,658	3,053‡
June	3,732	3,792	2,075	3,382	2,275	2,278	2,509	2,863‡
July	3,228	3,244	2,003	3,312	1,903	2,005	2,086	
August	3,426	2,668	1,788	3,141	1,580	1,630	1,560	
September	1,813	*	1,522	2,375	1,180	1,267	982	
October	1,259		1,338	2,039	868	791	542	
November	739		1,197	1,727	1,248	1,089	1,318	
December	1,900		2,103	2,258	2,077	1,951	2,364	

* No figures available between this date and March 1920.
† For this and subsequent years, figures relate to as near the first of the month as possible.
‡ Provisional.

Distribution of sugar stocks (1,000 tons)

Beginning of month	Germany	Czecho-Slovakia	France	Holland	Belgium	United Kingdom	Total Europe	United States (ports)	Cuba (ports)	Grand total
1922 January	808	425	177	158	128	176	1,872	45	844	2,761
April	495	262	104	177	71	218	1,327	222	930	2,479
July	216	83	61	90	30	368	848	193	862	1,903
October	37	6	45	52	12	272	424	128	316	868
December	772	470	176	185	51	334	1,988	40	49	2,077
1923 January	1,002	470	240	224	128	312	2,376	12	45	2,433
April	736	261	148	144	57	286	1,632	215	654	2,501
July	516	107	109	79	35	405	1,251	164	590	2,005
October	102	9	42	16	15	256	440	110	241	791
December	744	593	208	124	51	164	1,884	36	31	1,951
1924 January	908	546	291	154	143	164	2,206	27	22	2,255
April	718	378	127	83	63	264	1,633	167	660	2,460
July	488	113	78	67	38	322	1,106	192	788	2,086
October	2	7	47	22	11	150	239	76	227	542
November	345	337	151	115	61	118	1,127	46	145	1,318
December	874	706	305	198	62	154	2,299	24	41	2,364
1925 January	978	769	468	219	62	172	2,668	16	24	2,708
February	863	694	488	188	228	155	2,616	40	294	2,950
March	725	591	453	160	204	145	2,278	106	460	2,844
April	618	494	373	115	166	194	1,960	128	803	2,891
May	453	407	292	109	—	311	1,722*	173	1,158	2,053*
June	383	315	216	—	—	328	1,492*	277	1,094	2,863*

* Approximate totals.

Supply and consumption of sugar (tons)

	1920–1	1921–2	1922–3	1923–4	1924–5*
Stock carried over on 1 September	1,600,000	2,400,000	1,180,000	1,267,000	982,000
European beet crops	3,671,788	4,054,282	4,735,500	5,057,800	7,121,000
American beet crops	1,004,019	930,121	649,000	803,700	895,000
Cane crops	12,081,831	12,679,948	12,691,500	13,837,400	14,851,000
Total	18,357,638	20,064,351	19,256,000	20,965,900	23,849,000
Deduct visible supplies at end of season (1 September)	2,400,000	1,180,000	1,267,000	982,000	—
Total consumption	15,957,638	18,884,351	17,989,000	19,983,900	—

* Estimates only.

390

fluctuation, but, as the second table shows, this is really a compound of two variations, one for Europe, which is mainly concerned with beet sugar, and the other for America, which is dominated by the Cuban cane crop. Thus stocks in Europe are at a minimum about October 1st, and reach a maximum about January 1st, whereas American port stocks are at a minimum at about January 1st, and reach their maximum about May 1st. The fluctuation in the total visible supply figures is, of course, dominated by the European stocks, since only *port* stocks in Cuba and the United States are included.

In the second table the enormous carryover of the Cuban 1920–1 crop accounts for the very large amount in Cuban ports on January 1st, 1922. The steady increase in the maximum European stocks is also noticeable.

The table above gives a very rough idea of stocks, production and consumption in recent seasons:

Apart from the season 1922–3, the world's consumption has been steadily and greatly increasing, and the apparent decline in that year is in a sense illusory, for consumption in the previous year was, as it were, artificially stimulated by the abnormally low prices after the catastrophic break at the end of 1921. Production has clearly been responding to a considerable extent, and culminating in the present season, which will not improbably exceed last season's total by $2\frac{1}{2}$–3 million tons. Messrs Czarnikow on April 9th expressed the opinion that

it is too much to expect that the whole of this quantity will be accounted for by actual consumption, though it is reasonable to assume that at the present scale of prices, with a possibility of further slight reductions, sufficient confidence may be inspired for the building up of invisibles to a greater extent than has been done for some time past. Another point worth consideration is the fact that much sugar disappears into non-statistical countries in Europe, which it is impossible to trace, as was the case last year, when about one million tons were imperceptibly absorbed.

Some increase in recorded consumption can, of course, be confidently predicted. The following table shows consumption during

391

recent years by this country and the United States, which between them account for an extraordinary proportion of the exported sugar.

U.K. and U.S.A. consumption of sugar

	Consumption (raw values—tons)	
	United Kingdom	United States
1922	1,748,177	5,476,500
1923	1,602,029	5,141,000
1924	1,706,960	5,220,000

Taking all factors into consideration, there is every prospect of sufficient supplies of this commodity for the next twelve months, unless bad weather reduces the expected yield of the beet sugar crops, or the low price now prevailing proves deterrent to producers.

Tea in bond in the United Kingdom (1,000 lb)

End of month	1921	1922	1923	1924	1925
January	219,377	208,115	186,035	182,865	225,067*
February	223,179	221,362	176,681	188,559	234,557*
March	229,568	219,645	183,413	193,362	231,516*
April	233,018	214,484	167,763*	192,219	217,091*
May	228,793	192,396	141,659*	152,317	190,730
June	218,290	170,478	126,792*	138,691	
July	207,448	153,198	112,890*	121,097	
August	197,433	142,137	121,935*	128,266	
September	190,799	151,510	134,170*	136,694	
October	190,129	152,095	146,990*	150,721	
November	196,534	158,357	152,288*	174,414	
December	205,420	169,776	165,666*	205,859	

* Figures from April to December 1923, and January to May 1925, do not include stocks in the Irish Free State.

Figures from January 1921 to March 1924 represent revised stocks, while those from April 1924 onwards are subject to revision.

VIII. *Tea*

The only precise figures available for the stocks of tea are of those in bond in the United Kingdom. Since, however, about three-quarters of the total world production passes through this country, these stocks should form a fairly reliable index of the position.

IX. *Coffee*

About two-thirds of the supply of coffee for Europe and U.S.A. comes from Brazil. The table below is based on the figures

Coffee (1,000 bags)*

Year	Beginning of month	Visible supply of Europe	Visible supply of U.S.A.	Stocks in Brazil	Total
1913	July	6,480	1,848	1,947	10,275
	September	6,005	1,477	4,002	11,484
	October	6,019	1,393	4,769	12,181
1914	January	7,275	1,709	4,681	13,665
	April	8,702	2,172	1,743	12,617
	June	8,353	2,056	1,207	11,616
1919	January	758	1,010	9,296	11,364
	April	2,755	1,964	7,060	11,799
	July	3,124	1,508	5,704	10,336
	October	2,821	2,057	5,540	10,418
1920	January	2,843	2,007	5,020	9,870
	April	2,573	2,209	3,392	8,174
	July	2,509	2,293	1,948	6,750
	October	2,955	2,640	2,387	7,982
1921	January	2,588	2,442	3,735	8,765
	April	2,533	2,765	3,389	8,687
	July	2,562	2,100	4,038	8,700
	October	2,564	1,838	4,589	8,991
1922	January	2,399	2,056	4,948	9,403
	April	2,977	1,583	4,580	9,140
	July	3,068	1,456	4,115	8,639
	October	3,007	1,182	4,292	8,481

Table (*cont.*)

Year	Beginning of month	Visible supply of Europe	Visible supply of U.S.A.	Stocks in Brazil	Total
1923	January	2,839	1,385	3,756	7,980
	February	2,764	1,402	3,573	7,739
	March	2,443	1,625	3,312	7,480
	April	2,463	1,618	2,903	6,974
	May	2,438	1,197	2,488	6,123
	June	2,329	1,059	2,099	5,487
	July	2,296	1,075	1,969	5,340
	August	2,273	1,034	2,243	5,550
	September	2,449	1,387	2,016	5,852
	November	2,481	1,673	1,656	5,820
	December	2,453	1,750	1,182	5,385
1924	January	2,228	1,349	890	4,467
	February	2,153	1,088	979	4,220
	March	2,192	1,172	902	4,266
	April	1,935	1,075	954	3,964
	May	1,993	1,126	1,326	4,445
	June	2,215	1,096	1,443	4,754
	July	—	—	—	5,071
	August	2,140	1,110	1,128	4,378
	September	2,345	1,194	1,748	5,287
	October	2,255	1,337	2,135	5,727
	November	2,378	1,382	1,999	5,759
	December	2,158	1,358	2,115	5,631
1925	January	2,098	1,046	2,240	5,384
	February	2,072	1,112	2,072	5,256
	March	2,002	1,029	2,125	5,156
	April	2,028	1,116	2,245	5,389
	May	2,165	878	2,292	5,335
	June	2,192	779	2,257	5,228
	July	2,193	1,154	1,738	5,085

* G. Duuring & Zoon.

394

supplied by Messrs Duuring and Zoon, the most important omissions from which are the stocks in the East and Eastern ports, in the interior of Brazil, and coffee from the East afloat to U.S.A.

Deliveries during the last four years have been as follows:—

Deliveries of coffee (1,000 bags)

Year	To Europe	To U.S.A.	Total	From Brazil	Other kinds
1920	5,213	9,167	14,380	8,638	5,742
1921	8,094	9,958	18,052	11,356	6,696
1922	8,238	9,654	17,892	11,100	6,792
1923	9,240	10,585	19,825	13,516	6,309
1924	9,981	10,709	20,690	13,473	7,217

The position in the immediate future is dominated by the unknown amount held up-country in Brazil. On this no two authorities can agree, but according to a mean estimate the world's visible supply, inclusive of stock up-country in Brazil, will be on June 30th, 1925, no more than $4\frac{3}{4}$ million bags, or less than three months' supply. According to this authority, up-country stock will be negligible, whereas in 1924 it was probably as much as 3–4 million bags. Looking further ahead, the 1925–6 Brazil crop may be estimated at not more than 13 million bags, and the supply from other countries at about 6 million, or 19 millions in all. Consumption next year is put at 21 millions, which seems a conservative estimate. This would leave a total world's carryover of all coffee everywhere not exceeding $2\frac{3}{4}$ million bags, which is certainly too small a margin to be satisfactory. Unless unexpected supplies come forward, a definite shortage is in prospect, either sooner or later, for it is at least certain that production and stocks are shrinking, while consumption is rapidly increasing.

X. *Petroleum*

The only figures of stocks regularly available are those for the United States. Since, however, nearly 80 per cent of the world's oil stocks are held in the United States, these figures can be regarded as reasonably representative.

The following table of stocks of crude petroleum in the United States is that published by the American Petroleum Institute.

U.S.A. stocks of petroleum

Stocks at end of month	Crude petroleum (1,000 barrels)					
	1920	1921	1922	1923	1924	1925
January	127,164	117,099	180,984	282,875	364,954	391,233
February	126,329	121,713	191,471	283,498	368,901	392,029
March	125,597	128,754	202,906	289,871	373,561	392,373
April	124,991	134,719	213,371	295,970	378,214	393,222
May	124,689	143,614	224,388	304,668	383,488	
June	126,763	151,339	232,032	315,369	387,364	
July	128,168	159,030	238,233	326,635	391,919	
August	129,043	162,903	242,635	333,143	399,567	
September	128,788	164,076	244,778	339,961	401,478	
October	129,451	163,335	246,625	349,025	399,165	
November	131,325	164,073	247,942	350,000	396,516	
December	133,690	170,350	248,413	333,053	390,157	

These stocks at the beginning of 1925 represented about 158 days' supply, as compared with 162 days at the beginning of 1924, and 146 days at the beginning of 1923. But the recent* and prospective demand shows a considerable increase, and it seems likely that production in 1925 will be stationary, if not actually declining. There is still room, however, for a considerable

* For the first three months of 1925 American domestic consumption is estimated to have exceeded domestic production by 14 million barrels. Consumption of petrol in Great Britain is estimated to have been 29 per cent greater in 1924 than in 1923, as compared with a 15 per cent increase in 1922-3.

further reduction in stocks, and nothing approaching a shortage is imminent, whatever may be the case in the more distant future.

In addition to stocks of crude oil, there are also relatively smaller stocks (rather more than a month's supply) of the principal refined products. The half-yearly figures of these stocks in the United States have been as follows:

U.S.A. stocks of refined products (barrels)

End of month	Gasolene	Kerosene	Lub. oils	Fuel and gas oils
Dec. 1918	7,079,213	9,050,425	3,306,033	15,690,510
June 1919	14,140,396	6,012,915	4,175,828	19,328,348
Dec. 1919	10,637,939	8,079,040	3,269,498	17,002,963
June 1920	12,001,324	10,031,984	3,171,727	15,284,961
Dec. 1920	11,009,091	9,358,831	3,821,964	19,938,200
June 1921	17,872,487	10,358,493	6,211,503	29,730,097
Dec. 1921	13,954,456	8,119,251	5,161,084	31,696,796
June 1922	19,642,058	7,561,297	5,402,472	31,593,801
Dec. 1922	21,042,687	6,691,675	5,612,733	31,064,949
June 1923	30,085,000	6,293,000	5,360,000	31,524,000
Dec. 1923	25,590,000	6,742,000	5,780,000	36,072,000
June 1924	38,068,000	6,984,000	5,919,000	38,537,000
Dec. 1924	28,083,000	8,067,000	6,127,000	39,441,000
Mar. 1925	38,354,000	10,493,000	6,906,000	39,227,000

1,000 barrels

	Domestic consumption	Exports		Total
		General	Bunkers	
1919	349,565	62,853	14,031	426,449
1920	419,693	77,993	26,335	524,021
1921	418,963	70,723	27,027	516,713
1922	478,526	72,952	31,692	583,170
1923	589,631	100,436	37,643	727,710
1924	611,913	115,868	43,327	771,108

The relation of these stocks to current consumption of the various refined products (*not* consumption of crude oils by refineries) is shown by the table above.

XI. *Nitrate*

Nitrate statistics are comparatively simple, since they all come from one part of the world. Very reliable figures are regularly published by Messrs Aikman, and are quoted below [p. 399].

The figures for America include interior stocks, but not those held by the U.S.A. Government, which have gradually declined from round 300,000 tons in December 1921, to 60,000 tons at the present time.

In normal times there is a considerable reduction in the visible supply in the early part of the year, as the demand is somewhat seasonal.

The last column of the table opposite includes stocks in Japan and other countries, but excludes the following:

Stocks in the hands of the U.S.A. Government

31 Dec. 1921	300,000 tons	31 Dec. 1922	125,000 tons
28 Feb. 1922	210,000 ,,	31 Jan. 1923	85,000 ,,
30 April 1922	190–200,000 ,,	31 Jan. 1924	85,000 ,,
31 May 1922	175,000 ,,	31 Jan. 1925	60,000 ,,

Deliveries, year ending 30 June (1,000 tons)

	1914	1920	1921	1922	1923	1924
Europe and Egypt	1,984	861	706	895	1,030	1,104
U.S.A.	553	794	644	565	979	937*
Japan and others	92	227	84	84	150	151
	2,629	1,882	1,434	1,544	2,159	2,192

* Including 25,000 tons reserve stock consumed by American Naval Department.

Nitrate (1,000 tons)

End of month	Visible supply (including afloat)		Stocks in Chile	Total
	Europe and Egypt	U.S.A.		
1913 January	1,128	89	490	1,727
March	686	97	527	1,326
June	416	84	754	1,265
September	571	79	752	1,414
December	1,093	71	498	1,685
1919 July	140	28	1,594	1,780
September	152	49	1,705	1,925
December	430	95	1,576	2,134
1920 March	368	253	1,218	1,914
June	317	216	1,248	1,800
September	495	194	1,303	2,008
December	782	132	1,304	2,235
1921 March	868	218	1,283	2,384
June	836	249	1,317	2,405
September	828	41	1,453	2,370
December	903·5	260	1,441	2,622·5
1922 March	520	115	1,504	2,149
June	228·5	38	1,601	1,873·5
September	296	133	1,495	1,945
December	463·5	195	1,225	1,912·5
1923 March	379·5	238	889	1,310
June	173	54	997	1,250
July	234	114	960	1,357
August	316	135	913	1,400
September	365	96	927	1,415
October	405	71	966	1,469
November	463·5	103	981	1,561·5
December	573	200	852	1,639
1924 January	618	291	746	1,655
February	517·5	273	736	1,526·5
March	371	193	782	1,346
April	228	170	830	1,228
May	152·5	125	960	1,255·5
June	115	47	1,075	1,250
July	226	105	999	1,365
August	321	81	996	1,423
September	429	124	900	1,494
October	451	102	959	1,542
November	570	86	947	1,644
December	684	111	882	1,709
1925 January	711	121	855	1,718
February	586·5	247	768	1,601·5
March	379·5	233	756	1,368·5
April	245	233	754	1,232·5
May	179	93	875	1,147
June	227	122	869	1,218

Available supplies of wheat (1,000 qr of 480 lb)

	1 August–31 September				
	1920–1	1921–2	1922–3	1923–4	1924–5
Total available surplus in exporting countries	73–82,000	83,000	111,000	125,000	101,500
Shipments to importing countries	73,882	80,315	84,398	96,664	92,000
Apparent carryover in exporting countries at end of year	8,000	2,500	26,500	28,000	9,500
Total crops:—					
Exporting countries, Northern Hemisphere	194,300	218,980	236,440	244,890	216,640
Exporting countries, Southern Hemisphere	40,690	41,990	41,110	50,090	46,600
Importing countries	109,140	139,550	114,480	137,460	118,480
Total wheat crops	344,150	400,520	392,030	432,440	381,720
Supply for importing countries:—					
Crops	109,140	139,550	114,480	137,460	118,480
Imports	73,882	80,315	84,398	96,664	92,000
Total supply	183,002	219,865	198,878	234,124	210,480

XII. *Wheat*

Wheat is a baffling commodity to the compiler of comparative stock statistics, because it is a seasonal crop, coming from many different sources, and harvested at different times of year.

As in the case of other commodities, the statistics regularly available month by month are those of 'visible' supplies in 'second hands'; but, owing to the large amounts held on farms and elsewhere 'out of sight' and to the seasonal irregularity of supply, these figures are particularly unsatisfactory in the case of wheat.

For the purpose of a conspectus of the position as a whole, there is, perhaps, nothing better than the summary published weekly by Mr Broomhall in *The Corn Trade News*, of the supplies available in exporting countries during the cereal year and of the probable requirements of the importing countries during the same period. In the above table the figures for importers' requirements are based on the actual shipments, except in 1924–5, where Mr Broomhall's forecast is given, which takes account of actual shipments for the first three-quarters of the year.

These statistics may be supplemented by the quarterly figures of 'visible supply', i.e. the visible supply in elevators and public stores in the United States, Canada and Great Britain and the supply afloat for Europe:—

1,000 qr of 480 lb

	1919–0	1920–1	1921–2	1922–3	1923–4	1924–5
1 Aug.	18,370	17,950	16,800	15,091	17,340	20,270
1 Nov.	34,000	24,560	29,980	30,420	34,330	36,340
1 Feb.	28,120	23,750	26,520	35,660	39,350	37,900
1 May	23,870	19,660	23,730	28,500	34,750	29,900

Wheat supplies and their disposition in leading export countries, *1922–5* (million bushels)

	Approximations		Estimate
	1922–3	1923–4	1924–5
United States Year ending 30 June			
Stocks, 1 July	81·5	102·4	104
New crop	867·6	797·4	873
Supplies	949·1	899·8	977
Exports of wheat	154·9	78·8	—
Exports of flour	67·0	77·6	—
Imports (less re-exports), wheat and flour	19·7	27·9	—
Net exports, wheat and flour	202·2	128·5	260
Shipments to Possessions	2·8	2·9	3
Total for Abroad	205·0	131·4	263
Seed requirements	91·4	79·4	87
Domestic milling	}550·3{	496·1	505
Feed and waste		89·2	50
Total domestic use	641·7	664·7	642
Stocks, 30 June	102·4	103·7	72
Canada Year ending 31 August			
Stocks, 1 September	16·0	8·9	26
New crop	399·8	474·2	280*
Supplies	415·8	483·1	306
Exports, wheat and flour	279·1	342·8	184
Seed requirements	39·8	38·0	40
Milled for consumption	40·9	42·2	42
Feed and waste	47·1	33·6	25
Total domestic use	127·8	113·8	107
Stocks, 31 August	8·9	26·5	15
Argentina Year ending 31 July			
Stocks, 1 August	66·6	54·2	60
New crop	195·8	247·0	191
Supplies	262·4	301·2	251
Exports, wheat and flour	142·6	173·0	135
Seed requirements	18·7	20·6	21
Consumption, feed and waste	46·9	48·0	47
Total domestic use	65·6	68·6	68
Stocks, 31 July	54·2	59·6	48
Australia Year ending 31 July			
Stocks, 1 August	29·8	45·4	41
New crop	109·3	125·5	149
Supplies	139·1	170·9	190
Exports, wheat and flour	49·8	85·6	115
Seed requirements	8·9	9·4	10
Consumption	30·4	31·2	32
Feed and waste	4·6	3·5	4
Total domestic use	43·9	44·1	46
Stocks, 31 July	45·4	41·2	29

* Allowing for underestimate of Canadian crop.

The current available statistics relating to supplies and stocks of wheat are well summarised in the *Wheat Studies* (Vol. I, No. 5, April 1925), of the Food Research Institute of Stanford University, California, to which anyone who is interested in further details may be referred. The table above relating to wheat supplies in the leading countries of export, 1922–5, have been taken from this source.

From The London and Cambridge Economic Service, Special Memorandum No. 16 (February 1926)

STOCKS OF STAPLE COMMODITIES

The statistics given below are in continuation of Memoranda published in April 1923, June 1924, and July 1925.

The table below [pp. 404–5] is a summary of the figures given in detail afterwards for each separate commodity.

THE U.S. DEPARTMENT OF COMMERCE INDEX OF COMMODITY STOCKS

The advance recorded by this index during last winter has given way to a decline, and in July the total index was roughly the same as in July 1924, though this is the result of a balance between an increase in raw materials and manufactures, and a decline in foodstuffs, particularly manufactured foodstuffs. During August and September, however, there has been a sharp advance, but in view of the drop in October it is too early as yet to determine whether this means anything more than a temporary advance, such as took place last winter, though at a later date. The increase in stocks of raw materials is, nevertheless, very noticeable. [See pp. 406–7.]

Stocks of staple commodities

Beginning of month	Cotton 1,000 bales (1)	Copper 1,000 tons (2)	Tin 1,000 tons (3)	Lead 1,000 tons (4) U.K.	Lead U.S.	Spelter 1,000 tons (5)	Rubber 1,000 tons (6)	Sugar 1,000 tons (7)	Tea 1,000,000 lb (8)	Coffee 1,000 bags (9)	Crude oil 1,000,000 barrels (10)	Nitrate 1,000 tons (11)	Wheat 1,000 quarters (12)
1920 January	7,410	—	20	50·0	—	61	—	—	213	9,870	128	2,134	—
April	7,353	—	18	28·4	—	53	—	2,433	213	8,174	125	1,914	—
July	6,793	—	19	25·2	—	51	—	2,003	213	6,750	127	1,800	—
October	—	—	18	18·7	—	61	—	1,338	215	7,982	129	2,008	—
1921 January	—	399^A	18	19·0	—	81	219–229	2,313	214	8,765	134	2,235	183
April	—	—	16	23·9	—	88	—	3,331	230	8,687	129	2,384	—
July	—	—	17	13·3	—	99	—	3,312	218	8,700	151	2,405	—
October	9,534	—	21	9·9	—	89	—	2,039	191	8,991	164	2,370	—
1922 January	8,470	411^A	24	0·3	—	72	224–244	2,761	205	9,403	170	2,622·5	220
April	7,654	346^A	21	0·6	—	60	—	2,479	220	9,140	203	2,149	—
July	6,785	357^A	22	0·3	—	31	—	1,903	170	8,639	232	1,873·5	—
October	4,514	325^A	21	0·6	—	20	—	868	151	8,481	245	1,945	—
1923 January	—	347	22	0·5	—	17	286–306	2,433	170	7,980	248	1,912·5	199
April	3,111	350	22	0·4	—	10	249	2,501	183	6,974	290	1,310	—

July	2,765	352	17	0·2	—	17	278	2,005	127	5,340	315	1,250	—
October	2,699	391	17	1·4	—	21	244	791	134	5,835	340	1,415	—
1924 January	2,010	402	19	1·2	93	34	254	2,255	166	4,467	333	1,639	234
April	1,716	361	19	0·0	92	29	226	2,460	193	3,964	373	1,346	—
July	1,747	371	19	0·0	97	45	208	2,086	139	5,071	387	1,250	—
October	2,673	385	19	0·1	88	42	196	542	137	5,727	401	1,494	—
1925 January	2,563	389	23	0·1	78	19	181	2,708	206	5,384	390	1,790	210
April	1,904	403	18	0·0	94	16	151	2,891	231	5,389	528ᴮ	1,368·5	—
July	1,715	365	19	0·1	86	21	129	2,560	181	5,085	546ᴮ	1,218	—
October	—	347	17	0·0	—	11	141	1,211	181	5,230	545ᴮ	1,409	—
1926 January	2,681*	344	17	0·0	—	9	182	3,716*	204	5,164	538ᴮ	1,675·5	—

* Provisional. (1) Total supply, seasonally corrected, exclusive of European and Asiatic mill stocks. (2) Total supply outside hands of consumers. (3) Visible supply. (4) Visible supply in U.K., and stocks in U.S. (5) Visible supply in U.K. and U.S. (6) Total supply outside plantations. (7) Total visible supply. (8) Visible supply in Rio, Santos, Bahia, Europe and U.S. (9) Stocks in bond in U.K. (10) Visible supply in Chile, U.S., Europe and Egypt. (12) Supply available for importing countries. (11) Visible supply in U.S.

ᴬ (Copper). On 1 January 1921, Allied Government stocks amounted approximately to 82,000 tons, and stocks of scrap metal to 183,000; on 1 January 1922, the former had become trifling, and the latter had fallen to about 90,000 tons, and had become trifling by 1 January 1923. A decreasing allowance must be added to the figures shown on account of these stocks.

ᴮ (Crude oil). These figures now include heavy crude oil, below 20° Beaumé, including all grades of fuel oil, held on the Pacific Coast. They are not, therefore, comparable with the earlier figures.

Course of commodity stocks in the United States, by major groups (seasonal variations eliminated)

TOTAL INDEX

Year	Monthly average	Jan.	Feb.	March	April	May	June	July	Aug.	Sept.	Oct.	Nov.	Dec.
1919	100	103	103	100	104	102	97	97	96	101	100	100	97
1920	98	99	96	91	93	93	93	95	95	96	107	106	109
1921	138	124	134	141	136	139	145	145	148	138	137	132	131
1922	126	131	131	131	127	133	130	128	119	126	116	119	117
1923	118	121	116	117	117	111	115	114	125	118	118	122	125
1924	136	136	135	136	136	141	134	130	134	135	137	136	145
1925	—	155	152	149	141	143	140	133	142	149	133	—	—

RAW FOODSTUFFS

Year	Monthly average	Jan.	Feb.	March	April	May	June	July	Aug.	Sept.	Oct.	Nov.	Dec.
1919	100	125	120	99	101	89	86	91	101	108	94	99	87
1920	97	101	91	73	82	85	86	98	94	103	135	114	104
1921	174	121	147	164	147	154	171	171	198	184	212	205	209
1922	192	191	195	206	203	233	220	214	174	190	150	163	163
1923	142	165	157	161	169	143	146	134	133	119	113	122	141
1924	163	164	173	169	164	178	157	151	160	148	154	153	190
1925	—	192	187	192	176	195	187	149	158	160	113	—	—

RAW MATERIALS FOR MANUFACTURE

Year	Monthly average	Jan.	Feb.	March	April	May	June	July	Aug.	Sept.	Oct.	Nov.	Dec.
1919	100	106	105	107	111	110	100	100	85	85	95	98	98
1920	104	96	97	94	89	95	98	99	103	102	109	123	139

Year													
1921	158	154	166	171	176	178	184	189	176	151	124	118	110
1922	108	110	107	105	105	100	100	96	102	121	120	116	111
1923	108	111	102	101	96	93	95	94	111	118	130	123	119
1924	116	125	118	110	109	105	98	95	100	118	129	141	142
1925	—	149	139	130	120	100	98	104	124	161	151	—	—

MANUFACTURED FOODSTUFFS

Year													
1919	100	98	93	90	94	100	88	88	93	107	114	114	121
1920	95	113	114	115	113	99	95	87	85	82	78	79	78
1921	79	78	80	82	80	81	81	83	78	76	78	74	71
1922	72	66	68	63	58	66	75	80	80	77	75	76	75
1923	80	70	71	76	76	79	88	87	85	83	80	82	81
1924	84	74	74	79	86	86	87	89	87	90	87	84	88
1925	—	87	86	80	75	73	76	83	78	79	77	—	—

MANUFACTURED COMMODITIES

Year													
1919	100	88	95	103	110	110	109	107	100	100	98	92	89
1920	97	90	88	86	91	96	96	97	97	95	104	110	116
1921	136	141	142	144	143	144	145	141	140	133	124	120	120
1922	118	138	135	130	123	115	110	108	108	111	112	112	111
1923	129	124	121	117	113	117	121	128	136	140	141	147	146
1924	161	161	154	161	163	169	169	161	165	165	161	155	148
1925	—	175	174	171	171	171	168	171	183	181	176	—	—

Supplies other than European and Asiatic mill stocks (1,000 bales)*

End of month	Up-country	U.S. warehouse stocks†	U.S. mill stocks†	Total in U.S.A.	Correction for season	Corrected total in U.S.A.	Visible outside U.S.A.	Grand total, excluding mill stocks outside U.S.A.‡
1919 July	2,193	2,212	1,304	5,709	—	5,709	347	6,056
October	11,973	1,974	1,365	15,312	9,000	6,312	1,077	7,389
1920 January	3,780	3,760	3,677	11,217	6,000	5,217	2,082	7,299
April	3,252	2,967	1,809	8,028	3,000	5,028	2,034	7,062
July	1,703§	2,055	1,358	5,116	—	5,116	1,352	6,468
October	11,414	4,168	944	16,526	10,311	6,215	—	—
1921 January	6,788	5,645	1,273	13,706	6,874	6,832	—	—
April	4,961	5,029	1,316	11,306	3,437	7,869	—	—
July	3,713§	3,723	1,111	8,007	—	8,007	1,645	9,652
October	7,577	4,982	1,405	13,964	6,330	7,634	1,598	9,232
1922 January	4,550	4,618	1,675	10,843	4,220	6,623	1,581	8,204
April	3,484	3,214	1,458	8,156	2,110	6,046	1,436	7,482
July	964§	1,488	1,218	3,670	—	3,670	1,120	4,790
October	—	—	—	—	7,302	—	1,023	—
1923 January	1,569	3,486	1,988	7,043	4,868	2,175	1,295	3,471
April	667	1,966	1,878	4,511	2,434	2,077	804	2,881
July	280§	945	1,099	2,324	—	2,324	376	2,700
August	9,736	1,179	807	11,722	9,284	2,438	230	2,668
September	7,639	2,148	773	10,560	8,440	2,120	579	2,699
October	4,667	3,486	1,103	9,256	7,596	1,660	962	2,622
November	2,767	3,770	1,439	7,976	6,752	1,224	1,005	2,229
December	1,568	3,526	1,623	6,717	5,908	809	1,201	2,010

1924								
January	1,049	2,966	1,633	5,648	5,064	584	1,268	1,852
February	658	2,485	1,578	4,721	4,220	501	1,207	1,708
March	490	1,983	1,498	3,181	3,376	595	1,121	1,716
April	341	1,512	1,328	2,498	2,532	649	966	1,615
May	213	1,127	1,158	1,943	1,688	810	765	1,575
June	110	882	951	1,555	844	1,099	648	1,747
July	160§	674	721		—	1,555	528	2,083
August	13,217	811	553	14,581	12,518	2,063	373	2,436
September	10,833	2,073	514	13,420	11,380	2,040	633	2,673
October	7,008	4,225	731	10,242	10,242	1,722	1,021	2,743
November	4,226	4,914	1,047	10,187	9,104	1,083	1,444	2,527
December	2,666	4,624	1,319	8,609	7,966	643	1,920	2,563
1925								
January	1,780	3,863	1,434	7,077	6,828	249	1,956	2,205
February	1,174	3,075	1,546	5,795	5,690	105	1,958	2,063
March	656	2,237	1,645	4,538	4,552	−14	1,918	1,904
April	341	1,666	1,515	3,522	3,414	108	1,731	1,839
May	28	1,135	1,348	2,511	2,276	235	1,376	1,611
June	67	760	1,124	1,817	1,138	679	1,036	1,715
July	230§	487	878	1,504	—	1,504	764	2,268
August	14,634	1,040	680	16,354	14,303	2,051	556	2,607
September	—	—	—	—	13,003	—	1,044	—
October	7,467	4,499	1,216	13,191	11,703	1,488	1,280	2,768
November	4,817	5,206	1,456	11,479	10,403	1,076	1,660	2,736
December	2,602‖	5,608	1,718	9,928‖	9,103	825‖	1,856	2,681‖

* This table excludes linters, except that an insignificant quantity is included in the import figures.

† Figures for all kinds of cotton.

‡ Seasonally corrected and excluding European and Asiatic mill stocks.

§ The carry-over according to the above method was as follows: 1920, 2,171; 1921, 3,779; 1922, 2,615; 1923, 356; 1924, 6; 1925, 49.

‖ Provisional.

I. *American cotton*

At any given time stocks consist of the following:—

(1) Stocks up-country in the Southern States on plantations, railroads, and in 'uncounted'* interior towns.

(2) The 'visible' supply. This consists of (*a*) stocks in public storage and at compresses (warehouse stocks) in the more important interior towns and in the ports of the United States, (*b*) cotton afloat for Great Britain and the Continent, (*c*) warehouse stocks in the principal European ports, namely, Liverpool, Manchester, London, Havre, Marseilles, Genoa, Bremen, Ghent, Rotterdam and Barcelona.†

(3) Mill stocks in spinners' hands throughout the world, generally known as the 'invisible' or 'out of sight' supply.

In the first table the 'up-country' stock is taken as the 'up-country' carryover in the Southern States plus warehouse and mill stocks in the U.S. at the end of each season, plus the current year's crop, minus the U.S. consumption to any particular date, minus the net exports to that date (i.e. exports minus imports), minus warehouse and mill stocks at that date. By this means it is possible to estimate the location of all cotton in the U.S. month by month. But it follows that the whole of the new crop is suddenly added to the 'up-country' stock in August each year. This is corrected in the above table by the 'seasonal correction', which provides what would be the figure of total stock in the U.S. if the current crop came into existence at an even monthly rate through the year. The statistics of U.S. warehouse stocks and mill stocks are compiled by the U.S. Bureau of the Census, and may be regarded as reliable, as also may the 'visible' supply of Great Britain and the Continent.‡ The estimates of the current crop are reasonably accurate by the end of each calendar year. The 'up-country' carryover is the most

---

* I.e. towns not included in the figures of stocks in public storage and at compresses.
† Cotton afloat for Japan and in Japanese ports is not allowed for. All cotton consigned to Japan is considered by the leading exchanges as 'consumed' or 'out of sight'.
‡ As given by the Liverpool Cotton Exchange.

doubtful item, and is always liable to be under-, rather than over-estimated. The estimates of Mr H. G. Hester, the Secretary of the New Orleans Cotton Exchange, have been used until 1922, since when the estimates of the Shepperson Publishing Company (*Cotton Facts*) have been preferred. The monthly calculated figures for 'up-country' provide at best an estimate of the actual state of affairs, but in most years they tally reasonably well with the 'up-country carryover' estimates (see Note § below table).

At the beginning and in the middle of each season, statistics of European and Asiatic mill stocks, and of the world's actual consumption during the previous six months are available, and the position of the world's total stocks is shown in the two following tables.

As was anticipated in Special Memorandum No. 12, the world's consumption of cotton increased somewhat in the second half of the season 1924–5, and for the whole season amounted to 13,256,000 bales. This, however, left the fairly comfortable

Annual table of total stocks at the end of each season (1 August)
(1,000 bales)

	1919	1920	1921	1922	1923	1924	1925
Up-country carryover in interior cotton belt	2,193	1,703	3,713	964	280	160	230
U.S. warehouse stocks	2,212	2,055	3,723	1,488	945	674	487
U.S. mill stocks	1,304	1,358	1,111	1,218	1,099	721	787
Total in U.S.	5,709	5,116	8,547	3,670	2,324	1,555	1,504
European port stocks (including afloat for Europe)	1,247	1,394	1,695	1,120	376	528	764
European mill stocks	305	475	690	838	496	502	787
Asiatic mill stocks	?	267*	248	381	185	173	219
Total	7,261	7,252	11,180	6,009	3,381	2,758	3,274
Crop for year†	12,000	13,750	8,442	9,738	10,128	13,639	15,603
Total available	19,261	21,002	19,622	15,747	13,509	16,397	18,877
Total carried forward	6,990	10,386	7,066	3,081	2,554	3,141	—
Consumption for year	12,271	10,616	12,556	12,666	10,955	13,256	—

* Excluding China.

† For 1919–21 Hester's estimate of the actual growth, made at the beginning of the season, as the official figures for these years are questionable.

Annual table of total stocks in the middle of each season
(1 February) (1,000 bales)

	1920	1921	1922	1923	1924	1925
Up-country stocks	3,780	6,788	4,550	1,569	1,049	1,780
U.S. warehouse stocks	3,760	5,645	4,618	3,486	2,966	3,863
U.S. mill stocks	3,677	1,273	1,675	1,988	1,633	1,434
Total in U.S.	11,217	13,706	10,843	7,043	5,648	7,077
European port stocks (including afloat)	2,018	1,650	1,575	1,296	1,268	1,956
European mill stocks	597	675	740	637	578	755
Asiatic mill stocks	117*	166*	390	206	203	201
Total available	13,949	16,197	13,548	9,182	7,697	9,989
Total available 1 August preceding	19,261	21,005	19,622	15,747	13,509	16,397
Consumption for half-year	5,312	4,808	6.074	6,565	5,812	6,408

* Excluding China.

carryover of rather more than 3 million bales, for in view of the fact that, when prices are high, an unexpectedly large amount of cotton comes forward, we must assume that there is always some cotton in the interior of the U.S. which is not accounted for in the estimates of the up-country carryover. There was also a notable increase in European stocks.

The available supply of cotton for the current season amounts to not far short of 19 million bales, and therefore, allowing for the same carryover as last year, consumption can be increased to nearly 16 million bales. It becomes, however, increasingly clear as the season proceeds, that the current crop includes an unusually large proportion of low-grade cotton untenderable against the future contract. The stock of high-grade cotton may scarcely exceed the year's requirements of the mills. Moreover, a large carry-forward would be advisable in view of the present being a bumper crop and of the probability that if the existing low prices continue, the expenditure on labour and fertilisers will be curtailed, even if the acreage is maintained. Consumption in the U.S.A. already shows a substantial increase—2,594,000 bales from Aug. 1st, 1925, to Jan. 1st, 1926, as compared with

2,350,000 bales in the corresponding period last season. In this country demand for finished goods has not yet responded, but forwardings to the mills have been on a heavier scale. Prices have, of course, fallen sharply, and it is probably the uncertainty as to whether the bottom has yet been reached, which is restraining Lancashire manufacturing activity.

There are no statistics relating to finished cotton goods except for the United States. While not by any means complete, these statistics afford an interesting comparable series, as will be seen from the following table:—

Finished cotton goods in U.S.

| | 1,000 yards | | Cases | |
	Production	Orders grey yardage	Shipments	Stocks
1921 monthly average	85,385	90,154	44,935	36,226
1922 „ „	94,016	95,509	49,102	44,937
1923 „ „	95,098	91,504	48,116	46,166
1924 „ „	77,650	76,105	41,863	43,139
1925 January	81,174	84,459	49,319	36,925
February	81,650	83,293	47,961	36,101
March	94,039	86,776	48,879	36,121
April	88,986	76,505	45,776	39,296
May	75,463	63,128	40,573	40,460
June	70,593	65,103	40,133	41,461
July	69,281	69,364	39,153	40,710
August	63,994	69,176	37,903	41,151
September	72,257	81,079	42,608	40,711
October	85,859	85,907	47,556	39,917

II. *Copper*

Stocks of copper consist of (1) refined copper in the United States, which constitutes the main part of the world's floating supply, (2) rough and blister copper in transit to smelters and

Supplies and consumption of copper (tons of 2,240 lb)

	1 January 1920	1 January 1921	1 January 1922	1 January 1923	1 January 1924	1 January 1925	1 January 1926†
North and South America:—							
Refined	313,000	286,000	239,000	133,000	139,000	122,000	65,000
In process, etc.	175,000	58,000	142,000	175,000	226,000	212,000	215,000
Allied Govt. stocks	180,000	82,000	trifling	—	—	—	—
Scrap (approximate)	270,000	183,000	90,000	—	—	—	—
U.K., Havre, Japan stocks	46,000	55,000	30,000	39,000	37,000	55,000	64,000
Total	984,000	664,000	501,000	347,000	402,000	389,000	344,000
Production*	967,000	537,000	888,000	1,266,000	1,357,000	1,418,000	—
Available supply	1,951,000	1,201,000	1,389,000	1,613,000	1,759,000	1,807,000	—
Stock carried forward	664,000	501,000	347,000	402,000	389,000	344,000	—
Consumption	1,287,000	700,000	1,042,000	1,211,000	1,370,000	1,463,000	—
Price £	115 7 6	71 17 6	66 3 9	64 11 3	60 18 9	66 11 3	59 13 9
Cents	19	12¼	13¼	14¼	12¾	14¼	14

* American Bureau of Metal Statistics.
† Provisional figures.

refiners in North and South America, and on hand or in process at refineries, (3) refined and rough copper in European and Japanese warehouses. In the years immediately after the War there were also large stocks in the hands of the Allied Governments and in the form of scrap metal.

The estimates shown above for the past seven years have been revised by substituting the figures of the American Bureau of Metal Statistics, which have not been published until recently, in place of those of the U.S. Geological Survey.

The re-starting in 1925 of the regular publication of the figures of the American Bureau, which, in spite of being

Stocks of copper (tons of 2,240 lb)

Beginning of month	American refined*	American blister* (and in process)	U.K. all kinds	Havre	Japan	Total
1921 Jan.	286,000	58,000	11,646	5,968	37,500	399,000
1922 Jan.	239,000	142,000	16,655	4,138	9,300	411,000
1923 Jan.	133,000	175,000	26,780	3,345	9,072	347,000
Oct.	113,000	240,000	28,453	3,891	5,954	391,000
1924 Jan.	139,000	226,000	31,030	1,867	4,405	402,000
April	107,000	212,500	30,852	5,281	5,300	361,000
July	100,000	216,000	36,515	10,225	8,600	371,000
Oct.	122,000	209,000	37,387	7,885	9,000	385,000
1925 Jan.	122,000	212,000	38,419	7,180	9,992	389,000
April	109,200	233,000	44,276	8,341	7,743	403,000
July	81,500	223,500	47,984	6,389	5,832	365,000
Aug.	78,500	216,500	48,547	9,194	5,543	358,000
Sept.	69,000	214,000	49,900	10,316	5,406	349,000
Oct.	61,500	220,000	51,285	9,942	5,000‡	347,000
Nov.	65,000	218,000	53,352	7,376	5,000‡	349,000
Dec.	60,500	221,100	55,064	5,330	5,000‡	347,000
1926 Jan.	65,200	214,600	56,047†	3,013	5,000‡	344,000

* Includes North and South America.
† Of which 50,474 tons were rough copper and 5,573 tons refined.
‡ Provisional figures.

compiled, had been kept confidential hitherto and were the source of various partly inaccurate rumours, has put the compilation of Copper Statistics on a much more satisfactory basis. Certain figures have now been published retrospectively. The published figures were on a quarterly basis for the first half of 1925 and have been on a monthly basis beginning with July, 1925. In these returns 'American blister' includes all copper in first hands in North and South America which has not been refined and made available for delivery.

The table above supplies some more detailed statistics of the principal stocks.

In the quarterly and monthly reports the statistics for North and South America are not separated. In the Annual Report, however, stocks of blister copper in North and South America respectively are given separately, from which it appears that South America is responsible for from 10 to 20 per cent of the total.

The reduction in stocks of refined copper during 1925 has taken place in spite of new production on a record scale. For the first eleven months of 1925 the world's production of copper was estimated to be at the rate of 1,550,000 tons per annum. It is evident that copper can be produced in abundant quantity at a gold price about the same as before the War, which means a heavy fall in relation to commodities generally.

III. *Tin*

Stocks of tin mainly consist of:—

(1) The 'visible supply', as defined by the returns of Messrs Ricard and Freiwald, and of Messrs Strauss, namely, warehouse stocks in Holland, U.K. and U.S., and tin afloat from the Federated Malay States, Netherlands Indies and Australia.

(2) Stocks in the Federated Malay States and Netherlands Indies.

(3) Stocks of ore in Bolivia and Nigeria, and afloat from these countries to U.K., and in course of smelting in U.K.

(4) Stocks in China and afloat from China to U.S. and U.K.

Only in the case of (1), namely, the so-called 'visible supply', are detailed monthly figures regularly available. The returns of the two firms mentioned do not differ materially, if allowance is made for the slightly different bases on which they are compiled. The following table is based on the figures supplied by Messrs Strauss:—

*Visible stocks of tin** (tons of 2,240 lb)

End of month	1913	1921	1922	1923	1924	1925	1926
Jan.	14,875	18,104	25,346	22,598	21,173	21,155	15,602
Feb.	13,348	16,900	24,434	22,183	18,428	21,809	—
March	12,117	15,764	21,040	21,703	19,247	18,320	—
April	10,814	15,131	21,244	19,058	16,227	16,770	—
May	14,663	17,767	22,235	18,263	17,030	19,567	—
June	12,903	16,953	22,558	17,543	19,143	19,535	—
July	13,713	19,852	20,364	17,976	19,223	19,877	—
Aug.	12,841	19,037	21,753	16,170	20,321	19,539	—
Sept.	14,673	20,777	20,448	17,389	19,124	17,419	—
Oct.	13,049	22,891	19,975	18,479	17,769	15,402	—
Nov.	16,112	22,247	22,131	16,939	19,684	17,141	—
Dec.	15,543	24,273	22,155	18,596	23,374	16,709	—

* Figures of A. Strauss & Co.

These figures are apt, however, to be extremely misleading, even as a general indication of tendency, owing to their somewhat arbitrary character. The most important disturbing factor is to be found in the variation in the amount of refined and unrefined tin in the Straits itself. Considerable stocks of tin are held from time to time in the Straits Settlements which only become 'visible' when they are put on board ship for export. This impairs the value of the 'visible supply' figures from month to month, as well as over longer periods, since the comparisons between one month and the next may be sensibly affected by the accidents of sailings. But there may also be important variations in the amount of Chinese tin in China and afloat and in the amount of Bolivian tin awaiting shipment, afloat and in smelters' stocks in England.

Whilst no figures are available for the absolute amounts of these disturbing items, it is possible, nevertheless, to estimate *changes* in their amounts. The following is an attempt to get somewhat nearer to the net position than has been possible in earlier memoranda:

(1) *Stocks* (*refined and unrefined*) *in the Straits.*—As described in earlier memoranda, these stocks were abnormally swelled from 1920 onwards by tin held under the Bandoeng Agreement. The last lots of this tin were *sold* before the end of 1924, but the trade figures show that they were not *shipped*, and therefore did not enter into the 'visible supply' until some months later. Thus the figures which we gave in the last Memorandum on Stocks (and also the figures recently published by Messrs Strauss), under-estimated the total available stocks of tin, since they made no allowance under any heading for pool tin sold but not shipped. But apart from this there are from time to time quite considerable stocks held in the Straits, which are not included in any statistics. Since, however, the amount of the imports into the Straits from the Malay States and elsewhere are published regularly, and also the amount of the exports, it is possible to make some estimate as to the changes in the total stocks thus held.

Since the pool stocks held in the Straits at the beginning of

Tons

	Imports of tin into the Straits	Exports of tin from the Straits	Reduction of Straits stocks
1923	65,335	69,119	3,784
1924	74,109	79,940	5,831
1925	76,000*	78,819	2,819*

* Provisional.

418

1923 amounted to 13,600 tons (apart from 4,000 tons held in the Dutch Indies), these figures indicate that there were probably some surplus stocks, say 1,200 tons, still held in the Straits at the commencement of 1926, in addition to the normal quantities in transit and being refined. It follows, similarly, that at the beginning of 1924 there must have been some 4,000 tons of tin in the Straits which did not figure in any statistics.

(2) *Bolivian tin in transit and at the refineries.*—If we allow two months from the date of shipment from Bolivia to the time of delivery in refined form on the London market, some 5,000 tons of tin are normally thus in transit, but the actual figure may vary from (say) 4,000 tons to 8,000 tons. The irregularity of the shipments is illustrated by the fact that the shipments from Bolivia to England in 1923 and 1924 exceeded the arrivals by 4,200 tons, whilst in 1925 arrivals exceeded shipments by 4,400 tons, so that the quantity afloat on Jan. 1st, 1926, was 4,400 tons less than on Jan. 1st, 1925. On the other hand, smelters' stocks may have been appreciably heavier at the end of 1925.

(3) *Chinese tin.*—The production in Yunnan is at the rate of about 8,000 tons a year. A United States Consular report estimates the exports from this district during the first half of 1925 at about 4,600 tons as compared with about 3,100 during the first half of 1924. The shipments to Europe and the U.S. amounted to about 7,400 tons in 1925, which was about 100 tons less than in 1924. The arrivals in 1925, however, exceeded those in 1924 by about 600 tons.

The gradual exhaustion of the aggregate stocks is shown in the table below.

The warehouse stocks, exclusive of tin afloat, landing, or with smelters, were as below.

The quantity afloat at the end of 1925 was a good deal less than at the end of the previous year, and could not be much reduced; thus the true surplus stocks at the beginning of 1926 represented less than three weeks' requirements.

Turning to the demand side we find that the large reduction

of stocks during 1925 occurred in spite of some increase in production. The principal changes in the volume of production during the year were as follows:—

	Tons
Federated Malay States	+2,000
Bolivia	+ 850
Cornwall	+ 400
Total increase in production	3,250

The supply during the year from other sources was not much changed. Allowing for the reduction of stocks, of Bolivian ore afloat and of Chinese tin afloat, but for some increase of smelters' stocks, it seems that consumption may have increased during the year by as much as 16,000 tons. This is mainly accounted for

	1923	1924	1925
'Visible Supply'	−3,559	+4,778	−6,665
Stocks in Straits	−3,784	−5,831	−2,819*
Dutch Goverment pool stocks	−2,000	−2,000	—
Chinese tin in China and afloat	−1,700	+ 150	− 600
Bolivian ore afloat	+1,300	+2,900	−4,400
Total	−9,743	—	−14,484

* Provisional.

Warehouse stocks on 1 January (tons)

	1924	1925	1926
Straits	9,800	4,000	1,200
Dutch Indies	2,000	—	—
England	3,892	5,241	2,387
Holland	1,899	598	48
U.S.	732	669	439
Total	18,323	10,508	4,074

by consumption in the United States, which, at 76,455 tons, increased by 12,330 tons as compared with 1924, but only by 6,300 tons as compared with 1923. British consumption, at about 24,000 tons, was about 1,000 tons higher than in 1924. Thus consumption elsewhere appears to have increased by something more than 2,000 tons.

It does not seem probable that production this year can be greatly increased over the 1925 level. As regards the East, new properties will come into bearing capable of producing 2,000 tons or so per annum, but, on the other hand, some of the older properties will produce less. Some 1,500 tons net addition from the East, not more than 1,000 tons extra from Nigeria, and 1,500 tons from Bolivia—say 4,500 tons more production from the world as a whole seems to be about the maximum of reasonable expectation, and 3,000–4,000 tons a safer estimate.

We estimate recent production and consumption in the aggregate as follows:—

Tons

Year	Production	Consumption
1923	124,000	133,500
1924	134,500	134,500
1925	138,000	151,000
1926 (forecast)	141,500	—

It hardly seems possible that enough tin can be found in 1926 to satisfy a consumption on as high a scale as in 1925. On the other hand, there will probably be more than enough tin to satisfy a consumption on the scale of previous years. If consumption in 1926 shows signs of maintaining the 1925 level, the price may rise sensationally; but if it falls off to the level of 1924, the price may fall sensationally. Tin is a commodity of which both the consumption and the production are very inelastic in response to changes in the price of the metal, but of which the consumption is very sensitive to general trade influences—which explains its violent oscillations of price.

IV. *Lead*

Stocks in the United Kingdom are still negligible. Nevertheless there were probably a few thousand tons of lead in outside warehouses at the end of 1925, which do not appear in the statistics. Those in the United States and Mexico have remained steady at the moderate figure of round about 80,000 to 90,000 tons. The latter figures, however, are not for refined lead, but include lead in ore, base bullion, in transit and in process, as well as refined lead, which is only a small proportion of the total. Thus there have been in recent years virtually no surplus stocks of refined lead.

Stocks of lead in U.S., U.K., and Mexico (tons of 2,240 lb)

Beginning of month	1924			1925		
	U.S. and Mexico*	U.K.†	Total	U.S. and Mexico*	U.K.†	Total
January	93,005	1,183	94,188	77,854	58	77,912
February	89,759	296	90,055	90,112	130	90,242
March	90,376	57	90,434	94,475	136	94,611
April	92,292	27	92,319	93,557	14	93,571
May	98,585	20	98,605	90,146	34	90,180
June	98,145	7	98,152	87,020	74	87,094
July	97,107	6	97,113	86,319	141	86,460
August	94,161	3	94,164	81,776	102	81,878
September	92,372	19	92,391	86,580	5	86,585
October	87,747	65	87,812	—	5	—
November	87,028	1	87,029	—	95	—
December	87,822	3	87,825	—	5	—

* Stocks of ore, matte, base bullion and refined lead in the hands of those concerns which report to the American Bureau of Metal Statistics.
† Metal Exchange figures.

The following figures issued by the American Bureau of Metal Statistics apply to the principal lead-producing countries of the world, which, in 1924, furnished 79 per cent of the world's total lead output.

Production of lead (tons of 2,240 lb)

	1923	1924	1925*
United States	404,748	471,005	500,000
Mexico	164,502	158,796	180,000
Canada	48,124	75,298	109,000
Spain and Tunis	65,004	104,534	112,000
Italy	16,804	21,712	12,000
Australia	122,779	125,557	142,000
Burma	45,749	51,758	46,000
Rhodesia	10,859	6,253	3,000
Transvaal	4,816	4,477	2,000
Total	883,385	1,019,390	1,106,000

* At rate for first three quarters.

In the first four months of 1925 these same countries produced 365,800 tons, i.e. at the rate of 1,100,000 tons per annum. Thus the high prices recently prevailing have called forth increased production, sufficient to satisfy the high level of consumption. From the long-period point of view, the prospects of continued increasing production are not so favourable. The production of the seven countries, United States, Mexico, Canada, Spain, Australia, Burma, and Rhodesia (about 77 per cent of the world's output) has been approximately as follows in recent years:—

Production in principal areas

Year	Tons	Year	Tons
1920	629,464	1923	861,607
1921	615,178	1924	992,857
1922	762,500	1925*	1,092,000

* At rate for first three quarters.

V. *Spelter (Zinc)*

Monthly statistics are available of stocks in public warehouses in the United States and in the United Kingdom as given below.

423

U.K. and U.S. stocks of spelter (tons of 2,240 lb)

End of month	1921			1922			1923			1924			1925		
	U.S.	U.K.	Total	U.S.	U.K.	Total	U.S.	U.K.	Total	U.S.	U.K.	Total	U.S.	U.K.	Total
January	67,810	14,862	82,672	58,635	11,412	70,047	14,794	394	15,188	36,330	1,088	37,418	16,960	398	17,358
February	69,660	13,606	83,266	57,250	8,335	65,585	9,700	197	9,897	33,200	975	34,175	14,910	331	15,241
March	73,440	14,427	87,867	53,800	6,375	60,175	8,947	838	9,785	28,600	858	29,458	15,350	315	15,665
April	72,720	17,730	90,450	46,186	6,067	52,253	8,014	1,238	9,252	29,270	673	29,943	16,370	227	16,597
May	76,615	19,000	86,615	36,080	5,338	41,418	11,624	1,702	13,326	37,820	628	38,448	18,940	389	19,329
June	80,260	18,752	99,012	26,407	4,662	31,069	15,333	1,679	17,012	44,360	671	45,031	20,460	506	20,966
July	82,510	18,153	100,663	25,552	4,289	29,841	18,896	1,198	20,094	47,060	352	47,412	18,550	714	19,264
August	77,275	17,387	94,662	19,311	3,977	23,288	23,635	1,007	24,642	45,470	442	45,912	15,200	656	15,856
September	72,440	16,405	88,845	16,791	3,668	20,459	20,440	803	21,243	40,820	814	41,634	10,530	561	11,091
October	63,335	15,424	78,659	16,110	2,670	18,780	23,024	1,034	24,058	34,330	675	35,005	6,670	333	7,003
November	59,865	14,052	73,917	17,408	852	18,260	27,600	1,390	28,990	24,030	541	24,571	6,170	621	6,791
December	59,470	12,765	72,235	16,296	631	16,927	32,660	1,190	33,850	18,930	396	19,326	8,300	269	8,569

While these stocks in 1924 showed a distinct increase on the previous year, they have fallen during 1925 to the lowest figures recorded in recent years, representing not more than a few days' consumption.

This fall in stocks has been in spite of a very material increase in production in 1925, amounting to about 13 per cent in the principal producing countries as compared with 1924. According to Rudolf Wolff & Company the world's output of virgin spelter was 451,800 tons in 1921, 688,520 in 1922, 960,168 in 1923, 989,547 in 1924, and 1,123,592 in 1925.

According to figures issued by the American Bureau of Metal Statistics the production of spelter by countries, which in 1924 furnished about 87 per cent of the world's output, has been as follows:—

Production of spelter (tons of 2,240 lb)

	1923	1924	1925
United States	474,284	478,430	528,000
Canada	27,093	24,679	34,000
Belgium	145,733	160,411	169,000
Germany (including Polish Silesia)	110,396	102,989*	153,000
Australia	40,248	46,601	46,000
Great Britain	31,279	38,480	38,000
Total	829,032	851,591	968,000

* Probably under-estimated.

The increased production has been called forth by high prices. The shortage of stocks in U.S. and U.K. is not compensated by any material stocks elsewhere, Mr A. J. M. Sharpe, Foreign Correspondent of the American Zinc Institute, estimating world stocks at recent dates as below. Nevertheless, with any setback in industrial activity, the production of spelter, as of the other non-ferrous metals, would soon prove to be in excess.

World stocks 1925 (metric tons)

	1 Sept.	1 Oct.	1 Nov.	1 Dec.
United States	15,490	10,700	6,800	6,300
Germany and Poland	5,400	4,600	11,400	15,000
Canada	700	800	900	1,000
Great Britain	600	600	500	1,000
Belgium	1,700	1,600	1,800	1,900
France	800	700	800	800
Scandinavia	200	200	200	200
Australia*	2,000	2,200	2,200	2,000
Far East	500	500	500	500
Elsewhere	500	500	500	500
Total	27,890	22,400	25,600	29,200

* Including unsold shipments afloat.

VI. *Rubber*

The stocks of rubber are held mainly:—

(1) On plantations, etc., within the restricted area of Malaya.

(2) In Singapore and Penang.

(3) Afloat.

(4) In London and Liverpool.

(5) In U.S.A. warehouses and factories.

In addition relatively insignificant stocks are held:—

(6) In Ceylon and India.

(7) In Dutch East Indies.

(8) In Para (Brazil).

(9) In Amsterdam and Antwerp.

Monthly figures are only available for 3 and 4, but since 1923 quarterly figures are available for all except 1. The following table is based on yearly and half-yearly estimates of the total world stocks in the chief centres at the end of 1920, 1921, and 1922: for 1923 some quarterly returns are available also; and since

World's rubber stocks (exclusive of stock on estates) (1,000 tons)

End of:	United Kingdom*	United States†	Singapore and Penang	Ceylon and India	Dutch East Indies	Para (Brazil)	Amsterdam and Antwerp	Afloat	Approximate total
1920	56	76	35	?	?	?	?	37	(204)‡ 219§–229*
1921	80	52	40	?	?	?	?	37	(209)‡ 224§–244*
1922	81	90	55	?	?	?	?	45	(271)‡ 286§–306*
1923 March	79	87	21	3·5	9	0·6	1·0	48	— 249
June	64	101	46	?	?	?	?	52	(263)‡ 278§
September	68	90	27	4·0	10	0·9	1·2	43	— 244
December	75	73	38	4·0	10	?	2·5	52	— 254
1924 March	70	70	21	3·0	10	1·0	1·1	50	— 226
June	65	60	20	3·0	10	1·0	1·2	48	— 208
September	54	56	20	3·5	7	0·8	0·6	54	— 196
December	36	63	19	4·0	5	0·9	0·3	53	— 181
1925 March	23	55	17	4·0	5	1·2	0·1	50	— 155
June	7	40	16	3·0	3	0·5	0·2	59	— 129
September	7	45	16	4·0	5	1·1	0·3	63	— 141
December	7	74	20	4·5	5	1·5	0·2	70	— 182

* Including an estimate of stocks in private warehouses except in the figures for 1920, 1921, and 1922. The totals for these years were therefore certainly higher than the figures shown, and should perhaps be increased by 10,000 tons in 1920, and by 15–20,000 tons in 1921 and 1922.

† Returns cover 90–95 per cent of the whole.

‡ These figures in brackets give the actual total of stocks quoted.

§ These figures include an estimate of 15,000 tons for the unknown stocks in Ceylon, Dutch East Indies, Para, and at Amsterdam and Antwerp. This has been done in order to secure a more comparable series.

427

March 1924 the figures are reproduced from a table given in
The Rubber Quarterly.

There is fairly general agreement that consumption during
1925 has amounted to about 540,000 tons, and therefore the
aggregate stocks at the end of 1925 may be considered as
equivalent to about three months' consumption, as compared
with between four and a half and five months' consumption at
the end of 1924.

There are indications that the June figure for aggregate stocks
may be regarded as the lowest level, and with larger supplies
coming forward, a definite increase may be expected in the near
future.

While stocks of rubber in the United States have been at a

U.S. stocks of tyres and tubes (1,000,000)

End of month	Pneumatic tyres	Inner tubes
1921 September	3·3	3·8
December	3·7	4·7
1922 March	5·2	7·0
June	5·0	6·2
September	4·6	5·2
December	4·6	5·7
1923 March	5·7	7·7
June	7·0	8·9
September	5·4	6·5
December	4·3	6·3
1924 March	5·8	8·1
June	5·8	8·2
September	4·5	6·0
December	5·6	8·3
1925 March	7·1	10·7
June	5·4	7·8
September	5·8	7·5
October	5·0	6·5

relatively low level, stocks of tyres and tubes, which goods account for 80 per cent of the U.S. consumption of rubber, have not shown much more than the usual seasonal decline, and are still at a fairly high level.

The following are the estimates of production and consumption in recent years:—

Year	Production (1,000 tons)	Consumption (1,000 tons)
1919	339	335
1920	368	290
1921	293	292
1922	395*	408
1923	382	434
1924	420	475
1925	574	540

* This figure should probably be higher.

The estimates for 1925 have recently been made by the Rubber Association of America and must, of course, be regarded as provisional: the forecast of production made last spring by Messrs Symington & Sinclair, which was quoted in Special Memorandum No. 12, has, of course, been completely falsified by the greater release of rubber under the Restriction Scheme, due to the great rise in prices. The release of rubber under the Restriction Scheme will be raised to 100 per cent of standard production in February 1926, but it is unlikely that this will cause any great increase in supplies available for consumers before the end of 1926, as the present 85 per cent level is believed to be near the present potential productive capacity of many of the estates. The Rubber Association of America estimates production in 1926 at 606,000 tons, and consumption at 575,000 tons. The former figure is much less debateable than the latter. In recent years consumption has increased by roughly 10 per cent per annum: this would make the 1926 consumption as high as 594,000. The Rubber Association evidently considers that 'saturation point' is approaching. This may be true as regards the number of motor vehicles, but the consumption of petrol both in America and in this country shows that more and more mileage is being run per car per annum, which means a greater consumption of tyres. The development of balloon tyres has probably swelled consumption in the last year or two, not only because they contain more rubber, but also because cord tyres have been scrapped when only half-worn out. While balloon tyres probably wear out more quickly, higher prices may lead to a partial reversion to cord tyres not only for that reason, but also because cord tyres should be relatively cheaper since they contain less rubber. It is impossible to balance these and many other factors, especially the increased use of reclaimed rubber and of rubber substitutes; but the Rubber Association's consumption figure may easily be on the low side. On the other hand, their production figure is more likely to err in the same than in the opposite direction, for with the price of rubber at 2s. 6d. or higher, and costs of production at about 10d., supplies may be greatly increased by excessive 'tapping', or by an increase in the native output of the Dutch East Indies, or even of the wild rubber of the Amazon. Taking everything into consideration, the problem seems to resolve itself into the question whether supplies during the next year or so are going to be just adequate or a little more than adequate: there is nothing to warrant the idea of a glut, and equally nothing to warrant the idea of any real shortage. If supplies prove a little more than adequate, a wholly desirable increase in stocks will ensue: otherwise the existing hand-to-mouth level will continue to cause disturbing price fluctuations.

VII. *Sugar*

In the case of this commodity it is necessary to restrict ourselves to 'visible' supplies, accurate estimates of stocks held up by producers in the fairly numerous different sources of supply not being available. Nevertheless, this limitation is not so serious as it would be in the case of many commodities, because, on the one hand, sugar being a semi-manufactured product, the agricultural producers send the bulk of the output forward to the

Table I. Total visible supply of sugar (1,000 tons)

First half of month	1913	1914	1922†	1923	1924	1925	1926
January	3,234	3,711	2,761	2,433	2,255	2,708	3,716‡
February	4,043	4,323	2,543	2,511	2,357	2,950	
March	4,141	4,279	2,559	2,603	2,402	2,844	
April	4,006	4,192	2,479	2,501	2,460	2,891	
May	3,869	4,032	2,587	2,472	2,658	3,060	
June	3,732	3,792	2,275	2,278	2,509	2,950	
July	3,228	3,244	1,903	2,005	2,086	2,560	
August	3,426	2,668	1,580	1,630	1,560	2,013	
September	1,823	*	1,180	1,267	982	1,612	
October	1,259		868	791	542	1,211	
November	739		1,248	1,089	1,318	2,005	
December	1,900		2,077	1,951	2,364	3,265	

* No figures available between this date and March 1920.
† For this and subsequent years, figures relate to as near the first of the month as possible.
‡ Partly estimated.

centrals as soon as it is available, and, on the other hand, since it is in most countries a dutiable commodity, invisible supplies, on which duty has been paid, are not likely, as a rule, to be any larger than convenience dictates.

The total monthly figures of the visible supply are shown in Table I (up to December 1921 they were supplied by Messrs Bagot and Thompson, and since that date by Messrs C. Czarnikow, Ltd.: the two sets are only roughly comparable).

The distribution of the stock between the different countries is shown in Table II for selected dates.

The total 'visible' stocks naturally show a sharp seasonal fluctuation, but, as Table II shows, this is really a compound of two variations, one for Europe, which is mainly concerned with

Table II. Distribution of sugar stocks (1,000 tons)

Beginning of month	Germany	Czecho-Slovakia	France	Holland	Belgium	United Kingdom	Total Europe	United States (ports)	Cuba (ports)	Grand total
1922 January	808	425	177	158	128	176	1,872	45	844	2,761
April	495	262	104	177	71	218	1,327	222	930	2,479
July	216	83	61	90	30	368	848	193	862	1,903
October	37	6	45	52	12	272	424	128	316	868
December	772	470	176	185	51	334	1,988	40	49	2,077
1923 January	1,002	470	240	224	128	312	2,376	12	45	2,433
April	736	261	148	144	57	286	1,632	215	654	2,501
July	516	107	109	79	35	405	1,251	164	590	2,005
October	102	9	42	16	15	256	440	110	241	791
December	744	593	208	124	51	164	1,884	36	31	1,951
1924 January	908	546	291	154	143	164	2,206	27	22	2,255
April	718	378	127	83	63	264	1,633	167	660	2,460
July	488	113	78	67	38	322	1,106	192	788	2,086
October	2	7	47	22	11	150	239	76	227	542

November	345	337	151	115	61	118	1,127	46	145	1,318
December	874	706	305	198	62	154	2,299	24	41	2,364
1925 January	978	769	468	219	62	172	2,668	16	24	2,708
February	863	694	488	188	228	155	2,616	40	294	2,950
March	725	591	453	160	204	145	2,278	106	460	2,844
April	618	494	373	115	166	194	1,960	128	803	2,891
May	453	407	292	109	157	311	1,729	173	1,158	3,060
June	383	315	216	100	100	328	1,442	218	1,290	2,950
July	268	235	158	92	83	353	1,189	277	1,094	2,560
August	118	149	98	93	65	290	813	230	970	2,013
September	52	76	70	83	35	321	637	152	823	1,612
October	18	35	47	80	18	294	482	135	594	1,211
November	422	388	173	159	59	280	1,481	63	461	2,005
December	1,047	780	378	235	168	306	2,914	59	292	3,265
1926 January	1,210	934	487		223	434	3,523	61	132	3,716*

* Provisional.

Supply and consumption of sugar (tons)

	1920–1	1921–2	1922–3	1923–4	1924–5	1925–6
Stock carried over on 1 September	1,600,000	2,400,000	1,180,000	1,267,000	982,000	1,211,000
European beet crops	3,671,788	4,054,282	4,735,500	5,057,800	7,077,800	
American beet crops	1,004,019	930,121	649,000	803,700	1,010,400	
Cane crops	12,081,831	12,679,948	12,691,500	13,837,400	15,501,400	
Total	18,357,638	20,064,351	19,256,000	20,965,900	24,571,600	
Deduct visible supplies at end of season (1 September)	2,400,000	1,180,000	1,267,000	982,000	1,211,000	
Total consumption	15,957,638	18,884,351	17,989,000	19,983,900	23,360,600	

beet sugar, and the other for America, which is dominated by the Cuban cane crop. Thus stocks in Europe are at a minimum about October 1st, and reach a maximum about January 1st, whereas American port stocks are at a minimum at about January 1st, and reach their maximum about 1 May. The fluctuation in the total visible supply figures is, of course, dominated by the European stocks, since only *port* stocks in Cuba and the United States are included.

In Table II the enormous carryover of the Cuban 1920-1 crop accounts for the very large amount in Cuban ports on 1 January 1922. The steady increase in the maximum European stocks is also noticeable.

The above table gives a very rough idea of stocks, production, and consumption in recent seasons and the following table shows consumption during recent years by this country and the United States, which between them account for an extraordinary proportion of the exported sugar.

U.K. and U.S.A. consumption of sugar

	Consumption (raw values—tons)	
Year	United Kingdom	United States
1922	1,748,177	5,476,500
1923	1,602,029	5,141,000
1924	1,706,661	5,220,000
1925	1,818,089	5,925,000

During the season 1924-5 the world's consumption has again increased enormously. In part this may be due to the relatively low price-level, as was almost certainly the case in 1921-2, and it is further possible, though perhaps not probable, that there has been some increase in stocks in non-statistical countries. Production also increased enormously, but comparing the visible supply on Sept. 1st, 1925, with that in previous years, it has done

435

little more than keep pace with consumption. Estimates of production in the current season are still liable to considerable modification, but it is certain that there will be no such large increase as took place in 1924–5: at the most the increase may be put at three-quarters of a million tons, and it will very likely not exceed half a million. Allowing for some reduction in stocks, there is, therefore, room for consumption to increase by about three-quarters of a million tons. Judging by the recent course of events, consumption will increase more than this unless it is checked by a rise in price, but it is quite possible that a relatively small rise above the present level would considerably check consumption. Looking at the immediate future, therefore, it may be said that there are ample supplies to meet the demand at reasonable though hardly at present prices. Looking at the more distant future, however, it seems unlikely that production will even be maintained, for present prices are almost certainly below the cost of production; while production must, in fact, be increased, for there is no reason to suppose that consumption will cease its advance.

Tea in bond in the United Kingdom (1,000 lb)

End of month	1921	1922	1923	1924	1925
January	219,377	208,115	186,035	182,865	225,067
February	223,179	221,362	176,681	188,559	234,557
March	229,568	219,645	183,413	193,362	231,516
April	233,018	214,484	167,763	192,219	217,091
May	228,793	192,396	141,659	152,317	190,730
June	218,290	170,478	126,792	138,691	180,859
July	207,448	153,198	112,890	121,097	163,255
August	197,433	142,137	121,935	128,266	165,085
September	190,799	151,510	134,170	136,694	180,621
October	190,129	152,095	146,990	150,721	181,683
November	196,534	158,357	152,288	174,414	189,080
December	205,420	169,776	165,666	205,859	203,654

VIII. *Tea*

The only precise figures available for the stocks of tea are of
those in bond in the United Kingdom. Since, however, about
three-quarters of the total world production passes through this
country, these stocks should form a fairly reliable index of the
position.

IX. *Coffee*

Coffee (1,000 bags)*

Beginning of month	Visible supply of Europe	Visible supply of U.S.A.	Stocks in Brazil	Total
1913 July	6,480	1,848	1,947	10,275
September	6,005	1,477	4,002	11,484
October	6,019	1,393	4,769	12,181
1914 January	7,275	1,709	4,681	13,665
April	8,702	2,172	1,743	12,617
June	8,353	2,056	1,207	11,616
1919 January	758	1,010	9,296	11,364
April	2,755	1,964	7,060	11,799
July	3,124	1,508	5,704	10,336
October	2,821	2,057	5,540	10,418
1920 January	2,843	2,007	5,020	9,870
April	2,573	2,209	3,392	8,174
July	2,509	2,293	1,948	6,750
October	2,955	2,640	2,387	7,982
1921 January	2,588	2,442	3,735	8,765
April	2,533	2,765	3,389	8,687
July	2,562	2,100	4,038	8,700
October	2,564	1,838	4,589	8,991
1922 January	2,399	2,056	4,948	9,403
April	2,977	1,583	4,580	9,140
July	3,068	1,456	4,115	8,639
October	3,007	1,182	4,292	8,481
1923 January	2,839	1,385	3,756	7,980
April	2,463	1,618	2,903	6,974

Table (*cont.*)

Beginning of month	Visible supply of Europe	Visible supply of U.S.A.	Stocks in Brazil	Total
July	2,296	1,075	1,969	5,340
October	2,449	1,387	2,016	5,852
1924 January	2,228	1,349	890	4,467
February	2,153	1,088	979	4,220
March	2,192	1,172	902	4,266
April	1,935	1,075	954	3,964
May	1,993	1,126	1,326	4,445
June	2,215	1,096	1,443	4,754
July	—	—	—	5,071
August	2,140	1,110	1,128	4,378
September	2,345	1,194	1,748	5,287
October	2,255	1,337	2,135	5,727
November	2,378	1,382	1,999	5,759
December	2,158	1,358	2,115	5,631
1925 January	2,098	1,046	2,240	5,384
February	2,072	1,112	2,072	5,256
March	2,002	1,029	2,125	5,156
April	2,028	1,116	2,245	5,389
May	2,165	878	2,292	5,335
June	2,192	779	2,257	5,228
July	2,193	1,154	1,738	5,085
August	2,274	1,213	1,727	5,214
September	2,426	1,349	1,462	5,237
October	2,367	1,269	1,594	5,230
November	2,525	1,188	1,496	5,209
December	2,289	1,391	1,448	5,128
1926 January	2,163	1,484	1,517	5,164

* G. Duuring & Zoon.

About two-thirds of the supply of coffee for Europe and U.S.A. comes from Brazil. The preceding table is based on the figures supplied by Messrs Duuring & Zoon, the most important omissions from which are the stocks in the East and Eastern

Deliveries of coffee (1,000 bags)

Year	To Europe	To U.S.A.	Total	From Brazil	Other kinds
1920	5,213	9,167	14,380	8,638	5,742
1921	8,094	9,958	18,052	11,356	6,696
1922	8,238	9,654	17,892	11,100	6,792
1923	9,240	10,585	19,825	13,516	6,309
1924	9,981	10,709	20,690	13,473	7,217
1925	9,481	9,488	18,969	11,868	7,101

ports, in the interior of Brazil, and coffee from the East afloat to U.S.A.

Deliveries during the last six years have been as described above.

X. *Petroleum*

U.S.A. stocks of petroleum

Stocks at end of month	Crude petroleum (1,000 barrels)					
	1920	1921	1922	1923	1924	1925
January	127,164	117,099	180,984	282,875	364,954	391,233
February	126,329	121,713	191,471	283,498	368,901	521,417*
March	125,597	128,754	202,906	289,871	373,561	527,865
April	124,991	134,719	213,371	295,970	378,214	531,699
May	124,689	143,614	224,388	304,668	383,488	542,057
June	126,763	151,339	232,032	315,369	387,364	546,378
July	128,168	159,030	238,233	326,635	391,919	548,330
August	129,043	162,903	242,635	333,143	399,567	546,946
September	128,788	164,076	244,778	339,961	401,478	—
October	129,451	163,335	246,625	349,025	399,165	545,396
November	131,325	164,073	247,942	350,000	396,516	544,161
December	133,690	170,350	248,413	333,053	390,157	538,000†

* From this date the figures take in heavy crude oil below 20° Beaumé, including all grades of fuel oil, held on the Pacific Coast.
† Provisional.

The only figures of stocks regularly available are those for the United States. Since, however, nearly 80 per cent of the world's oil stocks are held in the United States, these figures can be regarded as reasonably representative.

The table on p. 439 of stocks of crude petroleum in the United States is that published by the American Petroleum Institute.

These stocks in September represented about six months' supply at the present general rate of consumption. During the winter months of 1924–5 it seemed that production and consumption were approaching equilibrium, and that by the present time a much-to-be-desired reduction of stocks might have taken place. This prospect has not been realised, owing to miscalculations on the supply side. Last spring production seemed likely to decline; in fact it increased rapidly until the end of May, and

U.S.A. stocks of refined products (barrels)

End of month	Gasolene	Kerosene	Lub. oils	Fuel and gas oils
1918 December	7,079,213	9,050,425	3,306,033	15,690,510
1919 June	14,140,396	6,012,915	4,175,828	19,328,348
December	10,637,939	8,079,040	3,269,498	17,002,963
1920 June	12,001,324	10,031,984	3,171,727	15,284,961
December	11,009,091	9,358,831	3,821,964	19,938,200
1921 June	17,872,487	10,358,493	6,211,503	29,730,097
December	13,954,456	8,119,251	5,161,084	31,696,796
1922 June	19,642,058	7,561,297	5,402,472	31,593,801
December	21,042,687	6,691,675	5,612,733	31,064,949
1923 June	30,085,000	6,293,000	5,360,000	31,524,000
December	25,590,000	6,742,000	5,780,000	36,072,000
1924 June	38,068,000	6,984,000	5,919,000	38,537,000
December	28,083,000	8,067,000	6,127,000	39,441,000
1925 June	36,839,000	10,863,000	6,528,000	51,992,000
September	36,051,000	8,396,000	6,760,000	60,033,000

at the end of October it was still above the rate at the beginning of the year. In addition the extension of 'cracking' plants has provided an increased yield of gasolene, to an extent greater than was anticipated. The expectations of a greatly increased consumption have in the main been realised, but production has apparently been capable of speedy increase, and, as is often the case under such circumstances, competition inevitably causes too large a response. Recently production has been curtailed, but it is as yet impossible to say whether this represents anything more than greater caution on the part of producers, following on their recent excess of optimism.

In addition to stocks of crude oil, there are also relatively smaller stocks (rather more than a month's supply) of the principal refined products. The half-yearly figures of these stocks in the United States have been as above.

The relation of these stocks to current consumption of the various refined products (*not* consumption of crude oils by refineries) is shown by the following table:—

1,000 barrels

Year	Domestic consumption	Exports		Total
		General	Bunkers	
1919	349,565	62,853	14,031	426,449
1920	419,693	77,993	26,335	524,021
1921	418,963	70,723	27,027	516,713
1922	478,526	72,952	31,692	583,170
1923	589,631	100,436	37,643	727,710
1924	611,913	115,868	43,327	771,108

XI. *Nitrate*

Nitrate statistics are comparatively simple, since they all come from one part of the world. Very reliable figures are regularly published by Messrs Aikman, and are quoted below.

The figures for America include interior stocks, but not those held by the U.S.A. Government, which have gradually declined from round 300,000 tons in December 1921, to 60,000 tons at the present time.

In normal times there is a considerable reduction in the visible supply in the early part of the year, as the demand is somewhat seasonal.

Nitrate (1,000 tons)

End of month	Visible supply (including afloat)		Stocks in Chile	Total
	Europe and Egypt	U.S.A.		
1913 January	1,128	89	490	1,727
March	686	97	527	1,326
June	416	84	754	1,265
September	571	79	752	1,414
December	1,093	71	498	1,685
1919 July	140	28	1,594	1,780
September	152	49	1,705	1,925
December	430	95	1,576	2,134
1920 March	368	253	1,218	1,914
June	317	216	1,248	1,800
September	495	194	1,303	2,008
December	782	132	1,304	2,235
1921 March	868	218	1,283	2,384
June	836	249	1,317	2,405
September	828	41	1,453	2,370
December	903·5	260	1,441	2,622·5
1922 March	520	115	1,504	2,149
June	228·5	38	1,601	1,873·5
September	296	133	1,495	1,945
December	463·5	195	1,225	1,912·5
1923 March	379·5	238	889	1,310
June	173	54	997	1,250
September	365	96	927	1,415
December	573	200	852	1,639
1924 January	618	291	746	1,655
February	517·5	273	736	1,526·5

Table (*cont.*)

End of month	Visible supply (including afloat)		Stocks in Chile	Total
	Europe and Egypt	U.S.A.		
March	371	193	782	1,346
April	228	170	830	1,228
May	152·5	125	960	1,255·5
June	115	47	1,075	1,250
July	226	105	999	1,365
August	321	81	996	1,423
September	429	124	900	1,494
October	451	102	959	1,542
November	570	86	947	1,644
December	684	111	882	1,709
1925 January	711	121	855	1,718
February	586·5	247	768	1,601·5
March	379·5	233	756	1,368·5
April	245	233	754	1,232·5
May	177	102	868	1,147
June	227	122	869	1,218
July	318	172	819	1,309
August	366	121	832	1,319
September	408	105	896	1,409
October	466	70	906	1,442
November	575	147	893	1,615
December	682·5	115	878	1,675·5

XII. *Wheat*

Wheat is a baffling commodity to the compiler of comparative stock statistics, because it is a seasonal crop, coming from many different sources, and harvested at different times of year.

As in the case of other commodities, the statistics regularly available month by month are those of 'visible' supplies in 'second hands'; but, owing to the large amounts held on farms

443

Available supplies of wheat (1,000 qr of 480 lb)

	1 August–31 July					
	1920–1	1921–2	1922–3	1923–4	1924–5	1925–6
Total available surplus in exporting countries	73–82,000	83,000	111,000	125,000	101,500	92,000
Shipments to importing countries	73,882	80,315	84,398	96,664	89,400	80,000
Apparent carryover in exporting countries at end of year	8,000	2,500	26,500	28,000	12,100	12,000
Total crops:—						
Exporting countries, Northern Hemisphere	194,320	218,980	236,440	244,890	216,640	229,040
Exporting countries, Southern Hemisphere	40,690	41,990	41,110	50,090	46,600	44,500
Importing countries	109,140	139,550	114,480	137,460	118,480	145,160
Total wheat crops:—	344,150	400,520	392,030	432,440	381,720	418,700
Supply for importing countries:—						
Crops	109,140	139,550	114,480	137,460	118,480	145,160
Imports	73,882	80,315	84,398	96,664	89,400	80,000
Total supply	183,022	219,865	198,878	234,124	207,880	225,160

and elsewhere 'out of sight' and to the seasonal irregularity of supply, these figures are particularly unsatisfactory in the case of wheat.

For the purpose of a conspectus of the position as a whole, there is, perhaps, nothing better than the summary published weekly by Mr Broomhall in *The Corn Trade News*, of the supplies available in exporting countries during the cereal year and of the probable requirements of the importing countries during the same period. In the above table the figures for importers' requirements are based on the actual shipments, except in 1925–6, where Mr Broomhall's forecast is given, which takes account of actual shipments for the first five months of the year.

These statistics may be supplemented by the quarterly figures of 'visible supply', i.e. the visible supply in elevators and public stores in the United States, Canada and Great Britain and the supply afloat for Europe:—

1,000 qr of 480 lb

	1919–20	1920–1	1921–2	1922–3	1923–4	1924–5	1925–6
1 Aug.	18,370	17,950	16,800	15,091	17,340	20,270	16,330
1 Nov.	34,000	24,560	29,980	30,420	34,330	36,340	29,150
1 Feb.	28,120	23,750	26,520	35,660	39,350	37,900	—
1 May	23,870	19,660	23,730	28,500	34,750	29,900	—

The current available statistics relating to supplies and stocks of wheat are well summarised in the *Wheat Studies* of the Food Research Institute of Stanford University, California, to which anyone who is interested in further details may be referred. The following table relating to wheat supplies in the leading countries of export, 1922–5, has been taken from this source.

Wheat supplies and their disposition in leading export countries 1922–25* (million bushels)

| | Approximations | | Estimate |
	1922–3	1923–4	1924–5
United States Year ending 30 June			
Stocks, 1 July	81·5	102·4	106·2
New crop	867·6	797·4	872·7
Supplies	949·1	899·8	978·9
Exports of wheat	154·9	78·8	195·5
Exports of flour	67·0	77·6	62·5
Imports (less re-exports), wheat and flour	19·7	27·9	6·1
Net exports, wheat and flour	202·2	128·5	251·9
Shipments to possessions	2·8	2·9	2·8
Total for abroad	205·0	131·4	254·7
Seed requirements	91·4	79·4	87·6
Domestic milling	} 550·3 {	496·1	484·6
Feed and waste		89·2	65·2
Total domestic use	641·7	664·7	637·4
Stocks, 30 June	102·4	103·7	86·8
Canada Year ending 31 August			
Stocks, 1 September	16·0	8·9	39·1
New crop	399·8	474·2	279·0
Supplies	415·8	483·1	318·1
Exports, wheat and flour	279·1	342·7	192·1
Seed requirements	39·8	38·0	38·8
Milled for consumption	40·9	42·2	39·0
Feed and waste	47·1	33·6	24·6
Total domestic use	127·8	113·8	103·4
Stocks, 31 August	8·9	26·3	22·6
Argentina Year ending 31 July			
Stocks, 1 August	66·6	54·2	59·6
New crop	195·8	247·0	191·1
Supplies	262·4	301·2	250·7
Exports, wheat and flour	142·6	173·0	123·1
Seed requirements	18·7	20·6	23·1
Consumption, feed and waste	46·9	48·0	47·3
Total domestic use	65·6	68·6	70·4
Stocks, 31 July	54·2	59·6	57·2
Australia Year ending 31 July			
Stocks, 1 August	29·8	45·4	41·2
New crop	109·3	125·5	164·0
Supplies	139·1	170·9	205·2
Exports, wheat and flour	49·8	85·6	123·6
Seed requirements	8·9	9·4	9·4
Consumption	30·4	31·2 }	36·6
Feed and waste	4·6	3·5 }	
Total domestic use	43·9	44·1	46·0
Stocks, 31 July	45·4	41·2	35·6

* From *Wheat Studies of the Food Research Institute*, Stanford University, California vol. II, no. 1.

COMMODITIES

*From The London and Cambridge Economic Service Special Memorandum
No. 22 (March 1927)*

STOCKS OF STAPLE COMMODITIES

The statistics given below are in continuation of Memoranda published in April 1923, June 1924, July 1925, and February 1926.

The table below is a summary of the figures given in detail afterwards for each commodity.

THE U.S. DEPARTMENT OF COMMERCE INDEX OF COMMODITY STOCKS

In December 1925, and again in January 1926, this index rose sharply. The new high level was then more or less maintained until midsummer, when a further sharp though somewhat irregular advance took place. The increase has been almost entirely in stocks of raw foodstuffs, though all the other groups show a small tendency to rise.

STOCKS OF AGRICULTURAL AND INDUSTRIAL COMMODITIES IN THE U.S.A.

The Federal Reserve Bulletin for February 1927 gives the following comparison of the volume of the stocks of certain agricultural commodities at the end of the last three years.

It is also stated that the value of these reported stocks on December 31, 1926, was $200 million smaller than at the end of 1925, and $300 million smaller than at the end of 1924.

A similar comparison of the stocks of industrial commodities is given in the table below [see pp. 452–3].

447

Stocks of staple commodities

Beginning of month	Cotton 1,000 bales (1)	Copper 1,000 tons (2)	Tin 1,000 tons (3)	Lead 1,000 tons (4) U.K.	Lead U.S.	Spelter 1,000 tons (5)	Rubber 1,000 tons (6)	Sugar 1,000 tons (7)	Tea 1,000,000 lb (8)	Coffee 1,000 bags (9)	Petroleum 1,000,000 barrels (10)	Nitrate 1,000 tons (11)
1920 January	7,410	—	20	50·0	—	61	—	—	213	9,870	—	2,134
April	7,353	—	18	28·4	—	53	—	2,433	213	8,174	—	1,914
July	6,793	—	19	25·2	—	51	—	2,003	213	6,750	171	1,800
October	—	—	18	18·7	—	61	—	1,338	215	7,982	—	2,008
1921 January	—	399^A	18	19·0	—	81	219–229	2,313	214	8,765	182	2,235
April	—	—	16	23·9	—	88	—	3,331	230	8,687	—	2,384
July	—	—	17	13·3	—	99	—	3,312	218	8,700	221	2,405
October	9,534	—	21	9·9	—	89	—	2,039	191	8,991	—	2,370
1922 January	8,470	411^A	24	0·3	—	72	224–244	2,761	205	9,403	235	2,622·5
April	7,654	346^A	21	0·6	—	60	—	2,479	220	9,140	—	2,149
July	6,785	357^A	22	0·3	—	31	—	1,903	170	8,639	302	1,873·5
October	4,514	325^A	21	0·6	—	20	—	868	151	8,481	—	1,945
1923 January	—	347	26	0·5	—	17	286–306	2,433	170	7,980	319	1,912·5
April	3,111	350	25	0·4	—	10	249	2,501	183	6,974	—	1,310

	(1)	(2)	(3)	(4)	(5)	(6)	(7)	(8)	(9)	(10)	(11)	^
July	2,765	352	21	0·2	—	17	278	2,005	127	5,340	396	1,250
October	2,699	391	20	1·4	—	21	244	791	134	5,835	—	1,415
1924 January	2,010	402	21	1·2	93	34	254	2,255	166	4,467	414	1,639
April	1,716	361	23	0·0	92	29	226	2,460	193	3,964	463	1,346
July	1,747	371	20	0·0	97	45	208	2,086	139	5,071	481	1,250
October	2,673	385	20	0·1	88	42	196	542	137	5,727	487	1,494
1925 January	2,563	389	25	0·1	78	19	181	2,708	206	5,384	478	1,790
April	1,904	403	20	0·0	94	16	151	2,891	231	5,389	491	1,368·5
July	1,715	365	20	0·1	86	21	129	2,560	181	5,085	505	1,218
October	—	347	18	0·0	94	11	141	1,211	181	5,230	473	1,409
1926 January	2,927	344	18	0·0	93	9	182	3,709	204	5,164	469	1,675·5
April	3,193	361	14	0·4	105	19	183	4,064	195	4,786	503	1,549
July	4,068	370	16	0·2	106	24	193	3,452	156	4,571	483	1,659
October	5,396	351	15	0·1	106	15	213	1,428	175	4,856	468	1,772
1927 January	4,916	367	16	1·7	—	20	259	3,307	207	4,911	476	1,806

(1) Total supply, seasonally corrected, exclusive of European and Asiatic mill stocks. (2) Total supply outside hands of consumers. (3) Visible supply. London Metal Exchange figures from 1923. (4) Visible supply in U.K. and stocks in U.S. (5) Visible supply in U.S. (6) Total supply outside plantations. (7) Total visible supply. (8) Stocks in bond in U.K. (9) Visible supply in Rio, Santos, Bahia, Europe and U.S. (10) Stocks of crude and refined oils in U.S. (11) Visible supply in Chile, U.S., Europe and Egypt.
^ (Copper). On 1 January 1921, Allied Government stocks amounted approximately to 82,000 tons, and stocks of scrap metal to 183,000; on 1 January 1922, the former had become trifling, and the latter had fallen to about 90,000 tons, and had become trifling by 1 January 1923. A decreasing allowance must be added to the figures shown on account of these stocks.

Course of commodity stocks in the United States, by major groups (seasonal variations eliminated)

TOTAL INDEX

Year	Monthly average	Jan.	Feb.	March	April	May	June	July	Aug.	Sept.	Oct.	Nov.	Dec.
1919	100	103	103	100	304	102	97	97	96	101	100	100	97
1920	98	99	96	91	93	93	93	95	95	96	107	106	109
1921	138	124	134	141	136	139	145	145	148	138	137	132	131
1922	126	131	131	131	127	133	130	128	119	126	116	119	117
1923	118	121	116	117	117	111	115	114	125	118	118	122	125
1924	136	136	135	136	136	141	134	130	134	135	137	136	145
1925	145	155	152	149	141	143	140	133	142	149	132	134	153
1926	170	167	164	154	157	162	162	167	184	172	174	198	186

RAW FOODSTUFFS

Year	Monthly average	Jan.	Feb.	March	April	May	June	July	Aug.	Sept.	Oct.	Nov.	Dec.
1919	100	125	120	99	101	89	86	91	101	108	94	99	87
1920	97	101	91	73	82	85	86	98	94	103	135	114	104
1921	174	121	147	164	147	154	171	171	198	184	212	205	209
1922	192	191	195	206	203	233	220	214	174	190	150	163	163
1923	142	165	157	161	169	143	146	134	133	119	113	122	141
1924	151	164	173	169	164	178	157	151	160	148	154	153	190
1925	169	192	187	192	176	195	187	149	158	160	113	128	171
1926	272	228	227	198	206	235	240	256	310	256	263	346	303

RAW MATERIALS FOR MANUFACTURE

Year	Monthly average	Jan.	Feb.	March	April	May	June	July	Aug.	Sept.	Oct.	Nov.	Dec.
1919	100	106	105	107	111	110	100	100	85	85	95	98	98
1920	104	96	97	94	89	95	98	99	103	102	109	123	139

Year													
1921	158	154	166	171	176	178	184	189	176	151	124	118	110
1922	108	110	107	105	105	100	100	96	102	121	120	116	111
1923	108	111	102	101	96	93	95	94	111	118	130	123	119
1924	116	125	118	110	109	105	98	95	100	118	129	141	142
1925	138	149	139	130	120	100	98	104	124	161	151	150	165
1926	144	169	163	153	141	134	132	120	127	130	143	160	158

MANUFACTURED FOODSTUFFS

Year													
1919	100	98	93	90	94	100	88	88	93	107	114	114	121
1920	95	113	114	115	113	99	95	87	85	82	78	79	78
1921	79	78	80	82	80	81	81	83	78	76	78	74	71
1922	72	66	68	63	58	66	75	80	80	77	75	76	75
1923	80	70	71	76	76	79	88	87	85	83	80	82	81
1924	84	74	74	79	86	86	87	89	87	90	87	84	88
1925	78	87	86	80	75	73	76	83	78	79	77	74	75
1926	82	74	74	80	95	85	81	89	88	88	84	76	72

MANUFACTURED COMMODITIES

Year													
1919	100	88	95	103	110	110	109	107	100	100	98	92	89
1920	97	90	88	86	91	96	96	97	97	95	104	110	116
1921	136	141	142	144	143	144	145	141	140	133	124	120	120
1922	118	138	135	130	123	115	110	108	108	111	112	112	111
1923	129	124	121	117	113	117	121	128	136	140	141	147	146
1924	161	161	154	161	163	169	169	161	165	165	161	156	148
1925	173	175	174	171	171	171	168	171	183	181	176	170	160
1926	175	179	174	170	169	170	169	172	177	183	180	180	182

Reported stocks of industrial commodities in December*

Commodities	1924	1925	1926	Per cent of change in 1926	
				1924	1925
Metals					
Iron ore (1,000 long tons)	36,360	36,898	38,426	+ 5·7	+ 4·1
Copper, refined (short tons)	136,434	73,082	85,501	− 37·3	+ 17·0
Copper, blister (short tons)	237,528	249,278	272,342	+ 14·7	+ 9·3
Zinc, slab, at refineries (short tons)	21,208	9,295	21,887	+ 3·2	+ 135·5
Lead, crude (short tons)	87,197	105,629	120,871†	+ 38·6	+ 14·4
Fuels					
Bituminous coal (1,000 short tons)	44,000‡	45,000‡	44,000‡	0·0	− 2·2
Petroleum, crude (1,000 barrels)	312,725	292,288	278,077	− 11·1	− 4·9
Gasolene (mn. gallons)	1,294	1,648	1,639	+ 26·7	− 0·6
Gas and fuel oil east of California (mn. gallons)	774	1,037	1,046	+ 35·1	+ 0·9
Building materials					
Yellow pine, southern (mn. board feet)	1,042	1,166	1,164	+ 11·7	− 0·2
Yellow pine, western (mn. board feet)	921	902	1,145†	+ 24·4	+ 27·0
Hardwoods (mn. board feet)	667	806	922	+ 38·2	+ 14·4
Flooring, oak and maple (1,000 board feet)	69,815	73,155	102,562	+ 46·9	+ 40·2
Common brick, burned (1,000)	354,477	316,023	453,452	+ 27·9	+ 43·5
Paving brick (1,000)	102,993	108,638	79,709	− 22·6	− 26·6
Cement (1,000 barrels)	13,857	18,429	20,555	+ 48·3	+ 11·5
Enamelled sanitary ware (1,000 pieces)	652	666	893	+ 37·0	+ 34·1
Textile materials and products					
Cotton, raw, at warehouses (1,000 bales)	4,617	5,584	6,479	+ 40·3	+ 16·0
Cotton, raw, at mills (1,000 bales)	1,320	1,721	1,766	+ 33·8	+ 2·6
Cotton goods (yards)	—	229,817	210,122	—	− 8·6
Cotton fabrics, finished (cases)	42,162	42,315	38,398	− 8·1	− 8·3

Wool, raw, manufacturers (1,000 lb)	211,515§	182,506§	161,943§	− 25·4	− 11·3
Wool, raw, dealers (1,000 lb)	179,733§	190,504§	213,770§	+ 18·9	+ 12·2
Wool, raw, in Boston (1,000 lb)	49,259	62,251	81,419	+ 65·3	+ 30·8
Silk, raw, at warehouses (bales)	61,533	49,824	52,478	− 14·7	+ 5·3
Hosiery (1,000 dozen pairs)	5,752	5,834	6,856‡	+ 19·2	+ 17·5
Knit underwear (1,000 dozen garments)	954	1,096	1,011†	+ 6·0	− 7·7
Leather					
Sole leather (1,000 backs, bends and sides)	6,467	6,310	3,660	− 43·4	− 42·0
Upper leather, cattle (1,000 sides)	4,305	4,004	3,142†	− 27·0	− 21·5
Upper leather, calf and kip (1,000 skins)	6,537	6,517	6,126†	− 6·3	− 6·0
Upper leather, goat and kid (1,000 skins)	18,925	18,493	19,170†	+ 1·3	+ 3·7
Rubber					
Rubber, crude (long tons)	49,645§	33,131§	58,883§	+ 18·6	+ 77·7
Pneumatic tires	5,571	6,106	7,847	+ 40·9	+ 28·5
Inner tubes	8,289	8,485	12,150	+ 46·6	+ 43·2
Wood pulp and paper					
Wood pulp, chemical (short tons)	54,372	37,774	41,688	− 23·3	+ 10·5
Wood pulp, mechanical (short tons)	179,466	191,911	195,926	+ 9·2	+ 2·1
Newsprint (short tons)	23,838	16,238	12,030	− 49·5	− 25·9
Book paper (short tons)	39,398	44,534	43,835	+ 11·3	− 1·6
Wrapping paper (short tons)	64,760	44,177	37,827	− 41·6	− 14·4
Fine paper (short tons)	41,714	40,090	42,521	+ 1·9	+ 6·1
Paper board (short tons)	42,534	45,600	52,758	+ 24·0	+ 15·7

* Stocks in every case are as of 31 December unless otherwise noted. These figures are derived from various sources, and all, except those referring to bituminous coal and to raw wool in Boston, are published regularly in the Survey of Current Business of the Department of Commerce. Coal stocks are compiled at irregular intervals by the Bureau of Mines, and those of wool in Boston are reported at the end of each year by the wool merchants of that city.

† Stocks as of 1 December.
‡ Stocks are of report dates nearest the end of the year—1 March 1925, 1 February 1926, and 1 October 1926.
§ Stocks for all years are as of 30 September.

Reported stocks of agricultural commodities in December

Commodity	1924	1925	1926
Cotton (1,000 bales)	5,937	7,326	8,245
Cotton seed (1,000 tons)	1,231	1,416	1,292
Wheat (1,000 bushels)	96,114	55,024	68,125
Corn (1,000 bushels)	19,693	19,095	36,412
Oats (1,000 bushels)	76,343	66,762	46,341
Cheese (1,000 pounds)	49,187	58,457	54,495
Apples (1,000 barrels)	5,232	7,051	9,282
Butter (1,000 pounds)	65,694	52,785	34,355
Frozen poultry (1,000 pounds)	133,990	111,501	144,230
Beef (1,000 pounds)	142,862	84,996	101,016
Pork (1,000 pounds)	642,981	472,219	475,576
Lard (1,000 pounds)	60,243	42,478	49,498
Eggs (1,000 cases)	1,050	1,683	1,111
Tobacco (mn. pounds)	1,714	1,819	1,842

I. *American cotton*

At any given time stocks consist of the following:—

(1) Stocks up-country in the Southern States on plantations, railroads, and in 'uncounted'* interior towns.

(2) The 'visible' supply. This consists of (*a*) stocks in public storage and at compresses (warehouse stocks) in the more important interior towns and in the ports of the United States, (*b*) cotton afloat for Great Britain and the Continent, (*c*) warehouse stocks in the principal European ports, namely, Liverpool, Manchester, London, Havre, Marseilles, Genoa, Bremen, Ghent, Rotterdam and Barcelona.†

(3) Mill stocks in spinners' hands throughout the world, generally known as the 'invisible' or 'out of sight' supply.

In the first table the 'up-country' stock is taken as the 'up-country' carryover in the Southern States plus warehouse and

* I.e. towns not included in the figures of stocks in public storage and at compresses.
† Cotton afloat for Japan and in Japanese ports is not allowed for. All cotton consigned to Japan is considered by the leading exchanges as 'consumed' or 'out of sight'.

mill stocks in the U.S. at the end of each season, plus the current year's crop, minus the U.S. consumption to any particular date, minus the net exports to that date (i.e. exports minus imports), minus warehouse and mill stocks at that date. By this means it is possible to estimate the location of all cotton in the U.S. month by month. But it follows that the whole of the new crop is suddenly added to the 'up-country' stock in August each year. This is corrected in the table below by the 'seasonal correction', which provides what would be the figure of total stock in the U.S. if the current crop came into existence at an even monthly rate through the year. The statistics of U.S. warehouse stocks and mill stocks are compiled by the U.S. Bureau of the Census, and may be regarded as reliable, as also may the 'visible' supply of Great Britain and the Continent.* The estimates of the current crop are reasonably accurate by the end of each calendar year. The 'up-country' carryover is the most doubtful item, and is always liable to be under-, rather than over-estimated. The estimates of Mr H. G. Hester, the Secretary of the New Orleans Cotton Exchange, have been used until 1922, since when the estimates of the Shepperson Publishing Company (*Cotton Facts*) have been preferred. The monthly calculated figures for 'up-country' provide at best an estimate of the actual state of affairs, but in most years they tally reasonably well with the 'up-country carryover' estimates (see Note § below table).

At the beginning and in the middle of each season, statistics of European and Asiatic mill stocks, and of the world's actual consumption during the previous six months are available, and the position of the world's total stocks is shown in the two tables below.

For the year 1925–6 the available supply of cotton was rather over 19 million bales, and therefore, allowing for a comfortable carryover of at least 3 million bales, consumption could have been increased to as much as 16 million bales. Actually it barely amounted to 13¾ million bales, or only half a million bales more

---

* As given by the Liverpool Cotton Exchange.

Supplies other than European and Asiatic mill stocks (1,000 bales)*

End of month	Up-country	U.S. warehouse stocks†	U.S. mill stocks†	Total in U.S.A.	Correction for season	Corrected total in U.S.A.	Visible outside U.S.A.	Grand total, excluding mill stocks outside U.S.A.‡
1919 July	2,193	2,212	1,304	5,709	—	5,709	347	6,056
October	11,973	1,974	1,365	15,312	9,000	6,312	1,077	7,389
1920 January	3,780	3,760	3,677	11,217	6,000	5,217	2,082	7,299
April	3,252	2,967	1,809	8,028	3,000	5,028	2,034	7,062
July	1,703§	2,055	1,358	5,116	—	5,116	1,352	6,468
October	11,414	4,168	944	16,526	10,311	6,215	—	—
1921 January	6,788	5,645	1,273	13,706	6,874	6,832	—	—
April	4,961	5,029	1,316	11,306	3,437	7,869	—	—
July	3,713§	3,723	1,111	8,007	—	8,007	1,645	9,652
October	7,577	4,982	1,405	13,964	6,330	7,634	1,598	9,232
1922 January	4,550	4,618	1,675	10,843	4,220	6,623	1,581	8,204
April	3,484	3,214	1,458	8,156	2,110	6,046	1,436	7,482
July	944§	1,488	1,218	3,670	—	3,670	1,120	4,790
October	—	—	—	—	7,302	—	1,023	—
1923 January	1,569	3,486	1,988	7,043	4,868	2,175	1,296	3,471
April	667	1,966	1,878	4,511	2,434	2,077	804	2,881
July	280§	945	1,099	2,324	—	2,324	376	2,700
October	4,667	3,486	1,103	9,256	7,596	1,660	962	2,622
1924 January	1,049	2,966	1,633	5,648	5,064	584	1,268	1,852
April	341	1,512	1,328	3,181	2,532	649	966	1,615
July	160§	674	721	1,555	—	1,555	528	2,083
August	13,217	811	553	14,581	12,518	2,063	373	2,436
September	10,833	2,073	514	13,420	11,380	2,040	633	2,673

October	7,008	4,225	731	10,242	10,242	1,722	1,021	2,743
November	4,226	4,914	1,047	10,187	9,104	1,083	1,444	2,527
December	2,666	4,624	1,319	8,609	7,966	643	1,920	2,563
1925 January	1,780	3,863	1,434	7,077	6,828	249	1,956	2,205
February	1,174	3,075	1,546	5,795	5,690	105	1,958	2,063
March	656	2,237	1,645	4,538	4,552	−14	1,918	1,904
April	341	1,666	1,515	3,522	3,414	108	1,731	1,839
May	28	1,135	1,348	2,511	2,276	235	1,376	1,611
June	67	760	1,124	1,817	1,138	679	1,036	1,715
July	230§	487	878	1,504	—	1,504	764	2,268
August	15,135	1,040	680	16,855	14,762	2,093	556	2,649
September	—				13,420	—	1,044	—
October	7,977	4,499	1,216	13,692	12,078	1,614	1,280	2,894
November	5,318	5,206	1,456	11,980	10,736	1,244	1,660	2,904
December	3,139	5,608	1,718	10,465	9,394	1,071	1,856	2,927
1926 January	2,223	5,176	1,811	9,210	9,052	1,158	1,707	2,865
February	1,560	4,744	1,831	8,135	6,710	1,425	1,636	3,061
March	1,103	4,163	1,768	7,034	5,368	1,666	1,527	3,193
April	816	3,531	1,639	5,986	4,026	1,960	1,388	3,348
May	656	2,965	1,450	5,071	2,684	2,387	1,306	3,693
June	559	2,408	1,268	4,235	1,342	2,893	1,175	4,068
July	510	1,936	1,096	3,542	—	3,542	985	4,527
August	17,721	1,716	921	20,358	16,214	4,144	920	5,064
September	14,777	3,293	937	19,007	14,740	4,267	1,174	5,441
October	10,425	5,470	1,216	17,111	13,266	3,845	1,551	5,396
November	7,079	6,479	1,766	15,324	11,792	3,532	2,397	5,929
December	4,780	6,517	1,498	12,795	10,318	2,477	2,639	4,916
1927 January	3,480	6,070	1,853	11,403	8,844	2,559	2,905	5,464
February||	3,165	5,044	1,668	9,877	7,370	2,507	2,821	5,328

* This table excludes linters, except that an insignificant quantity is included in the import figures.
† Figures for all kinds of cotton.
‡ Seasonally corrected and excluding European and Asiatic mill stocks.
§ The carryover according to the above method was as follows: 1920, 2,171; 1921, 3,779; 1922, 2,615; 1923, 356; 1924, 6; 1925, 0; 1926, 400.
|| Provisional.

Annual table of total stocks at the end of each season (1 August) (1,000 bales)

	1919	1920	1921	1922	1923	1924	1925	1926
Up-country carryover in interior cotton belt	2,193	1,703	3,713	964	280	160	230	510
U.S. warehouse stocks	2,212	2,055	3,723	1,488	945	674	487	1,936
U.S. mill stocks	1,304	1,358	1,111	1,218	1,099	721	787	1,096
Total in U.S.	5,709	5,116	8,547	3,670	2,324	1,555	1,504	3,542
European port stocks (including afloat for Europe)	1,247	1,394	1,695	1,120	376	528	764	985
European mill stocks	305	475	690	838	496	502	787	663
Asiatic mill stocks	?	267*	248	381	185	173	219	250
Total	7,261	7,252	11,180	6,009	3,381	2,758	3,274	5,440
Crop for year†	12,000	13,750	8,442	9,738	10,128	13,639	16,122	17,688
Total available	19,261	21,002	19,622	15,747	13,509	16,397	19,396	23,128
Total carried forward	6,990	10,386	7,066	3,081	2,554	3,141	5,666	—
Consumption for year	12,271	10,616	12,556	12,666	10,955	13,256	13,730	—

* Excluding China.

† For 1919–21 Hester's estimate of the actual growth, made at the beginning of the season, as the official figures for these years are questionable.

Annual table of total stocks in the middle of each season (1 February) (1,000 bales)

	1920	1921	1922	1923	1924	1925	1926	1927
Up-country stocks	3,780	6,788	4,550	1,569	1,049	1,780	2,223	3,480
U.S. warehouse stocks	3,760	5,645	4,618	3,486	2,966	3,863	5,176	6,070
U.S. mill stocks	3,677	1,273	1,675	1,988	1,633	1,434	1,811	1,853
Total in U.S.	11,217	13,706	10,843	7,043	5,648	7,077	9,210	11,403
European port stocks (including afloat)	2,018	1,650	1,575	1,296	1,268	1,956	1,707	2,905
European mill stocks	597	675	740	637	578	755	842	848
Asiatic mill stocks	117*	166*	390	206	203	201	192	269
Total available	13,949	16,197	13,548	9,182	7,697	9,989	11,951	15,425
Total available 1 August preceding	19,261	21,005	19,622	15,747	13,509	16,397	19,396	23,128
Consumption for half-year	5,312	4,808	6,074	6,565	5,812	6,408	7,445	7,703

* Excluding China.

than in the preceding season. In consequence the carryover on Aug. 1st, 1926, amounted to the large total of nearly $5\frac{1}{2}$ million bales. To this has been added a record crop estimated at 17·7 million bales. Thus the total supply of cotton available for the current season approaches 23 million bales. It is possible, however, that owing to the low prices and the lateness of the season, anything up to 500,000 bales may not be harvested. It was not until well on in October that the true magnitude of the current crop was realised, and there has therefore been little enough time for prices to reach a new equilibrium, or for manufacturers to adjust their plans accordingly, while in this country the effects of the coal stoppage caused further difficulties. In the six months to Jan. 31st, 1927, American manufacturers consumed over 254,000 bales more than in the corresponding period in the previous year, and as the increase may reasonably be expected to be of a cumulative nature, it seems likely that the U.S. will increase their consumption for the year by 500–600,000 bales. Owing to the coal stoppage, forwardings to the mills in Great Britain for the cotton year have not yet caught up those of a year ago ($-$146,000 bales up to March 18), but there is not much doubt that this will occur. Meanwhile the Continent has taken a considerably greater amount than last year ($+$461,000 bales up to March 11), and also Japan, etc. ($+$339,000 bales up to March 11), but not much of this has as yet passed into consumption, since the world consumption for the half-year ending Jan. 31st, 1927, was only some 250,000 bales more than in the half-year ending Jan. 31st, 1926. In other words the increase in world consumption is entirely accounted for by the increase in American consumption. It is little more than guesswork to suggest a possible increase in world consumption of about 2 million bales during the whole season 1926–7. This would mean a world consumption of about $15\frac{1}{2}$ million bales, leaving a carry-over of (say) 8 million bales. The price of cotton is now considerably below the cost of production to the average producer, and a campaign is on foot throughout the Southern States to secure a reduction of acreage in the coming season. A figure of 25 per cent is aimed at, but a reduction of 10 per cent will probably prove to be nearer the mark. Even so supplies should be ample through 1927–8 as well as 1926–7.

There are no statistics relating to finished cotton goods except for the United States. While not by any means complete, these statistics afford an interesting comparable series, as will be seen from the following table:—

Finished cotton goods in U.S.

	1,000 yards		Cases	
	Produc-tion	Orders grey yardage	Ship-ments	Stocks
1921 monthly average	85,385	90,154	44,935	36,226
1922 ,, ,,	94,016	95,509	49,102	44,937
1923 ,, ,,	95,098	91,504	48,116	46,166
1924 ,, ,,	77,650	76,105	41,863	43,139
1925 ,, ,,	78,756	76,558	43,691	39,640
1926 January	78,170	87,188	46,679	41,111
February	82,370	85,055	46,922	41,006
March	98,321	97,436	54,452	41,329
April	90,938	79,606	49,301	42,350
May	79,164	69,348	45,715	41,352
June	78,161	65,072	45,272	41,494
July	65,714	67,272	43,724	40,446
August	69,554	75,180	44,336	38,449
September	79,223	84,438	49,312	36,868
October	88,295	79,350	51,010	36,161
November	79,480	76,483	45,941	37,113
December	87,401	77,686	46,827	38,398

II. *Copper*

Stocks of copper consist of (1) refined copper in the United States, which constitutes the main part of the world's floating supply, (2) rough and blister copper in transit to smelters and

Supplies and consumption of copper (tons of 2,240 lb)

	1 January 1920	1 January 1921	1 January 1922	1 January 1923	1 January 1924	1 January 1925	1 January 1926	1 January 1927
North and South America:—								
Refined	313,000	286,000	239,000	133,000	139,000	122,000	65,000	76,000
In process, etc.	175,000	58,000	142,000	175,000	226,000	212,000	215,000	244,000
Allied Govt. stocks	180,000	82,000	Trifling	—	—	—	—	—
Scrap (approximate)	270,000	183,000	90,000	—	—	—	—	—
U.K., Havre, Japan stocks	46,000	55,000	30,000	39,000	37,000	55,000	64,000	47,000
Total	984,000	664,000	501,000	347,000	402,000	389,000	344,000	367,000
Production*	967,000	537,000	888,000	1,266,000	1,357,000	1,418,000	1,475,000	—
Available supply	1,951,000	1,201,000	1,389,000	1,613,000	1,759,000	1,807,000	1,819,000	—
Stock carried forward	664,000	501,000	347,000	402,000	389,000	344,000	367,000	—
Consumption	1,287,000	700,000	1,042,000	1,211,000	1,370,000	1,463,000	1,452,000	—
Price £	115 7 6	71 17 6	66 3 9	64 11 3	60 18 9	66 11 3	59 13 9	56 1 3
Cents per lb	19	12¾	13¾	14¾	12¾	14¼	14	13¼

* American Bureau of Metal Statistics.

refiners in North and South America, and on hand or in process at refineries, (3) refined and rough copper in European and Japanese warehouses. In the years immediately after the War there were also large stocks in the hands of the Allied Governments and in the form of scrap metal.

The table below supplies some more detailed statistics of the principal stocks. In these returns 'American blister' includes all copper in first hands in North and South America which has not been refined and made available for delivery.

Stocks of copper (tons of 2,240 lb)

Beginning of month	American refined*	American blister* (and in process)	U.K. all kinds	Havre	Japan	Total
1921 Jan.	286,000	58,000	11,646	5,968	37,500	399,000
1922 Jan.	239,000	142,000	16,655	4,138	9,300	411,000
1923 Jan.	133,000	175,000	26,780	3,345	9,072	347,000
Oct.	113,000	240,000	28,453	3,891	5,954	391,000
1924 Jan.	139,000	226,000	31,030	1,867	4,405	402,000
April	107,000	212,500	30,852	5,281	5,300	361,000
July	100,000	216,000	36,515	10,225	8,600	371,000
Oct.	122,000	209,000	37,387	7,885	9,000	385,000
1925 Jan.	122,000	212,000	38,419	7,180	9,992	389,000
April	109,200	233,000	44,276	8,341	7,743	403,000
July	81,500	223,500	47,984	6,389	5,832	365,000
Oct.	61,500	220,000	51,285	9,942	5,015	347,000
1926 Jan.	65,200	214,600	56,047	3,013	5,288	344,288
April	67,148	233,813	51,701	4,701	3,624	360,987
July	59,014	245,974	50,967	11,670	3,129	369,754
Oct.	62,622	235,656	39,029	10,682	3,468	351,457
1927 Jan.	76,340	243,871	34,636	8,650	3,500†	366,997
Feb.	83,913	245,923	32,533	8,804	3,500†	374,673
Mar.	93,769	239,563	28,848‡	8,283	3,500†	373,963

* Includes North and South America.
† Provisional figures.
‡ Of which 2,689 tons were refined and 26,159 tons rough copper.

The quarterly figures of American stocks, further analysed, were as follows:—

Stocks of copper in America (tons of 2,000 lb)

Beginning of month	Blister in North America	Blister in South America	In process of refining	Refined stocks	In ore and matte at refineries	Total
1926 Jan.	95,643	7,275	140,168	73,019	17,357	333,462
April	96,440	11,844	153,632	75,206	11,560	348,682
July	100,106	8,393	166,839	66,096	15,436	356,870
Oct.	98,595	7,083	157,074	70,137	13,730	346,619
1927 Jan.	104,927	9,910	157,505	85,501	11,549	369,392

The year 1926 was a somewhat eventful one for copper. The long-projected 'Copper Exporters Incorporated', by which controllers of copper supplies in America combined with the bulk, but not all, of the producers in the rest of the world to maintain a controlled price outside the United States, was successfully launched. This has not prevented copper, however, from falling to a lower price than for many years past—lower even than was usual before the War.

The figures for the year 1926 given above show that production again exceeded in volume all previous records, whilst consumption was maintained practically on the 1925 level. Increased output has come almost entirely from U.S., other countries showing reduced or stationary outputs. The African output from Katanga has not during 1926 fulfilled expectations. The normal increase in consumption was prevented by the slump in Germany early in 1926, the copper import surplus into Germany for 1926 falling from 193,000 metric tons to 121,000 metric tons. In Great Britain the apparent consumption, as deduced by the London Metal Exchange, increased from 115,189 long tons to 122,122 long tons, in spite of the coal strike. The net result has been a very slight increase in world stocks.

The fall in prices has been chiefly due, not to any real dis-equilibrium between demand and supply, but to an increasing appreciation of the low cost of production of a large part of the world supply of copper in modern conditions. Twenty years ago Jackling's processes brought the low-grade porphyry coppers within the field of supply, and for the past ten years the improvement of metallurgical practice has been producing a cumulative effect. There are still some high-cost producers to be squeezed out, but some authorities maintain that at least 60 per cent of the world's output is now produced at a cost as low as £45 per ton. Certainly it seems quite possible that the normal price for standard copper in the future will not exceed £50 per ton. The production costs of the big producers in South America are below 10 cents per pound, equivalent to well under £40 per ton for standard copper. During the period 1922–4, 55 per cent of the production in the U.S. cost under 12 cents per pound and averaged about 10 cents per pound.

The following table of the growth of the production and con-sumption of copper, based on the reports of the American Bureau of Metal Statistics (some of which differ slightly from those used above), is interesting:—

Rates of increase in world production and consumption of copper
(assuming 1923 production as 100)

	Production, per cent	Consumption, per cent	Average price, cents per pound
1923	100·0	95·8	14·421
1924	107·7	108·8	13·024
1925	112·1	115·1	14·042
1926	115·1	115·2	13·875
Annual average increase	5·03	5·07	—
Weighted average price	—	—	13·837

Country	1916*	1922	1923	1924	1925	1926†
United States	971,123	511,970	754,000	819,000	854,000	984,000
Mexico	60,751	29,842	60,538	57,139	59,123	42,600
Canada	52,880	25,300	40,230	50,072	56,239	33,700
Cuba	8,613	11,788	11,963	12,742	13,128	—
Bolivia	5,675	10,154	11,744	8,200	7,500	—
Chile	78,559	142,830	201,042	208,964	209,654	} 256,000
Peru	47,452	40,133	48,684	38,798	41,180	} —
Venezuela	1,300	1,075	1,175	1,230	1,500	—
Europe	105,434	86,950	115,492	120,618	130,957	104,000
Asia	110,900	60,825	66,227	71,300	77,013	77,000
Australasia	43,920	13,754	19,995	15,711	13,800	10,500
Africa	43,876	58,219	80,410	115,300	118,180	90,000
Other countries	3,307	3,307	3,307	4,409	4,409	52,200
World total	1,533,810	996,147	1,414,807	1,523,483	1,586,683	1,650,000

* War peak of production in United States was in 1916. War peak of world production was in 1917, the total being 1,580,475 tons.
† 1926 figures partly estimated; figures for individual countries not comparablewith figures for other years, as blister copper is not segregated according to countries of origin.

Estimates made by the American Bureau of Metal Statistics for consumption of copper in 1924 and 1925 are shown below in *metric* tons. (Most of the tables given above are in *long* tons.)

	1924	1925
United States	686,400	738,300
Canada	15,400	11,500
Total North America	701,800	749,800
Austria	13,900	17,000
Belgium	11,100	10,600
Czechoslovakia	12,300	15,700
France	132,300	121,600
Germany	131,600	232,700
Great Britain	135,900	137,100
Italy	52,900	63,500
Russia*	11,000	12,000
Spain	6,500	9,100
Sweden	18,100	18,000
Other Europe	27,500	25,000
Total Europe	553,000	662,300
Japan	63,500	67,900
Other Asia*	31,600	10,000
Total Asia	95,100	77,900
Africa*	12,000	12,000
Australia	9,700	9,000
Total world consumption	1,371,600	1,511,000
World production	1,373,600	1,440,300

* Metallgesellschaft for 1924.

Estimates of production of copper by the same authority, also in *metric* tons, are as above.

III. *Tin*

The total stocks of tin and tin ore are made up of:—

(1) The 'visible supply' as defined by the monthly returns of the London Metal Exchange, namely, (*a*) stocks landing or

warehoused in Great Britain, the United States and Holland, (*b*) tin afloat to Great Britain, the United States and Europe from the Straits, Batavia and China, and (*c*) tin afloat to Great Britain and the United States from China. Monthly returns of the 'visible supply' are also compiled by Messrs Ricard and Freiwald and by Messrs A. Strauss and Co., each on a slightly different basis from that of the Metal Exchange. The figures of the London Metal Exchange given below are in replacement of those of Messrs Strauss given in previous issues of this *Bulletin*.

(2) Stocks of tin and tin ore in the Straits Settlements, the Dutch Indies, China and Hong Kong.

(3) Stocks of tin ore afloat from Bolivia and Nigeria to Europe and in course of smelting.

(4) 'Invisible' stocks in the hands of consumers, etc.

(1) *The Visible Supply.* It will be noticed that the 'visible supply' figures, which are those commonly quoted, cover a wider field than that usually meant by 'stocks', since they include tin in transit which is in no sense available for consumption. It follows that the 'visible supply' of tin can never fall to zero, or even fall below (say) 9,000–12,000 tons, unless a total breakdown of current supplies is impending from the sources of production. On the other hand, they do not include the total aggregate of tin and tin ore in the widest interpretation. They represent a rather arbitrary compromise between prospective supplies and stocks available for consumption. The result is that they are highly misleading from month to month, fluctuating with the chance dates of shipments from the East, etc., which have no real bearing on the position. Figures for stocks in the limited sense, i.e. landing or warehoused in the countries of consumption, will therefore be given separately, and also some material to correct the misleading inferences which might be drawn from the 'visible supply' figures as to the short-period prospective supplies at any time.

The distribution of the immediately available stocks at the end of each year [month] was as follows:—

Available stocks of tin in the chief countries of consumption (U.K.,
U.S., and Holland) (tons of 2,240 lb)

End of month	1923	1924	1925	1926	1927
January	12,911	8,007	9,371	4,511	5,051
February	10,937	7,706	9,593	5,373	3,962
March	11,385	7,154	10,489	4,918	
April	10,373	10,189	7,313	3,494	
May	9,737	8,900	6,692	3,916	
June	8,954	9,091	8,554	4,908	
July	8,368	10,046	7,942	4,126	
August	9,004	10,185	8,596	3,994	
September	7,383	10,497	6,721	3,693	
October	8,588	7,721	5,896	3,344	
November	7,466	7,615	5,410	3,778	
December	7,870	9,262	5,863	4,170	

The distribution of these stocks at the end of each year was
as follows:—

31 December	1923	1924	1925	1926
U.K.: warehoused	3,892	5,241	2,387	1,179
„ landing	427	579	774	294
U.S.: warehoused and landing	1,652	2,844	2,654	1,909
Holland: warehoused	1,899	598	48	788

Since the total consumption of tin is 11,000–12,000 tons
monthly, the stocks available for consumers in 1923 amounted to
about 10 days' consumption, as compared with a month's supply
at the beginning of 1923. At the end of 1926 warehouse stocks,
i.e. excluding tin landing which was not, strictly speaking, available for consumption, amounted to 2,641 tons, and at the end
of Feb., 1927, to 1,823 tons, or less than a week's consumption.

469

Thus consumers of tin are entirely dependent on supplies coming forward regularly from the countries of production.

The 'visible supply' of tin (tons of 2,240 lb)*

End of month	1923	1924	1925	1926	1927
January	25,765	24,372	22,949	16,787	15,342
February	25,157	21,835	23,591	16,239	14,221
March	24,622	23,275	19,623	14,280	
April	22,116	19,023	18,105	15,516	
May	22,187	19,711	20,897	18,045	
June	21,297	20,094	19,797	15,831	
July	20,019	20,161	19,857	13,777	
August	18,754	21,302	20,000	13,352	
September	19,864	20,233	17,642	14,379	
October	20,567	18,971	15,770	14,841	
November	19,520	20,977	18,199	15,257	
December	21,011	25,088	18,029	16,326	

* London Metal Exchange figures.

(2) *Stocks in the East.* The main source of error in the figures just given as a true indication of the position is the fact that they neglect entirely the stocks of tin in the East, whence the bulk of the world's supplies are drawn. As described in earlier memoranda, these stocks were abnormally swollen from 1920 to 1925 by tin held mainly by the Straits and Dutch Indies Governments, under the Bandoeng Agreement. The last lots of this tin were sold before the end of 1924, but the trade figures show that some 3,000 tons were not shipped, and therefore did not enter into the 'visible supply', until 1925. Apart from the disposal of these exceptional stocks, the trade figures indicate that other more normal stocks of tin and of ore in the Straits were drawn upon in 1926, as shown below.

At the end of 1926 the tin carried over in the Straits was reported as being approximately 1,700 tons. Ore stocks in the

Tons of 2,240 lb

	Imports of tin into the Straits	Exports of tin from the Straits	Reduction of Straits stocks
1923	65,335	69,119	3,784
1924	74,109	79,940	5,831
1925	76,630	78,819	2,189
1926	74,362	76,474	2,112

hands of smelters in the Straits seem to have been reduced by some 500 tons during 1926. Thus the total stocks would appear to have been, roughly, as follows:—

	Tons		Tons
End of 1922	14,600	End of 1925	3,800
1923	10,800	1926	1,700
1924	5,000		

Of these stocks, at the end of 1922, 13,600 tons were held under the Bandoeng Pool, in addition to 4,000 tons held in the Dutch Indies.

As regard the Dutch Indies, part of the supplies (the tin from Billiton) is forwarded regularly to the Straits to be smelted there. The rest (the tin from Banca) is smelted locally and shipped direct, mainly to Europe. These shipments are more irregular than the production, depending on the selling policy of the Dutch Government. This is a further cause of error in the visible supply statistics, though probably not to the extent of more than (say) 500 tons in any month. But, apart from the Bandoeng Pool stocks now exhausted, there are no statistics.

As regards supplies from China, about half the production has found its way recently to U.K. and U.S.A. Estimates of stocks, mainly in Hong Kong, are only available irregularly. Some figures are given below.

471

Total stocks of tin (tons of 2,240 lb)

End of year	1922	1923	1924	1925	1926
Straits Pool tin	13,600	9,500	3,000	—	—
„ other stocks	500	1,800	2,500	3,300	1,700
„ surplus ore	500	500	500	500	—
Dutch Indies Pool	4,000	2,000	—	—	—
China	2,300	6,600	800	200	300
'Visible supply'	25,300	21,000	25,100	18,000	16,300
Grand total	47,200	35,400	31,900	22,000	18,300

This is the best available aggregate of tin supplies, apart from tin in the hands of smelters on the one hand and of consumers on the other. Apart from exceptional figures in isolated months, 13,000 tons is probably the lowest to which this total can fall, having regard to the amount of tin necessarily afloat. Thus the true surplus has fallen during the past four years from about 34,000 tons to 5,000 tons. A further fall of 5,000 tons, which is less than a fortnight's consumption, would therefore represent a total exhaustion of reserves.

(3) *Bolivian and Nigerian tin afloat and with the smelters.* If we allow two months from the date of shipment from Bolivia to the time of delivery in refined form on the London market, some 5,000 tons of tin are normally thus in transit, but the actual figure may vary from (say) 4,000 tons to 8,000 tons. The corresponding variations for Nigerian tin in transit are on a much smaller scale. These fluctuations average out, of course, over a period of time, but may considerably affect the statistics of visible supply between one month and another. During 1927 there may be some net addition to the supplies available over and above any increased production from the mines, on account of increased smelting capacity, owing to the resumption of operations by the German tin smelters, enabling the ore to be dealt with somewhat more rapidly. An addition of this kind, however, obviously happens once for all and cannot be repeated.

Shipments of Bolivian ore to Germany rose from 282 tons in 1925 to 3,734 tons in 1926. In 1927 German smelters may conceivably handle 5,000 tons of tin. Moreover, the German smelters may be able to deal with ore of a lower grade than the English smelters have cared to handle. There is also increased smelting capacity in the East, both actual and prospective. As regards the magnitude of this influence, it would be optimistic to expect in 1927 an increased supply of refined tin, at the expense of a corresponding reduction of ore stocks in smelters' hands, exceeding 1,000–2,000 tons at the most.

(4) *'Invisible' stocks in the hands of consumers, etc.* Probably a more important influence in accelerating supplies and decreasing the aggregate of 'invisible' stocks at all stages from the producer to the consumer is to be found in the development of a 'backwardation' on forward tin as against spot tin, i.e. in the fact that recently tin for delivery in three months has been standing at a price appreciably lower than tin for immediate delivery. This means on the one hand that the producers and smelters can gain the difference by hastening forward their supplies of refined metal, and on the other hand that consumers can save the difference by keeping their stocks as low as possible and covering their known prospective requirements by buying forward instead of keeping the actual metal on hand.

For short periods recently the 'backwardation' has amounted to as much as £17 per ton per three months and has recently averaged about £13. The average figures over each year have been as follows.

	Average price of spot tin	Average price of 3 months' tin	Spot tin above (+) or below (−) forward tin
	£ s. d.	£ s. d.	£ s. d.
1922	159 10 9	160 13 11	−1 3 2
1923	202 5 0	202 15 4	−0 10 4
1924	248 17 4	249 10 6½	−0 13 2½
1925	261 1 8½	262 5 9½	−1 4 1
1926	291 3 0½	284 7 7	+6 15 5½

The shift shown in these figures from a small 'contango' (i.e. a premium) on forward tin in previous years to a substantial 'backwardation' (i.e. a discount) in 1926 has afforded a considerable incentive during the year to economise stocks of ore in the hands of smelters and stocks of tin in the hands of consumers, with the result that the real excess of current consumption over current production has probably been somewhat greater than has appeared. Tin no longer 'pays for its keep', as it did in the days of a 'contango'. Indeed at present it costs £1 per ton a week to hold a reserve stock of tin in addition to the cost of interest, insurance and storage.

The principal changes in the volume of production have been approximately, as follows:—

World's tin production (tons of 2,240 lb)

	1923	1924	1925	1926
Malay States	39,500	46,500	48,000	48,000
Dutch Indies	28,000	30,000	31,000	31,500
Siam and Borneo	8,000	9,000	8,000	8,000
China	8,500	7,500	8,000	6,500
Australia	2,000	2,000	2,500	2,500
Nigeria	6,000	6,000	6,000	6,500
S. Africa	1,000	1,000	1,000	1,000
Cornwall	1,000	2,000	2,500	2,500
Bolivia	28,500	29,000	33,000	32,000
Elsewhere	1,500	1,500	2,000	2,000
Total	124,000	134,500	142,000	140,500

Thus the hopes expressed a year ago of a modest increase in supplies in 1926 have been disappointed.

On the side of consumption the situation in 1926 was saved by the slump in Germany in the early part of the year and the coal strike in Great Britain in the second half of the year. If Germany had taken tin in the first half of the year at the same rate as in the second half, and Great Britain had taken tin in the second half at the same rate as in the first half, the supplies would not have been sufficient to go round.

According to the London Metal Exchange figures of the 'apparent consumption' in Great Britain, the amount taken fell by 6,583 tons from 24,879 tons in 1925 to 18,296 tons in 1926. German net imports fell off by 2,600 tons and French imports by 700 tons. Deliveries in the United States, on the other hand, increased by 1,600 tons, and in the rest of the world were virtually unchanged, leaving the total consumption in 1926 about 7,000 tons less than in 1925, as follows:—

Consumption of tin (tons of 2,240 lb)

	1925	1926
Great Britain	25,000	18,500
United States	76,500	78,000
Germany	8,000	5,500
France	11,500	11,000
Asia	9,000	9,000
Other countries	22,000	22,000
Total	152,000	144,000

We estimate recent production and consumption of tin in the aggregate as follows:—

Tons of 2,240 lb

Year	Production	Consumption	Stocks at end of year
1923	124,000	133,500	35,500
1924	134,500	138,000	32,000
1925	142,000	152,000	22,000
1926	140,500	144,000	18,500*

* Of which 13,685 tons afloat or landing.

475

There seems to be no possibility of meeting a full demand for tin in 1927 from Great Britain, the United States and Germany simultaneously.

IV. *Lead*

Stocks in the United Kingdom in Metal Exchange warehouses are still negligible. Nevertheless there was probably as much as 20,000 tons of lead in outside warehouses at the end of 1926, which do not appear in the statistics. Those in the United States and Mexico have increased from round about 80,000 to 90,000 tons to over 100,000 tons. The latter figures, however, are not for refined lead, but include lead in ore, base bullion, in transit and in process, as well as refined lead, which is only a small proportion of the total. At the end of 1926 there were some surplus stocks of refined lead in the world for the first time for several years. Even so the aggregate surplus in all countries probably did not exceed 50,000 tons, that is to say, less than 5 per cent of the annual output. The existence of this surplus was chiefly due to a falling off in German consumption which, after rising from 84,000 metric tons in 1924 to 172,000 metric tons in 1925, fell to about 141,000 tons in 1926.

Production of lead (tons of 2,240 lb)

	1923	1924	1925	1926
United States	404,748	471,005	511,000	535,000
Mexico	164,502	158,796	181,000	199,000
Canada	48,124	75,298	111,000	124,000
Spain and Tunis	65,004	104,534	115,000	119,000
Italy	16,804	21,712	16,000	22,000
Australia	122,779	125,557	151,000	153,000
Burma	45,749	51,758	48,000	54,000
Rhodesia	10,859	6,253	3,000	4,000
Total	878,569	1,014,913	1,136,000	1,210,000

Stocks of lead in U.S., U.K., and Mexico (tons of 2,240 lb)

Beginning of month	1924			1925			1926		
	U.S. and Mexico*	U.K.†	Total	U.S. and Mexico*	U.K.†	Total	U.S. and Mexico*	U.K.†	Total
January	93,005	1,183	94,188	77,854	58	77,912	93,400	265	93,665
February	89,759	296	90,055	90,112	130	90,242	94,100	237	94,337
March	90,376	57	90,434	94,475	136	94,611	100,600	265	100,865
April	92,292	27	92,319	93,557	14	93,571	105,000	439	105,439
May	98,585	20	98,605	90,146	34	90,180	107,900	1,114	109,014
June	98,145	7	98,152	87,020	74	87,094	109,900	1,025	110,925
July	97,107	6	97,113	86,319	141	86,460	106,000	191	106,191
August	94,161	3	94,164	81,776	102	81,878	99,500	202	99,702
September	92,372	19	92,391	86,580	5	86,585	101,000	58	101,058
October	87,747	65	87,812	93,700	5	93,705	105,600	225	105,825
November	87,028	1	87,029	95,500	95	95,595	—	1,299	—
December	87,822	3	87,825	94,300	5	94,305	—	1,677	—

* Stocks of ore, matte, base bullion and refined lead in the hands of those concerns which report to the American Bureau of Metal Statistics.
† Metal Exchange figures.

The figures above issued by the American Bureau of Metal Statistics apply to the principal lead-producing countries of the world, which, in 1924, furnished 79 per cent of the world's total lead output.

The American Bureau estimates the total world production in 1926 at 1,537,000 tons as compared with 1,464,000 tons in 1925.

Thus high prices have called forth a production increasing, on the average of recent years, by about 10 per cent per annum, sufficient to satisfy the high level of consumption. It looks as if any further material increase in production would outrun demand for the time being and bring about a reaction in prices. The production of the seven countries, United States, Mexico, Canada, Spain, Australia, Burma, and Rhodesia (about 77 per cent of the world's output) has been approximately as follows in recent years:—

Production in principal areas

Year	Tons	Year	Tons
1920	629,464	1924	992,857
1921	615,178	1925	1,120,000
1922	762,500	1926	1,188,000
1923	861,607		

V. *Spelter (Zinc)*

Monthly statistics are available of stocks in public warehouses in the United States and in the United Kingdom as given below.

While these stocks fell during 1925 to the lowest figures recorded in recent years, representing not more than a few days' consumption, there was a slight recovery during 1926.

The material increase in production in 1925, amounting to about 13 per cent in the principal producing countries as compared with 1924, has been followed by a further increase of 11 per cent in 1926. According to Rudolf Wolff & Company the world's output of virgin spelter was 451,800 tons in 1921,

688,520 in 1922, 960,168 in 1923, 997,749 in 1924, 1,130,392 in 1925, and 1,231,762 in 1926.

The American Bureau of Metal Statistics estimates the world's output at 1,112,900 tons (2,240 lb) in 1925, and 1,225,400 tons in 1926.

According to figures issued by the latter authority the production of spelter by countries, which furnish about 86 per cent of the world's output, has been as follows:—

Production of spelter (tons of 2,240 lb)

	1923	1924	1925	1926
United States	474,284	478,430	528,000	570,000
Canada	27,093	24,679	34,000	55,000
Belgium	145,733	160,411	169,000	187,000
Germany (including Polish Silesia)	110,396	102,989*	153,000	171,000
Australia	40,248	46,601	46,000	47,000
Great Britain	31,279	38,480	38,000	18,000
Total	829,032	851,591	968,000	1,048,000

* Probably under-estimated.

The increased production was called forth at first by high prices. With the return of stocks, however, to a more normal level by the end of 1926, prices fell considerably and stood early in February 1927 at a lower figure than for some time past. Spelter is a commodity with a definite cost of production, and the output adjusts itself to the demand within a few months. It would seem that the great increase in output by as much as 25 per cent in 1926 as compared with 1924 has temporarily outrun demand by some small amount, perhaps by 2 per cent.

Mr A. J. M. Sharpe, Foreign Correspondent of the American Zinc Institute, has estimated world stocks at recent dates as below [p. 481].

479

U.K. and U.S. stocks of spelter (tons of 2,240 lb)

End of month	1922			1923			1924			1925			1926		
	U.S.	U.K.	Total	U.S.	U.K.	Total	U.S.	U.K.	Total	U.S.	U.K.	Total	U.S.	U.K.	Total
January	58,635	11,412	70,047	14,794	394	15,188	36,330	1,088	37,418	16,960	398	17,358	12,770	287	13,057
February	57,250	8,335	65,585	9,700	197	9,897	33,200	975	34,175	14,910	331	15,241	18,160	391	18,551
March	53,800	6,375	60,175	8,947	838	9,785	28,600	858	29,458	15,350	315	15,665	18,360	422	18,782
April	46,186	6,067	52,253	8,014	1,238	9,252	29,270	673	29,943	16,370	227	16,597	23,200	1,063	24,263
May	36,080	5,338	41,418	11,624	1,702	13,326	37,820	628	38,448	18,940	389	19,329	26,730	951	27,681
June	26,407	4,662	31,069	15,333	1,679	17,012	44,360	671	45,031	20,460	506	20,966	23,000	1,052	24,052
July	25,552	4,289	29,841	18,896	1,198	20,094	47,060	352	47,412	18,550	714	19,264	20,520	993	21,513
August	19,311	3,977	23,288	23,635	1,007	24,642	45,470	442	45,912	15,200	656	15,856	16,220	1,455	17,675
September	16,791	3,668	20,459	20,440	803	21,243	40,820	814	41,634	10,530	561	11,091	14,020	1,136	15,156
October	16,110	2,670	18,780	23,024	1,034	24,058	34,330	675	35,005	6,670	333	7,003	14,200	999	15,199
November	17,408	852	18,260	27,600	1,390	28,990	24,030	541	24,571	6,170	621	6,791	12,930	970	13,900
December	16,296	631	16,927	32,660	1,190	33,850	18,930	396	19,326	8,300	269	8,569	19,540	922	20,462

World stocks 1925-6 (metric tons)

	1 Sept. 1925	1 Dec. 1925	1 May 1926	1 July 1926	1 Nov. 1926	31 Dec. 1926
United States	15,490	6,300	23,600	23,400	14,400	19,800
Germany and Poland	5,400	15,000	7,500	6,500	6,000	9,500
Canada	700	1,000	2,200	2,100	2,300	3,200
Great Britain	600	1,000	1,800	1,200	1,000	1,000
Belgium	1,700	1,900	2,600	1,800	2,400	4,000
France	800	800	1,000	1,200	1,000	1,500
Scandinavia	200	200	200	200	200	200
Australia*	2,000	2,000	2,200	2,200	2,200	2,400
Far East	500	500	500	500	500	500
Elsewhere	500	500	1,500	1,500	1,500	1,500
Total	27,890	29,200	43,100	40,600	31,500	43,600

* Including unsold shipments afloat.

VI. *Rubber*

The stocks of rubber are held mainly:—

(1) On plantations, etc. within the restricted area of Malaya.

(2) In Singapore and Penang.

(3) Afloat.

(4) In London and Liverpool.

(5) In U.S.A. warehouses and factories.

In addition relatively insignificant stocks are held:—

(6) In Ceylon and India.

(7) In Dutch East Indies.

(8) In Para (Brazil).

(9) In Amsterdam and Antwerp.

Monthly figures are only available for 3 and 4, but since 1923 quarterly figures are available for all except 1. The table below is based on yearly and half-yearly estimates of the total world stocks in the chief centres at the end of 1920, 1921, and 1922: for 1923 some quarterly returns are available also; and since

World's rubber stocks (exclusive of stock on estates) (1,000 tons)

End of:	United Kingdom*	United States†	Singapore and Penang	Ceylon and India	Dutch East Indies	Para (Brazil)	Amsterdam and Antwerp	Afloat	Approximate total
1920	56	76	35	?	?	?	?	37	(204)‡ 219§–229*
1921	80	52	40	?	?	?	?	37	(209)‡ 224§–244*
1922	81	90	55	?	?	?	?	45	(271)‡ 286§–306*
1923 March	79	87	21	3·5	9	0·6	1·0	48	249
June	64	101	46	?	?	?	?	52	(263)‡ 278§
September	68	90	27	4·0	10	0·9	1·2	43	244
December	75	73	38	4·0	10	?	2·5	52	254
1924 March	70	70	21	3·0	10	1·0	1·1	50	226
June	65	60	20	3·0	10	1·0	1·2	48	208
September	54	56	20	3·5	7	0·8	0·6	54	196
December	36	63	19	4·0	5	0·9	0·3	53	181
1925 March	23	55	17	4·0	5	1·2	0·1	50	155
June	7	40	16	3·0	3	0·5	0·2	59	129
September	7	45	16	4·0	5	1·1	0·3	63	141
December	7	74	20	4·5	5	1·5	0·2	70	182
1926 March	16	61	18	4·5	7	2·0	0·2	74	183
June	28	60	19	4·5	7	1·8	0·8	72	193
September	42	62	26	4·5	8	2·1	1·3	67	213
December	59	72	26	5·5	7	1·5	1·1	77	259

* Including an estimate of stocks in private warehouses except in the figures for 1920, 1921, and 1922. The totals for these years were therefore certainly higher than the figures shown, and should perhaps be increased by 10,000 tons in 1920, and by 15–20,000 tons in 1921 and 1922.

† Returns cover 90–95 per cent of the whole.   ‡ These figures in brackets give the actual total of stocks quoted.

§ These figures include an estimate of 15,000 tons for the unknown stocks in Ceylon, Dutch East Indies, Para, and at Amsterdam and Antwerp. This has been done in order to secure a more comparable series.

March 1924 the figures are reproduced from a table given in *The Rubber Quarterly*.

The following are the estimates of production and consumption of rubber in recent years:—

Year	Production (1,000 tons)	Consumption (1,000 tons)	Apparent increase or decrease in stocks	Recorded change in stocks
1919	339	335	—	—
1920	368	290	—	—
1921	293	292	+ 1	+15
1922	395*	408	− 13	+62
1923	382	434	− 52	− 52
1924	420	475	− 55	− 73
1925	520	540	− 20	+ 1
1926	610	545	+65	+77

* This figure should probably be higher.

The reconciliation of statistics of production and consumption with the recorded changes in the world's stocks is no easy task, since not one of the three figures for any year can be regarded as strictly accurate. It is now, however, quite clear that the 1925 production figure of 574,000 tons, as quoted in the last *Bulletin* on the authority of the American Rubber Association, is enormously too high. A figure of round about 520,000 tons is now reasonably well agreed by the different authorities. With this correction the statistics of production and consumption in 1924 and 1925 can be reconciled with the total change in stocks over the two years together, though not for each year separately. In view of the fact that stocks were changing rapidly throughout these two years, and also in the months immediately preceding and following, insistence on particular dates is unreasonable, and therefore this reconciliation over the period as a whole may be regarded as satisfactory. But these figures do not, of course, take account of manufacturers' stocks, and if these stocks were considerably increased in 1925, it is possible that the 'actual' consumption into manufacture in that year was not as great as 540,000 tons. This possibility is of importance in the reconciliation of the figures for 1926. There appears to be tolerable agree-

U.S. stocks of tyres and tubes (1,000,000)

End of month	Pneumatic tyres	Inner tubes
1921 September	3·3	3·8
December	3·7	4·7
1922 March	5·2	7·0
June	5·0	6·2
September	4·6	5·2
December	4·6	5·7
1923 March	5·7	7·7
June	7·0	8·9
September	5·4	6·5
December	4·3	6·3
1924 March	5·8	8·1
June	5·8	8·2
September	4·5	6·0
December	5·6	8·3
1925 March	7·1	10·7
June	5·4	7·8
September	5·8	7·5
December	6·1	8·5
1926 March	9·0	14·3
June	9·0	15·2
September	7·0	11·5
December	7·8	12·1

ment on the production figure, but in view of the fairly steady annual increase of rather over 10 per cent in consumption during recent years, it is a little difficult to believe that an abrupt halt has occurred in 1926. Lieut.-Col. Kunhardt, in a recent review of the rubber position, adduces considerable evidence relating to the U.S.A., in support of the hypothesis that

it is far safer to try and estimate the real wear and tear consumption of the commodity on the assumption that it is increasing steadily at a fairly constant average rate per annum, rather than to allow oneself to be influenced too much by the imports of raw rubber into consuming countries, or its 'absorption' by manufacturers in a single year.

On this basis Lieut.-Col. Kunhardt estimates the true consumption in 1925 as 525,000 tons, and in 1926 as 580,000 tons. He believes that manufacturers have been drawing heavily on their stocks during 1926, which are now, therefore, very much below normal. If the statistics of visible stocks and production are in any way to be relied upon, a consumption figure of 580,000 tons necessitates the belief that manufacturers' stocks were as much as 50,000 tons higher at the beginning of 1926 than at the end. This seems hardly credible.

Lieut.-Col. Kunhardt seems to have underestimated the recently developed importance of reclaimed rubber. The American Rubber Association estimate the production of reclaimed rubber as follows: 1924, 76,000 tons; 1925, 124,000 tons; 1926, 165,000 tons. The hypothesis of an annual growth of rather over 10 per cent implies either that reclaimed rubber production is a constant, or that the actual consumption growth of new and reclaimed together has increased by much more than 10 per cent in the last two years. On the assumption that the normal expansion of total consumption is about 10 per cent, the increase would be about 47,000 tons in 1925 and 52,000 tons in 1926. In 1925 the increased production of reclaimed was 47,000 tons, and in 1926 40,000 tons. But in 1925 the apparent consumption of new rubber increased by 65,000 tons. In other words, either there was far more than a 10 per cent increase in 1925, or manufacturers must have built up their stocks to the tune of 50–60,000 tons. Since, as we have said of the reverse movement, this latter change is hardly credible, we come to the conclusion that the 1925 consumption was abnormally great.

Equally there was in reality no abrupt check to the total consumption of all kinds of rubber in 1926, since practically the full normal expansion was provided by increased supplies of reclaimed rubber. There was, however, an abrupt check to the consumption of new rubber.

Unless there can be some certainty as to the consumption figure for 1926, it is almost impossible to make any forecast of the position at the end of 1927. The production of reclaimed has varied more or less directly with the price of new rubber, though the time-lag is considerable. On the other hand, the wear of old rubber reclaimed by the newest methods has been found better than had been expected. On the balance of considerations, the 1927 production of reclaimed may not be much greater than in 1926. Any large expansion of consumption in 1927 must therefore be met by larger supplies of new rubber. The 10 per cent normal expansion would bring consumption in 1927 up to 600,000 tons. At present trade prospects in the U.S.A. do not suggest a year of such striking prosperity as 1925, and in general a 10 per cent expansion does not seem an under-estimate. Production in 1927 largely depends on the quotas allowed under the Restriction Scheme. It is now clear that Malaya cannot produce more than about 90 per cent of standard even with permissible exports at 100 per cent. In January the restriction was 80 per cent, and in the present period (Feb.–April) it is 70 per cent, but as the result of unused licences actual exports may show little decline. As the present accumulation of licences is used up, however, restriction will actually begin to operate. Taking all reasonably possible variations in average price with their effect on restriction, world production in 1927 must lie between 625,000 and 540,000 tons. The crude but serviceable method of splitting the difference gives production at about 580,000 tons. The deficiency of 20,000 tons as compared with the estimated consumption could easily be met from stocks, which could, in fact, be reduced by 60,000 tons and still leave more than two months' supply, excluding rubber afloat. Thus even if available

486

supplies sink to the minimum, which at the present level of prices in relation to the Restriction Scheme seems quite possible, there would be no inconvenient shortage.

Unless all the available statistics are quite untrustworthy, we do not see any reason to anticipate another acute shortage during 1927. On the other hand, the steady additions to stocks should soon come to an end. Thus it seems possible that the Colonial Office will achieve their ideal of stability within a few pence on either side of 1*s*. 9*d*. per pound.

VII. *Sugar*

In the case of this commodity it is necessary to restrict ourselves to 'visible' supplies, accurate estimates of stocks held up by producers in the fairly numerous different sources of supply not being available. Nevertheless, this limitation is not so serious as it would be in the case of many commodities, because, on the

Table I. Total visible supply of sugar (1,000 tons)

First half of month	1913	1914	1922‡	1923	1924	1925	1926	1927
Jan.	3,234	3,711	2,761	2,433	2,255	2,708	3,709	3,307
Feb.	4,043	4,323	2,543	2,511	2,357	2,950	3,802	
March	4,141	4,279	2,559	2,603	2,402	2,844	3,907	
April	4,006	4,192	2,479	2,501	2,460	2,891	4,064	
May	3,869	4,032	2,587	2,472	2,658	3,060	4,198	
June	3,732	3,792	2,275	2,278	2,509	2,950	3,882	
July	3,228	3,244	1,903	2,005	2,086	2,560	3,452	
Aug.	3,426	2,668	1,580	1,630	1,560	2,013	2,703	
Sept.	1,813	*	1,180	1,267	982	1,612	2,000	
Oct.	1,259		868	791	542	1,211	1,428	
Nov.	739		1,248	1,089	1,318	2,005	1,998	
Dec.	1,900		2,077	1,951	2,364	3,265	3,176	

* No figures available between this date and March 1920.
† For this and subsequent years, figures relate to as near the first of the month as possible.

Table II. Distribution of sugar stocks (1,000 tons)

Beginning of month	Germany	Czecho-Slovakia	France	Holland	Belgium	United Kingdom	Total Europe	United States (ports)	Cuba (ports)	Grand total
1922 January	808	425	177	158	128	176	1,872	45	844	2,761
April	495	262	104	177	71	218	1,327	222	930	2,479
July	216	83	61	90	30	368	848	193	862	1,903
October	37	6	45	52	12	272	424	128	316	868
December	772	470	176	185	51	334	1,988	40	49	2,077
1923 January	1,002	470	240	224	128	312	2,376	12	45	2,433
April	736	261	148	144	57	286	1,632	215	654	2,501
July	516	107	109	79	35	405	1,251	164	590	2,005
October	102	9	42	16	15	256	440	110	241	791
December	744	593	208	124	51	164	1,884	36	31	1,951
1924 January	908	546	291	154	143	164	2,206	27	22	2,255
April	718	378	127	83	63	264	1,633	167	660	2,460
July	488	113	78	67	38	322	1,106	192	788	2,086
October	2	7	47	22	11	150	239	76	227	542
December	874	706	305	198	62	154	2,299	24	41	2,364

1925	January	978	769	468	219	62	172	2,668	16	24	2,708
	April	618	494	373	115	166	194	1,960	128	803	2,891
	July	268	235	158	92	83	353	1,189	277	1,094	2,560
	October	18	35	47	80	18	294	482	135	594	1,211
	November	422	388	173	159	59	280	1,481	63	461	2,005
	December	1,047	780	378	235	168	306	2,914	59	292	3,265
1926	January	1,210	934	487	228	223	434	3,516	61	132	3,709
	February	1,143	900	425	236	205	477	3,386	52	364	3,802
	March	1,050	790	378	232	175	481	3,106	117	684	3,907
	April	927	680	325	164	148	505	2,749	208	1,107	4,064
	May	808	566	276	165	122	506	2,443	303	1,452	4,198
	June	694	447	234	135	85	475	2,070	370	1,442	3,882
	July	533	345	197	134	61	477	1,747	377	1,328	3,452
	August	351	204	136	95	37	398	1,216	291	1,196	2,703
	September	187	104	56	73	25	375	820	235	945	2,000
	October	80	44	51	47	18	366	606	219	603	1,428
	November	410	306	163	126	40	377	1,422	185	391	1,998
	December	985	628	398	210	129	349	2,699	251	226	3,176
1927	January	1,162	611	549	238	137	351	3,048	189	70	3,307
	February	1,065	561	505	238*	124	328	2,821	153	318	3,292

* Estimated.

489

one hand, sugar being a semi-manufactured product, the agricultural producers send the bulk of the output forward to the centrals as soon as it is available, and, on the other hand, since it is in most countries a dutiable commodity, invisible supplies, on which duty has been paid, are not likely, as a rule, to be any larger than convenience dictates.

The total monthly figures of the visible supply are shown in Table I (up to December 1921 they were supplied by Messrs Bagot and Thompson, and since that date by Messrs C. Czarnikow, Ltd.: the two sets are only roughly comparable).

The distribution of the stock between the different countries is shown in Table II for selected dates.

The total 'visible' stocks naturally show a sharp seasonal fluctuation, but, as Table II shows, this is really a compound of two variations, one for Europe, which is mainly concerned with beet sugar, and the other for America, which is dominated by the Cuban cane crop. Thus stocks in Europe are at a minimum about October 1st, and reach a maximum about January 1st, whereas American port stocks are at a minimum at about January 1st, and reach their maximum about May 1st. The fluctuation in the total visible supply figures is, of course, dominated by the European stocks, since only *port* stocks in Cuba and the United States are included.

The table below gives a very rough idea of stocks, production, and consumption in recent seasons and the table on page 492 shows consumption during recent years by this country and the United States, which between them account for an extraordinary proportion of the exported sugar.

During the season 1925–6 the world's consumption reached a new high record, though the rate of increase was much smaller than in the previous season. The greater part of the increase was due to increased buying by Far Eastern countries: consumption in the U.S.A. during the calendar year 1926 was only 173,000 tons greater than in 1925, while the total imported into the United Kingdom was actually less, though with the inclusion of

Supply and consumption of sugar (tons)

	1920–1	1921–2	1922–3	1923–4	1924–5	1925–6	1926–7
Stock carried over on 1 September	1,600,000	2,400,000	1,180,000	1,267,000	982,000	1,612,000	2,000,000
European beet crops	3,671,788	4,054,282	4,735,500	5,057,800	7,077,800	7,471,000	
American beet crops	1,004,019	930,121	649,000	803,700	1,010,400	836,900	
Cane crops	12,081,831	12,679,948	12,691,500	13,837,400	15,501,400	16,106,500	
Total	18,357,638	20,064,351	19,256,000	20,965,900	24,571,600	26,026,400	
Deduct visible supplies at end of season (1 September)	2,400,000	1,180,000	1,267,000	982,000	1,612,000	2,000,000	
Total consumption	15,957,638	18,884,351	17,989,000	19,983,900	22,959,600	24,026,400	

U.K. and U.S.A. consumption of sugar

Year	Consumption (raw values – tons)	
	United Kingdom	United States
1922	1,748,177	5,476,500
1923	1,602,029	5,141,000
1924	1,706,661	5,220,000
1925	1,854,594	5,925,000
1926	1,906,229	6,098,200

home-grown sugar there was an increase in consumption of just over 50,000 tons. In part the smaller increase in world consumption is presumably due to the considerable rise in price, which was well under way before Sept. 1st, 1926, though it developed on a much more important scale during the next four months: by the end of the year the price of raw sugars was nearly 40 per cent higher than at the end of 1925. Lately there has been some decline from this high level, but the market has been fairly firm, which is only to be expected in view of the position on the production side. In the season 1925–6, production increased by rather more than 800,000 tons. While a substantial increase was expected, the final result is somewhat surprising in view of the institution of the Cuban Restriction Scheme in May. This was made effective for the current crop by limiting the grinding of the cane, and the actual production was 4,884,000 tons as against expectations of nearer 5,500,000 tons. Despite this, however, the world's total cane crops were 600,000 tons greater. European beet crops were 400,000 tons greater, but the American beet crops 200,000 tons less. If production in 1926–7 were to be as great as in 1925–6, and if consumption were to continue to expand at the same rate, supplies would be ample in view of the very large carryover of 2 million tons. But there is, in fact, no possible chance that production will be maintained. By a decree signed in December, the Cuban crop is to be limited to 4,500,000 tons, and the world's cane crops are expected to be as much as 600–700,000 tons smaller. The European beet crop is also estimated to show a decrease of 400–500,000 tons; the American beet crop is estimated to show little change. While these estimates are still liable to very substantial modifications, the present outlook is for a decline in production of about 1 million tons. Stocks could comfortably be reduced by 1 million tons, but even so, this would only allow consumption to increase by about half as much as in the previous season. A further rise in price seems probable, though recent market fluctuations give some ground for the supposition that a small further rise may exercise a forcible check on consumption. If production estimates prove to be too low, the situation from the consumer's point of view will be eased, while the producer need not in any event entertain fears of a glut. If, however, production estimates prove to be too high, there is the distinct possibility of a shortage.

VIII. *Tea*

The only precise figures available for the stocks of tea are of those in bond in the United Kingdom. Since, however, about three-quarters of the total world production passes through this country, these stocks should form a fairly reliable index of the position. (See table below.)

Consumption in Great Britain and Northern Ireland has been as follows in recent years:—

Million lb	
1923	387·5
1924	396·5
1925	402·0
1926	408·8

World production during the marketing years July 1st–June 30th has been as given below (according to Messrs F. J. Denton, Ltd.). Some idea of the comparative changes of world consumption

493

Tea in bond in the United Kingdom (1,000 lb)

End of month	1921	1922	1923	1924	1925	1926	1927
January	219,377	208,115	186,035	182,865	225,067	209,655	222,636
February	223,179	221,362	176,681	188,559	234,557	202,300	217,413
March	229,568	219,645	183,413	193,362	231,516	195,388	
April	233,018	214,484	167,763*	192,219	217,091	179,891	
May	228,793	192,396	141,659	152,317	190,730	163,408	
June	218,290	170,478	126,792	138,691	180,859	155,595	
July	207,448	153,198	112,890	121,097	163,255	148,207	
August	197,433	142,137	121,935	128,266	165,085	156,850	
September	190,799	151,510	134,170	136,694	180,621	175,012	
October	190,129	152,095	146,990	150,721	181,683	186,861	
November	196,534	158,357	152,288	174,414	189,080	196,626	
December	205,420	169,776	165,666	205,859	203,654	207,003	

* Excluding Irish Free State from this month onwards.

Million lb

	1923–4	1924–5	1925–6
India	371·1	372·9	360·7
Ceylon	183·5	203·7	209·5
Java	90·1	104·9	94·6
Sumatra	16·5	17·9	16·6
Japan (exports only)	27·1	22·5	27·8
China (exports only)	106·8	86·5	89·0*
Formosa (exports only)	20·2	20·5	20·8
Elsewhere (estimated)	2·0	2·0	2·0
	817·4	830·9	821·1

* Estimated.

may be obtained from the following figures of total imports for home consumption into the principal consuming countries during recent calendar years. (The figures are partly estimated.)

Million lb	
1923	723·3
1924	738·1
1925	760·3

IX. *Coffee*

About two-thirds of the supply of coffee for Europe and U.S.A. comes from Brazil. The table below is based on the figures supplied by Messrs Duuring & Zoon, the most important omissions from which are the stocks in the East and Eastern ports, coffee afloat from the East to U.S.A., and stocks in the interior of Brazil. The last-named deficiency has, however, recently been made good, at least for practical purposes, by the publication of stocks in the interior of the State of Sao Paulo. It will be seen how very imperfectly the visible supply indicates the real position of available supplies.

495

Coffee (1,000 bags)*

Beginning of month	Visible supply of Europe	Visible supply of U.S.A.	Stocks in Brazil	Total	Stocks in interior of Sao Paulo	Grand total
1913 July	6,480	1,848	1,947	10,275		
September	6,005	1,477	4,002	11,484		
October	6,019	1,393	4,769	12,181		
1914 January	7,275	1,709	4,681	13,665		
April	8,702	2,172	1,743	12,617		
June	8,353	2,056	1,207	11,616		
1919 January	758	1,010	9,296	11,364		
April	2,755	1,964	7,060	11,799		
July	3,124	1,508	5,704	10,336		
October	2,821	2,057	5,540	10,418		
1920 January	2,843	2,007	5,020	9,870		
April	2,573	2,209	3,392	8,174		
July	2,509	2,293	1,948	6,750		
October	2,955	2,640	2,387	7,982		
1921 January	2,588	2,442	3,735	8,765		
April	2,533	2,765	3,389	8,687		
July	2,562	2,100	4,038	8,700		
October	2,564	1,838	4,589	8,991		
1922 January	2,399	2,056	4,948	9,403		
April	2,977	1,583	4,580	9,140		
July	3,068	1,456	4,115	8,639		
October	3,007	1,182	4,292	8,481		
1923 January	2,839	1,385	3,756	7,980		
April	2,463	1,618	2,903	6,974		
July	2,296	1,075	1,969	5,340		
October	2,449	1,387	2,016	5,852		
1924 January	2,228	1,349	890	4,467		
April	1,935	1,075	954	3,964		
July	2,152	1,387	1,532	5,071	4,592	9,663
October	2,255	1,337	2,135	5,727		

Table (*cont.*)

Beginning of month	Visible supply of Europe	Visible supply of U.S.A.	Stocks in Brazil	Total	Stocks in interior of Sao Paulo	Grand total
1925 January	2,098	1,046	2,240	5,384		
April	2,028	1,116	2,245	5,389		
July	2,193	1,154	1,738	5,085	1,786	6,871
October	2,367	1,269	1,594	5,230		
November	2,525	1,188	1,496	5,209		
December	2,289	1,391	1,448	5,128		
1926 January	2,163	1,484	1,517	5,164	4,383	9,547
February	1,974	1,229	1,599	4,802	4,329	9,131
March	1,964	1,314	1,510	4,788	4,214	9,002
April	2,041	1,258	1,487	4,786	3,902	8,688
May	2,092	998	1,443	4,533	3,531	8,064
June	1,991	1,031	1,427	4,449	3,144	7,593
July	2,028	1,065	1,478	4,571	2,833	7,404
August	2,119	1,205	1,377	4,701	3,098	7,799
September	2,179	1,428	1,320	4,927	4,011	8,938
October	2,190	1,448	1,217	4,856	5,255	10,111
November	2,238	1,582	1,029	4,849	6,144	10,993
December	2,106	1,651	1,022	4,779	6,397	11,175
1927 January	2,024	1,617	1,270	4,911	5,990	10,901
February	2,082	1,499	1,253	4,834	5,344	10,178
March	2,025	1,315	1,281	4,621		

* G. Durring & Zoon.

Deliveries during the last four years have been as below.

During the past year the Brazilian Coffee Defence Institute has exercised continuous control over supplies. There has been a slight decrease in the visible supply, but stocks in the interior of Sao Paulo were 1,600,000 bags higher on Jan. 1st, 1927, than a year previously. Consumption increased to the 1924 figure, but

Deliveries of coffee (1,000 bags)

Year	To Europe	To U.S.A.	Total	From Brazil	Other kinds
1920	5,213	9,167	14,380	8,638	5,742
1921	8,094	9,958	18,052	11,356	6,696
1922	8,238	9,654	17,892	11,100	6,792
1923	9,240	10,585	19,825	13,516	6,309
1924	9,981	10,709	20,690	13,473	7,217
1925	9,481	9,488	18,969	11,868	7,101
1926	9,984	10,665	20,649	13,164	7,485

despite a slightly falling price level,* the increase was not sufficient to prevent this piling up of interior stocks. If present expectations are realised, and the next Brazilian crop beats all records, it is clear that the Institute will have a formidable task. Its resources are probably adequate to prevent any serious fall in prices, provided that the planters continue their willing co-operation. Reports indicate discontent in some quarters, but it appears to be generally realised that defensive measures are all that is possible in the existing state of affairs, and that such measures cannot be expected to give the planter definite and positive gains: they can only save him from greater losses.

X. *Petroleum*

The only figures of stocks regularly available are those for the United States compiled by the U.S. Dept. of Commerce. Since, however, nearly 80 per cent of the world's oil stocks are held in the United States, these figures can be regarded as reasonably representative. Unfortunately, a change in the method of compilation has very greatly impaired the value of these American statistics. Since January 1925, stocks of fuel oil in California have been included in the figures of Californian stocks of crude

* There is, however, almost a shortage of really high-class grades, and all such supplies continue to command firm and relatively high prices.

Total U.S.A. stocks of crude and refined oils* (1,000 barrels)

End of month	1920	1921	1922	1923	1924	1925	1926
March	—	—	—	—	463,072	490,953	502,777
June	171,109	221,383	302,345	395,608	480,685	504,941	482,763
September	—	—	—	—	487,509	473,108	467,584
December	182,021	234,892	318,960	414,302	477,958	469,577	476,479
Monthly average run to stills	36,160	36,947	41,725	48,436	53,842	61,667	64,977

* The figures of refined oils are confined to liquid products, i.e., greases, etc., are not included.

petroleum. This change makes it impossible to ascertain the total American stocks of crude petroleum: only the total east of California is now available, and as this was not published separately before January 1925, no comparative series of any sort can be constructed. Similarly this change makes it impossible to ascertain the total American stocks of refined oils, because the stocks of fuel oil are exclusive of California. It is possible to give statistics of the total supply of crude and refined together, and to carry this series back beyond January 1925, but this is all that can be done. This series is as follows: in order to give some idea of the general growth of the industry, and therefore the relation of stocks to consumption, the monthly average for each year of crude petroleum run to stills is shown in the last line of the above table.

At the end of the last three years the total stocks of crude and refined oils have been approximately the same, but with the increase in consumption they have really, of course, become relatively smaller. The production of crude oil in the U.S. amounted to 714 million barrels in 1924, 764 million barrels in 1925, and 765 million barrels in 1926: stocks, including refined oils, at the end of 1926 still, therefore, represented nearly eight months' production. Commenting on production in 1926, Messrs Rowe and Pitman write:

Once again the American oilfields achieved the unexpected. Four important new fields were developed, and although the total output of crude oil for the first six months was well below that of the previous year, the flush production of the new fields in the second half of the year brought the year's total output to a new high record.

Production is still increasing, and though consumption will doubtless continue to increase, there is at present little prospect of any reduction in stocks, while prices are just as likely to fall as to rise.

1,000 barrels

	Crude petroleum stocks east of California	Crude petroleum and fuel oil stocks in California
1925 January	310,199	98,914
February	309,462	100,483
March	308,548	103,721
April	308,382	106,605
May	312,085	110,081
June	310,732	110,203
July	308,429	113,428
August	303,004	116,959
September	300,981	121,664
October	297,963	124,369
November	296,690	126,233
December	292,288	126,129
1926 January	291,400	131,194
February	287,975	131,638
March	287,710	131,678
April	286,208	124,290
May	284,009	125,359
June	281,432	122,794
July	278,184	121,344
August	277,486	119,893
September	277,771	117,964
October	277,014	117,928
November	277,099	117,497
December	278,077	118,330

Million gallons

End of month	Stocks of gasolene	Domestic consumption
1920 monthly average	464	354
1921 ,, ,,	631	376
1922 ,, ,,	791	448
1923 ,, ,,	1,186	549
1924 ,, ,,	1,483	647
1925 ,, ,,	1,614	782
1926 ,, ,,	—	—
1925 January	1,453	600
February	1,619	544
March	1,747	625
April	1,718	798
May	1,700	859
June	1,695	868
July	1,611	963
August	1,541	932
September	1,514	849
October	1,529	832
November	1,590	758
December	1,648	760
1926 January	1,749	720
February	1,859	651
March	1,936	780
April	1,927	831
May	1,802	989
June	1,713	969
July	1,609	1,015
August	1,451	1,104
September	1,400	943
October	1,416	986
November	1,508	850
December	1,639	900

The table on page 500 shows the stocks of crude petroleum east of California, and in the second column the stocks of crude and fuel oil in California, since January 1925.

Of refined products, kerosene and lubricating oils are now quantitatively unimportant. Since the statistics of stocks of fuel and gas oils are now exclusive of California, they are of very little significance, but the following brief summary may be given: no estimate of consumption is possible in the absence of adequate statistics of stocks.

Stocks of fuel and gas oils east of California (million gallons)

End of month	1925	1926
March	802	851
June	1,082	947
September	1,256	1,142
December	1,037	1,046

Fortunately the gasolene statistics are not affected by the change in statistical compilation. The table above [p. 501] shows the total stocks in the U.S.A., and the estimated domestic consumption.

XI. *Nitrate*

Nitrate statistics are comparatively simple, since they all come from one part of the world. Very reliable figures are regularly published by Messrs Aikman, and are quoted below.

The figures for America include interior stocks, but not those held by the U.S.A. Government, which have gradually declined from round 300,000 tons in December 1921, to 60,000 tons at the present time.

In normal times there is a considerable reduction in the visible supply in the early part of the year, as the demand is somewhat seasonal.

Nitrate (1,000 tons)

End of month	Visible supply (including afloat)		Stocks in Chile	Total
	Europe and Egypt	U.S.A.		
1913 January	1,128	89	490	1,727
March	686	97	527	1,326
June	416	84	754	1,652
September	571	79	752	1,414
December	1,093	71	498	1,685
1919 July	140	28	1,594	1,780
September	152	49	1,705	1,925
December	430	95	1,576	2,134
1920 March	368	253	1,218	1,914
June	317	216	1,248	1,800
September	495	194	1,303	2,008
December	782	132	1,304	2,235
1921 March	868	218	1,283	2,384
June	836	249	1,317	2,405
September	828	41	1,453	2,370
December	903·5	260	1,441	2,662·5
1922 March	520	115	1,504	2,149
June	228·5	38	1,601	1,873·5
September	296	133	1,495	1,945
December	463·5	195	1,225	1,912·5
1923 March	379·5	238	889	1,310
June	173	54	997	1,250
September	365	96	927	1,415
December	573	200	852	1,639
1924 March	371	193	782	1,346
June	115	47	1,075	1,250
September	429	124	900	1,494
December	684	111	882	1,709
1925 January	711	121	855	1,718
February	586·5	247	768	1,601·5
March	379·5	233	756	1,368·5
April	245	233	754	1,232·5
May	177	102	868	1,147
June	227	122	869	1,218
July	318	172	819	1,309
August	366	121	832	1,319
September	408	105	896	1,409
October	466	70	906	1,442
November	575	147	893	1,615
December	682·5	115	878	1,675·5

Table (*cont.*)

End of month	Visible supply (including afloat)		Stocks in Chile	Total
	Europe and Egypt	U.S.A.		
1926 January	683	135	906	1,724
February	575·5	235	861	1,671·5
March	447	196	906	1,549
April	359·5	259	987	1,605·5
May	305	221	1,145	1,671
June	314	117	1,228	1,659
July	325	149	1,220	1,694
August	335	146	1,279	1,760
September	334	150	1,288	1,772
October	313·5	166	1,295	1,774·5
November	330	204	1,273	1,807
December	337	201	1,268	1,806
1927 January	311	205	1,215	1,731
February	247	221	1,105	1,573

XII *Wheat*

Wheat is a baffling commodity to the compiler of comparative stock statistics, because it is a seasonal crop, coming from many different sources, and harvested at different times of year.

As in the case of other commodities, the statistics regularly available month by month are those of 'visible' supplies in 'second hands'; but, owing to the large amounts held on farms and elsewhere 'out of sight' and to the seasonal irregularity of supply, these figures are particularly unsatisfactory in the case of wheat.

The current available statistics relating to supplies and stocks of wheat are well summarised in the *Wheat Studies* of the Food Research Institute of Stanford University, California, to which anyone who is interested in further details may be referred. The following tables relating to wheat supplies in the leading countries of export, 1922–6, with a forecast for 1926–7, have been taken from this source.

These statistics may be supplemented by the quarterly figures of 'visible supply', published by Mr Broomhall in *The Corn Trade News*, i.e. the visible supply in elevators and public stores

Wheat supplies and their disposition in leading export countries, 1922–26; and a forecast for 1927* (million bushels)

	1922–3	1923–4	1924–5	1925–6	1926–7
United States Year ending 30 June					
Initial stocks	81·5	102·4	106·2	86·4	60·2
New crop	867·6	797·4	862·6	700·0	832·3
Total supplies	949·1	899·8	968·8	786·4	892·5
Net exports	205·0	131·4	254·7	93·4	170·0
Seed requirements	91·4	79·4	87·6	83·3	85·0
Consumption	}550·3{	496·1	484·6	510·0	505·0
Feed and waste		89·2	55·5	39·5	50·0
Total domestic use	641·7	664·7	627·7	632·8	640·0
Stocks at end	102·4	103·7	86·4	60·2	82·5
Canada Year ending 31 Aug. 1922–4 and 31 July 1925–7					
Initial stocks	16·0	8·9	45·2‡	26·5	35·6
New crop	399·8	474·2	278·0	437·8	405·8
Total supplies	415·8	483·1	323·2	464·3	441·4
Net exports	279·1	342·7	192·1	324·1	290·0
Seed requirements	39·8	38·0	38·5	40·0	41·0
Consumption	40·9	42·2	42·1	42·0	42·4
Feed and waste	47·1	33·6	24·0	22·6	25·0
Total domestic use	127·8	113·8	104·6	104·6	108·4
Stocks at end	8·9	26·3†	26·5	35·6	43·0
Argentina Year ending 31 July					
Initial stocks	66·6	54·2	59·6	57·2	59·1
New crop	195·8	247·0	191·1	191·1	215·3
Total supplies	262·4	301·2	250·7	248·3	274·4
Net exports	142·6	173·0	123·1	94·4	140·0
Seed requirements	18·7	20·6	23·1}	94·8	73·0
Consumption, feed and waste	46·9	48·0	47·3}		
Total domestic use	65·6	68·6	70·4	94·8	73·0
Stocks at end	54·2	59·6	57·2	59·1	61·4
Australia Year ending 31 July					
Initial stocks	29·8	45·4	41·2	36·2	28·4
New crop	109·3	125·5	164·6	113·4	154·0
Total supplies	139·1	170·9	205·8	149·6	182·4
Net exports	49·8	85·6	123·6	77·2	87·4
Seed requirements	8·9	9·4	9·4	9·4	9·4
Consumption	30·4	31·2}	36·6	34·6	36·0
Feed and waste	4·6	3·5}			
Total domestic use	43·9	44·1	46·0	44·0	45·4
Stocks, 31 July	45·4	41·2	36·2	28·4	42·0

* From *Wheat Studies of the Food Research Institute*, Stanford University, California, vol. II, no. I, and vol. III, no. 3.
† 31 August.   ‡ 1 August.

1,000 qr of 480 lb

	1919–20	1920–1	1921–2	1922–3	1923–4	1924–5	1925–6	1926–7
1 Aug.	18,370	17,950	16,800	15,091	17,340	20,270	16,330	17,400
1 Nov.	34,000	24,560	29,980	30,420	34,330	36,340	29,150	37,300
1 Feb.	28,120	23,750	26,520	35,660	39,350	37,900	33,710	
1 May	23,870	19,660	23,730	28,500	34,750	29,900	26,000	

in the United States, Canada and Great Britain and the supply afloat for Europe.

In the course of his commodity investigations and speculations, Keynes became seriously interested in the statistics available for tin. After extensive correspondence and inquiries, in September 1928 he prepared a note on 'The Production and Consumption of Tin'. Although it was never published in England, it did appear on the Continent in *Recueil Mensuel de l'Institut International du Commerce* on 20 October 1928. Below we reprint his original typescript.

THE PRODUCTION AND CONSUMPTION OF TIN

A certain amount of confusion has long existed in regard to tin statistics, because of the undue importance which it has been customary to attach to the figures of the so-called 'visible supply' which are published by the trade at monthly intervals. These statistics suffer from two serious defects:— they ignore the stocks of tin and tin ore in the Straits Settlements where a large proportion of the tin supply of the world is smelted, and they take no account, in their figures of supplies and deliveries, of tin which is sold direct by British smelters to consumers without passing through the Metal Exchange warehouses or the export returns.

Whilst it is not always practicable to make the necessary corrections immediately after the end of each month, it is always possible to do so after a little delay. For the authorities of the Straits Settlements publish figures of imports and exports from which the variations in the stocks of tin and tin ore can be deduced; whilst the addition which has to be made in respect of direct supplies from British smelters to British consumers in order to obtain the total British consumption can also be deduced from the official British export and import figures. Tables which make these necessary corrections are given below. Indeed the only serious obstacle in the way of getting fairly complete figures for the world production and consumption of tin is the lack of accurate figures for Chinese tin apart from what is shipped to Great Britain and the United States.

The broad outline of the history of the tin trade can be put quite tersely. The slump of 1920–1 caused enormous accumulations of the metal and a crisis in the producing countries which required the intervention of the Straits and Dutch Indies Governments in the market. From 1922, however, to the middle of 1927 the consumption of tin regularly exceeded the production and the redundant stocks were steadily absorbed. By the end of 1926 supplies had, indeed, reached a dangerously low level, and the price of the metal was correspondingly high. Meanwhile the steady improvement of the statistical position and the profitable price stimulated very active efforts to increase output both in Bolivia and in the Malay Peninsula. In Malaya in particular many new companies were formed and many old companies expanded in order to take over properties for exploitation by means of modern dredges. These new developments have been the occasion of many disappointments. The date at which metal has been won has nearly always been months after the scheduled date and the type of dredge ordered has not always been suited to the work it had to do. But by the end of 1927 there were 95 modern dredges at work in the Federated Malay States, Siam and Burma, 37 under construction, and 32 on order.

Thus the effects of increased development were slow. But they have been cumulative. Up to June, 1927 the net increase of output had not been very substantial, though it had been nearly enough to catch up with the then level of consumption. Since June, 1927, the output has been increasing with leaps and bounds. Fortunately consumption has also very greatly increased, with the result that the two were running fairly level up to about April, 1928. Since April, 1928, production has been definitely ahead of consumption in spite of the very satisfactory level of the latter.

The developments of the last two and a half years are sufficiently summarised in the following table:—

Long tons (2,240 lb)

Supplies*	Jan.– June 1926	July– Dec. 1926	Jan.– June 1927	July– Dec. 1927	Jan.– June 1928
Shipments from Straits†	37,533	38,943	38,773	43,997	45,994
Increase (+) or decrease (−) in Straits stocks	−1,595	−525	+408	+662	+1,105
Batavian shipments	8,155	8,290	8,081	7,496	6,261
Bolivian shipments‡	15,177	15,194	15,037	17,496	17,843
Chinese shipments to Europe and U.S.A.	2,182	840	1,125	210	577
British imports from Nigeria	3,408	3,664	4,068	3,524	4,423
Australian shipments	481	1,015	666	613	673
British production	1,090	1,110	1,100	1,130	1,120
Other production (estimated)	3,000	3,000	3,500	3,500	3,500
Total output	69,431	71,531	72,758	78,628	81,496

* London Metal Exchange Statistics employed whenever available.
† Includes tin mined in Siam, Burma and Dutch East Indies but smelted in the Straits.
‡ For periods beginning November and May respectively in previous half year.

	Jan.– June 1926	July– Dec. 1926	Jan.– June 1927	July– Dec. 1927	Jan.– June 1928
Change in stocks					
'Visible' supply*	−2,193	+495	−688	+95	+498
Straits stocks	−1,595	−525	+408	+662	+1,105
Total stocks	−3,788	−30	−280	+757	+1,603
Consumption deduced from the above	73,219	71,561	73,038	77,871	79,893

* London Metal Exchange figures.

These figures show how very narrowly balanced supply and demand has been up to a very recent date. In fact the price has had to rise to a point which would keep demand within the available supply. But in spite of the resilience of demand, it would seem that at last supply is getting ahead. The most up-to-date figures confirm this. In July and August 1928 total stocks increased by about 1,200 tons. On the basis of the figures for June to August 1928, the supplies from the Straits look like reaching 51,000 tons for the second half of 1928 which is 5,000 tons greater than for the previous half-year; and in this event total supplies in the second half of 1928 might reach 86,000 tons. Will consumption be capable of responding?

If we consider the matter in the light of trend, the result is as follows:—

(1,000 long tons)

	Production		Consumption	
	Actual	Trend	Actual	Trend
1922	130	130	132	132
1923	127·5	136	139	137
1924	136	142	140	142
1925	143·5	148	153·5	147
1926	141	154	145*	152
1927	151·5	160	151	157
1928 (estimate)	166	166	162	162

* British consumption greatly reduced on account of the coal strike.

Thus in the last six years the trend of production has been +6,000 tons per annum and the trend of consumption +5,000 tons per annum.

It is a peculiarity of tin that the greater part of the output is produced at a cost far below even the present reduced price. Thus the supply is very insensitive to price changes. There is, however, a fairly important amount of tin won by Chinese miners in the Malay peninsula employing

Stocks of staple commodities

Beginning of month	Cotton 1,000 bales (1)	Copper 1,000 tons (2)	Tin 1,000 tons (3)	Lead 1,000 tons (4) U.K.	Lead 1,000 tons (4) U.S.	Spelter 1,000 tons (5)	Rubber 1,000 tons (6)	Sugar 1,000 tons (7)	Tea 1,000,000 lb (8)	Coffee 1,000 bags (9)	Petroleum 1,000,000 barrels (10)	Nitrate 1,000 tons (11)
1920 January	7,410	—	20	50·0	—	61	—	—	213	9,870	—	2.134
April	7,353	—	18	28·4	—	53	—	2,433	213	8,174	—	1,914
July	6,793	—	19	25·2	—	51	—	2,003	213	6,750	171	1,800
October	—	—	18	18·7	—	61	—	1,338	215	7,982	—	2,008
1921 January	—	399ᴬ	18	19·0	—	81	219–229	2,313	214	8,765	182	2,235
April	—	—	16	23·9	—	88	—	3,331	230	8,687	—	2,384
July	—	—	17	13·3	—	99	—	3,312	218	8,700	221	2,405
October	9,534	—	21	9·9	—	89	—	2,039	191	8,991	—	2,370
1922 January	8,470	411ᴬ	24	0·3	—	72	224–244	2,761	205	9,403	235	2,622·5
April	7,654	346ᴬ	21	0·6	—	60	—	2,479	220	9,140	—	2,149
July	6,785	357ᴬ	22	0·3	—	31	—	1,903	170	8,639	302	1,873·5
October	4,514	325ᴬ	21	0·6	—	20	—	868	151	8,481	—	1,945
1923 January	—	347	26	0·5	—	17	286–306	2,433	170	7,980	319	1,912·5
April	3,111	350	25	0·4	—	10	249	2,501	183	6,974	—	1,310
July	2,765	352	21	0·2	—	17	278	2,005	127	5,340	396	1,250
October	2,699	391	20	1·4	—	21	244	791	134	5,835	—	1,415
1924 January	2,010	402	21	1·2	93	34	254	2,255	166	4,467	414	1,639
April	1,716	361	23	0·0	92	29	226	2,460	193	3,964	463	1,346
July	1,747	371	20	0·0	97	45	208	2,086	139	5,071	481	1,250
October	2,673	385	20	0·1	88	42	196	542	137	5,727	487	1,494

	(1)	(2)	(3)	(4)	(5)	(6)	(7)	(8)	(9)	(10)	(11)	
1925 January	2,563	389	25	0·1	78	19	181	2,708	206	5,384	478	1,790
April	1,904	403	20	0·0	94	16	151	2,891	231	5,389	491	1,368·5
July	1,715	365	20	0·1	86	21	129	2,560	181	5,085	505	1,218
October	—	347	18	0·0	94	11	141	1,211	181	5,230	473	1,409
1926 January	2,927	344	18	0·0	93	9	182	3,709	204	9,547	469	1,675·5
April	3,193	361	14	0·4	105	19	183	4,064	195	8,688	503	1,549
July	4,068	370	16	0·2	106	24	193	3,452	156	7,404	483	1,659
October	5,396	351	15	0·1	106	15	213	1,919	175	10,111	468	1,772
1927 January	4,916	369	16	1·7	113	20	259	3,643	207	10,901	476	1,806
April	5,211	367	15	2·7	130	33	273	—	194	8,446	499	1,415·5
July	4,942	346	16	2·4	152	41	263	4,090	145	8,032	521	1,175·5
October	5,540	—	15	2·1	143	32	271	1,780	164	14,555	532	1,202
1928 January	4,622	323	16	2·0	139	38	272	4,062	239	18,388	543	1,452·5
April	4,129	—	16	1·9	155	38	270	5,442	243	17,908	568	1,078
July	3,896*	—	16	1·3	146	41	222	4,303	179	17,401	571	1,135·5
October	4,012*	288	20	1·0	139	44	206	1,850	195	18,834	563	1,585·5
1929 January	3,404	298	25	0·9	144	42	239	4,271	241	18,138	571	2,036·5
April	2,879	281	27	1·3	—	35	245	6,190	260	15,383	599	1,794·5
July	2,919	—	24	0·8	—	34	—	—	203	—	—	1,653

* End of month. (1) Total supply, seasonally corrected, exclusive of European and Asiatic mill stocks. (2) Total supply outside hands of consumers. (3) Visible supply. London Metal Exchange figures from 1923. (4) Visible supply in U.K., and stocks in U.S. (5) Visible supply in U.K. and U.S. (6) Total supply outside plantations. (7) Total visible supply, exclusive of interior stocks in Cuba prior to October 1926. (8) Stocks in U.K. Comparability uncertain since April 1929. (9) Visible supply in Rio, Santos, Bahia, Europe and U.S., but exclusive of interior stocks in Brazil prior to January 1926. (10) Stocks of crude and refined oils in U.S. (11) Visible supply in Chile, U.S., Europe and Egypt. ∧ (Copper). On 1 January 1921, Allied Government stocks amounted approximately to 82,000 tons, and stocks of scrap metal to 183,000; on 1 January 1922, the former had become trifling, and the latter had fallen to about 90,000 tons, and had become trifling by 1 January 1923. A decreasing allowance must be added to the figures shown on account of these stocks.

primitive methods which probably shows little or no profit at the present prices of £210 to £220 a ton. No one seems to know at what point these marginal producers will fall away. But the future of the tin market in the near future mainly depends on this. So far there are no signs of these producers closing down on their operations.

Looking further ahead, it would seem very probable that consumption will again endeavour to outstrip production and will have to be kept within bounds by a high price. For no new tin-bearing ground is being discovered and many existing sources of supply have a short life. The present weakness of the market may become more accentuated, but it is essentially a passing phase due to new dredger production having matured a little faster than is wise.

From The London and Cambridge Economic Service, Special Memorandum No. 29 (August 1929)

STOCKS OF STAPLE COMMODITIES

The statistics given below are in continuation of Memoranda published by the London and Cambridge Economic Service in April 1923, June 1924, July 1925, February 1926, and March 1927.

The above table [pp. 510–11] is a summary of the figures given in detail afterwards for each separate commodity.

A NOTE ON WEIGHTS AND MEASURES

1. *Cotton.* All current statistics are given in 'running bales', i.e. regardless of exact weight and counting round bales as half-bales. At the end of each season the U.S. Department of

Commerce publishes the average weight of the bales produced in each State during that season, and this makes possible the conversion of running bales into equivalent 500-lb bales. Normally the average weight of the actual bales is within 6 or 7 lb above or below 500 lb, but recently the tendency has been to be above rather than below. In section I, crop figures are given in equivalent 500 lb bales, but all other figures refer to running bales.

2. *Metals.* Three different kinds of tons are in common use:
The British ton (often termed a long ton) = 2,240 lb.
The American ton (often termed a short ton) = 2,000 lb.
The Metric ton = 2,204 lb (approx.).

3. *Rubber, Sugar, Tea, Nitrate.* Statistics are usually given in British tons (=2,240 lb) and pounds.

4. *Coffee.* A bag (normally) = 60 kilos = 132·3 lb.

5. *Petroleum.* A barrel = 42 gallons.

THE U.S. DEPARTMENT OF COMMERCE INDEX OF COMMODITY STOCKS

This index has been completely recast and revised. It now includes 65 commodities as against 45 in the old index. Of the

Indexes of commodity stocks in the United States

	Total index	Manufactured goods	Raw materials
1919 monthly average	93	90	95
1920 ,, ,,	86	84	87
1921 ,, ,,	102	97	106
1922 ,, ,,	95	87	100
1923 ,, ,,	95	94	95
1924 ,, ,,	102	103	101
1925 ,, ,,	104	103	104
1926 ,, ,,	115	106	121
1927 ,, ,,	121	113	127
1928 ,, ,,	123	116	127

65 items, 46 cover manufactured goods and 19 raw materials. The index has been weighted by the relative value of the supply of each commodity in the years 1923 and 1925, ascertained by adding to the value of the amount marketed or manufactured the value of the amount imported. For manufactured products the values given are those shown in the census reports on manufactures, while for raw materials the weights used are those derived from the index of production and marketings. No adjustment has been made for seasonal variations. For further details, reference should be made to *The Survey of Current Business*, August 1928.

Total index

	March	June	Sept.	Dec.
1925	108	92	101	124
1926	115	104	108	136
1927	123	106	119	133
1928	127	108	116	140
1929	133			

Manufactured goods

	March	June	Sept.	Dec.
1925	108	105	99	101
1926	109	110	104	106
1927	111	114	113	111
1928	120	117	111	118
1929	121			

Raw materials

	March	June	Sept.	Dec.
1925	108	81	103	142
1926	119	99	112	159
1927	133	101	124	150
1928	132	102	120	157
1929	142			

I. *American cotton*

At any given time stocks consist of the following:—

(1) Stocks up-country in the Southern States on plantations, railroads, and in 'uncounted'* interior towns.

(2) The 'visible' supply. This consists of (*a*) stocks in public storage and at compresses (warehouse stocks) in the more important interior towns and in the ports of the United States, (*b*) cotton afloat for Great Britain and the Continent, (*c*) warehouse stocks in the principal European ports, namely, Liverpool, Manchester, London, Havre, Marseilles, Genoa, Bremen, Ghent, Rotterdam and Barcelona.†

(3) Mill stocks in spinners' hands throughout the world, generally known as the 'invisible' or 'out of sight' supply.

In the first table the 'up-country' stock is taken as the 'up-country' carryover in the Southern States plus warehouse and mill stocks in the U.S. at the end of each season, plus the current year's crop, minus the U.S. consumption to any particular date, minus the net exports to that date (i.e. exports minus imports), minus warehouse and mill stocks at that date. By this means it is possible to estimate the location of all cotton in the U.S. month by month. But it follows that the whole of the new crop is suddenly added to the 'up-country' stock in August each year. This is corrected in the table below, by the 'seasonal correction', which provides what would be the figure of total stock in the U.S. if the current crop came into existence at an even monthly rate through the year. The statistics of U.S. warehouse stocks and mill stocks are compiled by the U.S. Bureau of the Census, and may be regarded as reliable, as also may the 'visible' supply of Great Britain and the Continent.‡ The estimates of the current crop are reasonably accurate by the end of each calendar year. The 'up-country'

---

* I.e. towns not included in the figures of stocks in public storage and at compresses.
† Cotton afloat for Japan and in Japanese ports is not allowed for. All cotton consigned to Japan is considered by the leading exchanges as 'consumed' or 'out of sight'.
‡ As given by the Liverpool Cotton Exchange.

Supplies other than European and Asiatic mill stocks (1,000 bales)*

End of month	Up-country	U.S. warehouse stocks†	U.S. mill stocks†	Total in U.S.A.	Correction for season	Corrected total in U.S.A.	Visible outside U.S.A.	Grand total, excluding mill stocks outside U.S.A.‡
1919 July	2,193	2,212	1,304	5,709	—	5,709	347	6,056
October	11,973	1,974	1,365	15,312	9,000	6,312	1,077	7,389
1920 January	3,780	3,760	3,677	11,217	6,000	5,217	2,082	7,299
April	3,252	2,967	1,809	8,028	3,000	5,028	2,034	7,062
July	1,703§	2,055	1,358	5,116	—	5,116	1,352	6,468
October	11,414	4,168	944	16,526	10,311	6,215	—	—
1921 January	6,788	5,645	1,273	13,706	6,874	6,832	—	—
April	4,961	5,029	1,316	11,306	3,437	7,869	—	—
July	3,713§	3,723	1,111	8,007	—	8,007	1,645	9,652
October	7,577	4,982	1,405	13,964	6,330	7,634	1,598	9,232
1922 January	4,550	4,618	1,675	10,843	4,220	6,623	1,581	8,204
April	3,484	3,214	1,458	8,156	2,110	6,046	1,436	7,482
July	964§	1,488	1,218	3,670	—	3,670	1,120	4,790
October	—	—	—	—	7,302	—	1,023	—
1923 January	1,569	3,486	1,988	7,043	4,868	2,175	1,296	3,471
April	667	1,966	1,878	4,511	2,434	2,077	804	2,881
July	280§	945	1,099	2,324	—	2,324	376	2,700
October	4,667	3,486	1,103	9,256	7,596	1,660	962	2,622
1924 January	1,049	2,966	1,633	5,648	5,064	584	1,268	1,852
April	341	1,512	1,328	3,181	2,532	649	966	1,615
July	160§	674	721	1,555	—	1,555	528	2,083
October	7,008	4,225	731	10,242	10,242	1,722	1,021	2,743

Month								
1925 January	1,780	3,863	1,434	7,077	6,828	249	1,956	2,205
April	341	1,666	1,515	3,522	3,414	108	1,731	1,839
July	2,308	487	878	1,504	—	1,504	764	2,268
October	7,977	4,499	1,216	13,692	12,078	1,614	1,280	2,894
1926 January	2,223	5,176	1,811	9,210	8,052	1,158	1,707	2,865
April	816	3,531	1,639	5,986	4,026	1,960	1,388	3,348
July	510	1,936	1,096	3,542	—	3,542	985	4,527
October	10,425	5,470	1,216	17,111	13,266	3,845	1,551	5,396
1927 January	3,480	6,070	1,853	11,403	8,844	2,559	2,905	5,464
July	535	1,823	1,404	3,762	—	3,762	2,096	5,858
August	12,496	2,173	1,122	15,791	11,876	3,915	1,755	5,660
September	9,487	3,965	1,119	14,571	10,796	3,775	1,765	5,540
October	6,105	5,433	1,327	12,865	9,716	3,149	2,110	5,259
November	3,766	5,969	1,551	11,286	8,636	2,650	2,263	4,913
December	2,676	5,656	1,707	10,039	7,556	2,483	2,139	4,622
1928 January	2,061	5,014	1,707	8,782	6,476	2,306	2,087	4,393
February	1,651	4,313	1,669	7,633	5,396	2,237	2,061	4,298
March	1,395	3,510	1,593	6,498	4,316	2,182	1,947	4,129
April	1,093	2,921	1,508	5,522	3,236	2,286	1,915	4,201
May	740	2,305	1,331	4,376	2,156	2,220	1,789	4,009
June	632	1,646	1,158	3,436	1,078	2,358	1,590	3,948
July	335	1,189	1,007	2,531	—	2,531	1,365	3,896
August	14,075	2,646	782	16,046	13,080	2,966	1,087	4,053
September	11,396	4,636	720	14,762	11,891	2,871	—	—
October	7,223	5,253	1,195	13,054	10,702	2,352	1,657	4,012
November	4,158	5,315	1,567	10,978	9,513	1,465	1,966	3,431
December	2,400		1,741	9,456	8,324	1,132	2,272	3,404
1929 January	1,595	4,615	1,768	7,978	7,135	843	2,276	3,119
February	1,185	3,876	1,746	6,807	5,946	861	2,173	3,034
March	749	3,177	1,731	5,657	4,757	900	1,979	2,879
April	525	2,524	1,607	4,656	3,568	1,088	1,786	2,874
May	390	1,848	1,477	3,715	2,379	1,336	1,504	2,840
June‖	406	1,313	1,167	2,886	1,189	1,697	1,222	2,919

* This table excludes linters, except that an insignificant quantity is included in the import figures.

† Figures for all kinds of cotton.   ‡ Seasonally corrected and excluding European and Asiatic mill stocks.

§ The carryover according to the above method was as follows: 1920, 2,171; 1921, 3,779; 1922, 2,615; 1923, 356; 1924, 6; 1925, 0; 1926, 400; 1927, 274; 1928, 487.   ‖ Provisional.

Annual table of total stocks at the end of each season (1 August) (1,000 bales)

	1919	1920	1921	1922	1923	1924	1925	1926	1927	1928
Up-country carryover in interior cotton belt	2,193	1,703	3,713	964	280	160	230	510	535	335
U.S. warehouse stocks	2,212	2,055	3,723	1,488	945	674	487	1,936	1,823	1,189
U.S. mill stocks	1,304	1,358	1,111	1,218	1,099	721	787	1,096	1,404	1,007
Total in U.S.	5,709	5,116	8,547	3,670	2,324	1,555	1,504	3,542	3,762	2,531
European port stocks (including afloat for Europe)	1,247	1,394	1,695	1,120	376	528	764	985	2,096	1,365
European mill stocks	305	475	690	838	496	502	787	663	1,041	792
Asiatic mill stocks	?	267*	248	381	185	173	219	250	572	327
Total	7,261	7,252	11,180	6,009	3,381	2,758	3,274	5,440	7,471	5,015
Crop for year†	12,000	13,750	8,442	9,738	10,128	13,639	16,122	17,977	12,956	14,478
Total available	19,261	21,002	19,622	15,747	13,509	16,397	19,396	23,417	20,427	19,493
Total carried forward	6,990	10,386	7,066	3,081	2,554	3,141	5,666	7,637	5,020	
Consumption for year	12,271	10,616	12,556	12,666	10,955	13,256	13,730	15,780	15,407	

* Excluding China.

† For 1919–21 Hester's estimate of the actual growth, made at the beginning of the season, as the official figures for these years are questionable.

Annual table of total stocks in the middle of each season (1 February) (1,000 bales)

	1920	1921	1922	1923	1924	1925	1926	1927	1928	1929
Up-country stocks	3,780	6,788	4,550	1,569	1,049	1,780	2,223	3,480	2,061	1,595
U.S. warehouse stocks	3,760	5,645	4,618	3,486	2,966	3,863	5,176	6,070	5,014	4,615
U.S. mill stocks	3,677	1,273	1,675	1,988	1,633	1,434	1,811	1,853	1,707	1,768
Total in U.S.	11,217	13,706	10,843	7,043	5,648	7,077	9,210	11,403	8,782	7,978
European port stocks (including afloat)	2,018	1,650	1,575	1,296	1,268	1,956	1,707	2,905	2,087	2,276
European mill stocks	597	675	740	637	578	755	842	848	845	783
Asiatic mill stocks	117*	166*	390	206	203	201	192	269	331	349
Total available	13,949	16,197	13,548	9,182	7,697	9,989	11,951	15,425	12,045	11,386
Total available 1 August preceding	19,261	21,002	19,622	15,747	13,509	16,397	19,396	23,417	20,427	19,493
Consumption for half-year	5,312	4,805	6,074	6,565	5,812	6,408	7,445	7,992	8,382	8,107

* Excluding China.

carryover is the most doubtful item, and is always liable to be under-, rather than over-estimated. The estimates of Mr H. G. Hester, the Secretary of the New Orleans Cotton Exchange, have been used until 1922, since when the estimates of the Shepperson Publishing Company (*Cotton Facts*) have been preferred. The monthly calculated figures for 'up-country' provide at best an estimate of the actual state of affairs, but in most years they tally reasonably well with the 'up-country carryover' estimates (see Note § below table).

At the beginning and in the middle of each season, statistics of European and Asiatic mill stocks, and of the world's actual consumption during the previous six months are available, and the position of the world's total stocks is shown in the two tables above.

The history of the last two years has been the gradual reduction of the excessive supplies of raw cotton, which resulted from the large crop of 1925–6 and the record crop of 1926–7. Consumption was notably larger in the season 1926–7 than in previous years (the price was as low as 6–7 pence in the earlier part of that season), but there was some decline in 1927–8, and there is little probability of any substantially higher figure in the present season. Though consumption in the United States has recently been at a high level, elsewhere consumption is more or less stationary, partly on account of this increased use of Indian cotton. The position from the producer's point of view was saved by the small crop of 1927–8, and the moderate crop of the present season—another large crop like that of 1926–7 would have created an almost desperate situation in view of the steadiness of demand.

The present season opened with a world carryover of approximately 5 million bales, and with the current crop the total available was not much less than 19½ million bales. World consumption will probably total at least 15¼ million bales. The indications are, therefore, that on August 1st, 1929, the world carryover will be about 4 million bales. A carryover of less than

3 million bales would not be comfortable at the present level of consumption, and therefore to maintain consumption at $15\frac{1}{2}$ million bales, the coming crop must not be less than $14\frac{1}{2}$ million, or, in other words, at least as great as the present season's crop. It is quite impossible as yet to forecast the growing crop, for everything depends on the weather and the boll weevil, the two being, of course, to some extent interdependent. All that can be

Finished cotton goods in U.S.

| | 1,000 yards | | | |
| | | Orders grey yardage | Cases | |
	Production		Shipments	Stocks
1921 monthly average	85,385	90,154	44,935	36,226
1922 ,, ,,	94,016	95,509	49,102	44,937
1923 ,, ,,	95,098	91,504	48,116	46,166
1924 ,, ,,	77,650	76,105	41,863	43,139
1925 ,, ,,	78,756	76,558	43,691	39,640
1926 ,, ,,	81,214	78,565	47,352	39,641
1927 ,, ,,	84,458	81,710	49,428	38,243
1928 ,, ,,	75,100	74,299	46,563	37,829
1928 January	68,737	75,665	44,673	40,751
February	78,786	79,184	49,035	38,698
March	89,740	81,328	51,495	39,787
April	75,378	68,316	43,378	40,876
May	73,539	72,961	47,555	40,449
June	70,029	61,347	42,357	38,907
July	58,685	62,310	40,500	37,958
August	70,748	71,743	46,283	35,819
September	69,805	74,483	45,767	33,410
October	83,935	87,175	50,984	32,046
November	82,700	82,657	49,136	36,566
December	79,112	74,417	47,587	38,678
1929 January	81,676	86,302	53,196	36,374
February	81,418	88,460	54,391	37,153
March	98,495	94,872	65,112	35,478
April	96,707	90,469	57,030	34,920

said is that the acreage is 3–5 per cent greater than last year, while fertiliser sales have been good; on the other hand, the risks of damage from weevil are exceptionally serious. It is, however, tolerably clear that unless there is a bumper crop, there is no prospect of any great surplus, and if there should be a short crop, i.e. less than about 14 million bales, consumption will have to be curtailed.

There are no statistics relating to finished cotton goods except for the United States. While not by any means complete, these statistics afford an interesting comparable series, as will be seen from the table above.

II. *Copper*

Stocks of copper consist of (1) refined copper in the United States, which constitutes the main part of the world's floating supply, (2) rough and blister copper in transit to smelters and refiners in North and South America, and on hand or in process at refineries, (3) refined and rough copper in European and Japanese warehouses. In the years immediately after the War there were also large stocks in the hands of the Allied Governments and in the form of scrap metal.

The second table supplies some more detailed statistics of the principal stocks. In these returns 'American blister' includes all copper in first hands in North and South America which has not been refined and made available for delivery.

The copper market during the last two years has been largely under the control of the American 'Copper Exporters Incorporated', which was launched in 1926. The declared aim of this body was price stabilisation, and for a time it seemed as if this objective was being satisfactorily achieved. In 1926 copper fluctuated within the relatively narrow limits of £56 to £60 per ton. In 1927 the extreme limits were £53 and £61, and from January 1st to October 1st, 1928, prices fluctuated only between £60 and £64. But a marked change in the statistical position had been proceeding alongside this relative stability of prices.

Supplies and consumption of copper (tons of 2,240 lb)

	1 January 1920	1 January 1921	1 January 1922	1 January 1923	1 January 1924	1 January 1925	1 January 1926	1 January 1927	1 January 1928	1 January 1929
North and South America:—										
Refined	313,000	286,000	239,000	133,000	139,000	122,000	65,000	76,000	85,000	58,000
In process, etc.	175,000	58,000	142,000	175,000	226,000	212,000	215,000	244,000	221,000	224,000
Allied Govt. stocks	180,000	82,000	trifling	—	—	—	—	—	—	—
Scrap (approximate)	270,000	183,000	90,000							
U.K., Havre, Japan stocks	46,000	55,000	30,000	39,000	37,000	55,000	64,000	49,000	17,000	15,000
Total	984,000	664,000	501,000	347,000	402,000	389,000	344,000	369,000	323,000	297,000
Production*	967,000	537,000	888,000	1,266,000	1,357,000	1,418,000	1,475,000	1,495,000	1,711,000	—
Available supply	1,951,000	1,201,000	1,389,000	1,613,000	1,759,000	1,807,000	1,819,000	1,864,000	2,034,000	—
Stock carried forward	664,000	501,000	347,000	402,000	389,000	344,000	369,000	323,000	297,000	—
Consumption	1,287,000	700,000	1,042,000	1,211,000	1,370,000	1,463,000	1,450,000	1,541,000	1,737,000	—
Price £	115 7 6	71 17 6	66 3 9	64 11 3	60 18 9	66 11 3	59 13 9	56 3 9	61 1 10	74 12 6
Cents per lb	19	12¾	13¾	14¾	12¾	14¾	14	13½	14⅓	16⅜

* American Bureau of Metal Statistics.

Stocks of copper (tons of 2,240 lb)

Beginning of month	American refined*	American blister* (and in process)	U.K. all kinds	Havre	Japan	Total
1921 Jan.	286,000	58,000	11,646	5,968	37,500	399,000
1922 Jan.	239,000	142,000	16,655	4,138	9,300	411,000
1923 Jan.	133,000	175,000	26,780	3,345	9,072	347,000
Oct.	113,000	240,000	28,453	3,891	5,954	391,000
1924 Jan.	139,000	226,000	31,030	1,867	4,405	402,000
April	107,000	212,500	30,852	5,281	5,300	361,000
July	100,000	216,000	36,515	10,225	8,600	371,000
Oct.	122,000	209,000	37,387	7,885	9,000	385,000
1925 Jan.	122,000	212,000	38,419	7,180	9,992	389,000
April	109,200	233,000	44,276	8,341	7,743	403,000
July	81,500	223,500	47,984	6,389	5,832	365,000
Oct.	61,500	220,000	51,285	9,942	5,015	347,000
1926 Jan.	65,200	214,600	56,047	3,013	5,288	344,288
April	67,148	233,813	51,701	4,701	3,624	360,987
July	59,014	245,974	50,967	11,670	3,129	369,754
Oct.	62,622	235,656	39,029	10,682	3,468	351,457
1927 Jan.	76,340	243,871	34,636	8,650	5,500	368,997
April	91,640	235,150	28,089	6,797	5,330	367,006
July	86,036	230,021	22,032	3,333	5,000†	346,422
Oct.	77,226	220,104	17,659	1,720	—	—
1928 Jan.	85,084	220,836	10,912	1,236	5,087	323,155
April	77,939	216,536	9,092	1,980	—	—
July	52,507	224,727	7,957	1,189	—	—
Oct.	46,260	228,328	8,574	2,333	2,837	288,512
1929 Jan.	58,452	224,214	6,801	2,084	6,262	297,813
April	47,290	216,376	7,504	2,872	6,622	280,664
July	83,000	251,000	8,758	—	—	—

* Includes North and South America.
† Provisional.

Production in 1927 was only a little more than in 1926, and the United States' output actually declined, as the result of the combine's control over supplies. Consumption, though failing to increase as much as was expected, increased by nearly 100,000 tons, with the result that stocks declined about 45,000 tons. Even so the level of world stocks was not unsatisfactory, but stocks in Europe were seriously depleted, and consumers were living almost literally from hand to mouth. Apart from this potentially dangerous feature, the situation was reasonably sound at the beginning of 1928, and Copper Exporters held a firm grip on the market. European merchants and consumers were indignant at the system of quasi-rationing adopted by the combine, but fears were lulled by the absence of any signs that the combine had the intention of exploiting the position. During 1928 consumption increased at an accelerating rate, the total increase on the year amounting to nearly 200,000 tons. Production increased also, but not as much as consumption, and stocks declined by a further 26,000 tons to just under 300,000 tons. At the current level of consumption, these stocks represented less than two months' supply, and the stocks held in Europe were almost negligible at less than 9,000 tons. By January 1st, 1928, the price of standard copper was £74, a rise of roughly £10 since October 1st, but the price of electro as fixed by the combine had risen less, and the margin between the two was much smaller than the normal margin. While the London market was becoming apprehensive, there were still no signs of a real upheaval, and the statistical position, apart from the absence of stocks in Europe, which seemed on the way to becoming a new normal feature, cannot be said to have been immediately dangerous.

During January and February the slow rise in prices continued, and the margin between standard and electro began to widen. Trading was extremely active, and it was clear that consumption was increasing at a still faster rate. Then in the middle of March panic seized the market, and consumers became terrified of a shortage of supplies, particularly of electrolytic copper. A big buying movement developed, and Copper Exporters Incorporated substantially increased its quotation. This only added fuel to the flames, for consumers immediately concluded that the combine was out to exploit the situation to the uttermost in its own interest. Between March 14th and March 25th the price of electro rose from approximately £94 to £112, and the price of standard was dragged in its rear from £86 to £95 10s. For a week prices remained at approximately this level, and then, with the beginning of April, a decided fall began. By the middle of April, the price of electro had fallen to £84 and that of standard to about £77. This was the same level for standard as at the beginning of the year, but with the normal in place of a reduced margin for electro. Stability of a sort had been restored, and Copper Exporters appeared to have reasserted some measure of control over the market.

It is not easy to apportion the blame for this upheaval. European consumers roundly accuse Copper Exporters Incorporated of deliberately restricting production and attempting what amounts to a 'corner'. The combine, in a public rejoinder to remonstrances from Europe, has declared the fault to lie entirely with consumers, who needlessly became panic-stricken, and forced the combine in self-defence to raise prices in the hope of choking down the demand. It is asserted that the combine increased production 'as soon as the need could be foreseen', and that the probable demand could have been satisfied had not buyers 'insisted upon covering their requirements further ahead than necessary'. Judging by the statistical position of production and consumption, the combine has a solid basis for its defence, but it is also clear that in allowing stocks in Europe to fall practically out of existence, the combine made a great error. Assuming that its intentions have been and are solely to achieve price stabilisation, the combine is, in fact, faced with a big difficulty in this respect, for private traders cannot be blamed if they refuse to hold stocks when their value is at the dictation of a monopolistic combine, such as Copper Exporters undoubtedly is, even if it does not use its powers of extortion. It would appear that the combine must hold an adequate cushion of stocks in Europe if a repetition of recent events is to be avoided. A second, and an immediately graver, mistake was made by the combine when it raised prices with the aim of choking demand. The history of all such market upheavals shows unmistakably that in the early stages the rise in price is cumulative—every rise increases the consumer's fears, and leads to still greater buying and a larger and ever larger advance in price. Again assuming that the combine whole-heartedly desired to check the rise in price, its best policy would have been to have held its quotations steady, and publicly guaranteed the best rate of delivery which it could manage. The result might have been a speculative scramble little more edifying than that which actually took place, but consumers would then have had no excuse for their idea that the combine was an enemy and the cause of all the mischief. As it is, we are still in doubt as to the strict truth of the combine's assurances that their sole aim is stabilisation. While, as has been suggested, a good case can be made out on the lines that the combine was a victim of madness on the part of consumers, or at the worst a victim of its own unwitting mistakes and lack of experience, this defence is purely fictitious if the combine has other aims than stabilisation. At present there is no conclusive evidence either way, and European private merchants naturally think the worst of an organisation which in either case is depriving them of a living, while consumers still view any monopoly with natural distrust.

Since the end of April the price of electro has remained up to the moment (July 19th) at about £84, being virtually pegged by the unchanged quotation of Copper Exporters. The price of standard has, however, been slowly though irregularly sagging, and has now fallen to about £71. There is thus nearly double the normal margin between electro and standard, and it is becoming clear either that the London market's estimate is wrong, or that Copper Exporters will shortly have to reduce their quotation.

Country	1916*†	1922†	1923†	1924‡	1925‡	1926‡	1927‡	1928‡
United States	971,123	511,970	754,000	819,000	854,000	878,000	847,419	1,060,094
Mexico	60,751	29,842	60,538	57,139	59,123	62,303	63,760	50,556
Canada	52,880	25,300	40,230	50,072	56,239	64,124	70,698	63,040
Cuba	8,613	11,788	11,963	12,742	13,128	13,034	15,538	—
Bolivia	5,675	10,154	11,744	8,200	7,500	7,100	7,850	—
Chile	78,559	142,830	201,042	208,964	209,654	223,015	264,242 }	363,201
Peru	47,452	40,133	48,684	38,798	41,180	42,703	52,438 }	
Venezuela	1,300	1,075	1,175	1,230	1,500	—	—	
Europe	105,434	86,950	115,492	120,618	130,957	135,699	138,779	135,700
Asia	110,900	60,825	66,227	71,300	77,013	77,377	75,972	72,796
Australasia	43,920	13,754	19,995	15,711	13,800	11,244	12,800	10,912
Africa	43,876	58,219	80,410	115,300	118,180	108,010	120,763	124,172
Other countries	3,307	3,307	3,307	4,409	4,409	4,409	4,409	—
World total	1,533,810	996,147	1,414,807	1,523,483	1,586,683	1,628,018	1,674,818	1,916,471

* War peak of production in United States was in 1916. War peak of world production was in 1917, the total being 1,580,475 tons.
† Metric tons.
‡ Tons of 2,000 lb.

528

During the last three months European stocks have only risen to a very small extent, and buyers have been pursuing once again a hand to mouth policy. Stocks in the United States are now very definitely larger, though for safety's sake not nearly large enough even yet. But the will of the combine to build up a substantial reserve of world stocks is open to considerable doubt, for as early as May some of the big American producers announced a curtailment of output of ten per cent, while others are probably restricting their output without this open notice. Such curtailment of mine output does not, of course, take effect at once, but a policy of restriction at so early a date after the events of March–April casts further doubt on the true character of the policy of the combine. Apparently their intention is to try to hold the price of electro at £84 until the restriction takes effect. If so their true colours will soon be revealed, since at present costs stabilisation at £84 is stabilisation at a definitely monopolistic price.

Estimates of production of copper by the American Bureau of Metal Statistics are as above.

III. *Tin*

The total stocks of tin and tin ore are made up of:—

(1) The 'visible supply' as defined by the monthly returns of the London Metal Exchange, namely, (*a*) stocks landing or warehoused in Great Britain, the United States and Holland, (*b*) tin afloat to Great Britain, the United States and Europe from the Straits, Batavia and China, and (*c*) tin afloat to Great Britain and the United States from China. Monthly returns of the 'visible supply' are also compiled by Messrs Ricard and Freiwald and by Messrs A. Strauss and Co., each on a slightly different basis from that of the Metal Exchange. The figures given below are those of the London Metal Exchange.

(2) Stocks of tin and tin ore in the Straits Settlements, the Dutch Indies, China and Hong Kong.

(3) Stocks of tin ore afloat from Bolivia and Nigeria to Europe and in course of smelting.

(4) 'Invisible' stocks in the hands of consumers, etc.

Since the previous issues of this Memorandum, the Anglo-Oriental Mining Corporation has undertaken the monthly preparation of somewhat elaborate statistics, of which some use has been made below.

(1) *The Visible Supply*. It will be noticed that the 'visible supply' figures, which are those commonly quoted, cover a wider field than that usually meant by 'stocks', since they include tin in transit which is in no sense available for consumption. It follows that the 'visible supply' of tin can never fall to zero, or even fall below (say) 9,000–12,000 tons, unless a total breakdown of current supplies is impending from the sources of production. On the other hand, they do not include the total aggregate of tin and tin ore in the widest interpretation. They represent a rather arbitrary compromise between prospective supplies and stocks available for consumption. The result is that they are highly

Available stocks of tin in the chief countries of consumption (U.K., U.S., and Holland) (tons of 2,240 lb)

End of month	1923	1924	1925	1926	1927	1928	1929
Jan.	12,911	8,007	9,371	4,511	5,051	5,303	10,874
Feb.	10,937	7,706	9,593	5,373	3,962	5,238	12,076
March	11,385	7,154	10,489	4,918	3,919	4,166	11,305
April	10,373	10,189	7,313	3,494	3,767	3,919	11,767
May	9,737	8,900	6,692	3,916	3,183	5,273	12,213
June	8,954	9,091	8,554	4,908	2,876	4,304	12,046
July	8,368	10,046	7,942	4,126	3,157	5,877	
Aug.	9,004	10,185	8,596	3,994	3,938	4,564	
Sept.	7,383	10,497	6,721	3,693	3,030	6,797	
Oct.	8,588	7,721	5,896	3,344	4,120	9,352	
Nov.	7,466	7,615	5,410	3,778	3,458	9,103	
Dec.	7,870	9,262	5,863	4,170	4,109	10,382	

misleading from month to month, fluctuating with the chance dates of shipments from the East, etc., which have no real bearing on the position. Figures for stocks in the limited sense, i.e. landing or warehoused in the countries of consumption, will therefore be given separately, and also some material to correct the misleading inferences which might be drawn from the 'visible supply' figures as to the short-period prospective supplies at any time.

The distribution of these stocks at the end of each year was as follows:—

31 December	1923	1924	1925	1926	1927	1928
U.K.: warehoused	3,892	5,241	2,387	1,179	2,013	7,508
„ landing	427	579	774	294	523	446
U.S.: warehoused and landing	1,652	2,844	2,654	1,909	1,573	2,428
Holland: warehoused	1,899	598	48	788	Nil	Nil

Since the total consumption of tin is about 12,000 tons monthly, the stocks available for consumers in 1926 and 1927 amounted

The 'visible supply' of tin (tons of 2,240 lb)*

End of month	1923	1924	1925	1926	1927	1928	1929
Jan.	25,765	24,372	22,949	16,787	15,342	15,244	24,237
Feb.	25,157	21,835	23,591	16,239	14,221	17,645	26,402
March	24,622	23,275	19,623	14,280	15,441	15,586	26,632
April	22,116	19,023	18,105	15,516	13,849	15,001	26,353
May	22,187	19,711	20,897	18,045	14,655	17,064	24,765
June	21,297	20,094	19,797	15,831	15,638	16,231	23,751
July	20,019	20,161	19,857	13,777	15,377	18,022	23,789
Aug.	18,754	21,302	20,000	13,352	14,487	18,456	
Sept.	19,864	20,233	17,642	14,379	15,083	19,924	
Oct.	20,567	18,971	15,770	14,841	14,684	20,907	
Nov.	19,520	20,977	18,199	15,257	14,594	22,067	
Dec.	21,011	25,088	18,029	16,326	15,733	24,563	

* London Metal Exchange figures.

to about 10 days' consumption, as compared with a month's supply at the beginning of 1923; but by the middle of 1929 had recovered again to the equivalent of a full month's supplies.

(2) *Stocks in the East.* The main source of error in the figures just given as a true indication of the position is the fact that they neglect entirely the stocks of tin in the East, whence the bulk of the world's supplies are drawn. As described in earlier memoranda, these stocks were abnormally swollen from 1920 to 1925 by tin held mainly by the Straits and Dutch Indies Governments, under the Bandoeng Agreement. The last lots of this tin were sold before the end of 1924, but the trade figures show that some 3,000 tons were not shipped, and therefore did not enter into the 'visible supply', until 1925. Apart from the disposal of these exceptional stocks, the trade figures indicate that other more normal stocks of tin and of ore in the Straits have varied as follows:—

Tons of 2,240 lb

	Imports of tin into the Straits	Exports of tin from the Straits	Reduction of Straits stocks
1923	65,335	69,119	3,784
1924	74,109	79,940	5,831
1925	76,630	78,819	2,189
1926	74,362	76,474	2,112
1927	81,590	81,815	2,775*
1928	96,294	97,853	1,559

* Increase.

Total stocks in the Straits, including ore, would appear to have been, roughly, as follows:—

	Tons		Tons
End of 1922	14,600	End of 1926	1,700
1923	10,800	1927	4,500
1924	5,000	1928	3,000
1925	3,800		

Total stocks of tin (tons of 2,240 lb)

End of year	1922	1923	1924	1925	1926	1927	1928	1929 (30 April)
Straits pool tin	13,600	9,500	3,000	—	—	—	—	—
,, other stocks	500	1,800	2,500	3,300	1,750	1,350	1,225	1,450
,, surplus ore	500	500	500	500	250	2,470	1,025	1,200
Dutch Indies pool	4,000	2,000	—	—	—	—	—	—
China	1,500	1,400	1,000	500	600	300	300	300
'Visible supply'	25,300	21,000	25,100	18,000	16,300	15,730	24,550	26,350
Grand total	45,400	36,200	32,100	22,300	18,600	19,850	26,900	29,300

Of these stocks, at the end of 1922, 13,600 tons were held under the Bandoeng Pool, in addition to 4,000 tons held in the Dutch Indies.

As regards the Dutch Indies, part of the supplies (the tin from Billiton) is forwarded regularly to the Straits to be smelted there. The rest (the tin from Banca) is smelted locally and shipped direct, mainly to Europe. These shipments are more irregular than the production, depending on the selling policy of the Dutch Government. This is a further cause of error in the visible supply statistics, though probably not to the extent of more than (say) 500–1,000 tons in any month.

As regards supplies from China, about half the production used to find its way to U.K. and U.S.A.; but the exports recently have been on only a small scale. Estimates of stocks, mainly in Hong Kong, are available irregularly.

The best available aggregate of tin supplies, apart from tin in the hands of smelters on the one hand and of consumers on the other, is given above. Apart from exceptional figures in isolated months, 13,000 tons is probably the lowest to which this total can fall, having regard to the amount of tin necessarily afloat. Thus the surplus fell in 1926 almost to the minimum figure, but has since recovered to substantial proportions. Moreover, the true surplus in 1928 was probably a few thousand tons, and in 1929 several thousand tons, more than the figures given below, inasmuch as during these years a large amount was held privately by a 'bull' pool which was operating with a view to sustaining the market price of the metal.

(3) *Bolivian and Nigerian tin afloat and with the smelters.* If we allow two months from the date of shipment from Bolivia to the time of delivery in refined form on the London market, some 5,000 tons of tin are normally thus in transit, but the actual figure may vary from (say) 4,000 tons to 8,000 tons. The corresponding variations for Nigerian tin in transit are on a much smaller scale. These fluctuations average out, of course, over a period of time, but may considerably affect the statistics of visible supply between one month and another.

534

(4) *'Invisible' stocks in the hands of consumers, etc.* As stated above, there were in 1928 and 1929 some thousands of tons of 'invisible' stocks held privately by a 'bull' pool. Apart from such exceptional holdings, the most important influence in accelerating supplies and decreasing the aggregate of 'invisible' stocks at all stages from the producer to the consumer is to be found in the development of a 'backwardation' on forward tin as against spot tin, i.e. in tin for delivery in three months standing at a price appreciably lower than tin for immediate delivery. This means on the one hand that the producers and smelters can gain the difference by hastening forward their supplies of refined metal, and on the other hand that consumers can save the difference by keeping their stocks as low as possible and covering their known prospective requirements by buying forward instead of keeping the actual metal on hand.

For short periods during the time of acute shortage in 1927 the 'backwardation' sometimes reached or exceeded £12 per three months. The average figures over each year have been as follows:

	Average price of spot tin			Average price of 3 months' tin			Spot tin above (+) or below (−) forward tin		
	£	s.	d.	£	s.	d.	£	s.	d.
1922	159	10	9	160	13	11	−1	3	2
1923	202	5	0	202	15	4	−0	10	4
1924	248	17	4	249	10	6½	−0	13	2½
1925	261	1	8½	262	5	9½	−1	4	1
1926	291	3	0½	284	7	7	+6	15	5½
1927	289	0	0	282	4	0	+6	16	0
1928	227	6	0	225	14	0	+1	12	0

In 1929 the forward price of tin has again risen to a premium over spot tin, which is natural in view of the heavy stocks.

The principal changes in the volume of production have been, approximately, as below.

Production at last caught up with consumption towards the

World's tin production (tons of 2,240 lb)

	1923	1924	1925	1926	1927	1928
Malay States	39,500	46,500	48,000	48,000	54,000	64,500
Dutch Indies	29,000	32,000	31,500	31,500	35,500	35,000
Siam and Burma	9,000	9,000	8,000	8,000	9,000	10,000
China	8,000	7,000	9,000	6,500	6,500	6,500
Australia	3,000	3,000	3,000	3,000	3,000	3,000
Nigeria	6,000	6,000	6,000	7,000	7,500	9,000
S. Africa	1,000	1,000	1,000	1,000	1,000	1,000
Cornwall	1,000	1,500	2,000	2,000	2,000	2,500
Bolivia	29,500	31,500	32,000	32,000	34,000	40,000
Belgian Congo	1,000	1,000	2,000	2,000	2,000	2,000
Elsewhere	500	1,500	2,000	2,000	2,000	2,000
Total	127,500	140,000	144,500	143,000	156,500	175,500

end of 1926, and then, after keeping about level with it for a year, took a leap ahead, which consumption, although of record dimensions, has found it impossible to keep up with, as is shown by the following approximate estimates.

Consumption of tin (tons of 2,240 lb)

	1925	1926	1927	1928
Great Britain	25,000	18,500	23,000	31,000
United States	76,500	78,000	72,500	79,000
Germany	8,000	5,500	15,000	9,000
France	11,500	11,000	8,500	10,500
Asia	10,000	9,000	9,000	9,000
Other countries	23,500	24,500	27,000	27,000
Total	154,500	146,500	155,000	165,500

We estimate recent production and consumption of tin in the aggregate as below.

Production in 1929 is expected to exceed the amount mined in 1928 by a fairly substantial figure, with the result that, although consumption is also increasing and stands at a higher level than ever before, it is probable that production is still exceeding

Tons of 2,240 lb

Year	Production	Consumption	Stocks at end of year
1922	130,000	132,000	45,400
1923	127,500	139,000	36,000
1924	140,000	144,500	32,000
1925	144,500	154,500	22,000
1926	143,000	146,500	18,500
1927	156,500	155,000	20,000
1928	175,500	165,500	30,000

consumption by at least 500 tons a month. The price has naturally fallen heavily, but it would probably have fallen further if it had not been for the operations of a 'bull' pool which has accumulated very large stocks of metal and holds them off the market. The position is obviously dominated by this accumulation. Efforts are now being made to secure concerted measures by producers for an organised curtailment of output; but it is not easy to see how appropriate measures for the purpose could be devised.

IV. *Lead*

In the previous edition of this Memorandum (March 1927) it was pointed out that high prices of lead had called forth increased production, and it was suggested that any further increase in output would outrun demand and bring about a reaction in prices. The course of events over 1927 confirmed this diagnosis. Production continued its steady expansion, and with a falling off of consumption in America and France prices fell heavily over the year, while stocks were much above the level of previous years. This development continued well into 1928, but with increased American consumption stocks diminished and prices recovered.

The following figures issued by the American Bureau of Metal Statistics apply to the principal lead-producing countries of the

537

Stocks of lead in U.S., Mexico and U.K. (tons of 2,240 lb)

Beginning of month	1926			1927			1928			1929		
	U.S. and Mexico*	U.K.†	Total	U.S. and Mexico*	U.K.†	Total	U.S. and Mexico*	U.K.†	Total	U.S. and Mexico*	U.K.†	Total
January	94,300	5	94,305	113,400	1,677	115,077	139,500	2,014	141,514	144,100	917	145,017
February	93,400	265	93,665	120,300	2,516	122,816	140,600	1,931	142,531	139,400	1,586	140,986
March	94,100	237	94,337	124,800	2,596	127,396	149,700	1,975	151,675	143,400	1,403	144,803
April	100,600	265	100,865	130,200	2,732	132,932	154,800	1,873	156,673		1,304	
May	105,000	439	105,439	143,600	2,918	146,518	143,900	1,861	145,761		1,305	
June	107,900	1,114	109,014	156,400	2,467	158,867	142,300	1,383	143,683		945	
July	109,900	1,025	110,925	152,000	2,436	154,436	146,200	1,281	147,481		779	
August	106,000	191	106,191	147,800	2,165	149,965	141,800	1,383	143,183		773	
September	99,500	202	99,702	145,400	2,091	147,491	140,200	1,326	141,526			
October	101,000	58	101,058	143,000	2,136	145,136	138,800	977	139,777			
November	105,600	225	105,825	139,200	2,436	141,636	136,400	675	137,075			
December	107,200	1,299	108,499	139,000	2,278	141,278	140,600	400	141,000			

* Stocks of ore, matte, base bullion and refined lead in the hands of those concerns which report to the American Bureau of Metal Statistics.
† Metal Exchange figures.

world, which in 1924 furnished 79 per cent of the world's total lead output:

Production of lead (1,000 tons of 2,240 lb)

	1923	1924	1925	1926	1927	1928
United States	471	525	590	621	601	576
Mexico	164	159	181	197	245	223
Canada	48	75	111	126	139	147
Spain and Tunis	108	137	135	145	137	94
Italy	17	22	16	23	23	21
Australia	122	126	147	149	165	156
Burma	46	52	48	54	66	79
Rhodesia	11	6	3	4	6	5
Total	987	1,102	1,231	1,319	1,382	1,301

The American Bureau estimated world production in recent years as follows:—

	1,000 tons
1925	1,464
1926	1,570
1927	1,658
1928	1,624
1929 (6 months)	852

Thus the fall in prices which set in in 1927 brought about a check to production in the following year, and ended the long run of expanding output. Nevertheless, stocks at the end of 1928 were as large as a twelvemonth before. This year lead shared in the flutter and subsequent reaction of non-ferrous metal prices which occurred in March and April, but there are no signs yet of a revival of demand corresponding with the expansion of output indicated by the statistics for the first six months of the year.

V. *Spelter (Zinc)*

Monthly statistics are available of stocks in public warehouses in the United States and in the United Kingdom as given below.

539

U.K. and U.S. stocks of spelter (tons of 2,240 lb)

End of month	1926			1927			1928			1929		
	U.S.	U.K.	Total	U.S.	U.K.	Total	U.S.	U.K.	Total	U.S.	U.K.	Total
January	12,770	287	13,057	26,710	1,260	27,970	37,650	1,063	38,713	40,550	1,717	42,267
February	18,160	391	18,551	29,420	1,061	30,481	36,900	1,565	37,465	36,250	1,349	37,599
March	18,360	422	18,782	32,380	857	33,237	37,080	791	37,871	33,900	872	34,772
April	23,200	1,063	24,263	36,800	1,188	37,988	39,970	454	40,424	30,870	897	31,767
May	26,730	951	27,681	37,550	1,052	38,602	40,400	832	41,232	30,200	1,253	31,453
June	23,000	1,052	24,052	39,170	1,524	40,694	39,710	1,236	40,946	32,970	910	33,880
July	20,520	993	21,513	35,120	1,231	36,351	37,700	916	38,616	39,390	2,193	41,583
August	16,220	1,455	17,675	30,890	966	31,856	39,660	1,335	40,995			
September	14,020	1,136	15,156	30,610	1,017	31,627	42,800	1,343	44,143			
October	14,200	999	15,199	32,340	614	32,954	41,140	671	41,811			
November	12,930	970	13,900	35,120	1,160	36,280	41,570	1,486	43,056			
December	19,540	922	20,462	36,390	679	37,069	40,590	1,757	42,347			

From the lowest levels touched at the end of 1925 the figures have mounted almost uninterruptedly, and this easing in the stocks situation has been reflected in the price movement.

Annual production has continued to increase, but at a slower rate, and recently output has been restricted by organised action on the part of European producers. According to Rudolf Wolff & Co., the world's output of virgin spelter has been as follows:

World output of virgin spelter (1,000 tons of 2,240 lb)

1921	452	1925	1,132
1922	689	1926	1,238
1923	960	1927	1,305
1924	998	1928	1,384

The same authority gives the following figures for production of spelter by countries which furnish about 86 per cent of the world's output.

The falling off in U.S. production since 1926 has been more than offset by increases in other countries, and the development of new processes—differential flotation and electrical deposition —has undoubtedly favoured expansion of output. But any

Production of spelter (tons of 2,240 lb)

	1923	1924	1925	1926	1927	1928
United States	474,284	478,430	513,000	570,000	548,000	553,000
Canada	27,093	24,679	38,000	55,000	66,000	73,000
Belgium	145,733	160,411	171,000	190,000	199,000	205,000
Germany (including Polish Silesia)	110,396	102,989*	159,000	190,000	234,000	256,000
Australia	40,248	46,601	47,000	48,000	50,000	49,000
Great Britain	31,279	38,480	59,000	27,000	50,000	55,000
Total	829,032	851,591	987,000	1,080,000	1,147,000	1,191,000

* Probably under-estimated.

541

World stocks 1925–8 (metric tons)

	1 Sept. 1925	1 Dec. 1925	1 May 1926	1 July 1926	31 Dec. 1926	1 April 1927	1 July 1927	1 Oct. 1927	1 Jan. 1928
United States	15,490	6,300	23,600	23,400	19,800	33,000	39,871	31,100	37,000
Germany and Poland	5,400	15,000	7,500	6,500	9,500	6,800	6,800	7,600	6,100
Canada	700	1,000	2,200	2,100	3,200	3,000	2,600	2,600	2,400
Great Britain	600	1,000	1,800	1,200	1,000	1,200	1,500	1,400	1,100
Belgium	1,700	1,900	2,600	1,800	4,000	3,000	3,300	3,900	4,200
France	800	800	1,000	1,200	1,500	1,200	1,300	1,200	—
Scandinavia	200	200	200	200	200	200	200	200	200
Australia*	2,000	2,000	2,200	2,200	2,400	—	—	2,800	2,800
Far East	500	500	500	500	500	500	500	600	600
Elsewhere	500	500	1,500	1,500	1,500	1,500	1,500	1,500	1,700
Total	27,890	29,200	43,100	40,600	43,600	52,900	60,371	52,900	56,100

* Including unsold shipments afloat.

tendency for supply to outrun demand seems to have been checked before the end of 1928, and stocks showed very little increase over the year. It is not possible to say to what extent American producers are co-operating with the European restriction scheme, but for the moment producers seem to have the situation fairly well in hand.

Mr A. J. M. Sharpe, Foreign Correspondent of the American Zinc Institute, has estimated world stocks at recent dates as above.

VI. *Rubber*

The stocks of rubber are held mainly:—

(1) On plantations and with dealers within the restricted area of Malaya.

(2) In Singapore and Penang.

(3) Afloat.

(4) In London and Liverpool.

(5) In U.S.A. warehouses and factories.

In addition relatively insignificant stocks are held:—

(6) In Ceylon and India.

(7) In Dutch East Indies.

(8) In Para (Brazil).

(9) In Amsterdam and Antwerp.

Prior to 1928 no figures were available for (1). This omission became important during the interval between the announcement that restriction was to come to an end and its taking effect. Accordingly, a census of stocks within Malaya was taken. Use of this has been made in the table on page 545, which is the most useful available indication of total stocks in present circumstances.

It has been pointed out, however, in a recent issue of *The Rubber Quarterly* that the figures below for the rubber held within Malaya on October 1st, 1928, may have been seriously incorrect, and that the accumulations at that date were probably far greater than was admitted. For the shipments out of Malaya

543

World rubber stocks (exclusive of stock on estates) (1,000 tons)

End of	United Kingdom*	United States†	Singapore and Penang‡	Ceylon and India	Dutch East Indies	Para (Brazil)	Amsterdam and Antwerp	Afloat	Approximate total*
1920	56	76	35	?	?	?	?	37	(204)§ 219‖-229
1921	80	52	40	?	?	?	?	37	(209)§ 224‖-244
1922	81	90	55	?	?	?	?	45	(271)§ 286‖-306
1923 March	79	87	21	3·5	9	0·6	1·0	48	249
June	64	101	46	?	?	?	?	52	(263)§ 278‖
September	68	90	27	4·0	10	0·9	1·2	43	244
December	75	73	38	4·0	10	?	2·5	52	254
1924 March	70	70	21	3·0	10	1·0	1·1	50	226
June	65	60	20	3·0	10	1·0	1·2	48	208
September	54	56	20	3·5	7	0·8	0·6	54	196
December	36	63	19	4·0	5	0·9	0·3	53	181
1925 March	23	55	17	4·0	5	1·2	0·1	50	155
June	7	40	16	3·0	3	0·5	0·2	59	129
September	7	45	16	4·0	5	1·1	0·3	63	141
December	7	74	20	4·5	5	1·5	0·2	70	182
1926 March	16	61	18	4·5	7	2·0	0·2	74	183
June	28	60	19	4·5	7	1·8	0·8	72	193
September	42	62	26	4·5	8	2·1	1·3	67	213
December	59	72	26	5·5	7	1·5	1·1	77	259
1927 March	70	86	28	5·0	7	2·0	1·5	74	273
June	71	89	22	4·5	7	1·7	1·5	66	263
September	72	98	25	4	6	3	1	62	271
December	66	100	26	4	6	2	1	67	272
1928 March	60	114	21	4	5	2	1	63	270
June	41	90	18	4	5	2	1	59	222
September	34	69	15	4	5	3	2	74	206
December	23	66	34	5	5	3	1	102	239
1929 March	32	101	34	4	4	3	1	86	245

* Including an estimate of stocks in private warehouses from 1923 to June 1927. The true totals for 1920–2 were certainly higher than the figures shown, and should perhaps be increased by 10,000 tons in 1920, and by 15–20,000 tons in 1921 and 1922. From September 1927 the figures are the total published stocks in London and Liverpool.   † Returns cover 90–95 per cent of the whole.

‡ Including Wellesley, Dindings and Malacca from September 1927.   § These figures in brackets give the actual total of stocks quoted.

‖ These figures include an estimate of 15,000 tons for the unknown stocks in Ceylon, Dutch East Indies, Para, and at Amsterdam and Antwerp. This

	1 January 1928	1 April 1928	1 July 1928	1 October 1928	1 January 1929	1 April 1929	1 May 1929	1 June 1929
In London	63,793	58,272	38,611	31,462	19,727	27,656	31,213	31,539
In Liverpool	2,468	2,123	2,335	2,233	2,788	4,333	4,779	4,642
In the Straits	25,798	20,538	18,207	14,898	32,905	29,437	26,474	30,764
On Estates in Malaya	30,000	30,000	44,959	61,028	26,325	21,077	21,682	21,846
With dealers in Malaya	—	—	13,560	9,683	12,360	12,665	12,140	13,211
Ditto in Ceylon	7,000	7,000	9,300	13,100	7,000	7,000	7,000	7,000
In United States	100,130	114,061	90,198	68,850	66,166	100,537	107,659	97,191
Afloat to U.S.	47,938	39,324	40,001	48,566	68,764	56,476	55,408	55,404
Total stocks	277,127	271,318	257,171	249,820	236,035	259,181	266,355	261,597

between October 1928 and the end of March 1929 do not tally with the estate production during the period *plus* the reduction of stocks in Malaya as recorded in the above. It seems possible, indeed, that the stocks in Malaya on October 1st, 1928, may have been as much as twice the total given above, that is, 140,000 tons instead of 70,000. Some part of this discrepancy would be accounted for by rubber in transit and rubber on estates of less than 100 acres, which the published figure of 70,000 tons does not purport to include. But this can scarcely explain the whole of the difference.

The following are the estimates of production and consumption of rubber in recent years:—

Year	Production (1,000 tons)	Consumption (1,000 tons)	Apparent increase or decrease in stocks	Recorded change in stocks
1919	339	335	—	—
1920	368	290	—	—
1921	293	292	+ 1	+15
1922	395*	408	−13	+62
1923	382	434	−52	−52
1924	420	475	−55	−73
1925	520	540	−20	+ 1
1926	610	545	+65	+77
1927	630	590	+40	+38
1928	671	681	−10	−41

* This figure should probably be higher.

In the spring of 1929 the average of the guesses of those in the trade showed an expectation of production and consumption being approximately balanced during the year 1929 with consumption at 706,000 tons and production at 703,000 tons. More recently the sustained high level of consumption in the United States has led to increased estimates of consumption. On the other hand the very heavy shipments from Malaya are capable of being explained either by production in excess of the estimate, or, as suggested above, by a previous under-estimation of stocks. The latest estimates are for some excess of consumption over production in 1929 at a figure of about 750,000 tons for the former.

During 1928 the rubber market was, of course, dominated by the removal of restriction by the British Government, which, after about six months' notice, became effective on November 1st, 1928. It had become evident that the time was approaching for the gradual relaxation and eventual removal of restriction. But it would seem, in the light of after-events, that the time and manner of the removal actually chosen had the effect of sacrificing the fruits of restriction just when they were about to be secured; for the growth of world consumption was just about catching up with the growth of production.

The growth in the consumption of reclaimed rubber in the United States is shown below:—

United States consumption of crude and reclaimed rubber

	Crude rubber, long tons	Reclaimed rubber, long tons	Reclaimed-crude, per cent
1919	202,303	73,535	36·3
1920	196,270	75,297	38·4
1921	169,308	41,351	24·4
1922	283,271	54,458	19·2
1923	319,700	75,200	23·5
1924	336,600	78,500	23·3
1925	387,629	137,000	35·3
1926	366,000	164,500	45·0
1927	373,000	189,500	50·8
1928	437,000	223,000	51·0

VII. *Sugar*

In the case of this commodity it is necessary to restrict ourselves to 'visible supplies', accurate estimates of stocks held up by producers in the fairly numerous different sources of supply not being available, with the important exception of Cuba. Statistics of stocks in the interior of Cuba are now available since 1926, and the carryover of these stocks has recently been such as to make a considerable addition to the 'visible' carryover. With this deficiency made good, the limitation to 'visible' supplies is not so serious as it would be in the case of many commodities, because, on the one hand, sugar being a semi-manufactured product, the agricultural producers send the bulk of the output forward to the centrals as soon as it is available, and, on the other hand, since in most countries it is a dutiable commodity, invisible supplies, on which duty has been paid, are not likely, as a rule, to be larger than convenience dictates.

The following table shows the distribution of stocks in the seven most important European countries, and the total for Europe. This, of course, is predominantly beet sugar, and hence the stocks reach a maximum about the beginning of the calendar year, and a minimum in October. The remaining columns show stocks in U.S. ports, Cuba ports, and in the interior of Cuba. These are almost exclusively cane sugar, since the beet sugar crop of the U.S. is marketed internally. The harvesting of the Cuban crop is usually completed in May, and hence the grand total in the last column shows a somewhat different seasonal variation to the total for Europe, though the minimum is much the same, since by October the bulk of the Cuban supply has normally passed through the ports to the refiners.

The table below [p. 550] gives a very rough idea of stocks, production, and consumption in recent seasons and the table on page 551 shows consumption during recent years by this country and the United States, which between them account for an extraordinary proportion of the exported sugar.

The history of the sugar industry during the last two years may be summarised as a continuous struggle against excessive supplies despite a rapidly increasing demand; and the prospects for producers today are only a little, if at all, brighter. There

Distribution of sugar stocks (1,000 tons)

Beginning of month	Germany	Czecho-Slovakia	France	Holland	Belgium	Poland	United Kingdom	Total Europe	U.S. ports	Cuba ports	Cuba interior	Grand total
1925 January	977	769	468	195	228	237	162	3,036	32	42	—	—
April	591	494	373	86	166	171	192	2,073	128	860	—	—
July	269	235	158	66	83	93	357	1,261	277	1,095	—	—
October	17	36	51	17	18	—	300	439	135	594	—	—
1926 January	1,207	934	487	170	223	289	432	3,742	76	132	—	—
April	926	680	325	164	149	206	514	2,964	208	1,193	—	—
July	515	345	197	134	61	108	490	1,850	377	1,328	997	4,552
October	79	44	45	63	18	22	371	642	216	603	458	1,919
1927 January	1,176	611	547	238	137	291	380	3,380	181	70	12	3,643
April	855	413	393	172	105	189	362	2,489	219	1,324	1,041	4,090
July	535	178	269	58	71	98	411	1,620	259	1,170	464	1,780
October	80	9	67	29	14	4	258	461	183	672		
1928 January	1,231	846	587	192	183	293	277	3,591	179	218	74	4,062
February	1,127	803	560	176	166	273	341	3,446	172	306	291	4,215
March	1,021	730	488	166	150	241	338	3,134	254	851	750	4,989
April	889	623	409	146	142	200	320	2,729	315	1,203	1,195	5,442
May	783	521	347	127	135	178	310	2,401	517	1,325	1,224	5,467
June	643	406	304	103	124	147	323	2,050	551	1,258	1,073	4,932
July	502	292	221	92	102	121	310	1,640	544	1,159	960	4,303
August	337	196	159	67	71	80	227	1,137	490	982	826	3,435
September	174	110	108	41	46	40	168	687	386	828	617	2,518
October	101	47	62	33	25	14	136	418	343	630	459	1,850
November	482	343	188	136	63	108	180	1,500	272	475	314	2,561
December	1,225	702	439	249	180	286	190	3,271	204	287	177	3,939
1929 January	1,457	690	630	261	221	420	276	3,955	159	125	32	4,271
February	1,390	646	626	260	198	416	360	3,896	144	477	517	5,034
March	1,300	602	564	247	190	390	325	3,618	271	949	950	5,788
April	1,146	522	473	229	171	345	314	3,200	418	1,298	1,274	6,190
May	983	399	402	213	160	281	250	2,688	553	1,511	1,406	6,152
June	819	320	349	205	146	218	220	2,277	703	1,440	1,170	5,590
July												

Supply and consumption of sugar (tons)

	1920–1	1921–2	1922–3	1923–4	1924–5	1925–6	1926–7	1927–8	1928–9
Stock carried over on 1 September	1,600,000	2,400,000	1,180,000	1,267,000	982,000	1,612,000	2,657,000	2,439,000	2,518,000
European beet crops	3,671,788	4,054,282	4,735,500	5,057,000	7,077,800	7,453,000	6,860,000	8,031,000	8,337,000
American beet crops	1,004,019	930,121	649,000	803,700	1,010,400	836,900	829,000	965,000	949,000
Cane crops	12,081,831	12,679,948	12,691,500	13,837,400	15,501,400	16,293,700	15,901,000	16,330,000	17,298,000
Total	18,357,638	20,064,351	19,256,000	20,965,900	24,571,600	26,195,600	26,247,000	27,765,000	29,102,000
Deduct visible supplies at end of season (1 September)	2,400,000	1,180,000	1,267,000	982,000	1,612,000	2,000,000	2,439,000	2,518,000	—
Total consumption	15,957,638	18,884,351	17,989,000	19,983,900	22,959,600	24,195,600	23,808,000	25,247,000	—

550

* In this estimate by Willett and Gray the Cuban crop was put at 4,900,000 tons. Grinding has now been completed and the total crop is stated to be 5,156,000 tons. Assuming that this increase is not balanced by a decrease elsewhere, this raises the total for cane crops to 17,554,000 and the total available to 29,358,000 tons.

U.K. and U.S.A. consumption of sugar

Year	Consumption (raw values—tons)	
	United Kingdom	United States
1922	1,748,177	5,476,500
1923	1,602,029	5,141,000
1924	1,706,661	5,220,000
1925	1,817,869	5,925,000
1926	1,776,766	6,098,200
1927	1,681,351	5,695,700
1928	1,851,313	5,960,210

has also been the paradox of artificial limitation in Cuba, and an enormously increased production in the other great cane producing country, Java, despite a steadily falling price level. In the season 1926–7 the combined result of restriction in Cuba and a poor European beet crop was a substantial decline in production, which, however, was largely neutralised by a decline in consumption due, partly at least, to the relatively high price-level during the first part of the season, and stocks on September 1st, 1927, were only a little lower than a year previously. In the season 1927–8 production increased by 1·8 million tons, despite the still more drastic restriction of the Cuban crop to 4 million tons, and consumption also increased, though not sufficiently to prevent a further small addition to the enormous carryover. For the current season the production figures are still approximate, but can hardly fail to be at least 1 million tons greater. The low level of prices during the last twelve months and more appears to have restrained production in many of the smaller sources of supply, but this effect has been completely overlaid by the abandonment of all restriction or artificial control of any kind in Cuba, and by the enormous increase in Java, as the result of the widespread adoption of a new variety of cane which gives a very much higher yield than those formerly in cultivation. The Java crop last summer was 2,944,000 tons as compared with 2,359,000 and 1,959,000 tons in the two previous seasons.

As against an estimated increase of 1·5 million tons in production during the present season, there is no doubt that consumption has also been steadily and largely increasing, but it seems highly doubtful whether the carryover on September 1st next will show any reduction: a further increase of several hundred thousand tons is quite likely. It is therefore small wonder that prices have remained at an extraordinarily low level, a level at which probably only the Java producers can make any sort of reasonable profit; during June the cargo prices in the United Kingdom actually dropped to a figure which has not been reached since 1902. It is, of course, impossible, at this date, to forecast the crops of 1929–30, with the exception of the Java crop, which, though actually harvested during our summer months, is reckoned statistically as the crop for the season beginning on September 1st following, since very little of the new sugar moves into commerce before that date. The crop for 1929–30, which is now being harvested, is not likely to show an increase similar to that of the last two seasons, for the weather has not been so favourable, and though the new cane has been planted still more widely, it appears to be subject to certain weaknesses. The Java crop will probably not exceed 3 million tons by more than, say, 100,000 tons. Similarly the weather has not up to the present been too kind to the Cuban crop, and there appears to have been an appreciable restriction of new planting. These factors have helped to stir up a more bullish attitude and a little more activity in the futures market during the last few weeks. Such considerations, however, are of small importance beside two other factors of a more artificial kind. The first is whether there is to be a renewal of restriction in Cuba. Six months ago opinion in Cuba was decidedly adverse to restriction in any form, but the size of this year's crop and recent market conditions appear to have brought about a change, which has been further stimulated of late by the successful persuasion of the Dutch to take part in international conversations at Brussels, though they have not yet officially joined the Conference. It is rumoured that Cuba is trying to persuade the Java Sugar Producers' Association to agree to restrict their market to India and the Far East by offering in return to restrict Cuban production to 4 or 4½ million tons; at the same time Cuba would come to some marketing arrangement with the European Beet Cartel. It is also thought likely that even if there is no restriction Cuba may establish a central selling agency to market the entire crop, and thus endeavour to prevent undue price cutting. Should Cuban production be restricted, the whole situation would be materially different, for there is little reason to suppose a halt in the advance of consumption, and a gradual decline in the surplus stocks would almost certainly ensue. But against this favourable possibility, producers have also to consider the possibility of a much higher sugar tariff in the United States, if the present bill should be accepted by the Senate Finance Committee. According to present arrangements, no decision will be made on this question until October, and market opinion seems to be discounting pretty heavily the probability of any substantial increase in the tariff. Nevertheless, this is a very important factor in the situation, for a higher tariff would not only tend to reduce consumption in the biggest consuming country of the world, but it would also, of course, greatly stimulate production within the United States and its insular possessions. If, on the other hand, the tariff remains virtually unaltered, and if the producing countries come to some arrangement for restriction in Cuba and 'orderly' marketing, the sugar industry a year hence may be definitely in sight of less difficult times. Without some restriction of the Cuban crop, the approach to equilibrium will be a much slower process, but whether Cuba will again shoulder the burden without really strong and practical support from the other producing countries seems very doubtful, for once bit is twice shy, and with some reason, especially in this case.

Tea in bond in the United Kingdom (1,000 lb)

End of month	1921	1922	1923	1924	1925	1926	1927	1928	1929
January	219,377	208,115	186,035	182,865	225,067	209,655	222,636	254,957	251,387
February	223,179	221,362	176,681	188,559	234,557	202,300	217,413	252,704	253,716
March	229,568	219,645	183,413	193,362	231,516	195,388	194,362	242,771	259,651
April	233,018	214,484	167,763*	192,219	217,091	179,891	179,315	223,464	—
May	228,793	192,396	141,659	152,317	190,730	163,408	158,012	195,988	276,000
June	218,290	170,478	126,792	138,691	180,859	155,595	145,417	179,214	217,000
July	207,448	153,198	112,890	121,097	163,255	148,207	136,531	170,519	203,000
August	197,433	142,137	121,935	128,266	165,085	156,850	146,631	179,106	
September	190,799	151,510	134,170	136,694	180,621	175,012	163,838	194,681	
October	190,129	152,095	146,990	150,721	181,683	186,861	185,155	209,701	
November	196,534	158,357	152,288	174,414	189,080	196,626	213,808	224,717	
December	205,420	169,776	165,666	205,859	203,654	207,003	239,085	240,738	

* Excluding Irish Free State from this month onwards.

554

VIII. *Tea*

The only precise figures available for the stocks of tea are of those in bond in the United Kingdom. Since, however, about three-quarters of the total world production passes through this country, these stocks should form a fairly reliable index of the position. (See table above.)

With the removal of all duties on tea, the Customs Department have ceased to compile these figures. The Tea Brokers' Association of London are publishing returns of stocks in London public warehouses, which normally represent about 90 per cent of the total, but their efforts to obtain returns from private warehouses in London and from other ports have so far failed. In order to make the series more comparable the published figures have been raised by approximately 10 per cent, but it must be emphasised that the figures before and since March are not strictly comparable, while the degree of accuracy is now very uncertain.

During 1927, despite a steadily rising price level, stocks increased, and in the first two months of 1928 stood at the record amount of over 250 million lb. The result was a falling price level until towards the close of last year. Stocks at the end of January and February 1929 were approximately at the same level as a year previous, but against this allowance must be made for the increase in the rate of consumption. The further rise in stocks in March was probably due to Budget anticipations of an abolition or at least a reduction of the duty in England, which were duly realised. A marked feature of 1928 was the increased shipments direct to consuming countries such as Iraq (probably partly for Russia), Egypt, South America, etc., and there is little doubt that world consumption continues to expand not only in the present tea-drinking countries like Great Britain, but in countries hitherto of little account. Production in the season just ended seems likely to have been about equal to consumption, and stocks are only a little larger than convenience dictates, especially in view of the close balance between production and consumption.

Consumption in Great Britain and Northern Ireland has been as follows in recent years:—

	Million lb
1923	387·5
1924	396·5
1925	402·0
1926	408·8
1927	416·2
1928	423·7

World production during the calendar years has been as follows (according to Messrs F. J. Denton, Ltd.):—

Million lb

	1923	1924	1925	1926	1927
India	371·1	372·9	360·7	392·9	389·2
Ceylon	183·5	203·7	209·5	216·1	227·1
Java	90·1	104·9	94·6	118·7	126·7
Sumatra	16·5	17·9	16·6	17·4	17·6
Japan (exports only)	27·1	22·5	27·8	23·7	23·2
China (exports only)	106·8	86·5	89·0*	80·0*	83·0*
Formosa (exports only)	20·2	20·5	20·8	22·9	22·5
Elsewhere (estimated)	2·0	2·0	2·0	2·0*	2·0*
	817·4	830·9	821·1	871·9	891·4

* Estimated.

Some idea of the comparative changes in world consumption may be obtained from the following figures of total imports for home consumption into the principal consuming countries during recent calendar years. (The figures are partly estimated.)

	Million lb		Million lb
1923	723·3	1926	778·5
1924	738·1	1927	792·3
1925	754·6		

Coffee (1,ooo bags)*

Beginning of month	Visible supply of Europe	Visible supply of U.S.A.	Stocks in Brazil	Total	Stocks in interior of Sao Paulo	Grand total
1913 July	6,480	1,848	1,947	10,275		
September	6,005	1,477	4,002	11,484		
October	6,019	1,393	4,769	12,181		
1914 January	7,275	1,709	4,681	13,665		
April	8,702	2,172	1,743	12,617		
June	8,353	2,056	1,207	11,616		
1919 January	758	1,010	9,296	11,364		
April	2,755	1,964	7,060	11,799		
July	3,124	1,508	5,704	10,336		
October	2,821	2,057	5,540	10,418		
1920 January	2,843	2,007	5,020	9,870		
April	2,573	2,209	3,392	8,174		
July	2,509	2,293	1,948	6,750		
October	2,955	2,640	2,387	7,982		
1921 January	2,588	2,442	3,735	8,765		
April	2,533	2,765	3,389	8,687		
July	2,562	2,100	4,038	8,700		
October	2,564	1,838	4,589	8,991		
1922 January	2,399	2,056	4,948	9,403		
April	2,977	1,583	4,580	9,140		
July	3,068	1,456	4,115	8,639		
October	3,007	1,182	4,292	8,481		
1923 January	2,839	1,385	3,756	7,980		
April	2,463	1,618	2,903	6,974		
July	2,296	1,075	1,969	5,340		
October	2,449	1,387	2,016	5,852		
1924 January	2,228	1,349	890	4,467		
April	1,935	1,075	954	3,964		
July	2,152	1,387	1,532	5,071	4,592	9,663
October	2,255	1,337	2,135	5,727		

Table (*cont.*)

Beginning of month	Visible supply of Europe	Visible supply of U.S.A.	Stocks in Brazil	Total	Stocks in interior of Sao Paulo	Grand total
1925 January	2,098	1,046	2,240	5,384		
April	2,028	1,116	2,245	5,389		
July	2,193	1,154	1,738	5,085	1,786	6,871
October	2,367	1,269	1,594	5,230		
1926 January	2,163	1,484	1,517	5,164	4,383	9,547
April	2,041	1,258	1,487	4,786	3,902	8,688
July	2,028	1,065	1,478	4,571	2,833	7,404
October	2,190	1,448	1,217	4,856	5,255	10,111
1927 January	2,024	1,617	1,270	4,911	5,990	10,901
April	2,142	1,338	1,078	4,558	3,888	8,446
July	2,308	1,298	1,116	4,720	3,312	8,032
October	2,470	1,182	1,333	4,985	9,570	14,555
1928 January	2,277	1,479	1,512	5,268	13,120	18,388
February	2,297	1,390	1,412	5,099	13,354	18,453
March	2,253	1,243	1,421	4,917	13,211	18,128
April	2,442	1,409	1,404	5,255	12,653	17,908
May	2,545	1,361	1,528	5,434	12,115	17,549
June	2,718	1,374	1,346	5,438	11,714	16,152
July	2,841	1,381	1,507	5,729	11,672	17,401
August	2,823	1,351	1,547	5,721	11,986	17,707
September	2,740	1,202	1,579	5,521	13,018	18,539
October	2,608	1,193	1,564	5,365	13,469	18,834
November	2,650	1,286	1,396	5,332	13,669	19,001
December	2,431	1,244	1,594	5,269	13,205	18,474
1929 January	2,358	1,333	1,481	5,172	12,966	18,138
February	2,314	1,297	1,405	5,016	12,279	17,295
March	2,288	1,411	1,298	4,997	11,522	16,519
April	2,373	1,178	1,429	4,980	10,403	15,383
May	2,656	1,131	1,431	5,217	9,772	14,989
June	2,718	1,130	1,498	5,346	9,084	14,430
July	2,727	1,109	1,502	5,338		

* G. Duuring & Zoon.

In addition to the above stocks there were 1,180,000 bags in the interior of Rio de Janeiro on 1 July 1928. The stock has been regularly declining month by month, and on 1 June 1929, amounted to only 116,00 bags.

IX. *Coffee*

About two-thirds of the supply of coffee for Europe and U.S.A. comes from Brazil. The preceding table is based on the figures supplied by Messrs Duuring & Zoon, the most important omissions from which are the stocks in the East and Eastern ports, and until recently coffee afloat from the East to U.S.A. Until 1924, stocks in the interior of Brazil were omitted also, but since that year information as to stocks in the interior of Sao Paulo is available, and quite recently figures have been published of stocks held in the interior of Rio de Janeiro. The statistics have therefore recently become reasonably comprehensive. The visible supply has lately been only a fraction of the total supplies available, but this is, of course, due to the present valorisation scheme, whereby stocks are held in Government warehouses in the interior, and not, as in previous schemes, at Brazilian or foreign ports. The visible supply figures were not, therefore, so untrustworthy before 1924 as they have been recently.

Deliveries during the last four years have been as below.

Two years ago, with substantial stocks on its hands, and with the prospect of a record crop of 22 million bags for 1927–28, the Brazilian Coffee Defence Institute may well have wondered,

Deliveries of coffee (1,000 bags)

Year	To Europe	To U.S.A.	Total	From Brazil	Other kinds
1920	5,213	9,167	14,380	8,638	5,742
1921	8,094	9,958	18,052	11,356	6,696
1922	8,238	9,654	17,892	11,100	6,792
1923	9,240	10,585	19,825	13,516	6,309
1924	9,981	10,709	20,690	13,473	7,217
1925	9,481	9,488	18,969	11,868	7,101
1926	9,984	10,665	20,649	13,164	7,485
1927	10,656	10,933	21,589	13,834	7,755
1928	10,930	10,849	21,779	13,198	8,581

with its critics, whether it could ever achieve the colossal task which lay before it. Today this task has been achieved, and with a success which has surprised even its most ardent supporters. The bumper crop of 1927–8 was, as usual, followed by a very small crop, and by the end of the current season, stocks will probably have been reduced to about 8½ million bags from a peak of 13 million bags on July 1st 1928. Moreover this process of adjustment has actually been carried out to the accompaniment of a higher price level. At the present price level it is probable that all but the worst plantations are showing a satisfactory profit, while those in the new fertile districts which have recently been opened up are probably yielding fortunes to their owners. Nor at present is there much evidence that production is being stimulated in other countries to the material detriment of Brazil. Production in Colombia, Central America, Kenya and some other countries is certainly expanding rapidly, but it is probable that this would have taken place to a considerable extent under any circumstances short of a complete collapse of prices, which would certainly have been far more harmful to Brazil. Looking into the more distant future, Brazil has probably not much more to fear on this score, for the coffee area in these competing countries is limited, while they have to meet many difficulties in transport and labour.

At least as dangerous is the encouragement to new planting in Brazil itself under the stimulus of even present prices, but this factor will not make itself felt for another three or four years at least, and is at any rate within the control of Brazil if control is really required.

The real dangers to the continued success of valorisation lie not so much outside Brazil as within its own borders. The crop for 1929–30, now being harvested, is estimated at 17–18 million bags, a heavier crop than usually follows even in the second year after a bumper crop. Probably only 14 million bags at the most will be required for export, and therefore on July 31st, 1930, stocks may again be approaching 13 million bags. If the crop of

1930–1 is equally large the Institute will be faced with very serious difficulties. The flowering of the 1930–1 crop takes place this August and September, and Brazilians will welcome a frost, or later a drought; anything, in fact, which will materially reduce the crop and so lessen the prospective difficulties next year.

X. *Petroleum*

The only figures of stocks regularly available are those for the United States, compiled by the U.S. Dept. of Commerce. Since, however, nearly 80 per cent of the world's oil stocks are held in the United States, these figures can be regarded as reasonably representative. Unfortunately, a change in the method of compilation has very greatly impaired the value of these American statistics. Since January 1925, stocks of fuel oil in California have been included in the figures of Californian stocks of crude petroleum. This change makes it impossible to ascertain the total American stocks of crude petroleum: only the total east of California is now available, and as this was not published separately before January 1925, no comparative series of any sort can be constructed. Similarly this change makes it impossible to ascertain the total American stocks of refined oils, because the stocks of fuel oil are exclusive of California. It is possible to give statistics of the total supply of crude and refined together, and to carry this series back beyond January 1925, but this is all that can be done. This series is as follows: in order to give some idea of the general growth of the industry, and therefore the relation of stocks to consumption, the monthly average for each year of crude petroleum run to stills is shown in the last line of the table below.

The table on page 563 shows the stocks of crude petroleum east of California, and in the second column the stocks of crude and fuel oil in California, since March 1925.

Of refined products, kerosene and lubricating oils are now quantitatively unimportant. Since the statistics of stocks of fuel and gas oils are now exclusive of California, they are of very little significance, but the following brief summary may be given [p. 563]:

Total U.S.A. stocks of crude and refined oils* (1,000 barrels)

End of month	1920	1921	1922	1923	1924	1925	1926	1927	1928	1929
March	—	—	—	—	463,072	490,953	502,777	499,323	568,498	599,338
June	171,109	221,383	302,345	395,608	480,685	504,941	482,763	520,669	570,792	
September	—	—	—	—	487,509	473,108	467,584	531,658	562,914	
December	182,021	234,892	318,960	414,302	477,958	469,577	476,479	543,335	570,734	
Monthly average run to stills	36,160	36,947	41,725	48,436	53,842	61,667	64,977	69,070	75,850	

* The figures of refined oils are confined to liquid products, i.e. greases, etc., are not included.

1,000 barrels

	Crude petroleum stocks east of California	Crude petroleum and fuel oil stocks in California
1925 March	308,548	103,721
June	310,732	110,203
September	300,981	121,664
December	292,288	126,129
1926 March	287,710	131,678
June	281,432	122,794
September	277,771	117,964
December	278,077	118,330
1927 March	290,110	119,364
June	315,702	117,414
September	339,741	114,981
December	351,646	111,855
1928 March	368,744	114,117
June	370,751	113,431
September	366,652	113,433
December	368,431	116,970
1929 March	379,659	117,878

Stocks of fuel and gas oils east of California
(million gallons)

End of month	1925	1926	1927	1928	1929
March	802	851	948	1,225	1,268
June	1,082	947	1,117	1,513	
September	1,256	1,142	1,328	1,683	
December	1,037	1,046	1,343	1,467	

no estimate of consumption is possible in the absence of adequate statistics of stocks.

Fortunately the gasolene statistics are not affected by the change in statistical compilation. The following table shows the total stocks in the U.S.A., and the estimated domestic consumption.

Million gallons

End of month			Stocks of gasolene	Domestic consumption
1920	,,	,,	464	354
1921	,,	,,	631	376
1922	,,	,,	791	448
1923	,,	,,	1,186	549
1924	,,	,,	1,483	647
1925	,,	,,	1,614	782
1926	,,	,,	—	—
1925 March			1,747	625
June			1,695	868
September			1,514	849
December			1,648	760
1926 March			1,936	780
June			1,713	969
September			1,400	943
December			1,639	900
1927 March			2,201	943
June			1,838	1,167
September			1,249	1,193
December			1,357	996
1928 March			1,690	1,010
June			1,444	1,219
September			1,109	1,247
December			1,389	1,119
1929 March			2,025	1,155

The over-production which was already noticeable in the spring of 1927 had reached most serious proportions by the end of that year. Production increased from 765 million barrels in 1926 to over 900 million barrels in 1927. While consumption, especially under the stimulus of lower prices, also increased greatly, it could not, of course, keep pace, and the result by the end of 1927 was an addition of 67 million barrels to total stocks. In the late autumn, restriction of production began to be a reality, and was extended in the early part of 1928. The rate of output declined from nearly 2·6 million barrels a day in July 1927 to 2·3 million barrels in May 1928. In the summer of 1928 there was almost a shortage of gasolene, because the output of light crude oil in Oklahoma and California was especially reduced, and the existing 'cracking plants' were fully employed. The price of light crude oil rose, therefore, with the advance in gasolene prices from March to September last year, and though there was naturally some decline in the autumn, prices were very considerably higher at the end as compared with the beginning of the year. The supply of fuel oil, however, tended to become still more excessive (partly because the great fall in the price of coal had brought some return to coal as a fuel for ships), and the trend of heavy oil prices was steadily downwards throughout the year. This explains why the price of light oil was rising considerably at the same time that every possible effort was being made to extend a tighter restriction: though the demand for gasolene might have been still further increased if restriction had been relaxed, the result would have been an even greater decline in fuel oil prices, which were already below cost, and therefore gasolene would have had to bear a still higher proportion of the cost of crude oil.

In the second half of 1928, however, production began to increase again. Though restriction broke down in Oklahoma in September, the increased production was not in the main due to the failure of restriction, but to the development of new fields, in particular the Santa Fé Springs Field in California. By the end of the year, production was back again to 2·6 million barrels a day, and the result for the whole of 1928 was a production very nearly the same as 1927, but with the continued growth of consumption, stocks were only increased by about 27 million barrels as compared with 67 million during the previous year. (See table on page 562.)

During the first quarter of this year the situation seemed to be a little better: production appeared to be stabilised between 2·6 and 2·7 million barrels a day, and though the outlook for any extension of restriction was doubtful, the existing degree of restriction was being fairly well maintained. But in the second quarter there has definitely been a change for the worse. Restriction has broken down completely in Oklahoma, and partially in West Texas, owing to the defection of a large company in each case; while the President's conference of oil producing States at Colorado Springs, of which high hopes had been entertained, particularly in London, dispersed *sine die*, unable to come to any basis of agreement, and having served merely to reveal acute differences of policy between the leaders of the industry. With the beginning of June, production began to increase, as the result of unrestricted production in Oklahoma and West Texas. This would not be very serious, as the peak production of these fields has been passed, temporarily at any rate. But at the end of June restriction broke down in California, and there seems little doubt that production will increase still further. Given restriction, even as at the beginning of this year, the outlook was for the gradual re-establishment of an equilibrium between demand and a restricted supply, while the extension of cracking plants could have been relied upon to remove gradually the gap between heavy and light oil prices. Without restriction—and for the moment that appears to be the correct hypothesis—there is no sight of the end of over-production, and what is really a colossal waste of irreplaceable natural resources will continue.

In connection with the success of a restriction policy in the United States, as advocated by the Petroleum Institute, the following table of the world's output in 1927 and 1928 as computed by the U.S. Bureau of Mines, may be of interest. It should be remembered that outside the United States, the bulk of the productive capacity is under the control of big producers, most of whom have already promised co-operation with the Petroleum Institute, if the latter can make arrangements in the United States. Restriction of a kind is indeed being operated already in several countries, but production in most cases is expanding at the expense of the United States.

World's output of crude petroleum

	1927, million barrels	Per cent of total	1928, million barrels	Per cent of total
United States	901	71·5	902	68·2
Venezuela	63	5·0	106	8·0
Russia	77	6·1	88	6·7
Mexico	64	5·1	50	3·8
Persia	40	3·1	42	3·2
Roumania	26	2·1	31	2·3
Netherlands East Indies	26	2·1	28	2·2
Total of above countries	1,197	95	1,247	94·4
Rest of world	64	5	76	5·6
Grand total	1,261	100·0	1,323	100·0

XI. *Nitrate*

Very reliable figures for Chile nitrates are regularly published by Messrs Aikman, and are quoted below.

The figures for America include interior stocks, but not those held by the U.S.A. Government, which have gradually declined from round 300,000 tons in December 1921, to 60,000 tons at the present time.

In normal times there is a considerable reduction in the visible supply in the early part of the year, as the demand is somewhat seasonal.

Attention may be drawn to the agreement which has just been concluded between the Chilean nitrate industry and the two largest producers of synthetic nitrogen, the I.G. Farbenindustrie and Imperial Chemical Industries. These three groups control about 70 per cent of the world's nitrogen production, and it is expected that most of the remaining producers will enter the cartel, leaving outside only the American producers with some

Nitrate (1,000 tons)

End of month	Visible supply (including afloat)		Stocks in Chile	Total
	Europe and Egypt	U.S.A.		
1913 January	1,128	89	490	1,727
March	686	97	527	1,326
June	416	84	754	1,652
September	571	79	752	1,414
December	1,093	71	498	1,685
1919 July	140	28	1,594	1,780
September	152	49	1,705	1,925
December	430	95	1,576	2,134
1920 March	368	253	1,218	1,914
June	317	216	1,248	1,800
September	495	194	1,303	2,008
December	782	132	1,304	2,235
1921 March	868	218	1,283	2,384
June	836	249	1,317	2,405
September	828	41	1,453	2,370
December	903·5	260	1,441	2,622·5
1922 March	520	115	1,504	2,149
June	228·5	38	1,601	1,873·5
September	296	133	1,495	1,945
December	463·5	195	1,225	1,912·5
1923 March	379·5	238	889	1,310
June	173	54	997	1,250
September	365	96	927	1,415
December	573	200	852	1,639
1924 March	371	193	782	1,346
June	115	47	1,075	1,250
September	429	124	900	1,494
December	684	111	882	1,709
1925 March	379·5	233	756	1,368·5
June	227	122	869	1,218
September	408	105	896	1,409
December	682·5	115	878	1,675·5
1926 March	447	196	906	1,549
June	314	117	1,228	1,659
September	334	150	1,288	1,772
December	337	201	1,268	1,806
1927 March	224·5	106	992	1,322·5
June	139·5	52	989	1,180·5
September	395	86	721	1,202
December	803	130·5	519	1,452·5

Table (*cont.*)

| End of month | Visible supply (including afloat) | | Stocks in Chile | Total |
	Europe and Egypt	U.S.A.		
1928 January	820	214	459	1,493·5
February	661·5	256·5	409	1,327
March	524·5	168·5	385	1,078
April	458	154·5	422	1,034·5
May	359	162	535	1,056
June	349·5	114	672	1,135·5
July	415	139	753	1,307
August	487·5	129	838	1,454·5
September	550·5	112	923	1,585·5
October	726·5	131	922	1,779·5
November	814	179	922	1,915
December	956·5	206	874	2,036·5
1929 January	1,103·5	287	712	2,102·5
February	1,047	276	692	2,015
March	879·5	220	695	1,794·5
April	707·5	169	765	1,641·5
May	556·5	132	871	1,559·5
June	548	121	984	1,653

10 per cent, who cannot, of course, join, owing to the anti-trust legislation. The agreement provides for the fixing of agreed prices for all countries, and though the working of such a cartel will obviously be difficult, for the moment the nitrate war is, in a sense, over. This does not, however, mean an end but of course only an alleviation of the troubles of the subsidised Chilean industry and of the Chilean Finance Minister.

XII. *Wheat*

The current available statistics relating to supplies and stocks of wheat are well summarised in the *Wheat Studies* of the Food Research Institute of Stanford University, California, to which anyone who is interested in further details may be referred. The following table relating to wheat supplies in the leading countries of export 1924–9 with a forecast for 1928–9 has been taken from this source. The following extract from the Food

Research Institute's survey of the situation as it appeared in May of this year are [*sic*] of particular interest in view of recent developments in the wheat market.

The decline (in prices after mid-February) seems to have been due not only to accumulation of evidence tending to show that winter wheat had not suffered unusual damage in most countries, but also to the pressure of extraordinarily heavy stocks in exporting countries, especially after the new Argentine crop began to move in large volume. International trade was of record volume for the season. Low prices encouraged importation and consumption, especially in ex-European countries, which imported more wheat and flour than ever before. But in spite of the record shipments, the accumulation of stocks in exporting countries remained extraordinarily large. The prices of representative wheats in the United States were relatively too high to permit exportation in a volume consistent with the available supplies, and here the accumulation of stocks, principally in commercial channels, was most noteworthy. The volume of world trade for the crop year, as measured by net exports, now seems likely to approximate 950 million bushels, by far the largest in history; but year-end stocks also seem likely to be of record size. All told, stocks in the four principal exporting countries now seem likely to exceed 380 million bushels at the end of the crop year. Last year, when such stocks were previously the largest of post-war years, the total fell below 330 million. Hence the present crop year promises to end, as it has proved throughout its course, a year of extraordinarily heavy accumulations of wheat stocks in the major exporting countries.*

The situation as outlined above had resulted in a steady decline of wheat prices until by the end of May wheat was selling at nearly the pre-war price. The movement was then dramatically reversed as a result of poor harvest reports from all four of the leading export countries. Except in the case of U.S. winter wheat, which was damaged by excessive rains, the trouble in all the areas was attributed to drought. The Canadian crop has been estimated at as low as 340 million bushels, and in two months the price of Canadian wheat has risen by more than 70 per cent. Sharp, if less spectacular, increases have also occurred in American, Australian and Argentine prices.

* From *Wheat Studies of the Food Research Institute*, Stanford University, California, vol. v, no. 6; [as is the table on p. 571 (Ed.)].

Wheat supplies and their disposition in leading export countries, 1922–6; and a forecast for 1929 (million bushels)

	1924–5	1925–6	1926–7	1927–8	1928–9
United States Year ending 30 June					
Initial stocks	165	135	111	138	142
New crop	864	676	831	878	903
Total supplies	1,029	811	942	1,016	1,045
Net exports	258	95	209	194	140
Seed requirements	84	82	88	94	90
Consumption	479	492	492	505	507
Feed and waste	73	31	15	81	88
Apparent error in crop estimate	—	—	—	—	—
Stocks at end	135	111	138	142	220
Canada Year ending 31 July					
Initial stocks	41	26	35	48	75
New crop	262	395	407	480	534
Total supplies	303	421	442	528	609
Net exports	192	324	292	332	430
Seed requirements	38	40	39	41	42
Consumption	42	42	43	44	45
Feed and waste	22	18	31	43	43
Apparent error in crop estimate	−17	−38	−11	−7	−16
Stocks at end	26	35	48	75	65
Argentina Year ending 31 July					
Initial stocks	66	56	61	65	70
New crop	191	191	221	239	300
Total supplies	257	247	282	304	370
Net exports	123	94	143	178	215
Seed requirements	23	25	24	25	26
Consumption, feed and waste	55	64	60	62	65
Apparent error in crop estimate	—	+3	−10	−31	—
Stocks at end	56	61	65	70	64
Australia Year ending 31 July					
Initial stocks	38	36	30	41	40
New crop	165	115	161	117	159
Total supplies	203	151	191	158	199
Net exports	124	77	103	70	115
Seed requirements	11	11	12	14	14
Consumption	29	29	30	30	31
Feed and waste	3	4	5	4	5
Apparent error in crop estimate	—	—	—	—	—
Stocks, 31 July	36	30	41	40	34

Stocks of staple commodities [1930]

Beginning of month	Cotton 1,000 bales (1)	Copper 1,000 tons (2)	Tin 1,000 tons (3)	Lead 1,000 tons (4) U.K.	Lead 1,000 tons (4) U.S.	Spelter 1,000 tons (5)	Rubber 1,000 tons (6)	Sugar 1,000 tons (7)	Tea 1,000,000 lb (8)	Coffee 1,000 bags (9)	Petroleum 1,000,000 barrels (10)	Nitrate 1,000 tons (11)
1920 January	7,410	—	20	50.0	—	61	—	—	213	9,870	—	2,134
April	7,353	—	18	28.4	—	53	—	2,433	213	8,174	—	1,914
July	6,793	—	19	25.2	—	51	—	2,003	213	6,750	171	1,800
October	—	—	18	18.7	—	61	—	1,338	215	7,982	—	2,008
1921 January	—	399[A]	18	19.0	—	81	219–229	2,313	214	8,765	182	2,235
April	—	—	16	23.9	—	88	—	3,331	230	8,687	—	2,384
July	—	—	17	13.3	—	99	—	3,312	218	8,700	221	2,405
October	9,534	—	21	9.9	—	89	—	2,039	191	8,991	—	2,370
1922 January	8,470	411[A]	24	0.3	—	72	224–244	2,761	205	9,403	235	2,622.5
April	7,654	346[A]	21	0.6	—	60	—	2,479	220	9,140	—	2,149
July	6,785	357[A]	22	0.3	—	31	—	1,903	170	8,639	302	1,873.5
October	4,514	325[A]	21	0.6	—	20	—	868	151	8,481	—	1,945
1923 January	3,111	347	26	0.5	—	17	286–306	2,433	170	7,980	319	1,912.5
April	2,765	350	25	0.4	—	10	249	2,501	183	6,974	—	1,310
July	2,699	352	21	0.2	—	17	278	2,005	127	5,340	396	1,250
October	—	391	20	1.4	—	21	244	791	134	5,835	—	1,415
1924 January	2,010	402	21	1.2	93	34	254	2,255	166	4,467	414	1,639
April	1,716	361	23	0.0	92	29	226	2,460	193	3,964	463	1,346
July	1,747	371	20	0.0	97	45	208	2,086	139	5,071	481	1,250
October	2,673	385	20	0.1	88	42	196	542	137	5,727	487	1,494
1925 January	2,563	389	25	0.1	78	19	181	2,708	206	5,384	478	1,790
April	1,904	403	20	0.0	94	16	151	2,891	231	5,389	491	1,368.5
July	1,715	365	20	0.1	86	21	129	2,560	181	5,085	505	1,218
October	—	347	18	0.0	94	11	141	1,211	181	5,230	473	1,409

Period											
1926 January	2,927	344	18	0·0	93	9	182	3,709	204	9,547	469	1,675·5
April	3,193	361	14	0·4	105	19	183	4,064	195	8,688	503	1,549
July	4,068	370	16	0·2	106	24	193	3,452	156	7,404	483	1,659
October	5,396	351	15	0·1	106	15	213	1,919	175	10,111	468	1,779
1927 January	4,916	369	16	1·7	113	20	259	3,643	207	10,901	476	1,794
April	5,211	367	15	2·7	130	33	273	—	194	8,446	499	1,365·5
July	4,942	346	16	2·4	152	41	263	4,090	145	8,032	521	1,175·5
October	5,540	—	15	2·1	143	32	271	1,780	164	14,555	532	1,205
1928 January	4,622	323	16	2·0	139	38	272	4,062	239	18,388	543	1,452·5
April	4,129	—	16	1·9	155	38	270	5,442	243	17,908	568	1,091
July	3,948	—	16	1·3	146	41	222	4,303	179	18,581	571	1,135·5
October	4,029	288	20	1·0	139	44	206	1,850	195	18,834	563	1,583·5
1929 January	3,494	298	25	0·9	144	42	239	4,271	241	18,723	571	2,036·5
April	3,020	281	27	1·3	141	35	245	6,190	260	15,703	599	1,794·5
July	3,096	323	24	0·8	155	34	248	4,779	217	14,259	611	1,653
October	3,688	335	25	0·4	151	51	280	22,330	222	21,137	627	2,069
1930 January	3,622	414	28	2·0	135	73	321	5,473	286	25,063	624	2,515·5
April	3,870	490	33	6·8	129	89	397	6,982	274	27,470	628	2,387·5
July	4,970	—	43	7·4	—	117	394	6,156	221	28,424	631	2,249
October	—	—	40	6·2	—	—	—	—	—	—	—	—

(1) Total supply seasonally corrected, exclusive of European and Asiatic mill stocks. (2) Total supply outside hands of consumers. (3) Visible supply. London Metal Exchange figures from 1923. (4) Visible supply in U.K., and stocks in U.S. (5) Visible supply in U.K. and U.S. (6) Total supply outside plantations. (7) Total visible supply, exclusive of interior stocks in Cuba prior to October 1926. (8) Stocks in U.K. Comparability uncertain since April 1929. (9) Visible supply in Rio, Santos, Bahia, Europe and U.S., but exclusive of interior stocks in Brazil prior to January 1926. (10) Stocks of crude and refined oils in U.S. (11) Visible supply in Chile, U.S., Europe and Egypt.

A (Copper). On 1 January 1921, Allied Government stocks amounted approximately to 82,000 tons, and stocks of scrap metal to 183,000; on 1 January 1922, the former had become trifling, and the latter had fallen to about 90,000 tons, and had become trifling by 1 January 1923. A decreasing allowance must be added to the figures shown on account of these stocks.

*From The London and Cambridge Economic Service, Special Memorandum
No. 32 (September 1930)*

STOCKS OF STAPLE COMMODITIES

The statistics given below are in continuation of Memoranda
published by the London and Cambridge Economic Service in
April 1923, June 1924, July 1925, February 1926, March 1927,
and August 1929.

The table above is a summary of the figures given in detail
afterwards for each separate commodity.

INTRODUCTION

The present position in raw material industries generally is such
as to demand the most thorough and intensive study by economists. This would be quite beyond the scope of these memoranda, but a few brief observations and generalisations may be
attempted. In the first place, the present level of stocks is in
general comparable only with the aftermath of the post-war
slump in 1921, and in some cases even that peak is far exceeded.
An examination of the statistics of production reveals a fairly
general tendency to extremely rapid expansion since about 1924,
but consumption was also making great strides, and it cannot be
said that there was any serious lack of equilibrium until towards
midsummer 1929. Prices, however, had been tending downwards
for some time before that, if not throughout the period, and in
some industries control schemes disguised the true position,
since an unknown amount of producing capacity was shut down,
with the result that stocks were not accumulating as fast as they
would otherwise have done. This time last year the available
statistics of stocks did not by themselves indicate any serious
general excess of supplies, though they were certainly reaching
a high level in some cases. But when all factors are weighed

Production of staple commodities

Year (calendar or season)	American cotton 1,000 bales	Copper 1,000 tons	Tin 1,000 tons	Lead 1,000 tons	Spelter 1,000 tons	Rubber 1,000 tons	Sugar million tons	Tea million lb	Chile nitrates 1,000 tons
1924	13,639	1,357	140	1,298	998	420	23·5	831	
1925	16,122	1,418	146	1,464	1,132	517	24·6	821	
1926	17,977	1,475	143	1,570	1,238	620	23·6	872	1,297
1927	12,956	1,495	158	1,658	1,318	605	24·3	891	2,507
1928	14,478	1,711	176	1,649	1,401	650	27·1	948	3,228
1929	14,749	1,907	188	1,725	1,440	860	26·7	1,000	2,946

together—production, consumption and prices—it is now quite clear that there was a definite lack of equilibrium in tin, rubber, sugar, coffee and petroleum; with copper, lead, spelter, nitrate and cotton conditions were somewhat less out of line. The very fact that resort had already been made to artificial control schemes in sugar, coffee and petroleum is evidence of considerable maladjustment, and the relatively better conditions in copper, lead, spelter and nitrate were largely due to the temporary success of artificial control. If the wheat pools be accounted a form of artificial control, conditions of free production and marketing existed last summer only in cotton, tin, rubber and tea, out of the twelve commodities covered by this Memorandum, and the last-named was the only industry where conditions were still reasonably satisfactory. The number of these control schemes is direct evidence that producers generally were feeling the pinch long before midsummer 1929, though it would perhaps be more accurate to say that a large proportion of producers were thus affected, for in many industries the new capacity, which had come into existence since the War, was so much more efficient that even the prices of last summer were distinctly remunerative to these new low-cost producers.

What would have been the course of events if there had been no Wall Street crash is an idle question, but it may be stressed that the raw materials situation was disturbing before the Wall Street crash as well as after it. At the same time, the crash, as the herald of the present world depression, has, of course, entirely changed the situation in raw materials. Until last autumn little fault could be found with consumption, which in many instances was exceeding even the wildest expectations. The fault lay primarily on the supply, not on the demand side. But with the spread of the world depression, consumption has been definitely checked in its normal advance, and indeed sharply diminished. This temporary decline in consumption, coming on the top of already unsatisfactory conditions, would have been bad enough if it had not incidentally caused a fairly general breakdown of the power of restriction schemes to prevent a fall in prices. The combined effect has produced the present general crisis in raw material industries.

Since last October, and especially during the first quarter of this year, stocks have rapidly piled up to enormous proportions, even relatively to a normal consumption. Not only did the breakdown of the previous restriction measures temporarily increase the amount of active capacity, but the immediate effect of the fall in prices was that every producer strove for the maximum output in order to reduce costs. Early this summer in many commodities there was a further definite break to prices far below marginal total costs, and in some cases even below the prime costs of all but the most efficient producers. Stocks had in these cases piled up to such an extent that merchants and speculators were unable to carry any more, or unwilling to do so owing to their previous losses through prices continuing to fall when any further fall had seemed impossible. The function of stock-holding has thus been forced on producers, who in many cases have not the requisite financial resources to enable them to dispense with their usual supply of cash for current expenses of cultivation, even if they can pledge these stocks with banks on any reasonable conditions, which is not everywhere the case. The price of many commodities today (e.g. sugar, rubber, coffee, cotton and even wheat) bears little or no relation to total costs of production, and may rather be said to represent the current conditions on which the existing and prospective surplus stocks can be held. The present large stocks of many commodities in the hands of producers are at present being satisfactorily held, but it is doubtful in some industries whether this can continue for long, and therefore it is quite possible that prices will go even lower than at present, since there is really no limit to the potential fall when everything depends upon stockholding.

On the other hand, more recent attempts to operate restriction schemes are meeting with some measure of success, e.g. in copper, tin and nitrate, and this may prevent matters from becoming still worse, even if their ultimate benefit, either to producers or consumers, may be called in question. Again, in other cases, e.g. in sugar, coffee, copper and cotton, invisible stocks are probably extremely small, and some part of the recent decline in statistical consumption may have been due to a reduction of these invisible supplies, i.e. the rate of actual physical consumption may not have been so much reduced as statistical consumption would suggest. Against this, however, it must be admitted that the full effects of the world depression have probably not yet asserted themselves. If, however, consumption is really proceeding faster than the rate at which manufacturers and middlemen have been purchasing from producers, an increased demand will shortly materialise. Should this be sufficient to raise prices a little, or even to give a reasonable assurance against any further fall, there might well be a rush to rebuild invisible stocks at these lowest prices ever known in recent times, while speculators would at once regain their confidence and seek to recoup their losses. Prices may therefore recover with considerable rapidity to levels nearer the marginal costs of the supplies which the world will require in the immediate future.

Looking into the more distant future, however, the downward trend of costs, due to technical progress, of many raw commodities relatively to money incomes must not be overlooked or minimised. Producers may sigh, but they will be sighing quite in vain, for a return to the same relationship between the prices of their products and the general level of money incomes which prevailed even quite lately. Alongside the slump attributable to the credit cycle there is proceeding an adjustment of production to the lower relative price level consonant with the progress of technique. The rate of this advance varies greatly in different industries, and so, therefore, does the need and necessity to retire old high-cost capacity, which cannot either physically or profitably be modernised. Many industries have to undergo a pruning process sooner or later, and until that is accomplished, there can be no return to equilibrium. This is not, however, to deny that if the present price level continues for any length of time, that pruning may in some industries be too drastic, even from the point of view of the consumer and his ultimate interests.

A NOTE ON WEIGHTS AND MEASURES

1. *Cotton.* All current statistics are given in 'running bales', i.e. regardless of exact weight and counting round bales as half-bales. At the end of each season the U.S. Department of Commerce publishes the average weight of the bales produced in each State during that season, and this makes possible the conversion of running bales into equivalent 500 lb bales. Normally the average weight of the actual bales is within 6 or 7 lb above or below 500 lb, but recently the tendency has been to be above rather than below. In section I, crop figures are given in equivalent 500 lb bales, but all other figures refer to running bales.

2. *Metals.* Three different kinds of tons are in common use:
The British ton (often termed a long ton) = 2,240 lb.
The American ton (often termed a short ton) = 2,000 lb.
The metric ton = 2,204 lb (approx.).

3. *Rubber, Sugar, Tea, Nitrate.* Statistics are usually given in British tons (= 2,240 lb) and pounds.

4. *Coffee.* A bag (normally) = 60 kilos = 132·3 lb.

5. *Petroleum.* A barrel = 42 gallons.

THE U.S. DEPARTMENT OF COMMERCE INDEX OF COMMODITY STOCKS

This index includes 65 commodities, 46 covering manufactured goods and 19 raw materials. The index has been weighted by the relative value of the supply of each commodity in the years 1923 and 1925, ascertained by adding to the value of the amount marketed or manufactured the value of the amount imported. For manufactured products the values given are those shown in

Indexes of commodity stocks in the United States

	Total index	Manufactured goods	Raw materials
1919 monthly average	93	90	95
1920 ,, ,,	86	84	87
1921 ,, ,,	102	97	106
1922 ,, ,,	95	87	100
1923 ,, ,,	95	94	95
1924 ,, ,,	102	103	101
1925 ,, ,,	104	103	104
1926 ,, ,,	115	106	121
1927 ,, ,,	121	113	127
1928 ,, ,,	123	117	127
1929 ,, ,,	137	120	149

Total index

	March	June	Sept.	Dec.
1925	108	92	101	124
1926	115	104	108	136
1927	123	106	119	132
1928	127	109	116	142
1929	134	120	139	158
1930	142	125		

Manufactured goods

	March	June	Sept.	Dec.
1925	108	105	99	101
1926	109	110	104	106
1927	111	114	115	112
1928	121	118	111	121
1929	124	121	114	119
1930	127	125		

the census reports on manufactured, while for raw materials the weights used are those derived from the index of production and marketings. No adjustment has been made for seasonal variations. For further details, reference should be made to *The Survey of Current Business*, August 1928.

Raw materials

	March	June	Sept.	Dec.
1925	108	81	103	142
1926	119	99	112	159
1927	133	101	124	150
1928	132	102	119	156
1929	141	120	158	186
1930	152	125		

I. *American cotton*

At any given time stocks consist of the following:—

(1) Stocks up-country in the Southern States on plantations, railroads, and in 'uncounted'* interior towns.

(2) The 'visible' supply. This consists of (*a*) stocks in public storage and at compresses (warehouse stocks) in the more important interior towns and in the ports of the United States, (*b*) cotton afloat for Great Britain and the Continent, (*c*) warehouse stocks in the principal European ports, namely, Liverpool, Manchester, London, Havre, Marseilles, Genoa, Bremen, Ghent, Rotterdam and Barcelona.†

(3) Mill stocks in spinners' hands throughout the world, generally known as the 'invisible' or 'out of sight' supply.

In the first table the 'up-country' stock is taken as the 'up-country' carryover in the Southern States plus warehouse and mill stocks in the U.S. at the end of each season, plus the current

---

* I.e. towns not included in the figures of stocks in public storage and at compresses.

† Cotton afloat for Japan and in Japanese ports is not allowed for. All cotton consigned to Japan is considered by the leading exchanges as 'consumed' or 'out of sight'.

Supplies other than European and Asiatic mill stocks (1,000 bales)*

End of month	Up-country	U.S. warehouse stocks†	U.S. mill stocks†	Total in U.S.A.	Correction for season	Corrected total in U.S.A.	Visible outside U.S.A.	Grand total, excluding mill stocks outside U.S.A.‡
1919 July	2,193	2,212	1,304	5,709	—	5,709	347	6,056
October	11,973	1,974	1,365	15,312	9,000	6,312	1,077	7,389
1920 January	3,780	3,760	3,677	11,217	6,000	5,217	2,082	7,299
April	3,252	2,967	1,809	8,028	3,000	5,028	2,034	7,062
July	1,703§	2,055	1,358	5,116	—	5,116	1,352	6,468
October	11,414	4,168	944	16,526	10,311	6,215	—	—
1921 January	6,788	5,645	1,273	13,706	6,874	6,832	—	—
April	4,961	5,029	1,316	11,306	3,437	7,869	—	—
July	3,713§	3,723	1,111	8,007	—	8,007	1,645	9,652
October	7,577	4,982	1,405	13,964	6,330	7,634	1,598	9,232
1922 January	4,550	4,618	1,675	10,843	4,220	6,623	1,581	8,204
April	3,484	3,214	1,458	8,156	2,110	6,046	1,436	7,482
July	964§	1,488	1,218	3,670	—	3,670	1,120	4,790
October	—	—	—	—	7,302	—	1,023	—
1923 January	1,569	3,486	1,988	7,043	4,868	2,175	1,296	3,471
April	667	1,966	1,878	4,511	2,434	2,077	804	2,881
July	280§	945	1,099	2,324	—	2,324	376	2,700
October	4,667	3,486	1,103	9,256	7,596	1,660	962	2,622
1924 January	1,049	2,966	1,633	5,648	5,064	584	1,268	1,852
April	341	1,512	1,328	3,181	2,532	649	966	1,615
July	160§	674	721	1,555	—	1,555	528	2,083
October	7,008	4,225	731	10,242	10,242	1,722	1,021	2,743
1925 January	1,780	3,863	1,434	7,077	6,828	249	1,956	2,205
April	341	1,666	1,515	3,522	3,414	108	1,731	1,839
July	2,308	487	878	1,504	—	1,504	764	2,268
October	7,977	4,499	1,216	13,692	12,078	1,614	1,280	2,894
1926 January	2,223	5,176	1,811	9,210	8,052	1,158	1,707	2,865
April	816	3,531	1,639	5,986	4,026	1,960	1,388	3,348
July	510	1,936	1,096	3,542	—	3,542	985	4,527
October	10,425	5,470	1,216	17,111	13,266	3,845	1,551	5,396

Month								
1927 January	3,400							
July	535	1,823	1,404	3,762		3,762	2,096	5,858
August	12,496	2,173	1,122	15,791	11,876	3,915	1,755	5,660
September	9,487	3,965	1,119	14,571	10,796	3,775	1,765	5,540
October	6,105	5,433	1,327	12,865	9,716	3,149	2,110	5,259
November	3,766	5,969	1,551	11,286	8,636	2,650	2,263	4,913
December	2,676	5,656	1,707	10,039	7,556	2,483	2,139	4,622
1928 January	2,061	5,014	1,707	8,782	6,476	2,306	2,087	4,393
April	1,093	2,921	1,508	5,522	3,236	2,286	1,915	4,201
July	335	1,189	1,007	2,531	—	2,531	1,365	3,896
August	14,283	2,646	782	16,254	13,266	2,988	1,087	4,075
September	11,604	4,636	720	14,970	12,060	2,910	1,119	4,029
October	7,431	5,253	1,195	13,262	10,854	2,408	1,657	4,065
November	4,366		1,567	11,186	9,648	1,538	1,966	3,504
December	2,608	5,315	1,741	9,664	8,442	1,222	2,272	3,494
1929 January	1,803	4,615	1,768	8,186	7,236	950	2,276	3,226
February	1,393	3,876	1,746	7,015	6,030	985	2,173	3,158
March	957	3,177	1,731	5,865	4,824	1,041	1,979	3,020
April	733	2,524	1,607	4,864	3,618	1,246	1,786	3,032
May	598	1,848	1,477	3,923	2,412	1,511	1,564	3,015
June	415	1,376	1,289	3,080	1,206	1,874	1,222	3,096
July	275	985	1,052	2,312	—	2,312	1,005	3,317
August	14,064	1,387	802	16,253	13,519	2,734	785	3,519
September	11,038	3,225	792	15,055	12,290	2,765	923	3,688
October	6,510	5,312	1,361	13,183	11,061	2,122	1,454	3,576
November	4,211	5,842	1,672	11,725	9,832	1,893	1,673	3,566
December	2,639	5,914	1,844	10,397	8,603	1,794	1,868	3,662
1930 January	1,806	5,407	1,830	9,043	7,374	1,669	1,816	3,485
February	1,498	4,859	1,812	8,169	6,145	2,240	1,720	3,744
March	1,259	4,189	1,763	7,211	4,916	2,295	1,575	3,870
April	1,093	3,636	1,667	6,396	3,687	2,709	1,395	4,104
May	899	3,337	1,531	5,767	2,458	3,309	1,177	4,486
June	725	3,105	1,357	5,187	1,229	3,958	1,012	4,970
July	470	2,877	1,183	4,530	—	4,530	818	5,348
August‖	—	—		—	—	—	747	—

* This table excludes linters, except that an insignificant quantity is included in the import figures.

† Figures for all kinds of cotton.

‡ Seasonally corrected and excluding European and Asiatic mill stocks.

§ The carryover according to the above method was as follows: 1920, 2,171; 1921, 3,779; 1922, 2,615; 1923, 356; 1924, 6; 1925, 0; 1926, 400; 1927, 274; 1928, 487; 1929, 286; 1930, 575.

‖ Provisional.

year's crop, minus the U.S. consumption to any particular date, minus the net exports to that date (i.e. exports minus imports), minus warehouse and mill stocks at that date. By this means it is possible to estimate the location of all cotton in the U.S. month by month. But it follows that the whole of the new crop is suddenly added to the 'up-country' stock in August each year. This is corrected in the table on pp. 582–3, by the 'seasonal correction', which provides what would be the figure of total stock in the U.S. if the current crop came into existence at an even monthly rate through the year. The statistics of U.S. warehouse stocks and mill stocks are compiled by the U.S. Bureau of the Census, and may be regarded as reliable, as also may the 'visible' supply of Great Britain and the Continent.* The estimates of the current crop are reasonably accurate by the end of each calendar year. The 'up-country' carryover is the most doubtful item, and is always liable to be under-, rather than over-estimated. The estimates of Mr H. G. Hester, the Secretary of the New Orleans Cotton Exchange, have been used until 1922, since when the estimates of the Shepperson Publishing Company (*Cotton Facts*) have been preferred. The monthly calculated figures for 'up-country' provide at best an estimate of the actual state of affairs, but in most years they tally reasonably well with the 'up-country carryover' estimates (see Note § below table).

At the beginning and in the middle of each season, statistics of European and Asiatic mill stocks, and of the world's actual consumption during the previous six months are available, and the position of the world's total stocks is shown in the two tables below.

The 1929–30 season opened with a world carryover of about 4½ million bales, and with the current crop the total available was just over 19 million bales. The position was therefore approximately the same as at the beginning of the 1928–9 season, but before many months it was evident that consumption

* As given by the Liverpool Cotton Exchange.

Annual table of total stocks at the end of each season (*1 August*) (1,000 bales)

	1919	1920	1921	1922	1923	1924	1925	1926	1927	1928	1929	1930
Up-country carryover in interior cotton belt	2,193	1,703	3,713	964	280	160	230	510	535	335	275	470
U.S. warehouse stocks	2,212	2,055	3,723	1,488	945	674	487	1,936	1,823	1,189	1,052	2,877
U.S. mills stocks	1,304	1,358	1,111	1,218	1,099	721	787	1,096	1,404	1,007	985	1,185
Total in U.S.	5,709	5,116	8,547	3,670	2,324	1,555	1,504	3,542	3,762	2,531	2,312	4,530
European port stocks (including afloat for Europe)	1,247	1,394	1,695	1,120	376	528	764	985	2,096	1,365	1,005	818
European mill stocks	305	475	690	838	496	502	787	663	1,041	792	730	629
Asiatic mill stocks	?	267*	248	381	185	173	219	250	572	327	390	247
Total	7,261	7,252	11,180	6,009	3,381	2,758	3,274	5,440	7,471	5,015	4,437	6,224
Crop for year†	12,000	13,750	8,442	9,738	10,128	13,639	16,122	17,977	12,956	14,478	14,749	14,200‡
Total available	19,261	21,002	19,622	15,747	13,509	16,397	19,396	23,417	20,427	19,493	19,186	20,424‡
Total carried forward	6,990	10,386	7,066	3,081	2,554	3,141	5,666	7,637	5,020	4,417	6,163	
Consumption for year	12,271	10,616	12,556	12,666	10,955	13,256	13,730	15,780	15,407	15,076	13,023	

* Excluding China.
† For 1919–21 Hester's estimate of the actual growth, made at the beginning of the season, as the official figures for these years are questionable.
‡ Provisional.

585

Annual table of total stocks in the middle of each season (1 February) (1,000 bales)

	1920	1921	1922	1923	1924	1925	1926	1927	1928	1929	1930
Up-country stocks	3,780	6,788	4,550	1,569	1,049	1,780	2,223	3,480	2,061	1,866	1,806
U.S. warehouse stocks	3,760	5,645	4,618	3,486	2,966	3,863	5,176	6,070	5,014	4,615	5,407
U.S. mill stocks	3,677	1,273	1,675	1,988	1,633	1,434	1,811	1,853	1,707	1,768	1,830
Total in U.S.	11,217	13,706	10,843	7,043	5,648	7,077	9,210	11,403	8,782	8,249	9,043
European port stocks (including afloat)	2,018	1,650	1,575	1,296	1,268	1,956	1,707	2,905	2,087	2,276	1,816
European mill stocks	597	675	740	637	578	755	842	848	845	783	703
Asiatic mill stocks	117*	166*	390	206	203	201	192	269	331	349	219
Total available	13,949	16,197	13,548	9,182	7,697	9,989	11,951	15,425	12,045	11,657	11,781
Total available 1 August preceding	19,261	21,002	19,622	15,747	13,509	16,397	19,396	23,417	20,427	19,493	19,186
Consumption for half-year	5,312	4,805	6,074	6,565	5,812	6,408	7,445	7,992	8,382	7,836	7,405

* Excluding China.

586

was running well below the rate of the previous season in all divisions of the world cotton industry.

World consumption in the 1929–30 season was probably not much more than 13 million bales, giving a world carryover on August 1st, 1930, of about 6 million bales. The new crop has been estimated at over 14 million, giving a total of more than 20

Finished cotton goods in U.S.

		1,000 yards		Cases	
		Production	Orders grey yardage	Shipments	Stocks
1921 ,, ,,		85,385	90,154	44,935	36,226
1922 ,, ,,		94,016	95,509	49,102	44,937
1923 ,, ,,		95,098	91,504	48,116	46,166
1924 ,, ,,		77,650	76,105	41,863	43,139
1925 ,, ,,		78,756	76,558	43,691	39,640
1926 ,, ,,		81,214	78,565	47,352	39,641
1927 ,, ,,		84,458	81,710	49,428	38,243
1928 ,, ,,		75,100	74,299	46,563	37,829
1929 ,, ,,		79,795	75,198	48,716	36,433
1929 May		88,707	79,228	54,247	35,618
June		78,964	65,462	45,674	34,487
July		75,582	69,475	44,809	37,299
August		75,845	69,168	45,238	36,320
September		73,116	67,991	43,586	35,062
October		81,549	78,806	46,173	37,635
November		63,663	57,971	38,616	37,634
December		61,816	54,172	36,521	38,220
1930 January		63,457	71,723	41,793	35,428
February		64,271	57,834	37,014	32,967
March		66,246	60,526	39,459	32,528
April		65,364	56,641	34,308	40,741
May		59,384	46,699	39,307	34,571
June		50,933	39,249	32,986	34,477
July					

million bales as the available supply for 1930–1. At the current rate of consumption this is well in excess of the world's needs, and it is not surprising, therefore, that cotton prices have recently fallen to the lowest levels since 1915.

There are no statistics relating to finished cotton goods except for the United States. While not by any means complete, these statistics afford an interesting comparable series, as will be seen from the table above.

II. *Copper*

Stocks of copper consist of (1) refined copper in the United States, which constitutes the main part of the world's floating supply, (2) rough and blister copper in transit to smelters and refiners in North and South America, and on hand or in process at refineries, (3) refined and rough copper in European and Japanese warehouses. In the years immediately after the War there were also large stocks in the hands of the Allied Governments and in the form of scrap metal.

The second table supplies some more detailed statistics of the principal stocks. In these returns 'American blister' includes all copper in first hands in North and South America which has not been refined and made available for delivery.

On April 15th, 1929, Copper Exporters Inc. ended the speculative scramble of the previous few weeks by firmly fixing their quotation at 18 cents. For exactly one year this quotation remained in force, and was then reduced to 14 cents, on May 5th to 13 cents, and on May 7th to 12.50 cents, but on May 9th it was restored to 13 cents. Early in June further reductions were made to 12 cents, and after successive reductions during July, 11 cents was reached on July 21st. Towards the end of August further reductions began, and by the end of September 10.10 cents was reached. At the beginning of April last, stocks of refined copper in North and South America totalled 228,000 tons as compared with 47,000 tons a year previously, while stocks in Europe continued to be negligible. (The corresponding figures

Supplies and consumption of copper (tons of 2,240 lb)

	1 January 1920	1 January 1921	1 January 1922	1 January 1923	1 January 1924	1 January 1925	1 January 1926	1 January 1927	1 January 1928	1 January 1929	1 January 1930
North and South America:—											
Refined	313,000	286,000	239,000	133,000	139,000	122,000	65,000	76,000	85,000	58,000	153,000
In process, etc.	175,000	58,000	142,000	175,000	226,000	212,000	215,000	244,000	221,000	224,000	237,000
Allied Govt. stocks	180,000	82,000	trifling	—	—	—	—	—	—	—	—
Scrap (approximate)	270,000	183,000	90,000	—	—	—	—	—	—	—	—
U.K., Havre, Japan stocks	46,000	55,000	30,000	39,000	37,000	55,000	64,000	49,000	17,000	15,000	24,000
Total	984,000	664,000	501,000	347,000	402,000	389,000	344,000	369,000	323,000	297,000	414,000
Production*	967,000	537,000	888,000	1,266,000	1,357,000	1,418,000	1,475,000	1,495,000	1,711,000	1,907,000	
Available supply	1,951,000	1,201,000	1,389,000	1,613,000	1,759,000	1,807,000	1,819,000	1,864,000	2,034,000	2,204,000	
Stock carried forward	664,000	501,000	347,000	402,000	389,000	344,000	369,000	323,000	297,000	413,000	
Consumption	1,287,000	700,000	1,042,000	1,211,000	1,370,000	1,463,000	1,450,000	1,541,000	1,737,000	1,791,000	
Price £ (standard)	115 7 6	71 17 6	66 3 9	64 11 3	60 18 9	66 11 3	59 13 9	56 3 9	61 1 10	74 12 6	
Cents per lb (electro)	19	12¾	13¾	14¾	12¾	14¾	14	13½	14⅓	16⅔	

* American Bureau of Metal Statistics.

589

Table: *World's production as estimated by the American Bureau of Metal Statistics (tons of 2,000 lb)*

Country	1916*	1922	1923	1924	1925	1926	1927	1928	1929
United States	971,123	511,970	754,000	819,000	854,000	878,000	847,419	935,199	1,179,269
Mexico	60,751	29,842	60,538	57,139	59,123	62,303	63,760	72,579	63,678
Canada	52,880	25,300	40,230	50,072	56,239	64,124	70,698	96,634	79,919
Cuba	8,613	11,788	11,963	12,742	13,128	13,034	15,538	18,869	—
Bolivia	5,675	10,154	11,744	8,200	7,500	7,100	7,850	7,500	—
Chile	78,559	142,830	201,042	208,964	209,654	223,015	264,242	319,549⎫	392,795
Peru	47,452	40,133	48,684	38,798	41,180	42,703	52,438	57,830⎭	
Venezuela	1,300	1,075	1,175	1,230	1,500	—	—	—	—
Europe	105,434	86,950	115,492	120,618	130,957	135,699	138,779	138,489	146,500†
Asia	110,900	60,825	66,227	71,300	77,013	77,377	75,972	78,396	82,281‡
Australasia	43,920	13,754	19,995	15,711	13,800	11,244	12,800	12,846	12,980
Africa	43,876	58,219	80,410	115,300	118,180	108,010	120,763	141,131	142,599
Other countries	3,307	3,307	3,307	4,409	4,409	4,409	4,409	4,409	—
World total	1,533,810	996,147	1,414,807	1,523,483	1,586,683	1,628,018	1,674,818	1,883,431	2,136,021§

* War peak of production in United States was in 1916. War peak of world production was in 1917, the total being 1,580,475 short tons.
† Includes 36,000 tons estimated for the countries not detailed.
‡ Japan only.
§ Partly estimated.

Stocks of copper (tons of 2,240 lb)

Beginning of month	American refined*	American blister* (and in process)	U.K. all kinds	Havre	Japan	Total
1921 Jan.	286,000	58,000	11,646	5,968	37,500	399,000
1922 Jan.	239,000	142,000	16,665	4,138	9,300	411,000
1923 Jan.	133,000	175,000	26,780	3,345	9,072	347,000
Oct.	113,000	240,000	28,453	3,891	5,954	391,000
1924 Jan.	139,000	226,000	31,030	1,867	4,405	402,000
April	107,000	212,500	30,852	5,281	5,300	361,000
July	100,000	216,000	36,515	10,225	8,600	371,000
Oct.	122,000	209,000	37,387	7,885	9,000	385,000
1925 Jan.	122,000	212,000	38,419	7,180	9,992	389,000
April	109,200	233,000	44,276	8,341	7,743	403,000
July	81,500	223,500	47,984	6,389	5,832	365,000
Oct.	61,500	220,000	51,285	9,942	5,015	347,000
1926 Jan.	65,200	214,600	56,047	3,013	5,288	344,288
April	67,148	233,813	51,701	4,701	3,624	360,987
July	59,014	245,974	50,967	11,670	3,129	369,754
Oct.	62,622	235,656	39,029	10,682	3,468	351,457
1927 Jan.	76,340	243,871	34,636	8,650	5,500	368,997
April	91,640	235,150	28,089	6,797	5,330	367,006
July	86,036	230,021	22,032	3,333	5,000†	346,422
Oct.	77,226	220,104	17,659	1,720	—	—
1928 Jan.	85,084	220,836	10,912	1,236	5,087	323,155
April	77,939	216,536	9,092	1,980	—	—
July	52,507	224,727	7,957	1,189	—	—
Oct.	46,260	228,328	8,574	2,333	2,837	288,512
1929 Jan.	58,452	224,214	6,801	2,084	6,262	297,813
April	47,290	216,376	7,504	2,872	6,622	280,664
July	74,232	224,509	8,758	7,575	7,548	322,622
Oct.	84,600	225,580	7,782	6,978	10,144	335,084
1930 Jan.	152,678	237,500	6,504	4,612	12,657	413,951
April	228,571	238,392	7,070	5,547	10,147	489,727
July	282,812	229,045	7,118	6,225		

* Includes North and South America. † Provisional.

for July 1st were 283,000 tons and 74,000 tons.) Consumption in 1929 may be estimated at some 50,000 tons in excess of 1928, but production in 1929 increased by nearly 200,000 tons. These are the essential features of the history of copper during the past sixteen months.

It is clear that a new chapter is beginning, and though it is still too close to admit of final assessment, it seems worthwhile to try and review briefly the nature and activities of the Copper Exporters to date. In 1917 the world, under the stimulus of war requirements, succeeded in producing 1,580,000 short tons of copper, and it was not until 1927–8 that world consumption surpassed this rate of production. In 1917 the U.S. produced 961,000 short tons, a figure which was not approached again until 1928, but was exceeded by no less than 244,000 short tons in 1929. With the exception of Japan and Australasia, practically every other producing country in the world, however, had nearly equalled if not exceeded its 1917 output by 1923, and has continued to expand ever since. In other words, a large potential output capacity in the U.S. was dormant until 1929, because it could not be produced at a 13–14 cent level, though the rest of the world was finding that level profitable. In the formation of Copper Exporters in 1926, various factors played a part. There was the very strong desire of the Americans to end what was in their eyes the anomaly of world price-fixing by London when the U.S. had become by far the biggest producer and consumer. There was the belief that demand was inelastic, and that the excess productive capacity meant lower prices than were really necessary: some regulation of output and strict price control would therefore result in very considerable net advantages. There was also a widespread feeling that even if prices were appreciably raised, production in Europe and the other older sources of supply could not be expanded much further, owing to the approaching exhaustion of ore reserves, while African supplies would still take a long time to develop; hence what seemed to be required was careful nursing of the market, and the normal increase in consumption would sooner or later necessitate the recall into action of even the highest cost American mines. It was under some such ideas that the combine was floated, and during 1927 and 1928 its conduct could not be seriously arraigned from the consumer's point of view. During 1928 consumption expanded in a most gratifying manner, and despite some increase from Katanga and South America, the U.S. production could be expanded by 100,000 tons, while stocks were worked down to a very low level (too low for convenience, as was soon demonstrated), and by January 1st, 1929, price had been raised to over 16 cents. This price level must be considered as highly remunerative to any reasonably well-conditioned concern, but it was not so high as to check buying, or to excite serious accusations of monopolistic extortion. Consumption, in fact, continued to expand rapidly and price to rise slowly, while mine output was freely increased, though naturally it took time to increase refined supplies. Then in March 1929 occurred the speculative scramble which was discussed at some length in our last Memorandum. The initial blame may perhaps be opportioned equally between the combine and consumers, but in our view the combine certainly mismanaged the affair, if stabilisation, and not monopoly profits, was their true objective. By the middle of April 1929 this episode was over, but it produced a totally new situation. The combine had found it impossible, if indeed it tried, to maintain restrictions on output in the face of the high level to which prices had been carried, and the American mines were all in full swing. In May, Anaconda and some other groups were openly proclaiming a resumption of 10 per cent restriction, but many producers, having once regained their freedom, were loath to obey the call. The real weakness of the combine's control over production, inevitable, of course, owing to the anti-trust laws, was demonstrated, and the monthly figures showed little reduction until 1930, long after the period necessary for restriction of mine output to make itself effective. On the consumer's side there was an equally important change in the situation. The maintenance of the 18 cents price level could only be interpreted as clear evidence that the combine intended to try and make the world pay this definitely monopolistic price: in other words, that the policy of the combine was to finance the stocks which were inevitably piling up while restriction was being reintroduced, and to wait until demand revived at that price. Moreover, when there was some revival of buying last September, the Anaconda group broke away and endeavoured, though unsuccessfully, to obtain an even higher price. After the New York Stock Market collapse there was still no reduction in the combine's price, though it was now clear that the prospects for consumption had completely changed: on the contrary, the only result was still louder calls for more restriction. It was, in fact, clear that the combine had become a mere grasping monopoly, and that if stabilisation in the accepted sense of the term had ever been its true objective, it was so no longer. Meantime refined stocks continued to pile up as the world depression of trade spread and become intensified, until finally, last April, the combine accepted the inevitable.

An analysis of events in the above terms may be considered reasonably sound, but it is nevertheless inadequate, because it neglects the internal affairs of the combine. On this subject the true facts are known only to the inner circle of members, and the remarks which follow must be taken with considerable reserve. There are three big groups of American producers—Anaconda, the Morgan-Guggenheim (Kennecott Corporation, etc.) and the Phelps Dodge-Nicholls group, but the two last-named work in close liaison, and so there are really only two groups. Both these groups have their fair share of high-cost and low-cost producing units, and neither can obtain superiority over the other. It would take too long to review the evidence in detail, but it can be said with considerable certainty that, while the Morgan-Guggenheim interests have not been opposed to the general policy of price control and restriction, they desired to see the price stabilised at the highest level which the consumer could be made to pay and go on paying indefinitely, while Anaconda has wished to send prices soaring, irrespective of the ultimate effects. Rumour has it that Anaconda has been holding large blocks of shares which it desires to pass on to the public: hence their desire for a boom in prices, however transient. When Europe stampeded to buy in March 1929, it was playing into Anaconda's hands, and Anaconda's supremacy was still further increased. For the last eighteen months at least, it may be said that every move by the combine has been in the nature of a compromise; Anaconda, as the apostle of high prices, irrespective of the immediate cost or ultimate effects of the necessary output restriction, dragging after it the other groups of half-delighted, half-fearful producers, until finally the Morgan banking interests refused to finance any further accumulations of stocks, and abruptly called an end to such a game of folly.

The immediate future depends mainly upon the course of the world trade depression, and the degree to which the consumption of copper is affected. Production has been drastically curtailed in the United States, but even so, stocks continued to mount during the first half of the year, though there was a slight reduction in the August figure. This curtailment of production is undoubtedly in the main voluntary rather than enforced, though a large proportion of the reserve capacity cannot cover even direct costs at a selling price of 11 cents (£51 per ton). But at the same time the present requirements of consumption could probably be produced at direct costs considerably lower than 11 cents, and therefore there is no reason why the price should not fall even farther. Copper Exporters are, however, at present contriving to prevent a real collapse in prices such as has overtaken some commodities, and there are signs of a certain stability in the present position. Any further contraction in consumption may, however, make things too difficult for the combine, and a further fall in price is even now by no means impossible.

In copper production technique has recently made great strides, and the present excess capacity is mainly due to the introduction of new low-cost plants. The copper industry, more than most industries, has got to adjust itself to a new lower level of prices. Even if in the spring of 1931 consumption recovers its normal stride, it will take time to work off the accumulated stocks, and before the world needs increased production, there may well be time for a further expansion and development of low-cost sources of supply. Thus the centre of the world's copper production may shift with considerable rapidity away from the United States, while the establishment of two large new electrolytic refineries in Europe, and the development of African supplies, may in the not too distant future render Europe much less dependent on America. It is possible, therefore, that Copper Exporters will never again play so strong a hand, and it is certainly to be hoped that there will be no repetition of their history to date.

III. *Tin*

The total stocks of tin and tin ore are made up of:—

(1) The 'visible supply' as defined by the monthly returns of the London Metal Exchange, namely, (*a*) stocks landing or warehoused in Great Britain, the United States and Holland, (*b*) tin afloat to Great Britain, the United States and Europe from the Straits, Batavia and Australia, and (*c*) tin afloat to Great Britain and the United States from China. Monthly returns of the 'visible supply' are also compiled by Messrs Ricard and Freiwald and by Messrs A. Strauss and Co., each on a slightly different basis from that of the Metal Exchange. The figures given below are those of the London Metal Exchange.

(2) Stocks of tin and tin ore in the Straits Settlements, the Dutch Indies, China and Hong Kong.

(3) Stocks of tin ore afloat from Bolivia and Nigeria to Europe and in course of smelting.

(4) 'Invisible' stocks in the hands of consumers, etc.

Since the publication of the earlier issues of this Memorandum, the Anglo-Oriental Mining Corporation has undertaken the monthly preparation of somewhat elaborate statistics, of which some use has been made below.

596

(1) *The visible supply*. It will be noticed that the 'visible supply' figures, which are those commonly quoted, cover a wider field than that usually meant by 'stocks', since they include tin in transit which is in no sense available for consumption. It follows that the 'visible supply' of tin can never fall to zero, or even fall below (say) 9,000–12,000 tons, unless a total breakdown of current supplies is impending from the sources of production. On the other hand, they do not include the total aggregate of tin and tin ore in the widest interpretation. They represent a rather arbitrary compromise between prospective supplies and stocks available for consumption. The result is that they are highly misleading from month to month, fluctuating with the chance dates of shipments from the East, etc., which have no real bearing on the position. Figures for stocks in the limited sense, i.e. landing or warehoused in the countries of consumption, will therefore be given separately, and also some material to correct the misleading inferences which might be drawn from the 'visible supply' figures as to the short-period prospective supplies at any time.

Available stocks of tin in the chief countries of consumption (U.K., U.S., and Holland) (tons of 2,240 lb)

End of month	1923	1924	1925	1926	1927	1928	1929	1930
Jan.	12,911	8,007	9,371	4,511	5,051	5,303	10,874	16,937
Feb.	10,937	7,706	9,593	5,373	3,962	5,238	12,076	18,614
Mar.	11,385	7,154	10,489	4,918	3,919	4,166	11,305	19,893
April	10,373	10,189	7,313	3,494	3,767	3,919	11,767	23,962
May	9,737	8,900	6,692	3,916	3,183	5,273	12,213	26,558
June	8,954	9,091	8,554	4,908	2,876	4,304	12,046	30,207
July	8,368	10,046	7,942	4,126	3,157	5,877	12,401	30,623
Aug.	9,004	10,185	8,596	3,994	3,938	4,564	12,591	
Sept.	7,383	10,497	6,721	3,693	3,030	6,797	12,819	
Oct.	8,588	7,721	5,896	3,344	4,120	9,352	13,229	
Nov.	7,466	7,615	5,410	3,778	3,458	9,103	11,727	
Dec.	7,870	9,262	5,863	4,170	4,109	10,382	15,839	

The distribution of these stocks at the end of each year was as follows:—

31 December	1923	1924	1925	1926	1927	1928	1929
U.K.	4,319	5,820	3,161	1,473	2,536	7,954	13,019
U.S.	1,652	2,844	2,654	1,909	1,573	2,428	2,820
Holland	1,899	598	48	788	Nil	Nil	Nil

Since the normal consumption of tin is about 12,000 tons monthly, the supply stocks available for consumers in 1926 and 1927 amounted to about 10 days' consumption, as compared with a month's supply at the beginning of 1923; but by the middle of 1930 they had accumulated up to the substantial total of some ten weeks' supplies.

The 'visible supply' of tin (tons of 2,240 lb)*

End of month	1923	1924	1925	1926	1927	1928	1929	1930
Jan.	25,765	24,372	22,949	16,787	15,342	15,244	24,237	29,032
Feb.	25,157	21,835	23,591	16,239	14,221	17,645	26,402	33,581
Mar.	24,622	23,275	19,623	14,280	15,441	15,586	26,632	32,972
April	22,116	19,023	18,105	15,516	13,849	15,001	26,353	36,595
May	22,187	19,711	20,897	18,045	14,655	17,064	24,765	39,771
June	21,297	20,094	19,797	15,831	15,638	16,231	23,751	42,611
July	20,019	20,161	19,857	13,777	15,377	18,022	23,789	41,950
Aug.	18,754	21,302	20,000	13,352	14,487	18,456	26,400	43,805
Sept.	19,864	20,233	17,642	14,379	15,083	19,924	24,556	40,150
Oct.	20,567	18,971	15,770	14,841	14,684	20,907	25,580	
Nov.	19,520	20,977	18,199	15,257	14,594	22,067	25,171	
Dec.	21,011	25,088	18,029	16,326	15,733	24,563	28,140	

* London Metal Exchange figures.

(2) *Stocks in the East*. The main source of error in the figures just given as a true indication of the position is the fact that they neglect entirely the stocks of tin in the East, whence the bulk of

the world's supplies are drawn. As described in earlier memoranda, these stocks were abnormally swollen from 1920 to 1925 by tin held mainly by the Straits and Dutch Indies Governments, under the Bandoeng Agreement. The last lots of this tin were sold before the end of 1924, but the trade figures show that some 3,000 tons were not shipped, and therefore did not enter into the 'visible supply', until 1925. Apart from the disposal of these exceptional stocks, the trade figures indicate that other more normal stocks of tin and of ore in the Straits have varied as follows:

Tons of 2,240 lb

	Imports of tin into the Straits	Exports of tin from the Straits	Reduction of Straits stocks
1923	65,335	69,119	3,784
1924	74,109	79,940	5,831
1925	76,630	78,819	2,189
1926	74,362	76,474	2,112
1927	81,590	81,815	2,775*
1928	96,294	97,853	1,559
1929	104,490	102,019	2,471*

* Increase.

The imports into the Straits are in the form of ore, and are assumed in the trade returns to contain 72 per cent of fine metal. As time has gone by, it has become apparent that the actual contents are slightly greater than this. Thus the reduction of stocks has not been quite so great as indicated above. Total stocks in the Straits, including ore, would appear to have been, roughly, as follows:—

	Tons		Tons
End of 1922	14,600	End of 1926	2,000
1923	10,800	1927	5,000
1924	5,000	1928	4,000
1925	3,800	1929	7,700

Of these stocks, at the end of 1922, 13,600 tons were held under the Bandoeng Pool, in addition to 4,000 tons held in the Dutch Indies.

As regards the Dutch Indies, part of the supplies (the tin from Billiton) is forwarded regularly to the Straits to be smelted there. The rest (the tin from Banca) is smelted locally and shipped direct, mainly to Europe. These shipments are more irregular than the production, depending on the selling policy of the Dutch Government. This is a further cause of error in the visible supply statistics, though probably not to the extent of more than (say) 500–1,000 tons in any month.

As regards supplies from China, about half the production used to find its way to U.K. and U.S.A.; but the exports recently have been on only a small scale. Estimates of stocks, mainly in Hong Kong, are available irregularly.

The best available aggregate of tin supplies, apart from tin in the hands of smelters on the one hand and of consumers on the other, is given below. Apart from exceptional figures in isolated months, 13,000 tons is probably the lowest to which this total can fall, having regard to the amount of tin necessarily afloat. Thus the surplus fell in 1926 almost to the minimum figure, but has since recovered to substantial proportions. Moreover, the true surplus in 1928 was probably a few thousand tons, and in 1929 several thousand tons, more than the figures given below, inasmuch as during these years a large amount was held privately by a 'bull' pool which was operating with a view to sustaining the market price of the metal.

(3) *Bolivian and Nigerian tin afloat and with the smelters.* If we allow two months from the date of shipment from Bolivia to the time of delivery in refined form on the London market, some 5,000 tons of tin are normally thus in transit, but the actual figure may vary from (say) 4,000 tons to 8,000 tons. The corresponding variations for Nigerian tin in transit are on a much smaller scale. These fluctuations average out, of course, over a period of time, but may considerably affect the statistics of visible supply between one month and another.

Total stocks of tin (tons of 2,240 lb)

End of year	1922	1923	1924	1925	1926	1927	1928	1929	1930 (30 June)
Straits pool tin	13,600	9,500	3,000	—	—	—	—	—	—
,, other stocks	500	1,800	2,500	3,300	1,750	1,350	1,235	4,725	4,230
,, surplus ore	500	500	500	500	250	3,650	2,765	3,000	2,290
Dutch Indies pool	4,000	2,000	—	—	—	—	—	—	—
China	1,500	1,400	1,000	500	600	300	300	300	300
'Visible supply'	25,300	21,000	25,100	18,000	16,300	15,730	24,550	28,125	42,610
Grand total	45,400	36,200	32,100	22,300	18,600	21,030	28,850	36,150	49,430

(4) *'Invisible' stocks in the hands of consumers, etc.* As stated above, there were in 1928 and 1929 some thousands of tons of 'invisible' stocks held privately by a 'bull' pool. Apart from such exceptional holdings, the most important influence in accelerating supplies and decreasing the aggregate of 'invisible' stocks at all stages from the producer to the consumer is to be found in the development of a 'backwardation' on forward tin as against spot tin, i.e. in tin for delivery in three months standing, at a price appreciably lower than tin for immediate delivery. This means on the one hand that the producers and smelters can gain the difference by hastening forward their supplies of refined metal, and on the other hand that consumers can save the difference by keeping their stocks as low as possible and covering their known prospective requirements by buying forward instead of keeping the actual metal on hand.

For short periods during the time of acute shortage in 1927 the 'backwardation' sometimes reached or exceeded £12 per three months. The average figures over each year have been as follows:—

	Average price of spot tin			Average price of 3 months' tin			Spot tin above (+) or below (−) forward tin		
	£	s.	d.	£	s.	d.	£	s.	d.
1922	159	10	9	160	13	11	−1	3	2
1923	202	5	0	202	15	4	−0	10	4
1924	248	17	4	249	10	6½	−0	13	2½
1925	261	1	8½	262	5	9½	−1	4	1
1926	291	3	0½	284	7	7	+6	15	5½
1927	289	0	0	282	4	0	+6	16	0
1928	227	6	0	225	14	0	+1	12	0
1929 6 mos.	204	0	0	206	10	0	+2	10	0

The principal changes in the volume of production have been, approximately, as follows:—

World's tin production (tons of 2,240 lb)

	1923	1924	1925	1926	1927	1928	1929
Malay States	39,500	46,500	48,000	48,000	55,000	64,500	69,500
Dutch Indies	29,000	32,000	31,500	31,500	35,500	35,000	34,000
Siam and Burma	9,000	9,000	8,000	8,000	9,000	10,000	12,500
China	8,000	7,000	9,000	6,500	6,500	6,500	7,500
Australia	3,000	3,000	3,000	3,000	3,000	3,000	3,000
Nigeria	6,000	6,000	6,000	7,000	7,500	9,000	10,500
S. Africa	1,000	1,000	1,000	1,000	1,000	1,000	1,250
Cornwall	1,000	1,500	2,000	2,000	2,000	2,500	2,750
Bolivia	29,500	31,500	32,000	32,000	34,000	40,000	43,000
Elsewhere	1,500	2,500	4,000	4,000	4,000	4,000	4,000
Total	127,500	140,000	144,500	143,000	157,500	175,500	188,000

Production caught up with consumption towards the end of 1926, and then, after keeping about level with it for a year, took a leap ahead, which consumption, although of record dimensions in 1929, has found it impossible to keep up with, as is shown by the following approximate estimates.

Consumption of tin (tons of 2,240 lb)

	1925	1926	1927	1928	1929
Great Britain	25,000	18,500	23,000	33,000	35,000
United States	76,500	78,000	72,500	79,000	89,000
Germany	8,000	5,500	15,000	9,000	13,000
France	11,500	11,000	8,500	10,500	12,000
Asia	10,000	9,000	9,000	9,000	7,000
Other countries	23,500	24,500	27,000	27,000	25,000
Total	154,500	146,500	155,000	167,500	181,000

We estimate recent production and consumption of tin in the aggregate as follows:—

Tons of 2,240 lb

Year	Production	Consumption	Stocks at end of year
1922	130,000	132,000	45,400
1923	127,500	139,000	36,000
1924	140,000	144,500	32,000
1925	144,500	154,500	22,000
1926	143,000	146,500	18,500
1927	157,500	155,000	21,000
1928	175,000	167,500	29,000
1929	188,000	181,000	36,000
1930 (6 mos.)	90,500	77,000	49,500

It will be seen that the high prices which prevailed from 1921–7 stimulated a very substantial increase in output which, it is estimated, would have reached not less than 191,000 tons per annum in 1930 in the absence of restriction. Thus production caught up consumption in 1927 and exceeded it by 8,000 tons in 1928. In 1929, in spite of a consumption of record dimensions, especially in the United States, production was in excess by more than 500 tons a month. It was inevitable, therefore, that when the world-wide slump came in 1930 there should be a crisis of the first magnitude in the industry.

In fact the consumption of tin held up relatively well. The tinplate industry maintained its activity better than most, and outside the United States, where the slump in the motorcar industry caused a great reduction in takings, the set-back was moderate. In the aggregate, consumption fell back to about the level of 1927. But in the new conditions of output this meant an excess production of at least 2,000 tons a month. On the top of stocks which had already, since the end of 1928, grown to a total in excess of what was normal or necessary, this meant a steep fall in prices. By the middle of 1930 tin was selling at a price of about £135 per ton, which two years before would have been thought an impossibly low figure. At the end of September 1930 the price was below £130.

The position was complicated by the existence of the substantial speculative holding which had been built up in 1928-9 at much higher prices on the hands of persons who were also interested in the metal on the production side. Under these auspices feverish efforts were made to organise schemes of voluntary restriction on the part of producers, and a body known as the Tin Producers' Association was formed.

In April 1930 it was alleged that a restriction scheme had been agreed upon which would have the effect of reducing production by at least 2,200 tons a month, and perhaps by as much as 2,500 tons a month. But no such results were realised. Whilst Bolivian and Nigerian shipments showed some falling off, Malayan deliveries of tin remained at a figure which was virtually unabated. The statistics, which were adduced to show that, in spite of appearances to the contrary, the promised restriction was actually in force, commanded no confidence. If they were correct, it would follow that unrestricted production would have been appreciably greater than the 191,000 tons estimated above.

In July 1930 a more drastic, and also a more genuine, scheme was arranged by which a number of producers agreed to close down altogether for a period of two months, whilst others were to curtail output for the rest of the year. Officially this scheme is supposed to cut output by 17,000 tons between July and December 1930.

Even so, however, whilst stocks should cease to mount higher, the measures proposed are not calculated to make much of an inroad into existing stocks. In the absence of restriction production would probably exceed current consumption by fully 2,200 tons a month. Therefore, taken at its face value, the restriction scheme would only bring stocks at the end of December 1930 to a figure of 3,000 tons less than at the end of June 1930. Allowing for time lags, etc., the effect is likely to be still less than this, unless in the meantime consumption revives, which is not to be depended on. It would seem, therefore, that for any important price recovery, tin, like other commodities, must await a general revival of trade.

Failing this, low prices may do the work of restriction more surely than voluntary arrangements. Recent results show that most sound Malayan dredging companies can produce tin below £100 per ton, and some of them much below. These companies will not, therefore, be keen to continue closing down or restricting indefinitely so long as tin sells at £135 to £145 a ton. On the other hand, there seems to be fairly solid evidence that a price around £135 a ton seriously embarrasses producers in Nigeria, Australia and Cornwall, and goes a long way towards knocking out the majority of Bolivian producers. Thus the cost of production in Bolivia seems to hold the key to the position. For Bolivia has been producing some 40,000 tons a year. If, therefore, the majority of Bolivian producers begin to lose money when the London price falls below £150 a ton, as seems on the whole probable, equilibrium might be found, pending a general trade revival, somewhere in the neighbourhood of £135 even without organised restrictions. But this would be a disaster for Bolivia.

If we grant that Bolivian and Nigerian output will be needed in normal times, and that tin-mines are a wasting asset even for the cheapest producers, and, further, that a 20 per cent restriction will raise the price by at least 20 per cent (which is quite plausible), there may remain, nevertheless, a valid case for producers as a whole in favour of organised restriction.

IV. *Lead*

In common with many other commodities, the production of lead showed a considerable expansion in 1929. The following figures issued by the American Bureau of Metal Statistics apply to the principal lead-producing countries of the world, which in 1929 furnished 88 per cent of the world's total lead output.

Production of lead (1,000 tons of 2,240 lb)

	1924	1925	1926	1927	1928	1929
United States	525	590	621	601	580	618
Mexico	159	181	197	245	233	245
Canada	75	111	126	139	152	142
Spain and Tunis	137	135	145	137	121	103
Italy	22	16	23	23	21	22
Australia	126	147	149	165	163	173
Burma	52	48	54	66	78	80
Germany	44	49	75	80	86	109
Total for above	1,140	1,277	1,390	1,456	1,434	1,492

The American Bureau's figures for world production in recent years are as below.

In spite of the expansion in output and signs that production was in excess of requirements, prices were well maintained

1,000 tons

1924	1,298
1925	1,464
1926	1,570
1927	1,658
1928	1,649
1929	1,725
1930 (6 months)	[829]

during 1929 up to the time of the general break in the autumn, and the average for the year was well above the 1928 figure. The position was undoubtedly influenced by market control, since in August 1929 negotiations for the formation of a Lead Producers' Association were successfully concluded. Even after the autumn break, prices were pegged successfully for short periods, but subsequently have had to move down with the general trend of prices.

There were signs of accumulating stocks in the U.S.A. in the middle of 1929, but there was no significant change in the published figures for the U.K. until the beginning of 1930. The U.K. figures for official stocks have never, of course, represented anything like the total reserves in the country and have not the same value as the official copper and tin statistics. Reports this year have emphasised the piling up of stocks in private warehouses and consumers' yards. Nevertheless, on the assumption that there is some uniformity in the relation of official stocks to the general reserve, the huge increase in the official figures would imply a very weak position of the metal. It is asserted, however, that the figures have been swollen by the action of the Producers' Association in holding reserves in this country rather than at the producing points, a change of practice which entails the transfer of normal reserve supplies from the refineries to this country. The further suggestion that the smaller Continental demand has led to larger shipments to England, specially from America, is not inconsistent with the movement shown by the U.S. stocks

Stocks of lead in U.S., Mexico and U.K. (tons of 2,240 lb)

Beginning of month	1927			1928			1929			1930		
	U.S. and Mexico*	U.K.†	Total	U.S. and Mexico*	U.K.†	Total	U.S. and Mexico*	U.K.†	Total	U.S. and Mexico*	U.K.†	Total
January	113,400	1,677	115,100	139,500	2,014	141,500	144,100	917	145,000	135,300	2,036	137,300
February	120,300	2,516	122,800	140,600	1,931	142,500	139,400	1,586	141,000	133,400	4,466	137,900
March	124,800	2,596	127,400	149,700	1,975	151,700	143,400	1,403	144,800	125,700	6,684	132,400
April	130,200	2,732	132,900	154,800	1,873	156,700	141,200	1,304	142,500	128,900	6,845	135,700
May	143,600	2,918	146,500	143,900	1,861	145,800	140,000	1,305	141,300		7,626	
June	156,400	2,467	158,900	142,300	1,383	143,700	144,800	945	145,700		7,403	
July	152,000	2,436	154,400	146,200	1,281	147,500	155,000	779	155,800		7,366	
August	147,800	2,165	150,000	141,800	1,383	143,200	155,000	773	155,800		6,991	
September	145,400	2,091	147,500	140,200	1,326	141,500	156,800	658	157,500		5,720	
October	143,000	2,136	145,100	138,800	977	139,800	150,600	443	151,000		6,227	
November	139,200	2,436	141,600	136,400	675	137,100	149,300	422	149,700			
December	139,000	2,278	141,300	140,600	400	141,000	144,400	368	144,800			

* Stocks of ore, matte, base bullion and refined lead in the hands of those concerns which report to the American Bureau of Metal Statistics.
† Metal Exchange figures.

609

statistics. So far, the control of the market has been fairly effective, and there is some justification for the statement that the statistical position of lead is more sound than that of other metals.

V. *Spelter*

In spite of the restriction scheme operated by the European Cartel, the output of spelter showed a further increase in 1929, and at the end of the year the Cartel was in danger of breaking up. According to Rudolph Wolff & Co., the world's output of virgin spelter has been as follows:—

World output of virgin spelter (1,000 tons of 2,240 lb)

1921	452	1926	1,238
1922	689	1927	1,318
1923	960	1928	1,401
1924	998	1929	1,440
1925	1,132		

The same authority gives the following figures for production of spelter by countries which furnished about 90 per cent of the world's output [p. 611].

Monthly statics are available of stocks in public warehouses in the United States and in the United Kingdom as given below. These figures show that from the beginning of the second half of 1929 a rapid and serious accumulation of stocks occurred which is still unchecked. The price of the metal has fallen from the high point of £29 in March 1929 to under £16 at the present time.

During this year continuous efforts have been made to reconstitute the Cartel and to secure co-operation with American producers. Agreement was reached at Ostend in July. Under this arrangement, which is to last for two years in the first place, production quotas have been fixed based upon 1927–30 output in the case of European smelters and upon productive capacity

Production of spelter (tons of 2,240 lb)

	1924	1925	1926	1927	1928	1929
United States	460,000	513,000	570,000	548,000	553,000	561,000
Canada	25,000	38,000	55,000	66,000	73,000	77,000
Belgium	160,000	171,000	190,000	199,000	205,000	197,000
Germany (including Polish Silesia)	129,000*	159,000	190,000	234,000	256,000	266,000
Australia	44,000	47,000	48,000	50,000	49,000	52,000
Great Britain	53,000	59,000	27,000	50,000	55,000	59,000
France	59,000	67,000	68,000	78,000	95,000	90,000
Total for above countries	930,000	1,054,000	1,148,000	1,225,000	1,286,000	1,302,000

* Probably under-estimated.

U.K. and U.S. stocks of spelter (tons of 2,240 lb)

End of month	1927			1928			1929			1930		
	U.S.	U.K.	Total	U.S.	U.K.	Total	U.S.	U.K.	Total	U.S.	U.K.	Total
January	26,710	1,260	27,970	37,650	1,063	38,710	40,550	1,717	42,270	78,510	6,075	84,590
February	29,420	1,061	30,480	36,900	1,565	37,470	36,250	1,349	37,600	80,980	5,669	86,650
March	32,380	857	33,240	37,080	791	37,870	33,900	872	34,770	83,980	5,842	89,820
April	36,800	1,188	37,990	39,970	454	40,420	30,870	897	31,770	86,120	5,838	91,960
May	37,550	1,052	38,600	40,400	832	41,230	30,200	1,253	31,450	91,780	7,969	99,750
June	39,170	1,524	40,690	39,710	1,236	40,950	32,970	910	33,880	97,840	10,233	108,070
July	35,120	1,231	36,350	37,700	916	38,620	39,390	2,193	41,580	104,800	12,334	117,130
August	30,890	966	31,860	39,660	1,335	41,000	42,710	3,419	46,130	109,500	13,149	122,650
September	30,610	1,017	31,630	42,800	1,343	44,140	47,640	3,516	51,160		12,620	
October	32,340	614	32,950	41,140	671	41,810	51,000	3,535	54,540			
November	35,120	1,160	36,280	41,570	1,486	43,060	66,300	2,401	68,700			
December	36,390	679	37,070	40,590	1,757	42,350	69,000	4,440	73,440			

in the case of some of the overseas countries. Of the total world figure thus obtained, European producers will receive 77 per cent and overseas producers 23 per cent. A cut of about 30 per cent will be made on this basis, but this may not involve much reduction on recent actual output. The producers concerned represent about 87 per cent of the world's capacity, and negotiations are to be undertaken with the remaining 13 per cent. The announcement of this agreement had a temporary sentimental effect on prices, but the improvement was soon lost. In view of the weak statistical position, the expressed intention of the Cartel not to force up prices is perhaps superfluous, and the prospects of successful operation of the scheme are still very remote.

VI. *Rubber*

The stocks of rubber are held mainly:—

(1) On plantations and with dealers within the restricted area of Malaya.

(2) In Singapore and Penang.

(3) Afloat.

(4) In London and Liverpool.

(5) In U.S.A. warehouses and factories.

In addition relatively insignificant stocks are held:—

(6) In Ceylon and India.

(7) In Dutch East Indies.

(8) In Para (Brazil).

(9) In Amsterdam and Antwerp.

Prior to 1928 no figures were available for (1). This omission became important during the interval between the announcement that restriction was to come to an end and its actual withdrawal. Accordingly, a census of stocks in Malaya was then instituted. Use of this has been made in the table below, which is the best approximation to the actual stocks in existence which can be made, if an addition of approximately 15–20,000 tons is made for stocks in Ceylon, Dutch East Indies, Para and Continental European Ports.

World's rubber stocks (exclusive of stock on estates) (1,000 tons)

End of	United Kingdom*	United States†	Singapore and Penang‡	Ceylon and India	Dutch East Indies	Para (Brazil)	Amsterdam and Antwerp	Afloat	Approximate total*
1920	56	76	35	?	?	?	?	37	(204)§ 219–229
1921	80	52	40	?	?	?	?	37	(209)§ 224–244
1922	81	90	55	?	?	?	?	45	(271)§ 286–306
1923 March	79	87	21	3·5	9	0·6	1·0	48	249
June	64	101	46	?	?	?	?	52	(263)§ 278‖
September	68	90	27	4·0	10	0·9	1·2	43	244
December	75	73	38	4·0	10	?	2·5	52	254
1924 March	70	70	21	3·0	10	1·0	1·1	50	226
June	65	60	20	3·0	10	1·0	1·2	48	208
September	54	56	20	3·5	7	0·8	0·6	54	196
December	36	63	19	4·0	5	0·9	0·3	53	181
1925 March	23	55	17	4·0	5	1·2	0·1	50	155
June	7	40	16	3·0	3	0·5	0·2	59	129
September	7	45	16	4·0	5	1·1	0·3	63	141
December	7	74	20	4·5	5	1·5	0·2	70	182

1926 March	16	61	18	4·5	7	2·0	0·2	74	183
June	28	60	19	4·5	7	1·8	0·8	72	193
September	42	62	26	4·5	8	2·1	1·3	67	213
December	59	72	26	5·5	7	1·5	1·1	77	259
1927 March	70	86	28	5·0	7	2·0	1·5	74	273
June	71	89	22	4·5	7	1·7	1·5	66	263
September	72	98	25	4	6	3	1	62	271
December	66	100	26	4	6	2	1	67	272
1928 March	60	114	21	4	5	2	1	63	270
June	41	90	18	4	5	2	1	59	222
September	34	69	15	4	5	3	2	74	206
December	23	66	34	5	5	3	1	102	239
1929 March	32	101	29	4	4	4	1	86	261
June	36	92	32	4	4	3	1	76	248
September	55	84	32	5	4	4	2	94	280
December	77	105	33	6	4	3	2	91	321
1930 March	91	145	45	6	5	3	2	96	397
June	110	151	41	5	5	3	2	77	394

* Including an estimate of stocks in private warehouses from 1923 to June 1927. The true totals for 1920–2 were certainly higher than the figures shown, and should perhaps be increased by 10,000 tons in 1920, and by 15–20,000 tons in 1921 and 1922. From September 1927 the figures are the total published stocks in London and Liverpool.   † Returns cover 90–95 per cent of the whole.

‡ Including Wellesley, Dindings and Malacca from September 1927.   § These figures in brackets give the actual total of stocks quoted.

‖ These figures include an estimate of 15,000 tons for the unknown stocks in Ceylon, Dutch East Indies, Para, and at Amsterdam and Antwerp. This has been done in order to secure a more comparable series.

1,000 tons

	1 Jan. 1928	1 April 1928	1 July 1928	1 Oct. 1928	1 Jan. 1929	1 April 1929	1 July 1929	1 Oct. 1929	1 Jan. 1930	1 April 1930	1 July 1930
On estates in Malaya	30	30	45	61*	26	21	23	23	25	22	23
With dealers in Malaya	—	—	13	10*	12	13	15	16	16	17	14
” ” in Straits	26	20	18	15	33	29	30	34	33	39	37
In U.K.	66	60	41	34	23	32	36	55	77	91	110
In U.S.	100	114	90	69	66	101	92	84	105	145	151
Afloat to U.S.†	48	39	40	49	69	56	46	49	62	64	59
Elsewhere afloat†	19	24	19	25	33	30	30	45	29	32	18
Total	289	287	266	263	262	282	272	306	347	410	412

* Probably these figures should be much greater. See comment in Memorandum 29 [pp. 543–7].
† These figures are shown separately because the 'afloat to U.S.' figures are reasonably accurate, while the latter are rough estimates only.

The following are estimates of production* and consumption†
of crude rubber in recent years (1,000 tons):—

	Production	Consumption	Apparent increase or decrease in stocks	Recorded change in stocks
1919	398	330		
1920	354	310		
1921	300	265	+35	+15
1922	400	390	+10	+62
1923	407	435	−28	−52
1924	428	470	−42	−73
1925	517	560	−43	+ 1
1926	620	545	+75	+77
1927	605	590	+15	+23
1928	650	680	−30	−33
1929	860	795	+65	+82

During 1929 rubber once more did the unexpected, and not
one of the experts was even remotely correct in estimating either
production or consumption. The highest estimates for production ranged between 700 and 720 thousand tons. By July it was
clear that shipments from Malaya were exceedingly heavy, but it
was argued that this was primarily due to 'flush' production
after the enforced resting of the trees during the restriction years.
But month after month the shipments showed little reduction,
and by the end of the year had exceeded expectations by more
than 100,000 tons. Shipments from Ceylon were also nearly
20,000 tons in excess of expectations. The same rates of shipment
continued during the first three months of 1930. In view of the
fact that full tapping has now been in operation for two years, all
explanations in terms of flush production are becoming very
thin. The true explanation is that normal yields on estates have

* I.e. net exports as reckoned by the R[ubber] G[rowers'] A[ssociation].
† Estimated world absorption by manufacturers.

been greatly, and more or less permanently, increased. During restriction, nearly all estates maintained a labour force in excess of their actual requirements, hoping each quarter for a greater percentage release, and this surplus labour was used to improve drainage, soil conservation, aeration of the ground, etc. Systems of periodic tapping have been introduced in place of the continued daily tapping of the past. In addition, tapping tasks have been greatly reduced, and thus tapping is concluded at a much earlier hour, with consequent greater yields, while the actual tapping is less hurriedly done and so bark consumption is smaller. In these and many other ways, the normal yield has been greatly increased, and the falling off of shipments in April and May this year is mainly due to climatic conditions producing an unusually heavy leaf-fall, while the June figures reflect, of course, the results of the tapping holiday during May. Some small part of the huge yields on estates in 1929 may have been due to climatic conditions—so little is really known about the rubber tree that this cannot be with safety ignored—but the indications are that the increased yield will be more or less permanent. The increased yield on small-holdings (i.e. estates under 100 acres) is even greater than on the larger estates, and it is said that the native has been consuming his bark at a rate which will not permit sufficient time for its renewal. The general opinion of European planters is that there will be a big fall in native output by the end of this year, but some persons who are specially qualified to speak on this particular subject affirm that while this may be true on the basis of European methods of cultivation, the native will continue to make his trees yield at very nearly the present rate: and the planter has been so continuously wrong about native rubber that it will be rather surprising if he is right this time! The outlook is for very little if any reduction in Malayan output.

Production in 1929 was therefore approximately 150,000 tons more than was anticipated. Fortunately consumption followed suit, though nothing like so strongly. Consumption in the U.S.A.

increased by only 30,000 tons, though this must be considered good in view of the huge increase of 70,000 tons during 1928. But the new and most satisfactory feature was the increased takings by the rest of the world, and in particular by Europe. Doubtless this represents some rebuilding of manufacturers' stocks, but a total world increase of over 100,000 tons was most satisfactory.

The excessive increase of production involved a large addition to stocks by the end of 1929, and a further jump of no less than 60,000 tons took place during the first quarter of this year. After climbing back to 11*d.* and higher in the early spring of 1929, the price started declining again, and with a sharp break after the Wall Street crash had reached a level of 7*d.*–8*d.* by the end of the year. This level was held until the middle of May 1930, buoyed up to some extent by the May tapping holiday. But the lack of any immediate results from this expedient, and the positive evidence of reduced rubber consumption and of the low estimates of current motorcar production in the United States, sent the price to 6*d.* in mid-June. For the next three weeks, the negotiations between British and Dutch producers with a view to a definite restriction scheme postponed a further decline, but when the latter cast 40 per cent of their total votes against restriction, it became obvious that little was to be hoped for in that direction, and the price began dropping again until in the first week of August it passed below fivepence, and in September below fourpence. As with certain other commodities, the price of rubber now reflects the unwillingness or the inability of merchants and speculators to carry additional stocks, and there is no real reason why the price should not temporarily go even lower. Production capacity is not seriously out of adjustment with the trend of consumption, but consumption has declined sharply in the United States. The rest of the world was still buying in increasing quantities during the first quarter of this year—a somewhat striking fact, even if later statistics show the reverse. But nothing can, of course, outbalance the decline in the

619

United States, and the outlook for the future almost wholly depends on the recovery of American consumption. So long as prices remained above 6½d., very few estates were losing money, but certainly an appreciable proportion is being produced at a loss with the price below 5d. If the recovery of American consumption is long delayed—and there are no signs of recovery yet —a good many estates will close down in, say, six to nine months' time. A unanimous demand by producers on the British and Dutch Governments for restriction on the lines of the Stevenson Scheme seems most unlikely to materialise, for some of the most influential Dutch producers, including the Amsterdam Trading Company, have lately reiterated their opposition to restriction, at least until the high-cost, less efficient producers have been forced out of existence, while a recent circular by the Dunlop Company suggests that the low-cost British producers are not altogether sorry that restriction is off the map. If restriction comes at all, it will probably be enforced by the Governments on their own initiative as a remedy for the unemployment problems which will result from any large-scale abandonment of estates. Conversations have recently been proceeding between the Governors of Malaya and Java, but though Malaya is keen enough, Java naturally adopts the attitude of Holland, and the British Government will certainly not move without the Dutch, at any rate until conditions have proved to be as bad as the most pessimistic fear. From the consumer's point of view, the trouble is not the possible disappearance of some high-cost capacity, but the prevention of any addition of new low-cost capacity. While the consumer would gain little if restriction preserved this high-cost capacity, it is to be hoped that the price will not stay low too long, or the ultimate result will be another boom unless consumption greatly alters its trend.

One other feature of the position requires brief mention. Even the low price of crude rubber in 1929 has not ousted reclaimed rubber to any appreciable extent. American manufacturers are now firmly convinced of the utility of reclaimed for certain purposes, and have got accustomed to using a certain percentage in their compounds. Reclaimed has made a definite place for itself in commerce, and probably, unless the price of crude remains well below sixpence, the U.S.A. will continue to use nearly one-half as much as they do of crude, while reports indicate that European manufacturers are more inclined to follow this lead. It will be interesting to see whether even at threepence crude will oust reclaimed rubber to any appreciable extent. The following table illustrates these remarks:—

United States consumption of crude and reclaimed rubber

	Crude rubber, 1,000 long tons	Reclaimed rubber, 1,000 long tons	Reclaim-crude, per cent
1919	202	73	36·3
1920	196	75	38·4
1921	171	41	24·4
1922	283	54	19·2
1923	305	75	23·5
1924	340	78	23·3
1925	385	137	35·3
1926	358	164	45·0
1927	373	189	50·8
1928	442	223	51·0
1929	466	227	48·6

VII. *Sugar*

In the case of this commodity it is necessary to restrict ourselves to 'visible supplies', accurate estimates of stocks held up by producers in the fairly numerous different sources of supply not being available, with the important exception of Cuba. Statistics of stocks in the interior of Cuba are now available since 1926, and the carryover of these stocks has recently been such as to make a considerable addition to the 'visible' carryover. With this deficiency made good, the limitation to 'visible' supplies is

Distribution of sugar stocks (1,000 tons)

Beginning of month	Germany	Czecho-Slovakia	France	Holland	Belgium	Poland	United Kingdom	Total Europe	U.S. ports	Cuba ports	Cuba interior	Grand total
1925 January	977	769	468	195	228	237	162	3,036	32	42	—	—
April	591	494	373	86	166	171	192	2,073	128	860	—	—
July	269	235	158	66	83	93	357	1,261	277	1,095	—	—
October	17	36	51	17	18	—	300	439	135	594	—	—
1926 January	1,207	934	487	170	223	289	432	3,742	76	132	—	—
April	926	680	325	164	149	206	514	2,964	208	1,193	—	—
July	515	345	197	134	61	108	490	1,850	377	1,328	997	4,552
October	79	44	45	63	18	22	371	642	216	603	458	1,919
1927 January	1,176	611	547	238	137	291	380	3,380	181	70	12	3,643
April	855	413	393	172	105	189	362	2,489	219	1,324	—	—
July	535	178	269	58	71	98	411	1,620	259	1,170	1,041	4,090
October	80	9	67	29	14	4	258	461	183	672	464	1,780
1928 January	1,231	846	587	192	183	293	277	3,591	179	218	74	4,062
April	889	623	409	146	142	200	320	2,729	315	1,203	1,195	5,442
July	502	292	221	92	102	121	310	1,640	544	1,159	960	4,303
October	101	47	62	33	25	14	136	418	343	630	459	1,850
1929 January	1,457	690	630	261	221	420	276	3,955	159	125	32	4,271
February	1,390	646	626	260	198	416	360	3,896	144	477	517	5,034
March	1,300	602	564	247	190	390	325	3,618	271	949	950	5,788
April	1,146	522	473	229	171	345	314	3,200	418	1,298	1,274	6,190
May	983	399	402	213	160	281	250	2,688	553	1,511	1,406	6,152
June	819	320	349	205	146	218	220	2,277	703	1,440	1,170	5,590
July	644	247	288	186	123	183	163	1,834	673	1,299	993	4,799
August	411	155	242	149	93	123	125	1,298	645	1,051	832	3,826
September	211	92	203	101	69	80	100	856	608	740	600	2,804
October	103	34	130	73	36	34	180	590	926	504	510	2,530
November	486	362	271	126	53	161	241	1,700	879	327	395	3,301
December	1,305	743	502	226	157	375	280	3,588	793	255	310	4,946
1930 January	1,565	717	669	263	197	531	400	4,342	769	182	180	5,473
February	1,478	643	666	239	185	547	422	4,180	684	312	357	5,533
March	1,372	592	598	229	173	496	378	3,838	645	815	850	6,148
April	1,240	518	553	220	160	426	315	3,432	578	1,412	1,560	6,982
May	1,103	431	490	211	146	347	232	2,960	638	1,755	1,945	7,298
June	941	356	449	203	131	297	207	2,584	784	1,702	1,885	6,955
July	750	284	385	175	109	254	187	2,144	666	1,632	1,714	6,156

Supply and consumption of sugar (tons)

	1920-1	1921-2	1922-3	1923-4	1924-5	1925-6	1926-7	1927-8	1928-9	1929-30*
Stock carried over on 1 September	1,600,000	2,400,000	1,180,000	1,267,000	982,000	1,612,000	2,657,000	2,439,000	2,518,000	2,804,000
European beet crops	3,671,788	4,054,282	4,735,500	5,057,800	7,077,800	7,453,000	6,860,000	8,031,000	8,369,000	8,143,000
American beet crops	1,004,019	930,121	649,000	803,700	1,010,400	836,900	829,000	965,000	967,000	1,032,000
Cane crops	12,081,831	12,679,948	12,691,500	13,837,400	15,501,400	16,293,700	15,901,000	16,330,000	17,831,000	17,611,000
Total	18,357,638	20,064,351	19,256,000	20,965,900	24,571,600	26,195,600	26,247,000	27,765,000	29,685,000	29,590,000
Deduct visible supplies at end of season (1 September)	2,400,000	1,180,000	1,267,000	982,000	1,612,000	2,000,000	2,439,000	2,518,000	2,804,000	4,200,000†
Total consumption	15,957,638	18,884,351	17,989,000	19,983,900	22,959,600	24,195,600	23,808,000	25,247,000	26,881,000	25,390,000

* Crop figures are partly provisional estimates at present.
† Provisional.

not so serious as it would be in the case of many commodities, because, on the one hand, sugar being a semi-manufactured product, the agricultural producers send the bulk of the output forward to the centrals as soon as it is available, and, on the other hand, since in most countries it is a dutiable commodity, invisible supplies on which duty has been paid are not likely to be larger than convenience dictates.

The table on page 622 shows the distribution of stocks in the seven most important European countries, and the total for Europe. This, of course, is predominantly beet sugar, and hence the stocks reach a maximum about the beginning of the calendar year, and a minimum in October. The remaining columns show stocks in U.S. ports, Cuba ports, and in the interior of Cuba. These are almost exclusively cane sugar, since the beet sugar crop of the U.S. is marketed internally. The harvesting of the Cuban crop is usually completed in May, and hence the grand total in the last column shows a somewhat different seasonal variation from the total for Europe, though the minimum is much the same, since by October the bulk of the Cuban supply has normally passed through the ports to the refiners.

The tables on pp. 622–3 give a very rough idea of world stocks, production, and consumption in recent seasons, and the table below shows consumption during recent years by this

U.K. and U.S.A. consumption of sugar

	Consumption (raw values—tons)	
Year	United Kingdom	United States
1922	1,748,177	5,476,500
1923	1,602,029	5,141,000
1924	1,706,661	5,220,000
1925	1,817,869	5,925,000
1926	1,776,766	6,098,200
1927	1,681,351	5,695,700
1928	1,849,755	5,960,210
1929	1,952,034	6,248,380

country and the United States, which between them account for an extraordinary proportion of the exported sugar.

While the last Memorandum was in the press, the whole sugar situation was changed by the establishment of a Single Selling Agency in Cuba to take over the unsold balance of the 1928–9 crop on September 1st, and to dispose of the entire 1929–30 crop. The agency was to take the form of a compulsory co-operative institution, but pending its formation the Export Corporation was revived as a temporary selling committee. The objectives of the scheme may be said to have been threefold:—

(1) To prevent pressure on the market by sellers weak because in urgent need of cash, and, by holding back a certain tonnage, to give consumption a better chance to catch up supplies, thus raising the world price of sugar.

(2) To obtain for Cuba as much as possible of the 44 cents United States tariff preference by restricting supplies to the United States to the necessary extent (i.e. in the hope that the addition to the supplies of the rest of the world would not depress the world price so greatly as to lose on the swings what might be gained on the roundabouts).

(3) By thus raising the price in the United States market, to placate the U.S. domestic producers and induce them to modify their agitation for a higher tariff.

During September and October 1929 the Single Seller pursued a waiting policy in order to allow stocks of uncontrolled sugar in dealers' hands to reach their final destination. This took longer than was probably anticipated, and there were still appreciable supplies available from this source until December. The New York market was in general carefully nursed, and Cuba was obtaining a substantial proportion of the tariff preference, though this and the attempt to force a 2 per cent price from Europe undoubtedly resulted in a much larger carryover than was wise or even really necessary. But the ability to hold back supplies of the coming crop clearly depended on the provision of satisfactory arrangements for financing producers, and even the normal methods of financing were profoundly disturbed, since the merchants who made advances against the growing crop could not be given any assurance as to when the sugar could be sold, the sole power to sell being in the hands of the Co-operative Export Agency. As time went on, it became clear that the Export Agency was finding it difficult and even impossible to make satisfactory financing arrangements. The grinding of the new crop was prohibited by Presidential decree until January 15th, but when the new crop sugars became available just as the outlook for consumption was becoming daily worse in view of the onset of the world trade depression, the Export Agency found that prices still continued to decline even when it left the market almost completely alone. At the end of January sales began to be made by the Agency at 2 cents c. and f. New York with a guarantee that this would be the Agency's minimum price for a given period. The Agency appear to have staked everything on their ability to hold the price at 2 cents, for at the end of February they announced this as their minimum price throughout March. The result was virtually a cessation of business with the United States. Meantime, as grinding progressed, the problem of financing became more and more acute, especially for the Cuban-owned mills, which have not the same resources as those in American ownership. Rumours of the impending dissolution of the Agency became rife during March, and eventually a general meeting of the members was called to consider the situation. On April 3rd this meeting voted to continue the scheme by 12,918 to 11,139 votes. But this margin was obviously too narrow to be of practical use, and a fortnight later a second meeting was called, which voted heavily in favour of immediate dissolution. The Agency had succeeded in selling little more than one-tenth of the 1930 crop even at prices which averaged an equivalent of about $1\frac{3}{4}$ cents c. and f. New York.

The collapse of the Agency was the signal for a fresh break in prices and a subsequent slow decline. During May the long-drawn-out battle over the U.S. tariff was in its concluding stages, and the resulting uncertainty was blamed for this decline. But it was really having the reverse effect, for refiners were building up their stocks in anticipation of the expected increase in the duties, and when the tariff was passed and put into operation, they proceeded to work off these stocks, and their demand for fresh supplies temporarily declined below their current rate of melting. During June, Cuba could sell little sugar at all in New York, as the demand was mostly met by the holders of sugar which had paid the old duty and who now sold freely without any attempt to add the new higher rate of duty, counting themselves lucky to have such a chance of liquidation. In July business with Cuba was resumed at a level of 1.25 cents, but only those producers who can hold out no longer are accepting such prices. With the rest of the world Cuba did little better business, and on July 1st stocks in Cuba amounted to 3¼ million tons out of a total crop of 4·7 million tons.

A price level of 1¼* cents is, of course, far below the costs of the very cheapest producer. It represents not so much a serious excess of productive capacity, as the unwillingness of merchants and middlemen to hold stocks on the requisite scale. They have lost so much and so often by the decline of price below what seemed an impossibly low level, that they have virtually declined to hold stocks at all, and this function has been thrown back upon the shoulders of producers. The same thing has happened in Java, where the bulk of the crop is usually sold long before the harvest is complete. World production in 1929–30 has been approximately the same as world consumption in 1928–9, and it cannot be said, therefore, that productive capacity is much in excess of requirements. The trouble is that consumption in the current season appears to be falling behind that of last season by at least 1 million tons and probably more. It is the addition of this amount to the already enormous surplus stocks which has brought about the present crisis. Unless producers can hold out firmly, there is no reason why the price should not decline a great

* By 25 September the price was 1.13 cents c. and f. New York.

deal further—there is really no minimum limit when everything depends upon stock-holding. But at the same time it must be observed that invisible supplies are everywhere very small, and if the market received some assurance against a further price fall, or if prices once started rising, however slightly, buying might recommence on a substantial scale in order to take advantage of the present previously unheard-of prices. It seems likely that there will either be a further collapse caused by producers forced to sell, or a fairly rapid recovery of prices, and it is to be sincerely hoped for the sake of Cuba and other unprotected producers that the latter will occur first. Even so it will be some time before conditions become normal, unless the present world depression passes away with unexpected speed.

VIII. *Tea*

The only figures available for stocks of tea are those compiled by the Tea Brokers Association of London from returns supplied by the London tea warehouses. Previous to April 1929, official Customs statistics were available for tea in bond in the United Kingdom, and these furnished a complete record of stocks in this country. The current figures represent about 90 per cent of the trade, and for comparison with earlier years should be raised by about 10 per cent.

Even without this adjustment the stocks figures have run high since the middle of 1929, and the reduction this year is not more than the usual seasonal movement.

The general tendency of prices during 1929 was downward, and a recovery in the first quarter of this year has been followed by a renewed fall.

Consumption in Great Britain and Northern Ireland has been as below [p. 630] in recent years.

But the last is not comparable with previous years owing to the removal of the duty and the consequential lack of statistics of actual releases from bond for consumption. In view of the

Stocks of tea in the United Kingdom (1,000 lb)

End of month	1921	1922	1923	1924	1925	1926	1927	1928	1929	1930
January	219,377	208,115	186,035	182,865	225,067	209,655	222,636	254,957	251,387	266,633
February	223,179	221,362	176,681	188,559	234,557	202,300	217,413	252,704	253,716	267,028
March	229,568	219,645	183,413	193,362	231,516	195,388	194,362	242,771	259,651	248,948
April	233,018	214,484	167,763†	192,219	217,091	179,891	179,315	223,464	221,258	234,753
May	228,793	192,396	141,659	152,317	190,730	163,408	158,012	195,988	—	—
June	218,290	170,478	126,792	138,691	180,859	155,595	145,417	179,214	184,578	209,066
July	207,448	153,198	112,890	121,097	163,255	148,207	136,531	170,519	182,862	201,167
August	197,433	142,137	121,935	128,266	165,085	156,850	146,631	179,106	191,558	214,908
September	190,799	151,510	134,170	136,694	180,621	175,012	163,838	194,681	201,892	
October	190,129	152,095	146,990	150,721	181,683	186,861	185,155	209,701	221,439	
November	196,534	158,357	152,288	174,414	189,080	196,626	213,808	224,717	235,679	
December	205,420	169,776	165,666	205,859	203,654	207,003	239,085	240,738	260,427	

* Previous to April 1929, Tea in Bond in the U.K.
† Excluding Irish Free State from this month onwards.

[*U.K. consumption*] (million lb)

1923	387·5
1924	396·5
1925	402·0
1926	408·8
1927	416·2
1928	417·4
1929	465·6

previous trend it is extremely improbable that such a spurt in consumption occurred.

Some idea of the comparative changes in world consumption may be obtained from the following figures of total imports for home consumption into the principal consuming countries. (The figures are partly estimated.)

Million lb

1923	723·3
1924	738·1
1925	754·6
1926	778·5
1927	792·3
1928	817·9
1929	887·5

The large increase in 1929 is attributable to the United Kingdom (for which case, as mentioned above, the estimate is dubious) and to Russia (European). There was a large proportionate increase for Holland and a normal increase for many other countries. But the majority of the North and South American countries showed a decrease.

IX. *Coffee*

The table below is based on the figures supplied by Messrs Duuring & Zoon, the most important omissions therefrom are the stocks in the East and Eastern ports, and until recently coffee

Coffee (1,000 bags)*

Beginning of month	Visible supply of Europe	Visible supply of U.S.A.	Stocks in Brazil	Total	Stocks in interior of Sao Paulo	Stocks in interior of Rio de Janeiro	Grand total
1913 July	6,480	1,848	1,947	10,275			
Sept.	6,005	1,477	4,002	11,484			
Oct.	6,019	1,393	4,769	12,181			
1914 Jan.	7,275	1,709	4,681	13,665			
April	8,702	2,172	1,743	12,617			
June	8,353	2,056	1,207	11,616			
1919 Jan.	758	1,010	9,296	11,364			
April	2,755	1,964	7,060	11,799			
July	3,124	1,508	5,704	10,336			
Oct.	2,821	2,057	5,540	10,418			
1920 Jan.	2,843	2,007	5,020	9,870			
April	2,573	2,209	3,392	8,174			
July	2,509	2,293	1,948	6,750			
Oct.	2,955	2,640	2,387	7,982			
1921 Jan.	2,588	2,442	3,735	8,765			
April	2,533	2,765	3,389	8,687			
July	2,562	2,100	4,038	8,700			
Oct.	2,564	1,838	4,589	8,991			
1922 Jan.	2,399	2,056	4,948	9,403			
April	2,977	1,583	4,580	9,140			
July	3,068	1,456	4,115	8,639			
Oct.	3,007	1,182	4,292	8,481			
1923 Jan.	2,839	1,385	3,756	7,980			
April	2,463	1,618	2,903	6,974			
July	2,296	1,075	1,969	5,340			
Oct.	2,449	1,387	2,016	5,852			
1924 Jan.	2,228	1,349	890	4,467			
April	1,935	1,075	954	3,964			
July	2,152	1,387	1,532	5,071	4,592		9,663
Oct.	2,255	1,337	2,135	5,727			
1925 Jan.	2,098	1,046	2,240	5,384			
April	2,028	1,116	2,245	5,389			

Table (*cont.*)

Beginning of month	Visible supply of Europe	Visible supply of U.S.A.	Stocks in Brazil	Total	Stocks in interior of Sao Paulo	Stocks in interior of Rio de Janeiro	Grand total
July	2,193	1,154	1,738	5,085	1,786		6,871
Oct.	2,367	1,269	1,594	5,230			
1926 Jan.	2,163	1,484	1,517	5,164	4,383		9,547
April	2,041	1,258	1,487	4,786	3,902		8,688
July	2,028	1,065	1,478	4,571	2,833		7,404
Oct.	2,190	1,448	1,217	4,856	5,255		10,111
1927 Jan.	2,024	1,617	1,270	4,911	5,990		10,901
April	2,142	1,338	1,078	4,558	3,888		8,446
July	2,308	1,298	1,116	4,720	3,312		8,032
Oct.	2,470	1,182	1,333	4,985	9,570		14,555
1928 Jan.	2,277	1,479	1,512	5,268	13,120		18,388
April	2,442	1,409	1,404	5,255	12,653		17,908
July	2,841	1,381	1,507	5,729	11,672	1,180	18,581
Oct.	2,608	1,193	1,564	5,365	13,469		
1929 Jan.	2,358	1,333	1,481	5,172	12,966	585	18,723
April	2,373	1,178	1,429	4,980	10,403	320	15,703
May	2,656	1,131	1,431	5,217	9,772	186	15,175
June	2,718	1,130	1,498	5,346	9,084	116	14,546
July	2,727	1,109	1,502	5,338	8,785	136	14,259
Aug.	2,888	1,205	1,354	5,447	10,448	317	16,212
Sept.	2,858	1,197	1,261	5,316	12,531	654	18,801
Oct.	2,756	1,246	1,220	5,222	14,892	1,023	21,137
Nov.	2,619	1,211	1,239	5,069		1,407	
Dec.	2,383	1,113	1,473	4,969	17,251	1,542	23,762
1930 Jan.	2,285	1,107	1,702	5,094	18,357	1,612	25,063
Feb.	2,137	1,340	1,663	5,110	19,377	1,735	26,222
March	2,239	1,444	1,643	5,326	19,686	1,756	26,768
April	2,310	1,352	1,605	5,267	20,503	1,700	27,470
May	2,528	1,248	1,534	5,300	22,367	1,643	29,310
June	2,589	1,180	1,714	5,483	21,833	2,498	29,814
July	2,622	1,192	1,779	5,593	21,210	1,621	28,424

* G. Duuring & Zoon.

afloat from the East to U.S.A. About two-thirds of the supply of coffee for Europe and U.S.A. comes from Brazil. Until 1924, stocks in the interior of Brazil were omitted also, but since that year information as to stocks in the interior of Sao Paulo is available, and quite recently figures have been published of stocks held in the interior of Rio de Janeiro. The statistics have therefore recently become reasonably comprehensive. The visible supply has lately been only a fraction of the total supplies available, but this is, of course, due to the present valorisation scheme, whereby stocks are held in Government warehouses in the interior, and not, as in previous schemes, at Brazilian or foreign ports. The visible supply figures were not, therefore, so untrustworthy before 1924 as they have been recently.

Deliveries during recent years have been as follows:—

Deliveries of coffee (1,000 bags)

Year	To Europe	To U.S.A.	Total	From Brazil	Other kinds
1920	5,213	9,167	14,380	8,638	5,742
1921	8,094	9,958	18,052	11,356	6,696
1922	8,238	9,654	17,892	11,100	6,792
1923	9,240	10,585	19,825	13,516	6,309
1924	9,981	10,709	20,690	13,473	7,217
1925	9,481	9,488	18,969	11,868	7,101
1926	9,984	10,665	20,649	13,164	7,485
1927	10,656	10,933	21,589	13,834	7,755
1928	10,930	10,849	21,779	13,198	8,581
1929	10,800	10,881	21,681	12,814	8,867

In July 1929 the situation in Brazil showed such a marked improvement that it seemed as if the Coffee Defence Institute was more firmly in the saddle than it had ever been. Values had certainly been slowly declining for some months, and this continued throughout August and September, but there were no special developments affecting the current crop, though the frost so much desired by the planters did not occur, and hence the heavy flowering of the 1930–1 crop gave promise of a further large crop to come. Then at the end of the first week in October the Santos and the New York terminal markets collapsed with a sudden unexpectedness such as is almost unparalleled in the history of even speculative markets. The whole trade was taken completely unawares. Business came practically to a standstill, for no reliable news emanated from Brazil, and no one could be at all certain what was happening. Gradually it became apparent that, owing to the refusal by a firm of European bankers of a renewal of customary advances, due to the Hatry affair, the Institute was in financial difficulties, and could neither support the market as has been its practice, nor provide advances on the newly harvested coffee then being delivered in large quantities to the official interior warehouses. After innumerable rumours of all kinds, it was officially announced that the Bank of Brazil had undertaken to supply £2,500,000 to the Institute, but further rumours that the Institute had been refused a loan of £9,000,000 by European bankers sent the position from very bad to even worse. At the end of October the Santos No. 4 contract on the New York terminal market showed a decline from 20.5 cents a month previously to 13.4 cents, and the quotation for Santos Superior c. and f. Europe from 97s. per cwt to 80s. During November the terminal market was steady, but the Santos Superior quotation declined to 65s., and during December to 57s.; at the beginning of 1929 it had stood at 104s. In November an advance of £2,000,000 was made by the Federal Government to the Government of the State of Sao Paulo, and by the end of the year the Institute was clearly re-establishing its control over supplies, but its apparent inability to obtain loans from abroad still seemed to make its future very uncertain. Some small recovery in prices took place during January, and was more or less maintained during February and March, though it became evident that the Institute had resumed its supporting operations whenever prices sagged. At last, in April, the 1930 7 per cent

Coffee Realisation Loan was announced and successfully floated. This loan is for no less a sum than £20 million, and can hardly fail to satisfy the needs of the present and the immediate future. The loan is accompanied by conditions providing for a slightly more rapid release of the stocks of coffee, but the principle and general methods of valorisation are to be maintained.

With the flotation of the new loan the Institute is clearly subject to some measure of restrictive control. It seems to be assumed that the policy will now be to put on the market all the coffee it will take at a price equivalent of, say, 12–14 cents for Santos No. 4. The general opinion of the trade has always been that the demand for coffee is extremely inelastic, but it seems hardly conceivable that a halving of prices will not stimulate consumption appreciably, even taking account of the fact that the price of green coffee is but a small part of the price paid by the consumer for the processed article. Some increase in consumption may therefore be anticipated. But production in the mild countries may continue to expand for a time, though it is doubtful whether, even at the normal premium for milds, all the existing sources of supply can continue at the price level indicated above; and the prospects are for a very large Brazilian crop this summer. At a price level of 12–14 cents probably most of the Brazilian production could pay its way, apart from the financial burdens involved by valorisation, and the consequent delay in sales. But the need for financing stocks will remain for some time, and this is bound to continue to make a substantial addition to the expenses of production. The excess capacity in Brazil is, however, very large, and it seems likely that prices will have to go still lower before this excess is forced out of existence. As prices decline, a double process of relief ensues, for cultivation expenses will be restricted even on the better plantations in order to maintain profits, and this will bring about a decline in yields on these better plantations, while the high-cost old plantations will at the same time be abandoned. It will almost certainly take years to restore conditions of real equilibrium.

*Total U.S.A. stocks of crude and refined oils** (1,000 barrels)

End of month	1920	1921	1922	1923	1924	1925	1926	1927	1928	1929	1930
March	—	—	—	—	463,072	490,953	502,777	499,323	568,498	599,338	638,384
June	171,109	221,383	302,345	395,608	480,685	504,941	482,763	520,669	570,792	610,956	630,766
September	—	—	—	—	487,509	473,108	467,584	531,658	562,914	627,426	
December	182,021	234,892	318,960	414,302	477,958	469,577	476,479	543,335	570,734	623,798	
Monthly average run to stills	36,160	36,947	41,725	48,436	53,842	61,667	64,977	69,070	76,108	82,309	

* The figures of refined oils are confined to liquid products, i.e. greases, etc., are not included.

X. *Petroleum*

The only figures of stocks regularly available are those for the United States, compiled by the U.S. Dept. of Commerce. Since, however, nearly 80 per cent of the world's oil stocks are held in the United States, these figures can be regarded as reasonably representative. Unfortunately, a change in the method of compilation has very greatly impaired the value of these American statistics. Since January 1925, stocks of fuel oil in California have been included in the figures of Californian stocks of crude petroleum. This change makes it impossible to ascertain the total American stocks of crude petroleum: only the total east of California is now available, and as this was not published separately before January 1925, no comparative series of any sort can be constructed. Similarly this change makes it impossible to ascertain the total American stocks of refined oils, because the stocks of fuel oil are exclusive of California. It is possible to give statistics of the total supply of crude and refined together, and to carry this series back beyond January 1925, but this is all that can be done. This series is as follows: in order to give some idea of the general growth of the industry, and therefore the relation of stocks to consumption, the monthly average for each year of crude petroleum run to stills is shown in the last line of the table above [p. 636].

The table below shows the stocks of crude petroleum east of California, and in the second column the stocks of crude and fuel oil in California, since March 1925.

Of refined products, kerosene and lubricating oils are now quantitatively unimportant. Since the statistics of stocks of fuel and gas oils are now exclusive of California, they are of very little significance, but the brief summary below may be given: no estimate of consumption is possible in the absence of adequate statistics of stocks.

Fortunately the gasolene statistics are not affected by the change in statistical compilation. The table on page 639 shows the

1,000 barrels

	Crude petroleum stocks east of California	Crude petroleum and fuel oil stocks in California
1925 March	308,548	103,721
June	310,732	110,203
September	300,981	121,664
December	292,288	126,129
1926 March	287,710	131,678
June	281,432	122,794
September	277,771	117,964
December	278,077	118,330
1927 March	290,110	119,364
June	315,702	117,414
September	339,741	114,981
December	351,646	111,855
1928 March	368,744	114,117
June	370,751	113,431
September	366,652	113,433
December	368,431	115,914
1929 March	379,659	124,571
June	379,089	136,327
September	386,662	150,443
December	382,391	152,089
1930 March	380,007	152,124
June	377,822	146,321

Stocks of fuel and gas oils east of California (million gallons)

End of month	1925	1926	1927	1928	1929	1930
March	802	851	948	1,225	1,268	1,385
June	1,082	947	1,117	1,513	1,568	
September	1,256	1,142	1,328	1,683	1,707	
December	1,037	1,046	1,343	1,467	1,436	

COMMODITIES

Million gallons

End of month	Stocks of gasolene	Domestic consumption
1920 monthly average	464	354
1921 ,, ,,	631	376
1922 ,, ,,	791	448
1923 ,, ,,	1,186	549
1924 ,, ,,	1,483	647
1925 ,, ,,	1,614	782
1926 ,, ,,	—	—
1925 March	1,747	625
June	1,695	868
September	1,514	849
December	1,648	760
1926 March	1,936	780
June	1,713	969
September	1,400	943
December	1,639	900
1927 March	2,201	943
June	1,838	1,167
September	1,249	1,193
December	1,357	996
1928 March	1,690	1,010
June	1,444	1,219
September	1,109	1,247
December	1,389	1,119
1929 March	1,924	1,155
June	1,763	1,391
September	1,395	1,436
December	1,811	1,105
1930 March	2,319	1,303
June	2,109	1,508

total stocks in the U.S.A., and the estimated domestic consumption.

Despite efforts at restriction of output, stocks continued to increase throughout 1929 and during the first quarter of this year, though the rate of increase in itself was so small as to be of little account if it were not for the already high level of stocks, and the fact that the rise indicated that production was still in excess of consumption. In November, however, production suddenly dropped to a lower level, and if consumption had continued at the normal rate, a rapid improvement would have developed. But the normal increase in consumption appears to have been checked, though not much actually diminished, and hence there was little improvement in the stock position up till June. Recently, however, steps have been taken to enforce restriction more strictly and more widely, and if the forecasts prove true, production will be reduced still further. Consumption has so far been relatively little affected by the trade depression—that of gasolene shows even more than the normal increase—but prices have dropped considerably, and hence the desperation of producers which has led to more determined efforts at restriction. As compared with most other raw materials, however, petroleum is in a thoroughly happy condition, for even though it may take a long time to reduce the present accumulation of stocks, there has been no real breakdown of prices or diminished consumption.

XI. *Nitrate*

Very reliable figures for Chile nitrates are regularly published by Messrs Aikman, and are quoted below.* As in the case of so many other commodities, these also show a deterioration in the position from the middle of 1929 onwards, and we have to go back to 1921 for similarly high totals. By the end of 1929 it was obvious that estimated consumption would not be achieved, and successive measures were taken to meet the situation. These

* The issue of monthly statistical circulars by Messrs Aikman has now ceased.

involved the internal control of the Chilean industry, and subsequently arrangements with the synthetic producers.

On the internal side a restriction scheme was inaugurated to work from February 1st, 1930, with the object of reducing output by about 20 per cent through the closing down of the high-cost *oficinas*. Judging by the production figures for the first half-year, this proposed restriction was effective. A further step in control was taken when the Producers Association decided that from July 1st, 1930, the conveyance and sale of nitrate in Europe and the Mediterranean should be effected by the Association itself.

But the most drastic internal development was the consolidation of the whole industry into a single company, the Compania Salitera Nacional ('Cosana'). This merger is to absorb the present capital invested in the industry and, superseding the Nitrate Producers Association, to control production, distribution and propaganda. Details of the capitalisation and of the arrangements with the Chilean Government can be found in the reports of Messrs Aikman and in the financial press.

This rationalisation of the Chilean industry has facilitated negotiations with the synthetic producers. The understanding arrived at last year between the natural producers and the two largest synthetic producers, the I. G. Farbenindustrie and Imperial Chemicals Industries, was to some extent nullified by the unrestricted competition of other synthetic and by-product nitrogen producers, especially in Belgium, Holland, Czecho-Slovakia and Poland. This year an International Nitrate Conference was held at Ostend in June and continued in Paris, and in early August it was announced that a world-wide agreement had been concluded. Under this a 'European Convention of the Nitrate Industry' is to be established, and this Cartel is to unite with the Chilean producers in regulating output and prices (see financial press, August 11th, 1930).

Some rather optimistic estimates were made for the natural industry at the time of the 'Cosana' merger, and the latest

Stocks of nitrate (1,000 tons)

End of month	Visible supply (including afloat)		Stocks in Chile	Total
	Europe and Egypt	U.S.A.		
1913 January	1,128	89	490	1,727
March	686	97	527	1,326
June	416	84	754	1,652
September	571	79	752	1,414
December	1,093	71	498	1,685
1919 January	140	28	1,594	1,780
September	152	49	1,705	1,925
December	430	95	1,576	2,134
1920 March	368	253	1,218	1,914
June	317	216	1,248	1,800
September	495	194	1,303	2,008
December	782	132	1,304	2,235
1921 March	868	218	1,283	2,384
June	836	249	1,317	2,405
September	828	41	1,453	2,370
December	903·5	260	1,441	2,622·5
1922 March	520	115	1,504	2,149
June	228·5	38	1,601	1,873·5
September	296	133	1,495	1,945
December	463·5	195	1,225	1,912·5
1923 March	379·5	238	889	1,310
June	173	54	997	1,250
September	365	96	927	1,415
December	573	200	852	1,639
1924 March	371	193	782	1,346
June	115	47	1,075	1,250
September	429	124	900	1,494
December	684	111	882	1,709
1925 March	379·5	233	756	1,368·5
June	227	122	869	1,218
September	408	105	896	1,409
December	682·5	115	878	1,675·5
1926 March	447	196	906	1,549
June	314	117	1,228	1,659
September	324	152	1,303	1,779
December	328	192	1,274	1,794
1927 March	229·5	106	991	1,326·5
June	139·5	52	989	1,180·5
September	395	86	724	1,205
December	803	130·5	519	1,452·5

Table (*cont.*)

End of month	Visible supply (including afloat)		Stocks in Chile	Total
	Europe and Egypt	U.S.A.		
1928 March	526·5	170·5	394	1,091
June	349·5	114	670	1,133·5
September	549·5	112	922	1,583·5
December	956·5	206	874	2,036·5
1929 January	1,103·5	287	714	2,104·5
February	1,047	276	701	2,024
March	879·5	220	695	1,794·5
April	660	183	747	1,590
May	556·5	132	871	1,559·5
June	548	121	938	1,607
July	627	129	1,046	1,802
August	699	155	1,124	1,978
September	818	166	1,085	2,069
October	933	205	1,093	2,231
November	1,018	241	1,106	2,365
December	1,090·5	275	1,150	2,515·5
1930 January	1,086	358	1,209	2,653
February	957	378	1,268	2,603
March	786·5	307	1,294	2,387·5
April	626	174	1,447	2,247
May	546	121	1,568	2,235
June	466*	81*	1,702*	2,249*

* Provisional.

agreement should apparently fortify these claims. But this is not the first time that the end of the nitrate war has been proclaimed.

1,000 tons

	1924–5	1925–6	1926–7	1927–8	1928–9	1929–30
Synthetic nitrogen products	450	585	735	825	1,075	1,175
By-product sulphate of ammonia	275	300	310	390	405	425
Chilean nitrate	363	323	271	390	415	363
Total	1,088	1,208	1,316	1,605	1,895	1,963

According to Messrs Aikman the production of nitrate of soda in recent years has been as follows:—

Production of nitrate of soda in Chile twelve months ending 30 June (1,000 tons)

1927	1,297
1928	2,507
1929	3,228
1930	2,946

From the same source are quoted the consumption figures in terms of pure nitrogen over the past six years [p. 643].

XII. *Wheat*

The current available statistics relating to supplies and stocks of wheat are well summarised in the *Wheat Studies* of the Food Research Institute of Stanford University, California, to which reference is recommended. The following table relating to wheat supplies in the leading countries of export 1924–30 has been taken from this source. The following summary of the situation was published in the Food Research Institute's bulletin for August 1930.

At the close of the crop year 1929–30 international wheat prices reached their lowest post-war level, after a decline in two weeks of June induced by the pressure of large stocks of old-crop wheat in North America and an atmosphere of pessimism in the business world. . . .

Net exports in the crop year 1929–30 approximated only 625 million bushels. The decline in the volume of trade between 1928–9 and 1929–30, over 300 million bushels, was the largest change recorded in the twentieth century.

The world outward carryover was large, but not as large as that of 1929; it was heavily concentrated in North America. At the moment the wheat crop of 1930 appears to be about a normal one in size and distribution, if the Southern Hemisphere harvests good crops. Under the apparent distribution of world wheat supplies, international trade ought to prove much larger in 1930–1 than in 1929–30. Perhaps import requirements approximate 775–875

644

Wheat supplies and their disposition in four leading export countries, *1924–30** (million bushels)

	1924–5	1925–6	1926–7	1927–8	1928–9	1929–30
United States Year ending 30 June						
Initial stocks	165	135	112	137	143	264
New crop	864	677	831	878	915	806
Total supplies	1,029	812	943	1,015	1,058	1,070
Net exports	258	95	209	194	147	143
Seed requirements	84	79	84	90	82	83
Consumption	479	493	494	505	506	514
Feed and waste	73	33	17	83	59	40
Apparent error in crop estimate	—	—	—	—	—	—
Stocks at end	138	112	137	143	264	290
Canada Year ending 31 July						
Initial stocks	41	26	36	51	78	104
New crop	262	395	407	480	567	305
Total supplies	303	421	443	531	645	409
Net exports	192	324	292	332	406	185
Seed requirements	38	40	39	42	44	45
Consumption	42	42	43	42	44	44
Feed and waste	22	18	31	34	44	16
Apparent error in crop estimate	−17	−39	−13	+3	+3	+7
Stocks at end	26	35	51	78	104	112
Argentina Year ending 31 July						
Initial stocks	66	56	61	65	90	130
New crop	191	191	230	239	307	175
Total supplies	257	247	291	304	397	305
Net exports	123	94	143	178	224	151
Seed requirements	23	25	24	25	23	24
Consumption, feed and waste	55	64	60	62	65	66
Apparent error in crop estimate	—	+3	−1	−51	−45	—
Stocks at end	56	61	65	90	130	64
Australia Year ending 31 July						
Initial stocks	38	36	30	34	43	38
New crop	165	115	161	118	160	126
Total supplies	203	151	191	152	203	164
Net exports	124	77	103	71	109	62
Seed requirements	11	11	12	14	14	16
Consumption	29	29	30	30	31	31
Feed and waste	3	4	5	4	4	4
Apparent error in crop estimate	—	—	+7	−10	+7	—
Stocks. 31 July	36	30	34	43	38	51

* Estimates for 1929–30 preliminary.

million bushels. Requirements of this size can probably be met only with some reduction in the carryovers of exporting countries, but the statistical position can hardly be tight. Under the assumption that Argentina and Australia will harvest about 390 million bushels of wheat, that economic conditions throughout the world will improve, and that the feed grains and rye will prove to be less abundant in 1930–1 than in 1929–30, it seems reasonable to suppose that international wheat prices may rise from the low level of July–August 1930. But at the moment it is difficult to perceive elements of strength in the situation that would cause the level of prices in 1930–1 to be even a moderately high one.

According to the estimates above the total end of season stocks in the four major exporting countries declined, compared with the level at the end of the previous season. North American stocks showed a slight increase and the Australian figure was abnormally high, but the reduction in the Argentine carryover more than offset these increases. Other reports indicate an appreciable reduction in aggregate European stocks, although the French total on Aug. 1, 1930, was extraordinarily large. (These estimates for Europe do not cover Russia.)

As far as the new harvest is concerned the Northern Hemisphere wheat crop of 1930 is expected to prove an average one, in line with the post-war trend. The estimates are for a slightly larger crop in the U.S.A. than in 1929, a definitely larger crop in Canada, some increase for the Danubian exporting countries and a considerable reduction in the other (importing) European areas. For the last region the decline in 1929 has been estimated at 150 million bushels, France and Italy being the worst hit.

With regard to the Southern Hemisphere, calculations at the moment can only be based on acreage and sowing conditions, and these indicate a fairly large crop in 1930 if weather conditions during the remainder of the season are reasonably favourable.

Thus the harvest results and estimates suggest a larger volume of international trade in the current season than in the last, and this should reduce the existing high total of the carryover in the exporting countries. But import requirements would have to be very large to bring these stocks down to a normal level, and there is nothing in the immediate outlook to lift prices to even a moderately high post-war level.

The September 1930 Memorandum was the last in which Keynes was involved. Thereafter, the London and Cambridge Economic Service's work in the area took the form of a series of studies by J. W. F. Rowe of various schemes to control raw material prices during the 1920s. One more report on Stocks of Staple Commodities by H. Campion, A. G. Charles, J. Kahane and J. W. F. Rowe appeared in 1937.

Towards the end of 1930 Keynes summed up the significance of recent events in a brief contribution to an American daily paper. We print below from the initialled typescript copy in Keynes's papers.

From The Christian Science Monitor, *31 December 1930*

ECONOMIST ANALYSES YEAR

The most significant economic event of the year 1930 is, in my judgement, the catastrophic fall in the prices of the principal primary commodities. As measured by the wholesale index numbers, it has amounted to about 20 per cent. A long list of the principal commodities of the world stood 50 per cent higher a year ago than they do today—wheat, cotton, wool, silk, sugar, rubber, the leading metals, to mention only a few. The fall was as rapid in 1920, but that was from an exceptional peak. Apart from that, there has been nothing comparable in modern economic history. It is a disaster of the first order, for it renders the whole structure of established money incomes and many other forms of money payment inappropriate to the price level. It ruins innumerable producers throughout the world, and has brought somewhere between 10 and 20 per cent of the world's normal business activities to a standstill.

Chapter 4

THE TITHE

The tithe had long been a part of the English agricultural scene. This tax, levied in kind, of one tenth of the yearly produce of the land had originally been for the support of the clergy and the Church. However, in many cases, rights to receive tithes had passed from ecclesiastical to lay hands as a result of the dissolution of the monasteries by Henry VIII. In 1836 tithes were commuted and a rentcharge fixed instead. This rentcharge was based on an index of the prices of wheat, barley and oats averaged over the previous seven years. With the sharp rise in grain prices during the War, the rentcharge rose from £77 in 1915 to £109 3s. 11d. in 1918 per £100 par value in 1836. Such a rise, which most people expected to continue as grain prices would remain high after the war, led to an outcry which resulted in The Tithe Act, 1918, which pegged the rentcharge at its 1918 level for a further seven years. This pegging protected the farmer against the rising prices of the post-war boom, but it meant that the subsequent collapse in prices had no effect as well. True, tithe-payers could under earlier legislation redeem their liability by paying a capital sum of 25 times the par value, and many did so after 1917. Nevertheless, in the early 1920s more than £3 million per annum was being paid to tithe-holders. The resulting pressure from the payers produced further legislation in the form of The Tithe Act, 1925 which fixed the rentcharge in perpetuity at £105 per £100 nominal value, with a further £4 10s. paid annually to ecclesiastical persons or corporations as a sinking fund for the redemption of tithe after the year 2000. This Act did not remove the ill feeling caused by the tithe. Nor did further falls in agricultural prices. For example in 1935 there were 16,000 court cases concerned with non-payment of tithe and arrears totalled over £½ million.

In August 1934 the Government set up a Royal Commission on Tithe Rentcharge 'to enquire into and report upon the whole question of tithe rentcharge in England and Wales and its incidence, with special reference to stabilised value, statutory remission, powers of recovery, and method and terms of redemption'. Keynes, as Bursar of King's, provided the Commission with an appendix to the Statement of Evidence by a Committee of Cambridge Bursars referring to some earlier evidence before the Commission.

649

From the Royal Commission on Tithe Rentcharge in England and Wales, Minutes of Evidence.

ROYAL COMMISSION ON TITHE RENTCHARGE

Appendix III to the Statement of Evidence submitted by a Committee of Bursars of the Cambridge Colleges

Memorandum submitted by the Bursar of King's College on the case of Mrs Waspe, Ringshall, Suffolk and on certain other matters mentioned in evidence before the Royal Commission.

1. In the evidence given by Lady Evelyn Balfour to the Royal Commission on Tithe Rentcharge on the 11th January 1935, she cited in some detail the case of Mrs Waspe of Ringshall, Suffolk, where King's College, Cambridge, of which I am Bursar, owns the tithe. Since the particulars given in her evidence are incomplete and inaccurate, it may be useful that the Commission should have before them an outline of the facts, particularly as this case, though put forward as an example of the difficulties of tithe-payers, may be, perhaps, more appropriately regarded as an instructive example of the difficulties of tithe-owners.

2. Up to October 1930 the tithe on this farm was paid regularly, the year's tithe to that date being paid to the College in December 1930.

Since that date, namely some four years ago, Mrs Waspe has answered no communications addressed to her on behalf of the College; she has made no payments to the College; and she has not asked for relief. She has not even acknowledged letters from the College offering her relief, or an offer to pay the expenses of a visit of one of her sons to Cambridge to discuss the situation. Since the tithe had been paid regularly up to the end of 1930, the College allowed some time to elapse before taking any steps, beyond making repeated applications to Mrs Waspe to which she made no reply. But in June 1932, they put the matter in the hands of the College solicitors and obtained an Order for $1\frac{1}{2}$ years' tithe to April 1932. The College were now in a position to distrain, but still postponed doing so, and offered, through their solicitors, to make an allowance of 15 per cent, to which no reply was received. Eventually the distress was made in December 1932, certain agricultural machinery being impounded. But whilst it was in pound certain person or persons broke pound and removed certain essential parts of the machinery, thus reducing the value of what was left to little more than that of scrap iron. As a result the remainder of the impounded goods were sold for no more than £5 0s. 0d., leaving £2 10s. 0d. after deduction of costs towards the $1\frac{1}{2}$ years' tithe amounting to £48 11s. 3d.

3. The College then allowed a further six months to elapse, after which time they asked the Registrar to consider whether a further distress could be made. At the end of July 1933 the Registrar distrained on growing crops. The College, not wishing to proceed in a distraint of this kind, which had been made without their previous knowledge, made an offer to meet Mrs Waspe or her representative, and stated terms involving a concession. This offer was entirely ignored. Subsequently no tender having been received, the Judge directed the abandonment of the distress.

4. The College then allowed a further five months to elapse, after which a letter was written to Mrs Waspe proposing an interview, offering to pay the return fare of one of her sons and give him lunch in College if he would come for a discussion. No reply to this proposal was received.

5. After the elapse of another eight months the College felt that they must, in the circumstances, take some steps to establish their rights. Accordingly in March 1934 they applied for, and obtained, an order in respect of a further half year's tithe amounting to £16 3s. 9d. due on 1st October 1932. As a result of this five acres of cut wheat were distrained on in August 1934. Since the result of this distraint would involve the loss of the wheat bounty, it would have been well worth the while of Mrs Waspe

to release the wheat by making the payment. But she made no such proposal. The expenses of the distraint were naturally heavy out of all proportion and the result was a receipt by the College of £10 11s. 11d. out of which £8 2s. 9d. had to be paid for possession fees etc., leaving a net sum of £2 9s. 2d. though the loss to Mrs Waspe was, of course, much greater than this sum.

6. Thus the above sums of £2 10s. and £2 9s. 2d. are the only sums received by the College in respect of the four years tithe to October 1 last, namely £129 10s. 0d. The damage done to the machinery by the persons who broke pound on the occasion of the first distress and the loss of the wheat bounty and the expenses of sale and possession in the second case, mean that these receipts by the College have fallen very far short of the loss occasioned to Mrs Waspe. The College have naturally regretted this, but it is not obvious what alternative course was open to them in the circumstances.

7. For completeness, it should be added that owing to the failure of Mrs Waspe to reply to any communications, she, with the other executors of her late husband, was sued by mistake in November 1931 for tithe due from another Mr Waspe living in the same neighbourhood. Mrs Waspe made no attempt to point out that the letters addressed to her should have been sent to another person of the same surname, until after some interval the College solicitors carried the matter to Court, when, for the first time, evidence was brought that the applications had been sent to the wrong address. This tithe was subsequently paid by the tithe-payer who owed it.

8. If it is asked why the bailiff has selected for distraint such unsuitable assets as those referred to above, the explanation is as follows. The parish boundary cuts Mrs Waspe's farm into two portions. On one side lie her farm and farm buildings and her stock; on the other side lie the 108 acres of tithed lands on which there are no buildings and which, with the exception of one field, are arable. Now under the existing law the College is only entitled to distrain on lands lying within the parish to which the

tithe relates. Thus by moving her assets to the other side of the parish boundary, Mrs Waspe leaves the bailiff in the position of being limited to effecting a distress on assets lying in the arable fields. It is, therefore, natural that nothing but agricultural machinery or growing or cut crops can be available for distraint.

9. This case may be held to exemplify the following conclusions:—

(1) Although the College has been largely unsuccessful in obtaining tithe payments for some four years and have been ready to show consideration to the tithe-payer, the case has nevertheless lent itself to opposition and agitation and has been the subject of complaint against the College before the Royal Commission.

(2) The anomalies of the law have made it extremely difficult for the College to establish its just claims without taking measures extremely distasteful to them and unlikely to be fully effective.

(3) The steps which the College have felt compelled to take have involved the tithe-payer in far greater losses than are represented by the payments actually received by the College. Nothing could have been more vexatious and inefficient and expensive to all concerned than the application of the law in this particular case. I have not described the scenes which have attended the removal of the distrained goods and the several attempts which have been made to interfere by force with the course of the law. But it may be mentioned that on the last occasion the Chief Constables of the county considered it advisable to have some 200 police present on the farm. Yet for the College to have simply abandoned the attempt to collect its tithe would scarcely seem right in the circumstances.

10. I may take this opportunity of pointing out that two other references made to King's College, Cambridge, in evidence before the Royal Commission are inaccurate. In answer to question 3817 it was stated that King's College, Cambridge, sold certain farms when prices were high and subsequently

re-purchased the same farms when prices were low. There is no foundation for this statement.

11. In answer to question 4148 it was stated that King's College purchased a large estate from the late Captain Pretyman near Felixstowe and are developing it as building sites. This is a mistake for another purchaser. King's College have made no such purchase.

J. M. KEYNES

2 March 1935

Then on 8 March 1935, Keynes gave evidence to the Royal Commission. Previously he had provided the Commission with a written statement.

From the Royal Commission on Tithe Rentcharge in England and Wales, Minutes of Evidence.

ROYAL COMMISSION ON TITHE RENTCHARGE
NINETEENTH DAY
Friday 8 March 1935

Present:

Sir John Fischer Williams, C.B.E., K.C. (*Chairman*)
Lord Cornwallis, C.B.E., T.D.
Sir Edward R. Peacock, G.C.V.O., D.C.L.
Sir Leonard J. Coates
Sir John E. Lloyd, M.A., D.Litt., F.B.A.
    Mr E. Lawrence Mitchell, C.B.E. (*Secretary*)
    Mr A. S. Allen (*Assistant Secretary*)

Statement of Evidence submitted by Mr J. M. Keynes, C.B.

1. The question of tithe rentcharge has three main aspects— the relief of hard cases, the problem of an unpopular and mis- understood system, and certain legal perplexities and difficulties chiefly concerning recovery and rating.

2. If it was simply a question of relieving the hard cases, the problem could be handled without very great difficulty. These cases can be classified as being due to

(i) the tithe being an unusually high proportion of the Schedule B assessment;

(ii) the tithe-payer being a poor man with a very small income;

(iii) the tithe-payer being in financial difficulties (not, as a rule, chiefly or even appreciably on account of his tithe liabilities) owing to shortage of capital, abnormal losses, bad farming or old age.

3. Case (i) could be relieved by appropriate legislation; though legislation would involve individual tithe owners in hardship unless the reliefs were granted out of a central pool. Cases (ii) and (iii) are dealt with generously and with fair success under the existing system by the vast majority of tithe owners; though here also a central pool available for reliefs would be helpful.

4. The proper handling of the 'hard cases' involves a tithe-owner, who is anxious to be reasonable and humane without being imposed upon, in much trouble and loss of time. But what my tithe clerk calls the 'genuine' cases are not the real difficulty. If there were no other problem but these, there would have been no Royal Commission on Tithe. The real difficulties are due to a very small number of individuals, more often than not comparatively substantial, who, on grounds of principle or misunderstanding or an obstinate and litigious habit of mind, refuse to pay tithe except under compulsion and employ all the methods of obstruction, legal and otherwise, to which the historic tithe system unfortunately lends itself. These individuals seldom belong to the category of 'hard cases'. For their course of action is, as a rule, expensive. In the cases of this kind which have fallen within my personal experience, the tithe-payer has involved himself in costs and losses much greater than the amount of tithe in question; whilst at the same time the College, whose claims have been vindicated by the Courts in every case, has also suffered a loss through legal and other costs which are not

recoverable. And the same position is liable to repeat itself every half year.

5. Opposition of this kind, however, would never flourish if it were not for the background of the 'hard cases' and above all for the widespread unpopularity and misunderstanding concerning the exact nature of tithe rentcharge and its past history. The increased opposition in recent years is to be attributed partly to the great growth in the number of owner-occupiers through the break-up of large estates, partly to the agricultural distress which has made farmers a natural and proper object of general sympathy, and partly to the discovery of the confusion which surrounds the law and practice relating to the methods of recovery of tithe rentcharge.*

6. The position is much easier today, partly because the agricultural position is a little better and partly because a number of legal doubts have been cleared up in favour of the tithe-owner; with the result that, broadly speaking, tithe is now coming in very well. At the same time I am convinced both by my own observation and experience and by a perusal of the evidence presented to this Commission on behalf of tithe-payers and others, that the popular discontent with the system, the worry and expense and friction and bad temper generated, and the scandalous inadequacy of the existing law and practice to provide, smoothly and efficiently, for the satisfaction of just claims, will not be cleared away either by further legislative provision for hard cases, or by a modest all-round relief to the whole body of tithe-payers, which would only have the effect of depriving tithe-owners of income which is justly theirs without relieving them of the burden and recurrent anxiety of the system as a whole.

7. If, therefore, a means could be found of winding up the whole system in its present form whilst doing substantial justice both to the tithe-owners and to the tithe-payers, the advantages are manifest. I believe that a scheme to secure this is practicable.

* Several questions of law of the first importance had not, it seems, been decided by the Courts at any time in the last hundred years.

Moreover the evidence already given to the Royal Commission shows that a scheme along the general lines which I have in mind already has the support and sympathy of several important bodies representing different interests; though the actual figures I suggest are intermediate between those which would appear if detailed proposals were submitted by the different parties. It is, indeed, little more than an adaptation of the plan laid before the Commission by the Land Agents' Society.

8. It is fair, perhaps, that I should add that I have reason to believe that my proposals are considered by representative tithe-owners unnecessarily generous to tithe-payers and inequitable to the tithe-owners.

II

9. The essence of all these schemes can be expressed as follows:—

(i) The abolition of tithe rentcharge as such and the substitution of a charge of a different character is the only sound solution. The existing nature of the charge and of the laws determining it is so deeply rooted in past history, in the common law of a different age, and in the customs and practices of a form of society which has now passed away that it is very difficult to codify and simplify it into anything suited to modern practice; yet, on the other hand, to convert tithe rentcharge into a different kind of liability, whilst leaving the rest of the system substantially unchanged, would provoke much opposition.

(ii) It is not practicable to deal with the hard cases, widely interpreted, in a comprehensive way if ownership continues to be divided parish by parish as at present. It is necessary to create a central pool out of which reliefs can be granted.

(iii) Tithe rentcharge as at present constituted cannot be reasonably regarded as a gilt-edged security of the highest quality, if we allow for the trouble, expense and unpopularity involved in its collection, its liability (in the case of lay tithe) to the uncertainties of the rating system and the recurrent agitation for concessions; and this consideration provides a margin between the present annual value of tithe and the interest on the amount of government securities which it would be reasonable to ask the tithe-owners to accept in lieu of their present charge, probably sufficient to meet those claims for relief which can be substantiated on grounds of hardship.

10. The sort of scheme which would carry this out (only differing in detail from the scheme of the Land Agents' Society) can be summarised as follows:—

(i) Tithe rentcharge would be wholly discharged and in lieu of it there would be created an annuity charged on the land analogous to land tax, collected by Inland Revenue and recoverable by the usual methods.

(ii) Lay tithe-payers would be put on the same footing as payers of ecclesiastical tithe—that is to say they would pay an annuity of £109 10s. per cent of the commuted value for 76 years, in place of a perpetual annuity of £105 (plus, perhaps, a small additional sum to correspond to the sinking fund already accumulated out of payments of ecclesiastical tithe).

(iii) The future income of lay tithe-owners would be fixed as follows. From £105 there would be deducted the actual amount paid in rates and land tax by the tithe-owner concerned on the average of the last three years. For the purposes of illustration let us take this at £30. From the balance of, e.g., £75 there would be deducted one-sixth to represent the costs of collection and the loss of income which it would be reasonable to ask lay tithe-owners to sacrifice in view of the improvement in the quality of the security which they would obtain. This leaves an income of, e.g., £62 10s. I may mention in parenthesis that I do not accept the estimate of the Land Agents' Society that the lay tithe-owner does not now receive a greater net income than £60. I feel sure that this figure could not be substantiated. I believe that these tithe-owners as a body are successful, even to-day, in collecting 97 per cent of the tithe due to them. Thus the figure suggested above represents a substantial reduction, probably about 10 per cent, of the actual net income of tithe-owners.

(iv) In the case of ecclesiastical tithe, the deduction for rates would be £5, and I suggest that in this case one-seventh (instead of one-sixth as in the case of lay tithe) should be deducted to represent the costs of collection and the sacrifice of income which it would be reasonable to require. In the case of ecclesiastical tithe, it would be proper to pay some regard to the comparative poverty of many of the tithe-owners. Moreover, owing to the incidence of rates, a smaller sacrifice per cent of commuted value than in the case of lay tithe will provide an equally large pool to meet hard cases.

(v) To provide this income, tithe-owners would receive an amount of stock sufficient to yield an income of £62 10s. or £85 10s. as the case may be, per £100 commuted value in 3 per cent Guaranteed Stock (similar to Irish Land Stock), repayable by a cumulative sinking fund, operating through half-yearly drawings, over a period of 76 years.

(vi) Interest and sinking fund on the Guaranteed Stock would take about $3\frac{1}{3}$ per cent of the amount of stock issued leaving in the hands of the Revenue (apart from their costs of collection which, in the circumstances supposed, should be very small) about £39 10s. in the case of lay tithe and £14 10s. in the case of ecclesiastical tithe per cent of commuted value.

11. As regards reliefs to tithe-payers, I suggest that it is not unreasonable to ask tithe-owners in view of the improvement in their security, to provide a pool to meet hard cases, and the figures selected above have had this in view. The proposed reduction in the net income of tithe-owners (on the assumption that they continue to hold the Guaranteed Stock) should be sufficient to provide the following reliefs:—

(1) In any year in which the tithe exceeded two-fifths of the Schedule B assessment, the excess over two-fifths would be remitted. But this should apply, in my opinion, to the tithe-payer's holding as a whole, and not field by field. On the occasion of the recent projected legislation the cost of this was roughly estimated, I think, at about £7 per cent in present conditions,

and might be expected to cost much less in more normal conditions.

(2) Out of the balance (provisionally estimated at £2 to £3 per cent) individual tithe-payers whose total gross assessment to income tax fell below some stipulated figure might be exempted altogether from the payment of tithe.

(3) In addition to these reliefs for hard cases the above scheme represents an advantage to payers of lay tithe of about £3 per cent of commuted value, in as much as it turns a perpetual into a terminable annuity at the cost of a sinking fund of £4 10s. per cent of commuted value, whereas its actual cost, if it is assumed to accumulate at 3 per cent interest, would be £7 10s. per cent of commuted value.

12. I assume that tithe-owners would be entitled (as in the case of Irish Land Stock) to exchange the Guaranteed Stock into other approved investments, in so far as they desired to do so. By gradually re-investing the proceeds of some part in other suitable assets, less liquid and without the special attractions of a government security, it should be possible in present conditions largely to reinstate the existing income, with a degree of security and a freedom from anxiety, not inferior to what is now enjoyed. I have in mind the re-investment of the proceeds, in part at least, in, for example, debentures of public boards and in ground rents. It would be important to allow re-investment by tithe-owners, who are in the position of tenants-for-life or of trustees, in a somewhat wider category of securities than those prescribed in the existing obsolete Trustee Acts.

III

13. There remains the difficult question of the rates. In my own opinion, the decision that tithe rentcharge should be rateable was given in the first instance on doubtful grounds. But it is too late for tithe-owners to re-open this question today. I have assumed, therefore, in the above that they must accept a

permanent reduction in their incomes corresponding to the rates they now pay—namely, an assumed average of £30 per cent of commuted value in the case of lay tithe-owners and £5 in the case of ecclesiastical tithe.

When, however, tithe is redeemed under the existing law the corresponding assessable value is entirely lost to the rating authority, so that it is for them an uncertain and precarious source of income. If, moreover, tithe rentcharge were to be entirely redeemed as suggested above in exchange for a charge of a different character, it follows, presumably, that the new charge would cease to be rateable, just as is now the case with tithe rentcharge redemption annuities, unless express provision were to be made otherwise.

14. If, therefore, the settlement with the tithe-owner were to be on the lines proposed above, it would still remain for the Royal Commission to recommend in what way the equivalent of the sums now paid by tithe-owners to the rating authorities should be dealt with.

15. This is not a question in which the interests of tithe-owners would be involved. There would, however, be great advantages from the standpoint of securing an agreed settlement with tithe-payers, if the 76 year rentcharge of £109 10s. payable by all tithe-payers under the above scheme, whether impropriate or appropriate, could be reduced to £100 out of the above margin in the hands of the Inland Revenue. In this case any surplus would remain in the hands of Inland Revenue, and such compensation to the Rating Authorities, especially to those who now receive a substantial income from tithe-owners, as may seem advisable, would be merged in the next revision of the block grants.

IV

16. In the event of such a plan as this being rejected in favour of the retention of tithe rentcharge substantially in its present form, there are certain, comparatively minor, suggestions for change

which might be made. There is, however, one proposal to which I attach great importance.

17. If tithe rentcharge is to be retained, every encouragement should be given to its more rapid redemption. In particular the tithe should be compulsorily redeemed whenever land changes hands, part of the purchase price being compulsorily applied to the redemption of any tithe upon the land sold. The disclosure of tithe rentcharge by a vendor should be made obligatory and the purchaser should be authorised and required to pay over to the Ministry of Agriculture such part of the purchase price as represented the cost of redeeming the tithe. This would not apply, of course, to land passing by inheritance.

18. I submit that this plan has great advantages—indeed so much so that it might also be applied to any rentcharge substituted for tithe, as proposed above. If it had been in force since 1919, the tithe problem would have been largely cleared up by now. In particular

(1) It avoids the difficulties which the Ministry of Agriculture might find in collecting the money, and the individual hardships which might ensue, on any plan for the compulsory redemption of tithe at times when the land is not changing hands for cash.

(2) It would avoid the trouble and complexity of re-apportionments when a single ownership is broken up, and especially when land is being developed for building.

(3) It would avoid the hardship which occasionally results from a purchaser being ignorant that the tithe is charged on the land he is purchasing or from his misunderstanding the nature of the burden.

(4) It would bring about a fairly rapid liquidation of the tithe system.

19. Finally, if the tithe system is to be retained, I see no alternative to making tithe a personal liability on the tithe-payer. The present state of the law is uncertain, vexatious, inefficient, expensive and irritating to all concerned, and even at times a

threat to public order and the dignity of the Courts. It would be a great fault to leave it as it stands.

J. M. KEYNES

1 March 1935

Evidence of Mr J. M. Keynes, C.B.

6822 (CHAIRMAN) *I think you have a copy of your evidence in chief before you, but before dealing with that, perhaps I might just refer to the memorandum which has been submitted by you in regard to the case of Mrs Waspe. That has appeared as an appendix to the evidence submitted by the Committee of Bursars of the Cambridge College and printed in their evidence. I do not think any members of the Commission desire to ask you any questions about it, as our practice is not to pursue the details of individual cases?* That memorandum was put in officially on behalf of my College. My evidence is personal.

6823 *Your knowledge of the tithe question comes from your experience as Bursar of King's College?* Yes.

6824 *How long have you been Bursar?* For about 15 years, and I have been in sole charge of tithe for not quite the whole of that period.

6825 *We have had figures of the tithe you own. Do I understand rightly that a good deal of it lies in some of the highly tithed districts?* Yes.

6826 *Speaking generally, the result of your experience of the tithe question is that in your view it should be tackled by something in the nature of a general and drastic scheme?* Yes. I believe that concessions which would leave the main structure unchanged would not really get rid of the difficulties, so that the tithe-owners would have made their sacrifice to no purpose.

6827 *I do not know if you have had time to look through the evidence which has been given to the Commission so far?* Yes, I have done so.

6828 *We derived that impression from your memorandum. You tell us that in the cases in which you have had to take action the tithe-payer has often involved himself in costs and losses much greater than the amount of the tithe. I do not know if you saw one of the appendices to the evidence of the Oxford Colleges in which they gave particulars of a case and the expenses to which they as tithe-owners had been put. Have you had a similar experience?* We had a case where litigation was carried to the High Court and where, of course, the costs to the College were larger than the taxed costs and the taxed costs to the tithe-payer were very large in relation to the tithe involved. In addition to that, the costs of possession and so forth very often mount up, and, partly owing to the agitation, when distrained goods are sold by auction or by tender they very seldom fetch what they are really worth to the tithe-payer, so that when

663

matters proceed to that length both the tithe-payer and the tithe-owner are generally heavy sufferers. It is a system which in my opinion serves the interests of neither.

6829 *You tell us the position is much easier today?* Yes.

6830 *Can you give us any figures?* My impression is, although it is rather difficult to give exact figures, that in the last three or six months my College has collected as much tithe as in any similar recent period. Our arrears are diminishing and the real difficulties are limited to about half a dozen obstinate cases. In nearly all cases we are either collecting in full or we make reasonable concessions which satisfy the tithe-payer and the matter is cleared up, but there always remains this small number of obstinate cases which, as I have said in my memorandum, are seldom the poorest type of payer. In the case of the poorest type of payer we almost invariably succeed in coming to a settlement which we consider fair to them and which they accept.

6831 (SIR EDWARD PEACOCK) *In the case of the other type, he does not want a settlement?* No.

6832 (SIR JOHN LLOYD) *Do you think that improvement is due to an improvement in economic conditions, and not to any decline in agitation?* I think it is due partly to some improvement in agricultural conditions, but I also attribute it partly to the clearing up of certain legal doubts in favour of the tithe-owner, and the experience in certain localities that, if we are pressed to the farthest point, we can assert our rights, although, as I have explained, the cost is very heavy. I think if that had not been done, if we had not been prepared very occasionally to assert our rights, the position would have been more difficult than it is.

6833 (CHAIRMAN) *Do you think in the case of your College the opposition to the payment is based in any way on religious grounds?* I have come across very little that I could directly associate with religious grounds.

6834 *We have had, I think, one or two witnesses, who seemed to include lay tithe in more or less the same condemnation as the ecclesiastical tithe, as if it were in the nature of a tax to support the Church. I do not know whether you have found that particular belief is held to any extent?* I cannot remember any recent cases in which the tithe-payer has given that to me in writing as his reason. Sometimes one would have thought that it might in fact have had something to do with it, but I cannot attribute any substantial importance to that in the districts with which I have had to deal.

6835 *Perhaps we might now come to the scheme which you have been kind enough to sketch out, and Sir Edward Peacock would like to ask you some questions on that?* Certainly.

6836 (SIR EDWARD PEACOCK) *You begin by taking the view that tithe as such should disappear altogether?* Yes.

6837 *And you propose, on the one hand, that the charge remaining shall be in the nature of a land tax or something of that kind and, on the other hand, that the owner shall hereafter hold government stock and have nothing whatever to do with tithe?* Yes.

6838 *You take advantage of the difference in value between a government stock and a less good security to provide the cushion, if I may so call it, required in adjusting the various difficulties that might arise over this change?* Yes.

6839 *To come to the actual proposal, you first of all put the lay tithe-payer on the same basis as the ecclesiastical tithe-payer by raising his annual payment to £109 10s. per cent?* Yes.

6840 *And from that you first deduct £4 10s., which I suppose goes into a reserve fund for the moment?* Yes. I think in the Act of 1925 it was believed that the £4 10s. would form an adequate sinking fund. Certain assumptions had to be made as to the rate of interest and it looks doubtful as to whether they will be fulfilled. In the present circumstances a larger sinking fund has, in my judgement, to be provided. It is rash to forecast future rates of interest, but if a level 3 per cent is taken for the next 76 years then £4 10s. is not an adequate sinking fund.

6841 (CHAIRMAN) *Am I right in thinking that the £4 10s. was fixed for a definite period of years for better or worse and that if it did not yield an adequate amount nevertheless the ecclesiastical tithe-payer was relieved of any further payment at the end of the period?* Yes, that is right, it was fixed for better or worse in so far as the tithe-payer is concerned. Ecclesiastical tithe-owners may find themselves at the end of the period with a sum which will not bring in an income equal to their previous income from tithe.

6842 (SIR EDWARD PEACOCK) *Under your scheme the owner will have a government stock so that it will not concern him?* Yes, the question of the sinking fund would no longer affect the tithe-owner. In my calculations I have allowed for a sinking fund which is adequate; so that the Government would know that the sinking fund which it was applying would undoubtedly liquidate the stock within the period and the provision for drawings at par makes that an absolute certainty, whereas there was no similar certainty with the 1925 sinking fund.

6843 *The probability being, as you say, that under the Act of 1925 there will be a deficit?* That is the probability in the light of present conditions, though I think it was thought at that time that there would not be a deficit.

6844 *For the moment at any rate the £4 10s. goes to reserve?* Yes.

6845 *And we begin at £105 and from that we deduct the rates now payable which in the case of the lay tithe-owner you estimate at £30?* That is for rates and land tax.

6846 *And in addition you deduct one-sixth of the balance as a just deduction*

in view of the greater value of the new security to be owned by the tithe-owner?
Yes.

6847 *Leaving him with an income of £62 10s. per £100 of commuted tithe?* Yes.

6848 *The ecclesiastical tithe-owner goes through the same process, except that you take one-seventh off and only £5 rates, so that he gets £85 10s.?* Yes.

6849 *Then you point out, and I think it is a very interesting and important point, that the owner of the government stock, if he cares to do so, under present conditions could probably improve his income without taking undue risks by selling his government stock and buying other non-government stock for investment?* Yes.

6850 *That implies, of course, that the Government is going to make a proper issue of stock which is marketable?* Yes, that is essential to my scheme. It would be exactly analogous to the Irish Land Stock and the way that was done.

6851 *Under present market conditions dated stock with a sinking fund of this kind would doubtless sell at a premium?* It depends on which day of the week you are asking me the question!

6852 *But having regard to recent events and the trend of things it would at any rate produce par, even today?* If one is taking a view over an extended period, I think 3 per cent is a fair figure, but of course all the figures are for illustration rather than otherwise. Securities which were undated yesterday were yielding $3\frac{1}{8}$ per cent. If you compare it with Victory Bonds, this issue would have a life not very dissimilar from Victory Bonds, and Victory Bonds yesterday I think yielded £3 2s. per cent allowing for the loss on redemption over their average life.

6853 *This stock would have an advantage over Victory Bonds in not being subject to drawings which, to the individual owner, may cause a loss?* Yes, it would have that advantage, when it starts at par. If it started at 3 per cent at par, instead of 4 per cent stock standing appreciably above par, then that would possibly constitute an advantage. I am suggesting a lower rate of interest. I think this stock would be very comparable with Victory Bonds because there would be drawings and their average life would not be very different from Victory Bonds.

6854 *But I think your stock would be a little superior?* I agree.

6855 *Because of the high premium at which Victory Bonds stand?* Yes.

6856 *Coming to the sinking fund question, I take it that interest and sinking fund on the guaranteed stock would take $3\frac{1}{3}$ per cent of the amount of stock issued, leaving in the hands of the state about £39 10s. in the case of lay tithe and £14 10s. in the case of ecclesiastical tithe per cent of commuted value?* I am assuming the stock would be sufficient to produce £62. 10s. at 3 per cent and that would fix the amount issued, but the Treasury would have to meet not only that 3 per cent which would yield £62 10s., but also a further $\frac{1}{3}$ per cent to provide for the drawings.

6857 *So that if we are dealing with £100 you actually deduct £3 here but the amount the Treasury would have to find would be rather more than £3, would it not?* I am deducting rather more than £3. Perhaps I may go back to the beginning. The Treasury, the Revenue Authorities, receive £109 10s. They give £62 10s. of that in interest to the tithe-owner, which leaves £47. The sinking fund of ⅓ per cent I have taken at £7 10s., which leaves £39 10s.

6858 *Anyway in the sinking fund, whatever it is, the £4 10s. is included?* Yes.

6859 *In the case of the ecclesiastical tithe it works in the same way but on different figures. Turning to relief, you suggest that when the tithe exceeds two-fifths of Schedule B the excess should be remitted on the basis of the whole farm. It was estimated in connection with the 1934 Bill that this would cost £7 per cent. What would that be £7 per cent of?* Commuted value.

6860 *Of that particular land?* Of the whole amount of commuted value of tithes in the country, £7 per cent would be required to meet this concession. My belief is that it is a high estimate. It is extremely difficult to make an estimate because in the case of one's own tithe-payers one does not know what their Schedule B assessment is unless they claim under the Act of 1891 and, of course, the Act does not go down to two-fifths, but I believe some sample evidence was collected in 1934 which led to some such figure as this. I myself was surprised that it should be so high.

6861 *It might be expected to be less under more normal conditions?* Yes.

6862 *There would remain £2 to £3 per cent for cases which you suggest ought to be exempted from payment altogether?* I have had some such cases in my own experience. Elderly widows with a tiny holding, and in those cases I am accustomed to give certain relief and I should not like to hand them over to the Inland Revenue without any provision for the same sort of relief as they have had in the past. How high you could put the exemption point it is very difficult to say because the method by which agriculturists are assessed to income tax probably underestimates their real income, if one were to take the income in the ordinary sense, that is to say, their cash income plus the value of their dwelling house and the produce they raise for themselves. I should have liked to have seen the exemption limit somewhere in the region of the income tax limit, that is to say certainly £100 and possible £120 or £150, but the actual method of assessing the agriculturist is such that a figure of that sort might go a little too far. I have not sufficient knowledge of the average facts for the country to suggest what the figure should be.

6863 (CHAIRMAN) *Have you considered at all how the analogy of land tax would apply, because the right to exact land tax is, I think, subject substantially to income tax conditions, so that you have a machine already in existence in regard to land tax which gives exemptions. You must remember that there is a large number of agriculturists whose land is subject to land tax and as to whom you have got some sort of analogous machinery in force?* I was not aware of that.

6864 (SIR EDWARD PEACOCK) *Having dealt with the tithe-payers and tithe-owners the Government have a fund in hand of an unknown amount and you raise the question of the rates and of some concession to the tithe-payers. You suggest that the figure of £109 10s. could be brought down to £100 for all tithe-payers?* Yes. Perhaps I may say in regard to this that my feeling is that it is equitable to ask the tithe-owner to meet the main part of the claims for hard cases where in fact he has had to meet them one way or the other in the past and where general principles of equity may make it reasonable to throw it on to him, but when one goes beyond that one enters into a different field. In my opinion the whole body of tithe-payers have no really just claim to any relief at all, but it is the practice of statesmanship in this country where a grievance is sincerely felt to endeavour to do something to meet it even though, if the matter be viewed entirely objectively, it is doubtful whether any just claim for relief exists. I am convinced, on the one hand, that no just claim for relief, viewed objectively, does exist, but on the other hand that a grievance is genuinely felt. Relief given on that ground cannot, I think, properly be put upon the tithe-owners and is a subject for the state, either through the rate-payers or the taxpayers or partly through one and partly through the other. I have therefore endeavoured in my scheme to consider those two grounds for relief which appear to me to be of quite different quality and properly laid upon different contributors.

6865 *So that the concession of £9 10s., if it were made, would in your opinion be a concession to the tithe-payer which the general public should properly bear?* Yes.

6866 *There is a fund under your scheme of unknown amount and I understand your idea to be that the Government would draw upon it?* Yes.

6867 *And if, in the happy event of it covering more than the whole amount required for concessions to tithe-payers, the balance would be available for dealing with the question of rates?* Yes. The present position of rates is very anomalous, because when tithe is redeemed, either outright or by means of a tithe redemption annuity, it ceases to be a rateable hereditament and consequently the rating authority loses the whole amount of it, so they are now in the peculiar position of all or none. I think that has led to an unsatisfactory situation—that the rating authorities should suffer from a change of that kind, but it does seem that existing practice does not, so to speak, entitle them to the whole of the equivalent. If redemption were to be effected to a large extent, as it might quite well be done, by means of charges that were equivalent to redemption annuities, then under the existing law the rating authority would have lost the whole of their rateable value. But to put upon the rating authorities at one blow the loss arising from the extinction of the whole of the tithe would be a very serious thing in certain parishes. There are parts of the country where it could be lumped in with other changes that occur, but there are agricultural districts in which the tithe is now rather an important part of the rateable value of the area. So much else has been derated in one way or another that the tithe has become an important proportion and those are the areas which are already far from rich. I think there is a very strong case for compensating those authorities in their block grant or otherwise. It is difficult, I think, to say precisely how the cost of the concessions should be divided between the ratepayers and the taxpayers. My sympathies are, on the whole, with the ratepayer rather than with the taxpayer.

6868 *I gather that you would go so far as to say that even if the fund available from the payments made by the landowners were not sufficient, it would not be unjust that the Government should add something to meet those concessions?* I think it would be a wise act, having regard to the long past history of tithe and the advantages of getting rid of it in some way or other. I am sure the actual loss to the country through the friction and trouble generated, the trouble of the County Courts and so forth, is so great that it would be a real public gain to get rid of them apart from anything else.

6869 (CHAIRMAN) *I should like to know whether in your view the increased remission on the basis of two-fifths of the Schedule B values is something which can properly be charged against the tithe-owner, or whether you include that in the cost which you think the state, in one form or another, might fairly be asked to bear?* Having regard to the principle laid down in the Act of 1891 I think, on the whole, it is not unfair to ask the tithe-owner to meet that. It is a matter upon which opinions can very well differ and the precise two-fifths is in a sense rather arbitrary, but tithe-owners already have to bear the excess over two-thirds under existing legislation. Personally I believe that that is much the best test that can be devised of hardship in relation to the produce of the land, as distinct from the poverty of the individual tithe-payer.

6870 (SIR EDWARD PEACOCK) *That, I think, makes the general scheme which you propose quite clear. But I gather that a certain amount—a pool of some sort— would be set aside to deal with hard cases. Have you thought how that particular part of the machinery would be administered?* It was not my suggestion that a sum would be set aside in that way. My notion was that there would be certain stipulated reliefs namely in excess of two-fifths of Schedule B with some limit of income below which there would be total relief, that the Revenue would assume permanent liability for those reliefs, and that an estimate could be compiled of their cost. But in the event of that estimate proving to be wrong, I am not imagining that the tithe-payer would receive either more relief or less relief, but that it would be taken over by the Revenue, whether it was a plus or a minus figure.

6871 *Then one more point, the lay tithe-payer is to pay more than he pays now?* Yes, unless he receives some relief under the last clause.

6872 *But generally he is to pay more?* Yes, but although he pays more his perpetual annuity is transformed into a terminable annuity and the extra amount he has to pay is less than the sinking fund which would be required. Therefore, though he has to pay out more cash he is in fact getting a small actuarial advantage.

6873 *That is clear, but what do you think his frame of mind will be? Will he accept that actuarial advantage is a reasonable thing to set against the fact that he was paying more?* I think he would protest, and therefore if the Treasury could not find the full amount of relief down to £100 that I suggest in the last part of my memorandum, a reduction to £105 at any rate would be highly advisable, lest a grave sense of discontent might be aroused. On the other hand, there is no reason in the world, in history or equity, why the lay tithe-payer should be in a different position from the ecclesiastical tithe-payer.

6874 (CHAIRMAN) *At the present time he has this advantage, that when he comes to redeem his tithe he can do so on very much better terms from the tithe-owner because of the liability of tithe rentcharge to full rates. One therefore has to bear in mind that from the psychological point of view, if the lay tithe-payer is asked to pay something more, the hardship may appear to him to be greater in that his existing favourable position in regard to redemption will be affected?* I think that is quite true.

6875 (SIR LEONARD COATES) *I think you suggest that the tithe-owner under such a scheme should be allowed to invest in other classes of security?* Yes.

6876 *Would you tell me what rate of interest you anticipate from such investments?* It is very hard to say. I should think that some tithe-owners would be prepared to invest a certain proportion in investments such as ground rents, which might yield appreciably more than 3 per cent, but it is such a very personal estimate of risk, as to what proportion they would be ready to invest in that way. If you take Queen Anne's Bounty, which would be the largest interested party where very large sums would be involved, it would not be very easy for them to invest a high proportion of their funds in any one direction. The outlets for investment at better rates of interest are not unlimited and it would be unsuitable for many tithe-owners who are in the position of trustees to have large sums in certain types of security, though they might very properly have moderate sums in them, so that one has to make a guess as to the proportions which would be invested in different directions. There are debentures of certain public boards which could be taken as typical and my estimate is that there are investments, I do not say on an unlimited scale, of which the yield is 10 per cent more than that of government stocks of this kind and which would be perfectly suitable

oldings. That is why I say I believe that the tithe-owner could get very near to re-instating his income.

6877 *Aiming at a yield of 3⅓ per cent instead of 3 per cent?* Yes.

6878 *Not more than that?* That is a point upon which opinions differ so much. I have been told by some representative persons with whom I have discussed it that the figure I am suggesting to you of 3⅓ per cent is too high. You are asking me a question of professional investment and there is no subject upon which opinions differ so much.

6879 *I gather from your written evidence that if such investments were obtained for the tithe-owner you would regard them as quite as good as his present security?* Yes. I should regard first-class ground rents where the reversionary value did not play an important part, or the debentures of certain public boards which had a deferred date of redemption, as a security at least as good as tithe.

6880 *Of course your drawings would accrue over a period of 76 years, and during that period it might be possible to invest in alternative investments at a very much higher rate than we are now speaking of?* Personally I should expect the opposite.

6881 *So I have gathered elsewhere, but there is a possibility of that?* There is certainly a possibility of it, but I should say if that possibility is realised so many securities would become bad that there would not be a great deal of advantage in it.

6882 *Whether on that basis the tithe-owner, with a sinking fund which I believe was estimated under the Act of 1925 at an average yield of 3·7 per cent?* As I have provided in my scheme for a sinking fund with drawings, we are dealing with a certainty which does not involve any assumption as to future rates of interest.

6883 *I quite understand that; I was only putting the point to you that the kind of return I was asking you to contemplate was not different from that which has already formed the basis of tithe redemption finance?* Certainly. I am suggesting a very much lower rate of interest than ruled in 1925, but then one has to remember that if those rates of interest were to return the 3 per cent guaranteed stock would sell materially below par and, therefore, into those calculations the prediction of future rates did not enter at all. The only element that enters is the relative price of the Government Guaranteed Stock and the alternative investment, and, in point of fact, the re-investment could not have been done so favourably in 1925 as it could be done today, since the long-dated government securities have risen up by a percentage which is greater than the average percentage rise of the alternative investments I have been suggesting, and, therefore, the return to a higher rate of interest might very likely be disadvantageous. So that if one returned to the rates of interest of 1925 it would be more difficult and not less difficult for the tithe-owners to re-instate their income by moving from Guaranteed Stock to alternative investments.

6884 *On the other hand, if the capital transaction or the redemption were deferred and the higher rates of interest returned, it would then be a very much more feasible proposition from the tithe-payer's point of view than it is today?* It would make no difference. The capital sums I have taken for purposes of illustration really cancel out. We start with annuities paid by the tithe-payer and we end with annuities received by the tithe-owner. The capital sums which enter at certain stages of the argument really cancel out and it does not make very much difference to those calculations what the rate of interest is, except that it does to a certain extent affect the sinking fund. If you were to have 4 per cent Stock repaid by drawings at par, the provision I have made here for the sinking fund would be slightly altered, but otherwise it does not matter.

6885 *Does it not make a difference in this way, that the tithe-payer is being asked to put a government security in place of the capitalised figure for his tithe liability, or to become responsible for the interest and sinking fund upon it?* It is simply that one annuity is being substituted for another. The government security is really an annuity arranged on a certain scale over a certain period of years, and it does not make any difference to the tithe-payer at what number of years purchase, for convenience of exposition, you capitalise on the one hand his liability and on the other hand the assets of the tithe-owner.

6886 *That is the point I am unable to follow?* It is not as though the tithe-payer has to find a capital sum. What he pays is an annuity.

6887 (CHAIRMAN) *Might I interpose a question? Is it not of importance from the point of view of redemption during the 76 year period? If one conceives that the tithe-payer is to have a chance of redeeming the new imposition or tax, the prevailing rate of interest would then be very important, would it not?* It comes in in a sense, but if the rate of interest is higher the income which the tithe-payer is sacrificing by redeeming is correspondingly greater. If you look at it from the point of view of, firstly, as to how much income he sacrifices when he redeems, and, secondly, how much tithe liability he saves, if you assume him to be a gilt-edged investor, as you have to do in order to get a basis for calculation, it makes no difference to him.

6888 (SIR LEONARD COATES) *Let us assume he is an investor in land?* Then it depends upon whether the land is changing in value by a different percentage rate from that at which gilt-edged securities are changing in value. Of course, one could make whatever hypothesis one liked about that, but I think one has to assume that, while different forms of property have very different yields attached to them, there is no particular reason for expecting one to change in a different proportion from the other.

6889 *I do not quite follow why we have to look at the change. Why cannot we look at it at the present time, applying the present factor, which is I think 32 years' purchase? The tithe-payer who redeems is adding a value to the land which then is tithe redeemed land?* Yes.

6890 *If the value of the land has a much lower multiplier than 32, then surely he is making a bad investment if he pays 32 years' purchase for redemption of tithe?* You are not always making a bad investment if you change from an investment of one quality to another.

6891 *I am suggesting that what he does is to pay 32 years' purchase for something which when he has purchased it may only be worth 20 or 22 years' purchase?* I do not agree with you that that is necessarily the case, but even if it were so it would not affect these calculations because it is not as though the tithe-payer was asked to put up any capital sum whatever. He is now paying an annuity and under my scheme he will pay an annuity in the future.

6892 *Yes, but, of course, under your scheme someone has to see to the sinking fund to redeem the capital sum?* That is provided by the tithe-owner who accepts Government Guaranteed Stock which is subject to the liability of annual drawings at a prescribed rate and an amount is deducted in these calculations which exactly provides for that.

6893 *But we have somewhere to provide for the sinking fund?* It is provided by the tithe-owner.

6894 *I thought it was provided by the state or by the tithe-payer to whom we are going to add a liability of £4 10s.?* No. In these calculations the liability is put upon the tithe-owner. I can illustrate it in this way, that if the Treasury, if the Revenue Authorities, were to hand over to the Rating Authorities and to the Land Tax Authorities the same sums as the tithe-owner now pays, this scheme would exactly balance without costing anybody anything. If you take the first part of my memorandum, down to the end of the second section, I am putting no cost upon anybody. All the cost of the sinking fund and so forth is provided for up to that point, and up to the end of section two I am not putting any charge on the Revenue whatever. All the charges up to that point are provided by the tithe-owner.

6895 (SIR LEONARD COATES) *Might we take the illustration of the benefice tithe-owner. He receives £105 per £100 commuted value?* £105 plus £4 10s. for sinking fund.

6896 *We are going to deal with the sinking fund separately. £105, that is the true tithe, out of which he pays £5 to the Treasury for rating liability?* Yes.

6897 *And he is left with £100. I gather you say you would make a deduction as a contribution to the pool of one-seventh of the £100, just as the lay tithe-owner will make a contribution of one-sixth of £75?* He would have a deduction from his income of one-seventh to provide for the various things which follow.

6898 *A deduction from his income, in arriving at the annuity which he is to receive?* Yes.

6899 *Which I gather would be one-seventh of £100?* Yes. Sinking funds do not necessarily cost anybody anything if they are calculated at a correct figure, and a sinking fund is not a burden because a perpetual annuity is worth more than a terminable annuity.

6900 *I just wanted to see where it was coming from?* In a sense it does not come from anywhere, because I am transforming a perpetual annuity into a terminable annuity and am deducting the equivalent in sinking fund of the difference between the two, but there is no burden on anybody.

6901 *I want to see a balancing account. As I understand the scheme, the Government is to collect tithe on the same basis as hitherto, £105 plus £4 10s. sinking fund?* Yes. The sinking fund will take a little more than the £4 10s. It will take £7 10s.

6902 *In the case of ecclesiastical tithe it will take £9 or one-third of 1 per cent. This amount has to be provided on account of which the Government has a contribution of £4 10s. from the tithe-payer, so that the other £4 10s. has to be provided out of something which the Government receives from the tithe-payer?* I think I can give you a balance sheet. Taking the sinking fund in the case of ecclesiastical tithe at £9, I think I took it in my calculations at £9 10s., the tithe-payer pays £109 10s. and that sum is divided as follows. The ecclesiastical tithe-owner receives an income of £85 10s. £9 10s. is available for hard cases—that is the figure given in my memorandum: £5 represents the rates and £9 10s. is required for the sinking fund. That adds up to £109 10s.

6903 *My first point is that the tithe-payer provides £4 10s. for the sinking fund and another £5 is required out of what the Government receives from tithe?* Yes, and I have allowed for that in saying that the amount left over for hard cases would be £9 10s., otherwise it would have been £14 10s.

6904 *There is only £9 10s. left over for hard cases, but is it only for hard cases? You have not yet provided for the cost of collection?* As I say, it is for those two things, but in my opinion the cost of collection to the Government if done in this way would be very trifling. It would be done by the Inland Revenue along with all their other collections. I do not know what the Inland Revenue reckon the collection of land tax costs them, but it must be a very trifling percentage, and this would be similar. It is perfectly true, as I said in my memorandum, that I allowed no express sum in this calculation for the cost of collection by the Revenue Authorities and therefore it is true that to that extent I should qualify what I said a few minutes ago and should say that I am throwing on the Treasury, in my second section, the cost of collection.

674

6905 *I think you would probably agree that in Wales it is likely to be even more than 5 per cent?* I have no experience of Wales.

6906 *We have been told so. It may be that the experience of the Colleges is particularly favourable in this respect?* I cannot say how Wales compares with East Anglia, but it is possible to adapt this calculation to any assumed rate. Supposing the cost of collection is 1 per cent, I am either asking for a Revenue contribution of 1 per cent or else there is 1 per cent less available for hard cases.

6907 *I think the Welsh Church Commissioners told us their agents received 5 per cent commission to begin with.* (CHAIRMAN) *Some did?* My assumption was that it would not cost the Inland Revenue anything approaching that figure, having regard to their existing machinery and their effective powers of bringing pressure.

6908 (SIR LEONARD COATES) *Should we ever know what it cost the Inland Revenue?* We know what their expenses are in relation to the total sums they collect, an estimate could be made.

6909 *Do you think it would be fair to ask the tithe-owner to deduct 5 per cent for the cost of collection?* You will notice that I deduct in the first instance one-sixth of his income to cover hard cases and cost of collection. I admit his net income will not be reduced by as much as one-sixth. It is very difficult to estimate what it would be, but the estimate I give in my memorandum is that his actual net income will not be reduced by one-sixth, but by one-tenth.

6910 *I am trying to analyse this deduction of one-sixth or one-seventh. I think you say it is for cost of collection and bad debts. Is not that also supposed to cover the difference in the class of security which he is getting?* Yes, it covers three points. He escapes from his existing cost of collection, he escapes from his existing reliefs and bad debts and he gets a better security. My estimate is that the better security has to compensate for loss of 10 per cent of income, and the difference between one-sixth and one-tenth represents what he would save in cost of collection and in the reliefs he now gives.

6911 *If his net income is £100, as in the case of ecclesiastical tithe, you deduct from that . . .?* I bring him down from £100 to £85 10s.

6912 *£14 10s.?* Yes.

6913 *£10 of that, or a little more, you say he ought to allow for the better class of security he is getting?* Yes.

6914 *So that only £4 10s. represents the costs of collection and the risk of bad debts?* Yes. That I believe is actually very near. You are taking now ecclesiastical tithe where we possess more comprehensive figures than in the case of lay tithe. I think the evidence given by Queen Anne's Bounty shows that the actual cost of collection plus remittances over an average of years is very near that figure. I should have to refresh my memory to see exactly what it is.

I think the costs of collection of Queen Anne's Bounty are of the order of £3 10s. per cent in areas where they have had difficulty, and I think it was a smaller sum in more normal conditions, but the Commission have those figures before them. They can compare my £4 10s. or £5 with the evidence actually supplied by the Bounty.

6915 *I think those figures do not include quite all the expenses of the Bounty. The Bounty gives its central administrative services without charge?* Yes, I read the evidence concerning that.

6916 *That may account for the difference between the cost of collection as shown by Queen Anne's Bounty and the cost of collection shown to us, for instance, by the Welsh Church Commissioners?* It might. It is perfectly possible that the figure of £4 10s. might be estimated by different estimators as £5 or even £6, but I do not believe that the possible divergences in estimate would show a wider range than that.

6917 *You deduct £14 10s. from the ecclesiastical tithe-owner, and you deduct £12 10s., as I understand it, or one-sixth of £75, from the lay tithe-owner?* The latter represents a higher percentage. I deduct the £12 10s. from £75, and £14 10s. from £100, and what matters is the percentage reduction.

6918 *But are we taking the percentage on the right figure? Surely what matters is the £105 which the Government have to collect?* That is not what matters to the tithe-owner. What matters to him is what he eventually receives.

6919 *We were talking of collection and it is the gross not the net amount which is collected?* Certainly, and in reckoning my cost of collection I have taken that into account.

6920 *It seems to me that as between ecclesiastical and lay tithe it is fair to consider the figure of £105 in each case?* Yes, certainly. I have assumed approximately the same cost of collection and reliefs in the two cases, the same absolute amount per cent of commuted value.

6921 *But you seem to me to deduct for these things more from the ecclesiastical owner—£14 10s.—than from the lay—£12 10s.?* No, that will not be found to be the case if it is got out in detail. I am quite sure I have deducted the same amount in both cases. I do not give an exact estimate—because I have not one—of what the costs of lay tithe-owners are, but I am assuming an approximate figure when I say a reduction of one-tenth in their gross income is equal to a reduction of one-sixth in the net income, and the difference between those figures allows for the cost of collection. I have taken costs of collection and the other deductions that have to be made more or less on the same lines. I think I have in fact allowed a slightly larger figure.

6922 *That figure of £62 10s. is after deducting one-sixth of £75—£12 10s.?* Yes.

6923 *I am comparing the £12 10s. in the lay tithe-owner's case with the £14 10s.*

you just mentioned in the case of the ecclesiastical tithe-owner, and they both relate to a gross collection figure of £105? Yes, but I am ending with the same amount of reliefs. I think you are deceived by the fact that one has to move backwards and forwards from percentage to absolute calculation. I have given you a balance sheet in the case of the ecclesiastical tithe, and I could give you a similar one in the case of lay tithe, and I think you would see that these matters check arithmetically.

6924 *The balance sheet is another matter. That deals with the sinking fund, and so on, but the figures I am immediately asking about are for the same thing, as I understand it, in both cases?* No, they are not the same thing, because the net income of the two is a different percentage of the £105 from which we start, and therefore a given sacrifice would provide a larger pool per cent of commuted value in the case of ecclesiastical tithe than in the case of lay tithe. I am giving that back in part to the ecclesiastical tithe-payer by deducting one-seventh instead of one-sixth, and as I am taking that one-seventh from a larger figure than I am taking the one-sixth, the amount left over that for hard cases is approximately the same per cent of the commuted value in both cases.

6925 *Perhaps we shall see it from a closer examination of the figures later. Have you bought any lay tithe on behalf of your College?* Not in recent years.

6926 *Do you know its price?* I have seen no quotation for a very long time. I believe there have been cases of small amounts of lay tithe being sold by auction, but I do not think I have seen any price in recent times.

6927 (CHAIRMAN) *During your Bursarship has King's College bought any?* Prior to the Act of 1925 we bought some tithe, but not since the Act of 1925.

6928 *Can you tell us what price you paid?* From memory I could not say, it was many years ago.

6929 (SIR LEONARD COATES) *Do you think that so long a period of sinking fund—as long a period as is at present in force for ecclesiastical tithe, and as you suggest for the whole of tithe—would be generally acceptable?* I think the period is about right. I confess I have simply taken the period assumed in the Act of 1925 and have not given a great deal of thought to the possibility of altering the period. But if a much shorter period were to be taken the sinking fund becomes, of course, a very much larger amount, and you are then faced with the dilemma that you either have to charge the tithe-payer for converting his perpetual annuity, or his long-term annuity, into a short-term annuity, a sum which, although it would be its actuarial value, he might dislike paying, or else you would be throwing that burden on to some other authority on a scale which would be unreasonable. Of course, if the tithe-payer could have a long-term or perpetual annuity turned into a short-term annuity without charge to himself, clearly he would prefer the shorter period, but if he has to pay for it I think he would prefer a long period. It makes a very great deal of difference to sinking funds when one gets into the order of 70 years. It is after 50 years that the annual sum amounts up very quickly, because it is precisely in the latter part of the period that sinking funds accumulate at a greater rate.

6930 *Might I put it in this way? If it were thought to be necessary that the sinking fund period should be 50 years or less, would you regard any scheme of the kind you propose as practicable?* The extra expense would either have to be charged to the tithe-payer, or given to him.

6931 *But it would be a very much larger extra expense?* It would be a substantial extra expense, but of course he would be getting a substantial advantage. I think it is not a very good way in which to give him relief, because it is a way for which he would be insufficiently grateful, not having an actuarial mind. I think it is a method of granting relief which would cost the state, or whoever had to provide it, the maximum, while giving the minimum amount of satisfaction to the recipient.

6932 *That is what I meant by 'practicable'?* I think it is not expedient to give people reliefs in a form in which they will appreciate them least.

6933 *Quite. I think the Inland Revenue told us that they valued tithe on the basis of 12 to 14 years' purchase for the purpose of death duties?* I have no knowledge of their figures, but I should say that for the casual owner of tithe it is a very much worse form of investment than for the great tithe-owners. It needs great knowledge and experience to manage tithe to advantage, and for anyone who does not possess that knowledge and experience or the appropriate machinery, the ownership of tithe would be extremely unattractive. It would not be reasonable to calculate the value of tithe in the hands of bodies that have knowledge and experience and have built up that machinery in relation to what it would be worth to persons who entirely lacked those advantages.

6934 *Do you think that in the hands of experienced and large bodies lay tithe is worth a good deal more than 10 to 14 years' purchase?* Yes, of the net value. I do not know whether you are speaking of the net or gross value?

6935 *I believe it was of the net?* It makes a good deal of difference. If of the net I should say it is worth more than that. If it is of the gross, one would have to inquire what the rates were in the district concerned before one could answer whether it was a reasonable or unreasonable figure.

6936 *Quite. You have assumed, I think, 30 per cent of rates?* 30 per cent, of commuted value.

6937 *We were told yesterday afternoon that it runs up to as much as 40 per cent in the case of some of the Cambridge Colleges?* I would rather not speak on that without further investigation. I put the figure of 30 per cent in my scheme as an example rather than as an ascertained figure. I know there are

678

cases where it is higher, and under my formula where it is higher the tithe-owner would sacrifice the correspondingly greater amount. I am not suggesting 30, but whatever it actually is; but my belief is that those high figures mentioned are very exceptional. I think the Oxford Bursars have shown an aggregate not very far from my figure.

6938 *28 per cent, I think?* Yes, and from my own experience that is about right. I am at a loss at the moment for an explanation of the very high figures you quote. I was told of a figure approaching 50 per cent. That appears to my mind to involve some error, because the tithe-owner would only be liable for 50 per cent if the rates were more than 20s. in the pound, and I do not know of any district in this country where the rates are more than 20s. in the pound. It is not impossible that they should be. Therefore it appeared to me that the tithe-owner who made that return had either made a slip in the calculations, or else had allowed himself to be assessed on some method other than the proper legal basis. At any rate, if it turns out to be a figure higher than 30—this is not a flat figure for all tithe-owners—each tithe-owner would suffer such deduction as in fact he is now suffering.

6939 *On an average of three years?* Yes.

6940 *Would you deal with him in the same way as regards the amount of tithe uncollected? There may be tithe which has not been collected for some time. Do you mean that to be covered by a general percentage for risk of non-collection?* I should take the tithe to which he was legally entitled. I should not of course include lapsed tithe, but only tithe to which he was still legally entitled, and then in my various deductions I am allowing such part as is uncollectable. In my experience it is only of trifling sums that that is true. There are people sometimes who owe 5s. or 6s. a year, or possibly even 10s. or 12s. a year, of whom trace has been lost and where the tithe-owner has come to the conclusion that it would cost him more to run the tithe-payer to earth than the tithe would be worth. But I am not aware of any sums of tithe not collected except in such circumstances as those.

6941 *The casual owner of lay tithe who has not the experience of a large body may not be collecting his tithe to anything like the same extent as in your experience?* I have no experience of such tithe, but of course I should say that where it has been in the same hands from time immemorial there is usually the advantage of local knowledge. I was speaking of a tithe-owner not living in the district. Where, as used often to be the case, the ownership of lay tithe is associated with the great land-owning family of the district, then their agents will have the same sort of knowledge and experience as Colleges have, with the additional advantage of being on the spot. Both the Oxford and Cambridge Colleges and Queen Anne's Bounty have the disadvantage of being at a distance. The casual tithe-owner is an almost non-existent person, I think. I suppose there are such cases, but I should imagine the amount of tithe so held is a very trifling amount. I do not personally know of any such cases, but doubtless they exist.

6942 *Have not some odd groups of tithe been bought up and attached to schools in recent years?* It is not within my knowledge.

6943 *The whole of your scheme is based on the assumption that tithe continues to be collected at 105, and that 105 is a fair figure?* Yes.

6944 *You are definitely of that opinion?* At the time of the 1925 Act I was opposed to the stabilisation of tithe, but now that some time has passed I should be against any further alteration.[1] It seems to me that you must either have a tithe that fluctuates freely in accordance with prices so that the tithe-owner gets the smooth as well as the rough, or you must keep to a basis, and in my opinion the fluctuating relationship of prices was finally abandoned in 1925 and it would be highly inequitable to reopen it. That does not imply that I was in favour of that change when it was made.

6945 *But if it were reopened and put on a fluctuating basis, that basis would in your opinion require to be lower today than it is?* I do not think it would be just to start at a lower figure. If it was thought advisable to restore the fluctuating basis I should say you should start with a formula which would give the same figure as 105 at today's prices but might allow for fluctuation in the future. It seems to me that in equity the Legislature must be expected to maintain some continuity of policy, and to reopen this and start off the tithe-owner with a lower return would be a most inequitable act.

6946 *In saying that have you considered the purchasing power of tithe today as compared with immediately prior to the War?* I consider that in 1925 tithe was divorced from questions of purchasing power. What the actual purchasing power today is compared with previous dates is easily available.

6947 *Presumably it would be lower than 105 on a comparison of that sort?* I do not feel that the tithe-payer has a case for paying less whenever prices fall, and not paying more whenever prices rise.

6948 *That is of course the fluctuating basis. But you are going further and saying that if we were to revert to a fluctuating basis today, you would want to keep at 105?* Yes.

6949 *Even though 105 may be too high in relation to the value of tithe immediately prior to the War?* I think the tithe-payer cannot have it both ways. The 105 was a settlement at the time which I believed to be in favour of tithe-payers. As a tithe-owner I resisted that figure. It seems to me that the fluctuating basis having been abandoned and a fixed figure having been established which at that time was favourable to tithe-payers, you cannot reopen the whole thing as though that had never happened.

---

[1] See *JMK*, vol. XIX, pp. 451–3.

6950 (SIR JOHN LLOYD) *You said that the tithe-payer could not have it both ways. Does not he have it both ways at present in this respect, that the par value cannot be raised but he can get remission under the Act of 1891?* Yes, to the extent of the Act of 1891 he does get an advantage, but, as has been pointed that, that Act, while it is one which personally I think was a wise Act of the state, was a concession to tithe-payers which runs right across the general legal quality of tithe.

6951 *And it makes tithe something anomalous in that respect?* I regard the concession of the Act of 1891 as a concession which was justified on grounds of hardship and expediency, but it did run counter to the legal conception of tithe as it existed both before and after in other respects.

6952 (CHAIRMAN) *Do not you think there was something anomalous in the development from what was originally 10 per cent of certain, not the whole but certain, of the gross produce of the land, to something which might swallow up more than two-thirds of the total rental value?* One was on the gross, and the other was on the net.

6953 *Yes, but even so?* I think the original nature of tithe was entirely altered in 1836, and I should have doubted whether it could be usefully re-opened in any way. I am not a great authority on the history of tithe, and I have never thought very ancient history sufficiently relevant for it to be my duty to enter into any close study of it.

6954 *It was not so much a question of reopening ancient history as considering what one may look upon as the normal or natural, if that word be permitted, course of development of the money payment which was substituted for the old tenth of part of the gross produce?* I think the Commission have had evidence, with which I agree, as to the reasons why the Act of 1836 introduced fluctuating provisions. I think it was not an attempt to maintain in any sense 10 per cent of the gross, but to keep this charge fluctuating in accordance with the purchasing power of money.

6955 *No doubt, but in originally establishing it, it was intended to be something which was to be more or less equivalent in real value in 1836 to the net income which the tithe-owner was receiving; it was intended no doubt to set that as an upper limit?* It no doubt started from more or less the same figure, just as I suggest if it were to be reintroduced today you would have to start from what gave in the first instance substantially the same income.

6956 *I think there is no doubt that in 1836 the intention was to give the tithe-owner something which was reasonably equivalent to that which he was then receiving?* Yes.

6957 *But to prevent the tithe-owner increasing his income in the future in proportion to an increase in agricultural produce. Was not the intention to prevent his profiting by the labours of other people? Was not Adam Smith's criticism of the old tithe system based upon this, that every improvement which the agriculturist made was necessarily shared with the tithe-owner, and it was desirable to stop that system?* No doubt that entered into the motives of the settlement, but I have always understood a much wider field of reasons was covered than that.

6958 *No doubt: and in doing it it was desirable to give the tithe-owner an assurance of an income which should be more or less independent of the value of money?* I think all economists have always held that a tax on the gross is a bad form of tax.

6959 *That was certainly held in 1836?* And one of the motives that governed that legislation was the desire to abolish a tax on the gross.

6960 *There are one or two other questions which I should like to put. I see that in paragraph 10 (iv), you say, 'In the case of ecclesiastical tithe, it would be proper to pay some regard to the comparative poverty of many of the tithe-owners.' Can you amplify that?* I have read the evidence as to the number of incumbents with different ranges of income. I have not gone beyond that. I was impressed by the large number who had very moderate incomes.

6961 *Yes, but what form would 'regard to the comparative poverty of many of the tithe-owners' take?* I thought that as ecclesiastical tithe rentcharge could nevertheless provide an equally large pool I was justified in proposing a smaller reduction of ecclesiastical tithe than of lay tithe.

6962 *That is one of the things which were included in the allowance which you made?* Yes. I am not suggesting an additional allowance.

6963 *That is what I wanted to get at?* It is part of my reason for proposing one-seventh in the case of ecclesiastical tithe as compared with one-sixth in the case of lay tithe.

6964 *It is arguable that these questions of individual poverty hardly come within the scope of the Commission, and that one has to look at the incidence of tithe as a matter which has to be divorced from the particular circumstances of the people who are receiving it. For instance, in regard to ecclesiastical tithe it is quite conceivable that these hard cases should be met with something in the nature of a general reorganisation, or partial reorganisations, of Church finance?* I entirely agree in that, but I think even if there was to be an entire reorganisation there would still be what I call comparative poverty, and, if the poverty of the tithe-payers is allowed to weigh at all, I think in the case of the ecclesiastical tithe the fact that the beneficiaries are not rich men ought also to weigh.

6965 *On the question of redemption, you tell us that if tithe rentcharge is to be retained every encouragement should be given to its more rapid redemption. I see you put it as if it were a matter which was to be taken into consideration only if tithe rentcharge—by which I have no doubt you mean tithe rentcharge as it exists at the present time—is retained. Have you considered the question whether there ought to be any scheme for cash redemption of the new tax which will be substituted for tithe rentcharge under your plan?* Yes, I think it would be advisable.

6966 *Have you considered whether such redemption should be on terms more favourable to the payer than the figures which he at present has to pay if he wants to redeem tithe rentcharge?* In general, or in the event of the new scheme?

6967 *In the event of the new scheme. A practical difficulty which occurs to me in connection with your scheme is that the tithe-payer will be asked to pay in some cases more than he is paying at present. Have you considered whether the wind might be tempered to him by giving him a possibility of avoiding this higher payment by easy terms of redemption?* No, I have not considered that, but I should not be unsympathetic to such a suggestion. I think that is quite worth considering. The difficulty about making proposals for changes in the terms of redemption is that the formula has to be uniform, and if a concession is made the tithe which will probably be redeemed will be that which presents least difficulties as regards collection. Under the existing system I should consider it was right to give easier terms of redemption if an average parcel of tithe were to be redeemed, but if easier terms are granted and it is voluntary and you have a general formula, it is the most valuable tithe, the tithe which presents least difficulties, which would be redeemed. But if my scheme were adopted I agree with what you are suggesting.

6968 *You make a suggestion for dealing with some of the hard cases on the basis of relief analogous to that at present given in the case of land tax by reference to income tax. Have you considered whether that might complicate the calculations as to the sinking fund and as to the yield of the tax? The payers would doubtless include a large number of small agriculturists whose income certainly would not come up to the income tax limits, and the tax would yield nothing in their case?* It depends how high the exemption figure is. I assume in section II of my memorandum that it is put at such a figure as can be met out of the reduction in the income of tithe-owners. If the figure were to be fixed higher than that I do not think there would be difficulties over sinking fund and so forth, but there would be a higher charge on the revenue. I do not think it complicates the technical side of my proposals at all, but it makes it more expensive.

6969 *It makes the yield of the tax uncertain, because you have a fluctuating state of affairs—the land may be getting in the hands of small men, times may be bad, and you may get a larger proportion of land in respect of which you have got to remit your tax. On the other hand, if the tendency was the other way and more wealthy people were buying up land, the reliefs would be considerably less?* Certainly it makes it more uncertain what this scheme will cost the Revenue in future years, but I do not think it complicates the technical side of my proposal. It means the net charge on the Revenue in future years is problematical.

6970 *From the point of view of the Revenue that might be thought to be a point of some importance?* Except that the amount involved will not be substantial. The whole thing is not of the first order of magnitude, and the fluctuations arising out of this cause, unless the exemption limit were put very high indeed, ought not to be large enough, I think, to be a disturbing factor.

6971 *We have some information about land tax remission. Taking the total collectable amount of land tax at £866,500 odd a year, the remissions amount to £188,234, which I think is about 22 per cent of the total collectable amount. The basis of the remission is (a) when the incomes of owners do not exceed £160 a year, remission of the entire amount, (b) when the incomes of owners exceed £160 and do not exceed £400, remission of one-half the amount?* Those figures are new to me.

6972 *That would show that if you adopted that basis you would lose something over 20 per cent?* But this is a very high exemption limit.

6973 *It is the existing land tax limit, which was originally taken from the income tax?* I have not got in mind such high figures as those. I agree that if such high figures were taken the cost would be substantial. Partly of course because the payment of tithe and land tax overlaps to a considerable extent with people who pay under Schedule B, and Schedule B was devised to be very tender to the taxpayer as compared with Schedule D: and therefore many persons who would not be exempt on the principles of Schedule D fall within these limits on the principles of Schedule B. To allow these limits on Schedule B calculations is being very generous.

6974 *But you would think it possible that some rather different scale than that generous scale might be allowed?* Yes, at the start. It might be that, in future years, as experience was gained of the working of it, and possibly if the Revenue were feeling more affluent, a suitable time might arise for relieving taxation, just as in previous years when the revenue was coming in well the exemption limit of income taxpayers generally has been raised. I think these persons would fall in the general category of persons who might appropriately be relieved of heavy taxation when funds were available for the purpose.

6975 *Of course it would be introducing an entirely new principle, to turn tithe into this new tax; it departs altogether from the net annual value of the land or net annual value of the produce?* It does.

6976 *It has regard to the particular circumstances of the person who has to pay, which is a new system altogether as far as tithe is concerned?* I think that could not properly be adopted so long as tithe was in the hands of private owners. It is one of the advantages of my scheme, I think, that if it ceases to be tithe and becomes a charge of a different character like land tax for which the Revenue is responsible, then the general principles of taxation can be brought to operate. Might I perhaps call the particular attention of the Commission to section IV of my memorandum? No questions have been directed to the general principle of that, and I think it has not been put before the Commission from any other quarter. I may be wrong, but I myself attach great importance to it, although it is of less importance if the previous scheme is adopted. But even if the general scheme is adopted there is something to be said for this, I think, in the way of clearing things up, but I am really pressing its advantages if the general scheme is not adopted. I see no substantial objection to the proposals put forward in this section, and if they had been adopted 10 years ago immense progress would have been made by now.

6977 *May I put one difficulty which I felt on reading the particular proposal that tithe should be compulsorily redeemed whenever land changes hands. We have had particulars of cases in which the redemption price of tithe would actually exceed the purchase price of the land. In that case supposing the obligation to redeem were on the vendor, he would have actually to pay something more to the Revenue than he was getting from the purchaser?* I should have thought those were very exceptional cases.

6978 *In cases where the tithe is heavy and you have to redeem at 32 years' purchase and the value of the land is small, perhaps because drainage has been neglected or for some other reason—those cases do arise?* I should deal with that by giving the Ministry of Agriculture, or whatever the authority was that dealt with it, the same discretion that they have now in the case of compulsory redemptions. While under the law they can order compulsory redemption of any tithe rentcharge under £1, they are given a wide discretion as to whether they order redemption or not.

6979 *Would there not be considerable criticism from people who object to the increase of bureaucratic rule? Supposing there was a tithe of 5s. an acre (net value) which had to be redeemed at 32 years' purchase, that would mean a capital figure of £8 an acre. There is quite a good deal of agricultural land, I take it, the value of which, if it were brought into the market, especially at anything like a forced sale in the event of bankruptcy, does not exceed £8 by very much at any rate?* I see the difficulty. It would have to be dealt with, I think, by saying that the redemption money should not be more than a certain percentage of the purchase price.

6980 *Then if your scheme were not adopted you would in that case compel the tithe-owner to take something which would leave him very much worse off?* Yes, I should, but only in cases where his tithe was a very high percentage of the value of the land, and I think he would not be a real sufferer by getting his redemption money in those cases. But I see there is a difficulty which I had under-estimated.

6981 *I do not know if there is anything more to which you specially want to call our attention in that connection? You refer to the extraordinarily troublesome*

685

*question of reapportionment. I do not know how far you have had personal
experience of that. We have had a great deal of evidence of the trouble caused by
informal apportionments?* I have had great experience of that. The trouble
given sometimes is almost beyond belief. In the case of my own College we
take the utmost pains to satisfy everyone that they are being justly and
properly treated, and as the new purchaser, where an estate is broken up,
very seldom knows anything about tithe to start with, one of the troubles is
getting into their heads the nature of tithe and that the reapportionment is
being done properly, and getting them to show precisely the boundaries of
their property. We prepare draft maps and send them to them and ask them
to mark on the maps their boundaries, and we find they do not tally with
their neighbours, and it leads to interminable trouble.

6982 *You would be in favour of any system which enforced the redemption
of tithe where land was sold for building?* Yes.

6983 *We have been told of cases where whole streets of houses are jointly
charged with small amounts of tithe, and the result is that on redemption each
house would be liable for a sum in the neighbourhood of pence or even farthings?*
I think that reasonable consideration ought to be given to the circumstances
in which compulsory redemption could take place, but that leaves a great
deal untouched, and in the light of the objection to my proposal in section
IV which you have just raised, I feel even more strongly the advisability of
what I have proposed in the earlier sections as the only way of clearing
things up.

6984 *There is no question as to the nature of the liability in the case of your
new tax. It would be a personal liability to tax, just like any other tax is a personal liability?* Yes.

6985 *I notice that in your final paragraph you say that you see no alternative
to making tithe a personal liability on the tithe-payer if the tithe system is to be
retained. You know that that is one of the matters which arouses a great deal of
opposition when it is suggested?* I am aware of that, but all the same I think
it is a right proposal.

6986 (SIR JOHN LLOYD) *In paragraph 15 of your memorandum you express
the opinion, I think, that it would be a great advantage if the proposed figure
of £109 10s. could be reduced to £100?* Yes.

6987 *You feel it would be difficult to expect tithe-payers to pay more when
the payment had become a personal liability instead of being recoverable under
the existing system?* Yes, I do feel that, but of course there is no virtue in
the special figure of £100 except that it is a round figure.

6988 (CHAIRMAN) *You have not referred in your scheme to the question as to
whether any reductions in the amount payable by way of tithe or substituted tax
ought to extend to cases where the land is not agricultural?* No. I should be

sympathetic to the notion of limiting the concession to the cases of agricultural land. There is in my experience very little ground, I think, for concessions on urban land. I am only responsible for one tithe rentcharge which is mainly urban. That is tiresome and expensive to collect because it is in quite small parcels but it is never necessary to make concessions.

6989 *Do you have any tithe which is charged on railways?* Yes, it is generally quite small.

6990 *I think we have been told that the railway companies, being under no obligation to redeem tithe, have not, in fact, generally redeemed it?* I think I can remember small cases of redemption by railway companies. I actually had a case last week in which land was sold and there was a complicated reapportionment such as I have referred to, and it was found that although the railway company had not been paying tithe hitherto, they actually owned a piece of the apportioned area but the tithe on it had been paid by an adjoining owner, either to save trouble or without knowing it, but when the whole area was subdivided in ownership and the exact boundaries of every one's property was gone into in detail it was discovered there was a small piece for which a railway company was liable and we are now applying to them to pay, and I should rather expect that if they admit liability they will redeem. There is no difficulty in regard to their redeeming. I do not know how far it goes back, but it not infrequently happens that a tithe-payer for many years will pay the whole tithe on some small area of which he owns a portion only. He is, of course, liable as long as it has not been officially reapportioned. Any of the owners within the apportioned area is liable, and as far as the college is concerned, we are entitled to collect from any one owner to whom we apply.

6991 *I think he has a right of contribution from the other owners?* Yes.

6992 (SIR EDWARD PEACOCK) *Do you regard that tithe-owner's right as a proper one?* I think it is fair that when an area is not legally apportioned the man who is called upon to pay should have the right of recovery from his neighbours for a reasonable period.

6993 *Is it fair that you should have the right to call upon one man to pay another man's portion?* It is his business to get the reapportionment. He can always avoid this liability by going to the trouble of the reapportionment. I think it is quite right that that trouble should be put on him.

6994 *In many cases the particular person chosen is one of a great many people. Why should the trouble be placed upon him specially?* I think the practice of most tithe-owners in such a case is to apply in rotation, one year to one man, the next year to another. I quite agree that the existing law in relation to reapportionment is very unsatisfactory both in respect of the parties who have a right to apply for it, and the quite excessive costs sometimes involved. I do not say they are excessive in relation to the trouble caused to the Ministry,

687

which is very great, but they are a real hindrance to reapportionment. I have known cases in which the expense was really out of all proportion to the interests involved.

6995 (CHAIRMAN) *Would you think it reasonable that the Government should be asked to make no charge for these expenses?* I think it would ease matters.

6996 *It would undoubtedly ease matters, but do you think it reasonable to expect the Government to do it?* I think it is reasonable for the Government to ease matters if it can do so without undue expense.

6997 *Without making a charge? The Government are already prepared to carry out the transaction, but they do it at a price?* I think it is a question of the way in which the total expenses of the Tithe Department are allocated. I do not know that, as long as the existing system goes on, there is any reason why tithe-owners and tithe-payers between them should not pay the expenses of administering the system, but I think the actual rule by which they are allocated in particular cases is one which stands in the way of reapportionments which ought to be carried out. I think it is a case where there is no real justification for a claim, but nevertheless it would be wise and expedient to accede to it.

(CHAIRMAN) *It only remains for me to thank you for your evidence.*
(The witness withdrew)

The Royal Commission's Report was published on 27 February 1936. It recommended that the existing system end and that tithe-holders receive 3 per cent stock redeemable over 40 years in return for their claims. At the same time, these claims were adjusted downwards from the level set in 1925 to £91 11s. 2d. per £100 nominal value. Adjusted for taxes, collection costs and greater security, the values put on various classes of tithe varied between £76 12s. 6d. for benefice tithe and £51 19s. 9d. for lay tithe-holders. The Government accepted the Royal Commission's recommendations except for the 40-year redemption period, which it extended to 60 years. Following the Tithe Act, 1936 the Government issued its 3 per cent Redemption Stock, 1986–96 in 1937.

Chapter 5

KEYNES'S EARLY LECTURES

In the six years before the outbreak of War in 1914, Keynes carried a reasonably heavy lecture load. A table outlining his lecture subjects appears below. In addition, in 1910/11 he took papers in political economy for one hour a week for two terms and gave revision lectures in the final term.[1]

From these years, a number of sets of his lecture notes survive, as well as students' notes by D. H. Robertson and C. W. Guillebaud. Below we print two sets of Keynes's own notes. The first would appear to come from his Principles of Economics lectures, while the second came from his Theory of Money course. For each course of lectures we include his reading list of books suited to the standard of the class, and the test papers which, following a tradition set by Alfred Marshall that continued down to the 1920s, he set for students taking the course, marking, and then returning them in a later lecture. Throughout, we include Keynes's reminders to himself of the place he reached at the end of particular lectures, and the relevant newspaper clippings with their sources.

Subject	Years taught	Number of terms[2]	Number of hours per week
Money, Credit and Prices	1908/9–1909/10	2	2
The Stock Exchange and the Money Market	1909/10–1913/14	1	1
The Theory of Money	1910/11–1913/14	1	2
Company Finance and the Stock Exchange	1910/11–1912/13	1	1
Currency and Banking	1910/11–1913/14	1	2
The Currency and Finances of India	1910/11	1	1
Money Markets and Foreign Exchanges	1910/11–1912/13	1	1
Principles of Economics	1910/11–1913/14	3	2
The Monetary Affairs of India	1912/13	1	1

[1] Where newspaper clippings appeared in the original notes, we have not printed them unless Keynes's text referred to them. Rather we simply indicate the nature of the clipping.
[2] A term lasted eight weeks.

ELEMENTARY LECTURES ON MONEY

MONEY (ELEMENTARY) I

1. What are the chief requisites of a good currency?

2. Supposing that the amount of gold in a sovereign were halved, what would be the probable effect on the nominal price of (i) wheat; (ii) gold bracelets; (iii) Consols; (iv) railway ordinary stock; (v) cab fares?

3. In considering the probable movement in the general level of prices in this country during the next ten years, what are the principal factors of which you would take account?

4. What is an Index Number? What are the principal uses in which it can be employed?

5. Bring out the difficulties involved in the attempt to make a numerical comparison between the purchasing power of money at the present time in Germany and England.

6. Discuss the principal factors affecting fluctuations in the price of Consols at the present time. Illustrate your answer by reference to the main movements in price since 1870. Bring out the contrast between the amount of influence exerted by different factors now and a hundred years ago.

MONEY (ELEMENTARY) II

1. Explain in outline the process through which an increased supply of gold affects general prices.

2. Who is likely to gain and who to lose in a period of rising prices?

3. Explain the meaning of Gresham's law, giving a historical instance of its operation. Does it constitute an objection (i) to international bimetallism, (ii) to bimetallism in a single country?

4. Explain briefly the nature of the currency system now existing in each of the following countries:— France, Germany, U.S.A., India.

5. Discuss the principal differences between the banking systems of England and Germany.

6. Explain at least four different methods of regulating issues of paper currency.

MONEY

Marshall :—

I myself use the term currency to include everything which passes from hand to hand as a means of purchasing, without requiring any special or trade knowledge on the part of those who handle it.[3]

Roscher :—

The person who takes money as such must always harbour the hope of being able to dispose of it again as money.[4]

Uses of money:—

Medium of exchange
Measure of value, both for immediate and for deferred payments.

Use as a store of value not strictly monetary.

The following main topics:—

1. The social utility of money.
2. The causes determining the value of money.
3. Methods of measuring the value of money.
4. Consequences of fluctuations in the value of money.
5. Systems of currency.

---

[3] Evidence to the Royal Commission on the Values of Gold and Silver, 1887, Question 9630.
[4] W. Roscher, *Principles of Political Economy*, Book II, chapter III, section CXVIII, n. 2, p. 351. (Chicago, Callaghan, 1882.)

Books

F. W. Taussig. *Principles of Economics*, Book III

D. Kinley. *Money: A Study of the Theory of the Medium of Exchange* (excluding chapter VIII)

Marshall—Evidence [to the Royal Commission on the Values of Gold and Silver, 1887, 1888]

H. Withers—*The Meaning of Money*

G. S. Goschen—*The Theory of the Foreign Exchanges*

C. F. Dunbar—*Chapters on the Theory and History of Banking*

U.S. Monetary Commission—*English Banking System* (Withers, Palgrave, R. M. Holland)

1. *The social utility of money*

Adam Smith :—

The gold and silver money which circulates in any country may very properly be compared to a highway, which, while it circulates and carries to market all the grass and corn of the country, produces itself not a single pile of either.[5]

(a) Abolition of the inconveniences of barter. Hindrances to distant trade in the absence of a monetary system. Difficulty of producing in advance of consumption.

(b) Abolition of truck. Importance of money in securing the freedom of the individual and the possibility of modern industrial development. Truck Act of 1831. Change when money payments took the place of services. Process of adoption. Changes in India at the present time. Introduction of a money economy a definitely new step of development.

(c) Money is the chief means of enabling people to make the marginal utilities of their consumptions in different directions equal. For this reason, if for no other, money would be required in a communistic society. Wastefulness of free services unless the comparative marginal utilities of different individuals approximately equal. Example of free dinners, free railway travelling.

(d) Facilitates both the transfer and the aggregation of capital. Without it investments would be more local in character. The

[5] *The Wealth of Nations*, Bk II, ch. ii.

costs of exchange are diminished, and the number of exchanges increased.

(e) On the other hand disturbance may be caused in the distribution of incomes by changes in the value of money. This will be dealt with later.

2. *The causes determining the value of money*

The value of money depends, like anything else, upon the interaction of supply and demand, and can be treated, therefore, as a special case of the general theory of value. But the theory of the value of money is worth treating separately because it is conditioned by certain special simplifying circumstances—on account of which the theory of value as applied to money is sometimes crudely described as the 'Quantity Theory of Money'.

In a sense the value of anything depends upon its quantity, that is upon its supply. But, as we shall see, the quantity of money influences its value in a peculiarly direct manner. The use of the name 'Quantity Theory', however, has certainly tended to overemphasise the influence of supply as compared with that of demand; and may be partly responsible for the unreasoning attacks against every form of the theory.

As Lord Goschen said, there are many persons who cannot hear the relation of the level of prices to the volume of currency affirmed, without a feeling akin to irritation.

The best and clearest statements of the theory are to be found in Professor Marshall's evidence before the Gold and Silver Commission of 1888[6] and the Indian Currency Com^ee of 1899.[7]

Meaning of the *value* of money:—

The value of money is measured by the 'general level of prices'; and to say that prices are high is exactly the same thing as to say that the value of money is low; to say that gold prices have risen is the same thing as to say that gold has depreciated in value.

[6] The Commission produced its first Report in 1887, the final one in 1888.
[7] See *Official Papers by Alfred Marshall*, Ed. J. M. Keynes (Macmillan, 1926).

Now it is true of all commodities, in virtue of the law of diminishing utility, that in a given state of demand the value of each unit varies inversely as the supply. But the rate of decrease is not generally proportionately so great as the increase of supply, i.e. the value of each unit decreases, but the *total* value of all the units, as a rule, *increases*.

The peculiarity of money is this: in a given state of demand, and supposing that the money concerned is not required for non-monetary purposes, the total or aggregate value of all the units of money, whether they be many or few, tends to be *constant*.

(*End of 1st Lecture, Lent 1912*)

It is this peculiarity of money which the Q [uantity] T[heory] embodies. More precisely stated it is as follows:—
The total exchange value of the money in circulation is independent of the *quantity* of money in circulation.
If we suppose, however, that this condition *by itself* fixes the value of money, we are involved in an evident fallacy. The total exchange value of the money in circulation is *not independent* of the demand for money.

What is the justification of the theory?
The value to us of a sovereign entirely arises out of the fact that we can *exchange* it for other things we want. Its utility to us and, *putting aside for the present its use in the arts*, to everybody arises *entirely* out of its exchangeability. Thus if a sovereign were of only half the bulk that it actually is, we should not be incommoded, so long as it purchased the same amount as before. Its *utility* would be unchanged. This is not true of most other things, e.g. food, houses, a railway ticket.

Now as money is a counter between exchanges of real wealth, the total value of these exchanges is dependent, not on the composition of the counters, but on the amount of the real wealth to be exchanged. Thus the total value of the exchanges, which people desire to effect through the medium of money, is

694

fixed independently; and the total value of the commodity employed as money must be equal to this. If, therefore, the *amount* of the money-commodity is increased, the value of each unit is proportionately decreased.

(*End of 8th Lect. 1913*)

Let us measure the total value of the exchanges to be effected by means of money in terms of some standard of value other than money, e.g. bushels of corn

Let this value be D; let x be the number of units of money, and y the number of times each is used;
Let V be the value of each unit
Then we must have $xyV = D$
That is to say $V = 1/xy \, D$.

A complication arises out of the fact that the commodity which we use for money sometimes possesses utility apart from its exchangeability. This will be dealt with later. In the case of an inconvertible paper currency this difficulty does not arise.

We can now restate the theory again: *given* the value of the demand for purchasing power in the form of money, *given* that the commodity used as money is useful for no other purpose, and *given* that the average number of times each coin is used suffers no change; then the value of each unit of currency is inversely proportional to the number of units.

In this form the Q.T. of M. is *absolutely valid*.

The Quantity Theory of Money, therefore, gives us a formula by which if we know
(i) the total demand for purchasing power in the form of money
(ii) the number of units used as currency
(iii) the rapidity of circulation
we can infer
(iv) the value of each unit.
We shall now consider

First what determines the demand for purchasing power
Second what determines the number of units used as currency
Third what determines the rapidity of circulation
The theoretical part of our problem will then be complete.

The Demand for Money

Dependent upon the following factors:—

(i) changes in the volume of things on sale

(ii) changes in the average no. of times each of these things changes hands during the year

(iii) changes in the extent to which purchases are effected otherwise than by currency, e.g. by barter or credit; or in expectations regarding this.

(i) is likely to be due to changes in population and wealth which increase or diminish the aggregate national dividend.

(ii) is likely to be due to changes in the methods of transport, production, and business generally, which affect the number of hands through which commodities pass in the processes of making and dealing.

If one person or firm works up a product from the raw material to the finish, no exchange occurs and no money is required until it is ready for retail sale. When a man makes things for his own use, no money is required at all. If greater specialisation is introduced and the product changes hands several times during the course of manufacture, it is clear that the need for the medium of exchange is increased.

(iii) is likely to be due to the growth of credit agencies, which substitute other means of payment for currency. But credit requires as we shall see later a monetary reserve, and this causes a demand which partially offsets the relief caused by the use of credit.

It will be noticed that some of these causes tend to increase the demand for money and some to diminish it. Commercial and financial progress tends to increase the volume of things on sale, and also the frequency with which these things change hands;

this increases the demand for money, and so tends to *lower* prices.

But progress also tends to perfect processes for the economy of money—by the substitution of other means of payment for currency, and, as we shall see later, by increasing the rapidity of circulation. These tendencies decrease the demand for money and counteract the tendencies mentioned first.

The fact that progress has brought into existence opposing tendencies has been—historically—very fortunate. If the expansion in trade and population and wealth during the nineteenth century had not been accompanied by an enormous advance in banking and commercial organisation, the consequent disturbance to the equilibrium of prices might have upset the existing currency system altogether.

In 1888 Marshall pointed out that 'it is a gradual change in the methods of business which has enabled us to do some 20 or 30 times as much business as we did before with a volume of gold and silver only two or three times as large as we had before'[8] *without* an enormous change in the level of prices.

The compensatory action of the different forces brought into existence by economic progress has been, therefore, very important.

(*End of 9th Lect. 1913*)

The Supply of Money

1st The amount used not for exchanges, but as a store of value, i.e. for hoarding

2nd The amount used for other purposes, i.e. the arts in the case of metallic money

3rd The total production, i.e. of the mines in the case of metallic money; of the Gov^t in the case of paper money.

(i) Hoarding

Almost extinct in G.B. but not in France.

Apt to spring into existence again very rapidly if there is any distrust of the mechanism of exchange.

[8] Evidence to the Royal Commission on the Values of Gold and Silver, Question 9646.

Hoarding by governments, or by banks beyond the proper requirements of a reserve.

Absorption of bullion by the East.

Pliny (A.D. 79) complained that India drew from the Roman Empire not less than 5,000,000 sesterces (£500,000) a year.

India during the past 75 years (1835–1910) has absorbed £m433 silver and during the last 5 (1905–1910). [MS. blank]
£m229 gold

Not more than half of the imports of silver since 1835 are in use as currency.

(*End of 2nd Lecture, Lent 1912*)

(ii) Use in the arts

Dentists, watches, jewels, gilding.

As the total output has increased (i.e. since 1900) the *proportion* going to the arts has, so far as one can estimate, steadily fallen off. But perhaps as much as one third of the total production is still used in the arts.

The *wear* of gold is very considerable.

Jevons' calculations.

French experiments in 1895 found the loss on coins 1 per mill. in 8 years.

The proportions in which gold goes to currency and to the arts must be such that its marginal value for each purpose is the same. If the demand for currency decreases or the supply from the mines increases, new uses become profitable—and vice versa.

It is a normal case of joint demand.

(iii) The supply of gold

As gold is slowly consumed, the annual addition is small relatively to the accumulated stock.

Two outstanding facts:

(a) the smallness of the total amount of gold mined

(b) the enormous increase in recent times.

De Launay :—

The output of gold from antiquity up to 1907 may be put at some 18,000 tons, representing 2,480 millions. Calculating on the basis of the annual output at 10 hours' labour a day, this is practically the weight of ferruginous products (iron, cast iron and steel) which the world produces in one hour.

Nevertheless, though in insignificant quantities, there is gold almost everywhere.

For instance in the sea—near the Isle of Man 64 milligrammes per ton (30 milligrammes = ·9*d*.).

Annual average	£m	Production in 1909	£m
1493–1520	¾	Africa	34½
1521–1660	1	U.S.A.	20½
1660–1720	1–1½	Australasia	14½
1720–1810	2¼	Russia	6½
1810–1840	2	Mexico	4½
1841–1850	7	Canada	2
1851–1860	26½	India	2½
1860–1872	25	Other countries	7
1873–1887	21		—
1888–1893	26		92
1894–1897	41		
1898–1902	56		
1903–1909	79		
1910	90		
1911	93		

The modern gold age:

1st period   California (1848) and Australia (1851)
2nd period   Transvaal (1887), W. Australia (1890), Alaska (1891), Cripple Creek, Colorado (1891)

Value of gold and its cost of production

Adam Smith :—

Of all those expensive and uncertain projects [however] which bring bankruptcy upon the greater part of the people who engage in them, there is none, perhaps, more perfectly ruinous than the search after new [silver and] gold mines. It is, perhaps, the most disadvantageous lottery in the world, the one in which the gain of those who draw the prizes bears the least proportion to the loss of those who draw the blanks.[9]

The value of gold depends upon its scarcity, and its scarcity depends, in a sense, upon its cost of production; in the long run, that is to say, gold tends to be mined up to the point when its marginal cost of production is equal to its value.

But the cost of production exercises a less important control over production than in the case of some other commodities

(a) because, as A.S.[10] points out, there is a constant tendency for gold to be mined even when the marginal cost of production (i.e. total cost—supplementary and prime) falls short of its value

(b) because important changes in the *conditions* of production can, on account of the accumulated stock, exercise only a slow influence on value

(c) because gold is often found under 'windfall' conditions to which the normal theory of value is inapplicable.

Rapidity of Circulation

We have now considered two factors—the demand for purchasing power—the supply of units of currency.

But the total supply of purchasing power is compounded of the supply of units of currency and the number of times each is used. This factor is termed the rapidity or velocity of circulation, or the efficiency of currency.

Very difficult to obtain *data* to calculate the amount.

Fisher has calculated that in U.S.A. in 1896 each coin was used on the average about 18 times a year—i.e. money was held on the average about 20 days.

I should suspect that in England the rapidity of circulation at the present time is very much greater than this.

It is plain, however, that *changes* in the rapidity of circulation can very greatly affect the total supply of purchasing power.

[9] *The Wealth of Nations*, Bk IV, ch. vii, section 1.
[10] *Ibid.*

The Equation of Demand and Supply for Money

We can now bring together in a single equation the separate factors which we have elucidated above.

The *Demand* is for a certain amount of *Value*, which is required in the form of purchasing power.

Let us suppose, for convenience, that this value is measured in terms of bushels of corn.

The *Supply* is measured by the *number* of unit coins available for monetary purposes multiplied by the average number of times each is used in the unit of time to which the demand refers.

(10th Lect. 1913)

Our equation is, then, as follows:—

(Value of consumption goods on sale × average number of times each element of their value changes hands in the course of production)−purchases effected by barter or credit+banking reserves supporting credit transactions

= Demand (D)

(output of mines−use in arts−hoarding)×rapidity of circulation = Supply (S)

Then by Quantity Theory $V = D/S$ where V is value of each unit of currency.

Inductive verification

of such a theory is evidently difficult. We cannot isolate the various contributory causes, or prepare experiments. It is, therefore, always difficult to refute a controversialist who points to one of the possible causes as the *sole* cause of what has occurred. But it is surely hardly an exaggeration to say that the proposition that 'the level of prices would be different from what it is if the supply of money were different from what it is' is at least as evident as the proposition that 'a shortage in the supply of sugar makes the price higher than it would have been with a good harvest'.

701

The popular opinion that an advance of prices is to be attributed to the development of trade arises out of a confusion between the development of trade and the expansion of credit.

(*End of 3rd Lecture, Lent 1912*)

Two possible methods of inductive verification seem to be open to us:—

(i) To make independent estimates of each item in the equation of value, and to discover whether the equation is satisfied when these values are substituted.

I do not myself believe that we possess at present sufficiently accurate *data* to make this method of any practical value.

Professor Irving Fisher has attempted to apply it to the U.S. of America (where the *data* are certainly more ample than they are here). His results are to be found in his book on *The Purchasing Power of Money*. I shall discuss this in my advanced lectures, but not in these.

(ii) To study some period when the items most difficult to calculate can be safely assumed constant.

These conditions are much best fulfilled in illustrations drawn from the history of inconvertible currencies. But we may also perhaps obtain a little light from the general history of prices during the 19th century.

As an example of the former let us take the history of the French assignats.

Belief that the value of money 'if properly secured' is independent of its quantity.

Mirabeau :—

Paper money, we are told, will become superabundant. Of what paper do you speak? If of a paper without a solid basis, undoubtedly; if one based on the firm foundation of landed property, never . . . There cannot be a greater error than the fear, so generally prevalent, as to the overissue of assignats. . . . Reabsorbed progressively in the purchase of the national domains, this paper money can never become redundant, any more than the humidity of the atmosphere can become excessive, which descends in rills, finds the river, and is at length lost in the mighty ocean.

The Assembly successively violated pledges to limit the issues. Towards the end of 1794 there had been issued 7,000 million francs in assignats.

	Number		Value of 24 livres in assignats
May 1795	10,000 million	April 1795	238
end of July 1795	16,000	June	439
beginning of 1796	45,000	September	1,101
of which	36,000 in circulation	November	2,588
		January 1796	4,658
		February	5,337

At the last a paper note professing to be worth £4 sterling, passed current for less than 3*d.* in money.

In 1796 territorial mandates were ordered to be issued for assignats at 30:1, the mandates to be directly exchangeable for land, at the will of the holder, on demand. For a brief time after the first limited emission, the mandates rose as high as 80 per cent of their nominal value. Soon they were worth but 1/1000 part. So that the depreciation of the coinage was measured by 1:30,000. (But this is not really a satisfactory or exact verification of the quantity theory; for the depreciation was *much more* than in proportion to the quantity.)

The history of prices and gold production during the 19th century affords *prima facie* a singularly exact verification of the Quantity Theory, and is commonly quoted for this purpose.

But there is, I think, good reason to hold that the exactness of the apparent verification is largely fortuitous and due to the chance balancing of other larger changes.

The level of prices depends, as we have seen, mainly upon the supply of gold, the volume of trade, and the system of banking and credit.

There were during the 19th century enormous changes in the two latter which seem, through the merest accident, to have more or less counterbalanced one another, thus leaving to variations in the gold supply the balance of power.

Apparently, therefore, the curve of prices and the curve of gold supply show a remarkable agreement; but we must not agree from this that the one is directly and solely due to the causal influences of the other.

However let us examine the history of the two for what it is worth.

1820–50   general tendency of prices to fall and very small gold production
1848   Californian discoveries
1850   Australian discoveries
1850–6   very rapid rise of prices, giving rise to the second grand discussion amongst economists and even the public on the theory of currency—Chevalier, Cairnes, Jevons.
(The first grand discussion being the Bullionist controversy—Ricardo, Tooke, Lord Liverpool, McCulloch.)
1856–70   ups and downs of prices but no general tendency to rise or fall. Gold supply, which was somewhat diminished, being no more than sufficient to meet natural increase at the higher level of prices.
1876   began the great fall of prices which continued without sensible intermission until 1896. During the earlier part of this period no increase and even some diminution of gold production. At the same time demand for gold greatly increased both by natural growth and through the demonetisation of silver.
⎰Latin Union—limitation '73; suspension '78;
⎱Scandinavia '73; Netherlands '77;

U.S. '93 and '98; India '93 and '99; Spain 1901;
Mexico 1903; Austria-Hungary '92; Japan '93;
Russia '99

Thus all the whole of the world except China had in some manner or other replaced a silver standard by a gold standard (although by no means all adopted a gold *currency*).

This gave rise to the bimetallic controversy and the Gold and Silver Commⁿ of 1888.

1886   Gold Discoveries in the Transvaal.

The force of the fall of prices was broken in 1888, but there was no real recovery until the new supplies began to make themselves felt about 1897.

Since then, apart from a temporary cessation due to the closing of the mines during the Boer war, the movement has been upwards; and the movement, which is likely to continue, has now become so far obvious to the ordinary man that we may possibly be on the brink of the Fourth Grand Discussion.

The course of prices during the 19th century can, therefore, be accounted for by reference to the statistics of gold production in a fairly plausible manner.

And if we construct an index number of the estimated stock of gold employed in monetary uses and another of the course of prices we find a remarkable tendency to correspondence.

But as I have already explained the closeness of this correspondence is, probably, largely illusory and fortuitous.

The means by which money affects prices

By far the best verification of the conclusions of the Quantity Theory is to be found in an examination of the actual means through which alterations in the volume of currency affect prices. This is part of the argument which is most often omitted. It was first elaborated by Professor Marshall in his evidence before the G. and S. Commⁿ of 1888.

I shall deal with it in these lectures very briefly, because it would lead me otherwise too far into matters of detail; in my advanced lectures I shall say rather more about it.

A rise of prices always *appears* to be due to 'conditions of trade' and in the case of every article taken by itself a rise in its price is always due to an increase in the demand for it or to a decrease in the supply of it, as its proximate cause.

This is the chief reason why some bankers and many business men have always been inclined to doubt the connection of the level of prices with the volume of money—because they cannot perceive through what channels the influence of the one upon the other is exerted.

Additional money can, therefore, only raise prices by increasing the demand at a given price for individual commodities. It is clear that the amount of commodities that people will seek to buy at a given level of prices depends upon their purchasing power—the amount, that is to say, of their cash in hand or of what they can borrow. If they find themselves in possession of more funds, they will at the old level of price either buy more themselves or lend more to others thus enabling these others to buy more.

But as there is no reason why the supply of goods should be any greater than before at the old level of price, prices rise until at the new level of price the additional supply of funds is absorbed in purchasing practically the same volume of actual goods as before.

Let us proceed to more detail.

In some states of society a fresh supply of money might actually influence prices through individuals having more money in their pockets than before with which to affect purchases. When adventurers came back to England or Spain from America with gold and silver in their pockets, it was in this manner that prices rose.

(*End of 4th Lecture, Lent 1912*)

(5th Lecture answering Paper 1)

But with the existing monetary mechanism of England the train of events is somewhat more complicated. The new gold does not go into the pockets of individuals, but swells the reserves of bullion at the Bank of England. This as you all know tends to lower the rate of discount and increases the willingness of the Bank to lend. It is, therefore, through the greater volume of loans which are obtainable that new supplies of gold now tend to increase the demand at the former price level. The existence of the machinery of banking tends, in the first instance at any rate, to accentuate the influence of the new supplies. For the receipt of £1,000,000 enables the Bank to increase its loans by a great deal more than that amount.

Thus in the first instance those who are in the habit of borrowing from the B. of E. find their resources more ample. They are a particular class; and it follows, as a consequence of this, that the prices of different commodities are affected unequally. The prices of those commodities which this class is likely to purchase are the first to rise. Such commodities we may term the speculative commodities; and with them we may group Stock Exchange securities.

In England at the present time the most important speculative commodities are probably the metals.

The boom in securities tends to bring about the launching of new companies, and in general the rise of prices, by increasing temporarily the profits of entrepreneurs, gives an apparent fillip to trade.

For the moment employment will improve, wages tend to rise and the purchasing power of the working classes at the old level of prices is increased. A new class of commodities is now affected in price.

In time nearly all commodities will be affected in some degree; and at the new level of prices, partly in the form of bank reserves, partly for the payment of wages and in retail purchases, the *former* volume of trade will require the whole of the new supply of gold to finance it.

The outline of events is, therefore, as follows:

The new gold in the vaults of the B[ank] of E[ngland] brings about a tendency of the Bank rate to fall. This enables speculators and entrepreneurs to increase their purchases. This stimulus gradually spreads through all parts of the community, until the new gold is needed to finance a volume of real trade no larger, except through other influences, than before.

It must be noticed that the new money begins by increasing the demand for *some* commodities; but only on the part of the entrepreneur or dealer or middleman; the consumer must *pay* more and must therefore divert some part of his consumption of other things. There is no reason for supposing that in the long run the new gold affects the *total* demand—though of course the money value of the commodities is permanently increased, and the money value of the volume of credit outstanding.

(*11th Lecture 1913*)

Thus if we measured our wealth in *money*, the aggregate wealth of the community naturally *appears* to be greater than it was before.

This is no more than an outline account, and I have made no attempt to meet all possible objections or to fill in all the necessary details.

Index Numbers

No mystery about them.

An Index Number is in itself no more than the measure of an object at one time or in one place in terms of the magnitude of the same or a similar object at another time or place.

Example of the heights of the same or different people.

The coefficient 100 is introduced for the sake of arithmetical convenience. It is not essential to the conception—e.g. *The Economist*'s Index Number.

The difficulties arise because the quantities which we want in economics to compare by means of index numbers are very often not easily measured. If we are to compare them by means of index numbers, it is essential that we should first measure them in terms of some common unit. All the difficulties centre round this.

The difficulties are of two kinds. In the first kind the quantities in question are perfectly definite and capable of measurement, but the information at our disposal is incomplete; our task consists in making as accurate a measurement as we can by using what statistics we have. In the second kind the quantity itself is not, in the strictest sense, capable of numerical measurement at all; we must adopt some conventional, but practically useful, measure.

Instance of national money income and national utility income.

Index numbers can evidently be used for a great variety of purposes. The birth rate per mille is a kind of index number. We can have index numbers of foreign trade, of wages, of the price of corn, of suicides.

I shall be concerned in these lectures solely with what is usually termed the index number of the general level of prices.

This kind of index number involves both kinds of difficulties —the difficulty of actually obtaining the statistics we want, and the difficulty arising out of the fact that there is no strictly numerical quantity corresponding to the conception of a general level of prices. It is the second of these difficulties which I am specially anxious to make clear.

The fundamental difficulty can be expressed quite simply. If the prices of all commodities changed equally, if they all doubled for example, it would be clear that the general level of prices had risen twofold, and there could be no room for dispute.

But this is not what occurs in practice. In practice the prices of some commodities rise and the prices of others fall; and in order to judge whether the level of prices has risen or fallen on the whole, we must balance the importance of a fall of price in one commodity against the importance of a rise of price in another.

If articles never varied in relative importance, there would be no difficulty, no theoretical difficulty at any rate, in settling this relative importance once and for all.

But the relative importance of different articles is constantly changing, and when their price changes their relative importance generally changes at the same time.

Thus there does not seem to be anything constant which we can compare from one period to another.

Cf. difficulty of comparing standards of life in different countries or under different physical conditions.

This then is the prime theoretical difficulty and it is one which cannot be surmounted. All that we can say is that, when the relative importance is not changing rapidly, we can make approximate comparisons of the level of prices from one period to the next by ignoring the change of importance and considering only the change of price. When the change of relative importance is too great to be neglected, I know of no exact numerical means of comparison which can be justified.

But there is also the practical difficulty of obtaining all the statistical data that we really require.

The prices of many things, which are practically important in determining the level of prices, are not easily ascertainable, e.g. rent and services especially.

We must also avoid counting the same article twice.

(End of 6th Lecture, Lent 1912)

Here again, therefore, we have to make an approximate, and select from amongst those articles whose prices are sufficiently well known those of them which seem most suitable to our purpose.

When we have selected the articles, we must then determine as accurately as we can the relative importance that ought to be attributed to each.

It is clear that, if the statistics are adequate, the more articles we can include the better and the less does the element of practical approximation enter in.

A good index number of the general level of prices satisfies, therefore, three principal criteria:—

(i) It includes, on the basis of adequate statistical data, as many as possible of those articles of commerce, which are most important absolutely and which have the greatest stability of relative importance.

(ii) This relative importance must be estimated as accurately as possible.

(iii) The base year of comparison must not be too remote, in order that the articles may have as little time as possible in which their relative importance can fluctuate.

An index number of this character can be suitably regarded as measuring the price of *a representative commodity*.

Suppose we take wheat, iron and cotton and suppose we assume that the relative importances of these commodities are in the ratios 55, 35 and 10, then let us take a quantity of wheat which is worth 55*s*. in the base year, a quantity of iron worth 35*s*. and a quantity of cotton worth 10*s*.

At present prices $1\frac{2}{3}$ quarters of wheat

$\frac{2}{3}$ ton of pig iron

22 lb of raw American cotton

Then in 1912 a composite commodity composed of the above would be worth 100*s*.; if by 1913 the price had risen to 103*s*., we should say that the index number of wheat, iron, and cotton, weighted in the proportions 55, 35 and 10 had risen from 100 to 103. We might, in the absence of better data, regard the prices of this composite commodity as some sort of index of the general level of prices, taking it, in fact, as our representative commodity.

If we had measured the relative importance of these commodities correctly, if their relative importance were much the same in 1913 as in 1912, and if absolutely they had a preponderant importance in our economic life, movements of this index number might give a very fair indication indeed of the kind of fluctuation in which we are interested when we speak of a general level of prices.

But if we could greatly increase the number of commodities of which we were taking account, our composite commodity would evidently become more representative still.

The relative importance which we attribute to the different articles must clearly be determined by the precise object we have in view. The general level of prices is not an absolute thing. It is not only to a time, but to a particular place and sometimes to a particular class.

There are, therefore, several sets of index numbers designed for different purposes with different sets of weights.[11]

I have given this account entirely from my own point of view without considering controversial points or other ways of looking at the question. I shall deal with these in my advanced lectures. I will conclude by saying a little about two index numbers— Sauerbeck for the U.K. and the Falkner-Aldrich index number for U.S.A.

Sauerbeck

Most frequently consulted because it begins as early as 1846 and comes down to the present day. [First published in 1886.]
Does not satisfy our criteria very adequately
(1) Remote base period 1867–1877
(2) Number of distinct commodities 37 too small
(3) Very slight attempt at weighting

(12th Lecture 1913)

(13th Lecture 1913 answering paper)

The Falkner-Aldrich Index Number

Prepared in 1893 for the Aldrich Com^ee of the Senate by Prof. Falkner.

---

[11] The sentence in the original began 'There is, therefore, for several...'.

Now issued each year in March number of Bulletin of Labour Bureau.

(1) For recent years the comparatively recent period 1890 to 1892 has been taken as base.

(2) The prices are *not*, as a rule, the average prices throughout the year.

(3) No less than 223 commodities taken into account.

(4) Index numbers of eight *groups* of commodities calculated separately.

(5) Both an equally weighted and a rationally weighted index number are worked out. (Weights according to the importance of articles in the consumption of 2561 family budgets.)

Consequences of Fluctuations in the Value of Money

(1) Effects on the rate of interest and on anticipated profits.

(2) Effects on the distribution of wealth between different classes; social effects.

(3) Effects on booms or depressions of trade; commercial effects.

(4) Political effects.

(1) When we incur a loan we do so in order to make certain purchases. What we bargain to repay at the end of a stated period is not the equivalent of these purchases, but a sum of money equal to the sum lent us and another sum by way of interest.

If, therefore, the sum of money representing the capital has a lower purchasing power at the end of the period than at the beginning, the debtor has evidently gained at the expense of the creditor, unless it is made up to the latter by an exceptionally high rate of interest.

When a fall in the value of money is *foreseen*, therefore, the rate of interest tends to rise in order to counterbalance the above influence.

The effect of anticipated changes on the rate of interest is much more marked when we are considering short loans (for which the term 'rate of discount' is commonly used), than when we are considering permanent investments.

In the second case the effect of the disturbance is shared between the capital value and the rate of interest; in the first case, since the amount of money capital to be repaid is fixed, the whole is borne by the rate of discount.

e.g. if in Feby 1908 $\begin{cases}$ The price of consols was 81 and the yield 3 $\\$ The rate of discount $\quad$ 7 $\end{cases}$

Feby 1909 $\begin{cases}$ 85 $\qquad\qquad$ 3 $\\$ 3 $\end{cases}$

The yield on consols is only altered fractionally; but the two transactions are equally profitable.

The point does not, of course, present itself to businessmen in quite this form.

Each is concerned with his own commodity only; if he anticipates that its price will rise he is anxious to buy now and is willing to pay a higher rate of interest for a loan which will enable him to do so.

If commodities in general are thought by businessmen generally to be likely to rise, this shows itself in a general willingness to pay a relatively high rate of discount for temporary loans.

It is thus through individual actions that the appreciation or depreciation of money, in so far as it is anticipated, influences the current rates of interest and discount.

(2) Social effects of rising or falling prices.
The first effect of a fall in the value of currency is, evidently, to lower all dues enforced by contract or custom. All these suffer, that is to say, the amount of whose incomes is more or less fixed in terms of money—
i.e. wage earners
    salaried classes
    those paid by fixed fee
    those who live on the interest from shares which pay a fixed rate of interest.

We have seen that, in so far as a fall is foreseen, creditors are able to defend themselves against injury; but such changes have been as a rule very imperfectly foreshadowed.

Where changes have not been foreseen, concessions, it is true, may sometimes be made.

It is always found that, when the rent which the farmer has contracted to pay is higher than the land is really worth, the landlord sees his way to making improvements that he would otherwise have left the farmer to make or to go without. (M[arshall])[12]

But employees cannot as a rule foresee; and they have less power of acting on their knowledge. The consequence is that a rise of wages is seldom or never as fast as that of prices when the cause of the rise is an increase of the currency, that is not accompanied by an increased command over nature. (M)[13]

Looking at the periods in England in which there has been the greatest distress, I find that they are periods of rising prices. There never has been, I think, anything like as much distress in England as under the late Tudors and at the beginning of the 19th century; and in each of these periods prices were rising very fast. (M)[14]

There is evidence of this in Bowley's investigations into the level of wages (*Ec.J.* Dec. 1898)[15]:—

Real wages have steadily risen, nearly doubling between 1844–53 and 1891; but the rise of real wages after 1873 when prices were falling was greater than before 1873 when prices were rising.

(*End of 7th Lecture, Lent 1912*)

With the rise of prices since 1900 something similar has occurred, and it is commonplace to ascribe the prevailing

---

[12] Evidence to The Committee Appointed to Inquire into the Indian Currency, 1898, Question 11,780.
[13] *Ibid.*, Question 11,780.
[14] Evidence to the Royal Commission on the Values of Gold and Silver, 1888, Question 9,816.
[15] A. L. Bowley, 'Comparison of the Changes in Money Wages in France, the United States and the United Kingdom from 1840 to 1891'.

tendency to strike and industrial unrest as partially due to the effect of rising prices on real wages.

It is an important part of the business of the employer to anticipate changes of price in his raw material or in his finished commodity and to take advantage of them. The employee naturally does not regard with the same keenness corresponding changes in the price of what his wages are to purchase.

Here then is a *prima facie* argument against rising prices. It is likely to redistribute wealth in an undesirable way by reducing real wages.

It is sometimes set against this that the relief of debtors at the expense of creditors is, on the other hand, a desirable redistribution of wealth.

If we look more closely we see that the class of creditors damaged are the holders of bonds and debentures and preference shares and gilt-edged securities generally; and that the debtors, i.e. the borrowers, who are benefited are the holders of ordinary and deferred shares, private merchants and the entrepreneur class.

So far as any generalisation of this kind can be safely made, we may say that the latter, i.e. the borrowers, represent on the whole the rich and the investors the comparatively poor.

We must not be misled by the terminology into thinking of the debtors as poor and the creditors as rich.

We may say, therefore, that the effect of rising prices on the distribution of wealth is likely, on the whole, to be undesirable —i.e. to increase rather than to diminish existing inequalities.

(3) Commercial effects of rising or falling prices.

Since we are accustomed to measure our wealth in terms of money, as though it were of constant value, all those whose capital or income is capable of fluctuating in terms of money appear to be richer. A businessman's profits measured in money must tend to be higher. If he has bought plant for £1,000,000 ten years ago and has kept it in good condition; and if prices have risen 50 per cent, it will now be worth £1,500,000. Similarly his profits, if they really remain constant, will appear to rise from £100,000 to £150,000. Either he will continue to regard his capital as being £1,000,000 in which case his profits will have risen from 10 per cent to 15 per cent; or he will reckon it as being worth £1,500,000, in which case he will seem to be £500,000 richer than he was before.

But booms of trade, in so far as they are due to monetary rather than to strictly commercial causes, although sometimes started by an abundant supply of gold, are generally due in the main to an expansion in the volume of credit.

This expansion of credit, which is the cause not the effect of high prices, may or may not prove a beneficial thing in the long run; higher prices might therefore be the symptom of something desirable, but there is little to be said for the view that high prices as such are directly 'good for trade'.

During a period of rising prices anyone who is buying now to sell later makes a bigger profit than he bargained for. And most businessmen will be in this position.

Improvements will be neglected and many businesses become established which can only hope to succeed under these specially favourable and necessarily temporary conditions.

Ultimately the reaction comes. Prices cannot go on rising for ever. But 'we must not attribute this social malaise to the fall of prices, instead of to the previous morbid inflation which caused it'. (M)[16]

On the other hand there is no need to deny that falling prices also bring evils in their train.

(7th Lecture, 1914)

Summing up we may say that it is unforeseen changes in the price level which diminish the productiveness of industry. For they lead to miscalculation, and miscalculation to waste.

There is no sufficient ground for preferring rising prices to

---

[16] Evidence to the Committee Appointed to Inquire into the Indian Currency, 1898, Question 11,781.

falling prices, and even some reasons for thinking the latter to be preferable. We are misled into the opposite opinion partly because businessmen obtain unusual profits during a period of rising prices, and partly because we have an inveterate habit of measuring industrial progress by the growth of money values. We can never quite clear our heads of the preconception that money is an invariable unit which remains a permanently safe measure of comparison, while commodities change.

CURRENCY

Meaning of Standard Coin

(a) Unrestricted legal tender
     Restricted legal tender
(b) Free Mintage
     Token
(c) Convertible
     Inconvertible

Inconvertible currency of unrestricted legal tender is the true standard.

(End of 8th Lecture, Lent 1912)

(End of 14th Lecture, 1913)

Classification of Currencies

One metal freely minted and one only full legal tender—Monometallism (1)

Two metals freely minted and both full legal tender—Bimetallism (2)

One metal freely minted and two full legal tender—Limping Standard (3)

No metal freely minted but maintained at fixed par through foreign exchanges—Exchange Standard (4)

718

1800 Most countries with regular currency (2)

1870 England (1). Most other countries theoretically (2).

1911 None (2). England, Germany, Russia, Japan (1). L[atin] U[nion], U.S. (3). India and the East generally, Holland (4). Austria-Hungary (3) and (4)

Bimetallism

A currency system in which both gold and silver are freely minted and are both unlimited legal tender at a ratio determined by the public authorities, the debtor having a right to pay at option in either of the two metals. A dead controversy.

Advantages

(1) To steady prices

(a) by lessening the fluctuations in the value of money by drawing it from two *independent* sources.

We should have, perhaps, more frequent fluctuations, but smaller ones.

Prof. Edgeworth has agreed that the steadying effect would not be very considerable.

Marshall:—

The main causes of fluctuations of prices have not been fluctuations in the supplies of the precious metals. Changes in the methods of business and the amounts of commodities, or, as we may say, changes in the commercial environment, are the principal agent in disturbing prices ... Prices were almost halved between 1809 and 1816. Thus during this period when the supply of the precious metals was approximately constant, there were violent fluctuations of prices.[17]

(b) because silver is an intrinsically better measure of value —as shown by its past history.

It is true that between 1873 and 1888 silver may have been, under the existing circumstances, steadier than gold.

But this was probably fortuitous and the balancing not very exact.

[17] Evidence to the Royal Commission on the Values of Gold and Silver, 1887, Question 9695.

(2) To minimise the troubles due to fluctuations in the foreign exchanges with silver-using countries.

The further demonetisation of silver and the spread of the Gold Exchange Standard have reduced this argument to no importance.

Great distinction between international bimetallism and bimetallism for a silver country.

(3) To raise prices generally and thus to stimulate trade possibility of this discussed already.

From this aim came the driving force of the movement.

For the immediate raising of prices it was necessary that the ratio should be fixed below the market rate.

(a) Market ratio bimetallism—which would not have the above effect.

(b) $15\frac{1}{2}:1$. If effective, would raise prices in gold-using countries and lower them in silver-using countries. Gold mining would be hindered and silver mining stimulated. Possibility of maintaining this ratio open to doubt. In the case of international bimetallism, it is improbable that one metal would go out of circulation altogether. But the amount of each metal in circulation would vary from time to time.

The chief danger to the stability of the ratio would be in the possibility of hoarding on the part of Gov^t or individuals.

The transition from bimetallism to a gold standard has not meant in all cases a transition to a gold currency.

The reasons for this have been principally three:—

(1) Countries already possessing a large silver currency could not have disposed of it and replaced it by gold except at a heavy loss.

(2) The people were used to silver—or paper.

(3) Gold would give too large a unit for the majority of purchases.

These circumstances led at first to the adoption of what has been termed the *Limping Standard*.

With this standard, silver is unlimited legal tender and is

widely used as the currency of the country, but is kept at a fixed par with the standard by limitation of quantity and is not freely minted.

Introduced into L[atin] U[nion] and U.S.A.

In France and U.S.A. silver about $\frac{1}{3}$rd of the currency.

In the course of time, however, a more complete and scientific method has been devised for combining a gold standard with a silver currency. What we may term the *Gold Exchange* Standard depends upon the circumstance that if our silver currency will always purchase drafts for gold payment on foreign countries we have substantially the advantages of a gold standard.

So long as gold is available for payments of international indebtedness at an approximately constant rate in terms of the national currency, it is a matter of comparative indifference whether it actually forms the national currency.

This standard, in one form or another, has now been adopted by Holland, Austria-Hungary, India, Philippines, Mexico, Straits Settlements, Siam, Java, and Panama.

I do not propose in these lectures to go into details respecting this standard.

Two essential differences between the limping standard and the exchange standard (Conant):—

(1) The exchange standard contemplates a circulation of token coins without any necessary concurrent circulation of gold.

(2) It contemplates definite and comprehensive measures to maintain the value of the token coins at par with gold instead of relying purely upon custom and scarcity to give them value.

The precise nature of these measures varies from country to country, but as a rule a notification is issued when necessary that drafts on some foreign monetary centre will be sold at a fixed rate in terms of the local currency, and reserves are maintained at some foreign centre to meet this eventuality.

The existing tendency, therefore, is towards a variety of local currencies, consisting of some cheap material, whose exchangeability in terms of the international standard (at present gold) is maintained by Gov^t.

(*End of 9th Lecture, Lent 1912*)

I do not propose to give any account in these lectures of
Banking
Systems of Note Issue
Foreign Exchanges
Stock Exchange
These are all in the main matters of detail and would lead me too far from Principles.

Keynes's notes for the second course of lectures are incomplete. From the plan below only sections I and II of the theoretical outline survive, as well as some notes on German and American banking. Below we print the surviving theoretical sections which Keynes kept together in two binders.

THE THEORY OF MONEY

I   Introductory
II   Causes determining the value of money
III   Methods of measuring the value of money
IV   Consequences of fluctuations in the value of money
V   Systems of currency
VI   Systems of credit and gold reserves
VII   English banking
VIII   German banking
IX   American banking
A new section to be written on
Causes determining local differences in the value of money

PRINCIPLES OF MONEY I

1. Suppose a country, whose full legal tender money is a freely minted metal, puts a heavy tax on the importation of this metal:

what effect would this tend to produce on its home prices, its foreign trade, and its foreign exchanges?

2. Examine the relation between the cost of production of gold and its value as money.

3. What is going to be the future of gold prices?

4. Discuss Mr H. G. Wells's view that 'the problems of economic theory would undergo an enormous clarification' if instead of measuring money values in a fluctuating gold standard, they were measured in terms of units of electrical energy.

5. Distinguish the methods by which an increased supply of gold affects prices (a) in gold producing countries, (b) in others.

PRINCIPLES OF MONEY II

1. Adam Smith says[18] 'When a tax on coinage is so moderate as not to encourage false coining, though everybody advances the tax nobody pays it, because everybody gets it back in the advanced value of the coin.' Examine this.
Consider the incidence of a tax levied on all gold mines (30)

2. Visualise and explain as precisely as you can the steps by which an increase of 10 per cent in the annual production of gold would effect the price of bread in this country.

3. 'The value of the sovereign depends on the value of the metal in it as jewellery and plate.' How far is this an adequate statement?

4. 'Every £100 of credit displaces coin to that amount.' Criticise this statement, and explain exactly what determines the amount of coin required by a people.

5. Give as clear an account as you can of the fundamental

---

[18] *The Wealth of Nations*, Bk IV, Ch. vi.

difficulty in the conception of 'a general level of prices' and in its statistical measurement.

6. If the price level in a particular country is rising faster than the price levels elsewhere, what kinds of causes would occur to you as a possible explanation of such a circumstance?

[7] Suppose a country, whose full legal tender money is a freely minted metal puts a heavy tax on the importation of this metal: what effect would this tend to produce on its home prices, its foreign trade, and its foreign exchanges?

We must assume importation would occur in the absence of a tax

1st effect prices lower than they would otherwise have been
exchanges more favourable than the old specie point
2nd effect exports stimulated
imports retarded until exchanges reach new specie point
Henceforward they fluctuate about new specie point in exactly the way they did about the old, except that the export specie point is much more below the new equilibrium than it was formally.

At the new equilibrium prices are nominally lower, but the sovereign is normally worth more than the world value of the gold in it; so that the prices measured in gold elsewhere are practically what they were before. The foreign trade will be unchanged, except that, less gold being required than before, the demand for imports other than gold will be slightly greater and the foreign demand for exports slightly less than before. There is also a clear gain to the community because they are using a less expensive material with which to conduct their exchanges. Instance of India.

General Remarks

Importance of doing written work

Nicholson[19]:—

The subject of money is in its nature difficult, but not obscure or mysterious —it requires, like mathematics, hard thinking and regular advance.

Conant (p. 7)[20]:—

In matters relating to money the hypothetical assumptions of deductive reasoning are more uniformly borne out by events than in almost any other (economic) field. The usual limitations apply less—i.e. those referred to by Cairnes—'There are few practical problems which do not present other aspects than the purely economical—political, moral, educational, artistic aspects— and these may involve consequences so weighty as to turn the scale against purely economic solutions'.

List of Books on Money, etc.

F. W. Taussig—*Principles of Economics*, Book III

D. Kinley—*Money: A Study of the Theory of the Medium of Exchange* (excluding chapter VIII)

Marshall—Evidence [to the Royal Commission on the Values of Gold and Silver, 1887, 1888]

E. W. Kemmerer—*Money and Credit Instruments in their Relation to General Prices*

I. Fisher—*Appreciation and Interest* or *The Rate of Interest: Its Nature, Determination and Relation to Economic Phenomena*, chapters V and XIV.

I. Fisher—*Purchasing Power of Money: Its Determination and Relation to Credit, Interest and Crises* (omitting the appendices)

W. S. Jevons—*Investigations in Currency and Finance*

British Association—*Report on Index Numbers*

D. Ricardo—*High Price of Bullion: Proposals for an Economical and Secure Currency*

W. Bagehot—*Lombard Street*

---

[19] *A Treatise on Money and Essays on Monetary Problems* (Fifth ed., 1901) p. 11.
[20] *A History of Modern Banks of Issue.*

H. Withers—*The Meaning of Money*

G. J. Goschen—*The Theory of the Foreign Exchanges*

G. Clare—*The A.B.C. of the Foreign Exchanges*

C. F. Dunbar—*Chapters on the Theory and History of Banking*

U.S. National Monetary Commission—*The English Banking System* (Withers, Palgrave, R. M. Holland)
   —*Miscellaneous Articles on German Banking*
   —*Interviews on the Banking and Currency Systems of England, France, Germany, etc.*

Viscount Goschen—*Essays and Addresses on Economic Questions 1865–1893* (our cash reserves and central stock of gold)

For reference

C. A. Conant—*A History of Modern Banks of Issue*

L. Darwin—*Bimetallism: A Summary and Examination of the Arguments for and against a Bimetallic System of Currency*

H. F. Howard—*India and the Gold Standard*

J. L. Laughlin—*Principles of Money*

R. H. I. Palgrave—*Bank Rate and the Money Market in England, France, Germany, Holland and Belgium, 1844–1900*

J. S. Mill—*The Principles of Political Economy*, Book III

C. M. Walsh—*Measurement of General Exchange Value*

G. F. Knapp—*Staatlichte Theorie des Geldes*

U.S. Report on Stability of International Exchange [Reports of the United States Commission on International Exchange (1903) and The Introduction of the Gold Exchange Standard into China and Other Silver-Using Countries (1904)]

Books

Recent books mostly American—because currency was for many years an important political issue there.

(Difficulty of recommending books. Principles. Art of reading)

No good English book of recent date

A good deal of the most important material to be found in official reports.

American

General and Theory (Note views of each on quantitative principle)

D. Kinley—*Money: A Study of the Theory of the Medium of Exchange*

J. F. Johnson—*Money and Currency in Relation to Industry, Prices and the Rate of Interest*

J. L. Laughlin—*The Principles of Money*

General. (See also other general treatises on economics.)

N. G. Pierson—*Principles of Economics*, Vol. I, Part II

English

General and Theory

Marshall's Evidence before G[old] and S[ilver] Commission 1888

J. S. Nicholson—*A Treatise on Money and Essays on Monetary Problems* (elementary)

W. S. Jevons—*Money and the Mechanism of Exchange* (v. elementary)

Financial and Money Market

G. J. Goschen—*The Theory of the Foreign Exchanges* (cf. with G. Clare, *A.B.C. of F.E.*)

W. S. Jevons—*Investigations in Currency and Finance*

H. Withers—*The Meaning of Money* (supplants Bagehot)

I. Fisher—*The Rate of Interest*, Chapter XIV

G. Clare—*A Money Market Primer* (elementary)

Banking

C. A. Conant—*A History of Modern Banks of Issue*

C. F. Dunbar—*Chapters in the Theory and History of Banking*

L. Darwin—*Bimetallism: A Summary of the Arguments for and against a Bimetallic System of Currency*

A. L. Bowley—*An Elementary Manual of Statistics*

More Advanced Books

Ricardo—[*High Price of Bullion, Proposals for an Economical and Secure Currency*]

Knapp—[*Stattliche Theorie des Geldes*]

F. Y. Edgeworth—British Ass[n] Report on Index Numbers

C. M. Walsh—*Measurement of General Exchange Value*

American Academy of Pol. and Soc. Science March 1908— lessons of the Financial Crisis

Gold and Silver Commission 1888

Indian Currency Comm[ee] 1898 (especially Marshall's evidence)

U.S. Report on Stability of International Exchange and the Introduction of the Gold-Exchange Standard into China and Other Silver-using Countries.

(I can put anyone in the way of borrowing any of the above)

Economics Library[21]

Definition of Money

Marshall[22] :—

I myself use the term currency to include everything which passes from hand to hand as a means of purchasing, without requiring any special or trade knowledge on the part of those who handle it.

Conant[23] :—

That commodity of intrinsic value acceptable in exchanges which has become by law or custom the usual tender for debt. (i.e. paper money excluded)
Derived from Julia Moneta, whose temple was near the first Roman Mint (Livy)

Roscher :—

The person who takes money as such must always harbour the hope of being able to dispose of it again as money (*Principes d'Econ. Pol.* p. 218)

[21] A cupboard of economics books provided by Marshall, later incorporated with his books in the Marshall Library.
[22] Evidence to the Royal Commission on the values of Gold and Silver, 1887, Question 9638.
[23] *A History of Modern Banks of Issue.*

J. F. Johnson:—

(1) Scientific use (—Conant, excludes paper)
(2) Popular use—cash, or ready money, i.e. all forms of currency alike
(3) Figurative use—wealth
(4) Financial use—capital, or loanable funds
(5) Legal use—legal tender

Distinction between *Money* and *Currency* common in American writers.

Uses of Money

See Jevons or Nicholson
    Medium of Exchange
    Measure of Value
Disputed by [F.] Walker [*Money* (1878)]
    Store of Value
    Standard of deferred payments

Walker [p. 12]:—

When a commodity comes to serve as a store of value, it ceases to be money. The fact that gold may be used as a store constitutes one of the important facts which qualify it for service as money, just as its usefulness in arts and industry does. But gold in hoards or as treasure is no more money than gold in plate, or on the roof of a temple, or in a statue of Jupiter.

Jevons:—historically gold esteemed
    1st for ornamental purposes
    2nd as stored wealth
    3rd as a medium of exchange
    4th as a measure of value

Desirable Properties of Money

See Jevons.[24]
Jevons' list: utility, portability, indestructibility, homogeneity, divisibility, stability of value, cognizability.
But these are very trifling and are rather the requisites of intrinsically valuable metallic money.

[24] *Money and the Mechanism of Exchange.*

Exchangeability is the only utility which need be possessed by money, *qua* money.

See question 26

(1) A serviceable, durable and agreeable coin with suitable units.

(2) Of an inexpensive material *cet.par.*

(3) Of wide currency.

(4) Popular, generally acceptable.

(5) Stable in general exchange value.

Each of these points can be usefully enlarged upon.

II   *Causes determining the Value of Money*

This part of the subject has been and is a question of acute controversy and is classed by many amongst the unsolved problems of Monetary Science.

As Lord Goschen said, there are many persons who cannot hear the relation of the level of prices to the volume of currency affirmed, without a feeling akin to irritation.

Amongst businessmen such persons are common, as the evidence before any Royal Commission on Monetary Questions clearly shows. (Incident of my speech at the R.S.S. December 1911.)[25]

It is also common in America, several distinguished economists (Laughlin, Scott, and in a different manner Kinley [omit Chapter VIII]) controverting what I regard as the orthodox doctrine. Perhaps because Prof. Marshall's evidence before G. and S. Commission is not generally known there (not even by Prof. Fisher).

But a powerful orthodox school now arising in America (Fisher, Kemmerer, Taussig).

Businessmen appear to doubt what they report as the doctrine of the economists because they have not analysed their experience and do not see *how* an alteration in the volume of currency can effect prices. Or because they are considering short periods,

[25] See *JMK*, vol. XI, pp. 216–19.

for which the influence of fluctuations of credit is so much stronger than that of fluctuations with supply of money proper, as to obscure its influence.

We must not only show, therefore, that the influences we allege are bound to be brought to bear by arguing from fundamental assumptions however justifiable. The forces underlying and justifying these assumptions can only act by influencing the actions of individual businessmen. And we must justify our theoretical conclusions by displaying the individual motives which, attentive only to specific commodities and specific prices, nevertheless bring about in the aggregate these theoretical conclusions. We must not only argue from first principles to conclusions. We must also make sure that we can *visualise* the forms in which they actually clothe themselves and through which they influence the minds of individuals.

(General importance for economists of visualising in this way the particular workings of principles.)

When economists doubt or misstate what is known as the Quantity Theory of Money, they do so because they do not remember its qualifications or think that they are successfully controverting it when, by omitting one of these necessary qualifications, they proclaim it to be contrary to experience.

It is also disputed not infrequently (Laughlin is the best example) as a result of the belief that the volume of credit is unrelated to the monetary reserves behind it. This will be dealt with later.

Controversies regarding the Quantity Theory very fruitless; I shall not argue it controversially.

I shall attack the problem first from the theoretical side, and then attempt to visualise the actual process.

This part of the subject is the central point of all monetary theory, and I shall occupy some time with it.

The value of money depends upon a variety of factors. We can state the theory complete—in a rather cumbrous form. Or we can begin by isolating one of the factors and work up from this beginning to the final theory.

Historically this has been the method usually pursued. The factor first isolated has been that of the quantity of money; and the theory enunciated from this standpoint—correct in itself but not a complete theory of the value of money—is termed 'the Quantity Theory of Money'.

This has sometimes led, no doubt, to overemphasis of this factor and inadequate explanation of the rest.

I will approach the complete theory in more than one way and endeavour to avoid partiality.

We will now return to the various factors upon which the ultimate supply of money depends:—

M the gold in monetary uses

p the proportion of subsidiary currency to standard currency

r the ratio of gold reserves to subsidiary currency

kk' the rapidities of circulation

Before considering each of these factors in detail, let us enumerate the various factors upon which the ultimate demand for money depends.

(i) The volume of consumption.

(ii) The average number of times each element of eventual consumption changes hands in the processes of production and exchange.

(iii) The extent to which exchanges are effected by barter or by any other means outside the currency system we are considering.

Changes in (i) are likely to be due to changes in population and wealth which change the aggregate income or national dividend.

Changes in (ii) are due to changes in the methods of transport, production and business generally, which affect the number of hands through which commodities pass in the processes of making and dealing. If one person or firm works up a product from the raw material to the finish, no exchange occurs and no money is required until it is ready for retail sale. If greater specialisation is introduced and the product changes hands several times during the course of manufacture it is clear that the need for the means of exchange is increased. Similarly if the amount of exchange between different parts of the world is increased.

(iii) Process of adoption now fairly complete in the West; in full swing in India; still very incomplete in China.

The determination of M, the gold in monetary uses

Let T = the total available supply of gold
    H = the amount used for hoarding—i.e. as a store of value
    A = the amount used in the Arts
    M = the amount used in monetary uses.

Then $T = H + A + M$.

The proportions in which gold goes to each of these three uses must be such that its marginal value for each purpose is the same. A case of joint demand. If the demand in monetary uses decreases or the supply from the mines increases, new uses become profitable—and vice versa.

The demand for hoarding obeys the same peculiar law as the demand for monetary uses—it is a demand, that is to say, for a certain amount of *value* in the form of gold, independent of quantity. We can, therefore, lump these two sources of demand together, and discuss the distribution of gold between the arts on the one side and money and hoarding on the other.

This may be explained algebraically or geometrically:
The amount A used in the arts is fixed relatively to the amount $H + M$ used otherwise, so that the value in bushels of wheat of a unit of the metal for the arts when the supply for this purpose is A is equal to the value of a unit for other purposes when the supply for these purposes is $H + M$.
As the total value of $H + M$ is, by the Quantity Theory, equal

733

to a constant V; we have $p = f(A)$ as the demand in the arts when p is the value in bushels of wheat of a unit for the arts when there are A units and $p(H+M) = V$.

Since $A+H+M = T$

$$f(A) = \frac{V}{T-A}$$

This determines the amount of A
Or thus:—

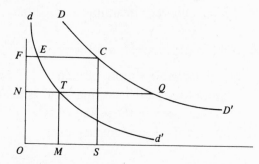

DD' Total demand for gold
  i.e. *NQ* amounts demanded when each unit is worth *ON* bushels of wheat.
dd' demand for hoarding and money
  i.e. *OM* amount of coin when each coin is worth *ON* bushels of wheat.

Then at this price *ON*, *TQ* is demand in arts. Hence if the stock of gold at any time is *OS* then *FE* is used for coin and *EC* in the arts.

(derived from Marshall's lectures)

The Supply of Gold, T

As gold is slowly consumed, the annual addition is small relatively to the accumulated stock.

Nevertheless as the amount absorbed by the East and by the Arts is *fairly* constant year by year and the balance goes to swell the currencies of Europe and America, the effect of new mines on these countries is more rapid than one might expect, as we

World's gold production (U.S. Mint)

	Total	£ million Average	Transvaal
1860–1872	326	25	
1873–1887	315	21	
1888–1893	156	26	
1894–1897	164	41	
1898		57	
99		61	
1900		50	
01		52	
02		59	
03		66	12
04		69	16
05		76	21
06		80	25
07		83	27
08		89	
09		91	
10		95	
1911		97	
1873–1907	1,288		
1860–1907	1,613		
Since discovery of America	2,500	(16,700 tons)	
(1908–11)	+360	+2,400	

	Annual average	
1493–1520	$\frac{3}{4}$	i.e. increased 22% in
1521–1660	1 (steady)	five years (1907–11)
1660–1720	$1–1\frac{1}{2}$	
1720–1810	$2\frac{1}{4}$	
1810–1840	2 (or less)	
1841–1850	7	
1851–1860	$26\frac{1}{2}$	
1881–1885	20	
1888–93	26	
1894–97	41	
1898–1902	57	
1907–11	90	

shall see when we come to the inductive verification of our theory.

The figures above compiled by the U.S. Mint show both the smallness of the amount of gold mined and the enormous increase in recent times.

End of 2nd Lecture, Lent 1912

Difficulty of accurate statistics

(1) Confusion between fine and crude gold (sometimes intentional for Stock Exchange purposes)

(2) Theft at mines (estimated in Transvaal at 5–10%
Siberia 20)

Graph of gold production of the world since 1851[26]

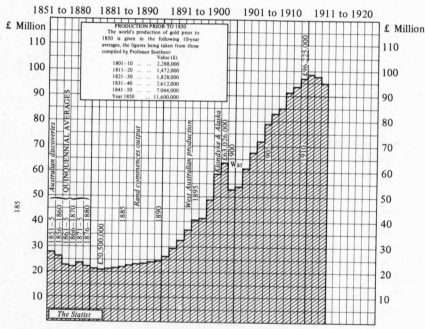

Note. The figures are according to the United States Mint estimates; those of 1912 and 1913, of course, only preliminary estimates.

[26] This chart and the tables on pp. 735–8 come from *The Statist*, 28 February 1914, pp. 436–7.

Table of the world's production of gold, 1850–1913

	Value of production £		Value of production £
1850	11,600,000	1883	20,640,000
1851	17,200,000	1884	20,830,000
1852	36,550,000	1885	21,250,000
1853	31,090,000	1886	21,430,000
1854	25,490,000	1887	21,500,000
1855	27,015,000	1888	21,985,000
1856	29,520,000	1889	23,835,000
1857	26,655,000	1890	24,260,000
1858	24,930,000	1891	26,700,000
1859	24,970,000	1892	29,900,000
1860	23,850,000	1893	32,600,000
1861	22,760,000	1894	37,228,000
1862	21,550,000	1895	40,842,000
1863	21,390,000	1896	41,559,000
1864	22,600,000	1897	48,509,000
1865	24,040,000	1898	58,949,000
1866	24,220,000	1899	63,026,000
1867	22,805,000	1900	52,311,000
1868	21,945,000	1901	53,629,000
1869	21,245,000	1902	60,974,000
1870	21,370,000	1903	67,337,000
1871	25,400,000	1904	71,380,000
1872	24,200,000	1905	78,143,000
1873	23,600,000	1906	82,707,000
1874	22,950,000	1907	84,857,000
1875	22,700,000	1908	91,030,000
1876	22,540,000	1909	93,376,000
1877	23,830,000	1910	96,225,000
1878	22,020,000	1911	97,274,000
1879	21,400,000	1912	97,000,000
1880	22,130,000	1913	94,720,000
1881	21,150,000	Grand aggregate	
1882	20,500,000	of 64 years	2,451,221,000

African production

	Transvaal £	Rhodesia £	West Africa £
1898	16,170,000	83,000	64,000
1899	14,263,000	206,000	51,000
1900	2,000,000	308,000	38,000
1901	1,014,000	610,000	22,000
1902	7,253,000	687,000	97,000
1903	12,589,000	828,000	255,000
1904	16,055,000	970,000	345,000
1905	20,802,000	1,450,000	657,000
1906	24,580,000	1,985,000	877,000
1907	27,406,000	2,218,000	1,160,000
1908	29,957,000	2,526,000	1,186,000
1909	30,926,000	2,624,000	956,000
1910	32,002,000	2,568,000	756,000
1911	34,991,000	2,648,000	1,069,000
1912	38,757,000	2,708,000	1,490,000
1913	37,000,000	2,903,000	1,635,000

United States production (according to the U.S. Mint estimates: $ at 4.85)

	£		£
1847	180,000	1901	16,220,000
1848	2,000,000	1902	16,500,000
1849	8,000,000	1903	15,173,000
1850	10,310,000	1904	16,590,000
1851–55 (average)	12,165,000	1905	18,390,000
1856–60 ,,	10,557,000	1906	19,458,000
1861–65 ,,	9,130,000	1907	18,646,000
1866–70 ,,	10,400,000	1908	19,500,000
1871–75 ,,	7,520,000	1909	20,550,000
1876–80 ,,	8,780,000	1910	19,860,000
1881–85 ,,	6,600,000	1911	19,840,000
1886–90 ,,	6,887,000	1912	19,268,000
1891–95 ,,	7,700,000	1913	18,206,000
1896–1900 ,,	13,400,000		

Australasian production (ooo's omitted)

	Victoria £	N.S. Wales £	N. Zealand £	Queensland £	Tasmania £	S. Australia £	W. Australia £	£
1851	851	468	—	—	—	—	—	1,319
1852	9,146	2,661	—	—	—	—	—	11,807
1853	10,976	1,781	—	—	—	—	—	12,757
1854	8,874	773	—	—	—	—	—	9,647
1855	11,277	655	—	—	—	—	—	11,932
1856-60	10,442	1,038	28	35	—	—	—	9,492
1861-65	6,955	1,721	1,771	315	—	—	—	10,773*
1866-70	6,066	1,014	2,514	546	3	—	—	10,142*
1871-75	4,829	1,242	1,384	672	19	20	—	8,669*
1876-80	3,296	473	1,339	962	116	48	—	6,234*
1881-85	3,194	465	988	929	178	73	—	5,829*
1886-90	2,489	394	819	1,819	126	97	35	5,790*
1891-95	2,652	830	986	2,190	188	140	486	7,472*
1896-00	3,293	1,228	1,211	2,565	290	97	3,976	12,661*
1901	3,158	731	1,754	2,184	295	93	7,238	15,459
1902	3,110	685	1,951	2,440	301	95	7,947	16,529
1903	3,259	1,080	2,037	2,930	254	90	8,770	18,332
1904	3,252	1,146	1,987	2,715	254	124	8,424	17,928
1905	3,174	1,165	2,094	2,517	280	86	8,306	17,654
1906	3,280	1,079	2,271	2,213	312	108	7,622	16,929
1907	2,982	1,051	2,027	1,944	255	50	7,211	15,536
1908	2,851	955	2,001	1,961	271	42	7,003	15,069
1909	2,778	869	2,007	1,935	256	30	6,776	14,589
1910	2,423	804	1,897	1,840	190	30	6,246	13,412
1911	2,139	915	1,926	1,600	172	30	5,823	12,613
1912	2,040	702	1,345	1,478	180	48	5,448	11,222
1913	1,847	636	1,460	1,119	160	46	5,582	10,850

* Averages.

World's production of gold, 1882, 1908, and 1913 compared

	1882 £	1908 £	1913 £
Africa	70,000	33,669,000	41,538,000
United States	6,500,000	19,500,000	18,206,000
Australasia	6,025,000	15,077,000	10,850,000
Russia	4,365,000	5,610,000	6,200,000
Mexico		3,330,000	3,610,000
Canada	3,540,000	1,970,000	3,155,000
India		2,664,000	2,390,000
Other countries		9,210,000	8,861,000
	20,500,000	91,030,000	94,720,000

(1908 bracketed group total: 15,112,000)

Aggregate gold outputs to 1913 inclusive

	£
Victoria	293,387,000
West Australia	114,880,000
New Zealand	82,461,000
Queensland	78,096,000
New South Wales	61,436,000
Tasmania	6,791,000
South Australia	3,556,000
Australasia (since 1851)	640,607,000
United States (since 1849)	722,294,000
Canada (since 1862)	63,994,000
India (since 1880)	42,381,000
West Africa (since 1880)	12,050,000
Transvaal (since 1884)	401,000,000
Rhodesia (since 1898)	25,282,000
All other countries	543,613,000
	2,451,221,000

I shall now make a short digression from the theoretical argument to the subject of *Gold*.

(L. De Launay—*The World's Gold*)

First we may note the extraordinarily small quantities of gold which have been obtained.

De Launay (p. 71):—

The output of gold from antiquity up to 1907 may be put at some 18,000 tons, representing 2,480 millions. Calculating on the basis of the annual output at 10 hours' labour a day, this is practically the weight of ferroginous products (iron, cast iron and steel) which the world produces in one hour.
(A similar calculation, which I reproduce for curiosity's sake, gives for the stock of diamonds counted in the rough, nearly 20 tons, representing a gross value of 140 millions.)

Nevertheless, though in insignificant quantities, there is gold almost everywhere. For instance in the sea.

Near Isle of Man	64 milligrammes per ton
San Francisco	32
N[ew] S[outh] W[ales]	32–64
30 milligrammes = ·9*d*.	

Although imaginative prospectors have taken out patents for the extraction of gold from the sea; this has not yet reached a practical stage.

Second, under what conditions is gold actually found?

(1) Sedimentary deposits (old detritus).

(2) Lodes (tissues in which the metals have crystallised after rising in solution in hot water).

(3) Alluvia (recent detritus).
Worked in the opposite order.

Nuggets of native gold and gold dust, which symbolise the idea of a gold mine to most people, are found in alluvia.

Alluvial gold is very easily detected, and is, therefore, only found now on the outskirts of civilisation, and deposits of this kind will soon be exhausted.

741

The workings of antiquity were of this character. Siberia, Yukon, New Zealand, Rhodesia at the present time supply alluvial gold.

The early Californian workings were alluvial. But such workings are soon exhausted and the time may soon come when the Californians will be as surprised to hear that gold was obtained from their rivers as the inhabitants of the Rhine, Po, Adous Valleys would be today.

Alluvian workings now unimportant (Siberia, Yukon, N.Z., Rhodesia, Guianas)
Sedimentary deposits in Transvaal
Elsewhere lodes

Per cent

	1848–75	1876	1890	1905
Alluvia	87·28	65·28	44·20	15·00
Lodes	12·02	34·76	47·80	57·50
Sedimentary	—	—	8·00	27·50

Third, The History of Gold Mining

Alluvial deposits are rich while they last, and there has been a tendency perhaps to depreciate unduly the gold workings of antiquity.

The gold discovered in tombs shows the real wealth in gold of the Mycenaean and Egyptian Kings.

The treasure of Montezuma and the Incas, discovered by the Spaniards, amounted according to the most recent estimates to 4 millions.

p. 84[27] 'The earliest centres of gold mining were evidently in the zone of the most ancient civilisations—Armenia, Chaldea, Asia Minor or Egypt.' . . .

'Greece herself was very poor in gold until the Persian Wars . . . The deposits . . . of Colchis, west of the Caucasus, gave rise to the fabulous legends of the Golden Fleece, which was perhaps [evidently] a method of collecting gold dust in the water-courses.'

[27] Of L. De Launay, *The World's Gold*.

Asia Minor the chief centre—Croesus King of Sardis
Midas [King of] Phrygia.

The Pactolus, Mt. Sipylus, north of Smyrna, once furnished gold to Tantalus. With the growth of commercial enterprise in Turkey, some of these workings may become again profitable.

In somewhat later times Thrace and Macedonia.

Egypt very rich. 'Ptolemy II derived from his mines an [large] annual revenue, estimated, perhaps rather highly, at £4,000,000. At the beginning of the Christian era the mines, although failing, were reputed to produce 3 [to 3·20] millions.' But the list could be made very long

Arabia

The legendary Ophir in the interior of Africa

Spain, the Pyrenees, Gaul

p. 89: 'Rome began, like Greece, by being very poor in gold, and a reference from Pliny has often been quoted to the effect that there was a difficulty in finding 1,000 lbs [of gold in the city to pay] as a ransom for [to] the Gauls.' . . . 'Rome had no gold mines till she expanded towards the Alps.'

p. 90: 'India had produced gold dust for ages; many centuries before Christ that far off country was already spoken of where ants brought up gold from under the earth.'

With the barbarian invasions the gold accumulated at Rome was scattered and disappeared.

'For several centuries Europe was very poor in precious metals . . . By the end of the Middle Ages it is estimated that not more than 12 to 16 million pounds' worth of gold remained in Europe.'[28]

Then came gold from Africa and the New World. In the 18th century the Brazilian output was important. At the beginning of the 19th the world's output v. small.

The modern Gold Age

	1848	1851

1st period   California and Australia

[28] De Launay, pp. 87, 89, 90. The words in square brackets are omitted in Keynes's handwritten notes.

                    1887
2nd [period] Transvaal
              quickly followed by
                 1893   1891   1891
              W. Australia, Colorado (Cripple Creek), Alaska

Steady expansion since 1850 in Russian Empire
1850–1888 Australia, N. America, Russia produced nearly all the gold.
We live in an age of exceptionally large gold production.

              In 1906   Transvaal 24·76
                        U.S.A.   20·20 millions
                        Australia 17·24

Mining much more concentrated in Transvaal than in U.S.A. or Australia.

Fourth, Methods of Mining

(1) Mining or quarrying
(2) Crushing
(3) Metallurgical extraction
In case of alluvial gold only washing required, gold falling by its weight and then retained by Mercury (The Golden Fleece)
Hydraulic Method first used in California The 'Giant' or 'Monitor'
    The difficulty of the method is the disposal of the debris; and it is now forbidden in California in the interests of the agriculturists. Elaborate mining and chemical methods (only lately perfected) required in Transvaal.
The Jaw-Breaker
The Tube Mill more modern, more complete crushing

What is or is not barren ore now entirely a matter of cost
Lehfeldt [*Economic Journal*, Sept. 1912, p. 488]:— In Transvaal 4 drs (17*s.*) per ton cost; if cost reduced to 3 drs, available is increased 50 to 100 per cent.

744

The future of gold mining

For some years at least production likely to be large. With modern methods poor ores can be worked, and there is plenty of poor ore in existence.

The largest gold mine in the world—Homestake, S. Dakota—annually crushes 1,400,000 tons containing less than 15*s*. 2*d*. a ton

Treadwell mine in Alaska 8*s*. 4½*d*.

Rand often as low as 24*s*.

Rand gold output[29]

	Number of mines	Number of stamps	Tons milled and yield per ton		Value £
			Tons	Yield s. d.	
1904	—	—	8,058,295	38/6	15,539,219
1905	—	—	11,160,422	35/9	19,991,658
1906	—	—	13,571,554	34/6	23,615,400
1907	—	—	15,523,229	34/0	26,421,837
1908	—	—	18,196,589	31/8	28,810,393
1909	—	—	20,543,759	29/0	29,900,359
1910					
January	9,225		1,754,140	28/1	2,462,591
February	9,265		1,614,730	28/11	2,338,043
March	9,303		1,767,059	28/0	2,471,749
April	9,205		1,763,104	28/8	2,524,591
May	9,240		1,785,821	28/11	2,577,201
June	9,250		1,761,034	28/10	2,541,584
July	9,215		1,814,686	28/7	2,593,934
August	—		1,834,105	28/0	2,646,888
September	—		—	—	2,639,163

Process of Distribution of Precious Metals

The following tables show that London is the distributing centre of the world.

[29] *The Statist*, 15 October 1910, p. 873.

Process of distribution of precious metals
(U.S. Mint figures for 1907)

	Silver			Gold		
	Imports	Exports		Imports	Exports	
U.S.	9	12	−3	29	11	+18
S. Africa				—	30	−30
Egypt				7	5	+2
France	13	8	+5	19	6	+13
Germany	1	1		10	11	−1
G.B.	18	16	+2	57	50	+7
B. India	16	1	+15	13	2	+11
Mexico	0	10	−10	0	3	−3
China	1	5	−4*			

In £million sterling

* Silver imported into Manchuria during Russo.-Japanese war was finding its way to the treaty ports and being sold for export.

Bullion market in London

Every Monday, the gold landed on Saturday is dealt with
£3 17s. 9d. the Bank's rate
£3 17s. 10½d. rate at which gold is coined into sovereigns

Exports of silver from London to India, China and Straits*

	India	China	Straits	Total
1898	4	1	—	5
9	5	1	—	7
1900	8	2	1	11
1	7	1	1	9
2	6	—	1	8
3	7	—	1	8
4	9	—	—	10
5	7	1	—	8
6	15	—	—	15
7	10	—	1	12

£ million

* U.S. Mint figures.

The destination of the Gold

Let us take the 10 years Dec. 31 1900–Dec. 31 1910

Total production	£m 758
Central banks and treasuries excl. India	£m 393 (52%)
Arts excl. India	£m 200
India	£m 60
	653

Leaving 105 for circulation, of this probably about 40 is accounted for by U.S.A.

Further increases in banks is mainly due to a few countries—i.e.

Argentine	+31	Italy	+32
Austria	+16	Japan	+17
Brazil	+19	Russia	+55
France	+38	U.S.A.	+140
Germany	+10		

Of these a large proportion have been engaged in changing their currency system during the period under review.

U.S.A. is likely to adopt some system more economical of coin, and in any case is unlikely to increase at the same rate.

(See next page.) Between 1895 and 1910 the per capita stock rose from $9.10 to $18.10.

The U.S. holds almost as much gold as the B. of France, the B. of England, the Imperial B. of Germany, the Austro-Hungarian B., and the B. of Spain all added together.

The U.S., Argentina and Brazil have increased their holdings in the ten years by £m190, which is 25 per cent of the world's production of the metal within the period.

During the last two or three years the demands of the principal state banks have begun to slacken.

It is difficult, therefore, to see how more new gold is to be absorbed without a considerable rise of prices.

India, Egypt, Turkey, S. Africa may not yet be satisfied; and more S. American republics (e.g. Chile) might adopt the plan of Argentina and Brazil.

Table of gold holdings of central banks and treasuries acting as central banks[30]

	1913 £	31 December 1910 £	31 December 1900 £	Increase or decrease £	Increase or decrease %	Increase per cent of total gold production %
Argentina: Caja de Conv.	46,629	37,033,000	6,272,000	+30,761,000	+488·3	4·0
Australasia		31,820,000	26,420,000	+5,400,000	+20·5	0·7
Austria	51,666	55,023,000	38,624,000	+16,399,000	+42·5	2·2
Belgium	9,960	8,252,000	2,843,000	+5,409,000	+193·2	0·7
Brazil: Caja de Convers.		19,000,000	Nil	+19,000,000	—	2·5
Bulgaria		1,296,000	500,000	+796,000	+169·2	0·1
Denmark	4,260	4,090,000	4,076,000	+14,000	+0·3	—
England	33,874	31,356,000	28,541,000	+2,816,000	+9·9	0·3
Finland		861,000	840,000	+24,000	+3·0	—
France	140,696	131,177,000	93,600,000	+37,577,000	+40·1	4·9
Germany	59,887	33,052,000	24,084,000	+8,968,000	+37·2	1·2
Greece		120,000	100,000	+20,000	+20·0	—
Holland	13,624	10,398,000	4,877,000	+5,521,000	+112·7	0·7
India: Currency Dept.	21,000	6,865,000	9,000,000	-2,135,000	-23·7	—
Do. gold standard reserve		Nil	1,200,000	-1,200,000	-100·0	—

Table (*cont.*)

	1913 £	31 December 1910 £	31 December 1900 £	Increase or decrease		Increase per cent of total gold production %
				£	%	
Ireland: banks of	4,500	4,462,000	3,798,000	+664,000	+17·5	0·1
Italy: National Bank	40,441	38,050,000	12,008,000	+26,052,000	+217·1	3·4
Do. other banks		10,308,000	4,092,000	+6,216,000	+151·6	0·8
Japan	2,657	24,192,000	6,864,000	+17,328,000	+251·1	2·3
Norway		1,997,000	1,720,000	+277,000	+16·2	0·03
Portugal		1,372,000	1,084,000	+288,000	+26·1	0·04
Roumania		4,756,000	1,592,000	+3,164,000	+197·8	0·4
Russia: State Bank and Treasury	168,255	130,476,000	75,540,000	+54,936,000	+72·7	7·2
Scotland: banks of		6,002,000	7,194,000	−1,192,000	−16·6	—
Servia		920,000	272,000	+648,000	+238·2	0·09
Spain	19,168	16,431,000	14,000,000	+2,430,000	+17·4	0·3
Sweden	5,627	4,461,000	2,076,000	+2,388,000	+113·7	0·3
Switzerland	6,817	6,224,000	4,004,000	+2,220,000	+5·5	0·3
Turkey		3,496,000	1,496,000	+1,700,000	+113·3	0·2
U. States: National Banks		29,804,000	21,512,000	+8,892,000	+41·2	1·1
Do. Treasury	258,546	233,437,000	102,038,000	+131,399,000	+128·8	17·3
Total		886,447,000	500,267,000	+386,180,000	+77·2	51·1

30 *The Statist*, 21 February 1911, p. 109. Keynes added in his own hand the figures for 1913, and a note that 'Total production of these ten years £m758'.

Above [pp. 748–9] we give a table setting out the gold holdings in the central banks of the world, and in the Treasuries which act as central banks, both at the end of 1900 and the end of 1910:—

We[31] have received from Mr C. Rozenraad a copy of his table comparing the stocks of gold and silver held by the principal banks of issue, their bank rate, the rate of exchange on London, and the price of the different government stocks of the various countries of Europe at the end of December and at the corresponding period of 1911. We append that portion of the table relating to stocks of gold and silver:—

Gold stocks of the banks

Bank of	Gold End of December		Silver End of December	
	1911 £	1912 £	1911 £	1912 £
England	32,438,162	31,300,487	—	—
Germany	36,388,000	38,832,400	14,003,900	13,019,350
France	128,257,920	127,748,600	32,165,040	26,831,080
Foreign bills	393,720	900,080	—	—
Russia	127,154,187	132,738,500	6,319,868	6,691,100
Balance abroad	15,826,597	22,556,600	—	—
Austria-Hungary	53,827,708	50,409,875	11,826,500	9,905,791
Foreign bills	2,500,000	2,500,000	—	—
Italy (three issue banks)	50,160,000	48,640,000	5,040,000	5,880,000
Foreign bills	2,922,100	2,760,000	—	—
Holland	11,690,635	13,481,100	986,984	673,485
Foreign bills	1,355,493	1,533,123	—	—
Belgium	7,563,680	8,559,800	2,403,640	3,006,880
Foreign bills	5,825,280	6,337,120	—	—
Spain	16,729,039	17,499,835	30,074,482	29,498,683
Foreign bills	5,707,859	8,175,857	—	—

[31] I.e. *The Times*, 11 January 1912, p. 13.

The U.S. holds almost as much gold as the Bank of France, the Bank of England, the Imperial Bank of Germany, the Austro-Hungarian Bank, and the Bank of Spain all added together.

The U.S., Argentina and Brazil have increased their holdings in the ten years by £190,000,000 which is 25 per cent of the world's production of the metal within the period.

(*End of 3rd Lect. Lent 1912*
4th Lect. Lent 1913
3rd Lect. Lent 1914)

Stock of gold in U.S.A.

		December 1907	£m June 1910	31 October 1912
Bullion in Texas	⎫	191	48	38
„ „ „ certificates	⎬		161	211
National Banks	⎫	132	44	
Private Banks and individuals	⎭		94	
		323	347	

Between 1895 and 1910 stock of gold increased by £m200, the *per capita* stock rising from $9.10 to $18.10.

Value of gold and its cost of production

Not much to add to what I have said in my general lectures. The relations between value and cost of production seems relatively unimportant in the case of the precious metals, because, the rate of consumption being slow, the value at any moment appears to be determined rather by the volume of the stocks in existence than by the cost of adding to the stock.

But the amount added to the stocks in any year is more or less regulated, more now than formerly, by the cost of production and the value at the moment. There is, therefore, an *equation* between present value and present cost of production.

Moreover in the long run the total volume is determined by the costs of production in the preceding years. Hence there is a sense in which it is true to say that the volume and, therefore, the value of money is governed in the long run by cost of production.

But inasmuch as at any moment the existing conditions of supply have a small effect on the value, it is misleading to say that the value at any time is determined by the cost of production *at that time*. It is true, of course, that we must nearly always add the qualification 'in the long run'; but when the long run is a *very* long run, so long that the ultimate event cannot be *foreseen*, the doctrine loses most of its importance.

If A and B react on another, if a large change arising on the side of A has a very small effect on B, whereas a large change arising on the side of B has a correspondingly large effect on A, then, though it is not strictly correct, we speak of B as being the cause of A rather than vice versa.

The following statement of Ricardo's (*High Price of Bullion*) is not, therefore, very illuminating, although, if properly interpreted, accurate:— 'Gold and silver, like other commodities, have an intrinsic value, which is not arbitrary, but is dependent on their scarcity, the quantity of labour bestowed in processing them, and the value of the capital employed in the procuring means which produce them.' [Sraffa, ed., vol. III, p. 52]

It is true that the value of money may often be determined by cost of production, in the sense that the cost of marginal production of gold tends to equal the value of gold, as in the case of other commodities. There is equilibrium between value and marginal cost. But value is not determined by cost of production in the sense that a considerable displacement of the curve of cost causes within a reasonable period a corresponding change in value.

We may put it thus: Given the demand, the value of money is determined by the supply; but a long time must elapse before the supply is much affected by changes in the cost of production.

Adam Smith :—

Of all those expensive and uncertain projects which bring bankruptcy upon the greater part of the people who engage in them, there is none, perhaps, more perfectly ruinous than the search after new [silver and] gold mines. It is, perhaps, the most disadvantageous lottery in the world, the one in which the gain of those who draw the prizes bears the least proportion to the loss of those who draw the blanks.[32]

Thus the influence of actual marginal cost is also modified by the speculative character of gold mining. On the one hand we have cases of windfalls, to which the normal theory of value does not apply. On the other hand it may be doubted whether on the average gold mining has paid—certainly in California and Australia it has not.

Under modern conditions of production, however, in S.A., as we have seen, the amount of gold annually produced does depend very sensibly on the cost of production.

Use in the arts

The amount of gold used in the arts is much greater perhaps than one would expect.

Of the amount sent to India, with which I have already dealt, it is difficult to distinguish between that part which one can properly regard as hoarded and that part which is used in the arts.

Dentists in America

Watches, watch chains, jewels, gilding, etc. etc.

Various estimates have been made of the amount. The most careful is that annually prepared by the U.S. Mint, which I quote below.

This Mint estimated an annual consumption of 140 tons from 1890 to 1900, i.e. 1,400 tons out of 3,000 produced or 40 to 46 per cent. The industrial demand is probably fairly steady and has, therefore, been consuming a decreasing proportion, as the total amount mined has increased.

De Launay estimates

Industry	40 per cent
Coinage	44
East and loss	16

[32] *The Wealth of Nations*, Bk IV, ch. vii, section 1.

Use of gold in the arts

£ million	1907	1909
U.S.	7	
G.B.	3	
France	3	
Germany	2	
India	7	
Total	22	
Other countries	5	
Grand total	27	28·5
Total production of gold	82	

The *wear* of gold is very considerable
Jevons' calculations
French experiments in 1895 found the loss on coins 1 per mille in 8 years.

Hoarding

Often difficult to distinguish from use in the arts on the one hand, and a preference for keeping monetary resources in hand rather than at a bank.

The distinction between hoarding and current monetary resources similar to that between deposit and current account at the bank.

Marshall (before Gold and Silver Commission, Question 9705):—

As the French peasants grow out of hoarding, other nations will grow into it. It is a stage, I think, through which nations pass when they become rich enough and settled enough to have gold to hoard, when their security from the taxgatherer is sufficient to enable them to save, and when they have not arrived at that extremely elaborate system which there is in England and France enabling the poor, if they wish, to buy small sums of Consols and Rentes.

Marshall (before Gold and Silver Commission, Question 9950):—

When a bank has more gold than it really wants as the basis of its currency, which, of course, the Bank of France is supposed often to have had, that gold

754

is to all intents and purposes hoarded. If gold comes out of the hoards of a country (i.e. for export) it does not act on prices at all. It seems to me that that is very important to bear in mind with regard to Indian prices.

So-called hoarding by banks will be discussed later with regard to the variation of gold reserves.

The extent to which gold is hoarded is partly dependent upon anticipations regarding its future value.

The fact that money is used, not only for the immediate purposes of exchange, but also as a store of value and for future exchange, renders its present value dependent, not only upon its *present* volume, but also upon beliefs which are held respecting its *future* volume and the future demand for it.

Marshall:—

There is, therefore, something fiduciary in the value of gold and silver; part of their value depends upon the confidence with which people generally look forward to the maintenance and extension of the monetary demand for them.[33]

The history of the French assignats and American paper, during the period of its forced currency, show that, if the credit of a currency falls, its value falls relatively to commodities, even when there is no change in its volume. (Marshall)[34]
Cf. also the attempt to introduce iron currency in China.

Hoarding in the East
Jevons (Investigations, p. 127):—

With a moderate rise (of price) the surplus of the precious metals flowed off to the East, where an immense metallic currency, an absence of any modes of economising it, and a general taste for their luxurious use, open a great sphere for their absorption and consumption. This current to the East was inevitably coincident with a low price of oriental produce.
Asia is the great reservoir and sink of the precious metals. It has saved us

---

[33] Evidence to the Committee Appointed to Inquiry into the Indian Currency, 1898, Question 11,762.
[34] A paraphrase of *ibid.*, Question 11,762.

from a commercial revolution, and taken off our hands many millions of bullion which would be worse than useless here. In the middle ages it relieved Europe of the excess of Spanish American treasure.

Pliny (A.D. 79) complained that India drew from the Roman Empire not less than 5,000,000 sesterces (£500,000) a year.

Absorption of bullion by the East

Imports of silver into India 1835 to March 1912   £m433+2½
Imports of gold into India 1835 to March 1912   £m229+25
Amount of gold mined probably about £m30+2
In 1909–11 India absorbed £m16.6 gold and £m6.3 silver
In 1910–11 India absorbed £m18.1 gold and £m5.8 silver
In five years 1906–1911 India absorbed £m65.5
Imports of silver units India during the 3 years ending 1907 (when the Gov^t was coining heavily) amounted to 71·4 per cent of total world production.
In 1907 price of silver in London rose to 32d.
1911 about 24d.
Now (Jan. 1912) rising in anticipation of I[ndian] G[overnment]'s demands.
Large speculative holdings, estimated at £m4.

Should China carry into effect measures for a large coinage of silver, there would be an improvement in the silver market. With the limited demands of U.S. and Europe for silver for coinage and use in arts, any permanent increase in the price of silver must chiefly depend upon the requirements of India and China.

Silver chiefly a bye-product of lead and copper ores—a disadvantage for it, regarded as a monetary standard, as it renders the supply really insensitive to changes of value.

(End of 5th Lect., 1913)

We have now considered the principal *data* which throw light on the determination of M—the amount of gold in monetary uses.

We will now take the other factors upon which the ultimate supply of money depends, namely:—

p   the proportion of subsidiary currency to standard currency
r   the ratio of gold reserves to subsidiary currency
k k' the rapidities of circulation

The proportion of subsidiary currency to standard currency

Dependent upon:
(1) the habits and tastes of the people
(2) the development of banking
(3) the degree of confidence felt in the subsidiary currency
(4) the strength of the motive (chiefly on the part of financiers and bankers sometimes on the part of Gov^t) to economise the use of standard currency
(1) This and (2) are in general the dominating influences, e.g. the use of the rupee in India; and the use of notes in Austria, in Brazil.
(2) The use of cheques turns partly on custom, but largely upon the spread of banking facilities, the number of bank branches and their willingness to take and manage small accounts without making charges.
General in English-speaking countries—England, Canada, Australia, U.S.A., S. Africa.
Notes, on the other hand, usual in Russia, Germany and Latin countries.
Metal in oriental countries.
I shall deal more fully with this when I come to systems of currency and systems of credit and gold reserves.
(3) If there is any lack of confidence in the subsidiary currency it is clear that the proportion may be rapidly changed in favour of the standard currency.

(*End of 4th Lecture, Lent 1912*)

(*4th Lecture, Lent 1913*)

(4) Gov^t pressure not always successful, e.g. Germany in forcing gold into circulation; India in pricing gold into circulation about 1900.

757

But by providing facilities Govts. and bankers may often slowly influence the monetary habits of a community, e.g. India now with 'universal notes'; bankers in England by offering numerous facilities to their customers free of charge.

The motive of Govts. will usually be the stabilisation of the currency; the motive of the bankers will be profit. The amount of each of the advantages thus to be obtained by increasing the proportion of subsidiary currency is thus relevant.

The proportion will also depend in some degree upon the ease with which the standard currency can be obtained—i.e. upon changes in its quantity (to be discussed later in connection with the real exceptions to the Q.T.).

Statistical investigations into proportion of cash and cheques in business transactions*

England:—

	Coin	Notes	Cheques and bills
1857 (Slater)	3%	7%	90%
1865 (Sir J. Lubbock)	6%	2·4%	97%
			(London only)

U.S.A.:—

Various investigations by Treasury previous to 1896 for National Banks, showing about 90% credit instruments.

Kinley in 1896 (1 July) elaborate estimates for 5,530 banks

	Money	Cheques
% in total deposits	7·4	92·5
wholesale deposits	4·7	95·3
repaid deposits	32·3	67·4
other deposits	4·7	95·1

* (Kemmerer, *Money and Credit Investments*, p. 100.)

Kinley concludes that '75 per cent is a fair estimate of the amount of business transactions of all kinds done with credit instruments'. Kemmerer thinks Kinley has underestimated importance of cash for wage payments and would regard 75 per cent as 'a great maximum' not (as Kinley calls it) 'a great minimum'.

The ratio of gold reserves to subsidiary currency

If the ratio is low, p is evidently very important; and conversely if p is large, the magnitude of r is very important. There are no theoretical considerations which help us to determine the proper magnitude of r. There is not, therefore, much to be said about it in a discussion of principles. I shall fill in the details later when I come to a more realistic account of systems of currency and credit. It is only necessary here to point out the importance of this factor and of variations in this factor for determining the relation of the value of money to its quantity under modern conditions.

Two important cases worth distinguishing:—
(i) when the subsidiary currency is in the form of notes
(ii) when the subsidiary currency is in the form of cheque currency.

The value of r is likely to be very different in the two cases— much greater in case (i) than in case (ii).

The rapidities of circulation

k, the rapidity of circulation of coin per annum is measured by the volumes of exchanges effected by means of it within the year defined by the number of coins in monetary use; i.e. it measures the *average* number of times each coin changes hands within the year.

We may also term it the 'efficiency of the currency'.
k', the rapidity of circulation of subsidiary money is measured in a similar manner.

In the case of credit currency we may measure its amount by the average aggregate of sums on current account at the banks (although it will often be difficult to draw the line between current and deposit accounts). This ambiguity, however, is not very important—because what we are usually interested in is

759

$k'C$—i.e. the aggregate of exchanges effected by means of credit currency—and this sum is determinate. The difficulty of separating $k'C$ into its component parts is in no way vital to the argument.

(5th Lect. 1914)

There is a somewhat different point of view from which we may also look at this factor.

The question of the rapidity of circulation is practically the same thing as the question of the proportion of their resources which people are in the habit of keeping in the form of purchasing power (whether in cash or at the bank); and is determined by the same considerations.

These are

(i) the frequency of a man's receipts in relation to the frequency of his outgoings;

(ii) distrust or unpopularity of the coinage;

(iii) banking facilities.

(i) It is clear that, if a man receives his wages on Saturday morning and pays his week's bills on Saturday night, the proportion of his income which he has *on the average* in his possession in the form of money is very small. (Fisher[35] notices effects of synchronising receipts and disbursements.) If he receives his salary quarterly and pays it out gradually in the course of the quarter, the proportion is very much greater. (Fisher—a change from monthly to weekly wage payments tends to increase the velocity.) Similarly if the unit of saving or investment is large in proportion to a man's income, the money he's accumulating in his hands and his average proportion in the form of money is great. (Fisher—*Regularity* of payment also facilitates the turnover.) The rapidity of circulation for the lower classes is, therefore, likely to be greater than for the upper:— though the habits of the latter may tend to economise money more than those of the former because they keep what they do keep in a cheap

[35] *The Purchasing Power of Money.*

subsidiary currency (banking accounts). (Fisher concludes the opposite (p. 169):— The rich have a higher rate of turnover than the poor. Statistics collected at Yale of a number of cases of individual turnover show this clearly. In other words, the man who spends much, though he needs to carry more money than the man who spends little, does not need to carry as much in proportion to his expenditure.) But none of those at Yale were wage earners. N.B. Fisher ought to mean by expenditure 'cash expenditure'.

(End of 6th Lect. 1913)

(ii) The level of prices which a given volume of currency will sustain is liable to be affected by any lack of trust and confidence in the currency itself. This influence will act through two or three agencies, but partly through increasing the rapidity of circulation,—because no one will wish to be left with the doubtful money in their possession and everyone will seek to pass it on as quickly as possible.

We see this in the case of a bad half crown. Its rapidity of circulation is probably much faster than that of a good half crown; so that in a sense the bad half crown performs the function of money the more 'efficiently' of the two.

The lower the credit of the currency, the lower will be the share of their resources which people care to keep in the form of currency. It is for this reason that a depreciated currency often raises prices *more* than in proportion to its excessive volume.

(iii) Banking facilities

Facilities for drawing out money rapidly when required, or for overdraft (thus avoiding the necessity of keeping large permanent balances for contingencies).

Influence of spread of banks in country districts.

When I go away from Cambridge and from the neighbourhood of my bank, slow circulation of my monetary resources.

The proportion of purchasing power one keeps ready in hand

closely dependent upon the speed and facility with which one can increase it *if necessary*.

Interesting statistical attempts recently made by American economists to estimate the actual rapidities of circulation and the amounts of cash which different classes actually keep in hand.

Jevons (writing in 1875)[36]:—

I have never met with any attempt to determine in any country the average rapidity of circulation, nor have I been able to think of any means whatever of approaching the investigation of the question, except in the inverse way. If we know the amount of exchanges effected, and the quantity of currency used, we might get by division the average number of times the currency is turned over; but the data, as already stated, are quite wanting.

In the case of England, the above still remains true. In the case of U.S.A. a few relevant data do seem to exist.
First attempt made by Kemmerer, who himself says:—'The data upon which it is based are so uncertain that it makes no other claim than that of being "better than nothing".'
His method is very roundabout.
On the basis of Kinley's investigation he estimates to the total cheque transactions for 1896 as $m143,000.
As already explained he thinks this represents 75% of total transactions, therefore cash transactions were $m47,700.
Circulation in 1896 exclusive of bank reserves was estimated as $m1,025; that we have 47 as the rapidity of circulation.

(*End of 5th Lecture, Lent 1912*)

Fisher's Method

Prof. I. Fisher has very recently[37] put forward an ingenious formula for *measuring* the rapidity of circulation, which is perhaps applicable in U.S. and England, though not elsewhere.
Roughly annual deposits in banks+wages = total volume of exchanges.
Refer for detail to *Stat. Journal* for September 1905 or p. 486.

[36] *Money and the Mechanism of Exchange*, ch. XXVI, p. 336.
[37] *The Purchasing Power of Money*, 1911.

For America in 1896	thousand million dollars
Money deposited in banks	11
Wage earners	$4\frac{1}{2}$
Other non depositors	$1\frac{1}{2}$ (say)
	17
Other small allowances	1

The amount of money circulating estimated at 974,000,000 which gives a velocity of about 18 times a year, i.e. money was held on the average about 20 days (Guesses in the past have varied from 4 to 150 times a year).

Fisher's experiments with Yale students

Two series of experiments:—
1st each student asked to estimate roughly his annual cash expenditure and average cash on hand.
Estimates from 128—
  average cash expenditure £100
  quotient 34
2nd 113 kept accurate accounts for one month
  average cash expenditure £150
  quotient 66
In this class 'the richer men averaged about three times as great an expenditure as the poorer, but carried only 50% more cash on hand'. 'This law of increasing velocity with increasing expenditure agrees with the general fact that the larger the scale of any business operation, the greater the economy.'
My own case velocity about 34 I should guess.
What is yours?
  Difficulties of calculation. Does one for instance, draw money out and pay bills in cash at the end of term?

The rapidity of turnover of bank deposits has been estimated by M. des Essars in 1895 (Kemmerer, p. 186)

B. of France	about	120
B. of Germany		160
B. of Belgium		130

According to Fisher the corresponding velocity for U.S.A. has increased between 1896 and 1909 from 36 to 54.

Summary

We have seen, therefore, a strong tendency for increased demand for purchasing power due to the growth of population, wealth, and the division of labour and to the process of adversation (we may take the transition from a silver standard to a gold standard under this head). The ultimate source of the supply of this purchasing power is gold. But the volume of purchasing power in the form of currency, which our unit of gold will support is not constant. It depends upon what stage of banking and monetary development has been reached.

We might put this shortly by saying that the supply of purchasing power depends upon banking and gold jointly. Good banking can affect the value of money

1st by increasing use of credit
2nd by decreasing proportion of necessary reserve
3rd by decreasing hoarding
4th by increasing rapidity of circulation

The influences at work may be represented diagrammatically.

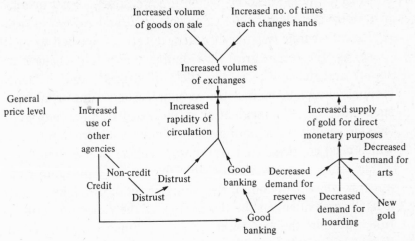

(*End of 6th Lecture, Lent 1912*)

(*End of 6th Lecture, 1914*)

Inductive verification

I have said something about this in my elementary lectures.
Two methods
(i) to study some period when the items most difficult to calculate can be safely assumed constant;
(ii) to make independent estimates of each item involved in the equation of exchange.

The first method

has been employed both for and against the Q.T. The inductive verifications of the adherents of the theory have been, I think, nearly as fallacious as those of its opponents.

Let us take the latter first.

Practical men are inclined to attribute a rise of prices to an expansion of trade (whereas, of course, according to the Q.T. precisely the opposite ought to occur) and it is easy for them to show that the two are in fact constantly associated.

This tendency was noted by Cairnes[38] at the time of the dis-

---

[38] See *Essays in Political Economy, Theoretical and Applied* (1873), ch. II.

cussions on these questions which followed the gold discoveries in California and Australia. The enhanced scale of wages and prices at that time was not disputed, but it was referred to such causes as 'the recent great development of trade', 'changes in supply and demand', or 'the effect of strikes'; and the facts seeming in each given instance to be traceable to one or more of such influences, the incident of an increased abundance of gold (was) regarded as something superfluous and irrelevant, and which need not be taken account of in seeking their explanation.

The same thing was noticeable during the bimetallic controversy which arose out of the falling prices of the eighties; and it has been evident in the discussions of the rupee question in India. Within the last three years the Financial Member of Viceroy's Council was able to assert that the rising prices were unrelated to the increasing volume of currency. But to show that an advance of prices is connected, for instance, with a development of trade, is not to prove that it is *not* due to increased supplies of gold. 'An increased supply of money does not, and cannot, act upon prices, or upon the value of the metal. Comparing it, in any other way than by being made the instrument of trade, by affecting demand and supply, or by furnishing employers with the means and the motives for advancing the wages of their workmen.' (Cairnes)

The fallacy is due

1st to ignoring the expansion of credit to which the rise of prices in such cases is in fact usually due

2nd to measuring 'an expansion of trade' by the expansion of money prices, in which case so far from being the cause of rising prices it is the same thing.

The adherents of the theory have attempted statistical verification either by taking examples from the history of inconvertible currencies, or by examining the history of gold prices and gold production during the past century.

Neither of these methods is really satisfactory, for the following reasons:—

Examples of inconvertible currencies (e.g. China, the French Assignats, the American Greenbacks, the suspension of cash payments in England) are not satisfactory because the depreciation generally tends to be a good deal more than in proportion to the increase of volume,—because of a change in the element of 'trust of the currency' since this factor has not remained constant, the conditions necessary for a valid verification are not present.

(End of 7th Lect. 1913)

In the case of the history of gold prices, to which defenders of the Q.T. usually refer with confidence, factors other than gold production have changed and fluctuated so hugely and so notoriously that the use of any apparent close coincidence between the level of prices and gold production in support of the Q.T. is a gross example of a *post hoc, ergo propter hoc* argument. Since other factors have *not* remained constant, the theory would only lead us to anticipate coincidence between prices and gold production if the other factors happened to balance one another; and one cannot easily prove this without assuming the theory itself.

I have quoted the example of inconvertible currencies and the history of prices in my elementary lectures for what they are worth.

Principles of Money III

(1. What are the principal difficulties involved in an attempt to make a numerical comparison between the general purchasing power of money at two periods as remote from one another as the middle of the 16th century and the beginning of the 20th? If you had to make as good a practical approximation as possible, how would you set about it?)

2. Write a memorandum for the Board of Trade setting forth the main principles by which they should be guided in the construction of index numbers of prices.

3. What precisely do you understand by 'a stable standard of value'?

Why is stability in this sense held to be desirable?

(Upon what grounds is it maintained that stability would be increased by the introduction of international bimetallism?)

4. The rise of prices during the last ten years is sometimes given as a part explanation of the fall of consols. Discuss fully, both from the theoretical and practical points of view, the validity of this explanation.

(1) Effect of rise of prices in divorcing nominal from real rate of interest

(2) Effect of rise on saving of those who invest in debentures

(3) Effect in making those who invest in deb. require a higher rate of interest

Principles of Money IV

1. In comparing the advantages, as Chancellor of the Exchequer, of issuing £10m consols or £10m Exchequer Bonds, by what considerations would you be chiefly guided?

See Lehfeldt p. 26[39]

2. Which is the more profitable to *bankers*—a period of rising prices or a period of falling prices?

	Cash	16	Deposits	100
	Money at call	$14\frac{1}{4}$		
	Investments	$18\frac{3}{4}$		
(1/5+4/5)	Discounts and advances	$58\frac{3}{4}$		
	Premises	$2\frac{1}{4}$		
		110		

3. If you were appointed as a Commissioner to investigate the rise of prices in India, what are the principal facts which you would seek to ascertain?

[39] R. A. Lenfeldt, 'Public Loans and the Modern Theory of Interest', *The Economic Journal*, March 1912.

4. Would it be a wise policy on the part of the British Govt. to buy up the South African gold mines and close them down?

One recent and ingenious attempt to use this method (Professor Cassel's) deserves a reference:—

Hooker—'The course of Prices at Home and Abroad 1890–1910', *Stat. Journ.* Dec. 1911, pp. 23–4.

The measurement of changes in the stock of the currency used as a standard of value presents very serious difficulties, especially when the increase of credit is also considered. But an exceedingly ingenious method has been evolved by Mr G. Cassel in the *Ekonomisk Tidskrift*,* and the results at which he arrives are so suggestive that I propose to utilise them here. Mr Cassel's method, which seems to me perfectly sound, is to take two periods during which prices generally were as nearly as possible at the same level. It is then assumed that whatever changes have taken place in the quantity of currency available for use in exchange have been just sufficient to cover any increase or decrease in the volume of commerce during the period. Mr Cassel thus takes the two periods about 1850 and 1900, when prices were on a similar level, and computes the expansion of monetary stocks of gold, including reserves, during the interval. This gives a 'norm' for the quantity of gold required annually to keep prices at the same level, after providing for the increase of trade, of credit, &c.

Although I am not quite prepared to accept the exact numerical result yielded on Mr Cassel's basis, the general direction of the curves at different periods is sufficiently shown by his method to make the accompanying diagram (VII)† very convincing as to the general trend of events since 1850. The similarity of the movements of prices and stocks of monetary gold between 1850–70 and 1870–95 will also not escape attention.

---

* *Om förändringar i den allmänna prisnivån,* by G. Cassel. *Ekonomisk Tidskrift* (Stockholm), 1904, pp. 312–31.

† A reproduction of Mr Cassel's so far as regards the line of stocks of gold between 1850 and 1900, and continued to 1910. Mr Sauerbeck's index-number is reduced to the 1890–99 standard; and the base line of Mr Cassel's curve has been raised so that it corresponds approximately to the ordinate of 115.

Estimated monetary stocks of gold (smooth curve, Cassel) and index numbers of prices (Sauerbeck).

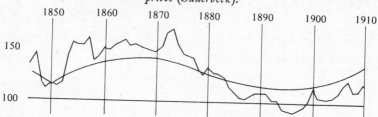

The figures from which Mr Cassel constructs his curve are, so far as the critical point of the available stocks of gold in 1850 and 1900 is concerned, as follows:—

For 1850 a stock of 500,000,000*l.* is assumed, for which figure Lexis' article in the *Handwörterbuch der Staatswissenschaften* is cited.

For 1900 a stock of 1,850,000,000*l.* is assumed, reference being made to a table in Helfferich's *Das Geld*, page 90.

These figures show an expansion at the rate of 2·65 per cent per annum; or, approximately, 30 per cent per decade. By 1910, therefore, the 'normal' requirements of the world would have expanded by nearly 555,000,000*l.*; while the estimated output of gold in the decade has exceeded this by fully 220,000,000*l.* The supplies needed to meet requirements at a steady price-level would be about 2,400,000,000*l.*, and the actual supplies about 9 per cent in excess of that figure.

In this last calculation, it will be noticed that the 2·65 per cent yearly has been treated as including provision for industrial and artistic uses. Mr Cassel quotes Lexis as estimating 2 per cent of the existing stock of gold to be required annually to meet the losses of this nature; but the fact that he allows for 1,350,000,000*l.* expansion of stocks in the half century, while the Director of the United States Mint gives tables showing only about 1,400,000,000*l.* as the total output of gold in that period, seems to show that the question of losses has been involved in some confusion.

As a matter of fact, a loss of 2 per cent yearly would leave the accumulated stocks at about 1,100,000,000*l.* in 1900, showing a growth of 1·57 per cent per annum on the average of the half century. At this rate the 'normal' requirements of 1910 would be about 1,275,000,000*l.*, while the actual supplies, allowing for the 2 per cent loss each year, would be about 1,600,000,000*l.*, or 25 per cent in excess of the 'normal' requirements.

It is probable that normal requirements have not increased at the same rate throughout, and that the losses have not represented a uniform percentage of available stocks, and may not, at any rate for a part of the time, have reached 2 per cent. The selected base years, 1850 and 1900, are, moreover, not the best possible, as the conditions of trade were very different; in especial, trade prosperity was producing its maximum effect in 1900.

The fundamental objection to this method is, of course, that it assumes that the other factors have changed uniformly throughout the period, an assumption for which there is very little foundation. Indeed Cassel's own diagram if it is examined in detail is sufficient to refute it.

It takes no explicit account, for instance, of the fact that at the beginning of the period England was almost alone in having a gold currency, whereas at the end of the period a gold standard was almost universal.

However the investigation and Hooker's continuation up to 1910 is not uninteresting.

One further criticism:

Having calculated PT and $MV+M'V'$ in this way, he brings them to equality for the year 1909 by multiplying PT by $\frac{399}{155}$. This is perfectly legitimate; since PT and $MV+M'V'$ are indexes, not absolute quantities.

He then works out a table of the ratio of PT to $MV+M'V'$ as calculated from 1896 to 1909.

If the verification were exact, this ratio would be unity in each case. In point of fact PT varies from 24 per cent in excess downwards.

Fisher now makes a further adjustment, through which he reduces the apparent error by about half, which seems to me to be entirely illegitimate.

It will be remembered that $T = \Sigma p_0 Q \qquad P = \Sigma pQ \div \Sigma p_0 Q$ where p_0 is the price in the base year 1909.

Thus P and T are each individually dependent upon the particular base chosen; but the product PT for any year is an absolute amount independent of the base year.

(*End of 7th Lecture, Lent 1912*)

771

Fisher, remembering that P is relative to the base year, but forgetting that T is also relative to it and PT independent of it, thinks he can adjust P to another base without T; i.e. he thinks he can alter P by any percentage he likes leaving T unchanged. He finds that if he reduces all the numbers for P by 11 per cent his final result comes out most satisfactorily. And he proceeds to do this.

I do not think, therefore, that this method of verification has yet been applied successfully.

The course of prices

There have been in last hundred years three principal crises in the history of currency; and the main developments of monetary theory have been in connection with these.

1st The Bullionist Controversy.

Suspension of cash payments by Bank of England 1796—the bank being *restrained* from paying in cash, though willing to. (Ricardo held that this was unnecessary.) No serious depreciation until 1809, which was the year of Ricardo's *High Price of Bullion*.

(7th Lect. 1914)

1810 Report of Bullion Committee, the doctrines of the Report being nearly those of R. (cash payments in 2 years).

War of pamphlets. Bullionists beaten in the House.

1811 Lord Stanhope's Act making it an offence to deal in guineas for notes above their nominal value.

1819 Bill on Bullionist lines.

1820–1821 Cash payments and Lord Liverpool's reform of the currency (Thornton, Tooke, McCulloch).

2nd The Californian and Australian discoveries gave rise to the second grant discussion amongst economists and even the public—Chevalier, Cairnes, Jevons.

3rd The demonetisation of silver in the Latin Union and Germany, combined with diminished production of gold, gave rise to the bimetallic controversy.

Very voluminous literature.

Marshall's evidence before G. and S. Commission of 1888.

McLeod, Taussig, Nicholson, Foxwell.

Indian controversy.

(End of 8th, Lent 1913)

We may possibly be on the brink of a fourth grand discussion. The recent rise of prices has caused discontent and embarrassed governments in many parts of the world. Several are at the moment conducting investigations into the recent rise in the cost of living; and a project of an International Commission of Enquiry has been launched.

Let us, therefore, consider briefly the future of gold prices. We have seen that the very greatly increased annual output of gold dates from the end of the Boer War when the South Africans were in a position to exploit their resources to the utmost. It is important to remember that, in spite of this huge output, prices are not yet high, if we have regard to long-period movements. For 1911 Sauerbeck's index number is 80. In the last 40 years it has been as high as 111 and as low as 61. At the present moment, therefore, we stand about midway between the limits of price known to this generation; and not more than half of the long fall from 1873 to 1896 has been recovered so far. Sauerbeck's index number has registered 80 in the years 1848, 1852, 1884, 1907, 1911. In 1900 the index number stood at 75, so that the immense gold output since that time has only raised it 5 points. The experience of the last 11 years should be sufficient to show that the volume of gold output is not always the dominating influence on prices.

The influence of this output has probably been neutralised by a variety of causes. It was needed, first of all, to counteract the tremendous fall of prices that must have occurred in its absence

773

on account of the enormous industrial and trade expansion of the last 15 years. The growth of wealth and the need of purchasing power to deal with it has probably increased at an unexampled rate and it has not been accompanied to the same extent as the growth of the '70's and '80's was by a corresponding development of banking and means of economising the use of money.

But it has also been neutralised by the number of new countries which have during this period adopted a gold standard —Russia, India, Brazil, Argentina.

We have already seen that these four countries took £m165 between 1900 and 1910 out of £m558 available.

Another potent cause has been the extravagant banking system of U.S.A. which has taken £m140.

Thus leaving only £m150 or £m15 a year to meet the increased needs, arising out of increased trade apart from higher prices, of the rest of the world.

Thus the greater part of the increased output since 1900 has been absorbed by exceptional sources of demand; and the great effect it must otherwise have had on prices has been neutralised.

But if we consider the future—what further exceptional sources of demand can we discover?

Let us suppose that the stock of gold now in monetary uses amounts to £m1,500—it does not [seem] likely that it can exceed this. It seems likely in the immediate future that the annual output will be about £m100, of which about £m70 will be available for monetary purposes.

If, therefore, the progress of banking about counterbalanced the increase of business, and there were no exceptional sources of demand, prices would rise by about $4\frac{1}{2}\%$ annually (though at a decreasing rate if the output were constant).

774

End of	Volume of currency	Index number		
1911	1500	100		80
1912	1570	104·7		
1913	1640	109·3		
1914	1710	114		
1915	1780	118·7		
1916	1850	123·3		
1917	1920	128		
1918	1990	132·7		
1919	2060	137·3	100	109·8
1920	2130	142	103·5	113·6

Thus even on these hypotheses Sauerbeck's index would not reach the level of 1873 until 1920.

And against this we have to set the following considerations:—
(i) There are sure to be some exceptional sources of demand
(ii) It is doubtful whether or not credit banking can increase fast enough to counteract the growth of business
(iii) Much gold mining is now on a narrow margin and an increase of prices by 10 per cent or 15 per cent might appreciably diminish the output.

With regard to (i)
China might possibly come on a gold basis—though there seems little immediate prospect of it.

Chile might adopt the Argentine and Brazilian system and require £m20 or £m30.

Turkey may require a good deal more gold.

With regard to (ii)
a great deal depends upon banking reform in U.S.A. where the demand for gold of late years has been enormous. There seems to be an immediate prospect of some improvement but not of any great improvement.

With regard to (iii)
it is possible, of course, that new and fertile gold mines may still remain to be discovered.

(*End of 8th Lecture, Lent 1912*)

We can, therefore, scarcely prophesy.

But it is just worthwhile to guess.

Apart from credit booms it seems likely that the annual rise of prices during the next few years can hardly be less than 2 or 3 per cent. Credit booms and depressions are likely, of course, to make the upward movement irregular.

I should anticipate, therefore, a prolonged period of dear money and a further fall of securities yielding a fixed money income.

Means through which money affects prices

The proof of the Quantity Theory has given us general grounds for supposing that an increased volume of currency tends to raise prices, but it supplies no indication of the actual steps by means of which this effect is produced.

A rise of prices always *appears* to be due to 'conditions of trade' and in the case of every article taken by itself a rise in its price is always due to an increase in the demand for it or to a decrease in the supply of it, as its proximate cause.

This then is the chief reason why some bankers and many businessmen have always been inclined to doubt the connection of the level of prices with the volume of money—because they cannot perceive through what channels the influence of the one upon the other is exerted.

To fill in this part of the argument is, therefore, essential for its completion. The only economist who, so far as I know, has made any attempt to do so is Professor Marshall. His theory of it, moreover, has only been published insofar as it appears in his evidence before the G. and S. Commission of 1888 and the Indian Currency Committee of 1898. It is not, therefore, so widely known as it should be, and you will find scarcely any allusion to it in works on the theory of money. It is a great misfortune that Prof. Marshall has never published his theory in a full and complete form. What I shall have to say is entirely derived from him, either from his printed evidence, to which I refer you, or in conversation.

The theory differs in detail according to the stage of economic organisation which exists in the countries to which it is to be applied.

I shall consider four typical cases
(1) Europe in the 17th century
(2) England 30 years ago
(3) England at the present day
(4) India at the present day.

I will consider, first and in detail, England at the present day and will then deal more briefly with the others.

At the present time new gold finds its way almost at once, in the manner which I have already described, into the vaults of the Bank of England. This, as is well known, at once increases the willingness of the Bank of England and of other banks to lend. Even if it is insufficient to lower the Bank rate at once, the knowledge of it increases the probability of the official rate's being lowered in the future, and so has an immediate influence on the market rate.

This increased willingness to lend enables people to increase their speculation with borrowed capital. And thus gives a fillip, though perhaps a very slight one, to trade, and hastens or renders more probable its revival.

Nevertheless the effect of more accumulations of gold at the state banks does not, at the present time, if it is unaided by any other agency, produce a very great or a very immediate influence of this kind.

This is not, perhaps, true of the B. of E. Gold cannot long accumulate there without exerting an influence. But other banks respond much more lethargically to the influence of such accumulation. The B. of F., for instance, deliberately aims above everything at a *steady* bank rate, rarely falling below and rarely exceeding 3 per cent. New gold, therefore, has a great tendency to accumulate in its vaults, for a time at any rate, in the form of what is practically a hoard and affects prices very slightly. This seems to have been happening during the last year or two. But the B. of F.'s gold, not yet in active circulation, is probably only biding its time.

Other state banks, Germany and Russia for instance, are always willing to strengthen their gold position when they can do it cheaply; and take the opportunity to fill up their hoards when gold is plentiful.

New gold does not, therefore, necessarily lower the Bank rate to the full extent which its quantity would justify at *once*. It bides its time. It bides its time until a plentiful harvest or some other of the rather mysterious agents which influence the cyclical fluctuations of trade sets on foot an expansion of commerce and industry. Then the influence of the Bank's hoards is fully felt. Directors who were unwilling to lower their rates are now unwilling to raise them, and the fact of the hoards prevents the new movement from being checked in its infancy by a too rapid rise of the rates of discount.

New gold, therefore, although it may not exert an immediate influence and may wait until other causes have *started* an expansion of trade, assists these causes, accelerates the revival of trade, reduces the period between the old boom and the new one, and eventually serves to keep the bank rate lower than it would have been in the absence of increased gold production.

We can now proceed to the next step in the argument. New gold, we have seen, helps to bring on or prevents the retardation of a boom in trade. It raises, therefore, the demand for the more speculative kinds of commodities, and so raises their prices. So far, however, there is no *general* rise of prices, and the commodities, which by being the first subject of speculative buying and selling rise first, are at the present time in England chiefly the raw materials of industry such as coal and iron. Ease of borrowing stimulates those expansions of industrial instruments and railways which chiefly require these commodities.

The increased demand for coal and iron rapidly raises wages in those industries and increases the number of men employed. *At the present time this is probably the principal channel through which the new gold is diffused through the community.*

The increased purchasing power of the working classes stimulates the demand for a greater variety of goods, and there is a tendency to rise on the part of all prices—some sooner, some later.

A tendency of most prices to rise is thus brought into existence. Ultimately this would have the effect of adding to the volume of the currency required for circulation; because prices having risen, a person who had found it answers his purpose to have on the average £17 in currency in his pocket, would now require £18 or £19; and so on for others. Except insofar as the methods of business change, a rise of prices requires people to use more currency for retail transactions (Marshall). In the new state of affairs, therefore, more coin is required partly for the conduct of retail transactions and partly for the payment of wages.

Furthermore the money value of the credit required to carry on a given volume of business increases when prices rise, so that bankers find it necessary to increase the amount of their cash reserve, held in case of panic and liquidation, when a sudden distrust of the credit instruments may lead to a widespread desire to replace them by coin.

(8th Lect. 1914)

Thus the new gold, by making bankers more willing to lend, results in an outflow into the country of some part of the new money. This causes some reaction and diminishes the willingness of lenders to lend, until a fresh equilibrium has been reached, the new money being divided into two portions, one for the basis of new credit, the other for the pockets of the people.

(9th Lect. 1912)

We have already noticed that not all commodities will be affected equally by an increase in the quantity of money; some will rise *sooner* than others. The first effect of an increase in the monetary stock is felt by those commodities whose prices are most sensitive to changes in the money market. (Conant) Some commodities will not feel the effect until long subsequently.

This makes it necessary to differentiate between the case of England at the present time and England 20 years ago or India. In all three cases the first influence of new money is felt I believe, through the greater willingness of lenders to lend. But after this stage of the argument the resemblance between the different cases becomes less.

Formerly in England the favourite subjects of speculation were not so much intermediate utilities, such as coal and iron, as articles of immediate consumption, such as wheat and coffee. When this was the case, the principal cause of the diffusion of the new gold through the community was not so much the increase of wages, as the greater amount of cash required for retail purposes, arising out of the direct effect of speculative activity on the prices of consumable commodities.

The order of events in India at the present day is of a complexity which would require more detailed knowledge than I possess for its unravelling. But I should suspect that a good deal of speculation is stimulated in directly consumable articles. Such commodities as jute and cotton receive, no doubt, their share of speculative attention. But speculation in food grains is probably a much more important factor in the situation than it is in England at the present day. The relative ease in the money market stimulates the natural tendency of Indian grain dealers to hold up and speculate for the rise.

The effect in India of new currency on the prices of many important articles of direct consumption is, therefore, unexpectedly rapid.

Suppose the new money, instead of going immediately, as it now does, from the bullion market to the Bank of England, was brought—for instance—in the pockets of travellers in small driblets,—this would make very little difference to the order of events. If through such a means there was more gold in circulation than people wanted to do that part of their business which they prefer to do with currency, they would simply send it to their banks, whence it would quickly find its way, as before, to the reserve of the Bank of England.

But when, as in the 17th century, no banking system is in existence to make this process possible, the course of the argument must be considerably modified. The progress of events is at once much simpler and much slower. Those who possess the gold must, if they do not hoard it, increase their purchases. As there is no reason, so long as prices have not risen, why other people should diminish theirs, there is, on the whole, an increased demand. The increased demand will raise the prices of those articles for which it exists. Those who have obtained no share of the new gold will then have to diminish their purchases; and we shall have eventually the same volume of purchases as before at a higher level of price. But this process may move slowly from commodity to commodity, and very slowly from district to district. I have heard Prof. Marshall say that the higher level of prices caused by the new bullion from S. America did not move from the European receiver of the new supply at the rate of more than 30 or 40 miles a year.

(9th Lect. 1914)

This primitive manner by which new money raises prices is probably partly operative in India at the present time, as well as the modern manner.

Where gold is newly discovered also, as in Australia or California during the '50's, we have interesting examples of the direct action of new currency on prices.
(Mention Cairnes, and enlarge slightly on this point)

The main outline of the argument is now complete. The following questions and answers from Prof. Marshall's evidence before the G. and S. Commission sum up the explanation of

the optical delusion, regarding the theory of money, by which
businessmen are sometimes deceived:—

Then do you think that the increase of gold acts in this way, that it rather
strengthens the influences which are at work to raise the prices of particular
commodities, and that, on the other hand, a reduced supply of gold rather
strengthens the influences which are at work to reduce prices?—Yes.[40]
So that, in the long run, although only trade influences appear to affect
prices, really the reduced or increased supply of gold tends to bring about
a lower or higher average level of prices?—Yes.[41]

In conclusion two possible misunderstandings must be
guarded against:—

First it must be noticed that the new money begins by increasing the demand for commodities; but there is afterwards a
reaction; and there is no reason for supposing that in the long
run it affects the total demand—though of course the money
value of the commodities is permanently increased, and the
money value of the volume of credit outstanding.

This involves the question of the general effect on trade and
social wellbeing of an appreciating or depreciating currency—of
which I shall treat with detail in a future lecture.

New gold and the rate of discount

It has been shown that, in the first instance, new money acts
by lowering the rate of discount. We might perhaps draw from
this the conclusion that a low rate of discount and rising prices
generally occur together.

This is not, however, the case. Although a new supply of
money causes for the moment a lowering of the rate of discount,
its supply exercises no permanent influence over the rate. The
average rate of discount permanently is determined by the
profitableness of business. All that the influx of gold does is to
make a wave on the surface which temporarily disturbs the
equilibrium.

[40] Question 9977—Marshall's answer was 'That is my opinion'.
[41] Question 9978.

When fresh money comes into the market it temporarily increases the resources of those whose professional business it is to lend, at the expense of others, and so for a time increases the facility with which loans can be obtained.

(End of 9th Lect. Lent 1913)

There is also a side issue. The *belief* that prices are going to rise, stimulates speculation, and raises the rate of discount.

M[arshall]:—

When the gold comes to the country it is known and people expect that prices will rise. Now if a person doubting whether to borrow for speculative purposes has reason to believe that prices will rise, he is willing to take a loan at 3 per cent, which before he would not have taken at 2½ per cent, and consequently the influx of gold into the country, by making people believe that prices will rise, increases the demand for capital and *raises*, therefore, in my opinion, the rate of discount.[42]

The right way to put this is:—

New gold raises prices by making borrowers more eager or willing to borrow. It does this for one of two reasons:—

(1) by lowering the rate of discount below the normal

or

(2) by raising an expectation of higher prices in the future more than in proportion to any momentary *rise* in the rate of discount which may take place.

Here follow

III Methods of measuring the value of money (Index Numbers)

IV Consequences of fluctuations in the value of money.

This completes the first term's lectures.

[42] Evidence to the Royal Commission on the values of Gold and Silver, Question 9981.

Chapter 6

EDITOR AND REFEREE

Keynes's editorship of *The Economic Journal* between 1911 and 1945 naturally brought him into discussions with most of the leading economists of his generation. We have already printed some of the resulting correspondence in other volumes, most notably XIV and XXIX.

Until the 1930s, Keynes's editorial files for the *Journal* are remarkably sparse. In the years before 1919, this reflects the fact that he did not have regular secretarial assistance, so only the in-letters survive. After 1920 there may have been some weeding to keep them down, but it is also clear from the correspondence with Bertil Ohlin reprinted in volume XI (pp. 462–4) that Keynes still conducted part of his *Journal* correspondence in longhand.

From the 1920s, however, much of both sides of the correspondence on one article survives, that from Frank Ramsey's 'A Mathematical Theory of Saving' which Keynes published in the issue for December 1928.

From F. P. RAMSEY, *28 June* [*1928*]

Dear Maynard,

Here is an article which I hope you will think suitable for *The Economic Journal*.

The mathematics is all very elementary, and the beginning part is fully explained for the sake of those who will read a little way.

Although the matter is terribly oversimplified, the equations must arise in any attempt to apply utilitarianism to saving and so far as I know they've never been treated before. The difficulty is to find simple results of sufficient generality to be interesting and yet not obvious. In this I think I've succeeded surprisingly well. To prove them is never hard, except when it comes to taxation which is very complicated and in which I've wasted a lot of time with only one achievement of any sort.

Of course the whole thing is a waste of time as I'm mainly occupied on a book on logic, from which this distracts me so that I'm glad to have it done. But it's much easier to concentrate on than philosophy and the difficulties that arise rather obsess me.

Yours ever,
FRANK RAMSEY

1. There seem to me to be two further assumptions implicit in this argument, namely (i) That the community will be always governed by the same motives in accumulation at all relevant future dates, so that there is no chance of accumulations being egotistically consumed by a subsequent generation; and (ii) That no misfortunes occur to sweep away accumulations at any point within the relevant future. I have no doubt that you would accept these assumptions. But it is important to make them explicit, because it is the fear or the probability that they will not be fulfilled which in fact makes it rational to save at a slower rate than your formula would indicate. We all know the incredible effect of compound interest over three or four hundred years. If the proceeds of one Spanish galleon seized by Drake had been invested abroad at 5 per cent compound interest, the value at the present day would be many times that of the whole of our actual foreign investments. Of course, this point could be dealt with by assuming that the true rate of interest over a long period is something immensely lower than 5 per cent. But I am sure that one of the reasons why in practice we are not influenced to set more money aside by reflecting on the magical consequences of compound interest over a long period is to be found in the fact that we do not rely on the accumulation continuing uninterruptedly. And indeed we are justified, on the basis of past experience, in expecting that something would happen to interrupt it.

2. Subject to these additional assumptions, your conclusion in Section I seems to me to be correct. But can it not be proved much more briefly, and indeed without any mathematics at all, as follows:—

Assuming compound interest to operate continuously at a positive finite rate, a sacrifice at any time of a finite amount, however small, will reach in time to any finite sum, however large. If, therefore, we assume the uninterrupted operation of compound interest and treat all points in time equally, it is worth while at any time to make a sacrifice equal to the maximum advantage which can be obtained at any future time. Now the sacrifice at any time involved in saving a given sum is equal to the amount saved multiplied by the marginal utility of money at that time; whilst the maximum subsequent gain is equal to the amount by which the present total net rate of enjoyment of utility falls short of the maximum possible rate of enjoyment. From which your result follows.

3. A small point on page 9. I think it needs more explanation why in your numerical example the marginal utility is measured by $\frac{5}{300}$.

4. Coming now to your Section II, in which you admit the possibility of future utilities being discounted. The defect of this section seems to me to be that you assume[1] [   ] to be independent of the time. That is to say, if [   ] is the rate of discounting next year, then [   ] is the rate of discounting n, n years hence. But of course this is not so. It is a characteristic of the actual discounting at future dates that the discounting is at a faster and faster rate as the time in question becomes more remote, so that [   ]

5. I have not yet had time to get quite to the bottom of your sections on the effect of taxation. How much would they be affected if you were to admit that [   ] is a function of the time. For this being a practical problem, it is essential that the assumptions should be in reasonable accordance with the facts.

Subject to that, one preliminary point occurs to me. Are you assuming that the proceeds of taxation which are 'exhausted' and not 'transferred' furnish the community with no utility. At first reading you seem to be assuming this. But is this correct? As I understand the distinction, revenue is exhausted when the actual expenditure is incurred by the government, as in the case

---

[1] Keynes's workings were on the top copy, but he did not transfer them to his carbon. The top copy has not survived.

of building a warship, and that it is transferred when the government merely act as a channel for taking the money from one tax-payer and handing it out to be spent by another, as in the case of old age pensions. I am not clear how the distinction between an expenditure which is made by an individual and an expenditure which is made socially differ from one another in a way relevant to your argument.

From F. P. RAMSEY, *Tuesday* [*3 or 10 July, 1928*]

Dear Maynard,

It is very kind of you to ask us on Thursday 19th we shall be delighted to come there, and will let you know the train later.[2] Thank you for taking such a lot of trouble over my article. I am a little handicapped in dealing with them by having no copy and having rather forgotten some of the details. Here, however, is what I think about your criticisms; don't bother to answer this but if you think worthwhile send my article back and I'll make some alterations according to what I now say.

Yours ever,

FRANK RAMSEY

From F. P. RAMSEY [*July 1928*]

(1) The extra assumptions you mention are, of course, presupposed and should be put in; thank you for seeing them.

(2) The argument that my first result is obvious is, I think, just a muddle; and when you think what it means you can see endless objections to it; e.g. you say it is worthwhile at any time to make a sacrifice equal to the maximum advantage which can be obtained at any future time. Against this one can say at once

(a) Why might not the maximum advantage be obtained with a less than equal sacrifice?

(b) It is essential to the rule that the sacrifice should be measured by marginal and the advantage by total utility; if both were measured in the same way we should get an absurdity.

(c) My present sacrifice is not the whole cause of my future advantage at one moment and cannot be equated to it.

and so on ad. inf. the whole conception being just a muddle.

(3) The argument that we ought to save even more is a similar muddle; but this is so natural that I ought I think to say something about it in my

---

[2] The Ramseys came to stay at Tilton on 19 July, 1928.

article to begin with. By sacrificing a penny now I can obtain bliss someday, yes, but all this proves is that I must obtain bliss someday, and it does not tell me how quickly I ought to obtain it, e.g. if it's worth sacrificing (1) now to obtain bliss sooner. If bliss is a finite amount this is a genuine quantitative problem.

Marshall saw this point right, but I haven't the reference.

(4) I don't see at all clearly that we discount that future at an *increasing* rate; I should have thought if anything at a *decreasing*, at any rate in the far future. Remember it is *compound* discount. Suppose we took utility 100 years hence as $\frac{1}{2}$ what it is now, i.e. about 15 per cent per annum discount. Then   200 years hence would be   1/4 present
300 years hence would be   1/8   „
1000 years hence would be   1/1024   „
1100 years hence would be   1/2048   „
Surely you don't want the rate accelerated as we go on; what happens in 1000 years' time isn't more than twice as important as what happens in 1100 years' time.

Really the rate is large to begin with, e.g. next week is distinctly less important than this say 1 per cent, i.e. 1 per cent per week = 50 per cent *p.a.* and then falls until our own death becomes probable, when it is enormous for a bit then falls again until our children's death where there is a large rise and a subsequent fall to *zero* (600 years hence = 500 years hence).
N.B. p is not your $Q(t)$ which is present value. (Present value at constant rate of discount $p = e^{-pt}$ and in general $p = -Q'(t)/Q(t)$

(5) The differential equations can easily be modified, much as you suggest, to let p be variable; in fact simply put in the $p = -Q'(t)/Q(t)$, where $Q(t)$ is present value. But then they have no intelligible solution, they can be solved formally but not in a way that conveys anything, and I've aimed at leaving out such matter of purely manipulative interest.

Graph of $Q(t)$ and $p(t)$

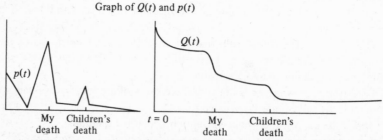

| | My death | Children's death | $t=0$ | My death | Children's death |

(6) With regard to taxation I don't remember exactly what I said, but the argument that exemption of savings causes no sacrifice when work is fixed and all taxation transferred, would still hold for a variable rate of discount.

(7) The distinction between transferred and exhausted revenue for my purpose is this.

Transferred revenue is itself subject to tax, and whether it is saved or spent depends on the tax system, just like any other income; this is not true of exhausted revenue.

Exhausted revenue is not really taken to have no utility, although its utility is left out of account. It is supposed to have a separate utility which could be just added to the utility of private consumption. The government may be supposed to need certain funds for parks, warships, etc. which it takes from the public and gives no option to the public as to whether they are saved or spent. The government saves or spends them as it thinks fit borrowing or lending in the market provided it doesn't have an indefinitely increasing debt, and from a definite revenue discounted to present value at the rate of *interest* not at the rate of discount of future utility. If you think, you will see this is right as it can borrow and lend at the rate of interest supposed constant. It gets, we suppose, a definite utility. The question is by what 'announcement formula' it shall raise that revenue from the public in order to diminish as little as possible the utility of private consumption.

But I see I ought to have explained this properly.

F.P.R.

From F. P. RAMSEY [*postmarked 12 July 1928*]

Yes your proof is quite right, sorry I ought to have seen it; stupid of me; if you send my manuscript back I will try to alter it. Your proof corresponds to changing the indep[enden]t. variable from time to capital which is anyhow simpler in the first case (no discount and infinite time) but not in the others.

F.P.R.

The second set of letters concerns Michal Kalecki's 'A Theory of Commodity, Income and Capital Taxation' which eventually appeared in *The Economic Journal* for September 1937.

From M. KALECKI, *4 February 1937*

Dear Mr Keynes,

I beg to send you enclosed my paper 'The commodity tax, income tax and capital tax in the light of the Keynesian theory' and to ask whether it might be published in *The Economic Journal*.

Yours sincerely,

M. KALECKI

P.S. I tried to do my best as concerns the English but the curve of my 'marginal productivity' in this 'production' is steeply falling.

To M. KALECKI, *16 February 1937*

Dear Kalecki,

I am happy to accept the enclosed, which I find very interesting, for *The Economic Journal*. The English is not bad, and the corrections required mainly affect the order of the words. The argument would be easier for an English reader to follow if the sentences were somewhat rearranged into our more habitual order. Could you, do you think, pass the article on to some English friend and get him to dictate from it in a more flowing order.

There is only one small suggestion I have to make in the text. I think it would be advisable, in the first part, to make quite explicit your assumption that the consumption of the capitalists is entirely directed to goods other than wage goods. It is clear to a careful reader that you are assuming this, but since the assumption is a very unrealistic one, it is desirable to make it clearly.

I have been conscious for some time of the relevance of the theory you refer to to the choice between income tax and a capital tax, but I had not myself worked out the conclusions as rigorously as you have done.

I return the article herewith for revision. You are too late for the March *Journal* and in plenty of time for the June one.

Yours sincerely,
[copy initialled] J.M.K.

From M. KALECKI, *20 March 1937*

Dear Mr Keynes,

I beg to send you the revised version of my paper. The style was corrected by one of my friends according to your kind advice. I also acted on your suggestion to state explicitly that the capitalists consume only goods other than wage goods in putting the footnote on page 4. I consider there besides the probable effect of this assumption's not being fulfilled.

I enclose the reprint of my paper 'A Theory of the Business Cycle'[3] and I should like very much if possible to hear your opinion on it.

Yours sincerely
M. KALECKI

P.S. I use the opportunity to thank you for the reprint of your article 'The General Theory of Employment'.[4]

My address after April 1st is: c/o The Rockefeller Foundation, 20 rue de la Baume, Paris 8e.

To M. KALECKI, *30 March 1937*

Dear Kalecki,

Thank you for the revised version of your article, which I now find quite clearly written.

I have, to begin with, one or two passing criticisms, mainly the following:—

1. There is something wrong at the bottom of page 2. It looks like a misprint in the last complete sentence.

2. I am not clear that the top of page 5 is quite satisfactory. If the capitalists assume that their income subject to tax will remain the same, the effect of the tax will surely be to reduce their spending. It is only if they have read your article and are convinced by it that their profit will rise by the amount of the tax that they will maintain their spending as before.

3. You are, I think, assuming throughout that there is a surplus of the factors of production. If this is so, it should perhaps be emphasised. Modifications might be required as soon as any type of labour or type of equipment is in short supply.

I have, however, one more fundamental point which I should like you to think over. Reading your article again, it appears to me that your assumption to the effect that the consumption of

---

[3] *Review of Economic Studies*, February 1937.
[4] *Quarterly Journal of Economics*, February 1937 (*JMK*, vol. XIV, pp. 109–23).

capitalists is entirely directed to goods other than wage goods goes a good deal further than you have admitted in the footnote at the bottom of page 4. Does not your argument require that the factors of production required to produce capitalists' consumption-goods shall be totally distinct from the factors of production required to produce wage goods, no substitution of any kind being possible between the two. If so, this is, of course, a hopelessly unrealistic assumption. It may be that capitalists live in quite different sorts of houses from workers. But this does not prove that they do not both use bricks and mortar and the services of plumbers and painters. And there is the obvious case of raw materials.

If this is right, you are obviously in a very strange world. For example, if you are assuming that every factor of production is in surplus supply and that there is no possible substitution between the factors relevant to capitalists' consumption and the factors relevant to workers' consumption, it follows that, however much the capitalists consume, their incomes will rise correspondingly. I am well aware that there is an element of truth in this paradox applied to the real world. But your conclusions purport to be applicable to affairs and, if I am not mistaken, you ought to make more emphatic the peculiarities of the assumptions.

Now my impression is that your assumption about the consumption of capitalists, whilst technically convenient for the particular method of exposition you have adopted, is not really required to establish your main conclusions about the effect of various taxes on output. It is required, on the other hand, to establish your conclusions as to the effect of the taxes on the distribution of real income between capitalists and workers. The latter, however, is a matter in which you are only secondarily interested. Will you think this over? My impression is that your conclusions as to the effect of taxes on output could be established without such special assumptions. I am inclined to think that the very pretty technique which you use in the section on short-period equilibrium in your article in the *Review of Economic Studies* would serve your purpose.

You ask me what I think of the above-mentioned article. The first two sections I like very much. But I am not convinced by the section on 'The Inducement to Invest', particularly pages 84 and 85.

In the second complete paragraph on page 84 you seem to be assuming not merely that the current rise of prices will have a disproportionate effect on expectations as to future prices, but that future prices will be expected to rise in exactly the same proportion. Surely this is an extravagant over-emphasis of the effect of the immediate situation on long-term expectations? It appears to me that it is only if future prices are expected to rise *in the same proportion* as present prices that you have established the result that 'equilibrium is not reached and the investment continues to rise'.

In the same way on page 85 you point out that the current increase of wealth does something to diminish the marginal risk. But to establish your conclusion you appear to be making some quantitative assumption that the effect will be just of the right degree, which appears to be unjustified. I might mention, in passing, that the risk relating to prospective profit is already allowed for in my formula for the marginal efficiency of capital.

In general, therefore, I do not feel that you have sufficiently established the conclusion italicised at the bottom of page 85.

Yours sincerely,
[copy initialled] J.M.K.

From M. KALECKI, *4 April 1937*

Dear Mr Keynes,

Thank you very much for yours of March 30. I am very sorry for the bad misprint at the bottom of page 2 which I have now corrected.

Much more difficult is the question of my assumption about the behaviour of capitalists following immediately the introduction of income tax (top of page 5). I do not think they must necessarily read my article in order not to curtail at once their expenditure on consumption and investment. The matter is treated at first on page 3 in connection with commodity tax. After the introduction of new tax the entrepreneurs even if they expect their incomes to fall *cannot* immediately reduce their investment because it is the result of previous investment decisions which require a certain time to be completed. Thus their savings remain unaltered in the first period of new taxation régime. Their consumption remains also unaltered, if their propensity to consume is not changed. This latter *is* of course an additional assumption for the expectation of future fall of income can influence the present propensity to consume. I think however that the capitalists' consumption is rather insensitive to *expectation*: and that it is only the *actual* fall of their income which can compel them—and this also often only with a time lag—to reduce their standard of living. (I have now added a footnote on this matter.)

I think that this assumption is essential not only for the problems of taxation, but for the whole of *The General Theory*. If for instance the rise of money wages caused the capitalists to reduce immediately their consumption in expectation of future fall of profits, the result would be rather in accordance with the classical theory. Of course my analysis of taxation problems also must be fundamentally changed if I reject the assumption of insensitiveness of capitalists' consumption to expectations of changes in income. The income taxation for instance is then unlikely to raise employment.

I wonder whether it is necessary to emphasise the existence of a surplus of the factors of production. I do not need this assumption at all for the case of commodity tax. For the case of income tax (and capital tax) I think I have paid due attention to this problem in discussing the influence of the elasticity of supply of wage goods (at the bottom of page 6).

I come now to your last question concerning the assumption about capitalists consuming only goods other than wage goods. I fully agree that this assumption is unrealistic. (As concerns however the problem of connection between prices of wage goods and prices of goods subject to capitalists' consumption through the channel of common raw materials it does not arise if the commodity tax is levied on *finished* wage goods. For as I have shown in the paper the output of these goods is unaffected by such taxation and thus the prices of raw materials remain unaltered.) Therefore I have not only stated in the footnote on page 4 this assumption explicitly but also tried to show what corrections are needed if this special assumption is *dropped*. (I have now altered a little this footnote.)

I think however that [on the] whole this problem is not so important in reality. The commodity taxes are usually levied not on all wage goods but only on some articles e.g. sugar, cigarettes, matches and so on. The effect of

794

such taxes will be similar to the effect of those examined in the paper. The capitalists' consumption of these goods—being a small part of total consumption of them—does not interfere much with the process examined. (I have made a corresponding addition to the footnote on page 4.)

May I yet make some remarks on your criticism on my paper in the *Review*? I think that my statement in the second complete paragraph on page 84 you refer to is independent of *how much* expectations improve under the influence of the present rise of prices. I state in this paragraph only that the increase of prices of investment goods which equates the marginal efficiency based on the *initial* state of expectations to the rate of interest, does not create an 'equilibrium'; for at the same time expectations improve to some extent and thus investment increases further. I do not deny that this increase may be convergent and then the point A in the Fig, 3 corresponding to this 'equilibrium' may be reached without increase of the rate of interest (see the bottom of the page 88); whilst if the reaction of the entrepreneurs to 'the present state of affairs' is strong enough full employment will be reached and then the rise of the rate of interest would perform the task of stopping 'inflation' and create the 'equilibrium' represented by point A.

In any case however the process of reaching this equilibrium will be in general spread over many τ periods. Thus it is interesting to know what determines the rate of investment decisions *during* this process. I sought of solving this problem by introducing the 'principle' of increasing risk and this enabled me to describe the course of reaching point A (Fig. 6).

I think however that the reference to increasing risk (or something like that) is necessary also for adequate explanation of various positions of 'equilibrium' (positions in which the rate of investment has no tendency to change). For the facts show the prices of new investment goods are relatively rigid. It follows from the statistics of Mr Kuznets about gross capital formation that the prices of new investment goods have fallen in U.S.A. between 1929 and 1932 only by 15 per cent. Thus it is clear that the gap between prospective rate of profit and the rate of interest was much lower in the depression than in the prosperity. But then some thing besides the prices of investment goods is required for the formation of 'equilibrium'.

You question also my explanation of why it is the *rate* of investment decisions which is dependent on the gap between prospective rate of profit and the rate of interest. If in first τ period all capitalists have decided to invest, say, £1.000.000.000 the savings of second τ period will be £1.000.000.000 too. Thus precisely this amount can be freely reinvested in the second τ period—if the gap between prospective rate of profit is the same as in the first τ period—because the investment of *new accumulated capital* does not increase the risk. (The existence of pure rentiers creates some complication but does not affect the argument; if the relation of the net indebtedness of an entrepreneur to his wealth is δ and his saving during a given period s—he can invest without increasing risk the amount $s(1+\delta)$. The sum of this amounts is $\Sigma s(1+\delta) = \Sigma s + \Sigma \delta s$ where Σs is the total saving of entrepreneurs and $\Sigma \delta s$ is the total saving of 'pure' rentiers, or the sum of amounts to be invested without increasing the risk is the total saving S.)

I am very sorry for troubling you with this long discussion.

Yours sincerely,

M. KALECKI

My address is: c/o The Rockefeller Foundation, 20 rue de la Baume, Paris 8e.

To M. KALECKI, *12 April 1937*

Dear Kalecki,

I have your letter of April 4th. We have now got to the point where I must distinguish between what I am entitled to say to you as editor, and any remarks I am moved to make as a private critic.

From the former point of view, the only essential is that you should state your assumptions quite fully and clearly. In the light of your letter, they seem to be the following:—

1. It is assumed that within the period in view the volume of investment is unalterable.

2. It is assumed that the consumption of capitalists is insensitive to their expectations as to their future income.

3. It is assumed that there is a surplus of all factors of production.

4. It is assumed that the consumption of capitalists is directed to entirely different articles of consumption from those of workers.

5. In some parts of the argument, but not in all, it is assumed that no substitution is possible between factors of production and raw materials which produce for capitalists and those which produce for workers. I am not sure whether it has to be assumed that factors and raw materials which are used for investment goods cannot be used for consumption goods.

These points ought to be made quite clear and emphatic in the manuscript.

As a private critic I add the following, though please take no notice of this.

1. I regard the assumption that investment is fixed as unplausible. Firstly, because it ignores the possibility of fluctuation in stocks. Secondly, because it ignores the possibility of altering the pace at which existing investment decisions are carried out, and thirdly, because at best it can be overcome after a time lag, which may be very short indeed.

2. I think it unplausible to suppose that capitalists' consumption is insensitive to their expectations, for the latter are affected by a change in the taxes on their incomes.

3. Much more important than the above, with all these assumptions you can prove something much more drastic and general than you have put down, from which your particular conclusions can be easily derived. But, of course, these more drastic conclusions would not look very plausible if applied to real life.

4. Whilst some of your conclusions may require these assumptions, I do not believe that your main conclusions do require them. The assumptions are mainly brought in to facilitate the exposition. But as long as they are there, they are there; and very much impair the generality of the argument.

5. I hope you are not right in thinking that my *General Theory* depends on an assumption that the immediate reaction of a capitalist is of a particular kind. I tried to deal with this on page 271, where I assume that the immediate reaction of capitalists is the most unfavourable to my conclusion. I regard behaviour as arrived at by trial and error, and no theory can be regarded as sound which depends on the *initial* reaction being of a particular kind. One must assume that the initial reaction may be anything in the world, but that the process of trial and error will eventually arrive at the conclusion which one is predicting.

One word about pages 4 and 5 of your letter. On page 4 your argument seems to me a version of Achilles and the tortoise, and you are telling me at the bottom of the page that even though Achilles does catch the tortoise up, it will only be after many periods have passed by. At the bottom of page 5 I feel that you are making too much of a discontinuity between your periods. I quite agree, however, that the amount of unexecuted decisions which the entrepreneurs are ready, so to speak, to have at risk, is an important element in holding up the pace of investment and cannot be neglected. It is only the precision of your conclusion which I was criticising.

Meanwhile I return the article in the hope that you will preface it with a catalogue of your assumptions. For it is not fair to the reader that he should be forced to disentangle them for himself and then wonder whether or not you really are making them.

Yours sincerely,
[copy initialled] J.M.K.

The third set of letters concerns two publications of Colin Clark's—his 'The Determination of the Multiplier from National Income Statistics', *The Economic Journal*, September 1938; and, with J. G. Crawford, *The National Income of Australia* (Sydney, 1938).

From COLIN CLARK, *1 February 1938*

Dear Maynard,

All the news that has reached Australia has been that you are progressing slowly but favourably and I take it that by the time this reaches you, you will be alright.

At the moment I'm paying a short visit to New Zealand $\frac{3}{4}$ politics and $\frac{1}{4}$ scenery and the latter at any rate is magnificent. At this far end of South Island there is a huge granite mountain range running down to the ocean, cut up into great fiords and lakes. Norway and Switzerland look tame beside 6000 feet rising sheer out of the fiords.

Incidentally tourism here is a nationalised industry. Hotels, ships, tracks, buses and tourist agencies are all Govt. run, and they have recently taken over most of the remaining private services (except this hotel which is a little island of private enterprise). It works very well. The conservation of natural beauties is obviously only safe in public hands and it is clearly unjust for the Govt. to conserve the amenities and construct the roads and then leave the profits of tourism to private enterprise; and there are great advantages in a centralised travel service. You get full choice of routes and stopping places. This goes for England too, I think. After the retail distribution of necessaries, the next most advantageous field of public enterprise should be the establishment of national parks for areas of particular natural beauty or historic interest, and a publicly run tourist service.

I am having an excellent time in Australia where economics ranks next after cricket as a topic of public interest. In collaboration with Crawford of the Rural Bank in Sydney I have been preparing a booklet on national income statistics in Australia, a copy of which will be posted to you as soon as it is off the press. The part which will interest you most however is a verification of the multiplier over the period 1928–1936: the verification is very close. But while you and Kahn dealt with an *employment* multiplier, this is a *money income* multiplier.

Australia being anything but a closed economy, changes in imports and exports must be allowed for. We decided to treat changes in export income as exactly on all forms with changes in gross investment. Imports generally follow changes in national income with a 'marginal propensity to import' of 0·25; when however they move otherwise than in accordance with this linear relation, such 'excess imports' are regarded as a further factor tending to depress national income.

Kahn allowed for 'saving on the dole' as an ingredient of the multiplier. We have included Govt. deficits with investment.

The result is that we get four determinants of money income:

> Gross investment
> Exports
> Govt. deficit (or negative if surplus)
> Excess imports (negative)

Marginal propensity to import being ·25, and to save ·23, we get a multiplier of 2·1, and the sum of changes in the above form determinants, multiplied by 2·1, gives almost exactly the changes in national income.

I have been keeping up with the British national income figures through the medium of Richard Stone (who incidentally has been searching the world's literature for data bearing on Marg. Prop. to Cons. and has got an interesting collection). The difficulty in England arises from the great time lags in the spending habits of our rentiers (who maintained their 1929 level of expenditure till 1931, and their slump level of expenditure till 1935). But I have been trying to overcome this by multiple correlation analysis and think I have got the situation fairly determinate.

Do you think there would be room in the June *Economic Journal* for an analysis of developments of national income during the past year?

My address till August will be University of Western Australia. If you airmail me in reply it will reach me by mid to end March, and I will airmail the article about 19 April to reach you on 1st May.

I am reaching the conclusion that I want to stay in Australia. People have minds which are not closed to new truths, as the minds of so many Englishmen are: and with all the mistakes Australia has made in the past, I still think that she may show the world, in economics, politics, education, and technology, in the next twenty years.

Yours,
COLIN

To COLIN CLARK, *5 March 1938*

My dear Colin,

I have much enjoyed getting your interesting letter to February 1st. I should certainly like to have the article you suggest for the June *Journal*. I assume you will be prepared to do without seeing a proof. But, even so, I hope you will do your best to let me have the article not later than the date you mention.

I can see that there is something to be said for your new conception of a money-income multiplier. But I shall have to see your text before I am quite sure what difficulties or assumptions are raised. You are assuming, I imagine, that price changes in the 'four determinants of money-income' give a sufficiently satisfactory index to price changes in money-income taken as a whole. And I see no reason why this should not be a fairly satisfactory approximation. But are you assuming that the marginal propensities to import and to save are constant for your nine-year period? If so, this would arouse my suspicions.

I am rather dismayed with the last paragraph in your letter, though not taken entirely by surprise. Don't make too quick a decision. Come back here in the first instance anyhow. You will be able to get back to Australia at any subsequent moment you may choose. The problem of doing anything here might be more difficult—indeed it is—but it may be more important. It is very necessary to lay the foundations for a proper department of statistical realistic economics[5] at Cambridge. If such plans are met with discouragement, then it would be difficult to dissuade you from going away. But I do hope you will come back and test the possibilities of satisfactory work here.

Yours ever,
[copy initialled] J.M.K.

From COLIN CLARK, *28 March 1938*

Dear Maynard

Thank you for your letter. I will make sure that the stuff reaches you by May 1st.

News seems to have reached England that the Queensland Government have appointed me Director of their Bureau of Industry and State Statistician. So far as Cambridge is concerned I am very sorry. Having in mind considerations similar to those urged in your letter, relating to the statistical work which could and should be done at Cambridge, I had already refused an £1100 a year professorship at Adelaide. But when Queensland made their offer I thought it was too remarkable an opportunity to be missed for putting economics into practice. My job is to advise the Premier on practically everything connected with economic matters, to plan the public works programmes, and to manage the state statistical office. Queensland has the highest standard of living of the six Australian states, has considerable undeveloped natural resources, has had Labour governments for years, a remarkably able and intelligent politician at the head of it in Mr Forgan-Smith, and complete freedom of legislation, having abolished its Upper Chamber. I believe you yourself would have thought twice before rejecting an opportunity like that for putting some of your conclusions into practice.

Enclosed are extracts from a booklet which I am publishing in Australia on national income and related questions, the extracts relating to the multiplier. I think you will agree that a 'money income multiplier' works very well. My treatment does not involve any assumption that prices in the

[5] This refers to plans to found what became the Department of Applied Economics.

'determinants' are the same as prices in national income as a whole, and in fact they often move differently. The essence of my idea is that a given rise in exports or investment will generate a given rise in money national income as a whole, comprising (as in Australia in 1933–5) an increased output of consumption goods at stable prices, or (as in Aust. from 1935–7) higher prices for a virtually unchanged output of consumption goods. In other words, I can sail my multiplier much further into the wind of full employment than you can yours.

Would you show this to Joan, Kahn and Harrod if you think they would be interested, and also to Stone (416 Fulham Road, London S.W. 6).

I feel rather paternal about the present depression. Is it true that the British Government's economic advisers told them the peak of the boom would come in 1938, and that they were planning to hold an election then?

Yours,
COLIN

On receiving Clark's article, Keynes commented to Austin Robinson, his assistant editor for *The Economic Journal*.

From a letter to E.A.G. ROBINSON, *4 May 1938*

3. I have just received an extremely interesting article from Colin Clark,—the one he promised. But I hesitate to print this without giving him any opportunity for revision in proof. As so often happens with his stuff, it seems to me full of mistakes, obscurities and misapprehensions, some of them by no means vital, but in the aggregate very tiresome to the reader, and I should like to send him my criticisms, for what they are worth, which would be prevented if we were to put this into June.

Before replying to Clark, Keynes also consulted Richard Kahn on the history of the multiplier doctrine. He then commented on both the article and the booklet.

To COLIN CLARK, *31 May 1938*

My dear Colin,

I received with the greatest interest your two communications —the extract from the Australian booklet and the article for the

Journal. As regards the former, I am sending it on to the people you mention. The latter reached me just too late for the June *Journal* which I had had to fill up, being uncertain just when your article would arrive. It has, however, gone to the printer with a view to the September *Journal*. I am instructing the printer to send you out one proof by air mail, which ought to give plenty of time for corrections.

I am anxious that there should be time for corrections because I have a good many points on the article which I should like you to consider in proof. I have written these out at length on the enclosed paper. A portion of them really only affects your Australian booklet. But there is so much popular confusion about what the multiplier means that I do not want it to be added to any further by there being an unnecessary appearance of you and me being at cross purposes about it. It seems to me there are passages in the early part of the article which may encourage what seem to me to be existing misunderstandings about the formulation of the doctrine.

I have also added a few words about its history, which were stimulated by what you say in the extract from the booklet.

I imagine that a certain amount of British statistics are reaching you promptly, and it may be that apart from the points I want you to consider in the proof you will be able to bring certain matters a bit up to date. The most disturbing feature in the situation at the moment, as I see it, is that commodity prices seem to have come completely unstuck. The weekly index number fell last week by 5 per cent, which must be almost a record for a week's movement, isn't it?

My health being a bit better, I have come up here [Cambridge] for a fortnight, and was given the opportunity of seeing Giblin[6] who is still in residence.

Yours ever,
[copy initialled] J. M. K.

---

[6] L. F. Giblin, Ritchie Professor of Economics, University of Melbourne, 803 Australia; in 1938 he was Supernumerary Fellow of King's College, Cambridge.

Comments on *Journal* article
(and incidentally extracts from Australian booklet)

Page 1, 1. When there is an unforeseen change of conditions the propensity to consume temporarily departs from its normal value and there is a time lag before it resumes it. Investment also does not adjust itself to the revised expectation instantaneously. It is *not* that there is a time lag in the operation of the multiplier theory. What happens is that the parameters on which the multiplier theory operates temporarily depart from what their values would be if all had been foreseen.

Page 2. The phenomena of hoarding surely have to do with changes in liquidity preference and not with a definition of income. Here again it is not a change of income as such, but an *unexpected* change which is relevant. If income changes unexpectedly there is a temporary disturbance in liquidity preference. This applies equally whether it is actual current income or the expectation of prospective income which has changed.

In short an unforeseen change in the situation leads to temporarily anomalous values of propensity to consume, rate of investment and liquidity preference; and there is a time lag before these anomalies cure themselves. Indeed this is obvious. How long these anomalous values persist is, as you point out, a matter for enquiry, and is a matter of practical importance for forecasting; but it does not really affect the central theory.

Page 3. It seems to me that there is here a serious confusion (as also in the Australian booklet) between Kahn's employment multiplier and my investment multiplier. You are mistakenly attributing the former to me. Your money income multiplier is substantially identical to my investment multiplier except that yours is in terms of money and mine of wage units. I see no advantage and on the contrary much disadvantage in using a money measurement. It saves very little trouble, and the marginal propensity to consume is likely to be much more stable in terms of real income than of money income whenever prices and wages are suffering significant changes in terms of money.

Page 4. Are you not overlooking the fact that my analysis is adapted to an open system by reason of the fact that the favourable trade balance constitutes a part of investment. In this way foreign trade enters indirectly into my main formulation. Indeed in the case of Great Britain you treat foreign trade just as I have. It remains true, of course, that changes in the terms of trade may lead to correlated changes in the propensity to consume, and indeed the other parameters.

This does not mean that I object to your separating out foreign trade in the way you do, which I agree has advantages—it only means that I have not neglected it. And if it is true—e.g. in Australia—that the marginal propensity to import is often stable your technique is instructive.

Similarly Government deficits are regarded by me as part of investment.

Money income multiplier

I like your analysis of the multiplier into several factors. But I can see no possible advantage in your calculating in terms of money undeflated by wages or prices. As I have said above, there is surely a *greater* presumption of stability of marginal propensity to consume or to import in terms of wage units or composite commodity units than in terms of money. In fact your Australian figures do not work out at all well on the assumption of a stable marginal propensity to consume in terms of money; though I cannot say whether the correspondence would look better if you were to deflate money by reference to wage units.

It is of course true that if the marginal propensity to consume is a constant and equal to the average propensity to consume, then it would be just as satisfactory to assume a stable marginal propensity in terms of money income as in terms of real income. But in so far as different classes spend different proportions of their incomes, and particularly in so far as the same person spends a different proportion on the margin than on the average, your assumption is wrong. Now surely we are pretty certain that the average propensity to consume and the marginal propensity to consume at various levels of income are *not* equal. Thus you are introducing a possible serious source of error without, so far as I can see, gaining any advantages.

History of the multiplier doctrine

One must distinguish here between some sort of formal statement such as was given in Kahn's *Economic Journal*[7] article and the general notion of there being such a thing as secondary employment.

If one is to include unpublished memoranda then it must be remembered that the original draft of Kahn's theory was contained in a memorandum which he wrote (as you will remember) for the Economic Advisory Council in the late summer of 1930. He tells me that he thinks there was something analogous published by the Berlin Institut für Konjuncturforschung some time in the same year.

The general notion of secondary employment, however, must go back much further. For example, it is clearly explained in *Can Lloyd George do it?*[8] by Hubert Henderson and myself, where we used the argument that because of secondary employment the aggregate saving on the dole would pay half the capital cost of public works. Joan adds that an early reference to the idea of secondary employment is to be found in a report of the Cunliffe Committee who gave the correct explanation of the effect on prices of a high Bank rate.

And in one passage have you not forgotten your own earliest treatments of the subject (page 99 of the extract from the booklet —middle paragraph)? Your *National Income and Outlay* contained a whole chapter on the multiplier, where you anticipated the practical application of it long before your present contribution.

[7] 'The Relation of Home Investment to Unemployment', *The Economic Journal*, June 1931.
[8] *JMK*, vol. IX, pp. 111–12.

Kahn adds a point as perhaps explaining why you think that your money income multiplier is quite different from my investment multiplier. There are two quite distinct senses of the multiplier that are constantly confused. There is, first of all, the multiplier you use in forecasting the effect of a public works programme (or of a tariff) making due allowance for consequential changes of imports etc.; and in the second place there is the multiplier you use in correlating *total* investment (home and foreign) with income. The second kind of multiplier is worked out for an open system exactly as for a closed system, and is greater than the multiplier in the first sense. And it is the second kind of multiplier that statisticians like you are employing whether you are dealing with Australia or any other country. Of course, however, the difference between this and the other kind of multiplier is greater the more open the system.

J. M. K.

From COLIN CLARK, *16 July 1938*

Dear Maynard,

I have been able to bring some of my conclusions up to date though I thought it better not to put emendations into the tables at this stage.

British Government public finance seems to be designed, taking all circumstances into account, to reduce the national income as rapidly as possible, and at the end, you notice, I reach a very gloomy conclusion. A lot depends on the behaviour of imports and exports. A really overwhelming movement of the terms of trade in Great Britain's favour, accompanied by a quantitative restriction of imports, might mitigate the slump in Great Britain. But that would only make things far worse for us primary producers.

Yours truly,
COLIN CLARK

At the top of his next letter to Clark, Keynes wrote: 'He forecast employment in first quarter of 1939 at 1,200,000 below first quarter of 1938.'

To COLIN CLARK, *10 August 1938*

Dear Colin,

Your proofs reached me in good time, and the article will appear in the September *Journal*. But there were two passages which troubled me a good deal, about which I should have pressed you strongly to make a change if you had been on the spot. It was for that reason that I sent you a cable. Having had no reply, I have assumed the necessary discretion. I hope very much that I have not gone against your considered wishes. But at any rate the changes are only negative.

The first point relates to the deletion of the passage on the first slip, which I enclose herewith.[9] I had not made it as clear as I should have done in my previous letter that this is surely a misunderstanding of the position, and I was most anxious not to get into a controversy with you about it or darken counsel by one more variant interpretation. There is enough muddle about the multiplier already. The point is that the theory of the multiplier leaves plenty of room for time lags; what doesn't allow for time lags is the theory of the multiplier based on the assumption of a constant propensity to consume. But that is your doctrine, not mine. I, as you know, always protest against assuming that the propensity to consume is constant. The multiplier is by definition an instantaneous phenomenon which has nothing to do with time lags one way or the other. But the theory of the multiplier provides for time lags in the propensity to consume which, when there is a sudden and unexpected disturbance, departs from its normal value and only resumes that value after an appropriate time lag. It is, of course, all only a matter of definition. But in my treatment I pack all the time lag business into fluctuations in the propensity to consume and am enabled in that way to get a perfectly clear and logical definition of the multiplier itself.

The second point relates to the new passage at the end which you supplied in MS, making a forecast of prospective unemployment. This seemed to me to be extremely dangerous, since it was based, I thought, on statistical information about the position here which is not up to date. The main point relates to the increase in the government deficit financed by loans. You assume that this might be £12,000,000 per quarter in excess of

[9] The galley proof, which has not survived.

last year. But this estimate made me suppose that you were not aware that the whole of the supplementary estimates are to be financed by loans and that these are likely to be substantial. My own guess would be that the increase will be more like £25,000,000 per quarter.[10] Nor is this altogether guess work. For the first four months of the financial year the increase in the deficit has worked out, I think, slightly higher than that, and it is, of course, the first part of the financial year which will be relevant to your forecasts. Now the difference between £25,000,000 and £12,000,000 is pretty significant, and would make a big difference to your result. That there is a possibility of some deterioration I do not at all dispute, but your quantitative calculation of it really did seem to be based on misapprehension. There were also other minor points where the latest figures might have slightly modified your views. So what I did was to soften that paragraph and leave out certain specific figures without altering more than I could help of its general tendency and complexion. I hope you will not feel when you see it that I misrepresented you.

Yours ever,
[copy not initialled or signed]

From a letter from COLIN CLARK, *19 August 1938*

I have much pleasure in enclosing the text of our book on *Australian National Income* which has been at the printers since January.

You will see that we have reprinted some of your notes on pp. 92–3.[11]

The question of whether the multiplier is applicable to real or to money incomes is obviously of basic importance and I will try out a series of tests, both on the Australian and other statistics, to see which gives the better

[10] In the margin of the copy Keynes noted 'at rate of £m35 for first quarter and a half'.

[11] The extracts from Keynes's note of 30 May, which Clark had re-arranged and edited ran as follows in the book:—

'In correspondence with Mr Clark, Mr J. M. Keynes has written:

"It seems to me that there is a serious confusion between Kahn's employment multiplier and my investment multiplier. You are mistakenly attributing the former to me. Your money income multiplier is substantially identical to my investment multiplier except that yours is in terms of money and mine of wage units.

'I can see no possible advantage in your calculation in terms of money undeflated by wages or prices. There is surely a greater presumption of stability of marginal propensity

fit. I take it that real consumable income rather than employment is the factor determining consumption and savings in your analysis. This distinction is of great importance in a country like Australia, which is subject to violent changes in the terms of trade. Employment in wool production in Australia is practically the same as it was two years ago, and 'real income produced' remains the same; but both money incomes and 'real income consumable' of wool producers have fallen heavily.

In November 1938, Charles Madge, a founder of Mass Observation with Tom Harrisson, began a series of enquiries into working class patterns of saving and spending. In April 1939, after reading Keynes's articles on 'Crisis Finance' in *The Times* (*JMK*, vol. XXI, pp. 509–18), Madge had written to Keynes on the effects of the crisis on working class savings (*ibid.*, pp. 519–22).

There matters rested until after the outbreak of war and the publication of Keynes's pamphlet *How to Pay for the War* (*JMK*, vol. IX, pp. 367–439). The correspondence that followed spawned several articles for *The Economic Journal* and also played a role in the formulation of the 1941 Budget (*JMK*, vol. XXII, pp. 215, 255, 274–6, 335).

From CHARLES MADGE, *17 March 1940*

Dear Mr Keynes

I'm sending you a short memo[12] on a piece of research that seems to me to be urgently necessary. As there set out, the assumption is made that the Government goes on relying on voluntary saving. But the problems it would investigate would still be important if your plan for deferred payment were adopted because, as you point out, it would still be necessary to keep the voluntary savings system going as well.

Questions just sent out to M.O.'s part-time observers include: 'If it is true that your war-time consumption must be cut by a third, would you prefer it to be cut (a) by more rationing (b) by more taxes (c) by higher prices (d) by

to consume or to import in terms of wage units or composite commodity units than in terms of money. In fact the Australian figures do not work out at all well on the assumption of a stable marginal propensity to consume in terms of money; though I cannot say whether the correspondence would look better if you were to deflate money by reference to wage units.

I like your analysis of the multiplier into several factors.

Separating our foreign trade in the way that you do, I agree, has advantages—I have not neglected it. And if it is true, e.g. in Australia, that the marginal propensity to import is often stable your technique is instructive.

Similarly government deficits are regarded by me as part of investment."'

For Keynes's original wording, see above pp. 802 and 803.

[12] Entitled 'Civilian Consumption and War Savings'. Not printed.

Mr Keynes's scheme (described in the article above), (e) by some other method? Give your reasons.'
Even with Trades Union approval, your plan is going to need careful 'putting over' for the mass of people. I would be intensely interested to discuss with you this side of the problem, if you can find time.

Yours sincerely
CHARLES MADGE

Madge met Keynes on 21 March before following up his visit with a further letter.

From CHARLES MADGE, *26 March 1940*

Dear Mr Keynes,

Here as promised is a memo for the National Institute.[13] I am sending two copies. If you think fuller information is needed please let me know.

I need hardly say how immensely grateful I am for this very timely help. We have reached a stage where it is pretty urgent to get some subsidy if the organisation is to survive. It would make all the difference if you could possibly advance us the £50 which you so kindly volunteered. We are most eager to get on with the job and your encouragement is the best thing that could have happened.

Yours sincerely,
CHARLES MADGE

To CHARLES MADGE, *28 March 1940*

Dear Madge,

Thanks for your memorandum, which will serve my purpose. I am sending it on to Geoffrey Crowther, who is now in charge of the National Institute, with my blessing and approval. I am suggesting to him that your enquiry should be considered by the National Institute as a suitable object of support.

Meanwhile, I enclose an advance of £50 for you to get on with.

Yours sincerely,
[copy initialled] J. M. K.

[13] For a research project entitled 'Spending and Saving in Wartime'.

Keynes's letters to Geoffrey Crowther ran as follows.

To GEOFFREY CROWTHER, *28 March 1940*

My dear Crowther,

You probably know by name at least the two lads who have been making themselves responsible for what they call Mass Observation—Tom Harrisson and Charles Madge. In my opinion they are live wires, amongst the most original investigators of the younger generation and well worth encouraging.

They are now proposing to undertake a new job of work of a more purely economico-scientific character than some of their previous enquiries, namely, the question of how individuals will behave if in a given situation they have more or less money to spend. This is an enquiry of first-class importance, which I have long wished to see undertaken. It works both ways. If a man's wages improve 5s. a week, what does he spend it on? If they fall 5s. a week, on what does he curtail? If meat rationing restricts his previous expenditure on meat, on what does he spend the balance thus released?

The answers to these questions are of importance in all sorts of economic contexts and are, of course, of first-class administrative interest at the present time.

This enquiry seems to me particularly well suited for the Mass Observation methods. It needs a fairly large number of trained observers who take certain sample districts and then do their best to produce a fairly large objective sample. Of course, they might fail, but if they were to succeed even in a modest degree, the results would be of high value.

Now they are, I understand, quite without resources of their own. Their method of working, whilst extremely economical for what they do, naturally involves some expenses. For this particular enquiry they want to have 20 whole-time investigators in the field, whom they would pay, I am told, the modest sum of about £2 each.

Now, the reason I write to you is to suggest that this is a proper object for assistance by the funds of the National Institute. I confess I was rather dismayed by the list of applications circulated in the last Minutes of the Council. It seemed to me that most of the applications were those which, left to my own judgement, I should turn down with very little hesitation. Some of them were quite proper as the subject of individual enquiry, but seemed to have no claim on funds intended for large-scale cooperative work. Others were of the dreariest description and contained very little hope of fruit.

Now, do not you think that the Mass Observation proposal is vastly more deserving? I enclose a memorandum of research, which Charles Madge has drawn up, to give you an idea of what they are driving at. I should like strongly to support a grant of, say, £500 to them from the funds of the National Institute.

The difficulty seems to me to be, not so much the value of what they are doing, which in my opinion is about ten times all the other proposed enquiries put together, but the technical one of how they can qualify for assistance, not being a university department. I suppose they would either have to be attached to headquarters, or some university would have to be prepared to father them. The former course would be much the most convenient, particularly as their head quarters are in London, so that they could be in touch with 32 Gordon Square. As a much less satisfactory alternative, I could, if necessary, ask the new Department of Realistic Economics at Cambridge if it would sponsor them. The only pretext there would be that Charles Madge was in fact at Cambridge all through his time and Harrisson was in residence for a brief period.

I believe that the next meeting of the Council has been called for April 8th, so that, if you approve the idea, it could be brought up then. Is that the date of the Annual Meeting? I had not intended to be in London on that date, but I could come up if you think it would be necessary and useful. In the following week I shall be in London, but that I suppose will be too late.

Yours sincerely,

[copy initialled] J. M. K.

From CHARLES MADGE, *1 April 1940*

Dear Mr Keynes

Thank you so very much for your cheque and exceedingly kind letter. It was particularly understanding of you to respond to what must have sounded like an S.O.S. I hope sometime I shall be able to tell you a bit more about the whole history of M.O., which is quite a remarkable story. I hope too that we shall do a job of work which will justify your gesture of confidence.

The above address and 'phone number will find me, or somebody, during all working hours.

Yours sincerely
CHARLES MADGE

To CHARLES MADGE, *16 April 1940*

Dear Madge,

The question of your enquiry was up before the Council of the National Institute yesterday, and we agreed to be benevolent, provisionally at least. So I expect you will be hearing from Crowther. We gathered that you are now also in touch with the Ministry of Information. If you can get off with them, that would be the best thing. But possibly we may be able to fill in a gap before you get officially adopted.

Could you put me on your list for *US*?[14]

Yours sincerely,
[copy initialled] J.M.K.

From CHARLES MADGE, *17 April 1940*

Dear Mr Keynes

Thank you so much for writing about the National Institute meeting. I went there yesterday and from what Miss Leontinoff told me it looks as if, thanks to your help, we shall be able to do the work we so much want to do. I see Crowther on Friday for a final decision about the conditions on which we should get the subsidy.

The Ministry of Information work only involves the unit working under the direction of Tom Harrisson. I am not involved in any way, nor is Mass-Observation as an organisation. Incidentally, the whole arrangement was supposed to be *highly* confidential, as one of the conditions on which the

[14] *US* was Mass Observation's weekly intelligence service.

Treasury agreed to make it! I'm personally very glad that M.O. will be working for the National Institute.

> With my best thanks
> Yours sincerely
> CHARLES MADGE

There the correspondence ended for five months, although in the interim Keynes published in *The Economic Journal* for June–September 1940 Madge's 'Wartime Saving and Spending: A District Survey' reporting on results from Islington and Coventry obtained under the grant from the National Institute.

The correspondence continued as Madge produced further results, which Keynes often fed into the Treasury machine in support of his 1941 Budget proposals.[15]

To CHARLES MADGE, *17 September 1940*

My dear Madge,

I have read with a great deal of interest your Report on Blackburn. I suppose you are now in Bristol, but you may be glad to have notes on certain points which have occurred to me.

(1) In Table I Column 8 is said to relate to savings in Trustee Savings Banks. I am wondering whether this is not a misdescription and whether Post Office Saving Banks are not also included in that column. Otherwise the latter seem to be missing altogether.

(2) When you come to consider the proportion who had a higher income before, the problem of earners called up, which you mention in passing on page 11, seems to me to deserve more emphasis and careful examination. After all the earner called up is himself earning something in cash or kind or both. Is the family income reckoned without taking this into account or after taking into account such amount as he remits home, including, e.g. separation allowance? In a good many contexts cases of falling income for this reason are irrelevant or at least confusing. Since they represent nearly a third of the whole number, it is

---

[15] See *JMK*, vol. XXII, pp. 215, 275-6, 302.

clearly important. By including these cases you seem to me to be decidedly understating the percentage of cases of increased income; or rather you are answering not quite the same question that people think you are answering. One imagines that this table relates to persons who both before and during the survey were in civil employment. I feel there is a lot to be said for dealing separately with cases of earners called up and working out your main tables with this category excluded.

(3) There is another question slightly analogous about your treatment of which I have been asked by someone who has been studying your work carefully. How do you deal with bachelors who have no household of their own? Where they are lodgers, are they excluded from the family with which they lodge and, if so, are they taken account of for their own sake, or do they slip through altogether? In any case, I suppose that bachelors employed within your district who sleep outside it slip through. For example, in the case of Coventry, I am told that a considerable number sleep in, e.g., Rugby. Since this class of bachelor is perhaps the one which is doing best of all out of the war, one wants to know just how it does or does not come into the figures.

(4) I am very distrustful of the calculation and argument which begins on page 15. In the first place, I think there may be a misunderstanding about withdrawals from the Trustee Savings Bank. I have been told by Trustee Savings Bank people exactly the opposite, namely, that withdrawals are far less than in the case of Savings Certificates. Moreover, their explanation of why this should be so sounds plausible. If a man wants half a crown he can only obtain it, if he holds a War Savings Certificate, by cashing out the whole 15s., but, if he has put his money in the Trustee Savings Bank, he can withdraw exactly what he wants. It is perfectly true, that especially in the early days, a very large proportion of the Savings Certificates were paid for by withdrawals from a Trustee Savings Bank, only a third or a quarter being really new money. But that is another matter, for it is merely a change in the form of saving. But, apart from this, I

find the argument rather hard to follow and not particularly plausible. I doubt if the explanation is to be found along that road.

(5) On the other hand, I should attach very great importance to what you say in the first complete paragraph on page 18.

The next issue of *The Economic Journal* is due to appear early in December, which means that most of it must be set up, at any rate in galley proof, as early as possible in November. May I have a further study from you on Blackburn and Bristol, supplementing your previous article? I have found your new study even more fascinating than the previous ones. You really have a genius for this sort of enquiry! Your previous contribution has had, as you have probably seen, quite an unusual press, including the attention of a leading article in *The Times*.

I am sending a copy of this letter to Miss Leontinoff.

Yours sincerely,

J. M. KEYNES

From CHARLES MADGE, *20 September 1940*

Dear Mr Keynes

Thank you for a most warming and encouraging letter, not the least flattering part being the detailed criticism, for which I am particularly grateful. Taking your points as they come:

(i) Column 8 in Table I should have been labelled '% of total savings saved in Post Office and Trustee Savings Bank'.

(ii) In my tables, men who have been called up are not included in the number of the families described; but Army allowances paid to their wives, and any other contribution which they make out of their pay to wives or other relatives are included in the income of these families. There are of course even more families affected in this way now in Bristol than there were six weeks ago in Blackburn, and I entirely agree that their position needs analysing more carefully. If members of families one or more of whose earners have been called up have less income per head as a result (taking Army allowances and other contributions into account), it seems as fair to include them in the 'incomeless' group as it would be to include, e.g., those whose earners had left home for other reasons, such as getting married. However, if the soldier members of the family were included, and their

817

Army pay, plus the value of the food, uniforms and other benefits provided by the army, were added to the family income, the effect would vary. In the case of a family consisting of soldier, wife and child, income might be taken as including:

Army pay	14s.
Value of Army food, etc (approx)	15s.
Army allowance to wife & child	24s.

or about £2 13s., probably less in most cases than what the husband was earning before he was called up, and giving an income per head of about 21s. The same family, if taken to consist only of the wife and child, would have an income per head of 16s.; or, if, as commonly happens, the husband contributed 6s. per week out of his pay, wife and child would have an income per head of 20s., nearly as much as by the other calculation. In the case of families where the earner called up was an unmarried son, there would be no Army allowance, and the decrease in income per head would be more marked. The best way to see what has happened would be, as you say, to analyse as a separate group all families where earners have been called up. For this group two calculations of income per head might be made, in one of which the soldier was included in the family, and not in the other.

(iii) Bachelors who have no household of their own have not entered into my figures at all, since my original instructions were to take a sample of families. I think this was a mistake and that we should have interviewed all lodgers in our sample households. So far lodgers have only been taken into account in so far as they provide income to the family with which they lodge. It is quite true that a great many people work in Coventry but sleep in other neighbouring places, though these people are not necessarily lodgers. A great many of the lodgers in Coventry were sending money to their families in other places. My impression was that the number of completely unattached bachelors would be small, but it should certainly be checked up. We could, if necessary, re-interview all households in our Bristol sample which are recorded as having lodgers, or rather go back and interview the lodgers, in order to find out more about this class. It would probably mean a few days' work beyond that at present budgeted for; I think it would be worth it.

(iv) I am sure that your criticisms of the calculation and argument which begins on page 15 are more than justified. It is not my job to attempt such calculations; my approach to them is naive in the extreme. However the evidence is that people who still prefer to save through Trustee Savings Banks rather than through War Savings say that their reason is that they can get money out of the T.S.B. more quickly and easily. I also know that where employers have organised Savings Groups, they usually make it as difficult as possible for their people to withdraw their money. I'll try to find out more about it, and leave the argument to others!

In Bristol we have been asking this question: 'To help pay for the war, would you rather (a) have everything rationed (b) have higher prices (c) have part of your wages saved for you till after the war?' There are of course a great many people who 'Don't Know', but a useful proportion of positive answers. A majority are in favour of more rationing, but about three in ten of the positive answers so far have been in favour of deferred wages, among working-class families with employed earners. This seems a high proportion to me, considering that most of the propaganda that most people have had about it has been hostile; and considering the immediate appeal of extended rationing as being a fair and equal method.

I am delighted that you should want a further study for *The Economic Journal*. I should be able to finish it by the end of October—I hope this will be in time. I have asked Miss Leontinoff to circulate a letter about my progress with Bristol, and my own tentative ideas about future work. We are doing very well in Bristol, but at a rather slower rate than before, because of the frequent sirens which waste a lot of time and stop the buses. At our present rate, the interviews should be finished by Oct. 12; if we also interview lodgers, it will take a few days more.

I hope that conditions will allow us to have another meeting soon.

Yours sincerely
CHARLES MADGE

To CHARLES MADGE, *29 September 1940*

Dear Madge,

Thank you for your letter of September 20th and the explanations you send. I do feel, in the light of them, that it is better to segregate the families of men called up. Everyone is well aware that in such cases there may easily be a decline in earnings per head calculated according to the formula, and the inclusion of such cases obscures the answer to the question whether the result of the war in a given district has been to raise materially the earnings of those who are at work above what they were previously.

In the matter of Savings Certificates versus T.S.B., it may

well be the case that the number of occasions on which money is drawn from the T.S.B. is greater, but the claim of the T.S.B. is that it adds up to much less money. If you want half-a-crown, you can draw out precisely that sum from T.S.B., but if you hold Savings Certificates, you have to cash in 15s. in order to get the 2s. 6d.

I am interested in what you report about the Bristol attitude towards proposals of deferred pay. I agree with you in thinking your result extremely satisfactory. I doubt, however, whether the majority who prefer a system of general rationing would continue to do so if they had any experience of it. They probably quite fail to realise the point that, owing to the great variety of tastes after one has moved away from a few staple commodities, the restrictive effect of general rationing and the waste involved through forcing people to change their habits is very considerable. At first sight it sounds a very fair system, but the practical inconveniences it involves are enormous.

If I can have your *Journal* article before the end of October, that will be time enough.

You may be interested in that connection to have the enclosed, sent me by Austin Robinson from the War Cabinet Office. I agree with him that this way of typing out your Table I is easier to read. You will notice the suggestion he makes for other interesting towns. I have sent on to him your own suggestion for further work in your letter to Miss Leontinoff. I hope we may be able to continue the grant on the basis suggested, but whether we shall feel free to do so for the whole six months in one bite I am not certain.

Yours sincerely,

J. M. KEYNES

To CHARLES MADGE, *15 October 1940*

Dear Madge,

You may be interested to glance at the enclosed article by

Menderhausen on differences in family savings.[16] I doubt
whether you will learn much from the statistical technique
employed, which seems to me too elaborate and adds little or
nothing to the proceedings. But you will be interested to see that
in America, just as here, there seem to be regional differences on
quite a large scale for which no obvious explanation is apparent.
Do not be terrified by the technique, but look at the table on
page 129 which, with its footnotes, tells you all there is in the
article.

I should like the magazine back some day, as it belongs to a
series which I keep.

Yours sincerely,
J. M. KEYNES

To CHARLES MADGE, *22 October 1940*

My dear Madge,

I had an occasion yesterday to mention some of the results
of your enquiry to the Chancellor of the Exchequer and
other people here. They showed themselves very much,
indeed surprisingly so, interested, and said that they would
like to have a summary of the Bristol results at the earliest
possible moment. They were particularly interested in the
results from the savings angle, both the amounts and the
ways in which people were saving and their responses to your
enquiry whether they preferred more rationing, higher prices,
deferred pay etc.

I daresay it will lead only to loss of time for you to attempt to
prepare anything in advance of what you will be letting me have
within a week for *The Economic Journal*. But, if you have an early
summary available with particular reference to the savings side
of the enquiry, I should be grateful if you could let me have it
here at the earliest opportunity.

Yours sincerely,
J. M. KEYNES

[6] H. Menderhausen, 'Differences in Family Savings between Cities of Different Size and
Location, Whites and Negroes', *Review of Economics and Statistics*, August 1940.

To CHARLES MADGE, *1 November 1940*

My dear Madge,

Thanks for your complete version, which arrived safely. I have been perplexed what to do in regard to its length. As you say, printed *in extenso* it is enormous, perhaps the longest article we should have ever printed. On the other hand, there is very little which is not interesting, and I think it loses materially by your cuts; though I am very grateful for these—few contributors are so conciliatory to the Editor!

In the end I have decided to print it intact and am, therefore, instructing the printer to ignore the cuts.

I am asking the printer to let me have 20 galley proofs as soon as possible, since the official interest in what you are doing has been by no means diminished by having read your earlier and shorter version, more particularly about savings. There are a good many points on which we are quite in the dark apart from your figures, which I only hope are right!

I have one or two small comments on the article which you might consider when it arrives in proof.

Table III would be clearer if in the column 'All Families' you put 'Families with men called up' so that one column would be all those except men called up, the other would be only men called up. If you lump them together, the latter category are swamped, and one really gets very little impression of what they would be taken by themselves. As before, you must explain the difference between Wage Earners A and Wage Earners B. These descriptions are not yet part of the English language.

Two matters arose in looking through the first version you sent which you might consider in Bradford. There is a passage in which you say that in Coventry 'more' in relation to incomes means 'much more', whilst in Blackburn it means 'not much more'. Can you quantify this a little more precisely? For example, it would interest us a good deal to know what percentage of the workers have an income which is increased by 20 per cent or more as compared with pre-war. At present you do not give us a clue to the dispersion of incomes or to the proportion who have actually increased their *real* income. In advance of collecting anything definite about this I should be interested to have your own personal impression in the towns so far visited as to the percentage whose money incomes have gone up by 20 per cent or more.

I have also been wondering whether your questionnaire about deferred pay could be improved. The question you asked does not cover the alternative of heavier taxation, whilst the alternative of universal rationing is perhaps rather an unreal one. What about the following?

'To help pay for the war would you rather (a) have higher prices (b) have higher taxes (c) have part of your wages saved for you till after the war?'

The point one really wants to get at is this. Let us suppose that a given sum has to be got somehow out of the wage earners which we might put at 5*s*. a week from a man earning £3 a week, 10*s*. a week from a man earning £4 a week, 18*s*. a week from a man earning £6 a week, and so on. Obviously this is a pretty steep figure. Would it make a great deal of difference psychologically if, instead of being taxation, this was to take the form of deferred pay? In other words would the offer of deferred pay mitigate considerably the psychological blow, or would it make, as some people say, precious little difference? If you could, particularly in the cases you interview yourself, try to elucidate this by means of some of your characteristic dialogues, one might get some faintly better indication than the views of gents who never meet any of those concerned.

There is also the question whether deferred pay would react on existing savings much more than an equal sum would taken in taxation. Suppose something of the order of 10 per cent of wages is taken from men earning more than £3 a week, what effect would this have on their savings from all sources? Would it reduce savings in other ways to a much greater extent if it were in the shape of deferred pay than if it were in the shape of an outright tax?

When you are passing through Cambridge, it would be worth while your ringing me up at my flat (Cambridge 54184) or asking the King's porter whether I am in residence. I shall be there next week-end, and I may occasionally sleep there next week; though, as I don't arrive as a rule until after 8 p.m. and leave at 8 a.m., this does not leave much of a gap for seeing people.

Yours sincerely,

J. M. KEYNES

To CHARLES MADGE, *7 November 1940*

Dear Madge,

I have just got from the Ministry of Labour early news of the increase in *Earnings* per head in industry shown by the Earnings Census of July last as compared with October, 1938. It seems to work out at about 31 per cent, which is, if I remember rightly, in close conformity with your Bristol results. So the criticism I made on this the other day does not seem to be justified.

The above figure is at present confidential and not for publication.

Yours sincerely,

J. M. KEYNES

From CHARLES MADGE, *10 November 1940*

Dear Mr Keynes,

We are arrived and comfortably installed here,[17] and I have gone over the proofs (enclosed) carefully.[18] I promised you gaily that I should be able to prune the formidable document, but I must confess myself stumped unless we revert to the method of cutting out several paragraphs, as in the cut version I sent you. I am returning this also.

A footnote to Galley 3 gives the result of a calculation made as you suggested of the percentage increase in those incomes that have increased. Though I was right in thinking there were a lot of small increases, there are enough big ones to pull the average up to 29 per cent. Mrs Robinson, and Rothbart, whom I met in Cambridge, were both worried about the apparent discrepancy between Table III and Table IV, but were reconciled to both tables when we remembered that Table III is a comparison with 1937,

[17] In Bradford.
[18] 'The Propensity to Save in Blackburn and Bristol', *Economic Journal*, December 1940.

Table IV with 1939. I put in another footnote to save anyone else this worry. Also as you suggested I have given the percentage above Standard Needs of the families with men called up. Even these show the apparently dominant Bristolian pattern of levels which comes out in the 1937–40 comparison for all families.

My team has already done half the Bradford interviews, and we have worked out a time-table according to which by Christmas we shall have finished Bradford, and also samples of 160 each in Huddersfield, Halifax and Wakefield. I suggest it would be best to make a report on all four wool towns which would be ready by about Jan. 15, 1941. I am writing to Mr Austin Robinson and Professor Bowley about their suggestion for further towns. A possible progress would be Doncaster, York, Ashington and a group of other mining villages, Carlisle. I want if possible to survey a heavy-industries town, on the hypothesis that the heaviest workers are on the whole the heaviest spenders. I think it will be possible, with the present efficient team, to cover these places pretty rapidly, as they are all smallish, and to write up one, while the team is interviewing the next one. I think I shall be able to preserve and even add to the detail, at the same time, covering more ground more rapidly, if we sample mainly smaller towns.

With very many thanks,

Yours sincerely,
CHARLES MADGE

To CHARLES MADGE, *14 November 1940*

Dear Madge,

Like you I have not found it easy to delete redundancies from the formidable document, so I am, after all, printing it intact.

Would you consider the following points, which I can still attend to in page proof if necessary:—

1) Surely the apparent discrepancy between Table III and Table IV is not chiefly due to the fact that the former is a comparison with 1937 and the latter with 1939, but to the fact that the former is a comparison of real incomes and the latter of money incomes. I have amended your footnote to this effect. Is that right?

2) I am not quite as clear as I should like to be in my own mind as to what is covered by standard means. Is there an allowance for rent? Does it in fact cover most of the items which

825

are in the cost of living index number? If it is mainly restricted to food, there ought to be some indication of that.

3) In Table VI I think it would tell one more if the figures given in brackets related to families *with* (instead of *except*) earners called up.

Glad to hear that you have made such rapid progress with Bradford. I agree that a composite report on the four wool towns is a good plan.

Yours sincerely,

[copy initialled] J.M.K.

The final letters concerned Madge's third article, 'Public Opinion and Paying for the War'.[19]

To CHARLES MADGE, *10 January 1941*

My dear Madge,

Very glad to get your latest document, which as usual has much that is interesting.

I am, of course, particularly interested in your questionnaire on page 21. I look forward to getting your subsidiary report on Deferred Pay. If this is to be of maximum utility, it ought to reach me at the earliest possible date. If I could circulate it next week, it might be very helpful indeed. Will you be able to bring it with you when you come to town on Wednesday?

I should like very much to have a talk with you before the Committee meeting which is called, I think, for Friday afternoon. Could you come to dinner, at 46 Gordon Square, on Wednesday evening, January 15th, at 7.30, or is that too soon after your arrival? We can provide you with an emergency bed for the night if the Blitz happens to prove bad that night, and, if you want to get to shelter, as is only sensible, before 7.30, come along there as soon as suits you. If that does not suit you, could you lunch with me at the United University Club on Thursday, January 16th, at 1.30?

Yours sincerely,

J. M. KEYNES

[19] *The Economic Journal*, March 1941.

From CHARLES MADGE, *26 January 1941*

Dear Mr Keynes,

I am enclosing a revised version of 'Public Opinion and Paying for the War'. I have inserted a passage at the end of the general introductory passage, and before the quotations begin, giving the proportions who voted for the different alternatives, and explaining the change in the question. I have cut out the final paragraphs and put two tables at the end. I haven't put in any acknowledgments to the National Institute—I imagine that other members of the subcommittee should be consulted, if the article is to appear under the Institute's auspices.

I also enclose a number of yellow documents which will explain themselves.[20] I should be very glad of your comments, at your leisure.

Progress in York has been expeditious, and I expect to be back in London on Jan. 31. I shall live in digs in London while Slough is being surveyed, as it is within easy reach by train, and congested with people. I have been promised a room at Chatham House to work in.

Yours,

CHARLES MADGE

To CHARLES MADGE, *5 February 1941*

Dear Madge,

Thanks for your letter of the 26th January and its enclosures. I am sending the revised version of 'Public Opinion and Paying for the War' to the printer, and you should get a proof shortly. I have ventured to make one or two changes, but use your own discretion when you see them in the proof. These changes are:

(1) To insert the two tables in the body of the text. I think they are more effective there in the right context than at the end. This means that Table I has to have a brief sentence introducing it.

(2) I have added a further sentence giving the opinion I expressed of the revised form of questionnaire.

(3) I have restored a part of what you deleted at the end. It seemed to me that one of your concluding sentences did make a very good peroration to the whole thing.

I have no criticism on your Slough programme. I am in

---

[20] These included draft questionnaires, proposals for future enquiries including one in Slough, and a book proposal.

favour of your proposal to make repeat enquiries, though it be at the cost of deferring the date of the completion of the Savings enquiry. I do not want you to be hurried about this or prevented from making a really good job of it. For it has the makings of a major work.

Your synopsis of the proposed book[21] is on more ambitious lines than I had been expecting, but no harm in that. I am more interested in your bringing the new material in its proper relation to the general problem. (You will have to be an industrious boy to finish all this by the dates suggested; but then you are an industrious boy.) And I assume that you mean to make the early general part subsidiary to the latter. As a matter of presentation it might be a mistake to keep the reader away from the new stuff by too many preliminary chapters. Your Chapter 4 I should certainly be inclined to put towards the end. And I think it might be worth considering whether Chapters 1, 2 and 3 should not be divided, being treated rather briefly at the outset and then returned to at the end in the light of your information. The point in my mind is that yours will be the book on this subject really based on facts. If you arrange it as you are proposing you will give the appearance of starting off with all the usual generalities unsupported. If you can make these and your criticisms of former writers emerge out of your material, it will be better. But if this is to happen the order of exposition needs reconsidering, so that the reader will be in possession of your material before he comes to your handling of the generalisations.

I am putting the problem rather than giving the solution, which is the author's job. But you will easily see what I mean.

The Slough questionnaire has now become a fairly formidable document for your staff. But the new questions are all interesting. I shall be interested to see whether you can really make much out of the study of the new sub-samples.   Yours,

J. M. KEYNES

---

[21] This eventually appeared as *Wartime Patterns of Saving and Spending*, National Institute of Economic and Social Research Occasional Papers IV (Cambridge, 1943).

The correspondence continued after Madge's 1941 article as Keynes read subsequent reports from the enquiry, made suggestions as to further implications and questions for research and the reactions of various people in Whitehall and the City to their results. The correspondence finally petered out as Madge moved into areas that interested Keynes less.

Keynes as editor could and did take advice on articles. Below we print what survives of the editorial exchanges on an article that Keynes did not publish, Michal Kalecki's 'A Theorem on Technical Progress'[22] which he received towards the end of January 1941.[23]

To JOAN ROBINSON, *4 February 1941*

My dear Joan,

Here is Kalecki's article. As I said the other night, after a highly rational introduction of a couple of pages my first impression is that it becomes high, almost delirious nonsense. I am ready to believe that there are some assumptions in relation to which his conclusions are correct. But so many of them are latent and tacit that no-one could say, I should have thought, whether he has proved his proposition. Indeed I do not feel perfectly sure whether the hypotheses may not be self-contradictory. Is it not rather odd when dealing with 'long-run problems' to start with the assumption that all firms are always working below capacity.

Or take his final conclusion that technical progress causes a reduction of output. I imagine that he really means by this that if, as a result of technical progress, two blades of grass grow where one grew before there would nevertheless be no increase in output, either because he measures output in terms of marginal wage cost or because he has made some assumption that leads to the conclusion that only half as many fields would be cultivated, the working day being reduced by half. But, if the former explanation is so, he gives no definition of output.

Has not the whole method been carried to ludicrous lengths?

---

[22] It appeared in *The Review of Economic Studies* for May 1941.
[23] No correspondence with Kalecki survives on this article.

However, I must not try to prejudice you but await your verdict. Yours ever,

J. M. K.

From JOAN ROBINSON, *4 February 1941*

Dear Maynard,

I am prepared to stick up for Kalecki. He is making an attempt to extend the *General Theory* beyond the short period—tho' not to the long period in the old sense, since that concept involves the whole Classical theory.

He is not saying that inventions leave output constant, for in his 'reference system' output is increasing as capital accumulates. He needs an indefinitely large reserve of labour in his reference system so that employment can increase as required. But granted that, he is all right. The trick is to make assumptions by which effective demand in terms of commodities is the same in the two systems. Then output is the same, and inventions by increasing output per head, reduce employment (relatively to the reference system). The case which he hints at at the end, where output falls (relatively) arises when inventions increase the share of capital relatively to the share of labour and so increase thriftiness. Two blades of grass grow where one grew before, but the demand for hay falls.

As for under-capacity working—that is part of the usual bag of tricks of Imperfect Competition theory. To say that price normally exceeds marginal prime cost sounds commonplace enough, but that is really the same thing.

Where Kalecki *is* barmy is insisting on writing articles in this inhuman style. It is a kind of sinful pride that makes him do it.

Perhaps you could find a spare moment in the week-end. I will keep the article till then and chew over it again. I enclose some notes addressed to Kalecki which I could send him if you approve. Yours,

JOAN

I am taking my parents to Merry Wives on Saturday dining at the Theatre at 7. It would be very nice if you and Lydia could join us.

J.

To JOAN ROBINSON, *12 February 1941*

My dear Joan,

Thanks for your notes on Kalecki. If he is extending the *General Theory* beyond the short period but not to the long period in the old sense, he really must tell us what the sense is. For I am still innocent enough to be bewildered by the idea that the assumption of all firms always working below capacity is consistent with 'a long-run problem'. To tell me that 'as for under-capacity working that is part of the usual pack of tricks of imperfect competition theory' does not carry me any further. For publication in the *Journal* an article must pass beyond the stage of esoteric abracadabra.

You tell me that it is a kind of sinful pride which makes Kalecki write like this. I think it is a sort of profound stupidity, though physical and aesthetic, perhaps, rather than intellectual. At any rate, he must write the article in such a style that it is fairly evident on the surface whether or not he is talking through his hat. I do not doubt that he is saying something. But I suspect him of being at one of his old tricks in an extreme form, namely, of taking artificial assumptions which have no possible relation to reality or any other merit except that they happen to lead up to a needed result.

All this does not mean that I am not most grateful to you for tackling him. I think much the best way would be if, as you suggest, you would write to him yourself, send him the enclosed notes, which I return, tell him that I, with my head much occupied in other directions, had asked you to look through it, and use all your influence to persuade him so to set it all out so that it is possible for some readers at any rate to exercise rational judgement on it.

Yours ever,

J. M. KEYNES

From JOAN ROBINSON, *14 February 1941*

My dear Maynard,

I have written to Kalecki as you suggest. I must protest at your calling Imperfect Competition an esoteric doctrine. It may be awful rot—as you have always suspected—but for better or worse it is in all the text books now.

Under Imp. Comp. there is surplus capacity even in full equilibrium

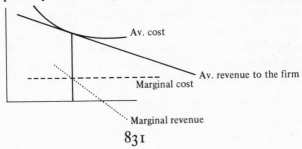

Under perfect comp. any firm which is working at all must be working bang up to capacity even in a deep slump. This is certainly more and not less ridiculous.

Yours,

JOAN

To JOAN ROBINSON, *18 February 1941*

My dear Joan,

That is not what I said or at any rate not what I mean to say. Imperfect competition as such has become quite the contrary of esoteric!—indeed one of the most fashionable subjects going, especially in U.S.A.

What I call esoteric is bringing in certain assumptions of this sort tacitly and assuming that the reader can be expected to supply out of his knowledge or imagination, not only the relevant assumptions, but the relevant consequences of them and, above all, the solution of how all this works in the 'long-run conditions'.

Kalecki must tell me exactly what he is assuming in his model, exactly in what respects it differs from the real world; in particular, he must justify for the purpose of his final comparison the assumption that there is no inconsistency between the assumptions governing each of the two states of affairs he is considering, so that it is legitimate to pass from one to the other.

The esoteric fault is to write subject to a whole contraption of secret knowledge, atmosphere and assumption, quite unknown to above half a dozen readers in the *Journal* at the outside.

Yours ever,

J. M. KEYNES

From JOAN ROBINSON, *24 February 1941*

Dear Maynard,

Kalecki has met the criticisms I made on his article, and I hope you will now find it publishable.

His conclusions differ from my Long-Period Theory[24] (which you swallowed all right at the time) only in showing that capital-using inventions do not reduce the share of labour in the Nat. Div. And this is a bull point

[24] 'The Long-Period Theory of Employment', *Zeitschrift für Nationalökonomie*, March 1936 reprinted in *Essays in the Theory of Employment*.

because the share of capital doesn't in fact rise as much as my original argument would lead one to expect.

In general I think Kalecki is explaining mysteries, not creating them.

Yours,

JOAN

To JOAN ROBINSON, *4 March 1941*

My dear Joan,

Thank you very much for taking so much trouble about Kalecki. The article is enormously improved in its present form and is not open to my previous criticisms, at any rate of presentation.

But, unfortunately, my complaints have become of exactly the opposite kind. Now that I believe myself to understand exactly what it says, it all seems plain as a pikestaff. Indeed, so much so that I cannot discover that the elaborate apparatus of the reference system leads to any conclusion which is not obvious from the start. Kalecki sums it all up on page 10 where he says— 'The significance of our theorem is to show that technical progress influences output only through the channels of invention stimulus, oligopoly and the general price level (or by overcoming scarcity of labour).' But in what other way has anyone ever supposed that it did operate?

Moreover, if the reference system led to a more interesting conclusion, is it not a highly dangerous and fallible method since it makes unsupported assumptions as to the legitimacy of superimposing one fact on another without any interaction.

Does the article tell you anything you did not know before? You say that it proves that capital-using inventions do not reduce the share of labour in the national dividend. Where does it show this? I have not discovered it. Don't you mean that, if it reduces it, it only reduces it through one or other of the agencies mentioned above?

I should like to send it to Kaldor for another opinion.

Yours ever,

J. M. KEYNES

To N. KALDOR, *4 March 1941*

My dear Kaldor,

As I have not now much spare brains for this sort of thing, I should be very grateful if I could have your opinion on the value of the enclosed article by Kalecki.

My *prima facie* criticisms on it are two.

1) I think that his method of a reference system is a dangerous one since it seems to me to make unsupported assumptions about the legitimacy of superimposing one fact upon another without any risk of interactions. I should, therefore, suspect it if it led to any conclusion not acceptable to my intuition on other grounds.

2) The conclusion which in fact it leads to seems to me to be obvious from the outset. It is summed up at the bottom of page 10, where he says, 'The significance of our theorem is to show that technical progress influences output only through the channels of invention stimulus, oligopoly and the general price level (or by overcoming the scarcity of labour)'. But how else has anyone ever supposed that it did operate?

However, I must not try to prejudice you against the article in advance.

Yours sincerely,

J. M. KEYNES

From JOAN ROBINSON, *6 March 1941*

My dear Maynard,

Yes, now you have gone to the other extreme. Surely if anyone asked you Do capital-using inventions increase capital per unit of output? You would have said Of course—what a dotty question.

It is the interplay of utilisation of capital with changes in technique that Kalecki brings out.

True it seems rather an elaborate mechanism just to add one point to our analysis, but it seems to me a gallant attempt to deal with the analysis of a developing economy without using pure short-period or full long-period assumptions—neither of which is adequate.

I think you are looking a gift horse in the mouth—after all even one valid proposition, extending the *General Theory*, throwing light on the old problem of the constancy of relative shares is something to be thankful for.

The real advantage of the theorem is to clear out of the way an unnecessary difficulty so that some progress can be made with long-run (but not full equilibrium) analysis. Without this theorem one is held up by thinking one has to allow for effects of changes in technique on thriftiness etc., as I thought when I did my Long-Period Theory. Kalecki is on to something important, and this is a necessary step on the way.   Yours,

JOAN

To JOAN ROBINSON, *12 March 1941*

My dear Joan,

What *am* I to do about the wretched Kalecki?

If you had asked me—'do capital-using inventions increase capital per unit of output?' of course I should have said 'yes', since I should have interpreted this to mean per unit of capacity output. If you make it clear to me that by output you do not mean capacity output, then I should say it obviously depends on whether their effect is to bring actual output nearer to or further from capacity. If you say you can invent an artificial system in which they would bring actual output on a lower level in relation to capacity than before, I should say it would be a balance as to what the answer was. (In Kalecki's notation it would depend on whether u was falling faster than c was rising.) If you assert as a dogma that in the actual world the effect of capital-using inventions is always to reduce u more than it increases c, I should probably have replied—'What a dotty idea!'

I had not realised that the whole object of the article was to make the above dogmatic assertion. For the last page scarcely seems to amount to a proof of this and, at the best, he will only be showing that u falls. I do not notice any discussion to lead one to suppose that in the actual world u must always fall faster than c rises. Certainly, if this is the whole purpose of the paper, it should be made a little clearer.

Meanwhile, I have sent the article to Kaldor and enclose his reply. You will see that, in his judgement, Kalecki has not made out your point; though I do not think Kaldor puts it quite strongly enough, since it might be true that technical progress necessarily raised the degree of oligopoly, and yet did not do so sufficiently to offset the other effects.

835

So I am inclined to return to the opinion that the article is pretentious, misleading, inconclusive and perhaps wrong. I would rather have cheese to a weight equal to the paper it would occupy in 5,000 copies of the *Journal*!

Yours ever,

J.M.K.

From JOAN ROBINSON, *13 March 1941*

My dear Maynard,

As you still do not get the point about inventions and relative shares, and Kaldor also failed to see it, I have to confess that Kalecki's article is not a success.

I have suggested to him to rewrite it much more briefly making the main point clear.

Yours,

JOAN

Hoping to see you at the weekend.

To N. KALDOR, *18 March 1941*

My dear Kaldor,

Thanks very much for your note on Kalecki which fell in with my ideas but not, you will have heard, with Joan's. Indeed I went a little further than you because it seemed to me that, even if Kalecki could establish that the effect of capital-using inventions was to increase the gap between actual output and capacity output, he would still have to show that this was quantitatively large enough to offset the opposite effect. I could not see that he made a trace of an effort to establish this. However, Joan has been able to discover that the article is really about something quite different, which neither you nor I noticed. So she is sending it back to Kalecki in the hope that he will elucidate it further. I do not doubt that in the end she will write quite a good article for him!

Yours sincerely,

J. M. KEYNES

The next exchange to survive relates to Michal Kalecki's 'A Theory of Profits'[25] which he sent to Keynes on 13 December 1941. On reading it Keynes replied.

To M. KALECKI, *2 January 1942*

Dear Kalecki,

I should like to have your article for *The Economic Journal*, though when I shall be allowed enough paper to publish it is rather uncertain. No chance, I am afraid, earlier than the August issue, and whether that will be possible remains to be seen. We have not yet got any paper allocation for 1942.

When you come to look at it in proof, there are one or two points which I should be glad if you would consider. I have a suspicion that a good many more assumptions are involved than you have explicitly stated. I mention two in particular:—

(a) Are you not in effect assuming constant prices? That would certainly facilitate the argument. If you are not assuming constant prices, then it seems to me a variety of particular assumptions have to be made. For example, suppose there was a policy of work or full maintenance at a constant real reward so that workers' real consumption is constant. Would not that disturb you?

(b) Is it not necessary for you to assimilate doles to capitalists' consumption rather than to workers' consumption? Your conclusions seem to me to relate to the sum of capitalists' consumption *plus* doles rather than to capitalists' consumption alone. For example, suppose a system of unemployed relief paid for by direct taxes on capitalists.

(c) As always in these cases, I am bothered about what assumptions are being made about the independence of factors. A rise in prices might affect the real weight of direct taxes owing to the nature of the tax system, though this particular difficulty you would get round if, as I suggest above, you are assuming constant prices.

[25] *The Economic Journal*, June–September 1942.

My other point is that by the time you have got to the end of the article you seem to have persuaded yourself that you are dealing with the real world. This makes it all the more important to emphasise the assumptions you are making which distinguish your model from reality.

I am retaining the article meanwhile.

Yours sincerely,
[copy initialled] J.M.K.

From M. KALECKI, *9 January 1942*

Dear Mr Keynes,

Thank you very much for your letter. To clear up the points you raise I should like to mention first that throughout the argument I consider profits *net* of direct taxes. (This I state on p. 1 but perhaps I did not stress it sufficiently). Accordingly capitalists' consumption is meant as their *personal* consumption *exclusive* of direct taxes (cf. footnote to p. 1). And the equation profits = capitalists' consumption + investment means that profits *net* of taxes are equal to personal capitalists' consumption + investment. Therefore doles paid by direct taxes on capitalists are *not* included in profits or capitalists' consumption. And the changes in the real weight of taxes dependent on price changes do not affect profits in my sense (they do, however, affect the non-profit incomes).

A system of work or full maintenance at a constant real reward so that workers' real consumption is constant does not disturb my results in any case because it does not affect the equality of profits net of tax and personal capitalists' consumption *plus* investment just as it does not affect the equality of saving and investment.

I am certainly *not* assuming constant prices. Nor am I aware of any assumptions which have not been clearly stated although some are introduced only in chapter II ('slowness' of long-run development p. 4, the relation between real capitalists' consumption and real capitalists' income p. 5).

Yours sincerely,
M. KALECKI

To M. KALECKI, *10 January 1942*

Dear Kalecki,

Yes, I did not appreciate that you were considering profits net of direct taxes. That makes a difference and ought to be emphasised.

I will not pursue further the question whether you are making unstated assumptions. The worst of your sort of procedure is that there is no means of knowing what assumptions are involved except by exercising intuition and trying to consider various possible cases. For example, suppose there is a system of E[xcess] P[rofits] T[ax] which keeps profits constant in terms of money, no doubt your equations regarded as truisms would hold good, but the practical conclusions one could draw from them would be widely different. For instance, in that case, capitalists' consumption would no longer be in any respect independent of their investment. Yet I think the reader would naturally assume that you were taking their consumption and their investment to be independent factors. One could probably go on like that for a long time. I believe that your conclusions are valid relative to some particular situation, but to decide exactly what that particular situation is you do not make one reader at least feel that he has full guidance.

Yours sincerely,
[copy initialled] J.M.K.

From M. KALECKI, *15 January 1942*

Dear Mr Keynes,

Thank you very much for your letter. The problem of E.P.T. you raise is solved by the fact that by taxes related to a certain period I mean taxes paid and not taxes due. The Government cannot collect E.P.T. and spend the proceeds (which is required by my assumption of a balanced budget) in the same period in which the profits accrue. There arises therefore in general a difference between tax liabilities and tax payments.

The capitalists cannot be prevented from spending in a certain short period on consumption and investment the amount they have decided.* But if E.P.T. tends to keep profits constant the excess of the sum of capitalists' consumption and investment over this fixed level will be just equal to the excess of tax liabilities over tax payments. One can ask whether this amount should be included in profits in the period considered, but if it is not, the

* Both capitalists' consumption and investment are determined by decisions dependent on factors which operated prior to the short period considered and therefore are not independent in this sense (cf. pp. 3-4 of my MS). But they *are* independent after the relevant decisions have been formed.

savings also are net of this amount, and they are clearly not equal to investment in that case.

One could imagine an Excess Saving Tax which tends to keep saving constant, and argue that savings in such a case are not determined by investment, and therefore the conclusions of the *General Theory* are valid only in relation to some particular situation. Such an argument would, of course, be wrong for reasons indicated above.

I admit, however, that E.P.T. would disturb my argument in section I— not because I make there any tacit assumption but because an assumption I make there explicitly becomes then unplausible. On page 5 I assume that the real capitalists' consumption is a function of real profits (with a time lag). Profits include, however, the excess of tax liabilities over tax payments, and capitalists' consumption will clearly depend not only on the total value of profits but also on what part of it is accounted for by this item. I shall therefore add there a footnote qualifying the assumption in question. (The argument in the *General Theory* pp. 90–96, 115, is subject to the same qualification.)

Yours sincerely,

M. KALECKI

To M. KALECKI, *20 January 1942*

Dear Kalecki,

In practice E.P.T. is retained by the concern and is at no stage transferred to the profit-earning consumer. Thus there is, I should have supposed, no time-lag in its effect.

If Excess Saving Taxes were in fact not infrequent events, I should, I think, have done well in the *General Theory* to call attention to their peculiar consequences.

Have you worked out your theory on what is today the more realistic assumption, that all or the bulk of the saving is done by the wage earning and salary earning class? The three broad conditions which prevail today are that profits are fixed in terms of money by E.P.T., so that any rise of prices reduces real profits and saving is preponderantly performed by the non-profit earning class.

Yours sincerely,

[copy initialled] J.M.K.

From M. KALECKI, *27 January 1942*

Dear Mr Keynes,

The time lag effect in the operation of E.P.T. arises simply because the

Government cannot collect and spend E.P.T. proceeds (the latter is required by my assumption of a balanced budget) before the profit for a certain period has accrued. The excess of capitalists' consumption *plus* investment over the level at which E.P.T. tends to fix profits makes for accumulation of tax reserves which are of course retained by the concerns.

If this accumulation of tax reserves is included in savings (namely, in undistributed profits) savings are always fully determined by investment whatever the method of taxation.

My theory is definitely not applicable to a war economy, not only because of my assumption that workers do not save, but also because I postulate a balanced budget and because of the complication which I mentioned at the end of my last letter.

Yours sincerely,
M. KALECKI

To M. KALECKI, *28 January 1942*

Dear Kalecki,

Thanks for your letter of January 27th. My letters were not meant to be merely teasing. I appreciate that there are certain assumptions on which your conclusions are correct. But, as I said before, the worst of your technique is that it is impossible for the reader as he goes along to know what those assumptions are. And when the conclusion is reached there is an atmosphere as though it had some application to the real world.

I regard it as a very interesting schematism and a useful tool of thought and I cannot but feel that the article would be a great deal better if it was represented like that. But there is also the point that, even regarded as a schematism, it is not much use unless the reader knows fairly precisely just what the assumptions are.

Yours sincerely,
J.M.K.

The final exchange of letters relates to Laszlo Rostas's 'Industrial Production, Productivity and Distribution in Britain, Germany and the United States'.[26]

[26] *The Economic Journal*, April 1943.

From L. ROSTAS, *20 October 1942*

Dear Lord Keynes,

I would like to submit the enclosed paper for *The Economic Journal*. It is a by-product of the research work on profit margins which I am now engaged in, in connection with Mrs Robinson and Kaldor and Stone. Although the paper is largely statistical in character, I thought that the comparisons between the capacity and efficiency of the German, British and American industries might be of sufficient interest, at the present time, to merit its publication in [a] non-statistical journal.

With comparisons of this kind, it is rather difficult to decide how far (i.e. in what detail) it is worth pursuing the matter. I have left out a certain amount of material which might be put in (such as the structure of costs in the different industries of the three countries etc.); on the other hand, it is quite possible to shorten the paper (from its present length) by leaving out some of the comparisons which are less important.

Yours sincerely,

L. ROSTAS

To L. ROSTAS, *24 October 1942*

Dear Mr Rostas,

Thank you for sending me the enclosed for *The Economic Journal*. I find it of the highest interest and am very glad to accept it. I fear, however, that there is no likelihood of my being able to find space for it in the forthcoming issue, nearly half of which will be occupied by articles in commemoration of Alfred Marshall's centenary. We shall be printing it, therefore, in April, which gives us a little time for considering one or two points.

First of all I should be grateful if you would consider carefully just what you mean by saying that industrial efficiency per head is more than twice as great in the United States as in Germany or this country, and even more if we calculate in terms of hourly efficiency. Unless I have misunderstood the way in which your tables are compiled, what you demonstrate is something rather different: namely that the value of output valued in terms of money is more than twice as great. In order that the two statements should mean the same thing you have to assume that the value of money is the same in the three countries, not merely in

842

general, but also for the particular products under examination. Was this really the case? There is first of all the question of date, which I think is fairly significant for price movements as between 1935 and 1937. Secondly there is the possibility that in some cases at any rate, having regard to the elaborate tariff system, domestic prices were not, as you seem to be supposing, identical through the three countries. Surely no direct observation would consent to the conclusion which would seem to follow from your figures, even allowing for the smaller proportion of value of output paid in wages in the U.S.A., that the standard of living is substantially double. If I am right about this it seems to me that you want to make it clear that it is money value of output you are talking about, and make any necessary reserves, qualifications or adjustments when translating this into comparisons of relevant efficiency.

The second question is whether the tables, which occupy a great deal of space, can be somewhat curtailed without too much loss. I agree with you that in comparisons of this kind it is most difficult to know when to stop. Practically speaking your tables, like the rest of the article, are of the highest interest; but space these days is a first class consideration and we must, I think, see what can be done to get something out.

My suggestions are as follows. Will you think them over? Table 5 seems to be on the whole the least interesting and might perhaps go. In any case, if it is printed, it would be more instructive if, after the number of persons employed, there was shown the percentage of the total industrial employed population in each of the industries in question. But perhaps better to cut this table out altogether. My next suggestion relates to table 7. Have I misunderstood you in supposing that these items in absolute quantities are the same material that table 6 gives in percentages? I agree that even so table 7 adds something to table 6 since it shows the importance of the industries relative to one another in the same country and not merely relatively to the same industry in the other countries. But on the whole I think

843

Table 7 could be omitted without much loss. An alternative might be to combine the absolute figures for certain industries give in Table 7 into Table 6, so that under the heading for each country in Table 6 there would be shown both the index number and also the absolute figure in pounds.

Yours sincerely,
[copy initialled] K.

From L. ROSTAS, *29 October 1942*

Dear Lord Keynes,

I thank you for your letter and for accepting my paper for publication in a later issue of *The Economic Journal*.

I am afraid that the explanatory text to my tables was not sufficiently clear. I attempted two different kinds of comparisons for 'output per head'. One is for a selected number of industries only, producing fairly homogeneous and comparable products, and is based on a comparison of *physical*, and not value productivity. (I.e. tons of steel, motor cars etc. produced per operative.) The other, which is more comprehensive and covers the whole field of manufacturing industry, is based on the *money value* of output per head, when German figures in terms of marks and American figures in terms of dollars are converted to £'s, on the basis of the approximate purchasing power parity rate. (The former, according to the German Institute of Business Research was 17.08 marks to the £ in 1935; the latter we selected the market rate.)

Thus Tables 6 and 7 differ not only that the one is in terms of percentages, while the other in terms of absolute values, but that the one is on a purely physical basis and the other on a value basis. The fact that the results nevertheless correspond fairly closely shows, I think, that the conversion rates chosen could not have been widely different from the true figures.

Hence the points raised in your letter—in particular, the question that the currency conversion rate should correspond to relative purchasing power in terms of the particular commodities compared, and not only in terms of commodities in general—refers only to the second method of comparison (Table 7) and not to the first method (Table 6). But the fact that the results are not significantly different (in most of the cases where both are available) suggests rather that these difficulties do not influence very much the results gained by the second method.

You mention in your letter that if output per head in America were everywhere twice as great as in England, real income per head would also be twice as great, which is certainly not the case. The explanation is, I believe (a) that a smaller proportion of the U.S. population is engaged in manufacturing industry, and a smaller percentage of the total population is gainfully occupied; (b) that in the other constituent elements of the national income, agriculture, transport, housing, distribution, the productivity relation is not so favourable to America. Thus the fact that Britain obtains a considerable part of its peacetime food supply from abroad on favourable terms, means, I think, that the amount of food obtained per British man hour is large relatively both to the United States and Germany.

According to Table 3, the value of output per head in the U.S. in 1935 was 195 per cent of Britain, while the percentage of wages in net output was 89 per cent of the British figure, according to Table 10. This would imply that American industrial earnings, when converted dollars to the £ at the rate of 4.90, ought to be 174 per cent of British industrial earnings. Now according Bureau of Labor and Ministry of Labour statistics (the latter adjusted to cover Census trades only), average industrial earnings in 1935 were 20.85 dollars and 46s. 2d. respectively; i.e. an earnings ratio of 184:100, when converted at 4.90 dollars to the £. The fairly close correspondence of these figures does not prove, of course, that the conversion rate of 4.90 dollars to the £ was the correct one; but it shows that the figures for productivity and distribution are consistent with one another.

The international cost of living inquiry of the I.L.O. for the Ford Motor Company, when adjusted for 1935, gives a purchasing power rate of about 6.70 dollars to the £. This index however is much influenced by the relatively high level of rents, etc., and contains few items which are products of manufacturing industry. It does not suggest that the rate of 4.90 dollars to the £ was too low for the wholesale prices of manufactured products.

I am quite ready, of course, to delete Table 5, and also Table 7, if you prefer it; though, in view of the above, I think you will agree that it is worth publishing both Table 6 and Table 7.

I return the article after deleting Table 5. I have added a sentence on p. 7 to make clear the difference between Table 6 and Table 7, and included separate figures for percentage relations as well as added a note to Table 7 in accordance with the suggestion in your letter. If you feel that further improvements or abbreviations may be advisable, I should of course be very willing to undertake them.

Yours sincerely

L. ROSTAS

To L. ROSTAS, *25 November 1942*

Dear Mr Rostas,

Your letter of October 29th convinced me that your results

are not unplausible. I must apologise for having overlooked the fact that one of the tables related to physical productivity. I do not feel that any further omissions or curtailments are advisable.

As I mentioned before, we shall not be able to print this article before the April issue; I am, however, sending it to the printers at once in order that we may get the proofs dealt with in good time.

Yours sincerely,

[copy initialled] K.

In 1940 the Royal Economic Society celebrated its fiftieth anniversary. As Editor of *The Economic Journal* Keynes marked the occasion with a note.

From The Economic Journal, *December 1940*

THE SOCIETY'S JUBILEE 1890–1940

The British Economic Association, of which the Royal Economic Society is the successor, was founded at a meeting held at University College, London, on November 20, 1890. The Jubilee of the Society fell due, therefore, to be celebrated shortly before the publication of this issue of the *Economic Journal*, whilst with this issue of the *Journal* the first fifty annual volumes are completed.

The celebrations and the reunion which otherwise would have been appropriate must be postponed until happier times. The Council of the Society have ordered the preparation of a complete subject index of the first fifty volumes of the *Journal*, which should be ready for publication immediately after the end of the war, although that also must be postponed for the time being. Meanwhile members may be interested to be reminded of those earliest proceedings of the Society which led to its foundation.

In 1890 Alfred Marshall was President of Section F (Economics and Statistics) of the British Association. In this capacity he took the lead in carrying into the field of action the subject of certain conversations amongst members of the Committee of Section F. On April 10, 1890, he circulated the following paper to members of this Committee.

After considering the tenour of the conversation on this subject at our last meeting, and after some consultation with Prof. Foxwell and Mr Palgrave I propose to move that on Tuesday next, as soon as the necessary business has been disposed of, we resolve ourselves into a special meeting for the discussion of the following questions:—

(i) Has the time come for founding an English Economic Journal somewhat similar in character to the American Quarterly?

(ii) Has the time come for founding an English Economic Society, or Association; which shall have as its main objects the encouragement of research and discussion, the publication of monographs, the translation of foreign works and the republication of English works that are out of print?

(iii) If so should its general lines be those of an English 'learned' society; or of the American Economic Association, which holds meetings only at rare intervals, and the membership of which does not profess to confer any sort of diploma?

(iv) Should the Journal be published by such Society or Association (if formed), and edited under the direction of a committee appointed for that purpose by this Council?

(v) Shall we appoint a small subcommittee to convene a meeting to discuss, and take action on these questions, and to invite to it (1) all members of the Council of the Royal Statistical Society; (2) all members of the Political Economy Club; (3) all who have been, or are, lecturers on economics in any university or public college in the United Kingdom together with ourselves and any other persons whose presence may seem to the Subcommittee specially desirable?

ALFRED MARSHALL

Balliol Croft, Cambridge:
10 April 1890

As a result of the discussions at that Committee the following paper was circulated over his signature, after having been discussed for several months and passed through several draft forms.

PROPOSAL TO FORM AN ENGLISH ECONOMIC ASSOCIATION

Dear Sir,

I have been requested to invite you to attend a private meeting at University College, London, on Thursday November the twentieth to discuss proposals for the foundation of an Economic Society or Association, and, in conjunction there with, of an Economic Journal, and to take action thereon. The chair will be taken by the Right Hon. the Chancellor of the Exchequer at 5 o'clock.

The need of an economic Journal has long been felt in England. Every other country in which economic studies are pursued with great activity, offers facilities for the publication of thorough scientific work by persons who have not the time, or are unwilling, to write a formal treatise. Since isolated pamphlets, however able, seldom obtain any considerable circulation, Englishmen who have something to say that is too technical for the ordinary magazines, and too short for a book, are sometimes compelled to give their views to the world in the columns of a foreign periodical, or as a publication of the American Economic Association; but more frequently they put it aside till an opportunity should offer for working it out more fully and publishing it as a book; and that opportunity too often does not come. A strong and widespread feeling that English economists, and especially the younger men among them, are thus placed at a great disadvantage through the want of any easy means of communication with one another, has led to the holding of many private meetings and discussions on the subject in Oxford, Cambridge, London, and possibly elsewhere; and lately the matter has come under consideration of the Committee of Section F (Economics and Statistics) of the British Association. It is as the result of these discussions that I have been requested to issue the present invitation to you.

It was at first proposed to collect a guarantee fund, and to issue the journal as a private concern. But latterly the feeling has been growing that some security should be afforded that the journal should always represent all shades of economic opinion, and be the organ not of one school of English economists, but of all schools; and it is thought that this end will be best attained by the publication of the journal under the authority of an Economic Association. It is suggested that it should be conducted by a salaried editor, who should have full power as to matters of detail, but should from time to time confer on matters of general principle with a Committee of the Association, appointed for that purpose.

It has been suggested that as a rule each number of the Journal might contain one long article, or monograph, and two or three shorter articles, together with reports from foreign correspondents, and a detailed bibliography of current economic literature, besides some miscellaneous matter. It is proposed also that extra numbers should occasionally be issued containing reprints of rare works that have historical interest, or translations of foreign pamphlets.

The Association might gradually enlarge the scope of its action. It might supply a common meeting place for English economists, and bring them together from time to time. It might increase its issues of economic publications. And lastly, if its funds sufficed for the purpose, it might do good service by promoting economic investigations, especially such as cannot well be undertaken by government departments, and yet involve considerable expense; for the ability, the inclination and the means to carry on investigations, such as that which is now being made on 'The Labour and Life of the People in London', are seldom united in one person.

Almost the only question on which a difference of opinion has so far shown itself is whether or not the Association should be open to all those who are sufficiently interested in economics to be willing to subscribe to its funds. If the Association should hold meetings for discussion, the further question would arise whether they should be at frequent intervals, say once a month, or more rarely, say once a year. There are some who think that the gene lines to be followed should be those of an English 'learned' Society, w others would prefer those of the American Economic Association, which holds meetings only at rare intervals, and the membership of which does not profess to confer any sort of diploma.

The meeting on November the 20th will be asked to decide Firstly, whether it is desirable to found an Economic Society or Association which shall undertake at once the issue of a journal; and (supposing this question to be answered in the affirmative) Secondly, whether, for the present, it shall hold any meetings other than business meetings; and if any, then at what intervals: Thirdly, what shall be the conditions of membership; and any other question that may arise. The meeting will further be asked to appoint a committee to give effect to its decisions.

It is proposed to invite to that meeting (1) all lecturers on economics in any university or public college in the United Kingdom; (2) the members of the Councils of the London, Dublin and Manchester Statistical Societies; (3) the members of the London Political Economy Club, together with a few other persons, besides members of the Committee of Section F of the British Association. I have the honour to remain,

Dear Sir,

Yours faithfully,

ALFRED MARSHALL

Cambridge, 24 Oct. 1890

It will be seen from the last paragraph but two of this circular that there had been some difference of opinion as to whether the proposed association should be open to all-comers or should be confined to a limited membership. One of those who at first was inclined to the latter opinion was Dr Bonar, who has transferred to the archives of the Society the following characteristic letter sent to him by Alfred Marshall on July 25, 1890, which gives an amusing indication of some of the arguments which were being used behind the scenes.

My Dear Bonar,

I am sorry you won't be present at the meeting; firstly because I think you might be converted to an open Society. No one, to whom I have spoken, except Foxwell, Edgeworth and yourself thinks a close society would be safe and the general opinion of those with whom I have conferred is that a close society would be inundated by Quacks, who could not be kept out, unless the society was so small as to be little more than a private club: but that Quacks would not care to come into a society which was open to all: and would not do much harm there, if they did come in.

Yours very truly,
ALFRED MARSHALL

25 July

As a result of the circular of October 24, 1890, the meeting to found the Association was held on November 20, 1890, under the presidency of Mr Goschen (as he then was), Chancellor of the Exchequer. A report of the proceedings at this meeting was printed at the beginning of the first issue of the *Journal* for March 1891. It is there mentioned that about 200 persons were present, of whom 63 were already sufficiently distinguished fifty years ago to be particularly mentioned by name. Of these 63 no fewer than 8 are, fifty years later, still with us—namely, James Bonar, Clara Collet, A. W. Flux, John Neville Keynes, Mrs Alfred Marshall, L. L. Price, Bernard Shaw and Hubert Llewellyn Smith. It is a further proof of the longevity of economists that 8 of the contributors to the first volume of *The*

Economic Journal are still living—namely, C. F. Bastable, Clara Collet, L. L. Price, F. W. Taussig,* Sidney Webb, James Bonar, H. Llewellyn Smith and J. N. Keynes—whilst one of the books reviewed (by James Bonar) was the first publication of Beatrice Potter (Mrs Sidney Webb). Miss Collet alone can claim that she has contributed both to our first and to our fiftieth volume.

From the full report of the proceedings in the first issue of the *Journal* the following extracts are worth reprinting. In introducing the motion of the day, Alfred Marshall said, amongst other things:—

It was remarkable that England was in these matters behind other countries; but this state of things was due not to want of careful consideration of the matter, but to sad accident. For although England in 1870 had a stronger array of economists than any other country—not more learned, but more full of creative power—within a few years the greater number of them were dead. Cairnes, Jevons, Bagehot, Cliffe Leslie, Toynbee, and Fawcett, whose power and originality placed them in the first rank, and who would have been the right men to take the lead in such a movement, died prematurely in the prime of life. Thus, though in 1870 England was remarkably strong, later on she was remarkably weak in economists of mark; and therefore he did not think they were to blame for not having started this movement long ago. Happily, however, in 1890 we had a large number of very able young men at Oxford, Cambridge, and elsewhere, who were at the age at which they might be expected to write papers suitable for a journal. Thus, while others, like Mr Palgrave and Professor Foxwell, had long taken a more cheery view of the situation, even he now felt that the time had come for the movement which they were beginning, and he no longer doubted whether it would be possible to maintain a journal at a high level of excellence. . . . He had received promises of assistance from almost every economist. Besides that, he had received a great number of suggestions from persons who were not economists, some of whom expressed the hope that the proposed Association would 'exert a wholesome influence'. That was the one thing which he hoped

---

* Since the above was written we have heard with the greatest regret of the death of Professor Taussig at the age of 80. As already Editor of *The Quarterly Journal of Economics*, he was consulted fifty years ago about the conduct of an economic journal and his reply is amongst our archives. No American economist commanded more confidence and affection than he amongst his British colleagues. A notice of his life and work will appear in the next issue of the *Journal*.

they would not set themselves to do. Their desire was not 'to exert a whole-some influence' in the sense of setting up a standard of orthodoxy, to which all contributors had to conform; economics was a science, and an 'orthodox science' was a contradiction in terms. Science could be true or false, but could not be orthodox; and the best way to find out what was true was to welcome the criticism of all people who knew what they were talking about. In that way, indeed, he did hope they would exercise a wholesome influence on the character of economic discussion. In the past, time had been wasted in controversies which ought never to have come into existence—controversies based upon a perversion of the words of some writer, the critic interpreting them in the most foolish sense possible, and then writing long articles to prove that they were absurd when thus misinterpreted. All sciences in their early youth had been pestered by this sort of controversy, though economics had suffered more than others. The one influence which he hoped they would exercise would be that they would start from an absolutely catholic basis, and include every school of economists which was doing genuine work. He trusted that those who should control this journal would insist that all who wrote in criticism of others should take the writings of those others in the best possible sense, and in that way all schools might work amicably together, interpreting each other in the fairest and most generous manner; acting on that principle they would make sound progress.

Marshall's deprecation of orthodoxy grated a little on the ears of some of the more senior of those present, who seemed to think that this was going perhaps a little too far. Goschen remarked:—

He saw in certain quarters men who called themselves political economists, but who had not the slightest idea what economics were. He had been warned by Professor Marshall against saying that there was anything orthodox in any school of economics. But economists were entitled to say that there were—he would not call them schools, because they could not claim that title at all— but certain groups of men who seemed to disbelieve in the possibility of any economic science whatever.

Leonard Courtney could not refrain (and he might, perhaps, have found a more fortunate example) from saying:—

There were some things which must [be] taken to be finally fixed, and just as a mathematical journal would exclude contributions which affected to square the circle, so in the science with which they were then concerned there were some propositions for which they would scarcely be able to find room. They might, for example, discuss whether gold alone, or silver alone, or an amalgam of both should be the basis of our currency; but if a gentleman suggested that an unlimited supply of paper would cover all the difficulties of the world, Professor Marshall would say that there must be authority somewhere, and that some opinions must be excluded. There was a sense in which, notwithstanding what Mr Marshall had said, he hoped the Association would exercise a wholesome influence.

In the discussion which ensued, having apparently given up his previous preference for a limited Society,

Professor Edgeworth defended the almost indiscriminate admission of members which was proposed, on the ground that it was impossible to find any satisfactory test of orthodoxy in economic doctrine. If it were attempted to apply any such test, if some were to be excluded because they appeared to be unsound to others, he feared that the list of members would be very small—not much larger than the number of the elect according to David Deans.

After the Society had been founded and the first Council duly elected—

Mr G. Bernard Shaw, whilst fully agreeing with all that their chairman, Mr Goschen, had said that evening, suggested, with all respect to Mr Goschen, that the head of the Association should not be a gentleman who was identified with any political party in the State.

The Chairman and Professor Marshall both rose, but Mr Goschen gave way to

Professor Marshall, who asked to be allowed to intervene. He was not a political supporter of their chairman, but he was sure he was expressing the general opinion when he said that it would be impossible to find any more fair and impartial man to be at their head than the present Chancellor of the Exchequer.

The Chairman said that he thought there was considerable force in what Mr Shaw had said. He would propose that his nomination should not be decided upon at this meeting, but should be deferred to another meeting. It would probably be better if a political economist were chosen who had no avowed political views. He hoped, therefore, that the matter would be left open.

In the same month the Rules of the Society were drafted by H. S. Foxwell, Sir Thomas Elliott and J. B. Martin, the Treasurer. F. Y. Edgeworth was appointed Editor and Secretary at a salary of £100. In March 1891 the first issue of the first volume duly saw the light, with a list of original members and the Rules of the Society prefixed. It began modestly, the first article of the first number being entitled 'The Eight Hours Day in Victoria'. The text of the *Journal* proper began with the following Manifesto, signed by the Editor:—

The British Economic Association is open to all schools and parties; no person is excluded because of his opinions. *The Economic Journal*, issued under the authority of the Association, will be conducted in a similar spirit of toleration. It will be open to writers of different schools. The most opposite doctrines may meet here as on a fair field. Thus the difficulties of Socialism will be considered in the first number; the difficulties of Individualism in the second. Opposing theories of currency will be represented with equal impartiality. Nor will it be attempted to prescribe the method, any more than the result of scientific investigation.

Is it extravagant to hope that this toleration of the differences between the votaries of economic science may tend to produce agreement between them? 'A little generous prudence, a little forbearance for one another, ... might win all these diligences to join and unite into one general and brotherly search for truth.' What Milton hoped for theology in the seventeenth century may prove true of political economy in the nineteenth.

Meanwhile, it will be the task of the Editor and his coadjutors, unbiassed by their personal convictions, to select the ablest representatives of each important interest. The Association is to be not only 'British' in its love of fair play and free speech, but also 'Economic' in the character which the term suggests of special knowledge and scientific accuracy.

As a fuller and more authentic statement of the principles on which the Association is based, the report of the speeches which the promoters of the Association delivered on the occasion of its foundation is submitted to the readers of the journal by

THE EDITOR

The year 1890 saw not only the foundation of the Society, but the publication of Marshall's *Principles of Economics* and the completion of the *Dictionary of Political Economy*, which was published in the following year at the same time as the first issue of the *Journal*. The modern age of British economics can, therefore, be dated from that year. Its achievements, its undiminished controversies, its many fruits, its escape from the 'orthodoxy' which seems to have weighed so heavily on the previous generation, and a record of the life and work of many of our founders and of their contemporaries are to be read in the subsequent 50 volumes.

THE EDITOR

1891–1895	F. Y. EDGEWORTH—Sole Editor
1895–1905	F. Y. EDGEWORTH—Editor
	H. HIGGS—Assistant Editor
1905–1911	F. Y. EDGEWORTH—Sole Editor
1911–1918	J. M. KEYNES—Sole Editor
1918–1925	J. M. KEYNES ⎫ Joint Editors
	F. Y. EDGEWORTH ⎭
1925–1933	J. M. KEYNES ⎫ Joint Editors
	D. H. MACGREGOR ⎭
1933–1934	J. M. KEYNES ⎫ Joint Editors
	D. H. MACGREGOR ⎭
	E. A. G. ROBINSON—Assistant Editor
1934–1940	J. M. KEYNES—Editor
	E. A. G. ROBINSON—Assistant Editor

As well as editing *The Economic Journal*, Keynes edited a series of Cambridge Economic Handbooks from their foundation in 1922 until he passed the editorship on to D. H. Robertson in 1936. Each volume of the series carried a contribution from Keynes, normally in the form of a standard introduction. In four of the first five volumes published in 1922 and 1923, the standard introduction ran as follows.

From the Cambridge Economic Handbooks, *1922 and 1923*

INTRODUCTION TO THE SERIES

The theory of economics does not furnish a body of settled conclusions immediately applicable to policy. It is a method rather than a doctrine, an apparatus of the mind, a technique of thinking, which helps its possessor to draw correct conclusions. It is not difficult in the sense in which mathematical and scientific techniques are difficult; but the fact that its modes of expression are much less precise than these, renders decidedly difficult the task of conveying it correctly to the minds of learners.

Before Adam Smith this apparatus of thought scarcely existed. Between his time and this it has been steadily enlarged and improved. Nor is there any branch of knowledge in the formation of which Englishmen can claim a more predominant part. It is not complete yet, but important improvements in its elements are becoming rare. The main task of the professional economist now consists, either in obtaining a wide knowledge of *relevant* facts and exercising skill in the application of economic principles to them, or in expounding the elements of his method in a lucid, accurate and illuminating way, so that, through his instruction, the number of those who can think for themselves may be increased.

This series is directed towards the latter aim. It is intended to convey to the ordinary reader and to the uninitiated student some conception of the general principles of thought which economists now apply to economic problems. The writers are not concerned to make original contributions to knowledge, or even to attempt a complete summary of all the principles of the subject. They have been more anxious to avoid obscure forms of expression than difficult ideas; and their object has been to expound to intelligent readers, previously unfamiliar with the subject, the most significant elements of economic method. Most of the omissions of matter often treated in textbooks are intentional; for as a subject develops, it is important, especially in books meant to be introductory, to discard the marks of the chrysalid stage before thought had wings.

Even on matters of principle there is not yet a complete unanimity of opinion amongst professors. Generally speaking, the writers of these volumes believe themselves to be orthodox members of the Cambridge School of Economics. At any rate, most of their ideas about the subject, and even their prejudices, are traceable to the contact they have enjoyed with the writings and lectures of the two economists who have chiefly influenced Cambridge thought for the past fifty years, Dr Marshall and Professor Pigou.

For one early book in the series, Harold Wright's *Population*, Keynes dropped his general introduction in favour of a preface.

From Population *by Harold Wright* (*1923*)

PREFACE

A belief in the material progress of mankind is not old. During the greater part of history such a belief was neither compatible with experience nor encouraged by religion. It is doubtful whether, taking one century with another, there was much variation in the lot of the unskilled labourer at the centres of civilisation in the two thousand years from the Greece of Solon to the England of Charles II or the France of Louis XIV. Paganism placed the Golden Age behind us; Christianity raised Heaven above us; and anyone, before the middle of the eighteenth century, who had expected a progressive improvement in material welfare here, as a result of the division of labour, the discoveries of science and the boundless fecundity of the species, would have been thought very eccentric.

In the eighteenth century, for obscure reasons which economic historians have not yet sufficiently explored, material progress commenced over wide areas in a decided and cumulative fashion

857

not previously experienced. Philosophers were ready with an appropriate superstition, and before the century was out Priestley's view was becoming fashionable, that, by the further division of labour,—'Nature, including both its materials and its laws, will be more at our command; men will make their situation in this world abundantly more easy and comfortable; they will prolong their existence in it and will grow daily more happy.'

It was against the philosophers of this school that Malthus directed his *Essay*. Its arguments impressed his reasonable contemporaries, and the interruption to progress by the Napoleonic wars supplied a favourable atmosphere. But as the nineteenth century proceeded, the tendency to material progress reasserted itself. Malthus was forgotten or discredited. The cloud was lifted; the classical economists dethroned; and the opinions of the Vicar of Wakefield, who 'was ever of opinion that the honest man who married and brought up a large family did more service than he who continued single and only talked of population', and of Adam Smith, who held that 'the most decisive mark of the prosperity of any country is the increase of the number of its inhabitants', almost recovered their sway.

Nevertheless, the interruption to prosperity by the War, corresponding to the similar interruption a hundred years before, has again encouraged an atmosphere of doubt; and there are some who have a care. The most interesting question in the world (of those at least to which time will bring us an answer) is whether, after a short interval of recovery, material progress will be resumed, or whether, on the other hand, the magnificent episode of the nineteenth century is over.

In this volume of the *Cambridge Economic Handbooks* Mr Harold Wright summarises the data, and outlines the main features of the problem of population. It is no part of the purpose of this series to present ready-made conclusions. Our object is to aid and stimulate study. The topic of this particular volume is one about which it is difficult, for anyone who has given much thought to it, not to feel strongly. But Mr Wright has avoided propagandism and has been concerned to display in a calm spirit the extraordinary interest, difficulty and importance of his subject, rather than to advocate any definite policies. His object will have been accomplished if he can do something to direct the thoughts of a few more students to what is going to be not merely an economist's problem, but, in the near future, the greatest of all social questions,—a question which will arouse some of the deepest instincts and emotions of men, and about which feeling may run as passionately as in earlier struggles between religions. A great transition in human history will have begun when civilised man endeavours to assume conscious control in his own hands, away from the blind instinct of mere predominant survival.

When the series brought out two new volumes in 1928, Keynes altered his introduction to the form it remained in for all subsequent volumes published under his editorship.

From the Cambridge Economic Handbooks, *1928–36*

INTRODUCTION TO THE SERIES

The theory of economics does not furnish a body of settled conclusions immediately applicable to policy. It is a method rather than a doctrine, an apparatus of the mind, a technique of thinking, which helps its possessor to draw correct conclusions. It is not difficult in the sense in which mathematical and scientific techniques are difficult; but the fact that its modes of expression are much less precise than these, renders decidedly difficult the task of conveying it correctly to the minds of learners.

Before Adam Smith this apparatus of thought scarcely existed. Between his time and this it has been steadily enlarged and improved. Nor is there any branch of knowledge in the formation of which Englishmen can claim a more predominant part. This series, however, is not directed towards making original contributions to economic science. Its object is to expound its elements in a lucid, accurate, and illuminating way, so that the number of those who can begin to think for themselves may be increased. It is intended to convey to the ordinary reader and to the uninitiated student some conception of the general principles of thought which economists now apply to economic problems. The writers have been more anxious to avoid obscure forms of expression than difficult ideas. Most of the omissions of matter often treated in textbooks are intentional; for as a subject develops, it is important, especially in books meant to be introductory, to discard the marks of the chrysalid stage before thought had wings.

Even on matters of principle there is not yet a complete unanimity of opinion amongst professional students of the subject. Immediately after the War daily economic events were of such a startling character as to divert attention from theoretical complexities. But today, economic science has recovered its wind. Traditional treatments and traditional solutions are being questioned, improved and revised. In the end this activity of research should clear up controversy. But for the moment controversy and doubt are increased. The writers of this series must apologise to the general reader and to the beginner if many parts of their subject have not yet reached to a degree of certainty and lucidity which would make them easy and straightforward reading.

In the course of his career as an economist, Keynes was frequently asked to referee manuscripts for Macmillan, his own publishers. He seems to have done little refereeing for anyone else. Although his own papers contain a reasonable proportion of his referee's reports, Macmillan's records are more complete and are available for consultation in the British Library (Add. 55201). Most of the books he refereed were topical pamphlets or tracts for the times, but three of them became classics and his reactions to them are of some interest. All three were written in 1932.

The first was J. R. Hicks's *The Theory of Wages* which Harold Macmillan sent him on 15 April 1932.

To HAROLD MACMILLAN, *27 April 1932*

Dear Macmillan,

I am sorry to say that you should, in my opinion, get a second opinion on Mr J. R. Hicks's manuscript, which I have already returned to you under separate cover. I would suggest Mr D. H. Robertson, Trinity College, Cambridge.

My reason for this is that the method is to me so unsympathetic that I find it very difficult to be fair to him. Yet it ought not to be turned down for this reason, because my want of sympathy would extend to a good many other authors of the highest repute, who have written about this subject.

Subject to the above, and to a strong hope that you will, as I suggest, get a second opinion, I record my comments as follows.

It is a highly theoretical book, the serious and careful work of an unoriginal but competent mind. It fills something of the gap in the subject, and assuming the problem is to be tackled in this sort of way, the treatment is probably fairly good of its kind and would, I think, meet with exceedingly favourable reviews in many quarters, if it were to be published. But to me personally the book is extremely boring, and I feel that the author is incapable of adding to my knowledge or understanding of the subject, or of getting anywhere near a satisfactory solution; because he is using traditional technique for a problem which experience shows it is incapable of solving. I find the author's very indefinite and jejune conclusions a confirmation of my general expectation. In fact the book seems to me to assume that prices are fixed independently of wages, so that whatever happens to money wages may be assumed to happen, more or less to the same extent, to real wages. This assumption may be legitimate when one is dealing merely with equilibrium, but after the first chapter the author is avowedly dealing with disequilibrium, and such problems as unemployment. For these problems his method of approach seems to me, as I have said, quite hopeless. But then I should say much the same about a good deal of Pigou's treatment of this subject. So it would not be fair to turn Mr Hicks down because I, out of a purely personal view, feel this way about it.

Yours sincerely,
[copy initialled] J.M.K.

Macmillan sent the book out to Robertson. The firm published it. Hicks carries the story further in his preface to the second edition of the book (London, 1965, pp. 305–7).[27]

The second manuscript Keynes received was a proposed edition of Knut Wicksell's *Lectures on Political Economy* in a translation by E. Classen. Daniel Macmillan sent the manuscript to him on 26 September 1932.

To DANIEL MACMILLAN, *3 October 1932*

My dear Dan,

I enclose a report on the gigantic Wicksell manuscript. It will be some little time before I shall feel fit to tackle such a big one again. I might add to what I say in the report that I was under the impression that there had been some talk of a translation of the *Vorlesungen* under the auspices of the London School of Economics. It might be that Classen first of all offered them his manuscript and that this was the origin of the rumours which reached me. But if you think of accepting it, it might be well first of all to write to Professor Robbins to make sure that they have given up the idea of preparing a translation, if they ever had such a project.

[27] See also his 'Recollections and Documents', *Economica*, February 1973, reprinted as Chapter VI of his *Economic Perspectives: Further Essays on Money and Growth* (Oxford 1977).

I am returning the manuscript under separate cover.

Yours ever,

[copy initialled] J. M. K.

TRANSLATION OF WICKSELL'S 'VORLESUNGEN'

This substantial volume consists of a translation of the two volumes of what is usually known as Wicksell's *Vorlesungen*. The two volumes are in fact two quite separate works. They were published separately at widely different dates and neither is necessary to the understanding of the other. They are best regarded, therefore, as two independent works, the first of which is on the Principles of Economics and the second on Money and Credit.

The Swedish economist Wicksell died in 1926 at the age of 75. His main works appeared in Swedish and German; none have appeared in English hitherto. Since Wicksell's death his reputation has been steadily rising and he is now widely recognised as having been much in advance of his time and as being in many respects the forerunner of the ideas which underlie the most modern treatment of the subject. For this reason much more interest is being taken in his work, though more perhaps from the point of view of the history of theory than as a substantial contribution to the theory of the subject as it now is. Consequently there has been a good deal of talk of late of arranging for a translation of some characteristic piece of his.

His two principal works are *Geldzins*[28] and those *Vorlesungen*. Two or three years ago the Royal Economic Society decided on my suggestion to translate one or other of these. After taking the best advice we could get on the matter, we decided on the *Geldzins*. The translation of this is nearly complete, though not yet in the printer's hands, since it has been held up through pre-

---

[28] *Geldzins und Güterpreise (Interest and Prices)*. The English translation by R. F. Kahn was published by Macmillan in 1936.

occupations of Professor Ohlin who has promised to write an introduction. It will, however, appear at no distant date, and I shall be asking Messrs Macmillan to undertake its publication in the same way as other publications of the Royal Economic Society.

Whilst, however, we had decided on translating *Geldzins*, some people are of the opinion that the *Vorlesungen* would have been a better choice. The *Vorlesungen* represent Wicksell's later and most mature work, and therefore from that point of view might have the preference. On the other hand only a very small part of the *Vorlesungen* is devoted to Wicksell's characteristic contributions to the subject, since it is a general treatise which aims at covering the whole ground. Also it is doubtful whether it is much of an improvement on the earlier work; whilst from the point of view of economic theory it is better to have the ideas in their original form rather than in a work which was revised several times, the principal edition being as late as 1922, when the ideas in question were by no means such a novelty as they had been twenty-four years earlier, when the *Geldzins* was published. A good account of the *Vorlesungen* and of the relationship between the two books will be found on page 505 of *The Economic Journal* for September 1926.

The manuscript which Mr Classen submitted includes *both* volumes of the *Vorlesungen*, whereas most projects for translating this work have related, I think, only to the second volume. Reading the two volumes together, which I have now done in this translation for the first time, I feel that it would be going rather far to publish an English edition of the two volumes in their entirety. But a single volume selected from the two would certainly contain some matter of very considerable interest. The earlier part of Volume One contains comparatively little which is specially characteristic of Wicksell, until we reach the second chapter of Book Three, entitled 'Capitalistic Production'. This section is highly original and of very considerable interest. As regards the second volume, the translation has not unfortunately been supplied with a table of contents, which makes reference a little difficult, but the really interesting matter comes towards the end, somewhere about chapter Nine, though there is also a good deal of interesting matter earlier. If the book is to be republished at all, probably the whole of Volume Two should be included, with the exception of the historical portions.

I conclude that the last part of Volume One, and Volume Two minus the historical portions, would make a volume of real value. What the prospects of sale would be, especially with the Royal Economic Society volume coming out much at the same time, I should not like to say. We shall certainly be very well satisfied if we sell 500 copies of the *Geldzins*.

The translation strikes me as quite tolerable. It has obviously been dictated off the reel, and has the faults necessarily attendant on that particular manufacturing process. Also, as Mr Classen says, it needs revision by an economist. Here and there the meaning is not clear and there is probably an error in the translation, whilst a number of proper names are mis-spelt. But considering that this purports to be no more than an unrevised translation, it is certainly quite fair. Mr Classen is not, I think, an economist; but he has been known to me for some years as the London representative of various Scandinavian newspapers, particularly for economic and financial matters.

J.M.K.

Macmillans declined the manuscript. Classen's translation, edited and with an introduction by Professor L. C. Robbins, was published by Routledge in 1934.

The final manuscript Keynes commented on in 1932 which is of interest was Joan Robinson's *The Economics of Imperfect Competition* which Macmillan published in 1933. Harold Macmillan asked Keynes to take it on 16 November. At that stage it was entitled 'Monopoly'.

To HAROLD MACMILLAN, *25 November 1932*

Dear Harold,

Monopoly by Joan Robinson

I have no doubt that you ought to accept this book. It is not easy to judge its length in the present state of the manuscript, but it is obviously a substantial volume, the cost of which will be somewhat increased by the considerable number of diagrams. It is also an advanced work, which will only appeal to specialists. All the same, I think it might sell more copies than you would suppose at first sight, for the following reasons.

There has been a very considerable development of the theory of value in the last five years, starting from the basis laid by Marshall and Pigou. The nature of these developments can only be ascertained at the present time by studying a number of scattered articles, largely in *The Economic Journal,* but also in America and Germany. These articles are generally concerned with particular points and rather assume a knowledge of the technique employed and the general character of the diagrammatic methods in use. At present there is no convenient place where anyone who is interested in these developments can either find a clear statement of the nature of modern technique, or a summary of the recent work on the subject. Mrs Robinson aims at filling this gap, and in my opinion she has done it very well. She would claim, I think, that she has done more than this, namely that she has cleared up a number of obscure and doubtful points, and has made some important contributions of her own to the whole matter. I think that the book does indeed contain a number of discussions which are more or less new; on the other hand I should hesitate a little to stress too much the originality of the work. It appears to me to be predominantly a discussion of the development of ideas which have been started by others, and which are now widely current, not only for learned articles, but in oral discussion at Cambridge and Oxford. She is, in a sense, taking the cream off a new movement which has not yet found its own expositor in print.

My view is then that the book will be for a little while to come an essential one for any serious student of the modern theory of value. Whilst the book is in a sense advanced and puzzling at first sight, it is not essentially a difficult book. It has also considerable qualities of lucidity. I have found it much easier to read rapidly than much other work in the same school which has come to my notice in the last year or two.

I have not read the book critically, which would be a formidable task. I have, however, a good deal of confidence that it is reasonably free from minor slips and errors and fallacies because the authoress explains in the preface that it has been very elaborately and carefully criticised by R. F. Kahn; indeed, I suspect that he has played a very substantial part in getting it to its present form. Now he is the most careful and accurate of all the younger economists, and mistakes do not easily get past him. I should say that he is a long way the ablest and most reliable critic of this type of work now to be found. Knowing the part that he has played in the preparation of the book, I have much greater confidence in its being free from the blunders which so very easily creep into a treatment of this kind, than if it was Mrs Robinson's own uncriticised effort.

If, therefore, you are predisposed to accept the book through your old-established relations with the Maurice[29] family, I think you should certainly not hesitate to accept this, which is a serious and valuable work.

There are two minor points of criticism which I might mention.

I think that the quotation from *Sylvie and Bruno* should be deleted, not because it is not apposite, but because Dennis Robertson really must be considered to have a patent in quotations from Lewis Carroll in economic works.

In the second place, there is something about the tone of the Introductory Chapter (not in the Preface) which is not, I think,

---

[29] Joan Robinson's grandfather, F. D. Maurice, had helped to give Macmillan his start in publishing.

quite satisfactory. It is not exactly pretentious, but it seems to me to have some sort of flavour which might give readers that feeling. I think the matter can be remedied by a few omissions, but I feel that as it stands at present it is, as it were, a little out of character with the rest of the book.

I am returning the manuscript under separate cover.

Yours sincerely,

[copy initialled] J.M.K.

I have a doubt about the argument in chap. 25, but I will take an opportunity to speak to Mrs R. about this.

I think the title is rather a misnomer. I would suggest 'The Theory of Value under Monopoly and Competition'.

DOCUMENTS REPRODUCED
IN THIS VOLUME

869

ARTICLES AND CORRESPONDENCE

MEMORANDA AND COMMENTS

MINUTES OF EVIDENCE

PAMPHLETS, PROSPECTUS

SPEECHES, LECTURE NOTES

ARTICLES AND CORRESPONDENCE

ACKNOWLEDGEMENTS

In preparing this volume we have incurred a number of debts, in particular in regard to the chapter on Keynes's activities as an investor. Thus we should like to thank the following for advice and, in many instances, papers: the Provost and Fellows of King's College, Cambridge; Professors S. K. Howson, Lord Kaldor, Charles Madge and W. B. Reddaway; Sir Anthony Burney; the late W. H. Haslam; and Messrs A. G. A. Mackay, Ian Macpherson, R. E. Macpherson, J. Peters, Oliver Westall and J. J. H. Wormell; Messrs Buckmaster and Moore, Stockbrokers and the National Mutual Life Assurance Society. Jonathan Reizenstein and Wayne Lewchuck provided research assistance and Coral George coped wonderfully with typing several varieties of handwriting. The Social Sciences and Humanities Research Council of Canada and the Canada Council provided financial support.

INDEX

INDEX

Nitrate (*cont.*)
control scheme, 'Cosana', 576, 577, 641, 643
measurement, 513, 579
nitrate of soda, 644
synthetic nitrate, 567, 641, 643
North Africa: wheat production, 356
North America: copper consumption, 467
Norton, H. T. J., 3
Norway, 798
gold holding, 749
speculation in krone (JMK), 4
spelter stocks, 293
Nyasaland, tea production, 349

Ohlin, Bertil, 784, 864
Oil companies, 82, 157-8, 160
oil stocks, 268, 269, 317, 320, 358, 360, 404-5
see also Fuels; Petroleum
Omes, investment in, 66
Orthodoxy, 852, 853, 855
Ostend, International Nitrate Conference, 641
Oxford, 848, 851, 867; College Bursars, evidence on tithes, 663, 679

Paish, F. W., 234
Palgrave, R. H. I., 726, 847, 851
Panama, gold exchange standard, 721
Panic, in copper market, 525-6
Peacock, Sir Edward R., member, Royal Commission on Tithe Rentcharge, 654, 664-7, 668, 669-70, 687-8
Pearl Insurance Company, 72
Penang: rubber stocks, 339, 383, 385, 426-7, 481-2, 543-4, 613-15
Persia
petroleum output, 567
tea consumption, 349
Peru, copper production, 466, 528, 590
Peters, Jack, clerk, 10
Petroleum
stocks, 305-7, 320, 350-2, 396-8, 439-41, 448-9, 498-502, 510-11, 561-7, 572, 636-40
measurement, 513, 579
prices, 565
production and consumption, 307, 440-1, 499-500; overproduction, 566; restriction, 565-6, 576, 640
Phelps Dodge-Nicholls copper group, 594
Philippines, gold exchange standard, 721
Pierson, N. G., 727

Planning and management, 239, 249
Pliny, 698, 743, 756
Poland
spelter stocks, 291, 426, 542
sugar stocks, 549, 622
synthetic nitrate, 641
tea consumption, 349
Political Economy Club, 847, 849
Polyphon Gramophone Company, 55
Pooling system
for reformed tithe rentcharge, 657, 659, 669, 673, 682
for tin, 418, 472, 533-4, 535, 537, 600, 601-2
for wheat, 576
Population, 696
Portugal, 749
Post Office Savings Bank, 228, 815, 817
Potter, Beatrice (Mrs Sidney Webb), 851
P.R. Finance Company, 31-2; JMK director, later chairman of, 1, 4 n 3, 8, 30; investment in, 14; goes into liquidation, 32
Practical men, 765
Pretyman, Captain, 654
Price, L. L., 850, 851
Prices
and consumption, 436
general level of, 693, 709, 712, 723
and gold production, 703, 772-3; monetary stocks of gold and, 769
movements of, 85, 122, 184, 187, 267, 270, 706; high prices, 265
in quantity theory, 775-83
questions on, 690
of shares, London and New York, 113
see also under Raw materials
Priestley, Joseph, 859
Production, and consumption: interval between, 256-65; of staple commodities, 270
see also under individual commodities
Profits, 53, 63, 78, 83, 718
capital profits as object of investment, 80, 81-3
ploughed back, 250
profit margins, 823
Progress, 857-8
Propensity to consume, 804, 808; marginal, 799, 805-6
Prosperity, 140, 178, 212
and prices, 265
Provident Mutual Life Assurance Association, 151